Sharing Economy and the Impact of Collaborative Consumption

Iviane Ramos de Luna
Open University of Catalonia, Spain

Àngels Fitó-Bertran
Open University of Catalonia, Spain

Josep Lladós-Masllorens
Open University of Catalonia, Spain

Francisco Liébana-Cabanillas
University of Granada, Spain

IGI Global
DISSEMINATOR OF KNOWLEDGE

A volume in the Advances in Finance, Accounting, and Economics (AFAE) Book Series

Published in the United States of America by
IGI Global
Business Science Reference (an imprint of IGI Global)
701 E. Chocolate Avenue
Hershey PA, USA 17033
Tel: 717-533-8845
Fax: 717-533-8661
E-mail: cust@igi-global.com
Web site: http://www.igi-global.com

Copyright © 2020 by IGI Global. All rights reserved. No part of this publication may be reproduced, stored or distributed in any form or by any means, electronic or mechanical, including photocopying, without written permission from the publisher. Product or company names used in this set are for identification purposes only. Inclusion of the names of the products or companies does not indicate a claim of ownership by IGI Global of the trademark or registered trademark.

Library of Congress Cataloging-in-Publication Data

Names: Luna, Iviane Ramos de, 1964- editor.
Title: Sharing economy and the impact of collaborative consumption / Iviane Ramos de Luna, [and three others], editors.
Description: Hershey, PA : Business Science Reference, [2020]
Identifiers: LCCN 2019012881| ISBN 9781522599289 (hardcover) | ISBN 9781522599302 (ebook) | ISBN 9781522599296 (softcover)
Subjects: LCSH: Cooperation. | Economic development. | Consumption (Economics)
Classification: LCC HD2963 .S53 2020 | DDC 334--dc23 LC record available at https://lccn.loc.gov/2019012881

This book is published in the IGI Global book series Advances in Finance, Accounting, and Economics (AFAE) (ISSN: 2327-5677; eISSN: 2327-5685)

British Cataloguing in Publication Data
A Cataloguing in Publication record for this book is available from the British Library.

All work contributed to this book is new, previously-unpublished material. The views expressed in this book are those of the authors, but not necessarily of the publisher.

For electronic access to this publication, please contact: eresources@igi-global.com.

Advances in Finance, Accounting, and Economics (AFAE) Book Series

Ahmed Driouchi
Al Akhawayn University, Morocco

ISSN:2327-5677
EISSN:2327-5685

Mission

In our changing economic and business environment, it is important to consider the financial changes occurring internationally as well as within individual organizations and business environments. Understanding these changes as well as the factors that influence them is crucial in preparing for our financial future and ensuring economic sustainability and growth.

The **Advances in Finance, Accounting, and Economics (AFAE)** book series aims to publish comprehensive and informative titles in all areas of economics and economic theory, finance, and accounting to assist in advancing the available knowledge and providing for further research development in these dynamic fields.

Coverage

- Investments and Derivatives
- Risk Analysis and Management
- Fiscal Policy
- Accounting Standards
- Economic Downturn
- Applied Accounting
- Macroeconomics
- Economic Policy
- Entrepreneurship in Accounting and Finance
- Economics Geography

IGI Global is currently accepting manuscripts for publication within this series. To submit a proposal for a volume in this series, please contact our Acquisition Editors at Acquisitions@igi-global.com or visit: http://www.igi-global.com/publish/.

The Advances in Finance, Accounting, and Economics (AFAE) Book Series (ISSN 2327-5677) is published by IGI Global, 701 E. Chocolate Avenue, Hershey, PA 17033-1240, USA, www.igi-global.com. This series is composed of titles available for purchase individually; each title is edited to be contextually exclusive from any other title within the series. For pricing and ordering information please visit http://www.igi-global.com/book-series/advances-finance-accounting-economics/73685. Postmaster: Send all address changes to above address. Copyright © 2020 IGI Global. All rights, including translation in other languages reserved by the publisher. No part of this series may be reproduced or used in any form or by any means – graphics, electronic, or mechanical, including photocopying, recording, taping, or information and retrieval systems – without written permission from the publisher, except for non commercial, educational use, including classroom teaching purposes. The views expressed in this series are those of the authors, but not necessarily of IGI Global.

Titles in this Series

For a list of additional titles in this series, please visit:
https://www.igi-global.com/book-series/advances-finance-accounting-economics/73685

Financial Technology and Disruptive Innovation in ASEAN
Muhammad Anshari (Universiti Brunei Darussalam, Brunei) Mohammad Nabil Almunawar (Universiti Brunei Darussalam, Brunei) and Masairol Masri (Universiti Brunei Darussalam, Brunei)
Business Science Reference • copyright 2020 • 331pp • H/C (ISBN: 9781522591832) • US $195.00 (our price)

International Trade Policies in the Era of Globalization
Ahu Coşkun Özer (Marmara University, Turkey)
Business Science Reference • copyright 2020 • 363pp • H/C (ISBN: 9781522595663) • US $205.00 (our price)

Management Accounting Standards for Sustainable Business Practices
Ionica Oncioiu (Titu Maiorescu University, Romania) Gary Cokins (Analytics-Based Performance Management LLC, USA) Sorinel Căpuşneanu (Titu Maiorescu University, Romania) and Dan Ioan Topor (1 Decembrie 1918 University, Romania)
Business Science Reference • copyright 2020 • 350pp • H/C (ISBN: 9781799801788) • US $215.00 (our price)

Handbook of Research on Economic and Political Implications of Green Trading and Energy Use
Ramesh Chandra Das (Vidyasagar University, India)
Business Science Reference • copyright 2019 • 421pp • H/C (ISBN: 9781522585473) • US $225.00 (our price)

Emerging Research on Monetary Policy, Banking, and Financial Markets
Cristi Spulbar (University of Craiova, Romania) and Ramona Birau (Constantin Brâncuşi University of Targu Jiu, Romania)
Business Science Reference • copyright 2019 • 322pp • H/C (ISBN: 9781522592693) • US $195.00 (our price)

Modernization and Accountability in the Social Economy Sector
Augusta Ferreira (University of Aveiro, Portugal) Rui Marques (University of Aveiro, Portugal) Graça Azevedo (University of Aveiro, Portugal) Helena Inácio (University of Aveiro, Portugal) and Carlos Santos (University of Aveiro, Portugal)
Business Science Reference • copyright 2019 • 351pp • H/C (ISBN: 9781522584827) • US $215.00 (our price)

Foreign Business in China and Opportunities for Technological Innovation and Sustainable Economics
Anna Visvizi (Deree – The American College of Greece, Greece) Miltiadis Lytras (Deree – The American College of Greece, Greece) Xi Zhang (Tianjin University, China) and Jie Zhao (Anhui University, China)
Business Science Reference • copyright 2019 • 284pp • H/C (ISBN: 9781522589808) • US $195.00 (our price)

IGI Global
DISSEMINATOR OF KNOWLEDGE

701 East Chocolate Avenue, Hershey, PA 17033, USA
Tel: 717-533-8845 x100 • Fax: 717-533-8661
E-Mail: cust@igi-global.com • www.igi-global.com

Table of Contents

Detailed Table of Contents

The aim of this chapter is to analyze the different strategies that take Uber to join the global market successfully, positioning itself in different countries, and to analyze how these businesses and strategies that follow become successful to the extent that Uber is doing, not just one city but many in several countries around the world. In order to accomplish this, it is necessary to reference a previous literature review on collaborative economies business model that is appropriate to identify the different theories that may be applicable. As a result, the analysis of this work shows the determining factors that have placed Uber as one of the leading companies within its area of influence and ends with some recommendations on the conflicts that the firm presents when entering a new market.

Without an equivalent conventional form, reward-based crowdfunding (RBCF) brings in new concepts that demand deeper awareness by all stakeholders, so that they can acknowledge corresponding responsibilities. Despite famous intermediaries' nearly decadelong operations, the digestion of risks seems still incomplete, also hindering a solid evolution. This qualitative study is a step toward a more holistic understanding of success and manufactured risks of RBCF that have been left out of sight in studies so far. Lack of efficient visibility on projects' post-funding completion and limitless overfunding create potential conflicts of interest which threaten platforms' neutrality and sustainability. RBCF platforms must afford higher transparency and richer tools for managing the risks to tap their true potential. This chapter presents an overview of the major pitfalls of Kickstarter (KS) and Indiegogo (IGG) that can throw light on RBCF's general shortcomings, also offering a glimpse on two successfully funded but failed projects.

Sectors from hospitality, consumer finance, freelance services to taxis have been reshaped in the last few years due to the growth of online access-based sharing platforms. Notable examples of such platforms are Airbnb (accommodation services), Lyft (mobility), TaskRabbit (freelancing), and Kickstarter (peer lending). The chapter posits that access-based sharing platforms are subject to an evolution from "peer-to-peer" (P2P) to "integrated" forms, where the platform owner adopts a series of governance mechanisms aimed at providing effective safeguarding, adaptation, and measurement features to transactions. The level of transaction frequency, uncertainty, and specificity is a strategic decision taken by the owner to grow the platform. The management of transaction features generates transaction costs and determines the need, by the platform members and by the platform owner, to adopt specific mechanisms of platform integration. The chapter concludes with a call for scholars to intensify empirical evaluation of the important and growing phenomena identified in the chapter.

Section 3
Collaborative Consumption and Consumer Behavior

The recent proliferation of collaborative models of consumption has called attention of organizations, governments, and the academy to understand the impact of these new forms of consumption on the economic scenario. However, specific efforts to understand the changes in consumer behavior are so far scarce. This chapter compiles the available knowledge on how consumers are coping with these new forms of consumption exploring the motivators and obstacles affecting their behavior. Additionally, some relevant information on the current status of the adoption of different forms of collaborative consumption, the collaborative consumer profile, as well as some perspectives for the future are also explored.

The growth in the use of online platforms in the sharing economy is generating great interest in the scientific community. This study seeks to discover what causes travelers to use ridesharing platforms. A theoretical model of causal relationships, evaluated with data collected in an online survey, using partial least squares structural equation modelling (PLS-SEM) is proposed. The results show that attitude towards ridesharing is a critical antecedent of intention to use. Travelers develop positive attitudes mainly due to the economic reward of making savings in travel costs. In addition, attitude is also positively influenced, although to a lesser extent, by perceptions of security and by the moral motivation to help other people. In contrast, the influence of social motivation is not significant. Practical implications guide platform managers in the design of their commercial strategies.

With the development of new shared transportation services, changes are occurring in the habitual consumption of these kinds of services, and it is expected that this trend will continue in the coming years. Given the rise of public bicycle-sharing systems (PBSS) and the increase in their use as a new mode of transportation in many cities, it is considered necessary to analyze and understand the main aspects that determine satisfaction with PBSS. This chapter proposes 10 aspects related to PBSS, grouped according to service infrastructure and other factors that are typical of this service. The results show that all the variables maintain a significant relationship with the established levels of satisfaction. In addition, it has been demonstrated that concessionaires and town halls must take special interest in the quality of the city's bicycles, bike lanes, and network of stations.

The rise of the platform economy is rapidly changing the traditional economic and business environment. The phenomenon is being widely studied in academia, although so far this has taken a general approach. Lack of precise data and differences in markets hinder more specific analyses that could illustrate the real impact of these trends. This chapter offers an exploratory study of the impact of food-delivery platforms on urban logistics. The study is based on data scraped from the app of the Barcelona-based Glovo, consisting of affiliated restaurants, delivery times, and cost of the delivery. The physical premises identified for the restaurants were georeferenced to study how they are spread and clustered in the city. Restaurants were also matched to their parent companies to obtain economic data from the specialist SABI database. The research questions aim to provide understanding of what types of restaurants have joined the platform, how this has affected their annual turnover, where their physical premises are located, and how the consumer's location affects the service.

Using survey data from an online Spanish university, real and perceived financial literacy levels, social interactions and personal trust with the social network are measured as key elements for collaborative finance development. This is the first study regarding the factors that may affect the use of collaborative finance. Results show levels of financial literacy are quiet low as in prior studies and individuals consider that the bank manager, friends, and parents can manage financial issues better than them, with the last two peers being those who most trust to discuss financial issues. The findings also provide information about how little individuals trust online networks when it comes to financial matters. Besides, respondents interact moderately with their social network missing the benefits of peer-to-peer learning. Overall, lack of financial literacy, low social interaction, and personal trust may be affecting the short use of collaborative financial services.

As the sharing economy is transforming the profile, preferences, and expectations of travel and tourism demand, technology becomes an essential element in understanding how tourists change their behavior and consumption patterns. The digital nature of tourism is determined by 1) analogical by digital tourism

Preface

The emergence of new technologies in recent years has been something very disruptive in contemporary society. A fact that have been transforming people's behavior and that still promises great changes, both socially and economically.

As a consequence of the introduction of new technology and technology services around the world, as well as technological and information empowerment by the consumer, new business models have begun to emerge. Added to these factors, the literature shows that people are turned away from ethical consumption because of economical and institutional reasons (Hamari, Sjöklint, & Ukkonen, 2016; Bray, Johns, & Kilburn, 2011; Eckhardt, Belk, & Devinney, 2010), yet with the development of these new ways of consumption through the sharing economy, such as collaborative consumption, these issues are addressed and potentially overcome.

The so-called Sharing Economy not only brings business models that offer new services or products using technology, but also propose the mission of creating a cleaner, cheaper and more equitable world. However, the main innovation in the business model of the sharing economy lies in the technological platforms and mobile apps which bring demand and supply together and group them in a way which was not possible before, quicker, cheaper and on a larger scale, including geographically (Basselier, Langenus, & Walravens).

In this way, the sharing economy brings many benefits to consumers, entrepreneurs and the environment. For this reason, in the last decade, the sharing economy has grown from a marginal concept to an economic powerhouse. Statista (2019) predicts that the total value of the global sharing economy will increase to some 335 billion U.S. dollars by 2025, from only 15 billion U.S. dollars in 2014. However, this phenomenon has already generated a significant and extremely rapid impact in several sectors, especially tourism and mobility. For example, Hilton hotels took 93 years to build 600,000 rooms, while home-sharing site Airbnb added that number to its platform in just four years (Pennington, 2017).

Companies and entrepreneurs can see this significant change in people's behavior as both an opportunity and a threat. Experts claim that whatever your organization is today, sharing economic is a great opportunity to lose - or a too great risk to not mitigate. Moreover, in this new context, the real and immediate challenge for participants in mature industries is to avoid being interrupted.

On the other hand, the introduction of these new business models based on sharing has been very fast and as a consequence, many political and regulatory issues have arisen since it seems that existing ones are not suitable for these business models. Currently, the informal nature of collaborative consumption in many cases allows individuals to circumvent local regulations that companies offering similar services must follow. These companies may have to pay licensing or other regulatory fees to operate legally.

This reality together with the rapid development of the shared economy brings with it the need and the urgency to expand the knowledge related to the collaborative consumption, as well as to explore and discuss more deeply the impact that this industry has in the economy, industry and society of different countries.

For this reason, the purpose of this book is to present in different perspectives the impact that the sharing economy and collaborative consumption are having on society and markets. As well as the importance of the sharing economy development in the coming years, dealing with relevant issues such as regulations, the technological aspects involved in these sharing platforms, the impact in different sectors and the consumer behavior in relation to these services.

In this way, this book aims to be highly multidisciplinary, establishing links between economics, finance, marketing, sociology and information technology. This contribution synthesizes how the sharing economy is related to each field and will help researchers expand and improve their understanding of this topic and identify new research problems in all of these areas.

ORGANIZATION OF THE BOOK

The book is organized into three sections in which thirteen chapters are distributed. Section 1, "Sharing Economy and Its Impact on Society"; Section 2, "Digital Platforms as a Sharing Economy Channel"; and Section 3, "Collaborative Consumption as the Protagonist of Changes in Consumer Behavior" (see Figure 1).

The first section describes in three chapters the aspects related to the impacts generated by the shared economy in regulations, in business models and in the target of a more sustainable development.

Chapter 1 review and identify the success factor of sharing economy business model and discusses the unique features of sharing economy practices considering the concept of value sharing.

Chapter 2 analyzes not only the impact of a changing business model but, specifically, how stakeholders, cities and regulators, should approach this moving target called sharing economy and for that, introduce the regulatory hurdles that come associated with the previous and mapping out its different futures.

Chapter 3 aims present the impact of collaborative consumption on the 10 Sustainable Development Goals of the United Nations to better understand that new economic paradigm in the economic system.

The second section is composed of five chapters that describe how some of the most successful digital platforms, positioned themselves as part of the sharing economy, are coordinating supply and demand of products and services that in their present form were previously unavailable on the market.

Figure 1. Theoretical book structure

Chapter 4 studied how prices are formed in Airbnb, focusing the analysis on a wide sample of accommodations listed in Barcelona (Spain). Some of the results exposed indicate that contextual factors, lodging amenities and some hosts' attributes critically influence pricing in the digital platform

Chapter 5 provides reliable information from online platforms that quantifies the impact of tourist accommodation in Granada in relation to commercial activities, hotels and residential homes. The results of this research can be extremely useful for residents, local government and stakeholders in general in order to take action on this field.

Chapter 6 aims to analyze the different strategies that take Uber to join the global market successfully, positioning itself in different countries and analyze how come these businesses and strategies that follow to become successful to the extent that Uber is doing, not just one city but in several countries around the world.

Chapter 7 give a more holistic understanding of success and manufactured risks of reward-based crowdfunding (RBCF) and an overview of the major pitfalls of Kickstarter (KS) and Indiegogo (IGG) that can throw light on RBCF's general shortcomings, also offering a glimpse on two successfully funded but failed projects.

Chapter 8 present an overview on the governance strategies of sharing platforms, postulating that access-based sharing platforms are subject to an evolution from "peer-to-peer" (P2P) to "integrated" forms, where the platform owner adopts a series of governance mechanisms aimed at providing effective safeguarding, adaptation, and measurement features to transactions.

The third section consists of six chapters, which explore the impact of collaborative consumption in consumer behavior and how this new business model has changed indeed the way of consuming goods and services.

Chapter 9 recompile the available knowledge on how consumers are coping with these new forms of consumption exploring the motivators and obstacles affecting their behavior. Additionally, some relevant information on the status of the adoption of different forms of collaborative consumption, the collaborative consumer profile as well as some perspectives for the future are also explored.

Chapter 10 seeks to discover what causes travelers to use ridesharing platforms and for this purpose a theoretical model of causal relationships, evaluated with data collected in an online survey, using partial least squares structural equation modelling (PLS-SEM) is proposed.

Chapter 11 proposes ten aspects related to public bicycle-sharing systems (PBSS), grouped according to service infrastructure and other factors that are typical of this service. Based on results, the authors show implications to concessionaires and town halls about the quality of the city's bicycles, bike lanes and network of stations.

Chapter 12 offers an exploratory study of the impact of food-delivery platforms on urban logistics based on data scraped from the app of the Barcelona-based Glovo, consisting of affiliated restaurants, delivery times and cost of the delivery.

Chapter 13 measured the real and perceived financial literacy levels, social interactions and personal trust with the social network as key elements for collaborative finance development.

Chapter 14 makes an original contribution by proposing a classification of digital tourists based on the use of technology supporting the tourist experience based on a sample of tourists in Barcelona.

We hope the content of this book will be interesting to readers and will contribute to future research in this area as a source of relevant knowledge, allowing researchers to explore more deeply how sharing economy and collaborative consumption are transforming contemporary society and how companies, governments and users can adapt to this new reality.

Iviane Ramos de Luna
Open University of Catalonia, Spain

Àngels Fitó-Bertran
Open University of Catalonia, Spain

Josep Lladós-Masllorens
Open University of Catalonia, Spain

Francisco Liébana-Cabanillas
University of Granada, Spain

REFERENCES

Basselier, R., Langenus, G., & Walravens, L. (2018). The rise of the sharing economy. *NBB Economic Review*, 57-78. Retrieved from https://www.nbb.be/doc/ts/publications/economicreview/2018/ecorev-iii2018_h3.pdf

Bray, J., Johns, N., & Kilburn, D. (2011). An exploratory study into the factors impeding ethical consumption. *Journal of Business Ethics*, *98*(4), 597–608. doi:10.100710551-010-0640-9

Eckhardt, G. M., Belk, R., & Devinney, T. M. (2010). Why don't consumers consume ethically? *Journal of Consumer Behaviour*, *9*(6), 426–436. doi:10.1002/cb.332

Hamari, J., Sjöklint, M., & Ukkonen, A. (2016). The sharing economy: Why people participate in collaborative consumption. *Journal of the Association for Information Science and Technology*, *67*(9), 2047–2059. doi:10.1002/asi.23552

Pennington, J. (2007). *The numbers that make China the world's largest sharing economy*. World Economic Forum. Annual Meeting of the New Champions. Retrieved from https://www.weforum.org/agenda/2017/06/china-sharing-economy-in-numbers/

Statista. (2019). *Value of the sharing economy worldwide in 2014 and 2025 (in billion U.S. dollars)*. Retrieved from https://www.statista.com/statistics/830986/value-of-the-global-sharing-economy/

Acknowledgment

The editors would like to acknowledge the help of all the people involved in this project and, more specifically, to the authors and reviewers that took part in the review process. Without their support, this book would not have become a reality.

First, the editors would like to thank each one of the authors for their contributions. Our sincere gratitude goes to the chapter's authors who contributed their time and expertise to this book.

Second, the editors wish to acknowledge the valuable contributions of the reviewers regarding the improvement of quality, coherence, and content presentation of chapters. Most of the authors also served as referees; we highly appreciate their double task.

Finally, the editors would like to give special thanks to Maria Rohde and all members of Development Team of IGI Global for their support in this project.

Iviane Ramos de Luna
Open University of Catalonia, Spain

Àngels Fitó-Bertran
Open University of Catalonia, Spain

Josep Lladós-Masllorens
Open University of Catalonia, Spain

Francisco Liébana-Cabanillas
University of Granada, Spain

Section 1
Sharing Economy Beyond Collaborative Consumption

Chapter 1
A Conceptual Framework of Value Sharing in the Sharing Economy

Melissa Farboudi Jahromi
University of Central Florida, USA

Tingting Zhang
University of Central Florida, USA

ABSTRACT

The sharing economy is a fast-growing phenomenon that has significantly disrupted traditional businesses. In order to identify the success factor of this new business model, this chapter discusses the unique features of sharing economy practices considering the concept of value sharing. First, the theoretical foundation of value sharing is explained using the value co-creation literature, which is derived from the service logics. Next, four types of values, namely economic, social, functional, and hedonic, are discussed in sharing economy practices. Finally, a conceptual framework of value sharing that depicts the benefits and costs of participation in the sharing economy is provided. Based on this framework, sharing each aforementioned value has its own benefits, which acts as an incentive for both resource suppliers and consumers in the sharing economy. However, the sharing process has its own costs that may be considered as a deterrent for sharing economy participants.

INTRODUCTION

The mode of consumption has been changing from ownership to access during recent years because of the shift in consumers' perception of value and the advancement of technology (Frenken & Schor, 2017). With the advent of online platforms that has made unlimited number of tangible and intangible resources accessible, ownership has lost its value in the consumers' mind (Bardhi & Eckhardt, 2012). Consumers believe that access to resources is associated with fewer risks than ownership, for example, they believe that the potential financial and social loss is greater in the purchase of a product than in the

DOI: 10.4018/978-1-5225-9928-9.ch001

This chapter published as an Open Access Chapter distributed under the terms of the Creative Commons Attribution License (http://creativecommons.org/licenses/by/4.0/) which permits unrestricted use, distribution, and production in any medium, provided the author of the original work and original publication source are properly credited.

free or fee-based access to the product (Schaefers, Lawson, & Kular-Kinny, 2016). All these new changes and beliefs have created a sharing practice named "sharing economy" in which individuals share their resources with others through online networks and promote the culture of collaborative consumption (Bucher, Fieseler, & Lutz, 2016). Sharing economy practices, which are seen in different sectors such as Airbnb in the lodging sector and Uber in the transportation sector, have become very popular and started to disrupt traditional businesses (Henten & Windekilde, 2016). Thus, researchers and practitioners have become interested in knowing the success factors of these practices.

Prior studies on the success factors of sharing economy majorly investigated the factors that motivate consumers to participate in the sharing economy. For example, using Self-Determination Theory, Hamari, Sjöklint, and Ukkonen (2016) found that the economic outcome is the major extrinsic motivation and enjoyment and reputation are the major intrinsic motivations for individuals to participate in the sharing economy, or, using a sustainability framework, Böcker and Meelen (2017) found that economic, social and environmental factors are the major drivers of accommodation sharing, meal sharing, and ride sharing respectively. Although these studies identified the general motivation categories of the participation in the sharing economy (e.g., economic and social motivations), they didn't investigate the specific motivators of each category. In addition, although value is an integral element in the sharing economy (Zhang, Gu, & Jahromi, 2018a), the studies didn't address the concept of 'value sharing' and didn't explore the drivers of the sharing economy using a value sharing perspective. Furthermore, prior studies mostly focused on the consumers' motivation and overlooked the suppliers' motivation to participate in sharing economy practices. Thus, in order to address the gaps in the sharing economy literature, this chapter aims to provide a conceptual framework of value sharing in the sharing economy by discussing the general and specific values that may drive and the costs that may deter both suppliers and consumers to adopt/readopt the sharing economy.

To achieve the above-mentioned objectives, the current chapter is developed as follows: first, the background of the sharing economy including evolving definitions and industry practices will be reviewed. Second, the concept of value sharing and its relation with value co-creation will be discussed. Next, four types of economic, social, functional, and hedonic values that are intrinsic in the sharing economy activities will be explained from the perspectives of suppliers and consumers. Fourth, a conceptual framework of value sharing will be provided adopting the Social Exchange Theory (Figure 1). According to this theory, in addition to the perceived values of any exchange (i.e., the sharing economy), perceived costs should be considered as the antecedent of participation in that exchange. Thus, in this section, first, the benefits, and, then, the costs inherent in sharing economy practices will be discussed.

BACKGROUND

The sharing economy has changed the classic notion of economic transaction by promoting collaborative consumption of products and services (Schor, 2016). This new economy practice is defined as sharing under-utilized human and non-human resources with others typically at an affordable price or free through online platforms (Frenken & Schor, 2017; Kathan, Matzler & Veider, 2016; Stephany, 2015). The sharing economy is found in different types of businesses, for example, in transportation, when a car owner gives a paid/free ride to his peers (e.g., Uber); in lodging, when a condo owner rents his condo while he is not using it (e.g., Airbnb); and in dining, when a chef shares paid/free dining experiences with others (e.g., Feastly). These peer-to-peer businesses have significantly disrupted traditional firms recently (Henten & Windekilde, 2016); for example, Airbnb has 4 million listings in 191 countries worldwide, which is greater than the number of listings held by Marriott, Hilton, Wyndham, Hyatt, and Intercontinental hotels combined (Hartmans, 2017), or the value of Uber is estimated at $120 billion, which is almost equal to General Motors, Ford, and Tesla combined (Ivanova, 2018). The unquestioned success of sharing economy companies highlights the unique characteristics of their business model, which are not seen in the traditional business model.

Sharing, the core feature of the sharing economy business model, goes beyond what is mine and yours to something as ours (Belk, 2010), which necessitates a harmonious peer-to-peer interaction (Frenken & Schor, 2017). Thus, what differentiates the sharing economy from the traditional economy is the type and level of interactions among participants (Dillahunt & Malone, 2015; Hawlitschek et al., 2016). First, interactions occur among peers who typically do not know each other, so they need to build trust in the initial step to be able to develop interactions (Hawlitschek et al., 2016). Second, interactions occur in both online and offline environments (Möhlmann 2016). In the online environment, resource suppliers and consumers adopt an online platform to initiate the interaction. The boundary between suppliers/consumers is not clear in the online environment because both sides are considered as consumers of an online service (Grönroos & Voima, 2013). However, in the offline environment, the boundary between the suppliers and consumers is clear from the perspective of product/service provision but blurred from the perspective of sharing, which is a mutual relationship (Narasimhan et al., 2018). Thus, in the real sharing phase, both sides are required to cooperate harmoniously with each other to make the sharing practice agreeable.

The other key feature of the sharing economy is the mode of consumption (Frenken & Schor, 2017). In sharing, two or more individuals may receive the benefits and costs of possessing a product/service through having access to it without actually possessing it. Thus, the mode of consumption in the sharing economy is 'access' to resources enabled through digital technology (Frenken & Schor, 2017). Historically, access was considered as an inferior mode of consumption compared to ownership; however, with the emergence of online information societies, peer-to-peer communities, and access-based platforms, consumers' perceived value shifted from owning tangible resources to having access to an unlimited number of both tangible and intangible resources (Bardhi & Eckhardt, 2012). In addition, the digital world changed the solid consumers' identity and property relations to fluid ones. More particularly, consumers change desires and values constantly, and prefer access as the transient mode of consumption since it provides them with more temporality and flexiblity (Bardhi, Eckhardt & Arnould, 2012).

Considering the triple-p (people-planet-profit) framework of sustainability (Elkington, 1998), the access mode of consumption in the sharing economy is associated with different types of economic, social, and environmental advantages at the macro level. At the economic level, the sharing economy is able to break the boundaries of centralized bureaucratic entities by promoting decentralized peer-to-peer markets (Acquier, Daudigeos & Pinkse, 2017). Advocates of the sharing economy believe that this new model of business results in the decreased monopoly of big corporations, and an increased transparency and control over the economy (Hasan & Birgach, 2016). At the social level, the sharing economy may create new forms of social bonding and cohesion by providing cheap access to underutilized resources at the community level and by promoting a collaborative lifestyle (Acquier et al., 2017; Heinrichs, 2013). Finally, at the environmental level, the sharing economy involves the redistribution of resources and sustainable consumption, which are associated with the decrease of resource depletion, production, waste, and carbon emissions (Frenken & Schor, 2017). An example from prior research showed that car sharing in the US has reduced carbon emission by about 482,170 tons per year (Kathan et al., 2016).

In addition to the macro-level impacts of sharing economy practices, sharing economy suppliers and consumers share and enjoy different types of value at the micro level, which is the focus of the current chapter. These micro values will be discussed in the context of value co-creation in the following section, and, then, conceptualized as a value sharing framework using Social Exchange Theory.

THE SHARING ECONOMY AND VALUE CO-CREATION

The concept of value sharing is derived from value co-creation (Grönroos, 2012), which is based on the service logics (Service-Dominant Logic and Service Science Logic) (Vargo & Lusch, 2010), highlighting the transformative role of consumers from a merely external passive factor to a crucial active actor in production and consumption processes. The investigation journey of value co-creation should begin with defining the concept of value. There are many considerations in prior works regarding the definition of value in the process of value co-creation. The changing definitions mainly depend on various factors such as market trends and consumers' needs (Troisi, Carrubbo, Maione, & Torre, 2016). Scholars perceive value as an inherent factor in the production process (process value) (Cova, Dalli, & Zwick, 2011), the product produced (market value) (Cova et al., 2011), the service provided (service value) (Aarikka-Stenroos & Jaakkola, 2012), and consumers' perception (consumer value) (Prahalad & Ramaswamy, 2004). There are many other value terminologies such as the value for third parties (stakeholder value) (Hammedi, Kandampully, Zhang, & Bouquiaux, 2015), the value for investors (shareholder value) (Birch & Parulava, 2017), and the value of a network (network value) (Chung, 2017), or a system (system value) (Vargo & Lusch, 2010).

The use of the term value in the business management literature is elusive (Grönroos, 2008). Originally, value was embedded in the foundation of economics and the theory of market exchange (Saarijärvi, Kannan, & Kuusela, 2013). The terms 'value-in-exchange' and 'value-in-use' were identified reflecting the interpretations of value and value creation (Vargo, Maglio, & Akaka, 2008). Goods-Dominant (G-D) logic, known as traditional marketing theory, emphasizes the "value-in-exchange" nature of the term (Vargo & Lusch, 2008). In G-D logic, a company manufactures value and distributes value to customers and markets in exchange for monetary gains (Vargo & Lusch, 2008). Based on G-D Logic, value is in the form of goods exchanged through the market (Grönroos & Voima, 2013); therefore, value is measured by exchanging activities in transactions (Vargo et al., 2008). Later, the Service-Dominant (S-D) Logic was proposed, strengthening "value-in-use" in market mechanisms (Lusch & Vargo, 2006).

The S-D logic advocates that value is jointly created between companies and consumers: both parties apply their resources, for example skills and knowledge to manufacture (company side) or to utilize (consumer side) goods (Lusch & Vargo, 2006). Goods that are produced by companies are perceived by consumers to have value only when they are utilized by consumers who acknowledge that the adoption of these products has improved their well-being/welfare (Grönroos, 2011). For example, a car company applies knowledge, resources, skills, and capabilities to transform raw materials into cars. S-D Logic argues that these cars are mere inputs into the value creation process and if consumers use the cars, the process will be completed (e.g., for driving, self-identity, and other purposes). If consumers don't know how to drive or don't use the cars to identify their social status, then vehicles themselves have no value. S-D Logic suggests that value is always co-created jointly and reciprocally in interactions between suppliers and beneficiaries through integration of resources and application of competences (Grönroos, 2011); therefore, the roles of producers and consumers are not separated from each other in S-D logic

(Grönroos & Voima, 2013). Recently, researchers have proposed Service Science Logic on the basis of S-D Logic by emphasizing the collaboration and adaptation in value co-creation (Saarijärvi et al., 2013).

Service Science Logic also terms value as "value-in-use" and builds a balanced and interdependent ecosystem of reciprocal service provision (Grönroos, 2011). The systems in Service Science logic may refer to individuals or crowds that exchange and apply resources, skills, and knowledge with other systems (Saarijärvi et al., 2013). Therefore, these systems engage in value co-creation activities by communications (Vargo et al., 2008). It is critical to note that consumers are the center of the value creation in the Service Science Logic (Grönroos, 2011). Companies only create values when they work with consumers in a direct manner (Vargo et al., 2008).

The fast-growing market dynamics are increasingly driving the co-creation of value in the collaboration and interaction mechanisms, which foster the emergence of new business models. The sharing economy is one of these emerging business models that echoes the importance of value co-creation and collaborative consumption (Troisi et al., 2016). The sharing economy links all stakeholders, resources, skills, and services shared among suppliers and consumers. In this regard, the sharing economy is considered as a complex logic involving a plurality of parties which are not properly defined as mere suppliers or consumers, rather, as active participating actors in the whole value creation and sharing process (Akbar & Tracogna, 2018). This notion emphasizes that values should be shared in a collaborative approach, and self-interest should be replaced by collaborative interests (Troisi et al., 2016). Also, it promotes inclusive relations to enhance the sustainability of resource and value sharing.

Since value sharing is an important concept derived from the integration of value co-creation and the sharing economy, it is necessary to decompose the value propositions for further considerations. Prior researchers suggested different types of value considering the nature of the value generated by the consumption of a product. For example, Sheth, Newman, and Gross (1991) introduced five types of value associated with the consumption of a product: functional value for the perceived performance of a product, social value for the perceived sociability associated with the consumption of a product, epistemic value for the knowledge gained through the consumption of a product, emotional value for the feelings aroused by the consumption of a product, and conditional value for the value acquired through the consumption of a product in a specific condition such as emergency. Although this categorization is one of the most comprehensive ones, it was developed for the consumption of retailing goods and not for the sharing economy goods/services. Thus, the current chapter adopted the value propositions – namely economic, social, functional (technical), and hedonic (emotional) values-- developed by Zhang et al. (2018a) specifically for the sharing economy context.

Many business reviews and marketers declared that economic value was their selling point in the initial startup of sharing economy businesses in the 2000s (Blal, Singal, & Templin, 2018; Guttentag & Smith, 2017; Traum, 2015). Economic value transforms people's behaviors from owning one object/service to sharing goods/services to gain a wider accessibility and mutual benefits. For example, Airbnb has found a strong price sensitivity relating to consumer value and intention to repurchase the accommodation service (Blal et al., 2018). Another value proposition, social value, is seen in the consumption of the sharing economy goods/services. In today's interconnected world, facilitated with high-speed internet and communication tools, e.g., cell phones (Zhu, So, & Hudson, 2017), social networking sites (Edwards, Cheng, Wong, Zhang, & Wu, 2017), and wearable technologies (Lee, Chan, Balaji, & Chong, 2016), establishing social connections and mingling with like-minded peers is deemed inseparable from a quality and healthy life. Prior empirical research showed that consumers of Airbnb (Zhang, Jahromi &

Kizildag, 2018b) and Uber (Zhu et al., 2017), two popular sharing economy businesses, perceived the social value of the sharing economy when they made friends during their consumption.

Similar to economic value, functional value is a utilitarian aspect that plays an important role in the value sharing model of the sharing economy (Edwards et al., 2017; Zhang et al., 2018b). For example, many users tend to consider the functional value propositions such as convenience, problem-solving or flexibility features when sharing accommodations, rides, meals, and even pets,. In a study conducted by Zhang et al. (2018a), the qualitative interviews with sharing economy users indicated that participants seek sharing accommodation services because of the flexibility of booking/reservation schedules, detailed instructions, and professional service quality. The interview results revealed the important role of functional value in the sharing economy service renderings.

Last but not least, hedonic value, which is of a more subjective nature than other values (Holbrook & Hirschman, 1982) is grounded in the sharing economy (Zhang et al., 2018a). Zhang et al. (2018b) demonstrated that the feeling of joy and pleasant surprises from the sharing economy experiences were highly valued by users and were identified as one of the major influential factors in their decision-making process. Examples of hedonic value offerings include the occasions in which Airbnb hosts have hot and cold beverages available for consumers along with a fresh fruit assortment, or Uber drivers and consumers exchange pleasant conversational information.

A CONCEPTUAL FRAMEWORK OF VALUE SHARING IN THE SHARING ECONOMY

Zeithaml (1988) defines value as a *consumer's overall assessment of the utility of a product based on perceptions of what is received and what is given* (p. 14). This definition indicates that the notion of social exchange is inherent in value sharing. Thus, drawing upon the Social Exchange Theory, this section conceptualizes the benefits and costs of value sharing in sharing economy practices. According to the Social Exchange Theory, a social interaction is an exchange in which participants seek to maximize benefits and minimize costs (Homans, 1958). As mentioned earlier, the sharing economy involves peer-to-peer interactions in which peers use a cost-benefit analysis to assess if the benefits outweigh the costs. If so, peers will initiate and keep the interactions. Now, the question is what are the costs and benefits of economic, social, functional, and hedonic value sharing for resource suppliers and consumers in the sharing economy?

In the following section, a conceptual framework of value sharing in the sharing economy will be provided (Figure 1). The value sharing framework depicts suppliers' and consumers' motivation to participate in the sharing economy despite its associated costs. Considering this framework, the benefits inherent in each mentioned value will be discussed first. For economic value, monetary profits, time efficiency, and control over the transaction will be considered as participation incentives, adopting from the study by Seign and Bogenberger (2012). For social value, social connection and spontaneous sociability will be discussed as motivators. Prior studies show that making social connection is the primary social factor that motivate individuals to participate in the sharing economy (e.g., Cohen & Kietzmann, 2014; Tussyadiah, 2015). However, some scholars believe that social connections made through the sharing economy do not last long (Parigi & State, 2014), which implies the possibility of spontaneous sociability in the sharing economy experiences. For functional value, usefulness, ease of use, and service quality will be considered. Davis (1989) asserted that usefulness and ease of use are the major factors of functional value, while Zhang et al. (2018b) found that service quality also plays an important role in the experience of functional value in the sharing economy. For hedonic value, emotional and sensory arousal will be explained in the sharing economy. These two factors were proposed by Smith and Colgate (2007) as the primary dimensions of hedonic value. In addition to the benefits, the most important costs of participation in the sharing economy including safety issues (Frenken & Schor, 2017), threat to privacy (Lutz, Hoffmann, Bucher & Fieseler, 2018), and financial loss (Mithun, 2012) will be explained. The costs are not associated with a specific value since they are inherent in the whole process of sharing and may involve multiple economic and social notions at the same time.

Economic Value Sharing

Sharing goods and services is considered as a utility maximizing behavior which serves as a motivation tool to save economic resources and create economic values (Hamari et al., 2016). In the sharing economy, participants believe that 'saving money', 'saving time', and 'having autonomy' are the most prominent economic values of their sharing practices (Seign & Bogenberger, 2012). In the accommodation sharing, Airbnb owners shares an economic value with Airbnb guests by renting their extra rooms/apartments at lower prices than the ones offered by established hotels, while Airbnb guests generate a source of income for owners by staying in their underused rooms/apartments. Another example of monetary value of sharing is seen in the urban car-sharing. Decrease of vehicle mileage and savings in fuel and accidents allow car-sharing participants to decrease their transportation costs in half (Fellows & Pitfield, 2000). In addition, the elimination of intermediaries and direct flow of value between suppliers and consumers decrease costs in sharing economy practices (Schor, 2016). Airbnb owners, for example, are not required to pay to list their properties, and both owners and guests pay a small fee for the transaction. Thus, both parties enjoy low costs and monetary profits, which are considered as an incentive to participate in the sharing practice (Frenken & Schor, 2017).

Another economic value associated with sharing is making efficient use of time (Hamari et al., 2016). Resource suppliers such as Uber drivers typically use their free time to give rides to others, while Uber users may make time for other activities such as reading a book or responding to an email by using this service. Another example of time efficiency is found in LifeLearn, a platform for the skill sharing. Skill owners such as photographers, football players, and mathematicians may use their free time to teach and share their skills with others, while skill learners may save time by finding and learning their skills of interest quickly rather than taking long educational/academic courses. Thus, saving time as an economic resource motivates individuals to participate in sharing economy practices (Seign & Bogenberger, 2012).

Last but not least, the sharing economy allows its participants to control their transaction process (Kim, Yoon & Zo, 2015); for example, Airbnb owners can set the price for their holdings and decide how much to charge per night, week, or month, while Airbnb guests may compare the price of different properties and choose the best one based on their budget (Henten & Windekilde, 2016). They can also contact Airbnb hosts and ask for a discount. Another example of transaction control is found in the meal sharing economy. In Feastly or Eatwith platforms, hosts can set any price for the meals they provide, or even showcase their cooking skills for free, while guests can choose their favorite meal considering the price, time, and location. Kim et al. (2015) believe that having autonomy in sharing economy practices is a competitive advantage not seen in traditional economy practices.

Social Value Sharing

As discussed earlier, value is co-created via a mutually beneficial relationship (Grönroos, 2011), which necessitates the presence of at least two individuals and embraces their social interaction. In the sharing economy, when two strangers engage in a sharing practice, they have the opportunity to both develop a 'social connection' and experience 'spontaneous sociability', which act as an incentive to drive and continue sharing. Previous studies showed that people participate in the accommodation sharing because it allows them to have meaningful interactions with hosts and other guests and create memorable experiences with them (Tussyadiah, 2015; Tussyadiah & Pesonen, 2016). Airbnb consumers' experiences show that, in some cases, the hosts picked up the guests from the airport, prepared meals for them, provided them with local information, or even spent time socializing with them (Schor, 2015). These examples indicate the possibility of social connection through sharing, which can be found at a higher level in other sharing economy practices such as the meal or skill sharing, in which resource suppliers and consumers have less economic motivations (Böcker & Meelen, 2017). For instance, Fitzmaurice et al. (2018) found that TaskRabbit, an online marketplace that matches freelance labor with local demand, helped participants develop social networks they can trust.

All the above-mentioned social connections have a unique feature, the experience of self-expansion, which is not seen in social connections created in contexts other than that of the sharing economy. Belk (2013) believes that possessions are a part of individuals' extended selves; therefore, when sharing economy participants share their materialized (e.g., a room) and non-materialized (e.g., privacy) possessions, they, in fact, share their extended selves and expand their selves' boundaries to embrace others. If participants perceive this experience as pleasant, they may become more willing to participate in social value sharing. Some researchers believe that social connections created through the sharing economy are not durable (Parigi & State, 2014). If so, such casual connections are not valueless since they are embedded in the concept of spontaneous sociability, which is essential to today's fast-paced life.

Spontaneous sociability is defined as *the ability of strangers to trust one another and work together in new, flexible forms of organization* and is *the most important form of sociability from an economic standpoint* (Fukuyama, 1995; p. 91). The sharing economy involves economic transactions among strangers who need to trust each other, and so spontaneous sociability is critical to this phenomenon. Considering this feature, participation in the sharing economy is a dynamic activity which may vary by the level of intensity. For example, millennials who would like to have spontaneous experiences and assess them as they happen (Bottomley & Burgess, 2018), may trust strangers in the accommodation sharing easily, form transactions and interactions with them enthusiastically, and fulfill their needs using an intensive level of spontaneous sociability. The concept of spontaneous sociability has been discussed in the context of social media usage (Smith and Gallicano, 2015), which is similar to participation in the sharing economy in terms of the opportunity to interact with strangers spontaneously. However, the degree of interpersonal trust should be higher in sharing economy practices since interactions mainly involve strangers as opposed to social media, which involves both families/friends and strangers. All in all, the social characteristic of the sharing economy acts as a catalyst for resource suppliers' and consumers' participation and makes it distinctive from a traditional economy (Botsman & Rogers, 2011).

Functional Value Sharing

Functional value refers to the degree to which a product/service performs well (Smith and Colgate, 2007). In order to assess this value, researchers consider various dimensions from reliability to quality. In the sharing economy context, since participants engage with online and offline services, the functionality dimensions that apply to both environments are considered. In the online environment, individuals perceive 'usefulness', the degree to which the product/service enhances an individual's performance, and 'ease of use', the degree to which the usage of the product/service is free of effort, as the most important functional values (Davis, 1989). In the sharing economy, participants enjoy usefulness since online platforms allow suppliers to share their underutilized resources and allow consumers to find what they need easily. In addition, the possibility of online transaction enables both suppliers and consumers to accomplish their tasks quickly. Sharing economy participants also consider ease of use as a functional feature of the sharing economy since its online platforms are typically user-friendly and provide clear and understandable information, which make interactions and transactions effortless.

In the offline environment of the sharing economy, 'service quality', is the most critical functional value perceived by participants (Zhang et al., 2018b). Service quality, which is the extent to which the service level meets consumers' expectations, is assessed with five dimensions: reliability, assurance, responsiveness, empathy, and tangibles (Parasuraman, Zeithaml & Berry, 1988). Sharing economy consumers enjoy functional value when they receive their promised service dependably and accurately such as an on-time ride (reliability). This notion also applies to resource suppliers since they would like to have consumers who keep their promises about on-time show-up and payment. The other dimension of service quality is sharing economy participants' ability to convey trust and to assure each other of the shared service (assurance) (Parasuraman et al., 1988). For example, resource suppliers' and consumers' courteous and friendly behavior may instill confidence in both sides and allow them to enjoy the shared value.

Sharing economy participants' willingness to provide prompt service and help (responsiveness) is another dimension of service quality (Parasuraman et al., 1988). An example is the accommodation suppliers' willingness to provide guests with local information or guests' willingness to obey the accommodation rules and regulations. The other dimension of service quality is the provision of individualized attention (empathy) (Parasuraman et al., 1988). This notion is more applicable to the condition in which consumers interact with caring suppliers; however, considerate consumers who respect suppliers may be considered empathic as well. Last but not least, sharing economy consumers expect the shared tangible services, such as a room or a car, to have an acceptable quality (Parasuraman et al., 1988); on the other hand, resource suppliers expect to receive back the shared tangibles in their initial shape and quality (tangibles).If sharing economy participants assume that all the dimensions of service quality are met, they will be encouraged to (re)adopt the sharing practice (Zhang et al., 2018b).

Hedonic Value Sharing

Hedonic (experiential) value is the degree to which a product/service creates pleasant experiences and emotions for consumers (Smith & Colgate, 2007). Hirschman (1984) believed that all types of consumption are considered as an "experience seeking" phenomenon. The more engaging the experience, the more consumers perceive emotional arousal and, as a result, hedonic value (Spangenberg, Voss & Crowley, 1997). Prior studies showed that hedonic value may involve emotional (e.g., enjoyment, excitement) and sensory (e.g., aromas) values (Smith & Colgate, 2007). In the sharing economy context, resource suppliers may deliver services that exceed consumers' expectations and create a sense of joy and excitement in them (emotional value); for example, some Uber/Lyft drivers provide water and snacks in their cars, which may result in consumers' happiness. In addition, resource suppliers may provide tangibles that arouse consumers' five senses (sensory value); for example, some Airbnb hosts provide aesthetically pleasing paintings, wallpaper, or other decorations in their properties or light scented candles to create a more peaceful, pleasant-smelling atmosphere. All these efforts may create hedonic value for consumers and motivate them to continue their participation in the sharing economy (Zhang et al., 2018b).

Hedonic value may also be experienced by resource suppliers; however, the level of their perceived hedonic value depends on the level of their involvement with consumers and the service they provide. Prior research showed that hedonic value is correlated with the level of involvement with a product/service (Spangenberg et al.,1997). The higher the level of involvement, the higher an individual's affective reactions and experience of hedonic value. There are various extrinsic and intrinsic stimuli such as novel or unique experiences that result in involvement; however, *stimuli are not inherently involving, consumers possess the capacity to be involved and this involvement will necessarily fluctuate from consumer to consumer and product to product* (Spangenberg et al., 1997, p. 236). Thus, if resource suppliers eagerly become involved in the sharing process, make it unique for themselves and their consumers, and develop strong relationships with consumers, they may experience a high level of hedonic value (Zhang et al., 2018b). All in all, as discussed above, the sharing economy involves various types of value, which act as a motivator for both resource suppliers and consumers. On the other hand, this phenomenon is also associated with costs that may be considered as a deterrent to participation.

The Costs Associated With the Sharing Economy

Despite all above-mentioned benefits of the sharing economy, there are three types of costs that may demotivate individuals to participate in the sharing economy. First and foremost, resource suppliers' and consumers' personal safety is a serious concern in sharing economy practices since sharing occurs among strangers in unknown situations, which entails uncertainty and high degree of risk (Frenken & Schor, 2017). For example, in Airbnb, incidents of rape and sexual assault (e.g., Leiber, 2015; Levin, 2017), hosts and/or guests being threatened, drunken or belligernt hosts and/or guests, and the lodging located in an unsafe area (Fergusson, Ahlqvist & Smith, 2017) have been reported over the recent years. Other common unsafe conditions have been dirty rooms and the presence of insects, both of which have caused health problems for guests (Fergusson et al., 2017). In addition, the lack of safety amenities has exacerbated guests' concerns about the safety of Airbnb properties. Kennedy, Jones and Gielen (2018) conducted a study on safety amenities of 120 691 venues in 16 US cities and revealed that many properties do not have fire extinguishers and first-aid kits, which may put guests at risk in case of an emergency.

Safety issues are seen in other sharing economy practices such as the ride and meal sharing; for example, sexual assaults in Uber and Lyft (O'Brien, Black, Devine & Griffin, 2018) and the lack of food safety in Eatwith and BonAppetour (Kramer, 2015) are among the consumers' concerns. In addition, resource suppliers may also be the victim of unsafe conditions since there have been some cases of physical violence against Uber drivers during the last few years (e.g., Attanasio & Pagones, 2018). Although all mentioned sharing economy practices have tried to increase safety using various measures such as running resource suppliers and consumers against regulatory watchlists, running safety workshops, and embedding emergency assistance in sharing economy apps (Airbnb, 2019a; Uber, 2019), the practice of sharing with strangers implies a certain degree of risk that may act as a demotivator (Tussyadiah, 2015).

The other risk of participation in the sharing economy is the threat of physical and information privacy. Sharing increases the risk of the violation of the resource suppliers' or consumers' personal space (physical privacy) (Lutz et al., 2018). When Airbnb hosts share their properties, which are considered as a locus of their extended selves, they may perceive interpersonal contamination if consumers leave anything behind from a physical damage to an unpleasant smell in the shared space (Lutz et al., 2018). On the other hand, consumers may experience a privacy violation if resource suppliers enter their private space such as a rented room without permission or secretly spy on them using a surveillance device (Airbnb, 2019b). The other significant privacy threat is related to the disclosure and sharing of personal information in online sharing economy platforms (Lutz et al., 2018). Uber and Lyft struggled with data breach scandals recently, which could discourage individuals to continue the adoption of these services (Cox, 2017; Edelstein, 2018). Researchers believe that privacy concerns are negatively correlated with resource suppliers' and consumers' perceived economic, social, and hedonic benefits of the sharing economy, however, these concerns don't prevent them to participate in the sharing economy (Lutz et al., 2018).

Financial loss is the other serious threat in the sharing economy. Mithun (2012) believes that consumers are concerned about the quality of products/services since poor quality equals financial costs. There are several negative online reviews of sharing economy practices in which consumers complained about the lack of hygiene, lack of advertised amenities, charge of unnecessary fees, unsatisfactory service, and suppliers' improper behavior. On the other hand, there are negative reviews about property damage, missing/stolen amenities and inconsiderate consumers, showing that resource suppliers are also subject to financial loss. Kamal and Chen (2016) conducted a survey among sharing economy participants and revealed that theft, fraud, and non-payment are the major risk factors they perceive. Sharing economy practices have started to address all above-mentioned risks using various measures; however, participants' negative experiences with the sharing economy or similar practices may negatively affect their motivation.

CONCLUSION

The sharing economy is a new business model that involves participants who are not clearly separated as suppliers or consumers (Grönroos & Voima, 2013). The participants co-create and share economic, social, functional, and hedonic values in reciprocal relationships (Zhang et al., 2018a). Involvement in the value sharing is driven by some benefits and costs. During the economic value sharing, suppliers earn money by sharing their underused assets while consumers save money by having access to low-priced products/services (Seign & Bogenberger, 2012). Both sides make efficient use of their time by participating in the sharing economy in their free time or by making free time using sharing economy practices (Seign & Bogenberger, 2012). In addition, they may enjoy having control over their transactions during the sharing process (Kim, Yoon & Zo, 2015). In addition to the economic value, sharing economy participants enjoy the social value by socializing, making friends, and developing social ties (Cohen & Kietzmann, 2014). They also satisfy their needs through spontaneous sociability, which is the ability of trusting strangers and developing speedy social interactions with them (Fukuyama, 1995). In terms of the functional value, participants are motivated by the usefulness and ease of use of the sharing economy online environment and the product/service quality of the offline environment (Zhang et al.,

Figure 1. The conceptual framework of value sharing in the sharing economy

2018b). Participants may also be involved in the hedonic value sharing, during which they may experience emotional and sensory arousal (Smith & Colgate, 2007), and, as a result, pleasant feelings (Zhang et al., 2018b). All these benefits encourage individuals to (re)adopt sharing economy practices; however, they may experience some risks during the sharing process.

A critical obstacle to participation in the sharing economy is the threat to participants' safety (Frenken & Schor, 2017). Sharing an apartment or a car with strangers or eating food prepared by unknown people may put participants' life at risk (Frenken & Schor, 2017). For example, there were cases of violence, sexual assaults, and physical diseases reported by some participants. The other risk of participation in the sharing economy is the violation of privacy (Lutz et al., 2018). Since strangers share a space/meal/skill in sharing economy practices in an uncertain situation, they may experience violation of their physical privacy. In addition, since most transactions of the sharing economy occur in an online environment, identity theft is a major concern for most participants (Kathan et al., 2016). Furthermore, sharing economy participants are at risk for financial loss (Mithun, 2012). For example, Airbnb suppliers may be worried about potential damages to their properties, while consumers may be concerned about getting overcharged (Weber, 2014). In order to decrease the aforementioned risks, sharing economy online platforms allow participants to source information on other participants, using ratings, and reviews; however, the information may not be as reliable as it should be (Frenken & Schor, 2017).

Knowing about sharing economy values, and their associated benefits and costs has implications for both traditional and sharing economy practitioners. Traditional practitioners should note that the sharing economy has disrupted conventional businesses by shifting the consumers' preference from ownership to access-based consumption (Bardhi & Eckhardt, 2012). Thus, in order to keep their businesses successful, they should know about sharing economy features and the motivations of its participants. For example, one of the significant characteristics of the sharing economy is the opportunity of social value sharing, which is rarely seen in conventional businesses. Therefore, traditional practitioners should try to create online and offline occasions in which their consumers can have social interactions with suppliers and other consumers. At the same time, sharing economy practitioners should also be aware of the motivators and deterrents of participation to be able to highlight motivating features and alleviate obstacles. For example, sharing economy practitioners may make the participation in the sharing economy more communal and enjoyable or employ trust systems that monitor participants' behavior to increase trust among participants and reduce associated risks (Hamari et al., 2016).

FUTURE RESEARCH DIRECTIONS

Future studies should consider testing the value sharing conceptual framework empirically; for example, researchers may test the framework with the suppliers and consumers of a specific sharing economy practice such as Uber. Empirical testing could reveal whether there is a meaningful relationship between value sharing benefits/costs and motivation to (re)adopt the sharing economy and which benefit/cost has the largest contribution to (re)adoption. Another research question for further investigation is whether there are other types of benefits/costs, and if yes, whether they are specific to suppliers or consumers or both. Knowing about other benefits and costs help practitioners to develop sharing economy businesses rapidly and properly and help potential participants to make decisions about participation easily. Another interesting related research topic is the comparable study of value sharing in different sharing economy sectors such as accommodation, transportation, meals, and skills, and to identify the difference among the roles of economic, social, functional, and hedonic values and associated benefits/risks in participants' motivation (e.g., Böcker & Meelen, 2017). Finally, the detailed examination of sharing economy macro-level benefits and costs (e.g., environmental sustainability) may shed light on the true nature of this new business model and accelerate/decelerate its growth rate.

REFERENCES

Aarikka-Stenroos, L., & Jaakkola, E. (2012). Value co-creation in knowledge intensive business services: A dyadic perspective on the joint problem solving process. *Industrial Marketing Management*, *41*(1), 15–26. doi:10.1016/j.indmarman.2011.11.008

Acquier, A., Daudigeos, T., & Pinkse, J. (2017). Promises and paradoxes of the sharing economy: An organizing framework. *Technological Forecasting and Social Change*, *125*, 1–10. doi:10.1016/j.techfore.2017.07.006

Airbnb. (2019a). *Trust & Safety*. Retrieved from https://www.airbnb.com/trust

Airbnb. (2019b). *What are Airbnb's rules about electronic surveillance devices in listings?* Retrieved from https://www.airbnb.com/help/article/887/what-are-airbnb-s-rules-about-electronic-surveillance-devices-in-listings

Akbar, Y. H., & Tracogna, A. (2018). The sharing economy and the future of the hotel industry: Transaction cost theory and platform economics. *International Journal of Hospitality Management*, *71*, 91–101. doi:10.1016/j.ijhm.2017.12.004

Attanasio, C., & Pagones, S. (2018). *Uber driver says he was attacked by passenger who accidentally ordered carpool*. Retrieved from https://nypost.com/2018/10/25/uber-driver-says-he-was-attacked-by-passenger-who-accidentally-ordered-carpool/

Bardhi, F., & Eckhardt, G. M. (2012). Access-based consumption: The case of car sharing. *The Journal of Consumer Research*, *39*(4), 881–898. doi:10.1086/666376

Bardhi, F., Eckhardt, G. M., & Arnould, E. J. (2012). Liquid relationship to possessions. *The Journal of Consumer Research*, *39*(3), 510–529. doi:10.1086/664037

Belk, R. (2010). Sharing. *The Journal of Consumer Research*, *36*(5), 715–734. doi:10.1086/612649

Belk, R. W. (2013). Extended self in a digital world. *The Journal of Consumer Research*, *40*(3), 477–500. doi:10.1086/671052

Birch, D. G., & Parulava, S. (2017). Ambient Accountability: Shared Ledger Technology and Radical Transparency for Next Generation Digital Financial Services. In Handbook of Blockchain, Digital Finance, and Inclusion (vol. 1, pp. 375–387). Elsevier.

Blal, I., Singal, M., & Templin, J. (2018). Airbnb's effect on hotel sales growth. *International Journal of Hospitality Management*, *73*, 85–92. doi:10.1016/j.ijhm.2018.02.006

Böcker, L., & Meelen, T. (2017). Sharing for people, planet or profit? Analysing motivations for intended sharing economy participation. *Environmental Innovation and Societal Transitions*, *23*, 28–39. doi:10.1016/j.eist.2016.09.004

Botsman, R., & Rogers, R. (2011). *What's mine is yours: How collaborative consumption is changing the way we live*. London: Collins.

Bottomley, K., & Burgess, S. W. (2018). Millennials in Leadership: An Examination of the Practice-Immediacy Model. In *Engaged Leadership* (pp. 223–234). Cham: Springer. doi:10.1007/978-3-319-72221-4_13

Bucher, E., Fieseler, C., & Lutz, C. (2016). What's mine is yours (for a nominal fee)–Exploring the spectrum of utilitarian to altruistic motives for Internet-mediated sharing. *Computers in Human Behavior*, *62*, 316–326. doi:10.1016/j.chb.2016.04.002

Chung, J. Y. (2017). Online friendships in a hospitality exchange network: A sharing economy perspective. *International Journal of Contemporary Hospitality Management*, *29*(12), 3177–3190. doi:10.1108/IJCHM-08-2016-0475

Cohen, B., & Kietzmann, J. (2014). Ride on! Mobility business models for the sharing economy. *Organization & Environment, 27*(3), 279–296. doi:10.1177/1086026614546199

Cova, B., Dalli, D., & Zwick, D. (2011). Critical perspectives on consumers' role as 'producers': Broadening the debate on value co-creation in marketing processes. *Marketing Theory, 11*(3), 231–241. doi:10.1177/1470593111408171

Cox, J. (2017). *Hackers are using Uber's 57 million account data breach to steal passwords*. Retrieved from https://www.thedailybeast.com/hackers-are-using-ubers-57-million-account-data-breach-to-steal-passwords?ref=scroll

Davis, F. D. (1989). Perceived usefulness, perceived ease of use, and user acceptance of information technology. *Management Information Systems Quarterly, 13*(3), 319–340. doi:10.2307/249008

Dillahunt, T. R., & Malone, A. R. (2015, April). The promise of the sharing economy among disadvantaged communities. In *Proceedings of the 33rd Annual ACM Conference on Human Factors in Computing Systems* (pp. 2285-2294). ACM. 10.1145/2702123.2702189

Edelstein, S. (2018). *Lyft investigates claim that employees improperly accessed customer data*. Retrieved from https://www.thedrive.com/tech/17993/lyft-investigates-claim-that-employees-improperly-accessed-consumer-data

Edwards, D., Cheng, M., Wong, I. A., Zhang, J., & Wu, Q. (2017). Ambassadors of knowledge sharing: Co-produced travel information through tourist-local social media exchange. *International Journal of Contemporary Hospitality Management, 29*(2), 690–708. doi:10.1108/IJCHM-10-2015-0607

Elkington, J. (1998). Partnerships from cannibals with forks: The triple bottom line of 21st-century business. *Environmental Quality Management, 8*(1), 37–51. doi:10.1002/tqem.3310080106

Fellows, N. T., & Pitfield, D. E. (2000). An economic and operational evaluation of urban car-sharing. *Transportation Research Part D, Transport and Environment, 5*(1), 1–10. doi:10.1016/S1361-9209(99)00016-4

Fergusson, A., Ahlqvist, S. R., & Smith, E. (2017). *Is Airbnb safe for guests? What causes an Airbnb stay to turn into a horror story?* Retrieved from https://www.asherfergusson.com/wp-content/uploads/2017/11/Is-Airbnb-Safe-for-Guests_-Research-Study-Method-Results-Recommendations.pdf

Fitzmaurice, C., Ladegaard, I., Attwood-Charles, W., Cansoy, M., Carfagna, L., Schor, J. B., & Wengronowitz, R. (2018). Domesticating the market: moral exchange and the sharing economy. *Socio-Economic Review, mwy003*. Retrieved from https://academic.oup.com/ser/advance-article-abstract/doi/10.1093/ser/mwy003/4866062?redirectedFrom=fulltext

Frenken, K., & Schor, J. (2017). Putting the sharing economy into perspective. *Environmental Innovation and Societal Transitions, 23*, 3–10. doi:10.1016/j.eist.2017.01.003

Fukuyama, F. (1995). Social capital and the global economy. *Foreign Affairs, 74*(5), 89–103. doi:10.2307/20047302

Grönroos, C. (2008). Service logic revisited: Who creates value? And who co-creates? *European Business Review, 20*(4), 298–314. doi:10.1108/09555340810886585

Grönroos, C. (2011). Value co-creation in service logic: A critical analysis. *Marketing Theory, 11*(3), 279–301. doi:10.1177/1470593111408177

Grönroos, C. (2012). Conceptualising value co-creation: A journey to the 1970s and back to the future. *Journal of Marketing Management, 28*(13–14), 1520–1534. doi:10.1080/0267257X.2012.737357

Grönroos, C., & Voima, P. (2013). Critical service logic: Making sense of value creation and co-creation. *Journal of the Academy of Marketing Science, 41*(2), 133–150. doi:10.100711747-012-0308-3

Guttentag, D. A., & Smith, S. L. (2017). Assessing Airbnb as a disruptive innovation relative to hotels: Substitution and comparative performance expectations. *International Journal of Hospitality Management, 64*, 1–10. doi:10.1016/j.ijhm.2017.02.003

Hamari, J., Sjöklint, M., & Ukkonen, A. (2016). The sharing economy: Why people participate in collaborative consumption. *Journal of the Association for Information Science and Technology, 67*(9), 2047–2059. doi:10.1002/asi.23552

Hammedi, W., Kandampully, J., Zhang, T. T., & Bouquiaux, L. (2015). Online consumer engagement: Creating social environments through brand community constellations. *Journal of Service Management, 26*(5), 777–806. doi:10.1108/JOSM-11-2014-0295

Hartmans, A. (2017). *Airbnb Now Has More Listings Worldwide than the Top Five Hotel Brands Combined.* Retrieved from https://www.businessinsider.com/airbnb-total-worldwide-listings-2017-8

Hasan, R., & Birgach, M. (2016, June). Critical success factors behind the sustainability of the Sharing Economy. In *2016 IEEE 14th International Conference on Software Engineering Research, Management and Applications (SERA)* (pp. 287-293). IEEE. 10.1109/SERA.2016.7516158

Hawlitschek, F., Teubner, T., Adam, M. T. P., Borchers, N. S., Moehlmann, M., & Weinhardt, C. (2016). Trust in the sharing economy: An experimental framework. *Proceedings of the Thirty-Seventh International Conference on Information Systems (ICIS).*

Heinrichs, H. (2013). Sharing economy: A potential new pathway to sustainability. *GAIA-Ecological Perspectives for Science and Society, 22*(4), 228–232. doi:10.14512/gaia.22.4.5

Henten, A. H., & Windekilde, I. M. (2016). Transaction costs and the sharing economy. *Info, 18*(1), 1–15. doi:10.1108/info-09-2015-0044

Hirschman, E. C. (1984). Experience seeking: A subjectivist perspective of consumption. *Journal of Business Research, 12*(1), 115–136. doi:10.1016/0148-2963(84)90042-0

Holbrook, M. B., & Hirschman, E. C. (1982). The experiential aspects of consumption: Consumer fantasies, feelings, and fun. *The Journal of Consumer Research, 9*(2), 132–140. doi:10.1086/208906

Homans, G. C. (1958). Social behavior as exchange. *American Journal of Sociology, 63*(6), 597–606. doi:10.1086/222355

Ivanova, I. (2018). *Uber Reportedly Worth More than Ford, GM, Tesla – Combined.* Retrieved from https://www.msn.com/en-us/money/companies/uber-reportedly-worth-more-than-ford-gm-tesla--combined/ar-BBOtpab

Kamal, P., & Chen, J. Q. (2016). Trust in Sharing Economy. In *Pacific Asia Conference on Information Systems (PACIS)* (pp. 109-119). Association for Information Systems.

Kathan, W., Matzler, K., & Veider, V. (2016). The sharing economy: Your business model's friend or foe? *Business Horizons*, *59*(6), 663–672. doi:10.1016/j.bushor.2016.06.006

Kennedy, H. R., Jones, V. C., & Gielen, A. (2018). Reported fire safety and first-aid amenities in Airbnb venues in 16 American cities. *Injury Prevention*, 1–3. Retrieved from https://injuryprevention.bmj.com/content/injuryprev/early/2018/05/28/injuryprev-2018-042740.full.pdf PMID:29735746

Kim, J., Yoon, Y., & Zo, H. (2015). Why People Participate in the Sharing Economy: A Social Exchange Perspective. In Pacific Asia Conference in Information Systems (PACIS) (pp. 76-84). Association for Information Systems.

Kramer, A. (2015). *Meal-sharing apps fly under the regulatory radar.* Retrieved from https://www.bna.com/mealsharing-apps-fly-b17179934259/

Lee, Z. W., Chan, T. K., Balaji, M. S., & Chong, A. Y.-L. (2016). Technology-mediated sharing economy: Understanding user participation in collaborative consumption through the benefit-cost perspective. *Proceedings of the 20th Pacific Asia Conference on Information Systems (PACIS).*

Leiber, R. (2015). *Airbnb Horror Story Points to Need for Precautions.* Retrieved from https://www.nytimes.com/2015/08/15/your-money/airbnb-horror-story-points-to-need-for-precautions.html

Levin, S. (2017). *Airbnb sued by woman who says she was sexually assaulted by 'superhost'.* Retrieved from https://www.theguardian.com/technology/2017/jul/27/airbnb-guest-sexual-assault-allegation

Lusch, R. F., & Vargo, S. L. (2006). Service-dominant logic: Reactions, reflections and refinements. *Marketing Theory*, *6*(3), 281–288. doi:10.1177/1470593106066781

Lutz, C., Hoffmann, C. P., Bucher, E., & Fieseler, C. (2018). The role of privacy concerns in the sharing economy. *Information Communication and Society*, *21*(10), 1472–1492. doi:10.1080/1369118X.2017.1339726

Mithun, C. (2012). *National Study Quantifies Reality of the "Sharing Economy" Movement.* Retrieved from https://www.prnewswire.com/news-releases/national-study-quantifies-the-sharing-economy-movement-138949069.html

Möhlmann, M. (2016). *Digital Trust and Peer-to-Peer Collaborative Consumption Platforms: A Mediation Analysis.* Retrieved from SSRN: https://ssrn.com/abstract=2813367 or doi:10.2139srn.2813367

Narasimhan, C., Papatla, P., Jiang, B., Kopalle, P. K., Messinger, P. R., Moorthy, S., ... Zhu, T. (2018). Sharing economy: Review of current research and future directions. *Customer Needs and Solutions*, *5*(1-2), 93–106. doi:10.100740547-017-0079-6

O'Brien, S. A., Black, N., Devine, C., & Griffin, D. (2018). *CNN investigation: 103 Uber drivers accused of sexual assault or abuse.* Retrieved from https://money.cnn.com/2018/04/30/technology/uber-driver-sexual-assault/index.html

Parasuraman, A., Zeithaml, V. A., & Berry, L. L. (1988). Servqual: A multiple-item scale for measuring consumer perc. *Journal of Retailing*, *64*(1), 12–40.

Parigi, P., & State, B. (2014). Disenchanting the world: the impact of technology on relationships. In *International Conference on Social Informatics* (pp. 166-182). Springer. 10.1007/978-3-319-13734-6_12

Prahalad, C. K., & Ramaswamy, V. (2004). Co-creating unique value with consumers. *Strategy and Leadership*, *32*(3), 4–9. doi:10.1108/10878570410699249

Saarijärvi, H., Kannan, P. K., & Kuusela, H. (2013). Value co-creation: Theoretical approaches and practical implications. *European Business Review*, *25*(1), 6–19. doi:10.1108/09555341311287718

Schaefers, T., Lawson, S. J., & Kukar-Kinney, M. (2016). How the burdens of ownership promote consumer usage of access-based services. *Marketing Letters*, *27*(3), 569–577. doi:10.100711002-015-9366-x

Schor, J. (2015). *The sharing economy: Reports from stage one* (Unpublished paper). Boston College. Retrieved from https://www.bc.edu/content/dam/files/schools/cas_sites/sociology/pdf/TheSharingEconomy.pdf

Schor, J. (2016). Debating the sharing economy. *Journal of Self-Governance & Management Economics*, *4*(3), 7–22. doi:10.22381/JSME4320161

Seign, R., & Bogenberger, K. (2012, March). *Prescriptions for the Successful Diffusion of Carsharing with Electric Vehicles*. Paper presented at the Conference on Future Automotive Technology Focus Electromobility, München, Germany.

Smith, B. G., & Gallicano, T. D. (2015). Terms of engagement: Analyzing public engagement with organizations through social media. *Computers in Human Behavior*, *53*, 82–90. doi:10.1016/j.chb.2015.05.060

Smith, J. B., & Colgate, M. (2007). Customer value creation: A practical framework. *Journal of Marketing Theory and Practice*, *15*(1), 7–23. doi:10.2753/MTP1069-6679150101

Spangenberg, E. R., Voss, K. E., & Crowley, A. E. (1997). Measuring the hedonic and utilitarian dimensions of attitude: A generally applicable scale. *Advances in Consumer Research. Association for Consumer Research (U. S.)*, *24*, 235–241.

Stephany, A. (2015). *The business of sharing: Making it in the new sharing economy*. Hampshire, UK: Palgrave Macmillan. doi:10.1057/9781137376183

Traum, A. B. (2015). Sharing Risk in the Sharing Economy: Insurance Regulation in the Age of Uber. *Cardozo Pub. L. Pol'y & Ethics J.*, *14*, 511–544.

Troisi, O., Carrubbo, L., Maione, G., & Torre, C. (2016). The more, the merrier: Co-Working as practical expression of Value Co-Creation in Sharing Economy. In *XXVI RESER conference* (pp. 1130–1144). Naples: European Association for Research on Services.

Tussyadiah, I. P. (2015). An exploratory study on drivers and deterrents of collaborative consumption in travel. In *Information and Communication Technologies in Tourism* (pp. 817–830). Cham: Springer.

Tussyadiah, I. P., & Pesonen, J. (2016). Impacts of peer-to-peer accommodation use on travel patterns. *Journal of Travel Research*, *55*(8), 1022–1040. doi:10.1177/0047287515608505

Uber. (2019). *Our Commitment to Safety*. Retrieved from https://www.uber.com/safety/

Vargo, S. L., & Lusch, R. F. (2008). Service-dominant logic: Continuing the evolution. *Journal of the Academy of Marketing Science*, *36*(1), 1–10. doi:10.100711747-007-0069-6

Vargo, S. L., & Lusch, R. F. (2010). From repeat patronage to value co-creation in service ecosystems: A transcending conceptualization of relationship. *Journal of Business Market Management*, *4*(4), 169–179. doi:10.100712087-010-0046-0

Vargo, S. L., Maglio, P. P., & Akaka, M. A. (2008). On value and value co-creation: A service systems and service logic perspective. *European Management Journal*, *26*(3), 145–152. doi:10.1016/j.emj.2008.04.003

Weber, T. A. (2014). Intermediation in a sharing economy: Insurance, moral hazard, and rent extraction. *Journal of Management Information Systems*, *31*(3), 35–71. doi:10.1080/07421222.2014.995520

Zeithaml, V. A. (1988). Consumer perceptions of price, quality, and value: A means-end model and synthesis of evidence. *Journal of Marketing*, *52*(3), 2–22. doi:10.1177/002224298805200302

Zhang, T. C., Gu, H., & Jahromi, M. F. (2018a). What Makes the Sharing Economy Successful? An Empirical Examination of Competitive Consumer Value Propositions. *Computers in Human Behavior*, *95*, 275–283. doi:10.1016/j.chb.2018.03.019

Zhang, T. C., Jahromi, M. F., & Kizildag, M. (2018b). Value co-creation in a sharing economy: The end of price wars? *International Journal of Hospitality Management*, *71*, 51–58. doi:10.1016/j.ijhm.2017.11.010

Zhu, G., So, K. K. F., & Hudson, S. (2017). Inside the sharing economy: Understanding consumer motivations behind the adoption of mobile applications. *International Journal of Contemporary Hospitality Management*, *29*(9), 2218–2239. doi:10.1108/IJCHM-09-2016-0496

ADDITIONAL READING

Akbar, Y. H., & Tracogna, A. (2018). The sharing economy and the future of the hotel industry: Transaction cost theory and platform economics. *International Journal of Hospitality Management*, *71*, 91–101. doi:10.1016/j.ijhm.2017.12.004

Boxall, K., Nyanjom, J., & Slaven, J. (2018). Disability, hospitality and the new sharing economy. *International Journal of Contemporary Hospitality Management*, *30*(1), 539–556. doi:10.1108/IJCHM-09-2016-0491

Camilleri, J., & Neuhofer, B. (2017). Value co-creation and co-destruction in the Airbnb sharing economy. *International Journal of Contemporary Hospitality Management*, *29*(9), 2322–2340. doi:10.1108/IJCHM-09-2016-0492

Celata, F., Hendrickson, C. Y., & Sanna, V. S. (2017). The sharing economy as community marketplace? Trust, reciprocity and belonging in peer-to-peer accommodation platforms. *Cambridge Journal of Regions, Economy and Society*, *10*(2), 349–363. doi:10.1093/cjres/rsw044

Heo, Y. (2016). Sharing economy and prospects in tourism research. *Annals of Tourism Research, 58*, 166–170. doi:10.1016/j.annals.2016.02.002

Mody, M., Suess, C., & Lehto, X. (2018). Using segmentation to compete in the age of the sharing economy: Testing a core-periphery framework. *International Journal of Hospitality Management, 78*, 199–213. doi:10.1016/j.ijhm.2018.09.003

Phua, V. C. (2018). Perceiving Airbnb as sharing economy: The issue of trust in using Airbnb. *Current Issues in Tourism, 1–5*. doi:10.1080/13683500.2018.1440539

Zhang, T. C., Gu, H., & Jahromi, M. F. (2018a). What Makes the Sharing Economy Successful? An Empirical Examination of Competitive Customer Value Propositions. *Computers in Human Behavior, 95*, 275–283. doi:10.1016/j.chb.2018.03.019

Zhang, T. C., Jahromi, M. F., & Kizildag, M. (2018b). Value co-creation in a sharing economy: The end of price wars? *International Journal of Hospitality Management, 71*, 51–58. doi:10.1016/j.ijhm.2017.11.010

KEY TERMS AND DEFINITIONS

Economic Value: The degree to which a product/service is monetarily beneficial.

Functional Value: The degree to which a product/service performs well.

Hedonic Value: The degree to which a product/service arouses emotions and creates pleasant experiences.

Sharing Economy: An economic system in which tangible and intangible resources such as houses, cars, meals, and skills are shared among peers at an affordable price or free, using digital platforms.

Social Value: The degree to which a product/service creates positive changes in an individual's life.

Value Co-Creation: An initiative in which resource suppliers and consumers jointly produce a valued outcome.

Value Sharing: An initiative in which resource suppliers and consumers share a valued resource.

Chapter 2
The Politics of the Sharing Economy

David Murillo
Ramon Llull University, Spain

ABSTRACT

The current academic debate on the sharing economy (SE) seems to embrace three main discussions: its definition, its effects, and the role of regulation. A neglected topic here seems to be analyzing the specific implications of the changing nature of these firms boosted by private equity and venture capital. As the author points out, we need to analyze not only the impact of a changing business model but, specifically, how stakeholders, cities, and regulators should approach this moving target now called SE. In the following sections the author departs from a traditional definition of the sharing economy to start building the case for treating the SE at large as an epiphenomenon of the platform economy, and as a temporary condition based on a moveable business model. The chapter closes by introducing the regulatory hurdles that come associated with the previous and mapping out its different futures.

INTRODUCTION: THE SHARING ECONOMY AS A MOVING TARGET

Learning From Experience in the Sharing Economy

'We have to admit when the free market is not working' – Tim Cook, Apple CEO, November 2018

Ten years ago, Uber became synonymous with sharing mobility. Uber is now a conglomerate whose business model has evolved from ride-hailing to helping drivers lease, rent, or buy a vehicle. The company also delivers food and sells data insights (Bamberger & Lobel, 2017, p. 1090). Uber is also pioneering self-driving cars and vertical take-off and landing aircraft for on-demand urban transportation (Ganapati & Reddick, 2018). A similar path has been followed by Airbnb, the other tycoon of the sharing economy (SE), whose business model has been drifting slowly away from facilitating temporary access to shared apartments, to making rental opportunities from well-established property firms accessible on its platform and offering city tours. It is becoming a hospitality conglomerate at large.

DOI: 10.4018/978-1-5225-9928-9.ch002

Copyright © 2020, IGI Global. Copying or distributing in print or electronic forms without written permission of IGI Global is prohibited.

Another example that has seen a similar evolution is Coursera, another of the big brands in the sharing sector and known for giving free access to top-school online courses. Here too we find a moving business model in quest of monetisation. The company now sells user data to companies searching for talent – the most important current stream of income according to Van Dijck, Poell and Waal (2018, p. 128). A pertinent question is the following: could this missional drift be otherwise? Additionally, what does this drift say about the social expectations we set on the SE?

At this point, we need to take a careful look at the evolution of these sharing platforms and start exploring the societal consequences of treating *sharing* instrumentally. This is a phenomenon connected to the evolutionary nature of platforms that has huge societal implications, and which has been largely overlooked. We argue that understanding the sharing component as a temporary phase in the evolution of a business can help us understand a myriad of cases that exemplify the controversial societal impacts of the SE. From those bike-sharing firms that pop up in large cities, and evaporate overnight while leaving thousands of unwanted bikes clogging streets and canals (Rinne, 2018), to the gradual income downgrading of taxi drivers who were allegedly mislead by the earning potential of collaborative ventures (Kazmin & Ram, 2017). These are all part of the academic discussion that tries to frame the plausible expectations of what the SE can and cannot do (Murillo, Buckland, & Val, 2017).

Current Debates: Sharing Initiatives and Platforms

A broader discussion on the societal consequences of the SE is only one of the discussions that capture the interest of scholars in this field. Currently, academic debate on the SE appears to be embracing three main discussions: its definition; its effects; and the role of regulation (Frenken, 2017). It is beyond the scope of this text to reopen the terminological debate that has been addressed elsewhere (Murillo et al., 2017; Richardson, 2015) but we must set forward a minimal definition that encompasses our arguments. For this purpose we can depart from the common understanding of the SE used by Parente, Geleilate and Rong (2018) and add what we consider relevant missing features.

According to these authors, the SE is composed of: i) companies whose business focuses on unlocking the value of unused or underutilised assets; ii) where consumers pay for temporary access instead of ownership using an internet-based platform; and iii) C2C interactions and network effects are relied on for growth. There are two additional important key dimensions of the SE that must be included: iv) the SE centrally depends on internet platforms to enable peer exchange; and v) these assets are often rented rather than shared (Ganapati & Reddick, 2018, p. 78).

In our view, a common weakness in this type of discourse starts by understanding the SE as composed by static rather than dynamic, that is evolving, organizations. This contradicts the evidence amassed in more than ten years of experience and where the sharing component of what we see as SE has come to mean different things: a market niche; a commercial strategy; a rhetorical device; a phase in the evolution of a firm; or, more often than not, a combination of some of the above. Thus, an important topic in the academic debate should be the implications of the changing nature of these firms. As we will point out, we need to analyse not only the impact of a changing business model on the sharing business, but specifically how stakeholders, citizens, and regulators should approach this moving target we call SE.

This important discussion on the limits and boundaries of what the SE is and is not, following Frenken (2017), implies a major redrafting of societal expectations about the SE. It is the centrality of platforms in the SE what makes them dependent on the broader logic of the digital economy. As we have explained elsewhere (Murillo et al., 2017) it is important to stress the importance of treating the

SE first as an epiphenomenon of the platform economy; and as a temporary condition or state – that of the sharing business – that is contingent on the transformative nature of business models in the platform economy (Frenken, 2017; Srnicek, 2016, 2017). This is particularly relevant when observing the role of large firms investing in the SE – such as the Japanese Softbank which spent $93 billion through its Vision Fund (incidentally, backed by Saudi and Abu Dhabi sovereign wealth funds) on companies such as Uber Technologies Inc or the shared-office space firm WeWork (Reuters, 2018).

Thus, we plan to present SE platforms, first and foremost, as platforms. This implies understanding these digital devices as having a specific political nature that aims to create a specific type of society. Our initial aim will be to open the discussion on the role that private equity and, more specifically, venture capital plays in the development of its business model. This will enable us to unfold the type of political activism exercised by SE firms and observe the disparities in corporate power by the main SE platforms in comparison with that of alternative platforms more closely connected to the allegedly collaborative nature of the SE.

We are witnessing here a crucial power imbalance that has important political consequences and which is going to be determinant for the type of political future the SE will be able to convey. At this point we are dependent on the axiological worlds, or orders of worth, presented by the instrumental sharing platforms and alternative counterparts. The contours of the default future will follow the well-known pattern of default market liberalism without any collaborative or sustainable nature. We close this chapter by introducing the regulatory hurdles associated with the previous scenario and map the alternative futures. Our goal: to highlight the political implications of the various approaches and justify the need for a comprehensive public approach to the SE. In our view, only a form of concerted multi-stakeholder activism led by public institutions will offer an alternative future for the SE.

PLATFORM CAPITALISM, VENTURE CAPITAL AND POWER IN THE SHARING ECONOMY

The Politics of Platforms

Platform ecosystems are entrenched in their own ideological-political system (Van Dijck et al., 2018, p. 163). As stated by Gillespie (2010), we may understand platforms as firms which are working not just politically but also discursively to frame their services and technologies. Platforms is a word that generally implies some kind of neutrality towards use – typically flat, featureless, and open to all. These platforms suggest a progressive and egalitarian arrangement, promising to support those on the platform and projecting a sense of technical neutrality and progressive openness (op.cit, p. 348; 350; 360). However, what are the implications of understanding the SE within the digital economy? Should we accept the idea that these platforms are *political* by nature?

Approaching SE companies both as continuously evolving organisations and political entities, enables us to keep a critical eye on the alleged *sharing* element of the SE and to better understand the possible futures of a SE led by these big players. From this perspective, we must start our analysis by exploring the consequences of the replacement of middlemen, as indicated in the SE literature, by these new gatekeepers or *über-middlemen* platforms – i.e., monopolies with an unprecedented control over the markets they themselves create (Olma, 2014; Srnicek, 2016). We can already identify associated corporate practices that relate to societal problems such as the exacerbation of inequality or unsustainable consumption patterns (Ganapati & Reddick, 2018).

Srnicek gives us a good starting point for understanding the politics of platforms. He posits that if these big platforms want to remain competitive, they must necessarily intensify their extraction, analysis, and control of data; and to do so they must invest in fixed capital (Srnicek, 2016, p. 97). Fuelled by network effects, and access to large amounts of data, success in winner-take-all economies largely depends on the availability of external resources (Tirole, 2019). As expressed in a report published by the *New Economics Foundation* (McCann 2018, p. 3) the competition for data becomes a concentrating force that has important repercussions on how companies perform and compete. Capital requirements become essential to internet companies if they want to stay ahead in the game. Obviously, such capital is not neutral in the way businesses operate. The transformative nature of sharing initiatives must be seen as conditioned firstly by the role of venture capital (V.C.) and then by private equity. Hence, we need to dig into the political implications of external financial support to understand the competitive patterns of these firms.

Venture Capital, Private Equity, and Platforms

Much remains to be learned from the role of private equity, and V.C. particularly, in businesses. When discussing the transformative role of V.C. on firms it has been stated that 'in some cases, the unanswered questions have been posed for years, but lack of access to data has proved to be a major barrier. For instance, confidentiality concerns have made a thorough understanding of the risk and reward characteristics of venture capital elusive' (Gompers & Lerner, 2001, p. 166). This difficulty in analysing the role of V.C. in platform firms enhances the characteristic opacity of the main players (Frenken & Schor, 2017).

What seems clear is that V.C. introduces a distinctive rationality in early stage start-up firms in the SE that can be a cause for 'supporting the need to compromise on the principles to ensure the sharing economy's expansion' or *mission drift* (Ciulli & Kolk, 2019, p. 995). Even a rather optimist recent article on the role of V.C. on start-ups admits that: 'More often than not, venture capitalists promote a "winner-take-all" mindset, pushing expansion at the cost of impact on initial customer targets' (Taneja, 2019). The author remarks on the controversial role of V.C. as follows: 'Today when I talk with entrepreneurs about how quickly they can grow, I want to see them recognise that creating a "virtuous" product may require them to grow more slowly than they might otherwise'.

There is a common understanding on why this mission drift takes place. Morozov (2018) puts it in the following manner: 'When Uber, Airbnb and similar platforms were young and tiny, it was easy to believe that a global revolution would liberate more informal economic activity. The laudable aims of empowerment, localism, and horizontalism were to be achieved by cosying up to a mighty but treacherous ally – by synchronising the heartbeat and needs of digital platforms with those of global capital.' The final goal of long-term profitability is achieved by overpowering competitors through faster growth, externalising operational costs, and leveraging political power (Morozov, 2019).

A more general critique of V.C. is that made by Griffit (2019) in *The New York Times*. She describes a pattern were 'start-ups raise piles of money from investors, and then use the cash to grow aggressively — faster than the competition, faster than regulators, faster than most normal businesses would consider sane. Larger and larger rounds of funding follow. The end goal is to sell or go public, producing astonishing returns for early investors. Social media is littered with tales of companies that withered under the pressure of hypergrowth, were crushed by so-called "toxic V.C.s" or were forced to raise too much venture capital — something known as the "*foie gras effect*.""

We can now again recall the case of Uber. Waiting for its IPO, Uber was valued by the financial market at $120 billion, about the same as General Motors, one of the icons of the automotive industry. Uber has raised more than $24 billion in different rounds of financing from early stage V.C. to private equity sponsored by the main technology investors. However, the company has not yet earned a single net euro in profit. The dollars raised by Uber enables it to sustain huge losses for a long time (McCann, 2018, p. 14). As an example, Uber lost $4.5 billion only in the year 2017 (Morozov, 2019). Overall, the political implications of a SE relying on V.C. and private equity need to be discussed.

The Politics of Venture Capital

It seems clear that early reliance on V.C. has very specific impacts on the political nature of platforms. Accordingly, the politics of the SE – defined as the kind of society they seek to generate – will not necessarily emphasize the *sharing* component. We can observe a clear pattern where the practical constraints of a P2P business model become first subservient to the logic of monetisation and then profit maximisation. Under this logic, for firms operating in the SE – or more appropriately, as part of the platform society at large (Van Dijck et al., 2018, p. 2) – it is expected that a rather instrumental logic will be the outcome. To put it differently, how *collaborative* can a sharing platform remain under the conditions set by external profit-maximising funds?

Some recent media attacks on the pernicious effects of V.C. in start-ups indicate where these firms are going (Bravo, 2019). V.C.-backed firms have been described as operating under the logic of captivating business angels; sometimes selling freely acquired locations in cities to attract publicity – e.g. bike-sharing initiatives like Ofo or oBike in Madrid (incidentally relying on V.C. funds from China and Singapore) – with the aim of generating media attention through city-brand association. This means linking the platform to a city to viralise attention and sell shares before promises of profitability wane. As pointed out by the author of this piece, this seems to be a gambling mentality rather than an economic – or collaborative – rationale.

Therefore, the problem for a SE that is closer to its initial collaborative nature, or for sustainability in general, is how to understand the impact of the entry of profit-maximising capital in SE firms. The work done by Zvolska, Palgan and Mont (2019) on how sharing organisations create and disrupt institutions is pertinent for illuminating the type of political activism undertaken by the strongly capitalised main SE players in urban spaces. By making use of the literature on institutional work (Lawrence & Suddaby, 2006) the authors cite three types of work that actors of the SE can undertake: (a) political work by changing regulatory institutions; (b) reconfiguration of of the belief systems of actors by modifying normative institutions; and (c) changing the boundaries of meaning systems by altering cognitive institutions.

Political Activism in the Sharing Economy

Lawrence and Suddaby (2006) describe institutional work as phases of conflict and cooperation between actors who represent old and new institutions, where the outcome typically reflects the values and interests of dominant actors. What is interesting at this point is how Zvolska et al. (op.cit) explore specific instances of how the SE creates and disrupt institutions. The analysis made specifically on the political work of SE platforms is particularly suitable for understanding the politics of these firms. Political work has three components that must be seen as part of a reinforcing loop: advocacy; defining; and vesting.

Advocacy is the prerequisite for defining rules and refers to the mobilisation of regulatory and political support through direct techniques of persuasion. Interestingly, the authors only found examples of powerful for-profit urban sharing organisations (USOs) with sufficiently abundant resources to engage in advocacy. The authors give several examples of this type of political activism. A reliance on litigation is reflected in the legal appeal made by Uber against a decision by the London government body responsible for transport that Uber had to employ its drivers. Lobbying is exemplified by a number of these SE platforms joining *Sharing Economy UK*, a trade body lobbying the government and policymakers to protect their interests. Or, at a later stage, shifting from city to supranational lobbying, as evidenced by Uber and Airbnb leading the EU lobby organisation, the *European Collaborative Forum*, in 2016. When for-profit bike sharing USOs based in London faced criticism for 'littering' the streets with bikes, the criticism was confronted by praising the positive impact of cycling on people's health, and communicating their positive environmental impact.

Defining is a prerequisite for advocacy and can be exemplified by the attempts by USOs to define themselves and their place in the sharing economy – and this further helps them in their lobbying and litigation activities. In a typical case, Uber attempted to avoid being regulated as a taxi service by claiming that it should not be seen as a mobility, taxi, or ride-sharing organisation – but as a tech-company.

Vesting, finally, is the attempt made by platforms to receive a special favourable treatment. While the authors did not find government agencies directly offering grants or subsidies to companies in exchange for a sharing service, they found examples such as the city halls in London, Berlin, and Malmö designating parking spaces to support car sharing. The previous examples show specific instances of the type of corporate activism we can expect and from which segment of the SE it will come. However, its broader political implications go beyond these examples and need to be carefully understood.

THE PROMISE OF LIBERATION IN THE SHARING ECONOMY

The Power Gap: Discussing Its Implications

The absence of corporate activism by not-for-profit SE examples in Zvolska et al. (op.cit) could be due to several reasons, although an initial response might be the lack of power to engage in political work in comparison with the large firms. The analysis made is soundly built upon the logic of institutional work since power implies access to resources and only powerful organisations can create or disrupt institutions (Lawrence & Suddaby, 2006, p. 235). Some additional implications are salient here too. These political manoeuvres have a replicative effect, since SE newcomers also imitate other more successful sharing platforms and develop their business models in line with the institutional transformation led by the main SE firms.

An example of *uberisation* is that new start-ups and corporate ventures want to be made subject to the same rules (or lack of) that were applied to Uber in the mobility sector. The institutional consequence is the expansion of specific understandings of what sharing is, the desired role of government and regulation, and the rights of users, workers, or citizens. Hence, we are seeing a new political world unfolding under the icebreaking thrust of these powerful and resourceful platforms.

Here we need to recover our main question: what remains of *sharing*, or collaboration, under the principles of market competition led by big players fuelled by private equity and a profit-maximising logic that aims at institutional creation and disruption? The previously mentioned report published by the *New Economics Foundation* (McCann 2018, p. 13) reminds us how tech giants compete by acquiring companies to cement a position in a market or extend reach into new markets. An important reflection appears as we watch the assumption of the neutrality of these platforms being bypassed: what does this tell us about the possible futures of the SE?

Some additional indication of the path being taken can be found in the patterns observed in the sustainability orientation of sharing economy platforms (Geissinger, Laurell, Öberg, & Sandström, 2019, p. 427). The conclusion indicates that as platforms develop they lose their sustainability orientations. Societal pressure, professionalisation, and the injection of capital into these firms explain, according to the authors, this development.

Orders of Worth and the New Spirit of Platform Capitalism

If we understand the SE as an epiphenomenon of the platform economy and as a moving target, what is now required is a discussion of the liberation envisioned by the main SE players – meaning what type of society, values, and goals the pursue. If sharing in its inception was a concept close to collaboration, sustainability, and inclusion (Murillo et al., 2017) what follows is a discussion of the political futures to be expected. To do so, the 'orders of worth' described in Lafaye and Thévenot (1993), Boltanski and Chiapello (2005), and Boltanski and Thévenot (2006) offer a guideline to these different futures or worlds.

In modern capitalism, these authors see an axiological and rhetorical battle at play that bundles meanings and values around specific principles of evaluation that claim to be global and universally acceptable. Several distinct worlds can be seen. An inspired world focuses on the results of platforms, ventures, and projects that emerge from a burst of inspiration and creativity. The business world is full of consumers with needs and desires and revolves around free markets, competition, and setting the right price. In the world of fame the ultimate value is public recognition and reputation. The industrial world emphasises efficiency, performance, and productivity. And, finally, adaptability and flexibility are the paramount elements in the project world.

The axiological world of the SE and platform capitalism is a world that celebrates innovation, public recognition, market logic and individualism – and where Uber becomes the synonym of innovation by breaking barriers and vested-interests, winning praise from entrepreneurial talent, and recognition from venture capitalists and growing markets. The champions of a flexible and adaptable future fight against an old regulatory system that is captured by trade associations and petty powers and which works against the meritocratic and democratic power of consumers. This is one possible future.

In contrast, on the other side of our possible futures, we encounter the domestic world – the world of tradition and personal bonds; and a civic world where collective interests override individualistic ones. This is a world concerned with the community's well-being, with principles of solidarity and fairness, as well as respect for the rule of law. And, finally, there is a green world of environmental protection and sustainability.

This last set of worlds forms a somewhat do-goody, sombre, and old-fashioned set of values that rely on the community, protectionism, and regulation. On the surface, these worlds seem incompatible with the promising and invigorating futures of the first collection of worlds.

Our goal at this point should be that of framing the previous orders of worth in relation to some of the main perils of the SE and platform capitalism. There has been some recent literature on this area. Among the issues discussed we find: regulatory arbitrage; discrimination; privacy (Calo & Rosenblat, 2017, pp. 1645–1648); competition; anti-trust issues; consumer protection; and business and taxation laws (Van Dijck et al., 2018, p. 157).

How is this 'new spirit of capitalism' (to use the title of Boltanski and Chiapello's book) going to confront these problems? Here we should turn to the traditional political agents that deal with this area: state and local governments.

There are many examples of regulatory measures that confront the previous challenges. At the most basic level, we see cities around the world trying to deal with the problem of gentrification. Cities have imposed regulatory measures on home-sharing platforms that range from full prohibitions to quantitative restrictions, proximity restrictions, and operational and licensing requirements. In other sectors, we see cities like Seattle supporting worker rights by helping gig workers to unionise. Similarly, to break the opacity of these platforms, municipalities have been asked to force platforms to disclose information (Ganapati & Reddick, 2018, pp. 84–85).

It is not difficult to imagine how big platforms are going to react to some of these new regulations. If we look at the attempt to make user data on mobility part of the broader public monitoring system of transport, the initial reaction seems clear. Breaking into the silos of privatised data collected by platforms contradicts one of the main principles by which platform capitalism operates: that of converging competition across markets based on *data extractivism* (maximised extraction) and *infrastructural enclosure* (not sharing data nor servers nor cables) (Srnicek, 2016). Mandatory information disclosure and *data extractivism* exemplify two poles of regulation and competition by default and different political futures.

Platform Capitalism at a Crossroads: The Neoliberal Direction

We need to turn now to the different promises of possible futures made by the SE. This is a much-overlooked aspect when we consider the uneasiness with which scholars working on the SE – who are savvy in narrow fields such as economics, law, or organisations – deal with societal or political reflections. We must start discussing the consequences of envisioning a future shaped by monopolistic super-platforms as postulated by Frenken (2017) in one of his three futures for the SE – i.e. monopolistic super-platforms; state-driven (regulated); and cooperatively-owned.

The values of market globalism are revealed in Uber's strategy to identify and deny service to local government authorities and so thwart state regulators – as exposed by the Greyball software disclosures. This is the ideology behind a managerial culture that celebrates breaking the law, bypassing regulation under the label of market disruption (Edelman, 2017), and which tries to find market solutions to market-made problems. Paraphrasing Morozov (2019), as Margaret Thatcher famously said "economics is the method; the object is to change the soul".

This is a future attuned with *technosolutionism* and *dataism*, the promise of social hope in technology and data, where markets provide solutions to every societal problem. As explained by Morozov (2015, p. 66) we can foresee companies extending their reach ever further into everyday life. Or, in Zuboff's terms (2018), moving from predicting behaviour to engineering behaviour, with computation replacing the political life of the community as the basis for governance.

A future that Tim Cook, Apple CEO, seems dubious about because he sees regulation inevitable (Goggin, 2018). In practical terms, *technosolutionism*, as a political device, implies ignoring the root causes of problems and trying to alleviate impacts at a superficial level – while dismissing the defensive activism of governments in defence of citizens. Much of the digital social entrepreneurship, hackathons, and what is now considered as corporate digital social innovation, comes in this particular flavour.

This represents a SE closely connected with mounting social inequality and pernicious competition based on a strategy of dumping prices and sustaining continuous losses; where asymmetries of information and power come to the fore, and where some large companies are capable of monitoring, nudging, and shaping human behaviour at an unprecedented scale (Calo & Rosenblat, 2017). For employees of the SE, this is a corporate-driven race to the bottom (Edelman, 2017) as recent JPMorgan and ILO reports reveal (Bershidsky, 2018). This is a logic compatible with platform business models that rely on the externalisation of costs and the continuous siphoning of income for every transaction facilitated (Srnicek, 2017).

Based on its impacts on society, the term 'crowd-based capitalism' as used by Sundararajan (2016) can be an appropriate name for the SE. A crowdsourcing internet marketplace like Amazon Mechanical Turk is a prime example of this extractive logic and its possible political futures. As expressed by Supiot (2018), the *uberisation* of work bolstered by the power of these big platforms, can exacerbate the dehumanisation of work intrinsic to the extension of the logic of Taylorism.

It is the opacity of these platforms (Frenken, 2017; Frenken & Schor, 2017), many located offshore as part of a global trend for profit maximisation (Zucman, 2015), that gives us the final picture. The usual rhetorical frameworks that capture the political activism of platforms under mottos like '*there is no way round*', '*markets are the future*', '*governments should not cap innovation*' or treat all social opposition as a Luddite backlash against technological progress, do much more than sell a sense of inevitability. They implicitly embrace the abandonment of any form of politics other than that of markets, corporate political activism, and the shrinkage of a public debate on the goals, principles, and means of the digital economy.

A Sharing Economy True to Its Values?

This default scenario has specific consequences for the alternative players of the SE – namely, those who claim to be true to the *collaborative* nature of the SE, and are willing to bypass the allure of private equity and organise under *orders of worth* different to those sustained by the market. Under this prism, other things being equal, it seems inevitable that alternative organisational forms – e.g. the zebras movement[1] or platform cooperativism (Rinne, 2018) – will remain residual. Fukuyama (2014) offers a very graphic explanation of how narrowing competition across sectors is translated into corporate political actions that further reinforce inequality in markets and society. The result is that big five tech firms dominate US digital markets with equivalent champions in autocratic China. A trend that is part of a broader process of economic concentration that, for the United States at least, encompasses practically all sectors (Leonhardt, 2018).

Using the dictum coined by traditional incumbent companies now competing with the big tech: can a different regulatory approach compensate those ventures that integrate societal expectations in their business models and level the playing field with the big firms? Here we need to review the role of regulation. When discussing different appraisals for the future of the platform economy, Dufva, Koivisto, Ilmola-Sheppard and Junno (2017) envision three possible scenarios: sustainable development led by Europe; polarisation driven by China and the US; or a US-driven platform economy of fast but mostly unreliable growth. At present, the European approach to regulation seems to be the only one aligned in principle with the views sustained by the alternative players in the SE. This is a model where the sharing element does more than free-ride on the positive connotation of the term for the purpose of lobbying the regulator (Zvolska et al., 2019).

The recent billion euro fines issued by the European Commission to companies like Google, or the landmark EUGDPR regulation of May 2018, seem to be the precursors for a platform economy that is more respectful towards the law, users, and citizens. Hopes indeed seem to be placed on something like a European, that is *humane*, approach to bridle big tech power (Supiot, 2018). However, Europe remains a small player in global digital platforms. With the exception of a few platforms like BlaBlaCar,[2] platform competition is mostly led by American and Chinese firms. On top of this, many of these American firms are based in offshore territories because of a perfectly coherent principle of profit maximisation and law avoidance.

Van Dijck et al. (2018) sees hope for a platform ecosystem that protects diversity, liberty, and solidarity in the European Union (which is paradoxically technologically weak and divided). In this view, the EU is a coalition of countries able to confront the libertarian and autocratic futures envisioned by America and China. The authors (2018, pp. 163–166) refer to our 'post-democratic' scenario where the nexus of the political, corporate, and media elite create political regimes that overemphasise economic and corporate-friendly priorities over everything else. How promising can the European project be in comparison with that of its counterparts? More interestingly, what form should it take to rein in the current gallop towards a neoliberal future?

CONCLUSION: A CALL FOR ALTERNATIVE POLITICAL APPROACHES TO *SHARING*

Introducing the Techno-Economic-Regulatory Gap

There are specific limitations on the regulation of these platforms continuing in the same way as today. The most obvious limitation is the long list of societal dangers associated with the SE platform economy in a planet that lacks a solid governance architecture (Bamberger & Lobel, 2017; Murillo et al., 2017). One of the proponents of a regulatory approach, the Nobel-prize laureate in economics Jean Tirole (2019), bundles together globalisation and legal ineffectiveness. He observes that rapidly changing technologies and globalisation have made traditional regulatory tools less effective and so cause competition policy to lag. Supiot (2018) goes a step further and analyses how corporations take advantage of different jurisdictions to render laws ineffective: 'rule of law is thus replaced by law 'shopping', subordinating the law to economic calculations rather than vice versa.' At this point, it seems imperative to discuss what we should expect from governments if there is such a lag?

For regulation to tackle the observed imbalances, we need to start by addressing the implications of the growing distance between technological development, business model adaptation, and a regulatory framework condemned to lag behind. We can observe three different layers operating on the platform economy. The first is technological and can be represented by the collection of practical and technical solutions to any observed problem. This is the layer of technological innovation. Here we find the world of possibilities exemplified by the reduction of costs associated with production, automation, exponential increases in the capacity to process information at lower prices (the three Vs of big data: volume, variety and velocity) and algorithmic development. This is the world of Moore's law and technological progress as analysed in the works of technology economics (Brynjolfsson & McAfee, 2016).

Figure 1.

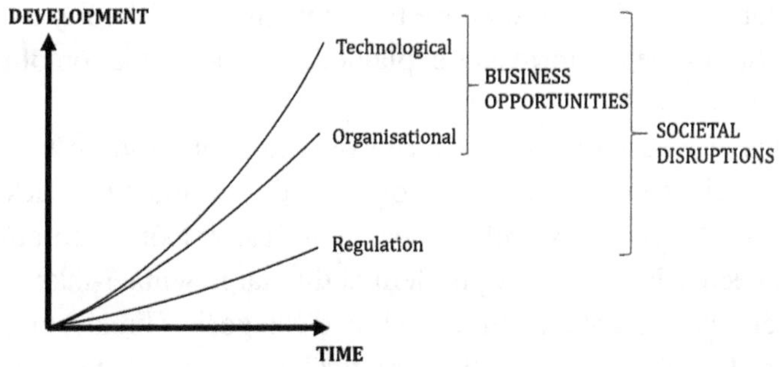

At a second deeper level, we find the transformation of technological solutions into market realities. Entrepreneurial projects aim to offer a viable business model, that is a market solution, capable of generating a paying demand for every given technological solution. It must be highlighted that it requires time to develop a viable solution capable of monetising a previous technological innovation and transform it into a real market opportunity. Additionally, as with any type of market innovation, we know that many of these projects fail or simply fail to reach a mature enough demand in time.

Thirdly, and lagging well behind the other two, comes regulation. Regulation is the result of political compromises that try to render effective measures for the goals set by the regulator. The effectiveness of such measures depends on the capacity of the regulator to collect the needed expertise, find a monitoring mechanism, and achieve the required enforcement capacity. Regulation typically involves a process of deliberation with the stakeholders and must be seen as reflecting the power and resources of the different parties. Using the classical argument set forward by Polanyi (1944), it is the expansion of market forces that determines a double movement for protection, which is to be found behind some forms of new regulation.

The distinctive nature of platform capitalism forces us to see the acceleration of technology in the digital world in parallel with the boost of entrepreneurial projects – backed initially by V.C. and then private equity – and with regulatory pressure lagging behind. It seems evident that societal disruptions, understood in the Polanyian sense as the space between the expansion of technology, markets, and the regulatory backlash, can only expand. In this process, following Morozov (2019), companies adapt to a rapidly changing environment, where capitalists must follow the imperatives of the new surveillance-based logic. At his point, governments must worry about the means of behavioural modification, not only about the means of production.

From Regulation to Political Activism

Contrary to what Taneja (2019) states, it is more than dubious that the era of 'move fast and break things' is over. The era of naive corporate humanism or regulation by default seems probably about to end too. Morozov (2018) suggests that 'many of these promises [the original promises of the SE] will look appealing. But without a robust political agenda – an agenda that harbours no illusions about the ability of global capital to promote social emancipation – they will produce the opposite effects'.

The question of how to address the imbalances and societal disruptions produced by the usual champions of the SE invites us to think about a new division of roles and responsibilities among the different stakeholders willing to offer alternative futures for the SE. It seems evident that it is not only the techno-economic-regulatory gap discussed above that explains the difficulty in finding a timely public action to tackle the politics of the platforms; as explained, it is the regulation of platforms itself that has become problematic.

The list of reasons why we need to find new forms of regulation to address the abovementioned controversies has recently received quite some attention. A major problem is a lack of imagination, which places regulation as being based excessively on past political responses to already identified market externalities. As it has been said, when the problem is that large winner-take-all markets give birth to single champions, policies can be grouped into two broad categories: break companies up or nationalise them (McCann, 2018, p. 16). To start, one rather practical problem is that discussed by this report: tech giants have become adept at focusing their exploitative power on the producer side while ensuring cheap or free services to users. This makes the case for reform hard to sell to the public since it is likely to impact on millions, if not billions, of people through potentially increased prices (McCann, 2018, p. 18).

Van Dijk et al. (2018, pp. 157–162) go a level deeper. The usual attempt to fix 'market failures' is going to fail for several additional reasons. Firstly, the sponsors of such attempts try to separately address the many controversial issues at stake – including privacy, competition, anti-trust issues, consumer protection, and business and taxation laws. Secondly, in many levels the sponsors of regulation lack the technological vocabulary and acumen to effectively address these problems. Thirdly, these sponsors lack information and the accountability mechanisms able to draw back the curtain of opacity that surrounds these platforms. [3] Fourthly, tech companies thrive in a vague space that cuts across sectors – and we should add countries – where market power helps them elude the radar of public scrutiny.

It seems clear that the regulatory approach needs to take a different turn. Governments must muster power by articulating the public value standards to which platforms must comply. This is, or more appropriately should be, the European approach to addressing problems with big platforms. Specifically, it means going beyond regulation and acting as a socio-political engineer instead. Following Lawrence and Suddaby (2006), and perhaps it is too obvious a reminder, governments can also create institutions that have the legitimacy, although not always the power, enjoyed by platforms. In these regard, van Dijck et al. (op.cit) make a call for governments to develop concerted, multiparty, collaborative efforts in which the state acts as both developer and partner.

There are already examples of this trend. New York is asking cab-hailing apps to share information on rides. E-Stonia gives citizens access to taxation services, identification, cadastral information, and personalised health information through a public platform. We could imagine an open calibrated taxi meter or a public identification service capable of bypassing big tech login apps. Interestingly, Harvard professor Shoshana Zuboff (2018) sees social movements as the only way out of surveillance capitalism, which she defines as a rogue mutation of capitalism based on a surveillance-based economic order that permeates the social fabric to an unprecedented extent.

Societies need a comprehensive regulatory approach that tackles the widespread disparities of power, welfare, and opportunity in an online world (Van Dijck et al., 2018, p. 157). Such an approach should lead the public debate on which digital infrastructure needs to be public and which not (Morozov, 2015, p. 63, 2019). Ultimately, this intrinsically political game goes well beyond mere regulation. Examples of these debates are becoming more and more common in the media: should police records be stored in a private cloud run by data extracting platforms or not? Should private medical records be in the hands of corporate conglomerates that spread across sectors and industries? Should platforms allow for personal and detailed analysis of the uses of the data we share with them?

A revival of the language of the commons is an indicator of the emerging political debate about technology. This political dispute should address issues like public/private digital infrastructure, fair competition, and above all, ownership of data and privacy rights in the digital era (Morozov, 2015, p. 64). Each country should have the capacity to enlarge the list. Again, this implies more than just regulating. A new form of activism is badly needed to confront the corporate political activism of the sharing platforms and platform capitalism. This activism needs to understand the challenges of big tech, the power of the prevalent surveillance technologies, and the intrinsically political nature of the corporate activism of big tech.

In this scenario, sharing platforms should be seen as crucial players in this competition which, away from the public eye, strives to create specific political futures. As we have discussed above, this political struggle is the result of a highly unbalanced mass of interests, power, and media attention which, in its present distribution, effectively narrows down the avenues for alternative political futures. The increasing alertness among citizens against big tech reveals a turn of the tide. The time is right for a different form of political activism that puts the interests of society at its centre.

REFERENCES

Bamberger, K. A., & Lobel, O. (2017). Platform Market Power. *Berkeley Technology Law Journal, 32*. Retrieved from https://heinonline.org/HOL/Page?handle=hein.journals/berktech32&id=1095&div=35&collection=journals

Bershidsky, L. (2018). *Gig-Economy Workers Are the Modern Proletariat*. Bloomberg.

Boltanski, L., & Chiapello, E. (2005). *The new spirit of capitalism*. Verso. doi:10.100710767-006-9006-9

Boltanski, L., & Thévenot, L. (2006). *On justification: economies of worth*. Princeton University Press.

Bravo, P. (2019, January 12). De las fake news a las empresas fake: cómo afecta la economía ficción a nuestras ciudades. *Eldiario.Es*. Retrieved from https://www.eldiario.es/desde-mi-bici/fake-empresas-economia-ficcion-ciudades_6_856074416.html

Brynjolfsson, E., & McAfee, A. (2016). *The second machine age: work, progress, and prosperity in a time of brilliant technologies*. W. W. Norton Company.

Calo, R., & Rosenblat, A. (2017). The Taking Economy: Uber, Information, and Power. *Columbia Law Review, 117*(6), 1623–1690. Retrieved from https://www.jstor.org/stable/44392959?seq=1#page_scan_tab_contents

Ciulli, F., & Kolk, A. (2019). Incumbents and business model innovation for the sharing economy: Implications for sustainability. *Journal of Cleaner Production, 214*, 995–1010. doi:10.1016/j.jclepro.2018.12.295

Dufva, M., Koivisto, R., Ilmola-Sheppard, L., & Junno, S. (2017). Anticipating Alternative Futures for the Platform Economy. *Technology Innovation Management Review, 7*(9), 6–16. doi:10.22215/timreview/1102

Edelman, B. (2017). Uber Can't Be Fixed — It's Time for Regulators to Shut It Down. *Harvard Business Review, 21*. Retrieved from https://hbr.org/2017/06/uber-cant-be-fixed-its-time-for-regulators-to-shut-it-down

Frenken, K. (2017). Political economies and environmental futures for the sharing economy. *Philosophical Transactions of the Royal Society A: Mathematical, Physical and Engineering Sciences, 375*. doi:10.1098/rsta.2016.0367

Frenken, K., & Schor, J. (2017). Putting the sharing economy into perspective. *Environmental Innovation and Societal Transitions, 23*, 3–10. doi:10.1016/j.eist.2017.01.003

Fukuyama, F. (2014). America in Decay: The Sources of Political Dysfunction. *Foreign Affairs*, 93.

Ganapati, S., & Reddick, C. G. (2018). Prospects and challenges of sharing economy for the public sector. *Government Information Quarterly, 35*(1), 77–87. doi:10.1016/j.giq.2018.01.001

Geissinger, A., Laurell, C., Öberg, C., & Sandström, C. (2019). How sustainable is the sharing economy? On the sustainability connotations of sharing economy platforms. *Journal of Cleaner Production, 206*, 419–429. doi:10.1016/j.jclepro.2018.09.196

Gillespie, T. (2010). The politics of 'platforms'. *New Media & Society, 12*(3), 347–364. doi:10.1177/1461444809342738

Goggin, B. (2018). Apple CEO Tim Cook on privacy: 'we have to admit when the free market is not working'. *Business Insider*. Retrieved from https://www.businessinsider.es/apple-ceo-tim-cook-on-privacy-the-free-market-is-not-working-regulations-2018-11?r=US&IR=T

Gompers, P., & Lerner, J. (2001). The Venture Capital Revolution. *The Journal of Economic Perspectives, 15*(2), 145–168. doi:10.1257/jep.15.2.145

Griffit, E. (2019, January 11). More Start-Ups Have an Unfamiliar Message for Venture Capitalists: Get Lost. *The New York Times*. Retrieved from https://www.nytimes.com/2019/01/11/technology/start-ups-rejecting-venture-capital.html

Kazmin, A., & Ram, A. (2017). India's Uber drivers feel taken for a ride on earnings promises | Financial Times. *Financial Times*. Retrieved from https://www.ft.com/content/12bf0cce-0d99-11e7-a88c-50ba212dce4d

Lafaye, C., & Thevenot, L. (1993). Une justification écologique?: Conflits dans l'aménagement de la nature. *Revue Francaise de Sociologie, 34*(4), 495. doi:10.2307/3321928

Lawrence, T. B., & Suddaby, R. (2006). Institutions and Institutional Work. In S. R. Clegg, C. Hardy, T. B. Lawrence, & W. R. Nord (Eds.), *The SAGE Handbook of Organization Studies* (2nd ed.; pp. 215–264). doi:10.4135/9781848608030.n7

Leonhardt, D. (2018). The Monopolization of America. *The New York Times*. Retrieved from https://www.nytimes.com/2018/11/25/opinion/monopolies-in-the-us.html

McCann, D. (2018). *Digital Power Players: Power and Accountability in the Digital Economy. Part 4: The Problem and the Power of Tech Monopolies*. Retrieved from https://neweconomics.org/uploads/files/Digital-Power-Players_181113_155656.pdf

Morozov, E. (2015). Socialize the data centres! *New Left Review*, (91): 45–66.

Morozov, E. (2018). From Airbnb to city bikes, the 'sharing economy' has been seized by big money. *The Guardian*. Retrieved from https://www.theguardian.com/commentisfree/2018/nov/27/airbnb-city-bikes-sharing-economy-big-money

Morozov, E. (2019). Capitalism's New Clothes. *The Baffler*.

Murillo, D., Buckland, H., & Val, E. (2017). When the sharing economy becomes neoliberalism on steroids: Unravelling the controversies. *Technological Forecasting and Social Change*, *125*, 66–76. doi:10.1016/j.techfore.2017.05.024

Olma, S. (2014). *Never Mind the Sharing Economy: Here's Platform Capitalism*. Retrieved from http://networkcultures.org/mycreativity/2014/10/16/never-mind-the-sharing-economy-heres-platform-capitalism/

Parente, R. C., Geleilate, J.-M. G. M. G., & Rong, K. (2018). The Sharing Economy Globalization Phenomenon: A Research Agenda. *Journal of International Management*, *24*(1), 52–64. doi:10.1016/j.intman.2017.10.001

Polanyi, K. (1944). *The great transformation: Economic and political origins of our time*. New York: Rinehart.

Reuters. (2018). SoftBank's Vision Fund says portfolio reached 65 companies so far. *Reuters*. Retrieved from https://www.reuters.com/article/us-saudi-investment-softbank-group-portf/softbanks-vision-fund-says-portfolio-reached-65-companies-so-far-idUSKCN1MX1DB

Richardson, L. (2015). Performing the sharing economy. *Geoforum*, *67*, 121–129. doi:10.1016/j.geoforum.2015.11.004

Rinne, A. (2018). The Dark Side of the Sharing Economy. *World Economic Forum*, 21. Retrieved from https://www.weforum.org/agenda/2018/01/the-dark-side-of-the-sharing-economy/

Srnicek, N. (2016). *Platform Capitalism*. Cambridge, UK: Polity Press.

Srnicek, N. (2017). The challenges of platform capitalism. *Juncture*, *23*(4), 254–257. doi:10.1111/newe.12023

Sundararajan, A. (2016). *The sharing economy: the end of employment and the rise of crowd-based capitalism*. MIT Press.

Supiot, A. (2018). A Labour code for the 21st century. *Le Monde Diplomatique*. Retrieved from https://mondediplo.com/2018/05/17-labourcode

Taneja, H. (2019). The Era of "Move Fast and Break Things" Is Over. *Harvard Business Review*. Retrieved from https://hbr.org/2019/01/the-era-of-move-fast-and-break-things-is-over

Tirole, J. (2019). Regulating the disrupters. *LiveMint*. Retrieved from https://www.livemint.com/Technology/XsgWUgy9tR4uaoME7xtITI/Regulating-the-disrupters-Jean-Tirole.html

van Dijck, J., Poell, T., & de Waal, M. (2018). *The platform society: public values in a connective world*. Oxford University Press. doi:10.1093/oso/9780190889760.001.0001

Zuboff, S. (2018). *The age of surveillance capitalism: The fight for a human future at the new frontier of power*. New York: Public Affairs. Retrieved from https://www.publicaffairsbooks.com/titles/shoshana-zuboff/the-age-of-surveillance-capitalism/9781610395694/

Zucman, G. (2015). *The hidden wealth of nations : the scourge of tax havens*. University of Chicago Press. doi:10.7208/chicago/9780226245560.001.0001

Zvolska, L., Palgan, Y. V., & Mont, O. (2019). How do sharing organisations create and disrupt institutions? Towards a framework for institutional work in the sharing economy. *Journal of Cleaner Production, 219*, 667–676. doi:10.1016/j.jclepro.2019.02.057 PMID:31080321

ENDNOTES

1 https://www.zebrasunite.com/

2 http://www.blablacar.com/

3 The role of International organisations like the OECD or the ILO could be that of providing information, data, potential policies and recommendations to guide and inform governments –i.e. on areas like taxation or decent work in digital platforms. However, we should not miss the powerplay that takes place between these organisations, its members and governments that pit their respective missional goals against the capacity to promote, enforce or resist those measures by the different individual countries. Existing international agreements and the legislative record promoted by institutions like the World Bank, the IMF and the WTO further limit the capacity of the previous states to oppose market forces.

Chapter 3
The Impact of Collaborative Consumption on Sustainable Development

Erhan İşcan
https://orcid.org/0000-0001-6068-6698
Çukurova University, Turkey

ABSTRACT

Excessive use of goods and services and industrialization progress of 20th century depleted resources and emerged the sustainable development as the main target of the policymakers, but past experiences and consequences of rapid economic growth of 20th century showed that there must be a change in the policies. Alleviating of poverty with inequalities and hunger in a degraded environment is needing sustainable cities and communities that have decent work for economic growth. In this context, perhaps, there must be a change in the economic paradigm beyond a policy change. Collaborative consumption is this new economic paradigm that has changed the understanding of the economic system. This new economic paradigm is depending on the sharing of idle resources with or without a fee that changed the importance of asset ownership. The main aim of this chapter is to present the impact of collaborative consumption on the 10 Sustainable Development Goals of the UN.

INTRODUCTION

The tremendous increase in consumption in the second half of the 20th century brought us a new term, hyper-consumption. Hyper-consumption can be defined as excessive consumption of goods and services that are seen especially in developed countries. Society is consuming beyond the needs and companies are encouraging this consuming behavior. This consumption pattern is threatening the world with new problems. Environmental pollution, excessive usage of resources, falling happiness of humankind and increasing inequality are the main problems that arose from this hyper-consumption pattern. Environmental pollution is increasing continuously that is induced by excessive use of resources. Many of the governments and international organizations agreed on the impacts of resource depletion with negative

DOI: 10.4018/978-1-5225-9928-9.ch003

Copyright © 2020, IGI Global. Copying or distributing in print or electronic forms without written permission of IGI Global is prohibited.

ecological impacts on economic growth (UNEP, 2015). Besides, the happiness of the humankind is falling especially for the last two decade and showed that consuming is not the way that is satisfying the consumers. Additionally, hyper-consumption is leading the increasing inequality with buying more than one can afford that is increasing the debt of lower and middle-income class. As a remarkable example, the level of US consumer debt raised over 4 trillion USD and 1 trillion USD of this debt is revolving credits used by consumers like credit cards (FED, 2019). This example showed us a very clear indicator of the hyper-consumption. On the other hand, overall happiness is decreasing year by year despite the high level of consumption. According to the World Happiness Report that is prepared by the New Economics Foundation, happiness is not related to the high income. Although the income of Costa Rica is low compared to the US, Japan or many European Countries, ranks the first place of the Happy Planet Index. US is the 108th with a score of 20.7 where the world average is 26.4 (Jeffrey et. al., 2016). Likewise Harris (2018) mentioned the same problem in his article at World Economic Forum's Agenda. Harris (2018) stated that there is a disparity between wealth and happiness for many of the developed countries. This disparity has started to affect policymakers' discussion radically for assessing the prosperity of the nation (Harris, 2018). The climate change, potential food crises in 2050, excessive use of resources, falling happiness and increasing inequality forced to find a new way of satisfying the needs.

In the last decade, an old solution with a new approach emerged to the hyper-consumption problem: Collaborative Consumption. Collaborative consumption is not a new concept but the progression of the internetworking, effect of the 2008 financial crisis, potential food crisis, and concerns about the environment gave a new pathway to collaborative consumption. Collaborative consumption is a new way of producing and consuming goods or services based on sharing all resources without ownership of an asset. This is a new socio-economic paradigm. This new paradigm allows people accessing, sharing, swapping, and consuming between individuals or through companies, with or without a fee. There are many different names of the collaborative consumption that define the same concept. The sharing economy, collaborative economy, on-demand economy, platform economy, and peer-to-peer economy are commonly used to define collaborative consumption.

In the WCED report, also called as Brundtland Report, defined the sustainable development and debates started (WCED, 1987). Sustainable development is still the most important debate of the third millennium that integrated economic and social development with environmental sustainability. Poverty, hunger, health, education, inequality, water, energy, climate, peace, and economic growth are the main goals of sustainable development for all developing and developed countries in global partnership. The 2030 Agenda for Sustainable Development of United Nations (UN) stated that 17 Sustainable Development Goals (SDG) provides a shared blueprint for peace and prosperity for people and planet from now to the future and adopted by all UN member states in 2015 (United Nations General Assembly, 2015, 1). Policymakers of the governments, international organizations, and supranational organizations are still dealing with unbalanced growth with the many sustainability problems that are threatening humanity. The worst problem for the policymakers is being at the end of old-school policies.

The main aim of this chapter is to assess the collaborative consumption in terms of sustainable development goals and to understand the impact of collaborative consumption on sustainable development. To achieve this goal, collaboration consumption will be examined within the framework of ten different sustainable development goal of the UN. Over the last decade, many researchers studied the definition, content, and sustainability of collaborative consumption but only a few of them linked the collaborative consumption with sustainable development. Therefore, this study will contribute to the literature and will suggest a framework for policymakers.

THE IMPACT OF COLLABORATIVE CONSUMPTION ON SUSTAINABLE DEVELOPMENT GOALS

Sustainable development is the main issue for the policymakers of the countries and international economic organizations for over three decades and they set many policies to achieve the goals of sustainable development. However, these policies are still the subject of discussion in terms of efficiency and performance of the current economic paradigm to achieve sustainable development goals is suspicious. Beyond the conventional economic paradigms, collaborative consumption is a remarkable one that has significant potential for achieving sustainable development goals over the last decade. Besides, because of the interlinked nature of the sustainable developments goals, collaborative consumption may be a new socio-economic paradigm that will make a difference due to the potential effect on the UN's sustainable development goals. UN indicated that environmental degradation, climate change, the persistence of hunger and poverty, increase in all types of inequality, and rapid urbanization are complicating the problems and new policies are requiring an integrating paradigm. Therefore collaborative consumption can be a new pathway to a sustainable future for all by changing the socio-economic paradigm.

In this study, the impact of collaborative consumption on poverty, hunger, gender equality, decent work and economic growth, sustainable cities and communities, responsible consumption and production, climate action, life below water and life on land will be analyzed. There are 17 sustainable development goals of the UN and 10 of them will be associated with collaborative consumption in this chapter. Interlinking these sustainable development goals with the collaborative consumption platforms is the strength of this new socio-economic paradigm.

No Poverty and Zero Hunger

Poverty is the main economic problem through the world for all times and due to this importance, the first goal of the UN is ending poverty within all its forms everywhere. Therefore, policymakers particularly setup policies to alleviate poverty in many countries. Poverty is not a problem for only the developing or less developed countries also it is affecting the developed countries. OECD mentioned that poverty rates increased in developed countries especially after the 2000s. OECD countries poverty rates are also very high especially in some countries for young people and some countries for old people. Figure 1 showed the poverty rates in OECD countries with two age groups and total and most of the countries have a rate of poverty over 0.1 for any groups or total. Some of the well-developed countries have interestingly high poverty rates especially for the senior citizen group while many of them have high poverty rates for the young. Global poverty is worse than this view and according to World Bank, 46 percent of the world population, 14 percent of Europe and Central Asia population and 85 percent of Sub-Saharan Africa population are living on less than 5.5 USD a day in 2015. This overview of the poverty indicators are only a part of the whole picture and it seems that extreme poverty is resisting to the conventional policies.

ILO reported that especially after the 2008 financial crises poverty is on the rise for Europe. Besides, ILO estimated that 300 million people were living in poverty in developed countries in 2012 and these trends can take the developed countries to higher poverty rates (ILO, 2016). For the developing and less-developed countries, the problem is much worse than the developed countries. While East Asia and the Pacific has lifted millions of people from poverty, South Asia also significantly decreased the number of poor people. On the other hand progress in Sub-Saharan Africa is relatively very slow and the number of the poor are increasing. In Eastern Europe and Central Asia the number of the poor is

Figure 1. Poverty rate in 2017 Source: OECD (2019), Poverty rate (indicator). doi: 10.1787/0fe1315d-en (Accessed on 03 March 2019)

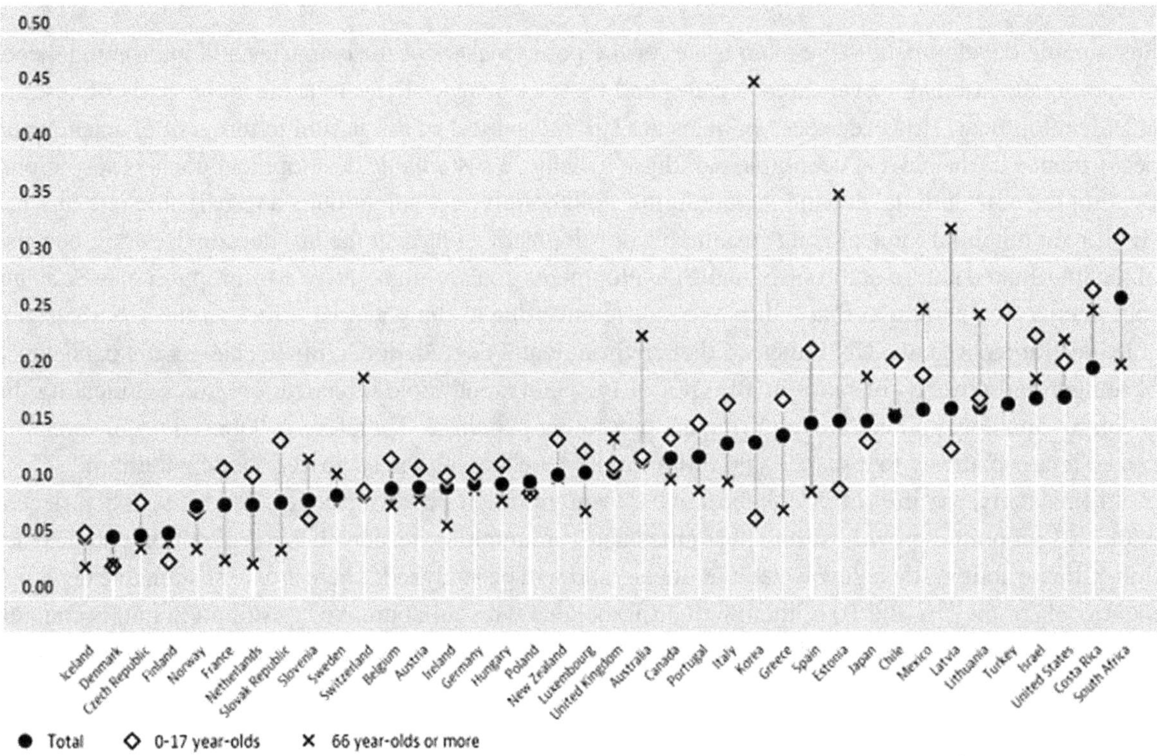

remarkable and a complex issue. Despite the remarkable progress in reducing extreme poverty still, there are over 3.3 billion poor in the world and it is getting harder to overcome the problem. It is very clear that policymakers are needing a new paradigm.

Hunger is the most disturbing problem for the humankind and second sustainable development goal of the UN. Researches have shown that there will be food crises due to the growing population and climate change in 2050. On the other hand, decreasing income of the lower and middle class is increasing the especially hidden hunger. FAO stated that 815 million people are suffering from hunger and this is not the worst case because hidden hunger –called as micronutrient malnutrition- is affecting over 2 billion people by now (FAO et. al., 2017; Hodge, 2016; Gödecke et. al 2018). After the food crises between 2007 and 2008 prices are still unstable that is threatening the world.

Poverty and hunger are seen together and suffering from poverty caused to hunger. At the same time undernourishing people also haven't got a chance to empower for work then poverty exists. This is an endless cycle of the two problems for humanity that are fostering each other. There are very different reasons for poverty and hunger but food shortages, climate change, economy, food waste, gender inequality may be counted as common reasons.

Many socioeconomic factors can cause poverty but property right is seen as an important factor especially in developing and less developed countries. In his seminal book, Hernando de Soto stated that capitalism's success in the West depends on property rights that are activating the capital (De Soto, 2000). Basically, property rights over resources reflect wealth and poverty. In this framework, ownership of the capital and natural resources is affecting the distribution of wealth among the citizens in every country. In his seminal book, Knight stated that most essential part of the economic progress is property rights because enjoyment of the use of the private property would give an incentive to use the goods effectively in production (Knight, 1971). This point is the beginning of the problem for poverty because insufficient land to live on and insecure access or rights over land are well-recognized factors in sustaining poverty. Many of the regions and countries that are suffering from poverty have the problem of property rights in parallel with the unequal distribution of property and without legal protection of the assets (UNDP, 2008).

Beside the other policies, collaborative consumption may be a useful socio-economic paradigm that will fight with poverty and hunger with various platforms. Collaborative consumption may empower individuals by solving the problem of owning the capital. The main contribution of collaborative consumption is depending on its sharing characteristics and this feature will enable to share the assets that are physical or human capital.

Collaborative consumption may transform some sectors and can create new job opportunities through online businesses. Besides, for these new job opportunities, there is no need to own an asset or a firm because online web sites are providing all of the needs. Airbnb is a remarkable practice that creates business opportunities for people. Airbnb is a website that anyone can rent an idle place with a few clicks and some photos by using only a smartphone. For the lower income group, Airbnb is creating an opportunity without any cost or bureaucracy. All of the legal works and payments are carried out by Airbnb and the host is responsible for only the condition of the place. There are many worldwide examples from developed, developing and less developed countries for the positive impact on people who have not an opportunity to rent the idle space. On the other hand, Airbnb is contributing to the tourism sector in every country by supplying idle resources or ideas of the local people. These idle resources or ideas are attracting tourists to new places and creating income for the local people. The tourism sector is very important for the world economy and producing 10% of the global GDP. These two effects are very important especially for the people that are suffering from poverty in all developed and less-developed countries. The effects of these interesting issues draw the attention of the Labour Market Committee of the Nordic Council of Ministers and published a report about implications of the sharing economy for the labor market and employment relations in the Nordic countries. Airbnb is not a unique example of collaborative consumption. There many different types of platforms that are serving on the same basis. Uber, Snapgoods, Dogvacay, Lyft, Tubber, Scotty, Lime, Grab, Zaarly, and Cargo are only a few examples of companies from different countries that are creating business opportunities, especially for the low and middle-income groups. These companies may have a remarkable effect for contribution to the alleviation of poverty by enabling the micro-entrepreneurs.

On the other hand, collaborative consumption may be lightening the hunger problem with innovative platforms. The main reason behind hunger is the lack of control over food resources. Controlling the resources for producing the food and creating connected food production systems between rural and urban or regions will have a chance to decrease hunger at least decrease the growth rate of hunger.

There are many kinds of collaborative platforms that can be useful for fighting with hunger. There are cases and policies in the report of Shareable that will affect the hunger problem. FoodCloud is linking up businesses and charities to redistribute surplus food to people in need. Seva Café is a pay-it-forward experiment in peer-to-peer generosity. Urban Agriculture Incentive Zone, Resolution to Support Seed Saving and Sharing, Agroecological Strategy to Increase Food Sovereignty and Creating a Vibrant Local

Food Ecosystem through Government-NGO Collaboration are the example of the policies (Shareable, 2017).

In addition, the moral pressure for the wasting of the food even packaged in supermarkets due to the best before the date and higher obesity population than hungry people will accelerate the collaborative consumption platforms. Governments started to support platforms that are targeting poverty and hunger across Europe. This is just the beginning.

Gender Equality and Reduce Inequalities

Gender equality is the fifth sustainable development goal of the UN and a key goal for achieving sustainable development. According to the World Bank CPIA data average Women, Business and Law Index increased to 74.7 but still, 48.4 percent of the women are participating to the labour force. Besides, CPIA gender equality rating decreased to 3.2 that indicated the increasing inequality (WB, 2019). Collaborative consumption may have a remarkable role for these two goals of sustainable development. International Finance Corporation of the World Bank published a report about the impact of collaborative consumption on gender equality and set out the potential of collaborative consumption (IFC, 2018). Collaborative Consumption companies are serving on a P2P basis and gave an opportunity to those who are unable to find a job in the current situation. According to Barzilay and Ben-David, there are two positive effects of collaborative consumption to gender equality. First one is having a greater degree of anonymity and potential inclusiveness that could offset bias, barriers, and discrimination against women. Especially gender-blinded platforms will encourage gender equality by reducing the barriers to entry especially of male-dominated industries and easier to negotiate for equal pay. The second one is the opportunity to provide flexibility in setting work schedules (Barzilay & Ben-David, 2016). This flexibility may be very valuable for single moms, caregivers, moms with disabled children or moms in the search for work-family balance and will give an opportunity to increase the income even changing the gendered roles of caretaking and breadwinning. Besides, collaborative consumption platforms may also provide a new basis for supplying goods and services that can be produced by women. Persistency of the labor market against women may diminish and will give equal chances to find new jobs with a man. This can be counted as a third effect and also will enable to fight with poverty simultaneously by empowering women (Barzilay & Ben-David, 2016). IFC stated that ride-hailing is an important example of contribution to gender equality. We can saw clearly this three effect in the ride-hailing industry on gender equality. Ride-hailing industry is, in fact, a male-dominated industry but these new collaborative consumption platforms reduce the barriers and boost the average income of women by working with a similar rate with a man. On the other hand, 91 percent of mothers that are driving with Uber is also the caregiver of their children. This is a clear example of the second effect that has a huge potential to empower women. A woman driver in Uber will have flexible working hours and care for her children in their daily life. There is no need permission for anything from a boss and finding extra hours by any reason will increase income. The third effect is directly about with participation of women to the labor force. Ride-hailing industry is also a brand new industry that increases female labor force participation and will help women to build and run their own business. Additionally, these new industries will encourage and give an opportunity to own the productive asset, i.e. a vehicle. In the IFC report stated that Uber arrangements offer new ways of vehicle ownership or access. There are many examples of women that are increasing the standard of living by the effect of collaborative consumption and its platforms all in developed, developing or less-developed countries (IFC, 2018). In the future women will be the most important economic agent for the collaborative platforms and disposable income of the women are expected to rise (WEF, 2019). This new economic paradigm will have a remarkable contribution by new ideas on empowering women to promote economic development.

Decent Work and Economic Growth

Sustainable development goals indicated that economic growth is not the only way of developing and exclusively must include decent work. The global unemployment rate decreased from 6.4 percent in 2000 to 5.6 percent in 2017 but still, youth employment was three times higher than adults. The average annual growth of the global working-age population is projected to fall 1.1 percent by 2030 (UN, 2018; ILO, 2019). Moreover, earning inequalities and informal employment are the main problem for the countries. Wages of men are 12.5 percent higher than those of women and 61 percent of all workers employed informally (UN, 2018). In other words, the economy must create good jobs while it is growing.

Collaborative consumption has changed the way of working from payroll working to on-demand working. Collaborative consumption platforms may have o potential to change the traditional employment forms to a self-employment form that is outsourcing the employer. Besides, the condition of the workplace, work or firm has changed or most of them disappeared and gave labor an opportunity to choose work-family balance. This kind of flexibility will directly affect the wage levels, working conditions and also the job itself. These changes in the labor market are not only important for disadvantaged groups or low-skilled workers. These platforms also provide an opportunity to enter the new markets for the high-skilled workers.

The problem for the mid-aged unemployed labor force is to engage new types of jobs because changing their education, learning curve, human capital, productive asset or personal specification is quite hard. Especially the mid-age workers in the labor force have an opportunity to find a new job after losing the old one. Collaborative consumption platforms provide a different kind of new jobs that are suitable with assets, desires, education, abilities or even hobbies of the mid-age labor force. Moreover, Corujo (2017) stated that this kind of work is a new phenomenon and called as uberization of the economy which is changing the workers to collaborators (Coujo, 2017). On the other hand, jobs that arise from collaborative consumption may be a transition job for the workers that give time for finding a suitable new job.

Collaborative consumption platforms have the potential to enable micro-entrepreneurship and crowdfunding may support to start-up new businesses. Especially unemployed youth and new job-seeking mid-aged labor will mostly benefit from these potentials. Platforms may increase the employment level while promoting the self-employment and lower the inequalities between all groups. Platforms also provide outsourcing to businesses and create new works that will promote micro-entrepreneurship.

On the other hand, initial barriers are the main problem for all the markets and the labor market is not exceptional. In fact, a barrier in the labor market is a crucial problem that is inducing the poverty and unemployment differences between all groups. Online labor markets that are allowing the labor a fair entry will promote the disadvantaged groups. Besides, these platforms are providing a fair credibility system for these disadvantaged groups that enabled them Collaborative platforms provide labor to enter the market with new ways of service supply and allow these groups to engage the labor force that will promote the decent work. Earnings of the disadvantaged group may rise with decreasing barriers and flexible working conditions. According to the Eurofound (2015), societal and economic developments labor markets will be more inclusive and give good access to work opportunities for all groups with flexibility and control on the working pattern (Eurofound, 2015).

Sustainable Cities and Communities

The rapid growth of the urban population inevitably increases the urbanization, slums population, need of infrastructure, solid waste, number of vehicles, air pollution, resource depletion, and crime rate. Therefore, sustainable cities and communities became very essential for sustainable development to provide healthy living space and therefore UN set as eleventh of the sustainable development goals. Healthy living space is not only about sufficient infrastructure, high air quality or low level of solid waste. Trust and social inclusion, developed a socio-economic environment and high sense of community and belonging are the main components for being sustainable cities. World Economic Forum stated that collaborative dynamics of this new socio-economic paradigm have creative implications and will create community among strangers, reduce overall use of resources for socio-economic development (WEF, 2017). Many cities have seen these significant potential benefits of collaborative consumption and developed different platforms. Especially, increasing digital inclusion, increasing population of the cities and smartphones accelerated the number and coverage of the platforms. Besides, awareness of the people about environmental, social, economic problems is higher than the past for now and this increasing awareness is also affecting the platforms. There is a very well definition of the cities in terms of collaborative consumption in a report of Sustainable Economies Law Center. *"Cities are built for sharing. It's what makes cities engines of prosperity, innovation, and cultural exchange."* (Orsi et. Al., 2013). There are many problems that are threatening the cities but collaborative consumption has a significant impact potential within eleven categories according to Shareable. Housing, mobility, food, work, energy, land, waste, water, technology, finance, and governance are the main collaborative categories that will promote the sustainability of cities and communities (Shareable, 2017).

Collaborative consumption may have a significant effect on cities to provide sustainability while there is no recommendation of new policies from conventional-type politicians. In these conditions, cities may be a stepping stone with globally-connected people to promote sustainable development. Many of the researchers stated that cities potential for improving the efficiency should carefully be managed to promote sustainable development. All of the policymakers and agents of the cities should share and accept the same aim to evaluate this potential.

Urbanization brought us a main problem that is concerning human right: Housing. Basic human rights are including an acceptable housing that is affordable. Housing is the primary condition for the prosperity and a requirement for a sound society. Besides, housing is not an issue for only the adults, seniors or families. Students are one of the main groups that need affordable and humane housing. Collaborative consumption Therefore; housing can be a tool for promoting the sustainable cities and communities. Collaborative Consumption provides a new and humane way of overcoming the housing problem. There are many case studies and policies in the framework of collaborative consumption in many cities that are promoting sustainability. For instance, Humanitas program bring the seniors and students together to share the same accommodation for solving the housing problem of students and social isolation problem of senior citizens in Deventer, Netherlands. This is a remarkable example of creating sustainable cities and communities that is also applied in Lyon, France and Cleveland, US. There are two sides of this intergenerational program; first, housing problem is solved for the students, and secondly, a contribution is made for stable community. Many single mother in US are employed in low-wage jobs and suffering from poverty with very small child. CoAdobe is another collaborative consumption application that is supporting single mothers among US by shared housing. Main idea of co-housing is sharing the financial and practical responsibilities of housing. The idea has twofold impact for single mothers. One is sharing the costs of the housing and collaboration against the life problems (Shareable, 2017).

Collaborative consumption has many policies or tools for promoting the sustainable cities and communities goal. Especially for this goal there are many experiences, case studies and policies among the world. There many case studies and policies form the world in the book "Sharing Cities: Activating the Urban Commons" that is edited by Shareable. Residents of the many cities are actively collaborating in 11 topics that are promoting the stable society. South Korea launched the Sharing City Seoul with many policies and programs that are about unemployment, pollution, and social isolation. This framework was a remarkable example for promoting the sustainable development and communities.

Responsible Consumption and Production

Collaborative consumption is fitting very well to this sustainable development goal because this is the basic definition and aim of this new paradigm. UN stated that economic growth is decoupling because of the excessive resource use and this is the most critical and complex problem for humanity (UN, 2018). Also, it is the same for production and half of the resource problem came from the production. In this decade all of the indicators are pointing out the decreasing quantity of the resources, environmental pollution and even decreasing happiness. Besides, producers can't utilize from present inventory stock for producing goods and services and that is inducing the excessive use of resources. Consumption and production have pressure on resources that are depleting. Especially after 2000s many of the researches talked about the green economy for decreasing the environmental damage of excessive consumption and production cycle. There were many debates and hopes about the green economy and green growth in the first decade of this era but after Rio+20 meeting it is revealed that green economy will not be a solution to worldwide problems because of the toughness of the consumption and production pattern change. There are many economic agents that need to change the consumption and production pattern. Countries, governments, multi-national producers, national producers, small and medium enterprises and citizens even opposition parties are the sides of the green growth and it is very difficult to create a green consensus with these agents at the same time. After Rio+20 the policymakers still had the problem of setting up a framework for responsible consumption and production. Similarly, Heinrichs (2017) stated that 20 years of discourse on sustainable development brought us mixed results and as a consequence, there is a need for new ways for sustainability (Heinrichs, 2017). While debates are ongoing at the end of the first decade of this era idea of collaboration consumption emerged and became a solution without the effects of policymakers.

This new idea collaborative consumption that is including the sustainable consumption and production in the core and based on accessing or reusing products to utilize from the idle capacity. This definition is the key for the responsible consumption and production because consumers become much less reliant and dependent on individual private ownership and this is a pattern change for being responsible (Frenken, 2017). Instead of buying new and more goods and services, consumers' access –with or without a fee- what they need with collaborative consumption platforms that are standing idle without using resources. This is a pattern change for sustainable development without implementing policies and decreasing excessive resource usage. Moreover, two important components of the economy, consumer and producers, changed the patterns and they became more responsible for sustainable development. The second decade of this era witnessed a two-sided, sustainable and rapid pattern change without the effects of international or national policymakers.

Collaborative consumption became an important framework for fighting against excessive use of resources for hyper-consuming. In fact, responsible consumption and production are interrelated with sustainable cities and communities. Creating sustainable cities are very essential for achieving the goal of sustainability and this will promote responsible consumption and production. There are 137 case studies and policies in 11 categories of collaborative platforms in the report of Shareable that will promote the sustainability of the economy and create responsible consumers and producers. A remarkable difference in collaborative consumption is the source of pattern change. Other policies, approaches or frameworks based on imposing the new pattern to consumers and producers but for collaborative consumption the source of the pattern change is themselves (Shareable, 2017). This pattern change may have a remarkable potential to increase the wealth and prosperity by decreasing the material footprint, use of resources, toxic materials, use of energy, pollutants without decoupling economic growth by environmental degradation.

On the other hand, Lane (2000) stated that there is a problem of the social recession of the developed countries despite there is an increase in consumption, wealth and prosperity (Lane, 2000). Collaborative consumption has a significant potential for affecting the social structure to increase the happiness of the people because this is not a policy imposed by a policymaker. This is an intrinsic behavior change that will make consumers happy and will change the producers aim from profit maximization to consumer utility maximization.

Climate Action, Life Below Water, and Life on Land

Last two decades are the worst years for climate change because humanity is encountering with the cost of economic growth of the 20th century. Policymakers are more aware of the environmental problems after the Brundtland report in 1987 due to the excessive use of the natural resource for rapid economic growth. Forests destroyed, productive drylands turned out to deserts, acid precipitation poisoned environment, populations of land and sea animals decreased, global warming became from theory to reality, industrial gases depleted ozone shield, new kinds of diseases raised, and underground water polluted after the middle of the 20th century. World Meteorological Organization stated that the five-year average global temperature from 2013 to 2017 was 1 Celsius above the pre-industrial period and the year 2017 is 0.46 Celsius above the 1981-2010 average as the warmest year (WMO, 2018). Besides, global mean CO2 surface mole fraction as an indicator for Greenhouse Gases was the highest on record in 2016 and rising sea levels with lower arctic sea-ice extent is a continuing problem. The global share of marine fish stock is decreasing every year with increasing marine acidity, pollution, and eutrophication. On the other hand, the earth's forest area is shrinking with declining productivity of lands and biodiversity got lost because of unsustainable agriculture. Almost all of the indicators about the environment are at emergency level and there are no positive signs for improvement. This brief explanation about the environment gave us the situation of the environment and this not in fact the worst part. The worst part is the low efficiency of the past policies and food will be scarcer after the next two decades. For this reason, the UN has different sustainable development goals due to the unprecedented change of the indicators.

Climate Action, Life below water and life on land are the three important sustainable development goal of the UN for protecting the environment. Policymakers are setting up their policies within the framework of these three goals. The rise of collaborative consumption may have the potential to serve these three goals. Especially, sharing city may have a chance to affect the environmental degradation trend to slow-down. Collaboration consumption provides a basis to share goods and services with high carbon emissions that will help to reduce GHG. In the report of Shareable every category is simultaneously serving for these three goals by increasing the excessive use of resources. In this context, ride-hailing, bike-sharing, car-pooling, tool sharing, housing, co-working, co-food, co-water, and co-energy cases or policies have a remarkable potential to fight against environmental degradation.

FUTURE RESEARCH DIRECTIONS

Impact of the collaborative consumption on sustainable development is a relatively new area for the researchers and there are still main debates about these impacts. Expected impacts are very well and seem to promote sustainable development. However, collaborative consumption is not well-understood or an inclusive economic paradigm that will solve all problems. There are many debates about all forms of collaborative consumption cases and policies. For instance, there is no clear evidence for the labor market that collaborative consumption has a positive impact. Moreover, the Nordic Council of Ministers reported that there may be significant negative impacts on the labor market. There is uncertainty about social security, retirement plans, rights, new discrimination codes because of ratings, protection of privacy, and so on. Likewise, there are debates about alleviating poverty. Future research directions should criticize and discuss the negative impacts of collaborative consumption.

Besides, there are debates about the impact of governmental regulations on collaborative consumption and the legal aspects of collaboration. In this context, tax evasion is an important debate issue for the governments. Collaborative consumptions platforms that are registered in tax heavens will be a problem for the host country by decreasing the tax revenues. On the other hand, there are legal concerns about housing and mobility platforms for obeying the law and regulating codes. Uber's legal situation in some countries is a clear example of the conflict between the platform and regulating codes. Because of the monopoly of taxi companies, Uber is controversial in some countries like Great Britain, Italy, Denmark, Hungary, Taiwan, and India. The core of the problem is the regulating codes. Airbnb has the same problems about city taxes or regulating codes in some cities like Paris, Berlin, Barcelona, New York, İstanbul and San Francisco. All of the problems arise from different issues like privacy policy, tax policy, a ban on short-term rentals and security reasons. Besides, the distortion of the competition is an important distorting factor for economies.

In this context, future researches are very important to highlight these questions and problems because unbalanced dispersion of the collaborative consumption platforms between the regions, cities, countries will decouple their economies. This new socio-economic paradigm may be exclusive as well as inclusive.

CONCLUSION

Past experiences and today's socioeconomic results showed that our consumption and production habits need to be changed. Poverty, hunger, inequalities, need for safe and secure working, problems of rapid urbanization and environmental degradation are worldwide problems. Many countries and international organizations set up many different policies but results have not changed as much as needed. At the beginning of the 21st century while humanity is dealing with those problems an old concept turned to a new socio-economic paradigm with the effect of technological advancement. This new socio-economic paradigm is "Collaborative Consumption" and refers to the economic paradigm without ownership of the asset. Collaborative consumption has a remarkable potential to affect the policies for sustainable development in various ways. However, it is not a magical solution to all life problems and it may be shaped with the policies for increasing the efficiency of the collaboration.

In general, sharing city cases and policies are the cornerstone of collaborative consumption and most successful platforms in terms of sustainable development. Shareable's report on sharing city revealed most of the potential for the UN's sustainable development goals.

It is very difficult to forecast the future of the collaborative platforms whether to progress or to stagnate, but it is certain that old and new kinds of trade will seem together.

ACKNOWLEDGMENT

This research was supported by the Research Fund of the Cukurova University [project number SBA-2019-12135].

REFERENCES

Barzilay, A. R., & Ben-David, A. (2016). Platform inequality: gender in the gig-economy. *Seton Hall L. Rev., 47*, 393.

De Soto, H. (2000). *The mystery of capital: Why capitalism triumphs in the West and fails everywhere else*. New York: Basic Books.

Eurofound. (2015). *New forms of employment*. Author.

FAO, IFAD, UNICEF, WFP, & WHO. (2017). *The State of Food Security and Nutrition in the World 2017. Building resilience for peace and food security*. Rome: FAO.

Gödecke, T., Stein, A. J., & Qaim, M. (2018). The global burden of chronic and hidden hunger: Trends and determinants. *Global Food Security, 17*, 21–29. doi:10.1016/j.gfs.2018.03.004

Harris, B. (2018). *These are the happiest countries in the world*. Retrieved from https://www.weforum.org/agenda/2018/03/these-are-t he-happiest-countries-in-the-world/

Heinrichs, H. (2013). Sharing Economy: A Potential New Pathway to Sustainability. *Gaia (Heidelberg), 22*(4), 228–231. doi:10.14512/gaia.22.4.5

Hodge, J. (2016). *Hidden hunger: Approaches to tackling micronutrient deficiencies. In Nourishing millions: Stories of change in nutrition*. Washington, DC: International Food Policy Research Institute (IFPRI). Retrieved from https://www.weforum.org/agenda/2019/01/sharing-economy/

ILO. (2019). World Employment and Social Outlook: Trends 2019. Geneva: ILO.

Jeffrey, K., Wheatley, H., & Abdallah, S. (2016). *The Happy Planet Index: 2016. A global index of sustainable well-being*. London: New Economics Foundation.

Lane, R. E. (2000). *The loss of happiness in market democracies*. Yale University Press.

OECD. (2019). *Poverty rate (indicator)*. OECD. doi:10.1787/0fe1315d-en

Orsi, J., Eskandari-Qajar, Y., Weissman, E., Hall, M., Mann, A., & Luna, M. (2013). *Policies for Shareable Cities: A sharing economy policy primer for urban leaders*. Shareable and the Sustainable Economies Law Center.

Shareable. (2018). *Sharing cities: Activating the urban commons*. Mountain View, CA: Shareable.

Suárez Corujo, B. (2017). The sharing economy: The emerging debate in Spain. *Spanish Labour Law and Employment Relations Journal*, *6*(1-2), 30–41. doi:10.20318llerj.2017.3923

UNDP. (2008). *Making the Law work for everyone* (Vol. 2). Working Group Reports.

UNEP. (2015). *Sustainable Consumption and Production: A Handbook for Policymakers*. Retrieved from http://wedocs.unep.org/bitstream/handle/20.500.118 22/9660/-Sustainable_Consumption_and_Production_a_Handbook_for_PolicymakersSustainable_Consumptio.pdf?sequence=2&isAllowed=y

United Nations. (2018). *The Sustainable Development Goals Report 2018*. New York: United Nations Publication.

United Nations General Assembly. (2015). *Transforming Our World: The 2030 Agenda for Sustainable Development*. Draft resolution referred to the United Nations summit for the adoption of the post 2015 development agenda by the General Assembly at its sixty-ninth session. UN Doc. A/70/L.1 of 18 September 2015.

WCED. (1987). *Our Common Future* (1st ed.). Oxford, UK: Oxford University Press.

World Bank Group. (n.d.). *CPIA database*. Retrieved from http://www.worldbank.org/ida

Section 2

Digital Platforms and Network Capitalism

Chapter 4
Pricing Rental Tourist Accommodation:
Airbnb in Barcelona

Josep Lladós-Masllorens
https://orcid.org/0000-0002-6236-5166
Universitat Oberta Catalunya (UOC), Spain

Antoni Meseguer-Artola
Universitat Oberta Catalunya (UOC), Spain

ABSTRACT

Digital marketplaces are rapidly flourishing, especially in travel and tourism services. Airbnb is providing one of the most evident examples of this successful evolution. Prices are a crucial factor to understand the business model and the economic performance in hospitality businesses. This chapter studies how prices are formed in Airbnb, focusing the analysis on a wide sample of accommodations listed in Barcelona (Spain). Contextual factors, lodging amenities and some hosts' attributes critically influence pricing in the digital platform. The accommodations located closer to the main tourist amenities concentrate most of the supply of rental services whereas consumer preferences for privacy and host identification give rise to higher prices. The research also confirms that commercial hosts exacerbate the upward movement of rental prices in the central districts of the city.

INTRODUCTION

The development and spread of information technologies has enabled the advent of highly-competitive digital platforms that promote user-generated content, sharing of goods and services and collaboration among members of the network (Kaplan & Haenlein, 2010). In particular, the sharing economy has emerged as a wide and diverse set of activities developed in digital platforms, facilitating the interaction between users and providers of goods and services to solve some market imperfections, regardless of whether they have commercial or unselfish purposes. These activities are addressing some situations

DOI: 10.4018/978-1-5225-9928-9.ch004

Copyright © 2020, IGI Global. Copying or distributing in print or electronic forms without written permission of IGI Global is prohibited.

Figure 1. Typologies of networks operating as digital platforms
Source: Oskam and Boswijk (2016)

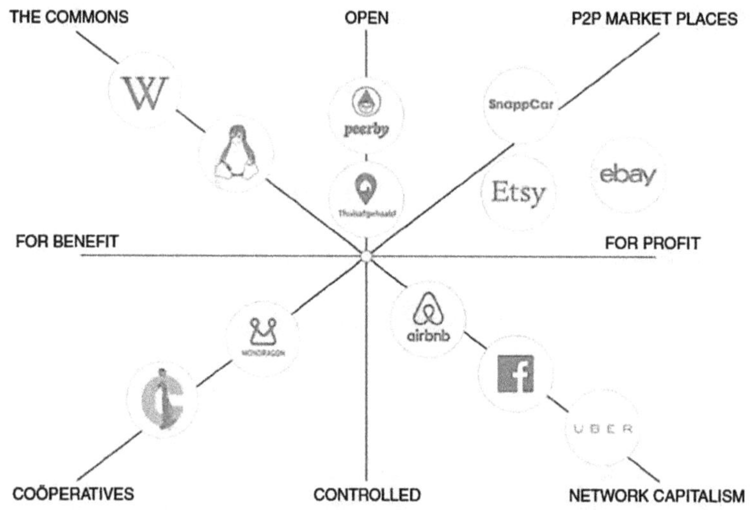

that conventional markets do not adequately resolve, both from a merely economic perspective as well as from social interest. Richardson (2015) reflects extensively the complex diversity of movements and ventures developed in this context.

In recent years, we have seen a proliferation of these online peer-to-peer marketplaces accompanied by the emergence of different business models. They are generating observable economic benefits associated with the decrease of transaction costs, the mobilization of idle resources or an increasing accessibility. Some of these digital intermediaries, promoting commercial networking activities through business models based on P2P, are transforming the market and tourist destinations, directly affecting the accommodation sector for tourism (Sundarajan, 2013). In particular, the emergence of Airbnb in many of the most populated destinations for tourism and leisure has disrupted the market for rental accommodation.

Although pricing is one of the most critical factors defining the business model and the economic performance in the hospitality business, the research on this topic is still scarce for rental accommodation services based on sharing economy models (Zhang et al, 2017). We focus our research on Airbnb listings in the city of Barcelona, one of the most successful tourist destinations in the Mediterranean region, to identify the key elements of price configuration.

AIRBNB IN THE UNIVERSE OF SHARING ECONOMY

Oskam and Boswijk (2016) represent the different types of value-generating networks that operate on the basis of digital platforms. Airbnb is placed in the field of network capitalism along with other major Internet operators, such as Facebook or Uber.

The company was created in 2008 and it has rapidly become a paradigmatic case of exponential organization, with a very fast evolution as its market was growing (Ismail et al, 2014). To understand this striking development, it is necessary to analyze the determining factors of economic success in networked accommodation. The platform acts like a two-sided market, facilitating transactions between individuals and adding value to both sides of the platform by providing a context of trust and reliability to both users and suppliers which otherwise would not be involved in the marketplace.

The company benefits from significant competitive advantages. On the one side, the cost savings derived from a minimal management structure and the coverage of expenses by the hosts who provide the accommodation. On the other, the network economies associated with the increase in the size of the market. The growth of the marketplace increases the visibility of the digital platform and makes it more attractive to the providers of accommodation services. The hosts are clearly motivated to join the network. Thus, the expansion of the marketplace yields higher returns to scale (Eisenmann et al., 2006). In addition, Airbnb exploits the experiential aspects of the rental accommodation in private houses and the sense of engagement and community. Users are encouraged to live a more authentic tourism experience (Ikkala & Lampinen 2015).

Obviously, the economic interests play a crucial role also both from the perspective of the users and the hosts. On the one side, guests obtain a better price and a higher flexibility. On the other, hosts benefit from the opportunity to increase the financial return of their properties (Botsmani Rogers 2011, Hamari et al., 2016, Zervas et al., 2017).

However, the Achilles' heel of this business model is trust, because when providers and consumers are facing a high level of risk and exposure, transactions between partners will only be effective if there is a substantial level of trust between them (Hamari et al, 2016). In the case of online transactions, there is a higher uncertainty about the behaviour of the involved agents (Riegelsberger et al. 2005). So, in contrast to the hotel industry, trust and reputation become the weaker link in the value chain of tourist accommodation rental, because these digital platforms lack the competitive advantages based on standardization, ranking and brand (Oskam & Boswijk, 2016). So, the mutual review system of hosts and guests could be the foundation of trust in Airbnb transactions, creating value as reputational capital allowing for higher prices (Finley, 2013; Wu et al., 2017; Ikkala & Lampinen, 2015; Teubner et al., 2017).

As a consequence, the P2P accommodation services face the necessity to create a user-friendly environment to offset the comparative disadvantage in terms of the lack of regulation and reputation, in a way that trust finally becomes one of the most critical elements for the value creation (Liang et al., 2017). This challenge to build a reputational capital could permit Airbnb to achieve even a greater economic performance. The initiatives of the company organizing and promoting an evaluation system by users should be comprehended in this context (Finley 2013).

The high-speed development and rapid implementation in many of the most populated destinations for tourism and leisure has disrupted the market for rental accommodation and generated a vivid and controversial debate about the negative economic externalities originated by its action in a context of ineffective regulation (Horn & Merante, 2017). Barcelona has not been an exception to this wave of critical approach. In several studies, the company is blamed for creating unfair competition, accelerating rents of housing for residents, increasing the cost of basic services or inducing urban gentrification and throwing resident population out from the downtown (Arias Sans, 2015; EY Spain 2015, Quijones 2015, Croft, 2015, Wachsmuth & Weisler, 2018). In fact, some authors point out a perfect political and regulatory storm has been detonated in the city (Dredge et al., 2016).

In turn, the company has provided alternative studies demonstrating that the improvement in efficiency and welfare has widely compensated the losses caused to some residents and the incumbent operators in the market (Airbnb 2013, Guttentag 2013, Lehr 2015). Whatever the case may be, it would be erroneous to consider Airbnb as a mere platform where private individuals exchange tourist accommodation services. The philosophy of sharing and reciprocity seems to be increasingly replaced by an

Figure 2. Airbnb: Evolution of the supply of rental accommodations in Barcelona
Source: Own elaboration from the information included in InsideAribnb.com

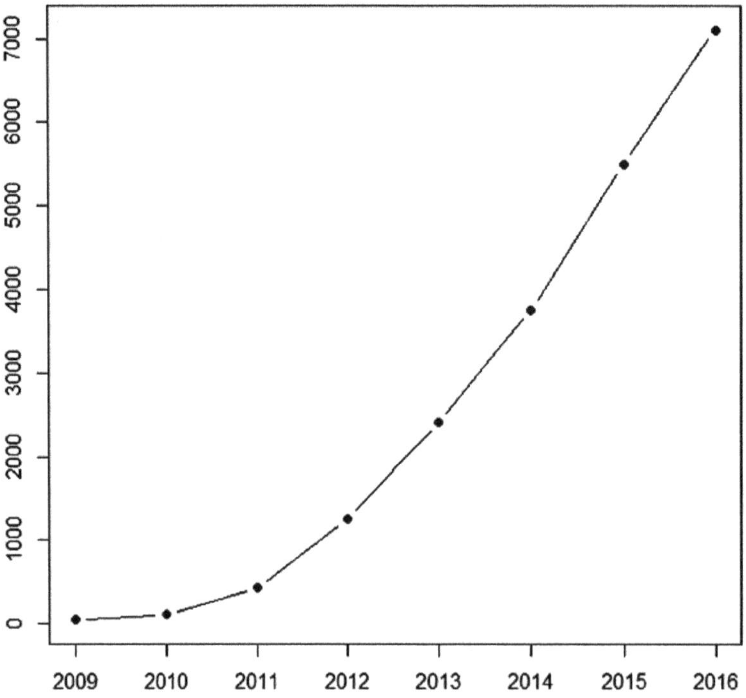

obvious commercial aim based on the concept of network capitalism and distant from the fundamentals of sharing economy (Belk 2014; Martin 2016).

The websitehttp://insideairbnb.com/ provides detailed information about many characteristics of the tourist rental accommodation services traded in the digital platform. The use of this database makes possible a better understanding of the activity developed by Airbnb in the city. The search was carried out with the data corresponding to October 2018. A significant sample of more than 6,890 registers (with ID number) has been analyzed to identify the main determining factors of prices, the importance of reputation and trust, the influence of professional hosts and the significance of location.

EMPIRICAL ANALYSIS

Location

The evolution of accommodations through the digital platform over time offers a clear evidence of Airbnb's defiance to the local hospitality business. As the platform is better known, it is also much more employed. The growth is continuous and violent, representing the increasing popularity of sharing economy in hospitality businesses.

The dispute becomes even more evident when comparing the geographical distribution of the accommodations included in the platform and the corresponding to the local hotel industry. Usually, the company has vindicated its activity on the presumption that is complementing the supply of the incumbent

Table 1. Distribution of tourist accommodation

Urban District	Airbnb	Hotels
Eixample	29.51	32.60
Ciutat Vella	26.05	33.42
Sants-Montjuïc	11.63	6.03
Sant Martí	10.91	9.04
Gràcia	10.01	1.37
SarriàSant-Gervasi	3.75	8.77
Horta-Guinardó	3.44	2.47
Sant Andreu	1.79	0.55
Les Corts	1.73	5.48
NouBarris	1.17	0.27

Source: Own elaboration from the information included in InsideAribnb.com and in the website infoturbarcelona.com

industry without falling into direct competition and providing a housing offer usually located in districts where the presence of hotel accommodation is limited.

Our analysis makes clear that, at least in the city of Barcelona, this would not seem to be the case. The correlation between the geographical distribution of both hospitality networks is very high (92.7%), since Airbnb's highest supply is lodged in the two most central districts where the hotel industry is also densely located.

Price Dispersion and the Role of Dimension

Next, we study the determining factors of prices in the selected sample through a descriptive analysis. The study of pricing configuration could provide relevant information about the business model and the economic consequences of this networked hospitality service.

From the standard deviation of this variable (78.10), we can infer that there is a high dispersion of prices in the city. In addition, we detect a clear asymmetry (3.51). In fact, the median value (49.0) is significantly lower than the mean (73.60). This high dispersion could be the result of a great disparity in the type of tourist accommodations. As a consequence, we proceed to a complementary descriptive analysis of prices according to the number of beds supplied in each accommodation.

The first column shows the variable "number of beds", ranging from 1 to 16. It shows how the majority of lodgings offer between 1 and 2 beds (53.10%). For the purposes of this study, the accommodations with more than six beds are removed, due to their insignificance. It is also demonstrated that rental prices move upward according to the number of accommodates and that the dispersion is higher among the larger accommodations.

An analysis of the variance of prices according to the type of housing has been also carried out. The results confirm that the differences observed between groups, depending on the size of accommodation, are statistically significant.

Next, we proceed to validate whether the fact that there is a positive relationship between the number of beds and the price of the home offered by Airbnb is the main determinant of the high variability

Table 2. Descriptive analysis of prices by number of beds

Beds	Price	s.d.	IQR	0%	25%	50%	75%	100%	N
1	44.63	32.13	21.00	8	29.00	40.00	50.00	575	4025
2	70.66	55.27	51.00	9	38.00	56.00	89.00	695	1334
3	111.99	84.03	66.00	9	64.00	90.00	130.00	600	688
4	145.39	111.48	90.00	9	80.00	110.00	170.00	633	476
5	178.19	135.80	140.00	9	85.00	135.50	225.00	550	234
6	192.74	137.90	158.50	20	96.50	149.00	255.00	635	133
7	216.40	136.80	201.25	25	96.25	190.00	297.50	545	40
8	233.06	110.39	150.00	10	150.00	210.00	300.00	595	31
9	297.20	115.51	139.00	75	229.00	295.00	368.00	545	15
10	222.67	180.90	296.25	38	63.75	184.50	360.00	570	12
11	320.00	113.14	-	240	240.00	320.00	-	400	2
12	332.50	187.18	282.50	20	192.50	362.50	475.00	550	6
13	390.00	-	0.00	390	390.00	390.00	390.00	390	1
14	221.75	192.84	349.75	47	71.50	172.50	421.25	495	4
15	420.00	-	0.00	420	420.00	420.00	420.00	420	1
16	95.00	77.78	-	40	40.00	95.00	-	150	2

Source: Own elaboration from the information included in InsideAribnb.com

observed in the prices of accommodations in Barcelona. A simple linear regression analysis has been performed between both variables.

The significant influence of size is fully confirmed. However, it is moderate as much as only 30.10% of the variability of prices is explained by differences in the size of rental accommodations. Consequently, other determining factors should be included into the analysis. We have considered other variables, related to the number of guests (people that can be hosted) or the quality of the accommodation (number of bedrooms and number of bathrooms).

The result of the multiple regression analysis shows how the number of beds is still relevant to explain price variability and that the three new variables incorporated into the model clearly improve the goodness-of-fit (up to 38.70%).

Table 3. ANOVA of differences in prices according to the number of beds

	Sum of Squares	df	Mean Square	F	Sig.
Between groups	11247360.750	5	2249472.150	600.524	0.000
Within groups	25786425.230	6884	3745.849		
Total	37033785.980	6889			

Source: Own elaboration from the information included in InsideAribnb.com

Table 4. Regression analysis between price and beds

	Coefficients	s.d.	T	p-Value
Constant	11.448	1.315	8.706	0.000
Beds	32.356	0.594	54.501	0.000
R-squared: 0.301				
F: 2970.379, p-value: 0.000				

Source: Own elaboration from the information included in InsideAribnb.com

Analysis of Airbnb as a Reliable Environment

As previously indicated, a critical in Airbnb's business model of Airbnb is reliability, since one of the main motivations of the company is to create a trusted environment, fully recognizable to users and customers of the marketplace. The rapid growth of tourism-related services based on the use of digital platforms is requiring a deep understanding of the trust mechanisms upon the marketplace is erected. With this aim, we have analysed the importance of the host identification on the prices of rental accommodation, regardless if this identity is or is not verified by the platform.

A contrast of hypotheses is conducted for the difference in average prices per accommodate. Although hosts with verified identity offer accommodations with a relevant higher unit price (25.35 euros) than non-identified hosts (24.97 euros), these differences are not statistically significant (t-statistic t = -0.932, p-value = 0.352).

However, despite differences are not important at the aggregate level, we detect significant divergences when we disaggregate the sample. In particular, as the presence of hosts managing multiple listings in the marketplace is growing over time (Li et al., 2015), we analyse the differences between professional and non-professional hosts, splitting the sample into two different subsamples. One of them containing information about those hosts having just 1 or 2 offers listed in Airbnb, and the other containing data about those commercial (or professional) hosts, having 3 or more housing offers in Airbnb. As a result of this split, we got that 37.70% of the listed offers came from professional hosts in Barcelona.

The results show a clear and statistically divergence. In the case of non-professional hosts (t-statistic= -2.073, p-value = 0.038) with verified identity the price is clearly higher (24.61 euros per accommodate

Table 5. Regression analysis between price and housing characteristics

	Coefficients	s.e.	t	p-Value
Constant	-15.144	2.141	-7.074	0.000
Accommodates	21.973	0.832	26.417	0.000
Bathrooms	7.296	1.676	4.353	0.000
Bedrooms	5.526	1.508	3.665	0.000
Beds	4.243	1.096	3.870	0.000
R-squared: 0.387, Adjusted R-squared: 0.386				
F: 1084.358, p-value: 0.000				

Source: Own elaboration from the information included in InsideAribnb.com

Table 6. Price per accommodate by host types and verification

	Total	Non-Professional	Professional
Host verified *(N)*	25.352 *(2261)*	24.608 *(1392)*	26.545 *(869)*
Host not verified *(N)*	24.975 *(4629)*	23.761 *(2947)*	27.102 *(1682)*

Source: Own elaboration from the information included in InsideAribnb.com

versus 23.76 euros). Hosts with verified identification in the digital platform usually benefit from premium prices because guests perceive this verification as a quality indication (Ert et al, 2016). Consequently, non-professional hosts are able to capitalize on a good reputation (Gutt et al., 2015; Wang & Nicolau, 2017, Teubner et al, 2017), because consumers' responsiveness to this hosts attribute is meaningful. In fact, online reputation is also gaining importance over the traditional star rating even for hotel industry (Abrate & Viglia, 2016).

However, in the subsample of professional hosts the differences in prices are not statistically significant according to the identity verification.

To build a trusted environment for the marketplace, Airbnb tries to reinforce reliability of users, both guests and hosts, through strategies based on the reputation of the accommodations. Consequently, Airbnb has defined a system of reviews and assessments on different characteristics of the accommodations. The company needs not only to engage users of the digital platform; it also requires the establishment of trust as a condition for transactions to take place. From this rating system, we have inferred the users' assessment about the following aspects connected with the accommodation:

- About the accuracy of the information provided in the marketplace ("Accuracy")
- About the cleaning conditions ("Cleanliness")
- About the register policy ("Check-in")
- About the connectivity options ("Communication"), and
- About the location ("Location")

The results demonstrate that these evaluations are very high: in all cases they are clearly above 9 in a scale from 1 to 10. Moreover, differences between professional and non-professional hosts are irrelevant.

Impact of Location on Prices

The position of lodgings plays a crucial role to justify the observed differences in prices. In Table 8 discernible divergences do exist among the different urban districts. With the exception of Sarrià-SantGervasi (the neighbourhood with the highest per capita income in the city), the most central districts (Ciutat Vella, Eixample and Gràcia) show the uppermost price per accommodate. Ciutat Vella is providing a wide sample of tourist resources closely related to historic heritage, while Eixample and Gràcia are quarters in which tourists can find most of tourist amenities and buildings connected with the art movement of modernism in Barcelona.

These urban districts are also the sites where most of accommodations are located (62.9%). Regarding to the perceived quality of guests, all the different dimensions obtain top results, bigger than 9 points,

Table 7. Mean value of the quality dimensions by host type.

	Non-Professional	Professional	Total
Accuracy	9.47	9.10	9.33
Cleanliness	9.25	9.02	9.16
Check-in	9.68	9.38	9.57
Communication	9.64	9.34	9.53
Location	9.55	9.38	9.49

Source: Own elaboration from the information included in InsideAribnb.com

with the exception of lodgings placed in Horta-Guinardó, Nou Barris and Sant Andreu, all of them peripheral districts. In these cases, the guests' evaluation of location is slightly inferior. As far as the accommodation move away from tourist amenities, the lower is its price. Contextual factors, as the location of the hospitality service, appear to be of paramount importance in terms of attractiveness for demand.

Although central districts are those with highest prices of rental accommodation, we should isolate the influence of the characteristics of the different lodgings to corroborate if central location, closest to the main tourist amenities, is the most determining factor of the price-making process in this digital platform.

Therefore, a discriminatory analysis is developed to find out if the variables associated with the price, related to the main characteristics of properties and previously identified and analysed in Table 5, or if the variables connected with the subjective valuations of users about the quality of lodgings and services (described in Table 7) permit the identification of the housing location. To perform this analysis, we define a new variable "City center": it takes value 1 in the case the offer is placed in one of the central districts (Ciutat Vella, Eixample or Gràcia) and 0 in the other cases.

The rate of success in the discriminant analysis is 59.16%. The results show that, for the whole tested variables, the highest differences in the mean values are those related to the characteristics of this kind of rental accommodations. This is the consequence of the lower size of lodgings located in the downtown

Table 8. Price per accommodate and quality perception for each urban district

Urban District	N	Price	Accuracy	Cleanliness	Checkin	Communication	Location
Ciutat Vella	1649	26.56	9.27	9.01	9.52	9.51	9.71
Eixample	2088	25.86	9.34	9.20	9.57	9.53	9.62
Gràcia	603	25.82	9.43	9.24	9.60	9.56	9.49
Horta-Guinardó	259	21.14	9.46	9.31	9.64	9.59	8.97
Les Corts	147	20.22	9.37	9.24	9.59	9.50	9.35
Nou Barris	99	17.61	9.41	9.15	9.65	9.58	8.77
Sant Andreu	138	19.67	9.25	9.12	9.55	9.38	8.99
Sant Martí	874	23.76	9.31	9.20	9.58	9.53	9.23
Sants-Montjuïc	836	23.74	9.40	9.24	9.60	9.55	9.40
Sarrià -Sant Gervasi	197	30.79	9.31	9.15	9.51	9.45	9.32
Total	**6890**	**25.10**	**9.34**	**9.16**	**9.57**	**9.53**	**9.49**

Source: Own elaboration from the information included in InsideAribnb.com

Table 9. Discriminant analysis of rental prices according to location

	Groups Mean		Discriminant Function
	No City Center	City Center	Coefficients
Accommodates	2.95	2.74	0.186
Bathrooms	1.25	1.19	0.296
Bedrooms	1.36	1.33	0.119
Beds	1.96	1.76	0.353
Accuracy	9.33	9.34	-0.212
Cleanliness	9.13	9.18	-0.296
Check-in	9.55	9.59	-0.113
Communication	9.50	9.54	-0.104
Location	9.46	9.51	-0.351

Source: Own elaboration from the information included in InsideAribnb.com

of Barcelona. Regarding to the valuations of users, we can observe that generally all the mean values are bigger in the case of lodgings placed in central districts. However, differences are not remarkable.

The Role of Professional Hosts

It has been shown that Airbnb's business in the city of Barcelona is essentially located in the central districts. Within these areas the concentration of supply is much higher because the rental activity is generally more profitable. Although the digital platform aspires to be recognized as part of the sharing economy universe, the fact is that this geographic deployment entails a direct and intense competition with the local hotel industry, also mainly located in the places with major tourist amenities. As Oskam and Boswijk (2016) point out, the company seems to act in Barcelona as a business-oriented and profit-searching digital platform, which means that the company would clearly enter into the field of network capitalism, based on hyperconnected and distributed platforms that have a clear commercial objective.

Significantly, not only private individuals are attracted to this marketplace to supply tourist rental accommodation. Many intermediaries and other players from the real state and tourism industries are taking advantage of the digital platform to expand their business opportunities and to optimize the returns and profitability of their properties portfolio. As a consequence, the platform could be hosting commercial networking activities that do not strictly fit nor with the business models based on P2P nor with the intrinsic constitution of collaborative consumption (Ke, 2017).

These professional hosts could be aggravating the observed concentration of tourist rental accommodation activities in the downtown of the city. A two-step analysis has been carried out to analyse the commercial functioning of these multiple hosts.

First, a contingency table has been calculated from centrality of location. We obtain results that confirm that the location and the fact of being a professional host are independent variables (Chi-squared = 0.329, p-value = 0.566). Although, most of lodgings in Barcelona are provided for non-commercial purposes (63.0%), both private hosts and professional hosts are distributed in a very similar way between the urban districts. Most of them are clearly located in the downtown (63.1% of accommodations). This

Table 10. Contingency table between location and type of host

	Non-Professional Hosts	Professional Hosts	Total
Non-central	23.1%	13.8%	36.9%
Central	39.9%	23.2%	63.1%
Total	63.0%	37.0%	100.0%

Source: Own elaboration from the information included in InsideAribnb.com

distribution manifestly puts pressure on the local hotel industry and the level of rents for residents, at least in this area of the city.

Second, a dependence analysis is also provided. We investigate the link between the variables price, location and type of host using the methodology of automatic detection of interactions. Results show that professionalization clearly has a more determining influence on prices than location. So, although the mean price in the city center is visibly superior to accommodations placed in the other districts, it can be seen that there is a much higher difference between the average price of non-professional hosts and the rental price of accommodations provided by hosts with multiple lodgings. Consequently, the stress on rental prices for residents in the downtown of Barcelona would seem to be closely related with the central location of many tourist accommodation facilities but even much more with the presence in the digital marketplace of professional hosts.

Therefore, localization and professionalization of the supply of rental accommodation for tourism in Barcelona using Airbnbn are two distinctive elements with a potentially disruptive impact in the business model of the incumbent industry that claim for an appropriate regulation. In particular, it becomes clear from our analysis that professionalization plays an important role as a determinant of price. However, pure utilitarian or economic motivations do not necessarily have to be considered as solely negative aspects and perhaps users with different motivations for participating could coincide in the digital platform in mutual beneficial ways (Hamari et al, 2016).

As a consequence, Airbnb is providing a disruptive innovation to the market that could be fostering different types of networked hospitality services, in the context of deep societal changes in the use of digital technologies and the preference for different experiences associated with tourism.

Figure 3. Segmentation tree according to host typology and place
Source: Own elaboration from the information included in InsideAribnb.com

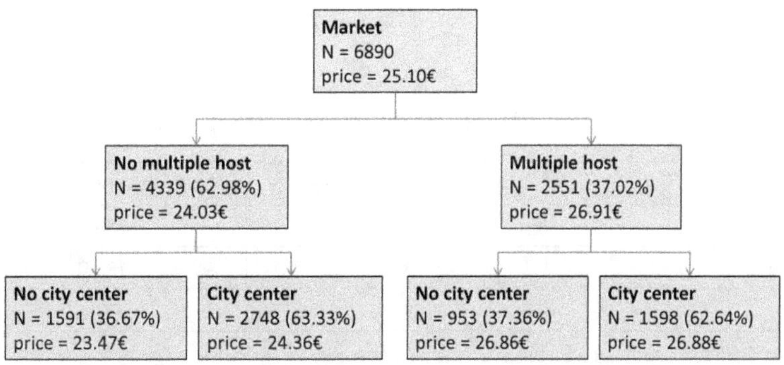

The large variety of offerings in the digital platform could also create market segmentation, based on the different consumers' preferences. In fact, hosts would employ marketing rational to target their listings for matching their supply with the predilections of some specific consumer segments and achieving a more efficient outcome (Lutz & Newlands, 2018).

In the database, there are two different types of lodgings related to the level of privacy provided to the users. On the one side, we have the supply of entire homes or apartments, and on the other side, the offer of private or shared rooms. The great majority of accommodations are private or shared rooms, while entire homes or apartments represent just a share of 32%. Since we have tested the relevance of professionalization, we are now interested in knowing its relationship with these two different types of accommodations. The results shown in Table 11 confirm that professionals are more inclined to offer entire homes and apartments in the Airbnb listings, meanwhile most of non-professional hosts in Barcelona provide accommodations in rooms (private or shared). The Chi-squared test show that both variables are not independent (Chi-squared = 535.23, p-value = 0.000).

Price Determinants of Airbnb's Housing Offers

We have already seen in previous sections that the accommodation's characteristics, related to the number of guests (people that can be hosted) or the quality of the accommodation (number of bedrooms, number of bathrooms, and number of beds), are important to explain price determination (see Table 5). However, results also showed that other factors had to be considered in order to improve the level of explained variability (38.7%). Later analyses permitted to discover other reliable candidates to be included in the list of significant factors. Among these factors, professionalization, location and type of housing exhibit the greatest potential to increase the variability of prices.

With the objective of testing this hypothesis, we include these three variables in the initial regression proposed in subsection II.II. Results in Table 12 prove that the inclusion of the new variables rise up the level of variance explained (41.1%). Individual significance analyses show that all variables are relevant except for "City center": while all p-values are clearly lower than 0.05, its p-value exceeds this bound. Again, professionalization emerges as a very significant factor that clearly overcomes the influence of location (as we already discussed in section II.V). Finally, the type of housing, followed by the number of accommodates, becomes the most important factor to explain price forming in the digital platform.

In fact, recent studies reveal that some attributes, as location, amenities or hosts are the most powerful influencers on Airbnb users' experiences, even surpassing the effect of rental prices (Mingming & Xin, 2019).

Table 11. Contingency table between housing types and host types

	Non-Professional Hosts	Professional Hosts	Total
Private or shared room	49.2%	18,9%	68,1%
Entire home or apartment	13.8%	18,1%	31,9%
Total	63.0%	37,0%	100.0%

Source: Own elaboration from the information included in InsideAribnb.com

Table 12. Determining factors of price forming

	Coefficients	s.e.	t	p-Value
Constant	-12.216	2.347	-5.205	0.000
Accommodates	15.415	0.909	16.967	0.000
Bathrooms	10.850	1.681	6.453	0.000
bedrooms	4.797	1.488	3.223	0.001
Beds	3.155	1.080	2.920	0.004
Professional	9.316	1.494	6.237	0.000
Entire home	31.941	2.145	14.894	0.000
City center	0.917	1.414	0.649	0.517
R-squared: 0.411, Adjusted R-squared: 0.411				
F: 686.804, p-value: 0.000				

Source: Own elaboration from the information included in InsideAribnb.com

Demand Side Analysis

In most part of this chapter, we have focused on the offer side. We have examined how the supply side fixes their housing prices, according to different factors related to the house characteristics, privacy, location and the hosts' profile. Although we have already studied in subsection II.III some specific issues concerning the demand side (i.e. the users' perceived quality about accuracy, cleanliness, check-in, communication and location), now we are interested in performing a more comprehensive analysis. We want to know, for example, if there exists a direct relation between offer (price) and demand. In other words, we would like to corroborate if the most demanded accommodations are also the most expensive.

As a proxy to measure the demand for an accommodation we will consider the number of reviews made by the users of that accommodation. In order to get a comparable measure, we will also consider the number of moths an accommodation has been listed in Airbnb. Table 13 contains the descriptive statistics of these two variables for each neighbourhood, jointly with the ratio between them.

The mean of reviews received by an accommodation listed in Airbnb is 31.6. We interpret this value as a proxy of the number of times an offer has been hired. Hence, we understand that the more demanded accommodations are those located in the city center (Ciutat Vella, Eixample and Gràcia) and also those placed in Horta-Guinardó, Sant Martí and Sants-Montjuïc. In average, offers in Airbnb have been listed during 19.6 months (approximately one year and a half). This represents that every lodging receives 1.8 reviews each month. In consequence, we consider that each accommodation is hired twice monthly.

Results for each urban district show that although accommodations in Gràcia are listed in average during 2 years (23.8 months), they are hired just 1.6 times each month. This data is clearly below the values obtained in the other two urban districts in the city center, Ciutat Vella and Eixample, which are clearly the most demanded: 2.0 and 1.9 respectively. The characteristics of tourist amenities could determine deeper centralities inside the city center. On the contrary, the accommodations located in the peripheral districts (as Les Corts, Sarrià-Sant Gervasi or Nou Barris) are the less demanded: 1.4-1.5 times each month.

The frequency analysis of the variable *number of reviews* shows that one third of the accommodations (33.3%) have received 5 or less reviews, meaning that they have had a very low demand among users.

Table 13. Mean value of the demand indicators for each urban district

Urban District	Number of Reviews	Moths Listed	Reviews per Month
Ciutat Vella	29.82	17.13	2.00
Eixample	33.71	20.26	1.89
Gràcia	35.95	23.77	1.60
Horta-Guinardó	30.65	18.74	1.82
Les Corts	21.05	18.09	1.42
Nou Barris	20.60	14.36	1.57
Sant Andreu	21.90	15.45	1.64
Sant Martí	29.89	20.46	1.76
Sants-Montjuïc	34.86	20.45	1.79
Sarrià-Sant Gervasi	26.53	21.22	1.52
Total	31.62	19.61	1.83

Source: Own elaboration from the information included in InsideAribnb.com

This low interest cannot be attributed to the location (these low demanded accommodations have around 2.5 reviews in average in all urban districts) nor is the consequence of the assessment process, because all dimensions obtain a very satisfactory value in the reviews (greater than nine). In our opinion, this scarce demand could probably be associated with to two other different factors:

- First, these low required accommodations have been listed recently, compared with the rest of the sample. In average, the low demanded accommodations have been offered during almost one year (10.9 months), whereas the other lodgings double this data (23.9 months). Accommodations need time in the market, a high rotation and a significant number of reviews to become more appealing for demand.
- Second, their average price per accommodate is higher than the average price of those accommodations with more than 5 reviews (26.6€ and 24.3€, respectively). This result makes clear the existence of an inverse effect between price and demand for these unconventional accommodation offers.

In fact the correlation analysis between price per accommodate and number of reviews (per month) confirms this suggested relationship: the Pearson correlation between them equals -0.14, with a p-value of 0.000. Although Airbnb does not focus on a single target group of users and the digital marketplace is segmented by the different qualities, amenities and location of properties, we can also verify that the most demanded rental accommodations for tourism and vacation in Barcelona are also the lodgings and homes with the lowest prices. This attribute would be providing the higher contribution to consumers' utility because tourists' satisfaction does not seem to critically depend on location.

CONCLUSION

In the hospitality business, Airbnb is becoming a direct rival for hotel industry and also a powerful driver for change. The digital platform is coordinating the demand and supply of tourist products and services that were previously unavailable on the market. But Airbnb's activities are also challenging many different policies, regulations and objectives of local governments, with the evolution of rents and the displacement of resident population from the central districts as the main concerns among policy-makers.

We have analysed one of the most populated destinations for tourism and leisure in the Mediterranean region, which also observed a dramatic increase in the number of listings offered in the digital platform. A great deal of information is revealed using Barcelona as a city lab. Our research provides some preliminary findings.

First, the identification of the digital marketplace as merely a P2P network that empowers individual consumers is clearly in question. Although transactions may be used for mutual benefit, the commercial intentions are undoubtedly present in the front line. The extractive nature seems to prevail over the collaborative consumption process. Significantly, the platform is attracting a growing number of multi-hosting players with an obvious commercial purpose. Airbnb would actually be more like a rental marketplace rather than a spare-room sharing platform. And, as home sharing is both a personal and a commercial enterprise, it should be appropriately regulated and taxed.

Second, the geographical distribution of the tourist rental accommodations included in the digital marketplace prevents Airbnb from playing a complementary role of the hotel industry. The patterns of distribution of lodgings in the city are very similar. Therefore, although the users of the platform benefit from a greater flexibility and favourable economic conditions, the emergence of negative externalities cannot be fully rejected. This networked hospitality business intensifies the stress of tourism on the level of rents and the supply of services in the central districts of the city.

Third, in Barcelona nearly 40% of the listing is in the hands of professional hosts. These agents seem to exercise a decisive influence on the evolution of rents in Barcelona, essentially due to their disproportionately high participation in the supply of entire homes and of accommodations located in central districts.

Fourth, Airbnb's efforts to build a reliable environment and to promote self-regulation policies are not only in the interest of protecting the users of the platform but of avoiding a direct negotiation and also inspiring trust, a critical condition for transitions to take place. This method needs the involvement of guests and seeks the profound complicity of hosts, because they are able to capitalize on the reputational dimension by means of higher prices.

Fifth, rental prices in Barcelona for tourist accommodation obviously depend on the quality and characteristics of the lodgings and their physical distance to the main tourist amenities but also of hosts' attributes. Clearly, contextual and reputational factors play a relevant role in the evolution of prices.

Finally, looking to the demand side, the analysis clearly confirms that both location and prices are the main determining factors for the selection of the accommodations services provided by the platform. The influence of these factors is probably very significant also for the local hotel industry. However, pricing is running the dominant segment of the sharing economy based market for rental tourism accommodation in Barcelona. As expected, the fast-growing supply of lodgings with affordable prices has decisively spurred the demand for short-term rental services in the digital marketplace.

In addition, more transparency should be demanded to the digital platform about hosts and properties, to properly identify commercial parties for preventing an excessive economic exploitation and some negative externalities on the domestic rental market. In particular, the upward trend to repurpose and reuse residential housing exclusively as tourist accommodation in Barcelona should be reverted.

The study has an important limitation. The effect of amenities and rental rules on prices has not been yet tested. Probably, some services provided by hosts and the degree of flexibility in accommodation rules could have a significant impact on prices. In addition, although this is not the specific aim of this research, the study does not focus on the demand side of the marketplace. Probably, some attributes of Airbnb's consumers could also influence the price of transactions.

REFERENCES

Abrate, G., & And Viglia, G. (2016). Strategic and tactical price decisions in hotel revenue management. *Tourism Management*, *55*, 123–132. doi:10.1016/j.tourman.2016.02.006

Airbnb. (2013). *New study: Airbnb community contributes $175 million to Barcelona's economy*. Available at: www.airbnb.nl/press/news/new-study-airbnb-community-contributes-175million-to-barcelona-s-economy

Arias Sans, A. (2015). *Desmuntant Airbnb. Apunts crítics sobre el cas de Barcelona*. Available at: http://latramaurbana.net/2015/07/01/desmuntant-airbnb-apunts-critics-sobre-el-cas-de-barcelona/#more-1245

Belk, R. (2014). Sharing Versus Pseudo-Sharing in Web 2.0. *Anthropologist*, *18*(1), 7–23. doi:10.1080/09720073.2014.11891518

Botsman, R., & Rogers, R. (2011). *What's Mine is Yours. How Collaborative Consumption is Changing the Way We Live*. London: Harper Collins.

Croft, A. (2015). Airbnb remains symbol of Barcelona's growing unease with tourism. *Skift*. Available at: http://skift.com/2015/08/26/airbnb-remains-symbol-of-barcelonas-growing-unease-withtourism/

Dredge, D., Gyimothy, S., Birkbak, A., Jensen, T. E., & Maqdsen, A. K. (2016). The impact of regulatory approaches targeting collaborative economy in the tourism accommodation sector: Barcelona, Berlin, Amsterdam and Paris. Impulse Paper, 9. Aalborg University.

Dredge, D. i S., & Gyimóthy, S. (2015). The collaborative economy and tourism: Critical perspectives, questionable claims and silenced voices. *Tourism Recreation Research*, *40*(3), 286–302. doi:10.1080/02508281.2015.1086076

Eisenmann, T., Parker, G., & Alstyne, V. W. (2006). Strategies for two-sided markets. *Harvard Business Review*, *84*(10).

Ert, E., Fleischer, A., & Magen, N. (2016). Trust and Reputation in the Sharing Economy: The Role of Personal Photos on Airbnb. *Tourism Management*, *55*, 62–71. doi:10.1016/j.tourman.2016.01.013

España, E. Y. (2015). *Impactos derivados del exponencial crecimiento de los alojamientos turísticos en viviendas de alquiler en España, impulsado por los modelos y plataformas ce comercialización*. Madrid: Exceltur.

Finley, K. (2013). *Trust in the Sharing Economy: An Exploratory Study*. Warwick, RI: Centre for Cultural Policy Studies, University of Warwick.

Gutt, D., & Herrmann, P. (2015). *Sharing Means Caring? Hosts' Price Reaction to Rating Visibility*. ECIS 2015 Research-in-Progress Papers. Paper 54.

Guttentag, D. (2013). Airbnb: Disruptive innovation and the rise of an informal tourism accommodation sector. *Current Issues in Tourism*, 1–26.

Hamari, J., Sjöklint, M., & Ukkonen, A. (2016). The sharing economy: Why people participate in collaborative consumption. *Journal of the Association for Information Science and Technology*, *67*(9), 2047–2059. doi:10.1002/asi.23552

Horn, K., & And Merante, M. (2017). Is home sharing driving up rents? Evidence from Airbnb in Boston. *Journal of Housing Economics*, *38*, 14–24. doi:10.1016/j.jhe.2017.08.002

Ikkala, T., & Lampinen, A. (2015). Monetizing network hospitality: hospitality and sociability in the context of Airbnb. *Proceedings of the 18th ACM Conference on Computer Supported Cooperative Work & Social Computing*, 1033-44. 10.1145/2675133.2675274

Kaplan, A. M., & Haenlein, M. (2010). Users of the world, unite! The challenges and opportunities of Social Media. *Business Horizons*, *53*(1), 59–68. doi:10.1016/j.bushor.2009.09.003

Ke, Q. (2017). Sharing Means Renting?: An Entire-marketplace Analysis of Airbnb. Cornell University. *Proceedings of the ACM on Web Science Conference*, 131-139.

Lehr, D. D. (2015). *An analysis of the changing competitive landscape in the hotel industry regarding Airbnb* (Master thesis). Dominican University of California, San Rafael, CA.

Li, J., Moreno, A., & Zhang, D. J. (2015). *Agent behavior in the sharing economy: evidence from Airbnb*. Working Paper 1298, Ross School of Business, University of Michigan.

Liang, Choi, & Joppe. (2017). Understanding repurchase intention of Airbnb consumers: perceived authenticity, electronic word-of-mouth, and price sensitivity. *Journal of Travel & Tourism Marketing*. doi:10.1080/10548408.2016.1224750

Lutz, C., & Newlands, G. (2018). Consumer segmentation within the sharing economy: The case of Airbnb. *Journal of Business Research*, *88*, 187–196. doi:10.1016/j.jbusres.2018.03.019

Martin, C. J. (2016). The sharing economy: A pathway to sustainability or a nightmarish form of neoliberal capitalism? *Ecological Economics*, *121*, 149–159. doi:10.1016/j.ecolecon.2015.11.027

Mingming, C., & Xin, J. (n.d.). What do Airbnb users care about? An analysis of online review comments. *International Journal of Hospitality Management*, *76*, 58–70.

Oskam, J., & Boswijk, A. (2016). Airbnb: The future of networked hospitality businesses. *Journal of Tourism Futures*, *2*(1), 22–42. doi:10.1108/JTF-11-2015-0048

Quijones, D. (2015). Barcelona just declared war on Airbnb. *Business Insider*. Available at: www.businessinsider.com/barcelona-just-declared-war-on-airbnb-2015-8

Richardson, L. (2015). Performing the sharing economy. *Geoforum*, *67*, 121–129. doi:10.1016/j.geoforum.2015.11.004

Riegelsberger, J., Sassei, M. A., & McCarthy, J. D. (2005). The mechanics of trust: A framework for research design. *International Journal of Human-Computer Studies*, *62*(3), 381–422. doi:10.1016/j.ijhcs.2005.01.001

Teubner, T., Hawlitschek, F., & Dann, D. (2017). Price Determinants on Airbnb: How Reputation Pays Off in the Sharing Economy. *Journal of Self-Governance and Management Economics*, *5*(4), 53–80. doi:10.22381/JSME5420173

Wachsmuth, D., & Weisler, A. (2018). Airbnb and the Rent Gap: Gentrification Through the Sharing Economy. *Environment and Planning A: Economy and Space, 50*(6).

Wang, D., & Nicolau, J. L. (2017). Price determinants of sharing economy based accommodation rental: A study of listings from 33 cities on Airbnb.com. *International Journal of Hospitality Management*, *62*, 120–131. doi:10.1016/j.ijhm.2016.12.007

Zervas, G., Proserpio, D., & Byers, J. (2017). The Rise of the Sharing Economy: Estimating the Impact of Airbnb on the Hotel Industry. *JMR, Journal of Marketing Research*, *54*(5), 687–705. doi:10.1509/jmr.15.0204

Zhang, Z., Chen, R. J. C., Han, L. D., & Yang, L. (2017). Key Factors Affecting the Price of Airbnb Listings: A Geographically Weighted Approach. *Sustainability*, *9*(1635).

Chapter 5
The Impact of Sharing Economy in Heritage Neighborhoods in Granada

Esteban Romero-Frías
https://orcid.org/0000-0003-2205-3560
University of Granada, Spain

Charalampos Leontidis
University of Granada, Spain

ABSTRACT

The objective of this chapter is to provide reliable information from online platforms that quantifies the impact of tourist accommodation in Granada in relation to commercial activities, hotels, and residential homes. To do so, the authors take into consideration economic and population variables. Particularly, they focus on offering evidence on the tourist pressure in the most touristic neighborhoods of the city, mainly Albaicín-Sacromonte, Centro 1, and Realejo. This type of research has been widely demanded by residents, local government, and stakeholders in general in order to take action on this field.

INTRODUCTION

The impact of the sharing economy on tourism is one of the most important challenges in the life of cities today (Schor & Charles, 2017). The incorporation of new types of accommodation to the tourist marketplace of cities has placed heavy pressure on historical neighborhoods, jeopardizing the living conditions of residents. Phenomena such as touristification or gentrification respond, among other factors, to the emergence of digital sharing economy platforms (e.g. Airbnb).

Residents have reacted to these changes in different ways, although negative responses are common and highlight negative externalities (Bakker & Twining-Ward, 2018). These include a fall in the number of houses available for permanent or long-term residence; higher rental and house prices; the transformation of local commercial activity and the loss of businesses that sustain everyday neighborhood life; the

DOI: 10.4018/978-1-5225-9928-9.ch005

Copyright © 2020, IGI Global. Copying or distributing in print or electronic forms without written permission of IGI Global is prohibited.

displacement of residents because of rising house prices; inconveniences generated by tourist flow; and unfair competition with hotels and other regulated sectors. Moreover, the problem is especially complex as residents themselves often benefit from these sharing economy platforms to obtain additional income.

To assess the impact of these new tourist practices on heritage cities, we need to map and quantify the current situation through data provided by the sharing economy platforms themselves. We believe this to be the optimal starting point for a comprehensive analysis of the situation in any given city in order to take informed decisions with regard to regulations and tourism management. In Granada, the lack of objective data on this topic is an issue residents, local government and other stakeholders frequently cite when seeking to take action and design policies. The aim of the present chapter is to provide reliable information gathered from a number of online platforms in order to quantify the impact of tourist accommodation on the city—one of the most frequently visited destinations in Spain—in relation to commercial activities, hotels and residential homes.

The background to this chapter includes a literature review of the most significant topics related to our research. Later, we focus specifically on the case of Granada, presenting data about the city and its neighborhood structure, the distribution of tourist flows, and local tourism management processes. The specific objectives and methodology of our study are detailed below. These are followed by our results, and a discussion on our research questions. Finally, we outline the limitations of the present study, future lines of research, and our conclusions.

BACKGROUND

The sharing economy phenomenon has attracted a growing amount of tourism-based research in recent years due to the popularization of services such as Uber or Airbnb, among others (Cheng, 2016; Juul, 2015; Heo, 2016; Leung, Xue, & Wen, 2019). Moreover, hospitality in particular has undergone a significant change given the new accommodation supply provided by Airbnb and similar platforms. As it has developed, the sharing economy has generated new sources of income for owners by exploiting their excess capacity (Heo, 2016), and offered tourists rental prices for apartments or rooms that are more competitive than traditional hotel prices (Fang, Ye, & Law, 2016). This has led to the redefining of concepts such as ownership and employment, and of tourist practices (Ferrell, Ferrell, & Huggins, 2017). Other positive effects include the environmental impact and social benefits (Gonzalez-Padron, 2017; Schor, 2016). However, these changes have generated negative impacts: the creation of a new class of worker insecurity, the concentration of supply in the hands of large corporations, and the lack of appropriate regulation of conditions for providing the service, among others. One highly significant factor, closely related to our research, is the fact that the increase in supply could negatively affect tourist destinations due to the lack of sustainability and growing massification (Guttentag, 2015; Oskam & Boswijk, 2016; Moreno-Izquierdo, Ramón-Rodríguez, Such-Devesa, & Perles-Ribes 2019), and the consequent negative impact on the residential market, leading to a progressive decline in population (Cócola Gant, 2016; Kesar, Dezeljin, & Bienenfeld, 2015).

In heritage cities in particular, the increase in tourism has generated phenomena such as touristification and gentrification. The term touristification refers to the impact of mass tourism on the commercial and social fabric of neighborhoods. It leads to services, facilities and shops being oriented towards and conceived of by reference to the tourist rather than the resident (Brauckmann, 2017). Gentrification entails the displacement of residents from neighborhoods that are revalued by the injection of public or private capital (Cócola Gant, 2016; Gravari-Barbas & Guinand, 2017; Lees, Shin, & López-Morales, 2016). Brauckmann (2017) considers touristification to be a kind of gentrification.

Amongst other factors, tourist pressure is determined by the volume of visitors a tourist destination receives, causing residents and tourists themselves difficulties in performing their daily activities. The main problem caused by massive tourism in cities is the loss of virtually all resources and basic services required by local residents (e.g. the closure of craft industries, local stores, small businesses, public services, etc.), which are replaced by hotels, tourist apartments, restaurants, souvenir shops and the like. Everything is dedicated to servicing the tourist in order to enhance economic performance.

The growing mass of tourism makes neighborhoods and/or cities uninhabitable for residents as escalating prices force them to move to districts they can afford. Brauckmann (2017) identifies Airbnb as a possible trigger to the displacement of inhabitants from the most attractive neighborhoods—mainly city center and heritage neighborhoods. Similarly, Edelman and Geradin (2015) indicate that Airbnb could be considered a threat to the safety and affordability of residential communities, causing an exodus of long-term tenants from specific neighborhoods and generating housing shortages. All of this has affected house purchase prices and rents, particularly in tourist cities. Studies such as that by Barron, Kung and Proserpio (2018) in the US have analyzed how residential sale and rental prices rise as the tourist apartment supply grows.

In the tourism industry, one of the most important debates centers on the substitute nature of the hosting offer of tourist apartments through sharing economy platforms such as Airbnb versus the traditional hotel sector. However, worldwide, research has found only limited evidence of this. Zervas et al. (2017) analyzed Airbnb's impact on the hotel industry in Texas and found that a 10% increase in Airbnb accommodation resulted in a 0.37% fall in hotel revenues. This was more than 1% lower than the 1.5% fall in revenue associated with a 10% increase in available hotel accommodation. These authors suggested that Airbnb's role as a substitute for hotels was marginal. Similar conclusions have been reached with regard to Nordic countries (Neeser, Peitz, & Stuhler, 2015). Heo, Blal and Choi (2019) indicated that P2P rentals and hotels in Paris are not in direct competition, as had previously been thought. The customer segments using each alternative appear to differ: holiday tourists have a positive approach to the Airbnb supply, whereas business tourists prefer hotels (Tussyadiah & Zach, 2015; Zervas et al., 2017).

Both the impact on residential housing and on the hotel sector justifies the need to measure tourist pressure and the impact of tourist apartments rented through online platforms (i.e. Airbnb). Several studies have pointed to specific problems (Owyand, Tran, & Silva, 2013; Belk, 2014; EU Innovation Observatory, 2014) that include conflict with the traditional tourist industry; uncertain regulation of sharing economy businesses (in relation to tax, competence, insurance); and resident opposition to this type of hosting activity.

Analysis of tourist accommodation impact has generally received more attention in large cities—e.g. Barcelona (Gutierrez, García-Palomares, Romanillos, & Salas-Olmedo, 2017) and Budapest (Dudás, Boros, Kovalcsik, & Kovalcsik, 2017; Boros, Dudás, Kovalcsik, Papp, & Vida, 2018)—and medium-large European cities (Coyle & Yeung, 2016). However, in small and medium-sized cities the phenomenon remains limited and research has focused on highly attractive tourist destinations like Venice (Seraphin, Sheeran, & Pilato, 2018), which have specific characteristics. Airbnb's own research on cities such as Madrid (Airbnb, 2015) has followed a similar pattern. Adamiak (2018) analyzed the distribution and characteristics of Airbnb activity across Europe, mapping and comparing some basic descriptive indicators for 432 European cities with at least 100 000 inhabitants.

Most of these studies have also focused on the city-wide distribution of Airbnb accommodation, finding that it is distributed unequally but significantly over the whole destination. Nevertheless, this requires close examination in every case. For example, in Barcelona Gutierrez et al. (2017) found that Airbnb accommodation is tightly concentrated in the historic city center, with a center-periphery pattern, whereas hotels show more complex patterns. In addition these authors concluded that Airbnb had been able to penetrate the city in closer proximity to tourist attractions than traditional hotels have. In Paris, Heo et al. (2019) explored the geographical distribution of Airbnb apartments across the Parisian districts and found that P2P rentals and hotels follow different patterns.

In the public sector, the sharing economy has raised a wide range of issues (Ganapati & Reddick, 2018). An uneasy balance exists between fostering innovative tourism and regulating practices that have created a hosting system that parallels the traditional hotel industry. Some of the most important issues relate to the fact that sharing economy companies bypass government regulations and their overheads have an impact on consumer rights, safety and quality, and disability compliance standards too (Juul, 2015; Rauch & Schleicher, 2015).

According to Acevedo (2016) and Ganapati and Reddick (2018), regulators have taken three main policy approaches to the sharing economy:

- **Regulate:** This approach ranges from treating the sharing economy like traditional services to banning these activities (e.g. Palma de Mallorca).
- **Don't Regulate:** This leads to self-regulation practices with the sharing economy platforms striving to balance the interests of both providers and customers, although generally leaving the interests of residents aside.
- **Wait and See:** This approach favors regulating sharing economy activities but argues that the time to do so has not yet come.

This third approach highlights the relevance of our research aim: to quantify the impact of sharing economy platforms on the city of Granada in order to help monitor the impact of short-term renting on communities. As Ganapati and Reddick (2018) state, local governments could set rules requiring platforms to participate, for example, by establishing home-sharing licenses. Mody, Suess and Dogru (2019) reject a one-size-fits-all approach to regulate Airbnb, given that the impact of its activity differs across and within destinations due to the diverse geographic distribution of supply.

TOURISM IN GRANADA

Granada in Spain and Europe

The city of Granada is located in southern Spain. It has approximately 232 000 inhabitants and is the center of an urban area with a population approaching 530 000. The 2018 INE (Instituto Nacional de Estadistica, n.d.) hotel occupancy survey ranked Granada sixth in Spain with 1 867 251 visitors, behind Madrid, Barcelona, Seville, Palma de Mallorca, and Benidorm. Granada's relatively low population and the fact that is not a beach destination (in contrast to Benidorm and Palma) highlight the importance of tourism, and its economic and social impact on the city are clear. In this context, the problems derived from the pressure exerted by tourism acquire particular interest, especially in those locations that concentrate the major tourist flow.

The Urbantur report (Exceltur, 2016)—which ranks Spanish cities in terms of their relevance as tourist attractions—placed Granada in 16th position. It asserted that the city's strengths lie in the range of leisure activities on offer, with special emphasis on cultural or Spanish language-oriented tourism, accommodation, and catering services. However, the report also revealed weaknesses in areas such as mobility, accessibility, governance, and strategic management of tourism.

In 2017, the European Commission published "The Cultural and Creative Cities Monitor" (European Commission, 2017) as a "tool to monitor and assess the performance of 'Cultural and Creative Cities' in Europe vis-à-vis their peers using both quantitative and qualitative data". The quantitative information, combining official statistics and experimental data from sharing economy platforms, is gathered into 29 indicators and 9 dimensions reflecting three major facets of the cultural, social and economic vitality of cities: Cultural Vibrancy, Creative Economy, and Enabling Environment. The first edition of the Cultural and Creative Cities Monitor covers 168 cities in 30 European countries (the EU-28 plus Norway and Switzerland). Granada—included in the Monitor as one of the UNESCO Creative Cities—ranks third in Spain, scoring 28.1 on their index. It is only surpassed by a very small margin by Madrid (28.6), and Barcelona (33.2), and stands well ahead of the fourth-ranking city, Santiago (23.7). At the European level it ranks slightly above cities such as Bruges (28.1), Cologne (28), and Porto (27.9), and surpasses capital cities such as Bucharest (27.7) and Rome (26.8). In global terms, Granada occupies 13th place in the European ranking of cities with between 100 000 and 250 000 inhabitants.

Granada is, therefore, a historic city with a valuable heritage and cultural life, the home of two large World Heritage attractions: the Alhambra and the Generalife gardens, and the Albaicín neighborhood (granted World Heritage status in 1984 and 1994, respectively).

Administrative Neighborhood Structure

The city of Granada is organized around 15 large neighborhoods or districts (identifiable by their postal codes), as shown in Table 1. The present study focuses on the three neighborhoods with historical heritage characteristics that concentrate the greater number of tourist attractions. These are: Albaicín-Sacromonte, Center 1, and Realejo.

In order to understand the different neighborhoods better, the authors have examined both income and population data. In terms of income, (Table 1), Center 1 is the neighborhood with the highest average income (€26 909 per year); Realejo stands in fourth place (€25 871) and Albaicín-Sacromonte in 11th (€22 685). If we estimate total population in absolute terms, none of these neighborhoods is among the most populous: Center 1 (11th: 11 741 residents), Albaicín-Sacromonte (12th: 9607) and Realejo (13th: 9466). In terms of population density, Center 1 is second with 22 250 inhabitants per square kilometer, whereas Realejo (2802.2) and Albaicín (285.2) have very low figures, which are explained by their urban structures. Although the space that corresponds to Center 1 is completely urbanized, this is not the case in either of the other two, with core populations that border the city center but territories that extend to the outskirts of the city into spaces protected for their historical and natural value. The Realejo, for example, includes the Alhambra, Generalife and the periburban park of the Dehesa del Generalife—one of the city's main green spaces.

Within the urban structure of Granada, tourist attractions are closely concentrated in historical and heritage neighborhoods which present highly specific challenges for mobility, accommodation, and ser-

Table 1. Descriptive data on the neighborhoods of Granada

Neighborhood	Average Income	Registered Voters	Estimated Total Population	Area in Square Kilometers	Estimated Total Population per Square Kilometer	Number of Monuments	Total Monument Visitors in 2018
Center 1 [18001]	26 909	9347	11 741	0.53	22 250.1	5	1 052 581
Center 2 [18002]	25 378	3767	4732	0.37	12 924.4	0	0
Ronda [18003]	23 813	9736	12 230	16.26	752.2	0	0
Ronda-Arabial [18004]	24 753	13 436	16 878	8.07	2090.8	1	12 202
San Antón [18005]	26 027	6435	8083	0.27	29 951.1	0	0
Fígares-Ciudad Jardín [18006]	23 004	17 126	21 513	1.63	13 186.9	2	904 370
Zaidín-Vergeles [18007]	17 616	17 187	21 589	3.21	6734.2	0	0
Carretera de la Sierra-Bola de Oro-Genil [18008]	23 990	25 186	31 637	8.10	3906.4	0	0
Realejo [18009]	25 871	7536	9466	3.38	2802.2	7	3 199 891
Albaicín-Sacromonte [18010]	22 685	7648	9607	33.69	285.2	7	354 819
Beiro-Norte [18011]	17 029	17 745	22 290	5.18	4301.3	1	44 494
Plaza de Toros [18012]	26 113	6464	8120	0.58	14 083.1	0	0
Polígono de Almanjayar [18013]	18 667	11 709	14 708	1.59	9248.6	0	0
Barrio de los Periodistas [18014]	24 767	17 770	22 322	3.45	6468.5	0	0
Chana [18015]	19 321	13 765	17 291	1.98	8723.0	0	0
Total		184 857	232 208	88.28	2630.4	23	5 568 357

vices. For example, mobility in the three neighborhoods under study is affected by restrictions to road traffic—mainly in Albaicín-Sacromonte—where access and exit routes are scarce and become congested several times a day. The difficulties of access are principally due to the orography of the neighborhood. The Albaicín is located on a hill facing the Alhambra and has an urban network of streets best-suited to pedestrians. The location of the Realejo, makes it a point of exit from the city to the east from the center or as an access to the Alhambra.

Reference to Figure 1 will help understand the city described in the coming sections. The map shows outlines of the neighborhoods and the main tourist attractions with information on the volume of visitors each receives.

The Distribution of the Tourist Flow

The hotel occupancy survey for 2018—published by the INE (Instituto Nacional de Estadistica, Spain's national statistics office)—reported that a total of 1 867 251 travelers (1 005 544 non-Spanish and 861 707 Spanish nationals) visited the city during the year. The INE (Instituto Nacional de Estadistica,

Figure 1. Neighborhoods of Granada and main tourist attractions

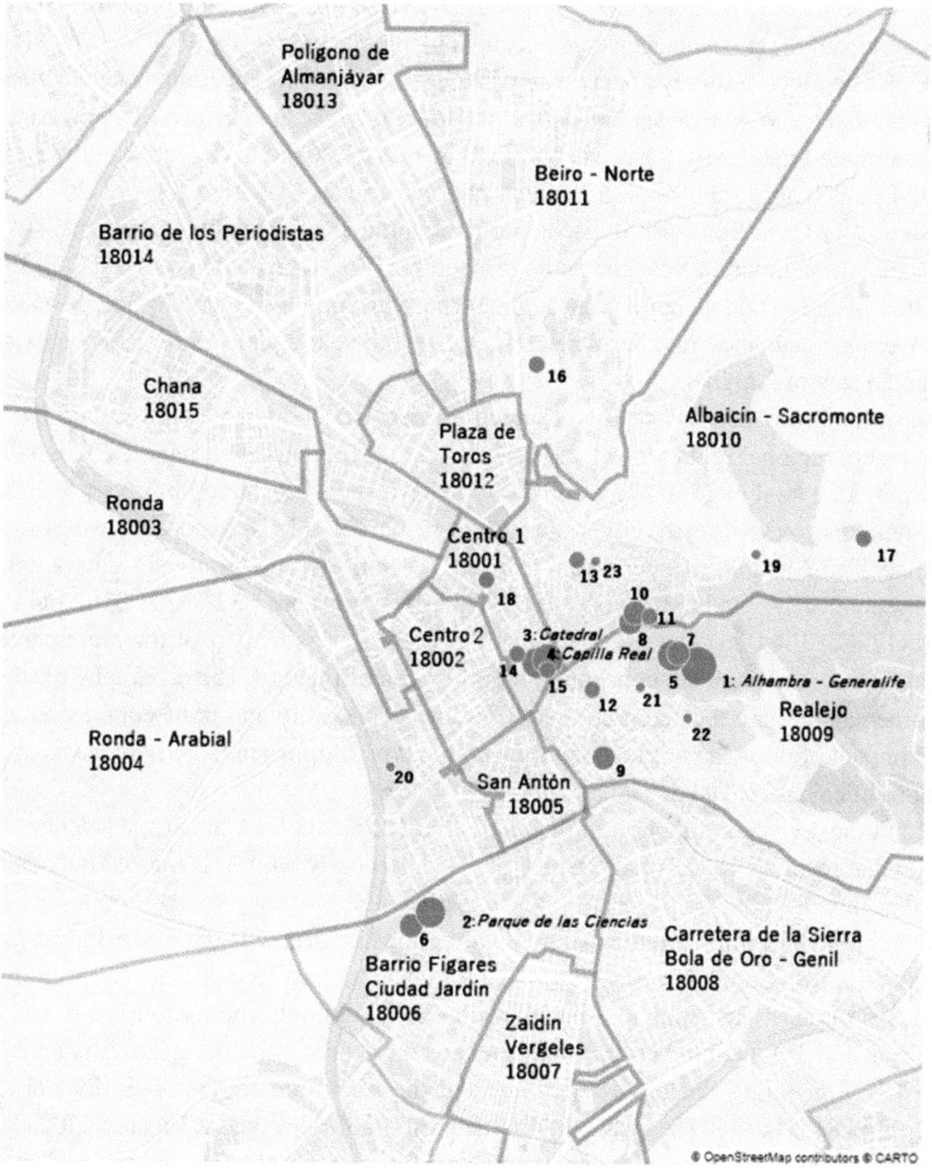

n.d.) defines travelers as "all those who make one or more overnight stay in the same accommodation" (translated from Spanish by the authors). In total, this corresponds to 3 363 539 overnight stays (each night a traveler stays at an establishment), of which 1 574 511 were Spanish and 1 789 028 were overseas visitors. The average stay was 1.80 nights per tourist. In 2018, the city had an average of 177 open hotel establishments on its records. These are defined as "establishments that provide collective accommodation services at a price with or without other complementary services (hotel, hotel-apartment or aparthotel, motel, hostel, pension, etc.)", and are also registered with the corresponding tourism councils of Spain's autonomous regions. This amounts to an average of 7431 rooms and 14 921 beds. In 2018, the average occupancy of available places was 60.79%, rising to 74.49% on weekends. The average occupancy rate per room was 67.38%. The average total of staff employed was 1764.17 people per month. From these data we determine that the total number of available overnight stays in hotel establishments was 5 433 047 (calculated from the percentage average occupancy by places).

The INE also conducts a survey of occupancy in tourist apartments (Instituto Nacional de Estadistica, n.d.) (*Encuesta de Ocupación en Apartamentos Turísticos*). These are defined as a "property the use of which is to be rented habitually for occasional lodging". The 2018 survey records 135 549 overnight stays (72 774 non-Spanish and 62 775 Spanish national travelers) with a total of 267 370 (142 778 non-Spanish and 124 592 Spanish). It also reports the number of available apartments—472 on average—increasing throughout the year and ending December 2018 on 514. This corresponds to an average total of 1576.3 places available per day throughout the year; amounting to 575 362 possible overnight stays. The average occupancy rate per place throughout the year equals 44.83% of the existing places with an average stay of 2 nights.

In contrast, data provided by the City Council tourism office indicates that, since the application of the most recent regional regulation change (Decree 28/2016, dated February 2 2016, on housing for tourism purposes), a total of 1250 homes of this type have been registered in the city.

Table 2 ranks data on visits to the city's main tourist resources in 2018, according to the city of Granada tourism office. The Alhambra-Generalife sites received 46.8% of the total visits computed in the year (2 610 549 people). If we add to the visits to the Alhambra museum (5.2%, 291 016) and the Museum of Fine Arts (2.4%, 134 076) located within the Palace of Carlos V, part of the aforementioned sites, we find that 54.4% of visitors are concentrated in this area of the city. The orography of the hill where these monumental sites are located presents difficulties of mobility and in its connection with the city center. The impact of the Alhambra on the city and the type of tourism the city receives are frequently the topic of political and social debate.

The second most visited attraction in the city is the Parque de las Ciencias, a science and technology museum that receives 13.6% of all visits (759 211). Recently built, it is located outside of the main tourist neighborhoods.

In third and fourth position are the two main attractions in Center 1: the Cathedral (8.7%, 485 478) and the Royal Chapel (Capilla Real) (7.9%, 442 693). The highest tourist flow concentration is found in Albaicín-Sacromonte, Realejo and Center 1, with 7, 7 and 5 outstanding tourist attractions, respectively (Tables 2 and 3). The numbers of visitors received by these attractions are: Albaicín-Sacromonte 354 819 (6.4% of the total), Realejo—which includes the Alhambra complex—3 199 891 (57.4%) and Center 1, 1 052 581 (18.9%). The only other neighborhood of relevance is Fígares-Ciudad Jardín with 904 370 visits which correspond to two contemporary attractions: the Parque de las Ciencias and the CajaGranada Museum.

Recent initiatives, organized by the city council and the University of Granada, and coordinated through Medialab UGR (n.d.), have strived to address the challenges posed by tourism in heritage neighborhoods—particularly the Albaicín-Sacromonte (Lab in Granada, n.d.)—through the organization of participatory processes to promote socially and environmentally sustainable practices (Midgett et al., 2017; Romero Frías, 2018a, 2018b). Residents and local associations coincide in their concern over an impoverished quality of life and the need for reliable data about tourist flows and tourist apartments in order for public institutions to make informed decisions. It is precisely this shared diagnosis that, together with the literature review, gives rise to the main objective of the present study and the research questions we seek to answer.

Table 2. Main tourist attractions per number of visits

Id	Tourist Attractions	Visitors in 2018	% of Total	Neighborhood
1	Alhambra-Generalife	2 610 549	46.8%	Realejo
2	Parque de las Ciencias	759 211	13.6%	Fígares-Ciudad Jardín
3	Catedral	485 478	8.7%	Centro 1
4	Capilla Real	442 693	7.9%	Centro 1
5	Museo de la Alhambra	291 016	5.2%	Realejo
6	Museo CajaGranada	145 159	2.6%	Fígares-Ciudad Jardín
7	Museo de Bellas Artes	134 076	2.4%	Realejo
8	El Bañuelo	90 756	1.6%	Albaicín-Sacromonte
9	Cuarto Real de Santo Domingo	86 128	1.5%	Realejo
10	Casa de Zafra	67 072	1.2%	Albaicín-Sacromonte
11	Museo Arqueológico	65 484	1.2%	Albaicín-Sacromonte
12	Casa de los Tiros	59 302	1.1%	Realejo
13	Palacio Dar al-Horra	53 126	1.0%	Albaicín-Sacromonte
14	Centro Lorca	49 039	0.9%	Centro 1
15	Centro José Guerrero	47 090	0.8%	Centro 1
16	Monasterio de Cartuja	44 494	0.8%	Beiro-Norte
17	Abadía de Sacromonte	41 207	0.7%	Albaicín-Sacromonte
18	Basílica de San Juan de Dios	34 281	0.6%	Centro 1
19	Museo Cuevas de Sacromonte	31 483	0.6%	Albaicín-Sacromonte
20	Huerta de San Vicente	12 202	0.2%	Ronda-Arabial
21	Fundación Rodríguez Acosta	11 434	0.2%	Realejo
22	Aljibe del Rey	7386	0.1%	Realejo
23	Casa Museo Manuel de Falla	5691	0.1%	Albaicín-Sacromonte

OBJECTIVES OF THE CHAPTER

The objective of the present chapter is to provide reliable information drawn from many sharing economy and other web platforms that will quantify the impact of tourist accommodation on the city in relation to commercial activities, hotels and residential homes. To do so, we will also consider economic and population variables. Particularly, we will focus on offering evidence of the tourist pressure in those neighborhoods that attract most tourists: Albaicín-Sacromonte, Center 1 and Realejo. Research of this type has been widely demanded by residents, local government and other stakeholders in order to take action.

The main research questions are:

RQ1: How are Airbnb tourist apartments distributed across the city in relation to neighborhood population density?

RQ2: How are Airbnb tourist apartments distributed in relation to traditional hotel activity in the neighborhoods?

RQ3: How are Airbnb tourist apartments distributed in relation to the real estate market in the neighborhoods?
RQ4: How are commercial services articulated in the neighborhoods?

METHODOLOGY

The project uses both quantitative analysis and georeferenced data visualization techniques, drawing on sources of information, such us: Airbnb, as a reference platform for tourist apartments; Booking.com, for the hotel offer; idealista.com, for the housing sales and rental market; and TripAdvisor, for restaurant services. Additionally, we draw on Google Maps for data on establishments closely related to residents' activities, such as supermarkets. Finally, population data from the electoral census have been taken into account, as well as data on average resident income by postal code.

Data Collection and Description

This study has used a wide variety of data from varied sources, involving a complex process of data gathering, processing and visualization. The following sections summarize these topics for each information source and describe the variables obtained for each element.

Airbnb: Tourist Apartment Data

On 14 January 2019, we obtained information relating to tourist apartments in Granada from the datahippo.org database. This information had previously been updated on 22 September 2018; the database contained a total of 3748 entries added since 2017. Given that some data had actually been deleted from the platform, a python script was implemented to verify those links that were functional. Final data parsing gave a total of 1833 records.

The information obtained for each hosting was as follows:

- Geographical location (longitude and latitude of the listing),
- Registration link,
- Accommodation type (single room, shared room, entire home),
- Number of bedrooms,
- Number of guests (maximum number),
- Host id (an identification number of the host offering the listing, in order to determine whether a few people were, in fact, managing a large number of apartments),
- Review count (number of reviews by guests), and
- Minimum number of nights.

Booking: Hotel Marketplace

On 4 December 2018, information was extracted from booking.com using a python script that scraped the site; 982 entries were recorded. Only 120 of them corresponded to hotels, hostels or pensions. The rest were mainly tourist apartments. Given that the volume of tourist apartments provided by Airbnb was greater, booking.com was only considered a source of professional hosting. For each of these records we gathered the name and geolocalization.

We also determined the volume of information available on other platforms, such as HomeAway (580 entries), Housetrip (212) and Only Apartments (175). However, this was discarded as they cover a much smaller volume than Airbnb.

TripAdvisor: Restaurants and Other Catering Services

Data from TripAdvisor was obtained on 18 January 2019 using the Google Chrome Web Scraper extension and a python script to gathered geolocalization data. In total, we obtained 1553 records of which 917 were restaurants, 253 cafés, 96 bars, 13 delicatessens and 274 establishments with no assigned category.

The information available for each establishment was:

- Link,
- Establishment type (restaurant, café, bar, etc.),
- Price range,
- Geographical location, and
- Number of reviews

Idealista: Properties for Rent or Sale

Idealista.com is one of the most important real estate web services in Spain. The data was collected on 24 January 2019 using the Google Chrome Web Scraper extension. Geolocalization was accomplished by using a python script, accessing the Google Maps API. In total there were 6510 records; 2863 considered rental offers and the remaining 3647 were properties for sale. Amongst the properties listed, 2396 were homes for sale, 1575 were homes for rent, and 440 individual rooms for rent. The remaining 2099 were other types of property, such as parking spaces, buildings, or land.

For each of the records we obtained the following variables:

- Offer type (for sale or to rent),
- Property type (in those to rent, the types included buildings, garages, rooms, commercial properties, offices and homes. In those for sale, the types included: buildings, garages, commercial properties, offices, land, storage rooms or homes.),
- Geographical location,
- Accuracy of geolocalization,
- Link,
- Price,
- Square meters,
- Number of rooms,
- Floor,
- Condition (new development, good condition or in need of renovation), and
- Garage (included or not).

Information about permission to smoke was also accessible and, in the case of rooms for rent, the number of people sharing was indicated. In the case of some properties for sale, an indication was given as to whether or not the property was still inhibited by the current owner.

Google Maps: Activities Relating to Residence

Google Maps was used as a geolocalization service to identify some activities related to permanent residence in a determined area: supermarkets and food supply stores (250 entries) and hairdresser's (225).

Electoral Registers: Population Information

The population data set corresponds to information provided by the electoral registers for Andalucía's regional elections, held on 2 December 2018. The population data per district and electoral section was taken from the carto.com database account of granadaimedia (Cart, n.d.), a local digital journal.

The total population on the electoral registers was 184 857 persons—lower than the current population—since not all citizens are necessarily eligible to vote, e.g. those aged under–18 years. According to recent INE (n.d.) data (updated at 1 January 2018), the city of Granada has a population of 232 208. This is 25.6% higher than that of the electoral registers. To estimate the population of each district and electoral section of the city, the available data was multiplied by 1.256.

The following information is available for each electoral section:

- Geolocalization,
- Electoral register,
- Corresponding neighborhood (by postal code), and
- Area in square meters

Tax Agency: Average Income

The data for average income correspond to 2016 and were obtained from the webpage of Spain`s national tax agency (Agencia Tributaria, n.d.), following their publication in January 2019. The database contains personal income tax returns for towns with over 200 000 inhabitants, grouped by postal codes.

Table 3 summarizes the aforementioned information, including data types, origin, number of records collected, number of variables for each record, date of extraction and method of collection.

Data Visualization

To provide a clear understanding of the issues involving tourism, visualization techniques are often used to portray the main variables relating to both tourism and residential activities.

The enormous growth in the volume of data generated through digital platforms and in the variety of information sources means we must explore new ways of managing, processing and visualizing information. Through data visualization, the present study aims to detect and analyze patterns hidden behind the mass of information, show the results, and make these data sets understandable. Several projects have sought to map the effects of tourism on cities or the flows generated by transport, tourists, and so on. Those which mainly focus on tourism include initiatives like the "Atlas of touristification in Madrid"

Table 3. Description of data

Data	Source	Quantity	Variables	Date	Method of Collection
Tourist apartments	Airbnb	1833	9	14/01/2019	Information available on datahippo.org. Validation of existing records with python script.
Hotels	Booking	120	3	04/12/2018	Scraping with python script.
Restaurants and other food services	TripAdvisor	1553	5	19/01/2019	Using Google Chrome Web Scraper extension. Geolocalization with python script.
Supermarkets	Google Maps	250	2	17/01/2019	Manual geolocalization on Google MyMaps.
Hairdresser's	Google Maps	225	2	17/01/2019	Manual geolocalization on Google MyMaps.
Homes and commercial properties for rent or sale	Idealista	6510	11	24/01/2019	Using Google Chrome Web Scraper extension. Geolocalization with python script.
Population of each district	Registered voters	184	4	02/12/2018	List of voters registered for the elections held on 02/12/2018.
Average income	Tax Agency	15	2	19/01/2019	Article published in *El País* on 19/01/2019

(http://turistificacion.300000kms.net/), a project which displays data from major tourism-centered internet platforms (TripAdvisor, Airbnb or Flickr amongst others), as well as other official sources. Other examples of flow visualizations include: Sense and the city (http://senseable.mit.edu/guggenheim/), which uses cameras to register pedestrian traffic, automatically recording individual routes and group dynamics; "Bostonography" (http://bostonography.com/bus/), which presents data on the positions and speeds of buses in Boston (USA), and Placemeter (http://www.placemeter.com/), which uses cameras to measure pedestrian traffic in cities.

In this chapter, data visualization was performed using CARTO builder (carto.com) to create maps. Carto is an SaaS cloud computing platform providing GIS and Web mapping tools for display in a web browser. CARTO builder also provides access to an SQL web interface that facilitates data manipulation.

One important goal was to use visualization to identify patterns relating different datasets in order to gain insights in relation to our research objectives. To facilitate the interpretation of maps, we tried to avoid information overload by creating several maps of the same size and using the same color codes, if possible, for comparative purposes. We used the same sized dots but changed the colors for each variable. In each map, we combined a maximum of four variables so as to make it easy to visually decompose it into its individual elements.

RESULTS

Our analysis focused on the construction of different visualizations of geolocated data on the city map and on a descriptive data analysis (Tables 4 and 5). Figure 1 shows the city neighborhoods and principal tourist attractions. Given that our analysis concerns the impact of Airbnb's tourist apartment marketplace on the city and, in particular, on the historic districts, Figure 2 relates this to traditional hotel establishments. Figure 3 shows the Airbnb marketplace in relation to residential housing for rent or sale. Finally, Figure 4 contrasts tourist- and resident-related services and local commercial stores in the city. In relation to the other maps, Figure 4 provides a global picture of the situation in Granada and, particularly, in its historic neighborhoods.

Figure 2 represents the different types of hosting in the city in relation to the population density of the fifteen neighborhoods. Population density is represented by shades of green, with the more intense green corresponding to higher population density. To provide more accurate data, information has been broken down to the level of electoral districts and each neighborhood has been outlined in black. The tourist accommodation depicted in these maps is: tourist apartments only (Airbnb; represented by black dots), rooms for tourist use (Airbnb; yellow dots) and hotel establishments (Booking; purple dots). This map allows us to respond to RQ1 and RQ2. In this study, we have assumed that both types of accommodation—that offered by Airbnb and that included on Booking.com—generally represent two different types, both of which are subject to different regulations that allow them to function properly as alternative or complementary services.

Table 4 shows that the city has a total of 1489 Airbnb apartments which could host up to 7072 people, plus 340 rooms with a capacity of 812 people. Consequently, if we consider the maximum daily occupation over 365 days, the city would have an annual accommodation capacity of 2 877 660 thanks to Airbnb.

The three historic neighborhoods concentrate 63.7% of the tourist apartment marketplace and 54.1% of Airbnb rooms. If Center 2 and San Antón—which occupy the more central part of Granada—are also added, these figures rise to 84% of apartments and 63% of rooms.

Albaicín-Sacromonte accounts for 489 apartments which, based on Airbnb data, amounts to a total capacity of 2193 people. Here, rooms for rent leads the rank order with 88; i.e. a potential capacity of 191 people. In second position lies the Realejo with 300 apartments and a total of 1334 people, and 59 rooms with a capacity of 147 people. These are followed by Center 2 and Center 1. In peripheral neighborhoods the supply is much more scarce, reducing the percentage difference between apartments and rooms or even inverting the relationship. Note that this accommodation is concentrated in the three historic neighborhoods of Granada—plus Center 2 and San Antón—which constitute the heart of the city: 84% of apartments and 63% of rooms.

Booking.com data records 119 establishments in the city, including hotels, hostels and pensions. The neighborhoods with most establishments are: Realejo (30), Albaicín-Sacromonte (25) and Center 1 (21). This contrasts with official data that indicate the existence of 177 such establishments in 2018. This suggests that Booking.com may have underestimated the real number, perhaps because not all of these establishments use this platform to commercialize their services. The difference may also be due to the fact that some establishments which were officially registered at that time were not actively advertising their services at the time of our study.

The Booking.com data available enable us to confirm the same geographical distribution pattern as for Airbnb accommodation. In those neighborhoods with no hotels, Airbnb does offer some accommodation, although very little.

Population density figures show that in Albaicín-Sacromonte and Realejo, where density is lower than in other central zones, the presence of Airbnb accommodation is striking.

If we focus on the number of residents per tourist apartment in the electoral districts, we find that among the 10 with the lowest numbers of people (and therefore greatest tourist pressure), are five dis-

Figure 2. Tourist accommodation in the city in relation to population density
Electoral districts in green indicating the higher (more intense green) or lower population density per square kilometer; tourist apartments (black dots), tourist rooms (yellow dots) and hotel establishments (purple dots)

tricts in Albaicín-Sacromonte (8, 9, 9.5, 19.8 and 22 persons per apartment) and 3 in Realejo (12.3, 14.1 and 14.1). If we consider rooms for tourist rental, the data is similar: amongst the first 10 we find 4 districts in Albaicín-Sacromonte (33.4, 57.9, 80.6 and 141.2 people per room) and 3 in Realejo (79.1, 91.2 and 108.4).

Figure 3 represents tourist accommodation in the city and residential homes for rent or sale in relation to the average income in each neighborhood. This map is related to RQ3. Data on residential homes for sale show that Center 1 has the most with 276 homes for sale (in good condition or in need of renovation), followed by C. Sierra-Bola de Oro-Genil (225) and Realejo (222)—third here, but in second place in terms of number of tourist apartments. Albaicín-Sacromonte (141) lies in ninth position but is first in terms of tourist apartments.

The average house price in Realejo and Albaicín-Sacromonte is clearly the highest. In the list of homes in good condition for sale, Realejo is first with 158 at an average price of €585 276, followed by Albaicín-Sacromonte with 106 homes at an average price of €330 928. In the list of homes in need of renovation for sale, Albaicín-Sacromonte has 35 at an average price of €454 685.7: the highest in the city. In third position, we find Realejo with 64 homes at an average price of €314 801.6.

In terms of the average price per square meter of homes in good condition for sale, Center 2 is in first place (€2492.3), followed by the central neighborhood of San Antón (€2392.3), Center 1 (€2382.1), Realejo (€2281.1) and, in sixth place, Albaicín-Sacromonte (€2197.5).

On the residential rental market, we find 1575 homes and 440 rooms for rent. Center 1 leads the list with 193 homes, followed by Realejo with 186. Albaicín-Sacromonte lies in seventh place with 110. In the rooms for rent list, Center 1 is first with 65 and Albaicín-Sacromonte third with 46. Again, the highest average price is found in Albaicín at €284, compared to an overall average for the city of €238.25. Center 1 is in fourth place (€257.6) and Realejo, fifth (€254.7).

The average rent for homes is €670.2 and Albaicín is one of the lowest at €546.6. The price of rental housing per square meter is €8.5 in Fígares-Ciudad Jardín, the most expensive neighborhood, followed by Center 1 (€8.4), Center 2 (€8.2), Realejo (€8.1) and, in sixth position, Albaicín-Sacromonte (€7.8). Given the historical nature of the neighborhoods under study, the average size of homes for rent in square meters is the smallest in the city: Albaicín-Sacromonte (70.21m^2, the smallest), Realejo (78.68m^2) and Center 1 (83.78m^2); far from the 117.13m^2 of Barrio de los Pajaritos, which has the largest homes.

Figure 4 shows some of the most important basic services for both tourists and residents. It allows us to respond to RQ4. Restaurants (TripAdvisor, yellow spots) are seen to be closely related to tourism, whereas two commercial activities are directly related to residents' interests: hairdresser's (purple spots) and supermarkets (red spots). Both were identified through Google Maps.

Restaurants are located mainly in Realejo (153), Albaicín-Sacromonte (131), Center 2 (116) and Center 1 (104). Consumer use of restaurants is indicated by the average number of reviews received for each neighborhood (Table 5). Albaicín-Sacromonte ranks first with an average of 238.3 reviews, while Realejo has an average of 173.6, compared to an average 89 per restaurant for all neighborhoods. The present study includes no qualitative analysis of the comments received. The situation of bars, cafés and other catering establishments is similar with the three historic districts having the highest numbers: Albaicín-Sacromonte (86), Realejo (84) and Center 1 (83); they also receive the most attention in reviews.

In relation to residential activity, the average number of supermarkets in the city is 16.4; in the neighborhoods under study we find Realejo (17), Albaicín-Sacromonte (14) and Center 1 (12). Note that this variable can be confusing because Google Maps includes under the same label small neighborhood stores often selling products destined to satisfy the needs of tourists passing by or staying in nearby apartments; these stores do not offer a range of products or prices to meet residents' needs. This is especially evident in Albaicín-Sacromonte where 6 of the 14 supermarkets are outside of the neighborhood's historic center, which further reduces the offer. Hairdresser's are also considered a resident-oriented service. The average per neighborhood is 14.9. Center 1 is just such an average neighborhood with 15 establishments, whereas Realejo is below average with 13 and Albaicín-Sacromonte (7) is the district with the fewest.

Finally, Table 5 includes information on commercial premises for sale or rent. The average number of stores for sale stands at 41.2. Center 1 is in third place with 58 whereas Realejo is below average with

Figure 3. Tourist accommodation in the city and residential homes for rent or sale in relation to average income

The city neighborhoods, indicating the highest (red) or lowest (yellow) average income; tourist apartments, both homes and individual rooms (black dots), homes for sale (purple dots) and homes and rooms for rent (green dots)

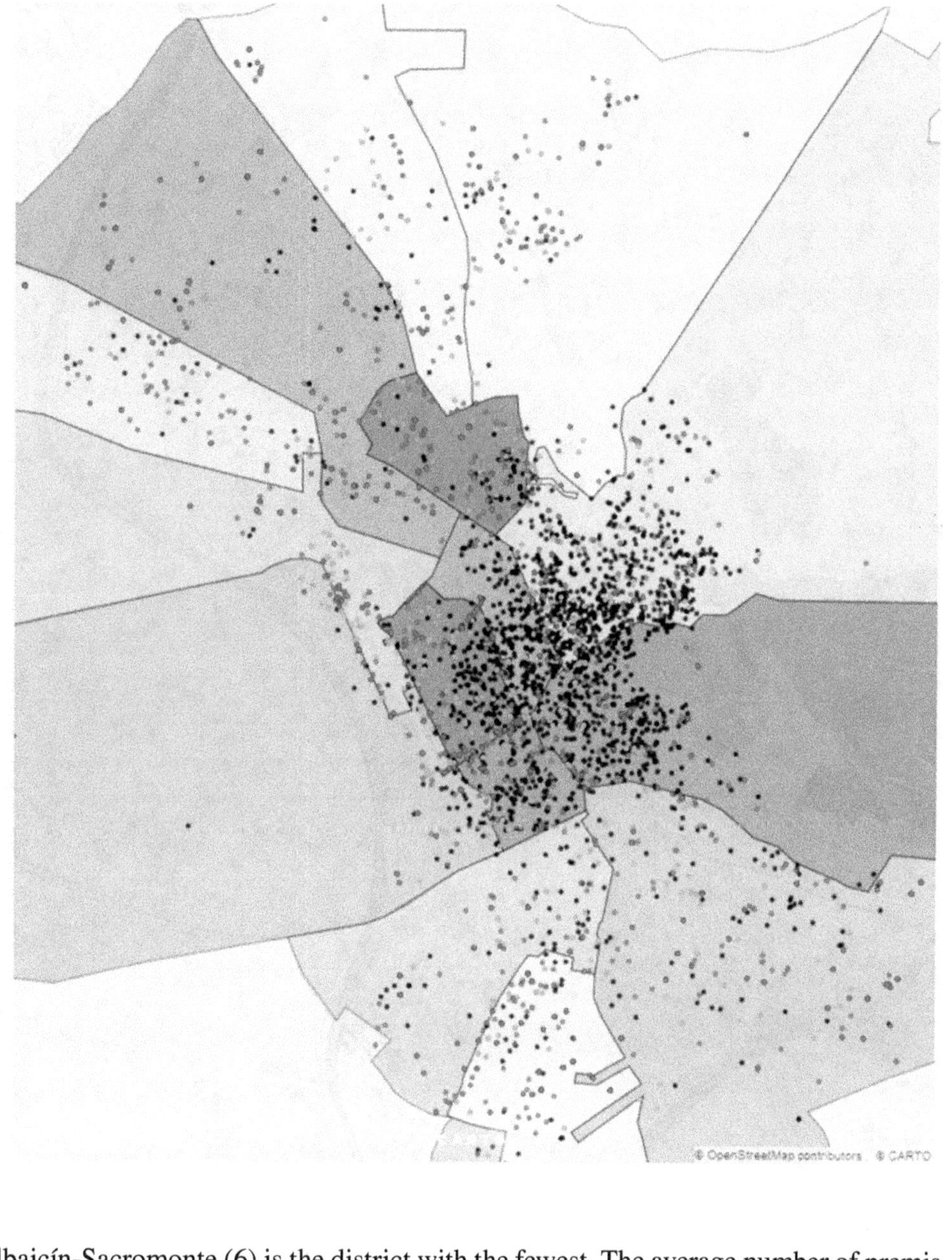

23 and Albaicín-Sacromonte (6) is the district with the fewest. The average number of premises for rent stands at 67.9. Center 1 is in first place with 78 whereas Albaicín-Sacromonte (13) and Realejo (11) have the fewest properties for rent in the city.

Figure 4. Services and their relationship to population density
The electoral districts are shown in green indicating the highest (most intense green) or lowest population density per square kilometer; restaurants (yellow dots), hairdresser's (purple dots) and supermarkets (red dots)

DISCUSSION

The above data corroborates the view that the historic districts of Albaicín-Sacromonte, Center 1 and Realejo are those that receive the greatest volume of tourist pressure as described by a variety of indicators—principally the Airbnb marketplace (63.7% of the tourist apartment offer in the city and 54.1% of individual rooms for rent). The geographical concentration of Airbnb supply has also been reported in other Spanish cities, such as Barcelona, Madrid and Palma de Mallorca (Gutierrez et al., 2017; Garcia-Ayllon, 2018).

By calculating at electoral district level the number of residents for each tourist apartment, we found that amongst the first 10 with the lowest numbers of people and, therefore, the highest tourist pressure, there are 5 districts in Albaicín-Sacromonte (8, 9, 9.5, 19.8 and 22 people per apartment) and 3 in Realejo (12.3, 14.1 and 14.1). Furthermore, if we look at rooms for tourist rental, the data is similar: amongst the first 10 we find 4 districts in Albaicín-Sacromonte (33.4, 57.9, 80.6 and 141.2 people per room) and 3 in Realejo (79.1, 91.2 and 108.4).

Clearly the concentration of individual rooms for rent is below that of apartments. Renting individual rooms is considered to be related to residents earning additional income, whereas renting homes is often an economic activity owners dedicate their home to permanently or on a seasonal basis to generate income. During 2018 Forum meetings on Sustainable Tourism in Albaicín and Sacromonte, the opinions of local residents were gathered. Findings indicated families resident in the neighborhood often rented out a second home in order to earn additional income. This issue should be explored via a more qualitative approach in future research.

In the historic districts, the proportion of apartments versus individual rooms is much greater than in more peripheral neighborhoods: Center 1 (9.4:1), Albaicín-Sacromonte (5.6:1), Realejo (5.1:1); downtown, in neighborhoods such as San Antón (7.3:1) or Center 2 (5.3:1), compared to neighborhoods such as Fígares-Ciudad Jardín (1.5:1), Zaidín-Vergeles (1.62:1), and Carretera de la Sierra-Bola de Oro-Genil (2:1). In two neighborhoods, more individual rooms are on offer than apartments: Beiro-Norte (0.9:1) and Polígono de Almanjáyar (0.5:1). These two are amongst the three neighborhoods with the lowest incomes so we would suggest that at the lower end of the income scale the incentive is to obtain additional income by renting individual rooms in homes. Adamiak (2018) indicated that the supply of entire properties (as opposed to rooms and shared rooms) is an indicator of the professionalization of Airbnb activity. This is particularly high in eastern and southern European countries. We need to investigate the extent to which owners are renting out more than one property in order to better understanding this professionalization in Granada.

Given the concentration of tourist apartments in the city center, we could question the dispersion of accommodation produced by Airbnb. However, we cannot give a conclusive answer to this question since Granada is surrounded by many smaller towns which add up to a population greater than that of the city itself and, therefore, the decentralization of tourist apartments may occur in other towns bordering the city. Similarly, we would need to contextualize other tourism resources, such as the Sierra Nevada ski resort which has a powerful seasonal component. How we define the units of analysis can generate different results. For instance, Adamiak (2018) in a comparison of European cities used various units: from municipal borders to urban regions or metropolitan areas.

Notwithstanding, data for neighborhoods with no or few hotel establishments shows Airbnb does have a presence there, albeit small. Differences in the distribution of hotel and Airbnb supply have also been reported in cities such as Paris (Heo et al., 2019).

Overall, the Airbnb accommodation capacity for apartments totals space for up to 7072 people (in 1489 apartments) plus 812 people in individual rented rooms (340). This amounts to 7884 overnight places, which means 2 877 660 places in a year. This contrasts with the INE survey of occupancy of tourist apartments data, which estimates an approximate annual total of 575 362 stays in tourist apartments. This is also lower than the 1250 homes registered for tourist use reported by Granada city council.

Since not all Airbnb apartments are registered in official records, the platform marketplace data is taken as a reference. Adding the 2 877 660 Airbnb stays to the estimated annual 5 433 047 hotel stays would increase the total offer by 53% above the capacity offered in hotels.

Despite this substantial Airbnb tourist apartment offer, the INE data on the evolution of the number of overnight stays in hotel establishments indicate an overall increase between 2013 and 2018 (with the exception of 2017). At the same time, the growth in the number of Airbnb apartments (Valdivia, 2017) since they first became available in 2010, has been very high. For example, in 2016 the offer grew by 105.42% in comparison with 2015.

The fact that the number of hotel establishments offering tourist accommodation has been maintained and, indeed grown in terms of overnight stays together with the new Airbnb marketplace implies that recent years have seen a significant increase in tourism in the city. Therefore, we cannot confirm that the demand for hotel accommodation is being replaced by the Airbnb supply, unlike the situation reported elsewhere (Zervas et al., 2017; Neeser et al., 2015; Heo et al., 2019).

Visitor numbers cannot be accurately measured by institutional instruments (Ganapati & Reddick, 2018). Hence, we need to improve measuring systems by including and regularizing, when this has not yet happened, the online tourist apartment marketplace.

The tourist pressure suffered by the city is confirmed through reports such as Urbantur (2016), which states that Granada ranks second after Santiago de Compostela in the tourist pressure index for accommodation, with 124.52 tourist places for each 1000 inhabitants.

In relation to the offer of homes for sale, data from the Idealista website shows that Center 1 and Realejo are two of the neighborhoods with the greatest numbers of properties available. The average prices of homes—both in need of renovation and in good condition—show Albaicín and Realejo are the most expensive. Similar results can be observed in terms of housing for rent. A key indicator, from the authors' point of view, is the ratio of homes offered for tourist rental compared to those offered for residential rental. The data shows that there are only 4 neighborhoods in which tourist rental exceeds residential rental. Two of them are: Albaicín, first, with a ratio of 4.4, and Realejo, with 1.6. Brauckmann (2017) analyzed the potential effects of sharing economy marketplaces on urban property markets and pointed out that increases in property prices due to growing city tourism may lead to the displacement of residents and businesses.

All this contributes as much to the touristification of city centers as to gentrification, which entails the expulsion of the population from neighborhoods that are revalued by an injection of public or private capital (Gravari-Barbas & Guinand, 2017; Grier, & Perry, 2018). In the historic districts, we find a greater volume of houses are only available to tourists and that prices are higher than those for residential rental. At the same time houses for sale also reach very high prices.

The touristification of downtown districts is also decisive because the total number of tourists in apartments and in hotels generates high flows that end up transforming the commercial nature of the city. We find a limited supply of basic services (e.g. supermarkets) which, together with the difficulties of access and mobility in historic neighborhoods, particularly Albaicín, discourages potential residents. Albaicín also has a lower average income than the overall average for the city and a smaller population.

LIMITATIONS, FUTURE INVESTIGATION, AND CONCLUSION

The present study involves a descriptive and quantitative exploration of current-day tourism in the city of Granada, taking the Airbnb supply as the main disruptive sharing economy factor.

The wide range of information sources used has introduced several limitations to our study: e.g. our capacity to update the data used; data quality; and the coverage different services have provided as approximations to the real situation, among others. Official data is currently obtained through procedures that clearly continue to exclude many of the phenomena relating to tourist apartments and therefore underestimate the real volume of tourist flows in cities.

Our results and their implications lead the discussion to the sustainability of tourism in historic and heritage cities. The concept of the "sharing city" has emerged to define the ways in which the sharing economy is implemented in urban areas (Agyeman, McLaren, & Schaefer-Borrego, 2013; McClaren & Agyeman, 2015). It is closely linked to achieving sustainability in cities by using digital technologies to activate underutilized resources in the face of growing resource constraints and environmental challenges. Cohen and Muñoz (2016) designed the Sharing Cities-SCP Plot, which seeks to provide a framework for understanding the emergence of sharing activity and its contribution to the generation of more sustainable urban economies. Sharing cities should definitely promote tourist practices that are both environmentally and socially sustainable. Currently, debates on sustainable tourism (Edgell, 2016) and the social responsibility of participants in tourist destinations are fundamental to the creation of interrelationships that satisfy the expectations of both tourists and local communities. This is a highly relevant approach for future research.

Additional lines of research in the context of sustainable tourism would involve the need to learn more about the nature of Airbnb tourist apartments: Are they registered with the public authorities? Who are the tenants? What are the profiles of the tourists that visit them? How well-satisfied are they? and so on. And the need to improve our understanding of the phenomenon of touristification in historic centers by making longitudinal studies that teach us about the evolution of shops and of neighborhood life. In cities with substantial metropolitan areas, as is the case of Granada, we need to incorporate these adjoining municipalities to gain a view of the city as a whole. The authors believe that it would also be appropriate to evaluate the development of explanatory models that allow us to integrate the variables in order to better understand the factors that determine tourist pressure and its effects on neighborhoods. Finally, comparisons of similar cities can help us understand the impact of the sharing economy on tourism at the national and European levels.

This would open up many opportunities to extend our work through different channels that might ultimately lead to better local management of tourism flows and a more adequate regulation of the reality of current problems.

The present study shows how the traditional accommodation marketplace together with the new alternatives on offer—which are much more flexible but difficult to quantify—increase the pressure that tourism exerts on urban centers. In Granada, this is mainly evident in the neighborhoods of Albaicín-Sacromonte, Realejo and Center 1. This represents a great challenge for our present and our future: namely, that of developing the awareness of residents and tourists in order to establish policies regarding the quality of the city's tourism sector so as to preserve the very nature of the neighborhoods and the lives of their people.

REFERENCES

Acevedo, D. D. (2016). Regulating employment relationships in the sharing economy. *Employee Rights & Employment Policy Journal*, *20*(1), 1–36.

Adamiak, C. (2018). Mapping Airbnb supply in European cities. *Annals of Tourism Research*, *71*(C), 67–71. doi:10.1016/j.annals.2018.02.008

Agencia Tributaria. (n.d.). Statistics of the taxpayers of the income tax of individuals of the largest municipalities by zip code. *Agencia Tributaria*. Retrieved from: https://www.agenciatributaria.es/AEAT.internet/datosabiertos/catalogo/hacienda/Estadistica_del_IRPF_por_codigo_postal.shtml

Agyeman, J., McLaren, D., & Schaefer-Borrego, A. (2013). Sharing cities. *Friends of the Earth Briefing*, 1-32.

Airbnb. (2015). *El impacto del alojamiento compartido en Madrid*. Available at: https://blog.atairbnb.com/el-impacto-del-alojamiento-compartido-en-madrid/

Bakker, M., & Twining-Ward, L. (2018). *Tourism and the Sharing Economy: Policy and Potential of Sustainable Peer-to-Peer Accommodation*. Washington, DC: World Bank. doi:10.1596/30452

Barron, K., Kung, E., & Proserpio, D. (2018). *The sharing economy and housing affordability: Evidence from Airbnb*. Available at: https://static1.squarespace.com/static/5bb2d447a9ab951efbf6d10a/t/5bea6881562fa7934045a3f0/1542088837594/The+Sharing+Economy+and+Housing+Affordability.pdf

Belk, R. (2014). You are what you can access: Sharing and collaborative consumption online. *Journal of Business Research*, *67*(8), 1595–1600. doi:10.1016/j.jbusres.2013.10.001

Boros, L., Dudás, G., Kovalcsik, T., Papp, S., & Vida, G. (2018). Airbnb in Budapest: Analysing spatial patterns and room rates of hotels and peer-to-peer accommodations. *Geo Journal of Tourism and Geosites*, *21*(1), 26–38.

Brauckmann, S. (2017). City tourism and the sharing economy–potential effects of online peer-to-peer marketplaces on urban property markets. *Journal of Tourism Futures*, *3*(2), 114–126. doi:10.1108/JTF-05-2017-0027

Cart. (n.d.). *granadaimedia. Cart*. Retrieved from: https://granadaimedia.carto.com/me

Cheng, M. (2016). Sharing economy: A review and agenda for future research. *International Journal of Hospitality Management*, *57*, 60–70. doi:10.1016/j.ijhm.2016.06.003

Cócola Gant, A. (2016). Holiday rentals: The new gentrification battlefront. *Sociological Research Online*, *21*(3), 1–9. doi:10.5153ro.4071

Cohen, B., & Munoz, P. (2016). Sharing cities and sustainable consumption and production: Towards an integrated framework. *Journal of Cleaner Production*, *134*, 87–97. doi:10.1016/j.jclepro.2015.07.133

Coyle, D., & Yeung, T. (2016). *Understanding Airbnb in fourteen European cities*. The Jean-Jacques Laffont Digital Chair Working Papers. Available at: http://www.lcii.eu/wp-content/uploads/2017/03/Yeung-Understanding-Airbnb-in-Fourteen-European-Cities-v4.1-1.pdf

Dudás, G., Boros, L., Kovalcsik, T., & Kovalcsik, B. (2017). The visualisation of the spatiality of Airbnb in Budapest using 3-band raster representation. *Geographia Technica, 12*(1), 23–30. doi:10.21163/GT_2017.121.03

Edelman, B. G., & Geradin, D. (2015). Efficiencies and regulatory shortcuts: How should we regulate companies like Airbnb and Uber. *Stanford Technology Law Review: STLR: An Online High-Technology Law Journal from Stanford Law School, 19*, 293–328.

Edgell, D. L. Sr. (2016). *Managing sustainable tourism: A legacy for the future*. Routledge. doi:10.4324/9781315688343

EU Innovation Observatory. (2014). *Collaborative Economy Collaborative production and the maker economy*. Business Innovation Observatory Contract No 190/PP/ENT/CIP/12/C/N03C01. Available at: https://ec.europa.eu/docsroom/documents/13423/attachments/1/translations/en/renditions/native

European Commission. (2017). *The cultural and creative cities monitor*. Available at: https://composite-indicators.jrc.ec.europa.eu/cultural-creative-cities-monitor/

European Commission. (2017). *The cultural and creative cities monitor*. European Commission. Retrieved from: https://composite-indicators.jrc.ec.europa.eu/cultural-creative-cities-monitor/

Exceltur. (2016). Urbantur 2016. *Monitor de competitividad turística de los destinos urbanos españoles*. Available at: https://www.exceltur.org/urbantur/

Fang, B., Ye, Q., & Law, R. (2016). Effect of sharing economy on tourism industry employment. *Annals of Tourism Research, 5*, 264–267. doi:10.1016/j.annals.2015.11.018

Ferrell, O. C., Ferrell, L., & Huggins, K. (2017). Seismic shifts in the sharing economy: Shaking up marketing channels and supply chains. *Journal of Marketing Channels, 24*(1–2), 3–12. doi:10.1080/1046669X.2017.1346973

Ganapati, S., & Reddick, C. G. (2018). Prospects and challenges of sharing economy for the public sector. *Government Information Quarterly, 35*(1), 77–87. doi:10.1016/j.giq.2018.01.001

Ganapati, S., & Reddick, C. G. (2018). Prospects and challenges of sharing economy for the public sector. *Government Information Quarterly, 35*(1), 77–87. doi:10.1016/j.giq.2018.01.001

Garcia-Ayllon, S. (2018). Urban Transformations as an Indicator of Unsustainability in the P2P Mass Tourism Phenomenon: The Airbnb Case in Spain through Three Case Studies. *Sustainability, 10*(8), 2933. doi:10.3390u10082933

Gonzalez-Padron, T. L. (2017). Ethics in the sharing economy: Creating a legitimate marketing channel. *Journal of Marketing Channels, 24*(1–2), 84–96. doi:10.1080/1046669X.2017.1347005

Gravari-Barbas, M., & Guinand, S. (Eds.). (2017). *Tourism and gentrification in contemporary metropolises: International perspectives*. Taylor & Francis. doi:10.4324/9781315629759

Gravari-Barbas, M., & Guinand, S. (Eds.). (2017). *Tourism and gentrification in contemporary metropolises: International perspectives*. Taylor & Francis. doi:10.4324/9781315629759

Grier, S. A., & Perry, V. G. (2018). Dog Parks and Coffee Shops: Faux Diversity and Consumption in Gentrifying Neighborhoods. *Journal of Public Policy & Marketing*, *37*(1), 23–38. doi:10.1509/jppm.16.230

Grier, S. A., & Perry, V. G. (2018). Dog parks and coffee shops: Faux diversity and consumption in gentrifying neighborhoods. *Journal of Public Policy & Marketing*, *37*(1), 23–38. doi:10.1509/jppm.16.230

Gutiérrez, J., García-Palomares, J. C., Romanillos, G., & Salas-Olmedo, M. H. (2017). The eruption of Airbnb in tourist cities: Comparing spatial patterns of hotels and peer-to-peer accommodation in Barcelona. *Tourism Management*, *62*, 278–291. doi:10.1016/j.tourman.2017.05.003

Guttentag, D. (2015). Airbnb: Disruptive innovation and the rise of an informal tourism accommodation sector. *Current Issues in Tourism*, *18*(12), 1192–1217. doi:10.1080/13683500.2013.827159

Heo, C. Y. (2016). Sharing economy and prospects in tourism research. *Annals of Tourism Research*, *58*, 156–170. doi:10.1016/j.annals.2016.02.002

Heo, C. Y., Blal, I., & Choi, M. (2019). What is happening in Paris? Airbnb, hotels, and the Parisian market: A case study. *Tourism Management*, *70*, 78–88. doi:10.1016/j.tourman.2018.04.003

Instituto Nacional de Estadistica. (n.d.). *Hotel occupation survey*. Instituto Nacional de Estadistica. Retrieved from: http://www.ine.es/dynt3/inebase/es/index.htm?padre=238&dh=1

Instituto Nacional de Estadistica. (n.d.). *Methodology*. Instituto Nacional de Estadistica. Retrieved from: https://www.ine.es/daco/daco42/ocuphotel/notaeoh.htm

Instituto Nacional de Estadistica. (n.d.). *Occupancy survey in tourist apartments*. Instituto Nacional de Estadistica. Retrieved from: https://www.ine.es/dynt3/inebase/index.htm?padre=231&capsel=231

Instituto Nacional de Estadistica. (n.d.). *Official population figures resulting from the revision of the Municipal Register on January 1*. Instituto Nacional de Estadistica. Retrieved from: http://www.ine.es/jaxiT3/Datos.htm?t=2871

Juul, M. (2015). *The Sharing Economy and Tourism*. Retrieved from http://www.europarl.europa.eu/RegData/etudes/BRIE/2015/568345/EPRS BRI(2015)568345 EN.pdf

Kesar, O., Dezeljin, R., & Bienenfeld, M. (2015). Tourism gentrification in the city of Zagreb: Time for a debate. *Interdisciplinary Management Research*, *11*, 657–668.

Lab in Granada. (n.d.). Retrieved from: https://labingranada.org/foroalbaicinsacromonte/

Lees, L., Shin, H. B., & López-MORALES, E. (2016). *Planetary gentrification*. Cambridge, UK: Polity Press.

Leung, X. Y., Xue, L., & Wen, H. (2019). Framing the sharing economy: Toward a sustainable ecosystem. *Tourism Management*, *71*, 44–53. doi:10.1016/j.tourman.2018.09.021

McLaren, D., & Agyeman, J. (2015). *Sharing cities: a case for truly smart and sustainable cities*. MIT Press.

Megalab, U. G. R. (n.d.). *Laboratory for research on culture and society digital*. Universidad de Granada. Retrieved from: https://medialab.ugr.es/

Midgett, C., Bendickson, J. S., Muldoon, J., & Solomon, S. J. (2017). The Sharing Economy and Sustainability: A Case for Airbnb. *Small Business Institute Journal, 13*(2), 51–71.

Mody, M., Suess, C., & Dogru, T. (2019). Not in my backyard? Is the anti-Airbnb discourse truly warranted? *Annals of Tourism Research, 74*(C), 198–203. doi:10.1016/j.annals.2018.05.004

Moreno-Izquierdo, L., Ramón-Rodríguez, A. B., Such-Devesa, M. J., & Perles-Ribes, J. F. (2019). Tourist environment and online reputation as a generator of added value in the sharing economy: The case of Airbnb in urban and sun-and-beach holiday destinations. *Journal of Destination Marketing & Management, 11*, 53–66. doi:10.1016/j.jdmm.2018.11.004

Neeser, D., Peitz, M., & Stuhler, J. (2015). *Does Airbnb hurt hotel business: Evidence from the Nordic countries.* Universidad Carlos III de Madrid.

Oskam, J., & Boswijk, A. (2016). Airbnb: The future of networked hospitality businesses. *Journal of Tourism Futures, 2*(1), 22–42. doi:10.1108/JTF-11-2015-0048

Owyang, J., Tran, C., & Silva, C. (2013). *The collaborative economy.* Altimeter. Retrieved from: http://www.collaboriamo.org/media/2014/04/collabecon-draft16-130531132802-phpapp02-2.pdf

Rauch, D. E., & Schleicher, D. (2015). *Like Uber, but for local governmental policy: The future of local regulation of the "Sharing Economy."* George Mason Law & Economics Research Paper (15-01).

Romero Frías, E. (2018a). «Granada Proyecta»: ciudadanía y funcionariado por un turismo sostenible. In C. Güemes, J. Resina, & C. Cruz-Rubio (Eds.), *Participación ciudadana: experiencias inspiradoras en España* (pp. 95–108). GIGAPP y Centro de Estudios Políticos y Constitucionales. Retrieved from http://www.cepc.gob.es/publicaciones/libros/colecciones?IDP=2738

Romero Frías, E. (2018b). Granada Proyecta: ciudadanía y funcionariado por un turismo sostenible. Medialab UGR. In *Gobernanza participativa local. Construyendo un nuevo marco de relación con la ciudadanía* (pp. 179-181). Federación Española de Municipios y Provincias. Retrieved from: http://femp.femp.es/files/3580-1936-fichero/GOBERNANZA%20PARTICIPATIVA%20LOCAL.pdf

Schor, J. (2016). Debating the sharing economy. *Journal of Self-Governance and Management Economics, 4*(3), 7–22. doi:10.22381/JSME4320161

Schor, J. B., & Attwood-Charles, W. (2017). The "sharing" economy: Labor, inequality, and social connection on for-profit platforms. *Sociology Compass, 11*(8), e12493. doi:10.1111oc4.12493

Seraphin, H., Sheeran, P., & Pilato, M. (2018). Over-tourism and the fall of Venice as a destination. *Journal of Destination Marketing & Management, 9*, 374–376. doi:10.1016/j.jdmm.2018.01.011

Tussyadiah, I. P., & Zach, F. (2015, May). *Hotels vs. peer-to-peer accommodationrentals: Text analytics of consumer reviews in Portland, Oregon.* Paper presented at the Travel and Tourism Research Association (TTRA) 46th Annual, Portland, OR.

Valdivia, A. (2017). *La turistificación en Granada.* Retrieved from: https://valdilab.wordpress.com/2017/07/18/turistificacion-en-granada/

Zervas, G., Proserpio, D., & Byers, J. W. (2017). The rise of the sharing economy: Estimating the impact of Airbnb on the hotel industry. *JMR, Journal of Marketing Research*, *54*(5), 687–705. doi:10.1509/jmr.15.0204

KEY TERMS AND DEFINITIONS

Cultural and Creative Cities Monitor: A tool, developed by the European Commission, to monitor, assess and compare the performance of 'Cultural and Creative Cities' in Europe from both the quantitative and qualitative perspectives. It consists of 29 indicators, 9 dimensions, and 3 major facets of the cultural, social, and economic vitality of cities: cultural vibrancy, creative economy, and enabling environment.

Gentrification: This entails the displacement of residents from neighborhoods that are revalued by the injection of public or private capital.

Sharing City: This refers to the application of sharing economy dynamics to urban areas in order to face social and environmental challenges within a scenario of growing resource constraints.

Sustainable Tourism: This is an approach to tourism that takes into account the many social and environmental impacts of tourism on a territory and the communities of residents living in it.

Tourist Apartments: This refers to those apartments that are for the use of tourists and includes those found on sharing economy platforms such as Airbnb.

Tourist Flows: This refers to the spatial patterns of tourists visiting a city. It provides information that is important in managing tourism and providing services and goods that are appropriate for tourists and residents.

Touristification: This refers to the impact of mass tourism on the commercial and social fabric of neighborhoods, causing services, facilities, and shops to be oriented towards and conceived of by reference to the tourist rather than the resident.

APPENDIX

Table 4. Main data on tourist and residential accommodation in the neighborhoods of Granada (the three neighborhoods with the highest indicators are highlighted by different intensities of red, from the highest to the lowest)

	Tourist Accommodation					Residential Accommodation			
	Hotels	Entire Homes		Rooms		Housing for Sale		Housing for Rent	
Neighborhoods		Quantity	Total Capacity	Quantity	Total Capacity	In Good Condition	In Need of Renovation	Entire Homes	Rooms
Center 1 [18001]	21	160	786	17	47	187	89	193	65
Center 2 [18002]	20	197	912	37	94	49	39	111	37
Ronda [18003]	4	20	100	4	8	75	42	85	18
Ronda-Arabial [18004]	4	25	158	11	24	112	96	51	34
San Antón [18005]	5	102	558	14	56	96	48	85	33
Fígares-C. Jardín [18006]	3	27	149	18	35	91	11	90	4
Zaidín-Vergeles [18007]	0	21	119	13	24	125	69	131	20
C. Sierra-Bola de Oro-Genil [18008]	2	52	329	26	67	183	42	61	11
Realejo [18009]	30	300	1334	59	147	158	64	186	36
Albaicín-Sacromonte [18010]	25	489	2193	88	191	106	35	110	46
Beiro-Norte [18011]	0	16	78	17	36	94	30	37	50
Plaza de Toros [18012]	2	45	193	20	41	99	56	154	35
Polígono de Almanjayar [18013]	0	2	12	4	10	52	10	22	13
Barrio de los Periodistas [18014]	3	22	97	7	15	125	44	173	31
Chana [18015]	0	11	54	5	17	77	38	86	7
Total	119	1489	7072	340	812	1683	713	1575	440

Table 5. Main data on tourist and residential accommodation in the neighborhoods of Granada (the three neighborhoods with the highest indicators are highlighted by different intensities of red, from the highest to the lowest)

Neighborhoods	Restaurants		Bars, Cafés and Others		Super-markets	Hairdresser's	Commercial Premises	
	Quantity	Average Number of Reviews Received	Quantity	Average Number of Reviews Received			For Sale	For Rent
Center 1 [18001]	104	114.46	83	107.3	12	15	58	78
Center 2 [18002]	116	167.10	72	90.2	12	14	23	49
Ronda [18003]	57	59.63	36	22.7	12	12	20	27
Ronda-Arabial [18004]	49	66.22	31	14.1	18	21	58	44
San Antón [18005]	45	85.49	41	89.8	18	11	58	69
Fígares-C. Jardín [18006]	42	41.38	43	18.2	22	14	51	32
Zaidín-Vergeles [18007]	21	66.19	15	6.7	17	14	72	38
C. Sierra-Bola de Oro-Genil [18008]	53	94.96	40	19.9	32	26	61	27
Realejo [18009]	153	173.60	84	131.5	17	13	23	11
Albaicín-Sacromonte [18010]	131	238.32	86	186.3	14	7	6	13
Beiro-Norte [18011]	1	59	5	3.8	10	10	29	8
Plaza de Toros [18012]	40	57.93	24	45.1	11	11	31	31
Polígono de Almanjayar [18013]	12	22.92	10	4.2	14	16	21	17
Barrio de los Periodistas [18014]	40	61.48	25	57.2	19	27	53	34
Chana [18015]	11	25.55	10	3.7	18	12	54	27
Total	875		605		246	223	618	1019

Chapter 6
Uber's Strategy as a Competitive Business Model of Sharing Economy

José G. Vargas-Hernández
University of Guadalajara, Mexico

ABSTRACT

The aim of this chapter is to analyze the different strategies that take Uber to join the global market successfully, positioning itself in different countries, and to analyze how these businesses and strategies that follow become successful to the extent that Uber is doing, not just one city but many in several countries around the world. In order to accomplish this, it is necessary to reference a previous literature review on collaborative economies business model that is appropriate to identify the different theories that may be applicable. As a result, the analysis of this work shows the determining factors that have placed Uber as one of the leading companies within its area of influence and ends with some recommendations on the conflicts that the firm presents when entering a new market.

INTRODUCTION

Uber is currently an international firm that offers its customers a private transport service, through its platform, an application for smartphones, which associates travelers with drivers of vehicles registered in the system to offer a service of private transportation through vehicles to people. The organization classifies travel in many urban communities around the world and its headquarters are located in California. Initially, drivers had vehicles that the company certified as appropriate.

As a result of these new ways of moving emerges UBER, which for several years start to mark a new trend in moving people from one point to another, especially in big cities around the world. It has its origins in a revised class concept of Strategic Management as it is born global that refers to those companies that are born in a global or international markets and are marking a new trend in the way of doing business, taking advantage of the technological changes that have occurred in the world in which today we live. This company considers having a relationship with the technological-based firms that are

DOI: 10.4018/978-1-5225-9928-9.ch006

Copyright © 2020, IGI Global. Copying or distributing in print or electronic forms without written permission of IGI Global is prohibited.

characterized by being innovative, enough reason to learn more about the same as it was able to study from approaches such as the theory based on institutions and global strategy.

Uber has its origins in 2008 as it tells the story in its page when Travis Kalanick and Garrett Camp could not get a taxi in Paris, which led to an idea to create an application where with just one button, could have a trip. What started with this simple idea is now changing the way people are transported in large cities? According to the Uber definition is the smartest way to move and luxury at low cost. After 2012, Uber includes a broader determination of cars for the market. The cars are assigned with the portable application. With this application, customers can track the area of accessible cars and the qualities of both the car and the driver. The company's operations begin in July 2014 in Mexico and Guadalajara, according to its official website.

The objective of this work is to reveal information about the Uber mobile application and its foray into the Mexican open transport market, in particular from Guadalajara. To begin with, the article shows a general outline of the idea of Uber and the administration it provides. First, there is a brief synopsis of how it has entered the global transportation showcase. In addition, the document delves into Uber from a strategic and competitive point of view (especially the taxi service), where an attempt is made to discover if the administration that provides this service, with its particularities and its competitive advantages, could possibly be considered as a component of the same important market of different types of public and private transport. It is intended to raise the advantages and disadvantages of this company in the market and what measures should be taken to solve the latter, as well as raise some competitive advantages that could be beneficial for the firm.

BACKGROUND OF THE PROBLEM

Today globalization plays an important process, because by this concept can be eliminated some barriers between countries. Through technology has been a way these barriers have been eliminated, since technological innovations often come equally to different countries and at different times around the world, so it can be seen different products with similar characteristics, which is called as a standard product, regardless of whether they are produced in different cultures.

The story so before it started this century tells that the common way to establish a company along the story is that the company or the plant reached the place where he would have operations, had a physical place, and was established formally. Now it is seeing a new trend in strategies and ways of doing business in enterprises as a platform generated by its operations, profits, sales and everything related to business dedicated activity. Which have started with this simple idea is now changing the way people are transported in large cities, according to the Uber definition is the smartest way to move and luxury at low cost.

Technology and innovation play an important role in the process of globalization. Adopting a comprehensive strategy for technology companies is essential and addressing new ways of doing business. Nowadays have been emerging these new companies of successful technology-based, born in markets international companies like Netshoes, Netflix, Google, Amazon and many other technological changes that have been created and have managed to be successful in their business segment. The creation of these new companies has diversified options that consumers have to purchase the good or service that require, with new technology and not in the common traditional form.

One problem faced by companies that wanted to provide the services of private transport in the country, were the unions of taxi drivers that prevent or put barriers to companies that wanted to provide these services faced, and who would provide the service had to join the unions of transportation in addition to the permits they had to acquire by the authorities to provide the service. Thus, the institutions were an impediment to a company that wanted to be in this area. But also, an advantage of same weaknesses they could have the same institutions, they have created companies like Uber and reaching nations that did not consider these businesses in their regulations. Taking advantage of those holes is how they have succeeded in entering the global market.

Within technology and new ways of doing business in the globalization process, it can be found different definitions and ways in which this process is changing. One of these definitions is that of Friedman (1970) and for example he says that globalization is a phenomenon characterized by technological innovation and its appearance in the world has been consolidated in stages. The initial stage of economic globalization, for some authors, is the industrial revolution the event that gave rise to this phenomenon. Most authors state that consolidation was given to a process of trade integration (Carbaugh, 2005).

In recent years this type of technology-based companies has increased their presence around the world and have led to the emergence of more of this type and have seen more and more not only born but become successful, not only in a nation but in the global market place.

Market Studied

In the beginning, the sector to which this company is directed should be established. Uber, in the country has three modes of service: UberX, UberPool and UberBlack; the two initial benefits are accessible or, rather, are typically taken by individuals who tend to use typical services, large space or shared use; UberX: it is Uber's most well-known and recurring alternative, it incorporates vehicles with a maximum 10-year model, although this depends on the Uber criteria for each city, it recognizes a maximum of four passengers and, alternatively, it allows the distribution of load between the traveler, Uber Pool: it was a simultaneous launch of UberX, delivering the door open to 3 customers from several areas to request an exit to a typical target that is close to all the customers who share the trip, thus saving a considerable sum of monetary resources.

On the other hand, UberBlack is a Premium administration, it was for clients with greater resources, it is part of the latest model of luxury cars, with a limit of four passengers, it is frequently used by associations and organizations for the transport of personnel (Uber, 2016).

Complementary to the above, the market area and its geographical coverage are clarified, for this case. In July 2014, Uber arrives in Guadalajara and later in other states of the Republic, where people can enjoy the benefits provided by the Uber application, registering on the Uber website. It is worth mentioning that the service is currently present in more than 38 cities in Latin America (Ferrer, 2016).

THEORETICAL: CONCEPTUAL REVIEW

A technology-based company can differentiate itself from other companies with the main feature innovation processes, either in the product or service offered. They base their activity on technological research, having scientific and technological knowledge.

For purposes of this research, the case of Uber is studied from the side of the strategies used to enter the global market, and succeeding in many countries, taking into account that each country and culture is different, the use of concepts as work global, technology-based companies, global strategy was considered a factor for growth and establishment of industries or companies of this type.

The technology-based companies like Uber have achieved their positioning in the limited control of institutions to such companies, in the absence of regulatory schemes both Uber and other companies have used this to establish their operations. Some features that make them different companies like Uber is that they have fewer staff operating or working for the company, since by creating the online platform and working and operating costs are lower than in a company established in a physical place also presented in the world with a standard or homogenized product.

Companies like Uber generate an advantage for users or consumers and have achieved different countries or states to consider making changes to their laws to fit the modus operandi of these companies. States allow or block entry of Uber and other companies in their type, having a power in the region where they arrive with their operations, thus having influence on decisions or regulations made in the laws for operation.

The research of these report wants to answer is on How technology-based companies with a global strategy have succeeded in entering and being successful in the new way of doing business?

The importance comes to have this work of serious research to understand the impact of the strategies of technology-based companies taking specific case of Uber. This is done using the theory of institutions and by applying the concept of global strategy came to succeed. Overall, a case of Uber especially as famous as the raised here in this paper case where the company has already been established in at least 20 countries, albeit with some adjustments as the nation where the product offering remains standard worldwide reaches, and despite having problems in some cities where he settled.

These problems especially with local competitors, called taxis are mainly due to they think is unfair competition and with innovation that the company Uber made in the product achievement that many people with common form move from side to side in public or private transport, now do differently and have changed the way they use the shuttle.

While we know that the group of people or consumers who can access this service is limited, because people who use it so far require at least two basic things to make use of the product. One of them is to have a cell phone where downloading the application, then also required to have a bank account as a credit card or debit card with which to pay the service they have. These basic elements are essential of this new business model and so far fundamental to acquire a service like what Uber offers, because without them they cannot access the transfer from one place to another. Thus, this is being a limiting factor that not all people can consume this good or service, so the service is intended for a specific sector of the population which operates the platform.

The technology-based companies today play an important role in the business world, which tries to capture this document as through its incorporation and importance have implemented a new way of doing business in companies of its kind, reducing costs, applying innovation in its services and creating a new business model, and in some cases, taking advantage of the weaknesses or gaps that exist in the laws and institutions of the nations where they arrive. Companies like Uber were not considered by institutions or legislation. Thus, taking advantage of the gaps, these companies have managed to enter the market and in some cases adapted in certain respects, but retaining the service innovation.

In the case of Mexico, so far is not entirely clear the legal fulfillments that must have this company. Mexico is working on making changes to laws, regulations roads and adaptations of the legal framework of the relevant institutions to consider Uber and companies of its kind in formal enterprises. In this case, some state laws are working to make adaptations to their traffic laws, such as the state of Jalisco and Mexico City that having already advanced and concrete proposals as to how to resolve this issue. However, at the time of writing this report, some of the proposals were being approved or published to make them official.

Moreover, companies offering the same service as Uber, in this case the taxis see it as an illegal and unfair to the service competition that for years have been offering and operating in some form as a monopoly. They do not pay taxes and have adopted certain aggressive strategies to try to reach the market to Uber through intimidation or aggression towards users or drivers of the business. Taking advantage of technological changes and the weakness of the institutions not considered. Also with the emergence years ago of other technology companies and carrying out a global strategy have been incorporated to market, different companies.

One of these technology-based companies with a comprehensive global strategy that has carried out these concepts in a successfully way is Uber because today it is seen with these strategies that has-been established in the market. After seeing this case have emerged more companies with the same features and offer the service of private transport, as are Cabify and City drive to name some of the same sector. Even its operations are similar to the case analyzed in this work. These firms are technology-based companies that offer a private shuttle service to their users through a platform. Although not all companies operate as such in the same cities, their strategies are like.

On the other hand, if it is seen the part where it operates each company taking the case of Mexico. For example, in Guadalajara operates Uber and City drive but not Cabify, leading to the conclusion that even with global strategies are not present in the same cities or arrive at the same time. Uber is in Guadalajara and 379 cities worldwide and is aimed at a specific segment of the population that is people with bank account, credit card or debit card to pay for the service they purchase, as well as having the application installed on their cell phone.

Within its business model, Uber does not accept payment in cash so far, this being an important innovation in the model, and this aspect is also part of the diversification of the service. Another important issue is quality standards for these keep the user since the end of each trip it can rate the service and the driver, this being another innovation in the service provided how had offered traditional way.

An important issue in such companies as already mentioned is the diversification of product or service offered, as it has been key to succeed and companies like Netshoes, Netflix, Amazon and the company analyzed in this case Uber. These technology-based companies have in common is that they are based on diversification and innovation in what they offer which is considered the most important to have successful operations in a globalized world.

An important segment is the population that has access to the good or service that is launched. when somebody wants to buy a product like shoes, food, books or any other product only they go to the market place where the product is sold and with money in hand it is acquired and anyone who can pay the price can buy it.

In the case of service Uber, this simply fact does not apply because it is a service that only is acquired it from a strict sense by people over 18, who are the people likely to have a bank account to pay for the service. Thus, the target population or that can be client f Uber, are people over 18 years with bank account. Uber on its website states that offers the service in five municipalities of the Metropolitan area of Guadalajara (ZMG), that is Guadalajara, Zapopan, Tlaquepaque, Tonala and Tlajomulco, taking a total of 2,745,260 potential customers broken down as follows the municipalities, and displaying data as much as by men and women. See Table 1.

According to data from the Metropolitan Transportation Institute Jalisco, taxis continue to maintain market power and Uber is positioned in second place in service of private transport as it is concerned. An advantage of Uber, considered by users is mainly the price and greater security.

Actors Studied

The characteristics of current and potential consumers are defined by the fact that Uber, all over the world, is a company that functions as a link between the driver and the customer. Whoever requests it has a need: to be transported. But not only a few individuals must be transported, as a whole. This type of service is required by society sooner or later, on a day-to-day basis. It is at that point, while there are alternatives to how to do it, for which numerous factors intervene, among which is the measure of cash that we can pay for the service, the speed of travel, comfort and security (Ávalos, 2015).

The above described consumers are around 18 to 40 years of age, since they are the closest to effectively manage the application that interacts with the driver. These customers are willing to pay for a trip at a reasonable price, as well as ready to share the road. In Mexico, more than half of the population agrees to travel with another person. No doubt, Uber came to achieve the Mexican market will pay through debit cards, understood that not all customers could access a loan, so, in its progress, has begun to cash in real money. At the end of the day, the buyers of this service are and have a habitual monetary position (Pallares, 2016).

It is worth mentioning that more than half of current customers, instead of using Uber, would use their own car. All consumers have a smartphone, less than half have a credit or debit card, however, they all have cash available. On the other hand, a relevant fact is that more than half would drive in a drunken state if it were not for Uber, implies that through this benefit accidents and conceivable deaths that happen every day are reduced. In the United States, Uber has coverage of 75% of the population, of which 22% of active drivers are women. In Mexico, more than 500,000 clients have joined the service (Pallares, 2016).

The company has recently implemented the issuance of invoices, that is, it still has this benefit unlike the competition, which different organizations need to produce charge credit, so current customers may require this voucher, be they moral persons, as well as to individuals, and thereby achieve a superior position in the market.

Table 1.

Municipality	Population 18 and over	Masculine population 18 and more	Feminine Population 18 and more
Guadalajara	1,031,902	482,713	549,189
Tlaquepaque	376,022	182,406	193,616
Tlajomulco de Zúñiga	235,703	115,015	120,688
Tonalá	289,679	147,418	142,261
Zapopan	811,954	388,501	423,453

Conflicts Studied

The dangers that threaten this company as an organizational entity that provides a private transport service, in the first place, is the professionalism with which it is handled, there is no guarantee that the driver can complete an expert driving, as is hypothetically guaranteed by the certification and in contrast to taxi drivers. The problem of the driving test and the basic requirements to acquire a driver's license in the corresponding modality shown to offer the service of taxis and other permits that are essential to deal with this specific car, which evidences legal shortcomings that decrease the safety of the traveler (Hernández, Galindo & Vicente 2015).

Another conflict is the certified identification of the driver, even though the driver must be a member of the firm and be registered as such in the application and the system, sometimes abusing the stipulated conditions, some drivers subcontract to others, to generate a business model in which the cars work on behalf of someone else and generate greater profits to the owner. On the other hand, another problem is the insurance coverage, since as the service provides a private car that is granted private transport benefits, the company's protection covers the accidents of the driver and not of the passengers in some cases (Hernández, Galindo & Vicente 2015).

According to Ávalos (2015), "another inconvenience is the lack of loyalty that some leading partners can have towards the company. Some taxi drivers claim that there is an unjustifiable lack and disadvantage, since Uber would not be obliged to accept all the needs that are expected from the other organizations that report to the SAT (Tax Administration Service). "

One aspect that was taken into account in writing this paper, it was to consider the different theories and revised concepts. One of the aspects that fit for this work was the subject where the importance of institutions is played and whether it can reach affect or influence strategies that take companies to conduct their operations. An aspect that Uber considered is the adaptation to the current legal framework, which call as the theory of institutions, and in this category it is found a definition of the Nobel laureate in economics, North (1990) who defined an institution as humanly planned restrictions that structure the interaction of people, which is popularly known as rules of the game.

Likewise, the same author classifies 2 different types of institutions and classifies them as follows (North 2005) formal and informal institutions. In the former are the laws, regulations and standards, and on the side of informal talks about rules, culture and ethics, including different ideas, values and attitudes of people in their behavior in society. Moreover, it is possible to distinguish three aspects the authors belonging to the first generation of institutionalisms, neo institutionalisms and the new institutional economics (Urbado and Hernandez, 2007). Moreover, Veblen (1965) also talks about the institutions and gives us another definition that by the end of this work is also acceptable. It is defined as common and predictable patterns of behavior in society, including the habits of thought and action generally shared.

One area where have failed Institutions are flaws in the regulations for these type of companies, i.e. not governments had considered the new e-business, category where Uber is characterized. Canals (1994) states that the objective of internationalizing a company are the opening of new markets, lower production costs, and a more efficient structure of production and distribution of the company.

The business model of this type of business is focused on a specific sector of the population and from this part gives a new way to operate, which is not available for all people who want to use the product or service this type of companies offer. The overall and global strategy adopted by these firms have advantages over competitors as it refers to how to compete, and focuses on providing standardized products and services worldwide (Peng 2000).

Within the theory of institutions see different regulations that have occurred around the world to allow the application to offer their services. For example, in the United States in the city of Chicago a new category of transportation calls service transport networks, just as in Mexico City was created have made regulations for the operation of the service, in New Orleans you will have to pay the city by permits, something similar happened in New York where the council of citizenship and Uber reached an agreement to set the number of vehicles that can circulate in the city.

Just as there are cities where they operate without any regulation of institutions, there are cases like the above where they operate with certain regulations by the institutions and authorities of the city, but is also the case of Florida in the United States because it does not operate in this city for failing to meet the requirements of city tax.

On the other hand, the phenomenon of globalization (Peng 2012) refers to the close integration of people and countries around the world, and today this concept is applied in different sectors and industries.

Within the theory of institutions are seen different regulations that have occurred around the world to allow the application to offer their services. For example, in the United States in the city of Chicago was created a new category of transportation called service transport networks, just as in Mexico City was created, both have made regulations for the operation of the service. In New Orleans the customer has to pay the city permits. Something similar happened in New York where the council of citizenship and Uber reached an agreement to set the number of vehicles that can circulate in the city.

Just as there are cities where they operate without any regulation of institutions, there are cases like the above where they operate with certain regulations by the institutions and authorities of the city. But, it is also the case of Florida in the United States, because it does not operate in this city for failing to meet the requirements of city tax.

On the other hand, the phenomenon of globalization (Peng 2012) refers to the close integration of people and countries around the world, and today this concept is applied in different sectors and industries.

COLLABORATIVE ECONOMIES BUSINESS MODEL

Bostman and Rogers (2010) (2010) argue that firms like UBER are part of a classic model of collaborative economy, being a disruptive innovation (Christensen & Raynor, 2003) that occurs when individuals share common interests and a common philosophy of life. In this case, they aim to rent cars in shared taxis or whole taxis through a social search and management system (Bostman & Rogers, 2010). So the emergence of this phenomenon is possible as the evolution of technology allows imitate the exchanges that usually or used to give face to face, on a larger scale thanks to the internet, together with the ability to create trust between strangers.

Rifkin (2014) points out that the decline in marginal costs, which tends to be near zero, is resulting in a dichotomous economy, partly capitalist market and on the other hand, collaborative commons gradually drawn out a new economic paradigm. Interian, (2016) argues that the sharing economy is credited with reducing transaction costs, increase efficiency and promote accountability and competence. This model does not require a centralized entity that should have an inventory and therefore is free of logistics, costs associated with maintaining inventory, product and geographic expansion for these purposes.

This model by allowing individuals to take advantage of the ability to take advantage of an asset that already possess, collaborative business model eliminates in an efficient and convenient way transaction costs. The specific characteristics of collaborative consumer of passengers and commuters are little known, although generally, it may try to travelers connected and experts, likely to responsible consumption, characterized by a high level of trust in the other members of the community and familiarity with internet and online commerce, demanding about the quality of its transport and commuting experiences (Russo & Quaglieri, 2014).

Despite its purported benefits, companies of collaborative economies have been strongly criticized for the way they operate, and in some cases have been forced to shut down operations. Critics argue that the laws are evading created precisely to regulate certain practices in which their companies are engaged; users sharing platforms become "prosumers" people who consume, like produce (Streitfeld, 2014)

Blurring the line between consumer and producer collaborative economy breaks with the traditional business model that companies own and people consume. On the other hand, the concept of sharing erodes the disinterested public regulation, substituting private regulation or leaving unattended regulated transactions. Because of this, business creation becomes more widespread and may even lead to displace their regulated and established counterparts some time ago. An example of this is Uber, which has become a ubiquitous service in major cities around the world (Interian, 2016). The most important cities in the United States and Europe have begun to implement regulations regarding share or rent cars and have initiated investigations with the goal of bringing the collaborative economy in accordance with existing laws (Chafkin, 2016).

On the other hand, information technologies have facilitated the exchange of user experiences, enabling the comments and product valuation objective and transparent manner. These valuations are perceived in the market as certain and are changing consumer behavior and redefining the role of influence during the buying process by providing more realistic expectations (Cañigueral, 2015). That is when the consumer can know the costs and perceived by others who have commented and valued their consumer experiences, which later will help to make a decision with some confidence, even if the consumer never had before contracted this service, reducing significantly benefits the perceived risk (Wen, 2009).

TECHNOLOGY-BASED COMPANIES, THEIR BEHAVIOR, AND MARKET PERFORMANCE

Today, economies have adapted to new business models or at least they try in some cases that have been created with this type of technology-based companies. For the same, now no longer have the need to have a physical space, plant or building in which to carry out its processes, but the base of their operations is through a platform in the network that can be accessed from any device with internet, what we call a new model of e-commerce business.

In its business model (Uber 2016) charges a 20% or 25% in the case the last drivers to register in the system to make use of the platform and the remaining is for the driver. According to the company in the metropolitan area of Guadalajara there are about 3,000 registered vehicles.

The success of Uber in the market is due to several factors. It is clear that neither it does not think and created anything new, nor does not offer a service that did not existed, or invented anything. But what it did was to apply an innovation to a service that already existed, introduced a new way of doing business and using technology achievement join and establish successfully its operations with a standard product around the world, keeping costs down and driven by different factors that in the analysis of results will be observed so more clear.

REVIEW OF THE EMPIRICAL LITERATURE

Strategic Reasons

Some of the competitive advantages that belong to Uber have to do with the fact of the price that the customer is willing to pay, and the methods of payment. In addition, requesting a taxi in Mexico, includes numerous circumstances. The first is the fare, in many parts of Mexico, including Guadalajara is common to be familiar with the idea that taxis have an excessive rate, since drivers not only take advantage of the lack of time that the traveler has, also of the region and the time for which the trip is made. A taxi does not charge the same in case it is requested it in different areas of the city.

The Mexican, therefore, pays a taxi of about 40 pesos when talking about a reasonable trip. In any case, normally the benefit is not what is really worth, since travelers run the risk of being robbed or arriving unpunctually at the established place. This is a serious disadvantage with respect to services such as Uber, because due to this circumstance of stress and uncertainty, it achieves its objective in the quality, speed and convenience of transport (Barranco & González, 2016).

Regarding the issue of the terms in which the payment is made, it must be emphasized that Uber (whose number of members increases at a rate of 20% each week in Mexico) only allowed payments with debit or credit cards and for that, the card should be linked with the application. But recently, Uber also cashes in cash, this is due to the way in which Mexico generally cannot get a payment by card or by fees and that the money used for transportation is a part of their daily spending plan (Uber, 2017).

Another important point that has been a strategic feature of Uber is the growth trend in the market. The development of Uber around the world has been exponential. It is available in more than four hundred cities, in seventy nations and makes more than five million departures per day. In Mexico, the company is available since 2014 and from then on its development is no less amazing. Each week the number of downloads of its application increases between 10% and 15%. It is also taken as a competitive advantage of the company's performance that around 30% of the drivers complement their common salary working with Uber (Ávalos, 2015).

For the case of the components that allow their development in the market, emphasis should be placed on the use of innovation. All consumers of the service in Mexico have a cell phone and know how to use it. From that point of view, where are the cars that work as Uber, it can be chosen a traditional car or a larger one, as mentioned above. In addition, the application allows to see the brand of the vehicle, the color and the image of the driver. It can also be seen the progress before and during the trip on the map of the application. The foregoing is how, progressively, Uber has taken this strategy to reach the client (Barranco & González, 2016).

Another factor that is additionally significant is the dynamism, transparency and accessibility of the rates, and these cannot change once the trip is accepted, these are not established through the channel. The cost of the trip is estimated not by meter, but by the GPS of the app, and the course is recorded in the application. When the consumer pays, as a client of Uber, when the company entered the Mexican market, it was important to enter a bank card number and at the end of the service, the application charged the agreed amount at the beginning, with the objective that the clients do not should deal with cash or stress over the fee or if the driver has enough change.

Likewise, in Mexico Uber saw that a large part of the clients could not access a credit, so the payment method has been updated to make it in cash. If the trip is shared, the application also allows to separate the passage. This clearly draws attention on the basis that the fees never exceed the desire to pay for a typical taxi (Barranco & González, 2016).

In the daily life of the consumer, when it is transported and the service provided causes some dissatisfaction, the company gives the option of accessing a driver rating system, an innovative and really useful aspect, which is that, upon completion of the travel, the app asks the consumer to value, through stars, how was the provision of transport service. With which, the company system records and evaluates the conditions and opinions of the consumer, in addition to checking if there is a conflict, taking some measures to receive the full satisfaction of the user, and can even reimburse the payment if it is the case. It is noted that these features are in no way presented in the taxi service.

Another factor that impacts its performance in the market is the advertising coverage it has. Uber manages the promotion through social networks, and with a recommendation method, and much of the Internet. The models and conditions of the cars also impact on the way to reach Mexican consumers, in contrast to taxis. Uber offers distinctive car models, regularly ventilated and substantially more current than regular taxis (Ferrer, 2015).

The competitive advantages that Uber has play an extremely important role, since derived from them this company is positioned as a leader in the market. The drivers enjoy that there are no established hours to work, also that the commission charged for the use of the platform is about one fifth of the ticket and a part is involved in the promotion costs with the objective that the system keep working.

The assignment of orders for trips is done automatically as the system will request the service depending on the vehicle that is closest to the customer. There are no fees for opening or registration fees. The collection of services is typically week after week and with automatic deposit. Finally, it provides a reliable environment for the driver, because the trip is recorded in the system and who is the passenger.

The consumer also has several strategic advantages that the company has established, for example, through the app that is user friendly and easy to use, the cost for the service is specified and does not change before requesting it, in addition the application is accessible to change the route. The client can also evaluate and provide feedback to the service. On the other hand, Uber intends that the user is in a reliable and comfortable environment, because whoever takes it knows that his order, the trip and the driver are registered in the system. It also allows to monitor the trip. And finally, a vehicle is available quickly.

On the contrary, to the above, it is relevant to establish what competitive disadvantages Uber has and analyze later what it can do to solve them. The driver may appreciate that, for example, he has no labor protection, unlike taxi drivers. The type of coverage provided by insurers in a lawsuit may be uncertain. One aspect that usually occurs when Uber enters a new city is that the company has to negotiate with the corresponding authorities, since they do not have the proper regulations for this type of service at present. Another disadvantage is that it is necessary to have data to connect with the platform.

RESEARCH METHOD

Analysis of Competitiveness in the Private Transport Business

For the projection of demand of the company to study, it is proposed to take as a reference the city of Guadalajara, which has a population of approximately 3 million citizens. It is in this sense that the projection of interest is expected to increase by one year around 35% in terms of the people who need and use the Uber in Guadalajara, as well as in different urban areas where the benefit of Uber is accessible (Uber, 2016).

Regarding the competence analysis, it is established that Uber works in a similar way to that of traditional taxis, causing direct rivalry with this type of transport; Be that as it may, it is not your most important rival. New applications that offer a feature such as Uber, for example, EasyTaxi or Cabify that have a place with a similar rank, qualify as immediate rivalry; It can also be said that car manufacturers could be displaced by this service, so they run the risk of reducing consumer demand.

Normally, in the market of public and private transport, the offer or chooses the places where the traveler is picked up and left, while, on account of the taxi, the client decides them. In other words, there are some significant differences between the types of public transport, for example, the train, the trolleybus, the ecobici or the buses, the taxis differ by choosing the stops. The variables that impact when choosing the service type of any option, for example, Uber, lie in the season, the amount of traffic and the speed of the service.

Analysis of Results

For the analysis of Uber's competence from a global point of view, it can be understood that Easytaxi is broad in 420 urban areas and in 30 countries, close to where Cabify has a reach only in Latin America, Spain and Portugal. Uber is on the five continents since 2011 and is developing as one of the most revolutionary organizations in the world sector. This firm registers a growth of 10% around the downloads that are made of the application.

In the case of allude to the classification of requested cars, it can be reasoned that there are two groups of consumers, the principal obtains the car by necessity and the second simply requests the car to acquire social status. The customer of need looks for a car for safety, comfort, quality, space and a lower price, so when choosing a car depends on the costs. However, the customer who only needs to have the car by status does not focus on the cost alone in the comfort and image of a luxurious year-round car.

Today many companies seek more customer satisfaction or give greater importance to this issue. Therefore, they carry out different strategies to accomplish this and satisfy their customers. According to the sector where companies unfold will make the appropriate innovations to the product or service offered by adaptations according to geographical area, with strategic advertising, by price or by improving product quality. Sometimes what the customer is looking for comfort, closeness or facility to acquire the asset or service. This is what UBER has done to offer its service. Uber implements innovations in the business model.

In finding that customer satisfaction, Uber relies to implement its innovations both in service and customer experience that maximizes utility when using the service. One of those innovations was the automatic payment. Also requesting service by an application installed on the user's phone that easily and at the touch of a button is the means to obtain the service. So consumers identify this innovation in service and thus the company could exercise monopoly power over its competitors once started. Uber to operate the platform seized market share by displacing the service that for years has been given in different parts of the world called taxis that were intended to transport people who had no car or prefer not to use it.

With all the technological changes that have occurred in recent years, it is common that most of the population have access to a cell where through download the application and use the platform can request their transportation service, regardless of whether they bring cash. Uber main advantages over its competitors and by its strategies just identified the customer, are:

1. Innovation in the way of providing the service.
2. No need cash (automatic payment).
3. The customer requires a cell with the application and a bank account where he will be charged by the service.
4. Cheaper than a taxi fare.
5. Provide a standard or homogenized product.
6. They offer a bonus in addition to transportation, like listening to the music the customer wants during the trip, water, air conditioning in the car.

An important aspect to consider is that many innovations and changes that a company has made if the service or product offered does not meet the quality standards of its customers would not be accepted. Bringing the theoretical aspects to the practice when technological innovations, prices and product quality were bad, Uber would not have achieved success that has today. In this way, it can be seen how by implementing a comprehensive and global strategy, a standardized product and application of technology in its service, Uber achieved to implement a new business model in the field of private transport service, and how this has given rise to emerging technology-based companies in different industries or sectors.

These technology-based companies begin to take an important role by having greater technological resources in their operations, with so many changes that have occurred in the way business enterprises have had to adapt to these technological changes and because of this have emerged companies like Uber.

On the side of the prices of the use of taxis in Guadalajara depend on many variables such as the price of gasoline, distance, time, supply, demand, traffic expectation, the area, the state of the car, insurance, etc. In a general average, the price per kilometer should be around 7.25 pesos with an increase of approximately one fifth at night. The tariffs in the different platforms are based on 5 variables mainly: time, distance, efficient route, traffic and demand.

According to Uber's behavior as a company, it is within an oligopolistic market structure. An oligopoly is a market governed by few organizations specialized in the sector. As a result of having two members in this type of market, each oligopolist knows the activities of its rivals. Since the choices of an organization influence or cause effects on the choices of others, a circumstance of equilibrium is established by the companies, with which the rivalry will not be exhibited. It is worth noting that, in an oligopoly of this type, there is no evident rivalry for the fact that organizations can collude to leave no space for another firm to position itself as a contender and to have communication between the companies involved in the oligopoly process can get the best benefits, or on the contrary if they compete with each other, what the leading company does will impact and cause a specific response from the rival.

According to what the game theory establishes, if an organization is a pioneer or leader (Uber) instead of waiting for an equilibrium in which all competitors simultaneously reach an equilibrium (Nash, for example), the advantage of the leader company over the followers, that is, having a dominant business advantage over the other firms, which results in first making a decision to which they respond, that is, they take it later, the followers. A clear example in this model is the decision Uber made when agreeing to an alliance with cell phone companies (Telcel and Movistar) to offer their free wireless Wi-Fi service with customers who hire a rate plan.

This leads the leader to consider, for each election, that the followers will react according to their decision, so they correct their method of positioning themselves in the market, taking into account what the others' choices will be, as if in some way I could control them and result in their own advantage.

One strategy of the oligopolies, in recent times, is to reduce the cost below costs in order that the other companies cannot compete and once they are built, they raise their prices indiscriminately. By establishing the oligopoly as a conceivable case, there would also be the possibility of collusion. This happens when the firms in the oligopoly agree to act in a planned manner when they offer their products or services and increase costs, in this sense they achieve a greater advantage more important for each of them than when they act independently.

If Uber or other platforms were prohibited, the oligopoly of the taxis would be maintained since they would impose their prices according to their criteria. In case they were allowed to enter these platforms without restrictions, either fiscal or monetary, these would include the new oligopoly that would replace the conventional taxi service. In this sense, it is understood that, in some way, no measure is reasonable for the current financial situation.

In spite of the above, it is not the only answer that could be shown by a competitor, it should be considered the scenario where Uber develops exponentially and becomes an imposing business model, that is, a Monopoly.

Beyond Uber building its market control as a monopolist, it is currently smaller and should be considered. Particularly in the possibility that the firm has strategies to evade rivalry. For example, the imposition of UberPool (accessible in Mexico City) represents a significant disadvantage for rivals with smaller market scales.

A relevant aspect related to the analysis of prices, the rates are different in each city. in Guadalajara the rates vary due to the types of trips, these are estimated by base rate, distance and time. The standard fare is 7.25 pesos per km and 3.50 pesos per minute, where Uber charges by commission between 20% to 25% of the final fare of all trips. The cost of the fare also depends on the type of car chosen, of which the most relevant ones were already mentioned.

This type of services uses the dynamic rate, which applies when there are numerous trips requested in a specific area of the city and there are not enough drivers. For example, if there are a couple of cars and numerous requests, the service estimate will be doubled by the estimation of the dynamic rate. The dynamic rate is calculated by increasing the base rate of the service by estimating the current dynamic rate.

The provision of this type of service works according to the law of supply and demand. The more consumers there are, the higher the cost to achieve a balance in the offer, or there would be an unstable demand. For example, if the cost is the same, but there are limited service providers. The waiting time would increase considerably, to the point where it will be unreasonably expensive, and customers would not wait much longer. This is solved by increasing the cost, so that customers who travel value the service even more. The above is shown in the following graph. See Figure 1.

The company has reasons to increase costs, and that means it can put more cars available for use, since drivers would get more cash on each trip, and they will be encouraged to activate the app and provide the service. That would suggest an expansion in the offer, so more users could travel, and therefore, Uber will have more benefits. Prices can go up well in times of high activity of people, big events. There are several cases of people who have paid four times more than normal for not risking public transportation in Guadalajara.

Figure 1.

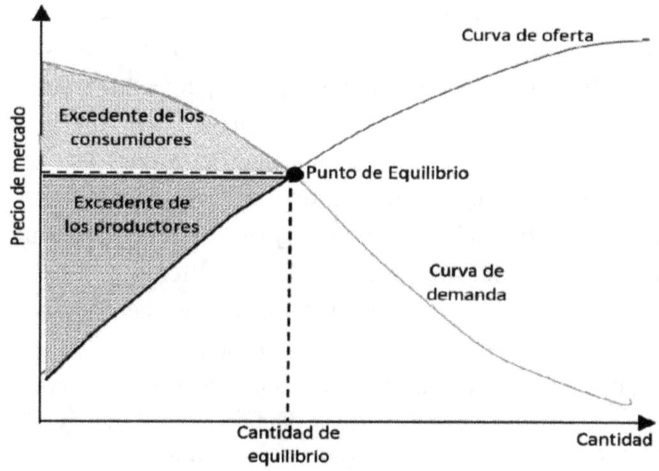

CONCLUSION AND RECOMMENDATIONS

One of the advantages of technology-based companies like Uber is to reduce costs and adapt to the new way they are giving businesses through different mechanisms and strategies that were studied for this case. It can be concluded that through a global strategy and technological adaptations companies like Uber have been successful and also taking advantage of the gaps that institutions not considering such firms have adapted to the country coming through a standard product offering in the world.

Companies of its kind have well defined characteristics as that base their operations through the use of technological resources, maintains a standard or homogenized product regardless of the region or geographical area and implements global strategies. However, a weakness that can have companies in their type and it is necessary to assess the institutional aspects, as in some countries are making changes to allow operation through restrictions or in some cases block and not allow its operation. It is important to consider carrying out a successful global strategy.

Another advantage that can have the technology-based companies over their competitors is that their operations are based on the use of technological resources, so it can be concluded that through technological innovations and through a global strategy, it is shown that there is an emerging new type of economic system or a new business model that emerged a few years ago and through successful cases like Uber. This new model begins to change the course of business.

The elements that the company included and considered fundamental are the implementation of automatic payment, request the service by installed on a cell application because without it cannot access the transfer from one place to another, thus being a limiting so that not all people have free access to the service.

Finally, it should be mentioned that innovations do not reach at the same time to all places. Where the technology-based company starts operations, a company is critical to have a successful experience away from and continue to apply the strategies used to bequeath to success in its home and then expand their horizons.

The netizen who has used applications that provide the private transport service, offered by organizations that work with pairing between the user and the driver, has clearly changed the act of its urban versatility.

Therefore, these organizations are also designing another method to offer the benefit of transportation, even though, first of all, the service was considered elitist and selective for a part of the population in its beginnings, for example, because of having credit cards. From now on, with the modifications and changes according to the collection system, the market opens up for a more prominent number of people,

Taking into account the previous analysis, it can be affirmed that Uber in the Mexican market has placed itself as an oligopoly that, little by little, has managed to control its competitors (followers) that provide a similar service. Without a doubt, the market that Uber covers to provide this service maintains the specific attributes identified with the simplicity of its platform, through the app, the low cost, the comfort it offers, its service monitoring interface, and its attention to the client. The latter is what differentiates it mainly from the taxi service. The above added to the effectiveness of the service have allowed users to start adopting this service from casual to usual.

Apart from the fact that Uber has its own market, it is not the only solution to satisfy the demand for transport, an example of this is its direct competitors. The economic theory of the producer, states that these options are called substitute goods and are one of the components that affect the demand for the service. For this situation, the demand for Uber could have been met with these substitute goods, for example, taxis, trains, trucks, or ecobici.

However, in the event that the client considers that the cost, ratio and quality of service are insufficient to choose another option, he chooses to pay the increase in the cost created by an increase in Uber's demand. The theory of the producer mentions that, instead of establishing a maximum tariff for the benefit of the consumer, the entry of competitors should be encouraged and the conditions of the alternatives improved. It is concluded that a maximum rate does not solve the problem of excess demand, competition does.

REFERENCES

Ávalos, M. (2015), Baby, you can't drive my car. El caso de Uber en México. Economía informa, (390), 104-112.

Barranco, M. C., & González, M. G. (2016). El transporte intracondominal en la movilidad cotidiana de la periurbanización: el enlace comunitario del Área Metropolitana de Guadalajara. *Revista Transporte y Territorio*, *14*, 167-188. Obtenido de http://revistascientificas.filo.uba .ar/index.php/rtt/article/view/2434/2092

Bostman, R., & Rogers, R. (2010). *What's mine is yours: the rise of collaborative consumption.* New York: Harper Business.

Bravo, M. (2015*). Caro y malo, el transporte público en México.* Obtenido de https://meganoticias.mx/tu-ciudad/guadalajara/especiales-meganoticias/item/85874-caro-ymalo- el-transporte-publico-en-mexico.html

Canals, J. (1994). *La internacionalización de la empresa.* Madrid: McGraw-Hill.

Cañigueral, A. (2015). Consumo colaborativo. *Leaners Magazine*, 18-22.

Carbaugh, R. J. (2005). La globalización de la actividad económica. In R. J. Carbaugh (Ed.), Economía Internacional (pp. 4-8). Thompson.

Chafkin, M. (2016). *Fast Company*. Obtenido de Fastcompany.com: http://www.fastcompany.com/3054873/can-airbnb-unite-the-world

Christensen, C., & Raynor, M. (2003). *The innovator's solution: creating and sustaining successful growth*. Boston: Harvard Business Press.

Ferrer, A. (2016). *Taxistas contra Uber: la pelea por los pasajeros en el DF*. Obtenido de http://www.milenio. com/df/conflicto_uber_taxis_df-pelea_uber_taxis_ciudad_mexico-apps_debate_taxis_df_0_647335583.html

Friedman, M. (1970, September 13). The Social Responsability of Business Is to Increase Profits. *The New York Times Magazine*.

Hernández, Y., Galindo, S., & Vicente, R. (2015). Conflictividad por la operación del transporte público de pasajeros (modalidad taxi) en conjuntos urbanos de Tecámac, Estado de México, *Revista Espacios Públicos. UAEM*, *18*(42), 135–156.

INEGI. (2010). *Mexico en cifras*. Recuperado de http://www.inegi.org.mx/

Interian, J. (2016). Up in the air: Harmonizing economy through airbnb regulations. *Boston College International and Comparative Law Review*, 129–161.

La Prensa. (2016). Uber recibirá pago en efectivo. *La Prensa*. Obtenido de http://www.prensa.com/economia/Uber-recibira-pago-efectivo_0_4543795641.html

MTJ. (2015). Estudio de oferta y demanda de los servicios de transporte de taxis y las nuevas empresas de redes de transporte UBER y CityDrive en el Área Metropolitana de Guadalajara. *El Informador*. Obtenido de https://issuu.com/el_informador/docs/estudio_taxis_uber

North, D. C. (1990). *Institutions, institutional Change, and economic performance*. New York: Norton. doi:10.1017/CBO9780511808678

North, D. C. (2005). *Understanding the Process of Economic Change*. Princeton, University Press. doi:10.1515/9781400829484

Olivares, E. M. (2014). *Sistemas económicos y modelos de economía moderna*. Bogotá: Universidad Autónoma de Colombia.

Pallares, M. A. (2016). Uber suma 1.2 millones de usuarios en México. *Periódico El Universal*. Obtenido de http://www.eluniversal.com.mx/articulo/cartera/negocios/2016/03/8/uber-suma-12-millones-de-usuarios-en-mexico

Peng, M. W. (2000). *Business strategies in transition economies*. Sage.

Peng, M. W. (2012). *Global Strategy*. Cincinnati, OH: Thomson South-Western.

Peng, M. W. (2012). *Estrategia global*. Cengage Learning.

Rifkin, J. (2014). *La sociedad de coste marginal cero: el internet de las cosas, el procomún colaborativo y el eclipse del capitalismo*. Barcelona: Paidós.

Russo, A., & Quaglieri, A. (2014). La lógica espacial del intercambio de casas: una aproximación a las nuevas geografías de lo cotidiano en el turismo contemporáneo. *Revista electrónica de georgrafía y ciencias sociales*, 324-331.

Streitfeld, D. (2014, October 15). Airbnb listing mostly illegal. *New York Times*.

Tiongson, J. (2015). Mobile App Marketing Insights: How Consumers Really Find and Use Your Apps. *Think with Google*. Obtenido de https://www.thinkwithgoogle.com/articles/mobile-app-marketing-insights.html

Uber. (2016a). *Uber mueve a Guadalajara*. Obtenido de https://www.uber.com/es-US/cities/guadalajara/

Uber. (2016b). Recuperado de https://www.uber.com

Uber. (2017). *Sala de redacción*. Obtenido de https://newsroom. uber.com/locations/#na-region

Urbado, D., Díaz, J., & Hernández, R. (2007). Evolución y principios de la teoría económica institucional. Una propuesta de aplicación para el análisis de los factores condicionantes de la creación de empresas. *Investigaciones Europeas de Dirección y Economía de la Empresa*, *13*(3), 183–198.

Veblen, T. (1965). *La teoría der la empresa de negocios (1904)*. Buenos Aires: Eudeba.

Villarreal, O. (2005). La internacionalización de la empresa y la empresa multinacional: Una revisión conceptual contemporánea. *Cuadernos de Gestión*, *5*(2), 55–73.

Wen, I. (2009). Factors affecting the online travel buying decision: A review. *International Journal of Contemporary Hospitality Management*, *21*(6), 752–765. doi:10.1108/09596110910975990

Yeung, E. (2012). How to Launch Your App in an International Market. *Mashable*. Obtenido de http://mashable.com/2012/02/13/mobile-apps-international/#aeYWOgIPIOq8

KEY TERMS AND DEFINITIONS

Business Model: It is a conceptual structure designed as a system to support the methods of business viability, the means to fulfill its purpose and goals, financing, resources, operations, customer base, generation of revenues and profits.

Collaborative Economy: It is a set of initiatives based on horizontal networks with the participation of a community and formed by individuals who have something to share and others who need them with the purpose of giving, swapping, borrowing, trading, renting, and sharing products and services based on distributed trust and decentralized power.

Private Market: The structure of transactions that are negotiated directly between two parties and can take any form.

Strategy: It is the orientation and delimitation given to resources and capabilities of a firm in relation to complex and uncertain competitive market environments in order to accomplish the vision and mission of the firm.

Technology-Based Company: Also known as tech company, it is a firm focusing on the development and manufacturing that uses leading edge scientific and technological knowledge systematically and continuously to produce new goods or services with high added value.

Transport Incorporated: The act or process of moving people or things through different means of transport from one place to another subject to a patronage or ridership refers to the number of people using a transit unit.

Uber: It is an acronym to mean ultimate, best for above in German. It also has the basic meaning of over, beyond, extremely good. As the trade mark and global brand of a private transportation incorporated company, Uber has been changing inner-city transport structure.

Chapter 7
Manufactured Risks of Reward-Based Crowdfunding Platforms

Selin Öner Kula
Independent Researcher, Austria

ABSTRACT

Without an equivalent conventional form, reward-based crowdfunding (RBCF) brings in new concepts that demand deeper awareness by all stakeholders, so that they can acknowledge corresponding responsibilities. Despite famous intermediaries' nearly decadelong operations, the digestion of risks seems still incomplete, also hindering a solid evolution. This qualitative study is a step toward a more holistic understanding of success and manufactured risks of RBCF that have been left out of sight in studies so far. Lack of efficient visibility on projects' post-funding completion and limitless overfunding create potential conflicts of interest which threaten platforms' neutrality and sustainability. RBCF platforms must afford higher transparency and richer tools for managing the risks to tap their true potential. This chapter presents an overview of the major pitfalls of Kickstarter (KS) and Indiegogo (IGG) that can throw light on RBCF's general shortcomings, also offering a glimpse on two successfully funded but failed projects.

INTRODUCTION

The novelty of the sharing economy puts all stakeholders into a learning process where certain grounds are not tested until they are stepped on, and the risks usually appear when things do not go as planned. The platforms themselves also learn and adapt through experience. Their sustainability will depend on how well they proactively address the weaknesses in their functioning and endow their users with systematic ways of managing risk and maintain trust in themselves.

Online sharing platforms address basic needs in a rather horizontal and decentralized manner. They mostly emerged in the last decade to provide a complementary solution for tackling the gaps in conventional channels, at least at the start. Some examples like Airbnb, Uber, and Lyft have evolved into giant corporations rising on peer-to-peer (p2p) service and losing the initial sharing essence—but this is the subject of another discussion. This chapter is about a pending improvement in "crowdfunding" platforms

DOI: 10.4018/978-1-5225-9928-9.ch007

Copyright © 2020, IGI Global. Copying or distributing in print or electronic forms without written permission of IGI Global is prohibited.

to sustain their birth spirit of collaborative p2p resource sharing, empowering micro-entrepreneurship, by implementing a sharing design that better addresses risks and information asymmetries and levels the playing field for users.

Serving as a marketplace where users in need of financial support can attract peers' funds for their projects in exchange for so-called "perks" (aka "rewards"), the reward-based type is one of the most widely known crowdfunding types, due to famous sites like KS and IGG. However, this is also a category for which one cannot find a previous counterpart. Despite some links with gift economy and cooperation structures for communal funding, contributing to imaginative projects of "strangers" through online platforms in exchange for to-be-created items is not like anything known before. This alone introduces some hard-to-define notions that, if not properly clarified, may not only inhibit this crowdfunding model from reaching its true potential but also threaten its sustainability. An understanding of peculiar risks is key for this collaborative model to advance in a credible fashion, which this study attempts to present. Since risks come forward in cases of failure, this chapter also investigates two "successfully funded" crowdfunding campaigns that disappointed in delivering on their promises.

BACKGROUND

With a surge in the means for sharing through the Internet, a new ecosystem encompassing different types of sharing (e.g., collaborative consumption, crowdfunding, and crowdsourcing) has shaped up, which is considered vital in many dimensions. Online collaborative platforms facilitate a shift from consumerism toward collaborative resource-sharing that feeds entrepreneurship, creation, and p2p collaboration. The sharing economy also carries the potential to revive a sense of "community" and "social cohesion" (Botsman & Rogers, 2010, p. 70), to similarly narrow the "widening gap between the rich and poor" (Siefkes, 2008, pp. 131-133) and to present a more ethical alternative to the market with "equality of access" (Stallman, 2002, pp. 59-64). Moreover, although its effectiveness is yet debated (Martin, 2016, pp. 149-159), this new ecosystem provides means for dealing with the concerns of "sustainability" (Heinrichs, 2013, p. 228).

Time will show whether these expectations of the sharing economy prove valid. On the downside, it may also "amplify worst excesses of the dominant economic model" (Morozov, 2013, para.10). Turning this ecosystem into its best form clearly requires systematic collaboration of stakeholders. Collective spaces distinctively mediated intentions of empowering the individual beyond the power centers of "organized capitalism," which, as Horkheimer (1974) argues, put "personal initiative" into ever smaller conventional boxes so that participation "remains at best a hobby" (p. 94). However, with the Internet, peers created or found the means to share in a different dimension than traditional daily life allowed, with more autonomy for participation and cooperation. As Jenkins (2006) considers, the participatory nature of the Internet lets small inputs matter.

"Crowdfunding" is a segment of the sharing economy in which minor contributions can really lead to major results by supporting the "creation of a specific product or the investment in a specific business idea" (Brabham, 2013, p. 37). Crowdfunding forms a funding model where peers with a challenge in funding use online platforms to gather financing from other peers to actualize projects or finance their companies. The project goals range from artistic to commercial, social, or technological ideas and products, and the production and distribution are in the project owner's hands.

In traditional finance, banks usually require a track record, while Angel Investors and Venture Capitalists, the usual investors in rather early-stage companies, are very selective. Independent artistic endeavors cannot easily find support in typical outlets either. Crowdfunding builds the means to resolve this mismatch by redistributing unused funds of the crowd to ideas lacking funding. This is similar to the "idle capacity" notion used by Botsman and Rogers' (2010) in collaborative consumption (pp.83-84).

RBCF sites became an important complement to prevailing funding sources, for new as well as renowned entrepreneurial and independent creators who found it even harder to raise funding following the 2008 financial crash. In the last decade, the KS platform intermediated US$3.7 billion in funds that successfully funded 159,000 projects (KS Stats). Annual revenues in 2017 were recorded as US$649 million (Kickstarter PBC 2017). IGG intermediated over US$1 billion of funds to nearly 800k projects (IGG for Entrepreneurs, IGG About). Such platforms have a value for their creators because of a built-in worldwide customer base, a "crowd" that any entrepreneurial endeavor would pursue, while contributors gain access to all kinds of creative projects early on and a chance to participate in their evolution.

While Kickstarter and Indiegogo are the most renowned crowdfunding examples based on rewards, Zopa (2005), Causes (2007), and Crowdcube (2011) are leading sites of lending-, donation-, and equity-based crowdfunding, respectively. A newer form is the membership-based crowdfunding platform, pioneered by Patreon (2013), which facilitates monthly continuing (subscription) support to creators.

Peculiar risks are prevalent for all types of crowdfunding platforms, but the analogies one can draw with the institutionalized examples can ease users' understanding of the related risks. For equity-based crowdfunding, the corresponding origin is the initial public offering or investing in listed shares of a company. In all three cases, investors receive a shareholding in a real entity, despite less rigorous due diligence for crowdfunding. In traditional counterpart of lending-based crowdfunding, borrowers raise money from lenders such as banks. The same goes for donation-based crowdfunding for social causes, through charities or NGOs. Online crowdfunding platforms carry the established methods to a diverse user range and emerge on the power of the crowd. This democratizes both the access to funds and the crowd's access to new ideas, social causes, and opportunities that would normally be reserved for certain groups.

These enhancements have come through the affordances of the internet, which also generates new uncertainties. Associated with Ulrich Beck's (1992) notion of "risk society," Giddens (1999) coined the term "manufactured risk" (p.3) that meddles in daily lives as a result of the advancement of "human development", specifically in "science and technology" (p. 4). The resulting new uncertainties and new decision-making processes, for which previous knowledge cannot really offer help, necessitate fresh awareness for allocation of risks and responsibilities.

Similarly, various online spaces and RBCF produce their own risks, widely unfamiliar from earlier exposure. Due to the absence of clear analogies with conventional equals, RBCF platforms must acquaint users more deeply with the uncertainties and provide tools to manage them, so that users can assume responsibilities for their decisions. The RBCF platforms Kickstarter and Indiegogo are selected as focal units of this chapter because of their long and more accessible history in both platform-crowd interaction and media coverage. Through online participant observation and online archival research analyzing publicly available data between 2015 and 2019, this chapter introduces the manufactured risks of RBCF, which pose uncertainty for current and potential users. The findings can shed light on the general pitfalls of RBCF, and well-known platforms like KS and IGG can lead the ecosystem in providing a healthier environment for addressing the intrinsic newborn risks through corrective measures.

MAIN PITFALLS OF REWARD-BASED CROWDFUNDING

Uncertainty About the Definition and Fulfillment of "Success"

Usually, the most discussed part of crowdfunding is how to successfully reach funding, in line with the name, not only on these platforms, but also through the whole sharing ecosystem on the net. At the latest check (15 March 2019), Google returns 11 million results on "successful crowdfunding campaigns," compared with 1.3 million and 150,000 on "failed crowdfunding campaigns" and "unsuccessful crowdfunding campaigns", respectively. The academic research has oriented itself to the determinants of funding success as well. A pick of the first 20 articles on elements of crowdfunding success through a search for keywords "reward" "crowdfunding" and "success" at ScienceDirect displays studies that all elaborate on marketing and funding success, looking from the fundraiser's perspective.

At Kickstarter, "unsuccessful" campaigns that do not reach the desired funding are searchable through the platform's own engine, but the platform delists them from external search engines Google or Bing (KS Help), which also lowers transparency. KS and IGG also usually educate on the funding part of the process, rather than on how to operationalize the project once funding is there. Nevertheless, some recent initiatives launched in 2017 by both platforms, such as the "Concierge"/ "Arrow" programs (IGG) and "Hardware Studio"/ "Creative Independent Magazine" (KS) are sensible steps for providing guidance on accomplishing projects, but they need higher visibility and applicability.

Indiegogo falls short of consistent and easily accessible operational data, while KS's frequently updated statistics disclose funding data in rich detail, including categorical results. This creditable transparency effort, however, only tracks the funding rate and supports the dominant rhetoric on funding success but fails to cover the full circle. As Oner Kula (2019) shows, unlike online collaborative consumption platforms which depend on accessibility of systematic p2p evaluation for management of uncertainties and "peer trust", Kickstarter and Indiegogo lack an organized self-monitoring system for projects' post-funding stage (p.212), except for KS's few one-off appreciable attempts to study failures. The crowd and the creators communicate through comments and creator's updates on project pages, yet, this channel does not provide a methodical screening despite technologic advances to absorb, store and present information.

This leaves the realization of a project as secondary and inaccessible, although it may show the real fulfillment of a project, representing a discrepancy between definitions of "success" and "failure" from different agents' perspectives in the crowdfunding transaction. What success means for the platform may not overlap with the meaning for the supporting crowd, but rather with that of the creator. A perfectly funded project appearing as a great success may fail in its promises, and the supporters see a "failure" instead. This would also hold in artistic projects that meet their goals of producing (i.e., a movie) but still neglect sending personal rewards out. Despite the centrality of the crowd in this ecosystem, the success from their perspective is left optional, also threatening a neutral middlemen role.

The ambiguity on creators' project-completion may also make risks hidden to a newcomer. With the increase of repeat campaigners, currently one-third of KS' creators (KS Blog, 2017), "a historical performance tool" is potentially to become even more needed for educated decision-making by backers (Oner Kula, 2019, p.212).

This mismatch is exacerbated also by the absence of accessible disclaimers on key risks on RBCF homepages. In contrast, on the equity crowdfunding platform—Crowdcube from UK, for instance—the users must accept the risks of losing their capital (in a separate statement than site terms) in order to invest in projects in the first place. This also complies with usually country-specific regulations, mostly treating equity-based crowdfunding as a more flexible but still an emerging part of capital markets. This study does not advocate an external regulatory intervention for RBCF, but rather platforms' self-regulatory initiatives for ensuring higher transparency, so that an impartial intermediation is ensured, and both the platform and the crowd can better grasp the downsides.

Furthermore, this chapter also does not encourage labeling projects that cannot deliver rewards as unsuccessful. This is also because what can be measured may not represent the full notion of "success." The impact of visibility on a platform with worldwide reach as well as interaction with smart users surely could add tangible and intangible benefits, such as gaining a user base and valuable feedback, regardless of the funding performance. Although this would be even harder to trace, this perspective would call for a holistic understanding of success factoring the publicity factor next to funding and fulfillment. Furthermore, a measure of post-funding deliveries may not fully capture "success" either, as the products may not meet the promised functionality.

The Specific Pitfall of Indiegogo: Partial Funding

KS has a strict funding rule that allows fundraisers to collect money only if the project meets its funding goal. IGG, however, allows partial funding, letting project owners collect funds below the target. Both have advantages and disadvantages for the crowdfunding spirit. Under a strict funding rule, backers need to say goodbye to a project that might not be realized in the first place with suboptimal funding, hence the crowd is protected. At the extreme opposite, a project raising 95% of the funding goal is not eligible to collect funds on KS but may do so on rival Indiegogo and kick off the project anyway. This directly protects the creator of a project, as well as the supporters indirectly. Filling minor deficits with funds from the "3 Fs" (friends, family, and fools) just to match the target could also be possible. According to KS statistics, projects funded within the 81%-99% of their goal represent already as small as 1% of the unsuccessfully funded projects.

The flexible funding rule is reflected in IGG's ratio of fully funded projects between its founding in 2007 and 2013, with only about 9.3% of projects fully funded, based on an analysis by the Verge under the headline "Indie no-go" (Jeffries, 2013a). IGG's funding ratio performs considerably more poorly than KS's funding success rate of 44% between 2009 and 2013 and compared with 37% currently (15 March 2019). Furthermore, based on IGG's 800,000 projects in its history, the author estimates the number of funded IGG projects at five times the number of KS's funded projects.

Comparatively, 80% of projects at Indiegogo collected only about 25% of their target, whereas 46% of Kickstarter's projects remained below the 20% level of fund-raising (currently 52%). Similarly, according to a more recent analysis by Crowdfunding Center, 69%-89% of projects in 2015 have not succeeded in reaching funding targets in the five largest crowdfunding platforms across the U.S., the U.K., and Canada, with IGG registering a full funding ratio of 13% compared with Kickstarter's 31% (Clifford, 2016).

KS has nearly 16 million backers and IGG 9 million, which could explain the former's higher funding rates to some extent. Also, KS has stricter guidelines on funding purposes, prohibiting projects from donating to a cause by requiring that all projects have creative output. IGG identifies itself as an "open platform" with "no application or approval process" in its own note on "Indiegogo vs. Kickstarter." Therefore, IGG can be thought of as an open-access square and KS like a shopping mall with x-ray screening at the entrance. IGG underlines its commitment to retaining the platform "safe" and "trusted"

(IGG Trust); yet, as a platform that proclaims letting in "any project," it lacks a clear explanation of its actions to ensure this trust.

Uncertainty About the Definition of "Contributions," "Rewards," and RBCF

The invisibility of projects' post-funding performance also leads to some obscurity in the crowd's true perception of what RBCF is about and blurs the definition of backers' contributions between pre-order and gift. Especially projects promising to deliver finished products appear as pre-sellers (usually in design and tech categories) and raise the crowd's expectations, and the platform looks like a pre-selling/pre-order platform to some users.

In all categories, both KS and IGG currently offer an address for projects at various levels of development status. Among KS's 15 categories, the top four sections— "games," "design," "technology," and "film & videos"— make up 75% of the total successful funding volume with 24%, 22%, 19%, and 10% shares, respectively (KS Stats). Table 1 shows the broad categories that may be associated with pre-order as they usually offer a complete product for each backer rather than a public output, such as a movie. Their funding volume amounted to US$1.9 billion between 2009 and March 2019, corresponding to about 52% of the total.

With obviously wider coverage of success stories on media, RBCF can easily become associated with famous successful projects such as Pebble watch, Coolest Cooler, Ouya game console or Pebble Time, which supplied millions of dollars' worth of products — US$10 million in 2012, US$13 million in 2014, US$8.6 million in 2013, and US$20 million in 2016, respectively, but the last one subject to partial refund (Gage, 2018). These can easily tilt the impression toward a pre-order site and create confusion: Is the crowd purchasing a product, just helping with its creation (like a gift), or both? Should the reward lie only in sending funds to a project, or should the crowd also await the output?

The question boils down to what the crowdfunders are really expecting. RBCF is an exchange that is embedded not only in monetary units, but also in certain goodwill. Backers look to get their rewards as well as the pleasure of seeing something materialize with their support. As the concept involves "reward" (Oxford: "a thing given in recognition of service, effort, or achievement") and promises delivery, the

Table 1. Kickstarter's project categories which mostly offer a complete product for each backer

Categories With Potential Pre-Order Features	Successfully Funded (US$ million)
Design	830
Technology	701
Fashion	144
Food	124
Comics	84
Photography	38
Crafts	14
Subtotal	1,935
Total successful funding	3,710
as % of total	52.2%

Source: The author compiled the table by using data provided by Kickstarter Statistics

funding cannot be considered as altruism or a "gift." Yet, with no systematic means to follow projects' realization, indifference arises that makes RBCF platforms look like living through an existential dilemma that would say, "Do not consider this as a gift if the project delivers its rewards but do consider it a gift if the project fails."

The deliverable "reward" aspect makes the performance of an RBCF campaign in meeting its promises more measurable than, say, in equity CF. In equity crowdfunding, it may take years until the crowd-investment pays off anything, if it ever does, making success also dependent on the exit timing of an investor, if there are no recurrent income streams like dividends. Yet, funders are entitled to a specified shareholding right away although it may yield zero value years later. Comparatively, RBCF users start their journey with an expectation of a reward, promised to be delivered within usually six to 12 months.

"The Pebble Time" was a clear extreme, raising over US$20 million from about 80,000 backers who were to receive perks in around two months from the campaign's finishing date. Shuptrine (2016) smartly interpreted this as evidence that Pebble must have used Kickstarter rather as a pre-order tool than for crowdfunding. Yet, in many technology projects, creators alleviate the burden of producing large volumes through crowdfunding, as accumulated orders contribute to economies of scale and lower unit production costs.

Until 2017, absence of a clear categorization of projects' development status made it difficult for the crowd to differentiate between projects' various distances to completion. IGG's efforts to introduce a "product stages" classification in technology projects may be helpful in this direction, which requires a tech project to pick the category into which it falls from among "concept, prototype, product, shipping" options. KS does not have a parallel device but incorporates a "risks and challenges section" at the end of each project page. Furthermore, IGG's novel section "Marketplace" separates pre-sellers from fundraisers, as it markets "ready-to-ship products" linked with a "buy now" click, rather than "fund". With these steps, IGG marked a divergent move from its competitor. KS consistently stands firm on its principle of "to help bring creative projects to life" (KS Mission), and spokesman David Gallagher underlined the platform's aim of supporting "the creation of something new" (Schleifer, 2017) rather than making a shop-like offering.

Still, at times, complaints arise, when campaigns cannot deliver the promises, or just suffer from delays. In many projects, user comments are mixed, from frustration to hopefulness. For instance, in an ongoing campaign on Indiegogo, the Piqo pocket projector, latest comments reflect serious concerns about some users' trust in RBCF in general, mentioning "low confidence," (Smets, 2019) and "If this projector doesn't fly this will be the last crowd source funded project I ever back. I've so far lost money on 9/10 projects…" (Poy, 2019). One user even calls many campaigns on Indiegogo "professional swindlers" but hopes this is not another case (Marin, 2019). Piqo project, at prototype stage, moved at the end of the campaign (January 2019) to the In-Demand section which allows campaigns meeting their funding goal "to keep raising funds" for a period "as long as they like" (IGG Support).

The online archival research covering such user comments, platform materials, blog posts, Reddit entries, and news reports, has demonstrated that even contributors cannot be aligned on what their support represents as rights, which forms the core struggle in RBCF. Bradford (2012), a law professor, considers that putting money into a project against a reward does not make a backer legally the owner of a "final product," because a backer only gets the promise of a reward (as cited in Gera, 2012, para.23).

RBCF platforms as a home for projects of various maturities qualify neither as a philanthropic platform nor a "pre-order" store, basically falling in between. It is a brand-new category with features of both. In an interview with Wallis (2017), Kickstarter's co-founder Strickler mentioned "three main ways money changes hands: commerce, investment, charity," and put reward-based crowdfunding into a fourth category with similarities to them all. This smart approach meets the necessity of opening a standalone new perception of RBCF.

Yet, even fitting RBCF into a hybrid category carrying notions of a gift does not rule out contributors wanting to see that their gift helps in the materialization of something. As Mauss (1990) and Derrida (1992) show, the "gift" also carries mostly an expectation of reciprocity. With the contribution not finding its purpose, the gift can become annulled anyway. Irrespective of whether the creator put out best efforts, perks never showing up can exhaust the good faith of a repeat backer, and some backers might shy away from the system altogether. In KS, for instance, this may explain why the repeat-backer ratio, is at 32.7% of total (KS Stats), and has not grown significantly through the years.

Uncertainty on Reward-Based Crowdfunding Platforms' "Accountability"

In September 2012, NPR's Business Correspondent Shahani inquired fairly: "When a Kickstarter campaign fails, does anyone get their money back?" mainly covering the Ouya game-console project after its remarkable funding of US$8.6 million from 63,416 backers while only seeking US$950,000. Both the campaign creator Julie Uhrman and Kickstarter's co-founder Yancey Strickler sounded confused. Strickler uttered a "probably no," naming this "new ground" not yet trodden, but when it was, it would not be his "favorite day." The platform was not prepared at all to face a big fail, hinting of a serious potential bump in the learning curve that lacked a clear direction.

Quite rapidly following the NPR coverage, Kickstarter's founders released a blog post briefly explaining its "accountability" and screening process (Strickler, Chen & Adler, 2012a). Projects are only screened through a "quick review" for accordance with "Project Guidelines" that primarily require "prototypes" for projects with a manufacturing process. The platform takes no responsibility for completion. Creators are expected to provide updates on project progress and deliver all perks or "refunds" to backers, also creating a "legal requirement for creators" and "recourse" for backers if creators fail to keep their promises. However, this recourse is only recommended as a last resort when backers feel that a creator has not made "a good-faith effort" to fulfill its promises.

Despite the explanations, further fluidity in users' minds turned the Comments section into a discussion forum under the Accountability post, moving KS after two weeks to post that it "is not a store" (2012). To counter the misconception that anything on Kickstarter is a secure campaign, brand new rules required each campaigner to elaborate on "Risks and Challenges" to highlight that the products are in development stage. For the sectors with most complications ("new hardware and product design"), special guidelines were integrated, prohibiting "product simulations" and "renderings": "Product images must be photos of the prototype as it currently exists." KS also emphasized the best rule of thumb as "under-promise and over-deliver" (Strickler et al., 2012b).

At the time, KS's announcement stirred a significant amount of both positive and negative user feedback again under the blog post (about 12 pages). Many supported increasing awareness of risks, but some complained about restriction on renderings, which presented the product vision. An impression also emerged that protecting the backers could come at the cost of killing the spirit of Kickstarter's own philosophy of encouraging creation. Kickstarter's labeling itself as "Kickstarter is not a store" led to over 65,000 Google results in about six months (Jeffries, 2013b), showing the initial resonance it had created. Currently, the "catchphrase" produces over 42 million Google results as of the latest data (15 March 2019).

Evidently, emphasizing its vocation as not a store is not only an attempt at clearing up confusion; it is also protection against all the liabilities that may be incurred through the day-to-day business. KS's efforts aimed to paint the "experimental" part of the crowdfunding by declaring the crowdfunding spirit as an uncertain bet on new ideas and by recommending that consumers looking for finished products buy them on Amazon (now actually also possible on Indiegogo's Marketplace).

Obviously, crowdfunding entails a creative essence that is a trial at best. However, this does not imply that the crowd can be left without stronger tools for managing the uncertainties and risks of experimentation in daily use, also given that not all users seem to be fully aligned with this "trial" principle. As of this date, the note on risks and challenges of KS projects appears at the very bottom of the page, making it considerably less accessible than the general project content. On IGG, the projects classification is right at the top of the page, hence more visible.

The Overstatements and the Overfunding Dilemma

Like most of the other peer platforms, Kickstarter and Indiegogo basically provide the infrastructure to make crowdfunding happen, assuming almost a passive intermediary role by denying any responsibility or guarantee for the completion or screening of a project. This platform stance and the invisibility of post-funding success, however, create a discrepancy with (for instance) KS's previous greeting message and mission of "bringing creative projects to life," as it sounds like the platform has an active role in the realization of a project. This kind of platform communication can feed controversy and inconsistency about the platform's role, despite all explanations.

KS's slogan and the mission statement became "to help bring creative projects to life" sometime between June 2018 and January 2019. Yet, KS's Instagram profile still carries the old message as of this date (15 March 2019). Moreover, in a recent news article, KS's outreach lead, Corcoran, mentioned the mission in the old form (Hill, 2019, para. 5). Indiegogo's mission statement is slightly more realistic, claiming "to empower people to unite around ideas that matter to them and together make those ideas come to life" (IGG About), while the second part is still stretching. IGG's summary of its accomplishments gives away the overstatement of its role: "Powered by curiosity, the Indiegogo community has helped bring more than 800,000 innovative ideas to life since 2008" (IGG About).

The impasse here is that neither of the platforms enable an organized and consistent mechanism for observing post-funding performance of crowdfunded projects. Hence, a valid statement would be that the crowd and the platform "attempted" on helping projects materialize. When successfully materialized, no user questions the viability of an RBCF project. Yet, when a 100k targeting campaign obtains a million in funds and fails to succeed, it highlights the manufactured risk of overfunding at RBCF sites.

The platform commission rates at RBCF platforms KS and IGG are at 5% flat of the total funding, which is not especially plentiful, but has become a market practice in the crowdfunding universe. However, with unlimited room for overfunding, RBCF platforms' incomes grow proportionally with the funding, even if a project never gets realized. Flat fees are also contrary to the traditional intermediary commission structure—also commonly known as the "Lehman Formula" that usually bases success-fee calculation on a reverse scale/ladder with deal size, sometimes applying defined absolute floors and/or caps.

IGG even uses the overfunding rate to promote its platform success, with the statement of "18,983% the most a campaign has exceeded its goal... so far!" (IGG About). Furthermore, currently the overfunding rates of projects that IGG endorses on the site under "The Top Ten Finds" range from 730% (in

"Snore Circle"—a snoring aid) to 52,653% (Vinpok Split-a monitor), demonstrating how extreme this overfunding can become (IGG Top Ten).

Another interesting number is revealed by KS's statistics. The successful funding volume as percentage of total dollars pledged is at 88.9%, substantially above the 36.7% funding success in the number of projects. This means that about one-third of projects on KS received nearly 90% of crowd funds since 2009. On US$3.7 billion successful funding, Kickstarter must have generated US$185 million in commissions since start—not outrageous, given that it translates into an average gross annual revenue of US$18.5 million and, given the size of its operations, hosting at any time almost 4,000 "live" projects. Recent years obviously yield a higher share in revenues and commissions. Based on platform data, the author estimates about US$30 million annual gross revenues on average between 2016 and 2018.

The magnitude of overfunding at RBCF is also alarming because it could pressurize the deliverables in crowdfunded projects, which already take a long time. In popular projects, funding success and excessive demand seem to excite backers, raising expectations as well as their involvement, and creators face thousands of comments and questions—a separate task and team effort on its own—that may distract them from the project's progress. The author interprets that this whole extreme overfunding success could manufacture further risk in some projects, where financial-,production-, and customer relations expertise may not be accessible.

In 2017, platforms introduced some special tools for creators: Indiegogo's special "Concierge" program for assisting projects achieving funding of more than US$500,000, and a similar program called "Hardware Studio" by Kickstarter for manufacturing support, respectively. Although these efforts can be useful, the infinite liberty in oversubscription and the resulting potential threat to platforms' unbiasedness may necessitate stronger initiatives to neutralize the middlemen role.

What exacerbates this neutrality issue is that RBCF sites do not appear so free of any impositions on projects, as they display some projects under "Projects We Love" (Kickstarter) or "Top 10 Finds" (Indiegogo) and "Team Favorites" (Indiegogo) listings. This directly conflicts with IGG's ToU statement on its role: "We do not pre-screen any Campaigns or endorse any User Content on our site" (IGG Terms; 6.a.). Marketed projects can also give the false impression that platforms sufficiently evaluate projects, on which basis the crowd may forego its own filtering and trust the platform picks.

Uncertainty on What Happens When Projects Fail Post-Funding

Aware of its shortcomings on visibility of project performance, Kickstarter invited the scholar Mollick to find out "how many projects fall short of delivering what was promised." Based on an extensive survey of 47,188 Kickstarter backers from a randomly selected pool of 456,751 contributors to 65,326 projects dating from KS's start year (2009) to May 2015, Mollick (2015) found an overall failure rate of 9% for projects ranging from 5% to 14% (p. 5), with the period 2009-2012 indicating higher failure rates of about 12.3%. In terms of dollars, 8.2% of contributions were directed to successfully funded projects that failed to deliver the promised perks.

In KS's history of 159k successfully funded projects, 341 raised US$1 million and above, among which games, technology, and design formed the bulk, with 120, 106, and 88 projects, respectively; while 5,523 projects attained between US$100,000 and US$1 million. The failure rate within this group would be a more critical metric for understanding the manufactured risks of reward-based crowdfunding, which could almost be called "reward-based overfunding." Without organized data on projects' performance, neither the general failure rate nor this high-worth segment's failure rate is possible to pinpoint. If the

8.2% rate in dollars found by Mollick for 2009-2015 were still valid, the size of failing projects would be calculated at US$304 million.

Despite all the wordy ToU contents, Help Center, or blog posts, various user comments under KS's key blog posts, as well as in project pages, expose that users seem mostly standalone and without a clear idea of what to expect from the platforms when the manufactured risks materialize. In case of no delivery, for example, should backers look for people in the Projects Comments section—the only space in which they can communicate with peers—who did not receive the rewards, and gather for a legal follow-up? Let's say that happens, as one user asks: should they come together and file litigation against a campaign owner who may have just spent the money (Bussema, 2012)—not necessarily with bad intentions.

This also looks rather exaggerated. When the contributions are compared with costs of litigation, it may not seem worth pursuing. Based on KS statistics, this study estimates average spending per backer of US$232 between 2009 and March 2019, while a more recent timeframe (November 2017-March 2019) indicates a higher average of US$350. Even KS board member Sunny Bates told to Polygon that the size of the contributions makes a potential scam negligible: "Here's the deal…It's one thing to be scammed like Bernie Madoff, where you've gone and you've been seduced by something and put in all your life savings. It's another thing for something not to come through for $25" (Gera, 2012), although US$25 example is far below the author's estimates.

This dilemma indicates that no one, including the platform and the contributors, has incentives to follow up with the aftermath of a successfully funded project. A platform that can still make money on the crowd's good faith and successfully funded projects, even if they fail to deliver on their promises because the contributions are too small to legally pursue, poses a conflict of interest and a question of sustainability in the long run. Even backers might find a lawsuit meaningless, and repeated failing experiences might lead them to find crowdfunding a throwaway too. Many users, in comments on projects as well as platform posts, shared how they lost their enthusiasm for contributing to crowdfunding projects, while some complaining that Kickstarter does not have enough accountability, and this is being exploited by some creators (Simon, 2015).

Although KS made clear that it cannot intervene for refunds, it frequently heard from backers in comments under its blog posts the question of "in what scenarios will Kickstarter refund the 5% fee?" This can be contemplated in the context of a failing project, Zano Drone, as an example. In this project, KS's commission would be US$180,000 on total funds collected of US$3.6 million. If KS's portion were distributed to backers, a backer would receive on average US$15 compared with the average spending of US$298. In view of this big divide, the redistribution of platform fees to backers does not seem satisfactory as an effective remedy. It could show the platform's goodwill; however, it will always fall short of closing the refund gap.

A system putting the liability for refunds on the fundraiser may also exert some exaggerated pressure on failing creators who with good intentions may have spent the funds. This can scare away creators from crowdfunding, as one creator complained on KS: "Why would anyone take that on their shoulders, especially when anyone with an Internet connection can back a project, including crazy litigious strangers?" (Garth, 2012).

Two Failing "Successfully Funded" Projects

The research selected two cases, one from each platform, of successfully funded projects that failed to deliver the rewards. Maybe not coincidentally, both projects involve high-tech products. Robot Dragonfly (a robot) was an Indiegogo project that raised US$1.1 million in 2013, while the Zano Drones on Kickstarter reached US$3.6 million in 2015.

Robot Dragonfly Project at Indiegogo

When the Robot Dragonfly campaign was initiated on IGG in 2012, the contributors seemed very excited, using remarks such as "the most awesome flying machine I've ever seen" (Paternot, 2012). As the creators stated, Robot Dragonfly was Indiegogo's first US$1 million-plus project. After three years of frequent updates and progress reports, the developers announced the failure and apologized to the supporters by November 2015. In their closing remarks, they outlined not only their "lack of experience in dealing with Asia to minimize expenditures," but also insufficient release of funds from PayPal and Indiegogo, who held the funds for about 14 months (TechJect Updates).

The creator, TechJect, pointed the finger at IGG's lack of transparency as the money "being wrongfully withheld," and some backers also complained, "PayPal didn't offer an option to demand a refund when money was with them for over a year. Classic fraud on both…I wish someone would sue PayPal and Indiegogo on our behalf" (Radcliff, 2017). This vivid reaction demonstrates also the ambiguity regarding IGG's funds-releasing process. Apparently, TechJect filed a lawsuit against PayPal on 13 October 2017 that resulted in favor of the defendant in August 2018, on which TechJect further filed an appeal (TechJect vs. PayPal).

On last campaign update, the creator team announced posting of all the details and failing parts of the project in a Wiki, so that supporters or anyone interested in learning the "pitfalls" could study it: "…For now, we will shift to making sure everyone has the complete WiKi with all designs uploaded for anyone to use as necessary, and we will continue our talks with PayPal and Indiegogo" (7 November 2015). Out of 3,203 backers, only 67 were hostile, and the team commented that it keeps pushing Indiegogo and PayPal to refund contributors.

From the start until suspension, there has been substantial interaction between the contributors and the project owners, especially at the time of the campaign and right after. The team thanked the backer community for feedback, some of which they planned to implement in production. These were the times when everything seemed achievable. With the absence of any cap on either orders or the amount of funding to raise, the project developers topped up the volume of rewards and continued to raise money beyond the funding goal: "DRAGONFLY Quantities increased! We have been overwhelmed by emails, complaints, and demands that we had no choice but to leave everyone with a happy weekend. We've increased the availability of the Dragonflies! Let your friends know!"

It is unknown whether the project could have delivered the rewards if the campaign had been restricted to the initial funding of US$110,000. However, the order expansion from about 300 pieces to about 2,800 units, as shown in Table 2, indicated an alarming shift whose impact on the workload and estimated delivery time, could not have been negligible.

An interesting note about this project is that it received much media coverage also, having originally received a US$1 million grant from the US Air Force, which apparently contributed to the trustworthiness of the project: "The research behind the dragonfly began with a $1,000,000 grant from the US Air Force. The dragonfly has been developed at the Georgia Institute of Technology, as a joint effort between 20+ researchers, PhDs, professors and students from multiple universities across the world." Burns from Techcrunch summarized the project's problem fairly: "good engineers do not always make good founders" (2015), which also represents a major risk of RBCF.

Table 2. Numerical analysis of Robot Dragonfly project's rewards and funding

Robot Dragonfly Funding Overview	US$
Funding goal	110,000
Funding raised	1,140,975
Number of backers	3,203
Average funding per backer	356
Smallest reward (perk)	99
Biggest reward (perk)	2,899
Number of comments	4891
Number of updates by creator	104

Source: The author compiled the table using data on Indiegogo Robot Dragonfly Campaign page

Zano Drones Project at Kickstarter

One of the biggest crowdfunding failures to date is "Zano drone" at Kickstarter, also labeled as the largest European campaign on Kickstarter (Cellon-Jones, 2016). In its campaign video, the presenters gave a rosy pitch for the Zano, showing off its technological capacity and background briefly, which seemed impressive, especially to someone without above-average tech know-how. The video finished with campaigners saying: "To make Zano truly accessible to everyone, we need to get volumes up so the price goes down. …The future of Zano is in your hands." Apparently, the crowd did its best to give a hand, even 20 times bigger in magnitude than the project owners had targeted. However, the Zano project announced liquidation toward the end of the same year.

The analysis run by this research on campaign numbers is provided in Table 3. The original rewards can be estimated as around 600 units, whose increase by 20-times would normally raise considerable concern about the feasibility relative to the initial scope, but the distribution timeline was maintained as six months without an adjustment in delivery schedule. Overall, the dominant problem seemed to be a typical working capital crisis of a rapidly and significantly growing company that both drowned under

Table 3. Numerical analysis of Zano Drones project's rewards and funding

Zano Drones	£
Funding goal	125,000
Funding raised	2,335,119
Number of backers	12,075
Average funding per backer	193
Smallest reward (perk)	5
Biggest reward (perk)	540
Number of comments	10415
Number of updates by creator	53

Source: The author compiled the table using data on Kickstarter Zano Drones Campaign page (£ is the original campaign currency, and funding raised corresponds to c.3.6 million in dollar terms)

the gigantic order it created and substantial mistakes in project management. Greater funds can also become a big hurdle when they land with people with limited know-how in business development and mean greater risks in meeting deliveries, as well as communicating with a huge backer force.

On Kickstarter's request for an independent review, technology expert and journalist Mark Harris (2016) published an inquiry on Medium covering the project chronology, including interviews with the project developers, Kickstarter team, and some contributors, in order to expose the major loopholes in the project. KS's efforts to mobilize an expert analysis, although in the aftermath of the funding, demonstrated the platform's ambition to learn from a significant bump in its learning curve. Still, the author could not find a link or reference on KS's website to this expert report.

Harris' examination was after a factual summary of where the money went and what lessons could be learned from a failing project that met its funding goal in only 10 days, received wide applause from the tech world, garnering certain prestigious awards like the Best of CES Award (Harris, 2016). The project was also Kickstarter's "staff pick" (Cellon-Jones, 2016). A big dose of optimism coupled with crucial false technical decisions, such as skipping a "pilot build" before going to mass production just to meet the deadlines loaded the campaign with a huge inventory of unfinished and semi-finished products that were not even functional, hence basically worth trash, reaping developers'—actually the crowd's cash piles—too early (Harris, 2016).

Furthermore, the developer company, Torquing, under Ivan Reedman, expanded into another duplicate pre-order campaign on its website beside the Kickstarter campaign, and pre-sold 3,000 more units. Non-KS users received their "barely operational" drones before the KS backers, as KS terms were not enforcing priority of treatment in order-handling contrary to IGG's terms. The campaign video contained a possible fake footage, as the prototype was not even fully functional. If so, there was discrepancy between the reality and the vision early-on, and it was violating Kickstarter's policy prohibiting "product simulations" (Harris, 2016).

The idea behind increasing the order size to reduce unit costs is a typical microeconomics fundamental called economies of scale. Still, it is hard to comprehend how initially a 600 piece-campaign can be feasible with only 125,000 pounds, but an order of 20x greater magnitude still does not reduce unit costs sufficiently. During the campaign, one user raised a red flag about the project by clicking the "Report This Project" button – a reporting mechanism for any user to submit a personal alarm to the platform through a button placed for the purpose. Although an analyst on KS's Integrity team reviewed the project, no evidence of fraud was found that would suspend the campaign; and KS expressed that "a single report is low for a project this size." This poses that the statistical significance criteria for red flags should be reviewed and plausibly based also on the original project size. After the funding, other complaints were received, reaching 62 at the end.

A key takeaway from Harris's exploration was that most of the contacted contributors stated that the Zano failure "soured them on Kickstarter itself and crowdfunding in general," although it was not the first time, they had lost money in "unsuccessful crowdfunding projects." This basically proves quite intensely that the trust that can be shaken with these failures is not only in the platform but also in the whole RBCF concept.

SOLUTIONS AND RECOMMENDATIONS

Making money on successful (over)funding regardless of projects' fulfillment creates potential conflicts of interest for RBCF platforms and challenges middlemen's neutrality. Crowdfunding sites KS and IGG do not actually need to take an active role in projects' completion but must actively create a healthier and unbiased environment where best efforts for materialization of projects can really be aligned without information asymmetries. Only with the correct means can the platforms and the crowd build a truer opinion on the manufactured risks of RBCF and manage them efficiently, and the passive intermediary role assumed by the platforms becomes viable as well.

Corrective devices should be designed case by case for each platform, covering all relevant aspects of the RBCF process from creator's submission process to filtering and overfunding so that a consistent and holistic remedy is formed. Obviously, an effective solution necessitates further information through discussion and collaboration with the platforms for a careful evaluation of their in-house accumulated lessons and considerations.

Still, the right initial steps would be reforming the sites for neutral presentation of projects and risks, and the development of a sustainable self-reporting tool for post-funding performance of successfully funded projects. The combination of this data, easily accessible and more organized than Comments on project pages, across projects can automatically yield a fulfilment statistic that speaks for itself and function as a risk warning for the creators and backers as well, also making platforms' mission and achievement statements – such as how many projects they helped come to life – concrete.

The benefits of these restructuring mechanisms for the platforms and the crowdfunding spirit would be addressing the risks that keep off potential users or estrange existing ones and creating a more trustworthy and sustainable environment which draws in a bigger, stronger and more conscious user base, hence solidifying and making the best of this rich collaboration potential.

FUTURE RESEARCH DIRECTIONS

The remedies mentioned above for RBCF may also compel a revisit of the platform fees, which can be adjusted upward if necessary, to afford a healthier infrastructure with stronger informative tools. The author finds the flat fees and unlimited overfunding more alarming than the level of commission rate itself, as they may cause a struggle with crowdfunding intermediaries' credibility over the long run, when failure stories of overfunded projects accumulate.

A restructuring would also fit in line with (for instance) KS's pioneering move to become a public-benefit corporation (PBC), which came with a concern about the effects of the business on society and a decision to donate 5% of the platform's net earnings to arts and culture education and initiatives addressing inequality (Strickler et al., 2015). However, solidifying KS's systems for backing the right creators to the right extent could be a more proactive daily public-benefit consideration.

Going forward, public-benefit structure adopted by KS can be also a helpful benchmark in sharing economy universe, for looking an alignment of platforms and users. Exploring the potential of this PBC model for sharing economy endeavors is critical, as the dominant for-profit route risks falling into the trap of the typical capitalist paradigm with significant ambitions on growth rather than on sustainability also on the back of expanding external funding and investor pressures. This makes some sharing economy examples more disruptive than others instead of providing complementary solutions. The applicability of ideal ownership structures that better conform to users' collaboration can enrich and strengthen the sharing ecosystem as well as platforms' and users' consciousness.

CONCLUSION

Reward-based crowdfunding sites, the Internet, and the academic literature so far have mostly focused on the funding part of the crowdfunding process, leaving on the periphery the main goal of a crowdfunding campaign: completion. While it is known that Kickstarter alone intermediated US$3.7 billion of crowdfunding, there is not a reliable data on what part of this funding culminated in successfully materialized projects.

Nevertheless, it is not that the crowdfunding ecosystem should be free of failures and risks, which would totally kill any need for self-monitoring and risk management. The idea should be to provide enough room for backers to make educated judgments on crowdfunding and campaigns, and to enable creators to learn from previous failure experiences on how to convert themselves from idea generators to project completers.

Absence of self-monitoring mechanisms makes certain platforms' rules on norms, limitations, and responsibilities unsustainable, also endangering the evolution of crowdfunding platforms into their ideal forms. If leading platforms such as Kickstarter and Indiegogo can truly eliminate information asymmetries and level the playing field for their users by facilitating better transparency, education, and risk management tools for the crowd, they can also set an example for the rest of the eco-system and ensure keeping this collaborative spirit free of regulatory intervention.

With one leg always with the crowd, an amateur spirit may prevail in most of the sharing-economy examples over the long-run, too. Still, while it is early enough, this collaborative ecosystem needs serious collaboration among all the stakeholders to pay due to its much richer potential than previous corporations, of aligning not only with shareholders but also with users.

Evidently, the impact of failures becomes more dramatic when risks are not thoroughly recognized. As Mitchell (1998) called it, "the uncertainties and dangers of the bitsphere frontier are great, but it is a place of new opportunity and hope" (p. 173). Seizing these prospects requires more efficient, consistent and sustainable tools smartly designed for each platform's own path and needs.

ACKNOWLEDGMENT

This research is based on the author's Ph.D. dissertation at Bilgi University (Turkey) and received no specific grant from any funding agency in the public, commercial, or not-for-profit sectors.

REFERENCES

About, I. G. G. (n.d.). Retrieved March 10, 2019, from https://www.indiegogo.com/about/our-story

Blog, K. S. (2017). Celebrating 100,000 Kickstarter Creators. Retrieved from https://www.kickstarter.com/blog/celebrating-100000-kickstarter-creators

Botsman, R., & Rogers, R. (2010). *What's mine is yours: The rise of collaborative consumption*. New York: Harper Business.

Brabham, D. C. (2013). *Crowdsourcing*. Cambridge, MA: The MIT Press. doi:10.7551/mit-press/9693.001.0001

Bradford, C.S. (2012). Crowdfunding and the Federal Securities Laws. *Columbia Business Law Review*, *1*(1), 1-150.

Burns, M. (2015, November 7). Another $1 million crowdfunded gadget company collapses. *TechCrunch*. Retrieved from https://techcrunch.com/2015/11/07/another-1-million-crowdfunded-gadget-company-collapses/

Bussema, C. (2012, September 5). *Accountability on Kickstarter*. Comment posted to https://www.kickstarter.com/blog/accountability-on-kickstarter

Cellon-Jones, R. (2016, January 20). Zano: The rise and fall of Kickstarter's mini-drone. *BBC.com*. Retrieved from https://www.bbc.com/news/technology-35356147

Clifford, C. (2016, January 18). Less than a third of crowdfunding campaigns reach their goals. *The Entrepreneur*. Retrieved from https://www.entrepreneur.com/article/269663

Derrida, J. (1992). *Given time: I. Counterfeit Money* (P. Kamuf, Trans.). Chicago: The University of Chicago Press.

Gage, D. (2018, April 30). The 10 biggest crowdfunding campaigns: where are they now? *The Wall Street Journal*. Retrieved from https://www.wsj.com/articles/the-10-biggest-crowdfunding-campaigns-where-are-they-now-1525140660

Garth. (2012, September 9). *Accountability on Kickstarter*. Comment posted to https://www.kickstarter.com/blog/accountability-on-kickstarter

Gera, E. (2012, June 27). Why Kickstarter 'can't' and won't protect backers once a project is funded. *Polygon*. Retrieved from https://www.polygon.com/gaming/2012/6/27/3099051/backers-rights-what-kickstarter-funders-can-expect-when-they-pledge

Giddens, A. (1999). Risk and responsibility. *The Modern Law Review*, *62*(1), 1–10. doi:10.1111/1468-2230.00188

Harris, M. (2016). How Zano raised millions on Kickstarter and left most backers with nothing. *Medium*. Retrieved from https://medium.com/kickstarter/how-zano-raised-millions-on-kickstarter-and-left-backers-with-nearly-nothing-85c0abe4a6cb

Heinrichs, H. (2013). Sharing economy: A potential new pathway to sustainability. *Gaia (Heidelberg)*, *22*(4), 228–231. doi:10.14512/gaia.22.4.5

Help, K. S. (n.d.). Retrieved January 24, 2019 from, https://help.kickstarter.com/hc/en-us/articles/115005135574-Are-projects-that-were-not-successfully-funded-browsable-on-Kickstarter-

Hill, D. (2019, January 10). How the world's largest crowdfunder for creativity is kickstarting sustainability. *Forbes*. Retrieved from https://www.forbes.com/sites/edfenergyexchange/2019/01/10/how-the-worlds-largest-crowdfunder-for-creativity-is-kickstarting-sustainability/#40ee17345b2b

Horkheimer, M. (1974). *Critique of Instrumental Reason*. New York: Seabury.

IGG for Entrepreneurs. (n.d.). Retrieved March 10, 2019, from https://entrepreneur.indiegogo.com/how-it-works/

Indiegogo vs. Kickstarter. (n.d.). Retrieved March 10, 2019, from https://entrepreneur.indiegogo.com/how-it-works/indiegogo-vs-kickstarter/

Jeffries, A. (2013a, August 7). Indie no-go: only one in ten projects gets fully funded on Kickstarter's biggest rival. A comparison of two crowdfunding platforms. *The Verge*. Retrieved from https://www.theverge.com/2013/8/7/4594824/less-than-10-percent-of-projects-on-indiegogo-get-fully-funded

Jeffries, A. (2013b, April 17). Kickstarter is not a store, except when it is: Ouya, Pebble, and the curse of the pre-order. *The Verge*. Retrieved from https://www.theverge.com/2013/4/17/4230440/kickstarter-is-not-a-store-except-when-it-is

Jenkins, H. (2006). *Convergence Culture: Where Old and New Media Collide*. New York: New York University Press.

Kickstarter is not a Store. (2012, September 20). *The Kickstarter Blog*. Retrieved from https://www.kickstarter.com/blog/kickstarter-is-not-a-store

KS PBC 2017. (n.d.). Retrieved from https://www.kickstarter.com/year/2017/benefit-statement

Marin, Y. (2019, March 17). *Piqo Pocket Projector*. Comment posted to https://www.indiegogo.com/projects/piqo-world-s-most-powerful-1080p-pocket-projector/x/151186

Marketplace. (n.d.). Retrieved February 11, 2019, from https://www.indiegogo.com/explore/all?project_type=product&project_timing=all&sort=trending

Martin, C. J. (2016). The sharing economy: A pathway to sustainability or a nightmarish form of neoliberal capitalism? *Ecological Economics*, *121*, 149–159. doi:10.1016/j.ecolecon.2015.11.027

Mauss, M. (1990). *The Gift, The Form and reason for exchange in Archaic societies*. London: Routledge.

Mission, K. S. (n.d.). Retrieved January 23, 2019, from https://www.kickstarter.com/about?ref=global-footer

Mitchell, W. J. (1998). *City of bits: Space, place, and the infobahn*. Cambridge, MA: MIT Press.

Mollick, E. R. (2015). *Delivery Rates on Kickstarter*. Retrieved from https://repository.upenn.edu/mgmt_papers/210

Morozov, E. (2013, October 14). *The 'sharing economy' undermines workers rights*. Retrieved from https://evgenymorozov.tumblr.com/post/64038831400/the-sharing-economy-undermines-workers-rights

Oner Kula, S. (2019). Responsibilities of sharing economy platforms for cultivating trust. In B. Tejerina, C. Miranda de Almeida, I. Perugorria (Eds.), *Proceedings of the International Conference Sharing Society. The Impact of Collaborative Collective Actions in the Transformation of Contemporary Societies* (pp. 207-222). Leioa: Universidad del País Vasco/Euskal Herriko Unibertsitatea.

Paternot, S. (2012). *Robot Dragonfly.* Comment posted to https://www.indiegogo.com/projects/robot-dragonfly-micro-aerial-vehicle#/

Poy, J. (2019, March 17). *Piqo Pocket Projector.* Comment posted to https://www.indiegogo.com/projects/piqo-world-s-most-powerful-1080p-pocket-projector/x/151186

Projects We Love. (n.d.). Retrieved March 12, 2019, from https://www.kickstarter.com/discover/recommended?ref=discovery_overlay

Radcliff, D. (2017, October). *Robot Dragonfly.* Comment posted to https://www.indiegogo.com/projects/robot-dragonfly-micro-aerial-vehicle#/

Reward. (n.d.). In *Oxford. Living Dictionaries, English.* Retrieved December 12, 2018, from https://en.oxforddictionaries.com/definition/reward

Robot Dragonfly. (2012). Retrieved December 21, 2018 from https://www.indiegogo.com/projects/robot-dragonfly-micro-aerial-vehicle#/

Schleifer, T. (2017). Crowdfunding site Indiegogo will now let you sell products as it shifts into commerce. *Recode.* Retrieved from https://www.recode.net/2017/10/16/16474794/indiegogo-crowdfunding-commerce-amazon

Science Direct. (n.d.). Retrieved March 11, 2019, from https://www.sciencedirect.com/search/advanced?qs=reward%20crowdfunding%20success&show=50&sortBy=relevance

Shahani, A. (2012, September 3). When a Kickstarter campaign fails, does anyone get the money back? *NPR.* Retrieved from https://www.npr.org/sections/alltechconsidered/2012/09/03/160505449/when-a-kickstarter-campaign-fails-does-anyone-get-their-money-back

Shuptrine, C. (2016). Kickstarter: Crowdfunding portal, or pre-order store? *The Huffington Post.* Retrieved from https://www.huffingtonpost.com/chris-shuptrine/kickstarter-crowdfunding-_b_9609322.html

Siefkes, C. (2008). *From exchange to contributions generalizing peer production into the physical world.* Berlin: Siefkes-Verlag.

Simon. (2015, January 12). *Accountability on Kickstarter.* Comment posted to https://www.kickstarter.com/blog/accountability-on-kickstarter

Smets, K. (2019, March 17). *Piqo Pocket Projector.* Comment posted to https://www.indiegogo.com/projects/piqo-world-s-most-powerful-1080p-pocket-projector/x/151186

Span, M. (2015, June 23). Indiegogo users raise $500 million. *Inc.com.* Retrieved from https://www.inc.com/maria-aspan/indiegogo-users-raise-$500-million.html

Stallman, R. (2002). *Free software, free society: Selected essays of Richard M. Stallman.* Boston, MA: Free Software Foundation.

Stats, K. S. (2019, March 15). Retrieved March, 15 2019, from https://www.kickstarter.com/help/stats?ref=global-footer

Strickler, Y., Chen, P., & Adler, C. (2012a, September 4). Accountability on Kickstarter. *The Kickstarter Blog*. Retrieved from https://www.kickstarter.com/blog/accountability-on-kickstarter

Strickler, Y., Chen, P., & Adler, C. (2012b, September 20). Kickstarter is not a store. *The Kickstarter Blog*. Retrieved from https://www.kickstarter.com/blog/kickstarter-is-not-a-store

Strickler, Y., Chen, P., & Adler, C. (2015a, September 21). Kickstarter is now a benefit corporation. *The Kickstarter Blog*. Retrieved from https://www.kickstarter.com/blog/kickstarter-is-now-a-benefit-corporation

Support, I. G. G. (n.d.). Retrieved March 19, 2019, from https://support.indiegogo.com/hc/en-us/articles/204092046-InDemand-FAQ

Team Favorites. (n.d.). Retrieved March 18, 2019, from https://www.indiegogo.com/campaign_collections/staff-picks

TechJect Updates. Robot Dragonfly Project. (n.d.). Retrieved November 27, 2017, from https://www.indiegogo.com/projects/robot-dragonfly-micro-aerial-vehicle/x/151186#/updates/all

TechJect vs. PayPal. (n.d.). Retrieved March 16, 2019, from https://www.pacermonitor.com/public/case/22748927/Techject,Incorporated_v_Paypal_Holdings,Incorporated

Terms, I. G. G. (2018, May 25). Terms of Use. Retrieved January 12, 2019, from https://www.indiegogo.com/about/terms

Top Ten, I. G. G. (n.d.). Retrieved March 11, 2019, from https://www.indiegogo.com/campaign_collections/top-10

Trust, I. G. I. (n.d.). Retrieved March 21, 2019, from https://learn.indiegogo.com/trust/

Wallis, O. F. (Interviewer) & Strickler, Y. (Interviewee). (2017). Kickstarter's Yancey Strickler: tech companies need to be better citizens. *Wired*. Retrieved from http://www.wired.co.uk/article/yancey-strickler-kickstarter-video-interview

Zano Drone. (2014). *Kickstarter*. Retrieved May 12, 2018, from https://www.kickstarter.com/projects/torquing/zano-autonomous-intelligent-swarming-nano-drone/community

ADDITIONAL READING

Bauwens, M., Mendoza, N., & Iacomella, F. (2012). A synthetic overview of the collaborative economy. *Orange Labs and P2P Foundation*. Retrieved from https://www.orange.com/fr/content/download/6834/101185/version/4/file/P2P+-+Synthetic+overview+of+the+collaborative+economy.pdf

Benkler, Y. (2006). *The wealth of networks: How social production transforms markets and freedom*. New Haven: Yale University Press.

Giddens, A. (1990). *The consequences of modernity*. Cambridge: Polity Press.

Jenkins, H. (2017). *Revisiting the Concept of "Sharing": An Interview with Nicholas John (Part One-Two-Three)*. Retrieved from http://henryjenkins.org/blog/2017/8/31/revisiting-the-concept-of-sharing-an-interview-with-nicholas-john-part-one

Mollick, E. R. (2016). Containing Multitudes: The Many Impacts of Kickstarter Funding. *SSRN*. Retrieved from SSRN https://ssrn.com/abstract=2808000 or doi:10.2139srn.2808000

Nissenbaum, H. (2003). Securing Trust Online. In B. Kolko (Ed.), *Virtual Publics: Policy and Community in an Electronic Age* (pp. 134–171). New York: Columbia University Press.

KEY TERMS AND DEFINITIONS

Angel Investor: Typically, a high net-worth person or sophisticated investor who offers early-stage capital for a startup usually against equity shares.

Average Spending/Crowdfunding Per Backer: Total funding volume divided by number of backers in a crowdfunding project.

Backer: The user of a crowdfunding platform who crowdfunds a project, also called "supporter", "contributor" or "crowdfunder".

Campaigner: The user of a crowdfunding platform who creates a project for fund raising, also called "project creator" or "creator."

Due Diligence: A thorough investigation of a company and its commercial, financial, legal records, and prospects that is primarily used as a basis for a business transaction including financing, merger, or acquisitions.

Economies of Scale: The economic principle of achieving lower unit costs through production or purchase of larger volumes of business.

Lehman Formula: A typically popular commission scheme for fund raising that lets an intermediary earn (success) fees in reverse proportion to size of funding (commission rate declining from 5% gradually by one basis points for each consecutive million raised, i.e., 3% of the third million).

Repeat Backer: A backer who has contributed to more than one crowdfunding project on a platform.

Sophisticated/High Net-Worth Investor: A financially acknowledged investor type that carries enough wealth and knowledge to invest in risky assets.

Success Fee: A commission that ties the amount paid to an intermediary in a transaction through a specified percentage rate on deal size. This acts as an alignment mechanism between the middleman and the party that usually raises the funding (through equity or debt).

Traditional Finance: This chapter calls typical and renowned methods of finance that usually involves financial institutions as "traditional," also interchangeably used with "conventional" finance.

Venture Capitalist: An individual or fund/institution that invests in startups at early-stage with higher risks in order to earn higher profits by a timely exit when the business is more mature.

Chapter 8
The Strategic Governance of Sharing Platforms:
Transaction Costs and Integration Mechanisms

Yusaf H. Akbar
Central European University, Hungary

Andrea Tracogna
University of Trieste, Italy

ABSTRACT

Sectors from hospitality, consumer finance, freelance services to taxis have been reshaped in the last few years due to the growth of online access-based sharing platforms. Notable examples of such platforms are Airbnb (accommodation services), Lyft (mobility), TaskRabbit (freelancing), and Kickstarter (peer lending). The chapter posits that access-based sharing platforms are subject to an evolution from "peer-to-peer" (P2P) to "integrated" forms, where the platform owner adopts a series of governance mechanisms aimed at providing effective safeguarding, adaptation, and measurement features to transactions. The level of transaction frequency, uncertainty, and specificity is a strategic decision taken by the owner to grow the platform. The management of transaction features generates transaction costs and determines the need, by the platform members and by the platform owner, to adopt specific mechanisms of platform integration. The chapter concludes with a call for scholars to intensify empirical evaluation of the important and growing phenomena identified in the chapter.

INTRODUCTION

Multiple industries, from accommodation services to car mobility, from freelance services to finance have been radically reshaped in the last few years due to the impressive growth of digital sharing platforms (European Commission, 2016). Among the most notable examples of such platforms are the cases of Airbnb (accommodation services), Lyft (car mobility), TaskRabbit (on-demand labor), and Kickstarter

DOI: 10.4018/978-1-5225-9928-9.ch008

Copyright © 2020, IGI Global. Copying or distributing in print or electronic forms without written permission of IGI Global is prohibited.

(peer lending). What accounts for the emergence and growth of sharing platforms across numerous industries today? How do these sharing platforms evolve over time and threaten the strategies and business models of industry incumbents? How can the platform evolution be effectively governed and strategically oriented? These are important and emerging questions for scholarly and policy-oriented research that have engaged multiple disciplines including anthropology, economics, law, management and sociology.

Our chapter contributes to this theoretical exploration from the perspective of platform governance using transaction cost theory (TCT) as the primary analytical lens. In doing so, we focus on three variables identified in TCT literature (Williamson, 1979): transaction frequency, transaction uncertainty, and transaction asset specificity. In particular, we analyze how such variables impact the strategic governance of sharing platforms by addressing three main transaction issues: 1. safeguarding of the assets invested by the parties in the transaction. 2. adaptation of the transaction to the changing circumstances. 3. measurement of the actual identity and performances of the involved parties.

In spite of the broad success of the TCT perspective, the extant literature has a scarcity of studies that have systematically theorized the general structural form of sharing platforms through an in-depth analysis of how economic exchange and transactions take place (Cheng, 2016; McIntyre and Srinivasan, 2017). By way of recent exception, Akbar and Tracogna (2018) have explored the role of TCT in explaining the strategic evolution and growth of sharing platforms in the specific context of the hotel industry. One of their main conclusions is that platform integration, defined as the increased involvement of the platform owner in the management of transactions and the minimization of transaction costs, represents an important option for the strategic governance of sharing platforms. The authors argue that, based on the market-hierarchy continuum implicit in TCT, there are two archetypes of sharing platforms. First is the peer-to-peer platform, where sharing involves three groups of participants: 1) goods and service providers who share physical or intangible (i.e., made of time or skills) assets; 2) users of these assets; and 3) platform owners who connect providers with users and facilitate transactions between them. The second type of sharing platform is the integrated platform, where the platform owner fully or partially integrates one side (typically the providers) and actively intervenes in the transaction mechanisms, directly addressing the issues of asset safeguarding, transaction adaptation, and identity/performance measurement. In this chapter, we draw parallels between sharing platforms and hybrid modes for governing economic transactions, since they both possess features of markets and hierarchies.

In common with markets, sharing platforms represent a marketplace that promotes transactions through the meeting of supply and demand. As with market settings, transactions can be repeated over time and the parties progressively learn how to deal with each other, thus activating mechanisms of relational contracting. As with hierarchies, sharing platforms directly influence transaction arrangements among the parties, through the formulation and enforcement of contractual conditions as well as the centralization of key administrative processes (payments, data collection, account management etc.). Further, we observe that sharing platforms are subject to a typical evolution: namely, they move from "peer-to-peer" (P2P) to "integrated" forms, where the platform owner—depending on transaction frequency (higher frequency justifies the investments in integration mechanisms), uncertainty level of transactions, and the required specificity of assets and services (based on preferences for specificity by platforms users)—adopts a series of governance mechanisms aimed at providing effective safeguarding, adaptation, and measurement features to transactions (which we call mechanisms of platform "integration").

The implications of theorizing transaction costs in sharing platforms and platforms as hybrid forms of transaction governance raise specific research questions which form the basis of this chapter. Specifically, how can frequency, uncertainty and asset specificity be governed and strategically managed in the context of sharing platforms? Can the governance structure adopted by a sharing platform be effectively defined with the aim of both economizing in transaction costs and also developing a competitive advantage for the platform itself? We believe that further detailed theoretical analysis of the core structural features of sharing platforms from the perspective of TCT could reveal dynamics of how sharing platforms function, perform, and evolve, offering valuable analytical findings for business strategy of firms and organizations confronted by the emergence of sharing platforms, as well as fostering a nuanced exchange of ideas among scholars on sharing platforms and their strategic implications.

Our chapter is organized as follows. A first section examines the factors and mechanisms that account for the recent evolution of sharing platforms. Further, we rehearse the key concepts of TCT and explore in more detail the main elements of frequency, uncertainty, asset specificity, and transaction governance structures, thereby describing sharing platforms as hybrid mechanisms of governance. Then, the key TCT constructs (frequency, uncertainty, and specificity) will be operationalized with reference to the strategic governance of sharing platforms. In the light of the above, the empirical section illustrates the strategic evolution of three sharing platforms: Airbnb, Lyft, and TaskRabbit. The final section concludes and sets the ground for further research.

THE EMERGENCE OF SHARING PLATFORMS: SOCIAL, TECHNOLOGICAL AND ECONOMIC DRIVERS

Social and Technological Drivers

A nuanced understanding of the key factors that account for the emergence of sharing platforms is an important and emerging issue for scholarly and policy-oriented research that has engaged multiple disciplines across anthropology, economics, business, law, and sociology. Thus far, this rich and broad multidisciplinary effort has uncovered a number of causes. Sharing is fundamentally considered to be rooted in a combination of ecosystem scale to reduce costs of production and digital distribution reducing the need for fixed assets (Belk, 2010; Benkler, 2004; Botsman & Rogers, 2010; Dervojeda et al., 2013; Olson & Connor, 2013; Owyang, 2014; Rifkin, 2014; Schor, 2016). Scholars have further identified radical structural changes in the nature of economic exchange that are shaping markets, societies, and communities more broadly. Here, three fundamental megatrends are worth emphasizing. The first — which may be partially driven by the socio-demographic characteristics of the so-called 'millennials' and 'post-millennials' (Hamari et al., 2015) — is represented by the rising preference to access socio-economic assets rather than owning the same assets (Bardhi & Eckhardt, 2012). Second, there appears to be a shift from an economy of scarcity to an economy of abundance, where the incremental (or marginal) cost of production and distribution of goods and services (particularly information goods) is close to zero; this is largely due to the emergence of digitization of economic value (Mason, 2015; Rifkin, 2014). Third, sharing platforms also appear to be a predominantly urbanized phenomenon due to the need for a critical mass of users (Davidson & Infranca, 2015).

Further, multiple technology-related forces contribute to the recent growth of sharing platforms. In particular, the evolution in digital technology related to the rapid growth of distribution and communication systems and the emergence of global online communities have enabled buyers to access and share knowledge, goods, and services in ways that were previously unavailable. Digitization has transformed services that previously required face-to-face interaction between suppliers and users. For example, travel agencies have now been mostly replaced by online travel portals that enable customers to design their own highly customized vacation plans (Law et al., 2004; Tse, 2003). Further, traditional distinctions between production and consumption have blurred, where digital goods and services are often produced by consumers themselves. For example, individuals can rent out their own homes on Airbnb while also renting out someone else's home on the very same platform. This has led to the emergence of the concept of pro-sumption (Tapscott & Williams, 2008).

With the aim of deepening the understanding of the structural features of this form of economic exchange, scholars have directed their research toward leading sharing platforms, such as Airbnb and Uber, as exemplars of the threat posed by sharing platforms to traditional sectors. For example, Varma et al. (2016) argue that Airbnb is a serious strategic threat to the hotel industry, and current hotel business models will have to adjust, as their "findings point to the need for the hotel industry to be more proactive, and to shake itself out of its stupor" (p. 263). Similarly, Wallsten (2015) provides evidence that Uber has created an alternative for consumers who would have otherwise complained to the regulator and encouraged taxis to improve their own service in response to new competition. In the same vein, Wallerstein and Shelat (2017) described how German truck manufacturer MAN established LoadFox in 2016 — a sharing platform to help smaller German logistics providers and carriers supplement their cargo trucks with less than a full truck load service for its clients.

Platform Economics

Platforms are an increasingly pervasive reality for both service sectors and manufacturing industries, particularly where partial or full digitization of the value proposition is a core feature. In particular, digital marketplaces where buyers and vendors of goods and services can meet and finalize their transactions have become a common feature of economic exchange (Schor, 2016) and a viable alternative business model to the traditionally integrated firm which comprise mechanisms for coordinating economic transactions and related activities that depart significantly from typical market governance mechanisms of the past. Hagiu and Wright (2011) define a platform as an organization that enables direct interactions among two or more distinct sides of users (typically, buyers and vendors), with each side being affiliated with and registered on the platform. Platforms are not a novelty: shopping malls have always connected buyers and sellers and newspapers have always connected readers and advertisers. Today, what is different is the central role of Information Technology (IT) in building marketplaces. IT allows for rapid scaling-up, reducing transaction costs and leveraging network effects. Furthermore, IT makes it possible to collect, analyze, and exchange large amounts of data, further increasing the value of the platform for members and enabling more effective targeting of users.

We can identify various types of IT-based digital platforms: First, trading platforms such as Amazon.com, a platform that facilitates the exchange of products (either physical and digital). Second, social media platforms, such as Facebook or Instagram, aimed at facilitating the interaction of people and advertisers within the framework of shared digital social interactions. Third, intermediation service portals, such as Booking.com or ctrip.com, which are leading platforms for booking travel and hospitality services. Fourth, there are platforms supporting collaborative production, which entails the collaboration of groups or networks of individuals to design, produce, or distribute goods; these platforms are related to the idea that it is the community that decides what to produce. Another type of platform is one that facilitates and monetizes shared allocation of durable assets (such as Airbnb, Blablacar, and Lyft) and facilitates supply of shared freelancer skills (such as TaskRabbit).

Prior research on platform economics (Baldwin & Woodard, 2009) describes a platform owner as being at the core of a strategic ecosystem (Iansiti & Levien, 2004) and as being responsible for mediating supply-side and demand-side users in a two-sided market (Parker & Van Alstyne, 2005; Rochet & Tirole, 2006). Users on both sides choose to interact through the platform when it is more efficient than transacting directly with each other (Eisenmann et al., 2006) and the platform offers more choices than would exist through traditional exchange. To fulfil the above role and to foster the long-term sustainability of the platform, platform owners take on multiple roles or functions. In addition to intermediation and integration of two-sided markets (supply and demand), they foster local agglomeration of demand and supply, generate positive network effects through price aggregation and the supply of an increased variety of products or services, manage contracts and administer payments, and facilitate information sharing and trust-generation mechanisms. Thus, the platform owner acts as a "regulator" (Farrell & Katz, 2000) and "market maker" supplying the needed trust in the platform ecosystem and attempting to lock-in users by increasing switching costs (Shapiro & Varian, 1999). This can also involve offering complementary and value-added services or products, as well as utilizing different pricing structures to build differentiated advantages into the platform.

The economics of platforms is heavily dependent on network size-effects: the larger the number of active users, the more efficient the platform becomes. This self-reinforcing dynamic (Arthur, 1989; Schilling, 2009) is exponential in nature, through network effects and economies of replication common to digital technologies; this frequently results in a "winner takes all (or most)" outcome, where the winning platform can benefit from zero (or close to) marginal costs and dominate the market to the extent of creating a durable monopoly which is hard to break by new entrants. This implies the importance of a platform attaining a minimum viable size in terms of number of users and volume of transactions (Hagiu, 2014; Eisenmann et al., 2006). In addition to cost advantages, by adding more users to the platform, owners can achieve higher diversified revenue sources: by understanding and harnessing both same-side and cross-side network effects, platform owners stimulate platform adoption by users (Katz & Shapiro, 1986). As platforms grow, owners are faced with increased platform complexity in both market and regulatory contexts which may pose challenges for the sustainability of the platform (Constantia et al., 2016).

While the emphasis in this chapter is on sharing platforms, it is important to emphasize that the above economic mechanisms and features apply to digital platforms in general and that the roles and functions of platform owners, as described above, are applicable to any type of platform, either in trading platforms that support the exchange of ownership of specific products or assets (such as eBay or Amazon) or in platforms that offer only shared access to products or assets (such as Airbnb or Uber). There are, of course, some specific differences between these platforms. In platforms where ownership is transferred, the extant property rights associated with the asset are also transferred, thereby creating flexibility, responsibility, and clear boundaries between the owner and others. In particular, the owner reserves the right to limit, regulate, or refuse access to others, as well as to use, sell, and retain any profits yielded from the use of an asset. In contrast, typical transactions in the sharing economy do not involve an exchange of ownership: access-based exchange does not transfer the same rights, thereby leading to more complex property contexts (Perzanowski & Schultz, 2015). Access-based exchange occurs so that users can access goods that they cannot afford to own or that they choose not to own due to living space constraints or concerns regarding the natural environment (Bardhi & Eckhardt, 2012). Because of their idiosyncratic nature, sharing platforms are commonly peer-to- peer (P2P) as they are based on the active participation of "peers" (i.e., the seller may also be the buyer in different transactions).

TCT AND THE GOVERNANCE OF SHARING PLATFORMS

In this chapter we adopt TCT, a well-established theoretical framework aimed at understanding how economic activity (transactions) can be governed through different institutional mechanisms (i.e. markets, hierarchies, or hybrid forms). This theoretical lens offers a broader and deeper understanding of the strategic governance of platforms. According to TCT, as will be made clearer subsequently in this chapter, sharing platforms are subject to a typical evolution: namely, they move from "peer-to-peer" (P2P) to "integrated" forms, where the platform owner—depending on transaction frequency (higher frequency justifies the investments in integration mechanisms), uncertainty level of transactions, and the required specificity of assets and services (based on preferences for specificity by platforms users)—adopts a series of governance mechanisms aimed at providing effective safeguarding, adaptation, and measurement features to transactions (which we call mechanisms of platform "integration"). We suggest that platform evolution occurs in parallel with increases in frequency, uncertainty and specificity of transactions, and this, in turn, involves the adoption of specific mechanisms of platform integration. Thus, a fuller understanding of the evolutionary paths and the strategic governance of sharing platforms requires a more precise definition of the nature and features of the transactions that occur on the platform.

TCT: Key Concepts

Drawing on the seminal work of Ronald Coase (1937), TCT has been developed mainly through the celebrated contributions of Oliver Williamson (1971, 1975, 1979, 1985, 1991). Within the TCT perspective, firms, markets, and other economic institutions are considered as bundles of contractual arrangements developed to administer economic exchange in the presence of transaction costs. There are two core assumptions that form the foundation of TCT and are related to the nature of economic agents and their behavior: *bounded rationality* (Simon, 1990) and *opportunism* (Williamson, 1975, 1985). Bounded rationality "designates rational choice that takes into account the cognitive limitations of the decision-maker—limitations of both knowledge and computational capacity" (Simon 1990, p. 15). Opportunism is defined as "self-interest seeking with guile" (Williamson, 1975, p. 255). He argues that, "Economic man is a much subtler and more devious creature than the usual self-interest seeking assumption reveals" (*ibid.*). Subsequently, Williamson elaborates the concept in terms of "the incomplete or distorted disclosure of information, especially to calculated efforts to mislead, distort, disguise, obfuscate, or otherwise confuse" (Williamson, 1985, p. 47).

Based on these assumptions, TCT develops three variables that constitute the core of the theory and describe the nature and features of economic transactions: frequency, uncertainty, and asset-specificity (Williamson, 1979). First, *transaction frequency* refers to the number of transactions that, over a certain period, occur among the same parties. In this respect, TCT typically distinguishes between occasional and recurrent transactions. Second, *transaction uncertainty* is closely linked to the identity of the parties (occasionally, exchange shall occur between relatively unknown counterparts) and the timespan of transactions that take place (which may be, at times, rather wide, thereby impacting the breadth of future contingencies for which contractual adaptations are required, as well as the risk of hard contracting and disputes in *ex-post* transaction governance). Third, *asset specificity* is the extent to which durable, specific investments in assets are needed to optimize transaction value. More precisely, asset specificity poses an issue of the return on investment, where this return is closely dependent on the specific context in which the transaction takes place. In several instances, this context is characterized by a "small numbers problem" (bilateral monopoly) where one party is asymmetrically dependent on the continuity of the transaction and this consequently increases the likelihood of exploitation, where the other party to the transaction may renege or hold up.

According to TCT, transaction costs are determined by the specific combination of the nature of the economic agents (bounded rationality and opportunistic behavior) and the transaction features themselves. More specifically, asset specificity and opportunism generate a problem of *safeguarding* the assets invested by the parties in the transaction, while bounded rationality and uncertainty pose problems of *adaptation* of the transaction to the changing circumstances and of *measurement* of the actual identity (*ex-ante*) and performance (*ex-post*) of the involved parties. In the presence of transaction costs, the two parties (or, in the case of platform-based exchanges, the platform owner) shall determine the most efficient contractual arrangements (i.e. organizational forms) for administering transactions (i.e., for the governance of economic activities). According to TCT, at the two extremes of a continuum of organizational forms stand markets and hierarchies. Markets are appropriate for administering transactions that are characterized by relatively low frequency, low uncertainty, and low asset specificity thus posing few problems of safeguarding, adaptation, and measurement. In contrast, hierarchies are most appropriate in the presence of high frequency, high uncertainty, and high asset specificity (Williamson, 1979). Improper governance of transactions creates significant consequences for economic activity: in the case of a lack of safeguarding mechanisms or difficulty in measuring the performance of parties or adapting to changing circumstances, economic agents may avoid transactions or invest fewer assets in the transaction, thereby decreasing the value exchanged. In the worst case, transactions fail to take place at all (market "failure").

In practice, few governance forms are of pure market or pure hierarchy form. Most governance systems adopted are hybrid in nature, incorporating both elements of market and hierarchy in conducting economic transactions. For example, strategic alliances or outsourcing relationships are examples of hybrid governance structures that use both autonomous (market-based) and coordinated (hierarchy-based) adaptations as well as both market price mechanism and hierarchical administrative controls. As observed by Rindfleish et al. (2010), hybrid (mixed) governance modes frequently arise in cases in which transactions are exposed to multiple exchange hazards (i.e., adaptation, measurement, and safeguarding problems). Their governance features can be based on two main complementary, contractual mechanisms (Williamson, 1979): *neo-classical contracting* (also known as trilateral contracting), where the assistance of a third party is introduced in the exchange; and *relational contracting*, when transactions are repeated over time and the parties progressively "learn" how to deal with each other. The working of such hybrid mechanisms is particularly significant in sharing platforms, as we will see in the next section.

Sharing Platforms as Hybrid Governance Structures

There are strong conceptual parallels between hybrid modes for governing economic transactions and sharing platforms, since they both possess features of markets and hierarchies and are both based on neo-classical (trilateral) contracting mechanisms and relational contracting processes. In common with markets, sharing platforms represent a marketplace that promotes transactions through the match-making of supply and demand. As with market settings, platform-based transactions can be repeated over time and the parties progressively learn how to deal with each other, thereby activating mechanisms of relational contracting. As with hierarchical governance mechanisms, sharing platforms directly influence transaction arrangements among the parties, through the formulation and enforcement of contractual conditions as well as the centralization of key administrative processes (payments, data collection, account management, etc.). In this perspective, sharing platforms adopt the typical mechanisms of neoclassical (trilateral) contracting.

Through the balancing of market and hierarchical characteristics platform owners are presented with choices on how to configure and manage their platform and support its evolution. TCT would suggest that while P2P sharing platforms appear to be relatively efficient for conducting transactions that are occasional, have intermediate levels of uncertainty, and have either idiosyncratic or mixed investment characteristics (Carter & Hodgson, 2006), as the actual level of frequency, uncertainty and specificity of sharing transactions varies in different environments and over time, sharing platforms evolve toward what we call "integrated" platforms by progressively adopting mechanisms of integration (safeguarding, adaptation, measurement) in response to high transaction costs. By contrast with P2P platforms, integrated platform owners actively intervene in transaction mechanisms, addressing the issues of asset safeguarding, transaction adaptation, and identity/performance measurement. Indeed, as platforms grow in size, transactions may be less occasional (e.g. the providers repeat the 'sharing' of the same asset more often; the same users access more assets, more often), uncertainty may be higher (in the cases of the activation of "marginal" transactions among unknown parties), and the specificity of the accessed assets may have higher degrees (this typically occurs when the sharing of assets becomes a professional activity and assets are specifically bought to be shared on a platform): such are the conditions where a progressive integration of the sharing platform may make sense to economize in terms of transaction costs. In particular, in the presence of medium-to-high frequency, uncertainty, and specificity, the transaction cost efficiency of integrated platforms over P2P platforms emerges clearly. This is because the transaction parties express a preference for the activation of mechanisms of integration of their transactions, aimed at ensuring appropriate safeguards for the assets, effective measurements of the parties' performances, and higher adaptability to unforeseen contingencies. This is in sharp contrast to the case where frequency, uncertainty, and specificity are relatively low and where P2P platforms may work well and guarantee higher effectiveness.

In sum, the shift from P2P toward greater or full platform integration is ultimately a strategic choice that is intimately related to the three dimensions of transactions derived from TCT: transaction frequency, transaction uncertainty, and asset specificity. This involves a determination by the platform owner to progressively introduce and balance different mechanisms of integration aimed at safeguarding assets, increasing transaction adaptability, and improving performance measurement.

THE STRATEGIC GOVERNANCE OF TRANSACTIONS ON SHARING PLATFORMS

While the salience of TCT to the integration of sharing platforms has been established above by focusing on the levels of transaction frequency, uncertainty, and asset specificity, a fundamental research challenge remains to be overcome: Can frequency, uncertainty, and asset specificity be purposely leveraged and calibrated in the context of sharing platforms to not only economize on transaction costs but also to create the basis for the development of sources of competitive advantage over other platforms and/or traditional firms?

From a strict TCT perspective, the selection of the governance mechanisms of transactions is *ex-post*: based on the transaction features (which represent an *ex-ante* condition), the more efficient platform is the one that economizes on transaction costs by offering adequate levels of safeguarding, adaptation, and measurement. However, platforms are also business models that are established and managed from the perspective of the platform owner. This implies that transaction features can also be considered as endogenous variables: they are not fixed and thus may be manipulated. The strategic rationale is straightforward. First, developing a higher frequency of transactions is the obvious avenue of platform establishment and growth. As with all business entities, platforms aim to grow and generate higher revenues while better spreading fixed costs of establishing and managing its infrastructure. In many cases, platform owners are trapped in market positions characterized by low frequency (low volumes), low uncertainty (platforms established in local and/or homogeneous communities), and low specificity (assets and services exchanged are of standard quality, without specific customization or adaptation to the buyer's needs). These platforms often lack the strategic intent and vision to grow in size and are operated in a manner that is similar to a neighborhood market, where everybody knows each other (low uncertainty), sales volumes are low (low frequency) and the same products are sold every day throughout the year (low specificity). The increase in frequency is a strategic goal for these platforms, which can only be achieved through direct and active intervention of the platform owner, such as via the acquisition of other platforms and/or the attraction of more platform users. Along the same lines, as frequency increases, the platform owner may accept an increase in transaction uncertainty (the new, marginal transactions will likely occur between little known parties). The platform owner may also find useful to manipulate asset specificity by launching new services and customizing existing ones aiming to better segment and target platform users.

Our chapter turns to exploring these strategic issues. We address the transaction features one by one, with the aim of further understanding their nature and deriving available options for their strategic governance by platform owners. In doing so, we draw on the broad TCT literature—over nine hundred empirical TCT articles have been published in the academic literature (Macher & Richman, 2008) to date. TCT's central tenet that governance choice is largely determined by the cost of transacting and that these costs are influenced by observable characteristics of the underlying transactions has received overwhelming support from extant literature. Empirical studies on TCT have also confirmed that transaction-level factors have an important influence not only on contracting and governance choice, but also on organizational performance and survival. Thus, we concur with Williamson (2000) that TCT "is an empirical success story" (p. 607). Yet, despite such success, considerable work remains to be done to more precisely test for the effects of key transaction cost variables (Macher & Richman, 2008) for the purposes of practically observing them and to aid managers in defining possible avenues for the strategic governance of transactions.

Managing Transaction Frequency

Despite its theoretical importance within TCT (Williamson, 1979), the role of frequency has rarely been studied empirically (Rindfleisch & Heide, 1997). Williamson notes that higher levels of transaction frequency provide an incentive for integration because "the costs of specialized governance structures will be easier to recover for large transactions of a recurring kind" (1985, p. 60). More precisely, the higher the frequency, the higher the incentive for the transaction parties to make the specific investments required and the higher the incentive for the platform owner to develop specific governance mechanisms aimed at reducing uncertainty and safeguarding assets. In their empirical work, Anderson and Schmittlein (1984) confirm this general prediction: "A specialized governance mechanism involves significant setup and maintenance costs. For rarely occurring transactions, losses from opportunism and inflexibility are likely to be lower than the integrated firm's incremental overhead. As a transaction recurs more frequently, however, integration becomes more desirable since potential losses from not integrating outweigh the overhead costs of integration" (p. 388). Despite the proposed advantage of internal organization in realizing scale economies related to transaction frequency, researchers have been largely unsuccessful in confirming this assertion. Several empirical studies show no positive association between transaction frequency and organizational mode (Anderson, 1985; Anderson & Schmittlein, 1984; Maltz 1993, 1994), while other studies dichotomize transaction frequency into one-time versus recurring exchanges and do find a significant relationship (John & Weitz, 1988; Klein et al., 1990).

In our chapter, we are interested in the application of the transaction frequency construct to the context of the governance of a sharing platform. Here, transaction frequency assumes a peculiar nature, because two distinct dimensions of frequency assume relevance: the repetition effect and the volume effect (Akbar & Tracogna, 2018). The repetition effect occurs at the single-transaction level and depends on the fact that an access-based sharing transaction (which implies the sharing of the same asset e.g., a bicycle, a car, or a room) may be repeated by the same vendor several times, both with the same buyers and with different buyers. Thus, as compared with one-off market transactions, such as those that imply the transfer of ownership, the repetition of access-based transactions increases transaction frequency. The volume effect is, in turn, to be considered from the perspective of the entire platform and is the outcome of two factors: the repetition of single transactions and the increase in the number of platform members (i.e., the number of buyers and sellers that actually meet on the platform or, seen from a sharing platform perspective, the number of assets that are actually shared through the platform). The volume effect has been extensively analyzed outside TCT, by scholars of platform economics (see the above section of this chapter), originating in research on network effects, a self-reinforcing dynamic (Arthur, 1989; Schilling, 2009). Among such network effects, increasing transactional frequency supports stronger reputation effects (Williamson, 2001).

The implications of the above for the strategic governance of platforms are straightforward. With regard to the transaction volume, given the fact that all transactions are conducted digitally, marginal transactions can often be executed at close to zero marginal cost. To exploit scale advantages, increases in the volume of transactions (and in the number of platform users) can be achieved both organically and via external lines, such as acquisitions and alliances. With regard to the repetition effect, it is obvious that there are strategic advantages for the asset owner if the assets are utilized extensively. This helps explain why platform members specialize in their role in an increasing number of cases and tend to become 'professional' users (for example, Uber drivers or Airbnb tenants), rather than remain 'peers among peers'. Consequently, growing platforms tend to generate a higher separation between supply and demand and progressively lose their P2P nature. As we will see in the next section, platform owners may facilitate this transformation by providing safeguards on the shared assets and/or increasing the use of mechanisms for the smooth administration of transactions and management of uncertainty.

Managing Transaction Uncertainty

Transaction uncertainty has been studied from multiple perspectives. For example, Anderson and Schmittlein (1984) distinguish between environmental unpredictability (which they measure in terms of transaction volume uncertainty, that is, with the expected deviation between forecast and actual sales) and behavioral uncertainty (i.e., the difficulty of evaluating performance, which they measure as the perceived difficulty of measuring the individual efforts equitably). Environmental uncertainty generally refers to "unanticipated changes in circumstances surrounding an exchange" (Noordewier et al., 1990, p. 82) and is typically related to future changes in the environment (Anderson, 1985). It generates unpredictability and the consequent need for adaptation. Behavioral uncertainty refers to the requirement, for the parties, to assess (measure) *ex-ante* the identity of the counterparts and to properly measure *ex-post* the performance of the parties. Operational measures of environmental uncertainty that have been employed in TCT empirical analyses are broad and include demand uncertainty (Heide & John, 1990), technological uncertainty (Walker & Weber, 1984; Balakrishnan & Wernerfelt, 1986), and supplier uncertainty (Walker & Weber, 1987). Behavioral uncertainty has seen far less operationalization: its measurement is often aimed at measuring and evaluating partner performance (Anderson, 1985; Heide & John, 1990; Stump & Heide, 1996).

Where opportunism and bounded rationality occurs, both environmental and behavioral uncertainty may be high due to asymmetric information, adverse selection, and moral hazard. This is particularly true when a platform rapidly grows in size, both organically or through mergers and acquisitions, as the "marginal" transactions may have very high levels of uncertainty. In other words, increases in a platform's transaction volumes may be achieved at the expense of transaction uncertainty. This may impede (or slow-down) the further growth of the platform and the generation of network effects described in previous sections. In such instances, direct and active intervention by the platform owner is required. Given that transaction uncertainty on sharing platforms has these two distinct components (environmental and behavioral), platform owners may develop specific tactics and processes to deal with each one individually. For example, with reference to environmental uncertainty, platform owners may exploit asset usage data. Systematic comparisons of planned (*ex-ante*) usage against actual (*real-time*) usage by platform owners allow them to select which types of assets are made available for sharing. For example, if a shared mobility platform notices a real-time spike in demand for electric vehicles or a shared accommodation platform observes a particular growth in demand for a specific location, it adjusts its 'inventory' available for sharing. With regard to behavioral uncertainty, in the context of sharing platforms, it mostly relates to the behavior of the user who pays for the shared asset ('the buyer'). Platform firms may assess 'buyer' behavior in both *ex-ante* and *ex-post* ways. Due diligence processes of the 'buyer' (production of valid ID, verified payment mechanisms, etc.) are an *ex-ante* tactic for reducing transaction uncertainty. The use of peer-ratings schemes *ex-post* serve as a means of managing behavioral uncertainty after the single transaction and to gauge the behavior of the 'buyers' over a sustained period of time if they are a repeat user. In the case of P2P platforms, behavioral uncertainty presents an additional complication for platform owners in that not only buyers of assets need to be assessed but also suppliers of shared assets need to be verified. In this case, platform owners extend the due diligence process (*ex-ante*) to suppliers of shared assets as well.

Managing Asset-Specificity

A key aspect of asset specificity is the degree of transaction-specific (nonmarketable) expenses incurred by the parties. As noted by Williamson, "items that are unspecialized among users pose few hazards, since buyers in these circumstances can easily turn to alternative sources, and suppliers can sell output intended for one order to other buyers without difficulty. Non-marketability problems arise when the specific identity of the parties has important cost-bearing consequences. Transactions of this kind are 'idiosyncratic' (Williamson, 1979, pp. 239–240). As reported by Macher and Richman (2008), measures of asset specificity in empirical TCT research are broad, often subjective (Minkler & Park, 1994), and include physical proximity (i.e., site specificity) between contracting parties (Joskow, 1985, 1987, 1990), idiosyncratic investments (Palay, 1984), product complexity (Masten, 1984), inter-firm co-specialization (Dyer, 1996), and spatial or temporal proximity (Masten et al., 1991; Pirrong, 1993). Barthelemy and Quelin (2006) suggest that perceived switching costs can be considered as a good measure of asset specificity (non-marketability).

Within the perspective of the sharing economy, asset specificity refers to the non-marketability of the assets (products or services) that are accessed through a transaction (e.g., rooms or apartments in the case of Airbnb; car use in the case of Blablacar or Uber). Asset specificity can be measured in terms of the losses incurred by the owner of the asset should he/she have to transfer the asset to another platform and/or to a different usage. As such, a higher degree of asset specificity may be considered mostly for its negative consequences. However, it must also be considered that a higher specificity of the shared assets can have positive consequences for the increase in frequency of their usage and the overall success of the platform. For example, higher specificity can support more granular segmentation of target markets and improve market positioning of a sharing platform. For example, Airbnb is targeting affluent customers and business people with its "Plus" service, which requires hosts to provide 'specific' investments in the shared property (such as furniture, amenities, and concierge services). In the same vein, the growth of the supply side of a sharing platform implies that it is increasingly represented by 'professional' members, who are sharing assets that they do not use by themselves and that are dedicated to the platform. Thus, the consequent increase in asset specificity can be strategically favored by the platform owner rather than merely representing an *ex-ante* condition. In sum, analogous to the strategic positioning model (Porter, 1980), platform owners may decide whether to stake out a niche position focusing on specific shared assets or to compete as a general-purpose shared asset provider. An example of the former is a shared accommodation provider that also offers luxury villas for sharing in order to differentiate itself from its broader competitors. An example of the latter is a car-sharing service that offers vehicles for sharing that can be used by many different types of drivers, thereby leveraging scale economies in asset sharing and limiting the switching costs entailed by asset specificity.

The Governance of Transactions: Strategic Platform Integration

In preceding sections, we described and discussed the possible options available to the platform owner for the management of transaction features. The definition of the appropriate level of frequency, uncertainty, and specificity is considered a strategic decision, which ultimately reflects the preference by the owner to grow the platform by developing either cost-based or a differentiation-based sources of competitive advantage. In turn, the management of transaction features generates transaction costs and determines the need, by the platform members and by the platform owner, to adopt specific mechanisms of platform integration. The balance of mechanisms adopted by the platform to manage transaction costs is here called *transaction governance*, while the process to achieve this balance is here called *strategic platform integration.*

Transaction governance is a multidimensional phenomenon, which can be usefully described as comprising specific clusters of features, particularly within hybrid forms such as sharing platforms. However, there is "little consensus as to the dimensions that characterize the construct" (Heide & John, 1990, pp. 24-25). Building on TCT, we now direct our attention to the specific mechanisms that characterize this construct in sharing platforms. TCT does not help us to directly identify specific dimensions of governance. To approach the matter, we observe that governance structures economize on transaction costs by addressing three main transaction issues:

1. Measurement of the actual identity and performances of the involved parties.
2. Adaptation of the transaction to the changing circumstances.
3. Safeguarding of the assets invested by the parties in the transaction.

Accordingly, we have identified a set of mechanisms that can be introduced for the progressive integration of the sharing platform. The first group of integration mechanisms pertain to the *measurement* issue, that is, to the control of uncertainty. Here, platform owners can focus on the pre-selection or pre-screening of assets or products to be accessed through the platform, that is, the owner of the platform may decide to limit platform access only to a specific set of goods or services that meet a predefined standard of quality; further, the platform can promote the collection and sharing of information among users to encourage platform participation (such as rating the services provided) and promote the exchange of feedback on the members' ratings (both sellers and buyers) to build reputations and attract additional members onto the platform. Indeed, as the platform grows in size, so does the average level of uncertainty of transactions (marginal transactions may take place between unknown parties): thus, the increased use of the sharing platform is related to the building of trust mechanisms into the platform. Platform owners enhance trust by developing systematic and reliable review functions on the platform, which emphasize the role of normative pressures and trust-building mechanisms. In this context, inter-organizational trust and relational exchange can function as additional governance mechanisms that, in platforms, can replace hierarchical devices and reflect the extent to which negotiations are fair and commitments are upheld (Anderson & Narus, 1990).

A second group of integration mechanisms pertains to the *adaptation* issue, as with measurement mechanisms, associated with the control of uncertainty. These mechanisms mostly refer to the administrative role of the platform, as a third party between the sellers and buyers. In particular, in their capacity as "regulators" of the marketplace, sharing platforms can establish and administer contracts between users, manage payments, define the terms of service, and manage rules and standards (regarding safety, health, and quality). Further, platform owners may develop active arbitration mechanisms to facilitate dispute resolution in platform transactions.

A third group of mechanisms refer to the issue of *safeguarding*, that is, the control of asset specificity. Here, also based on the evolution of emerging regulatory climates, sharing platform owners are increasingly obliged to provide insurance and warranties to protect the assets or products accessed through their platform. Another dimension of platform integration refers to the degree of internalization of transactions by the platform itself, in response to the preference expressed by users/providers to directly transact with the platform owner for access to the desired assets/services. In the extreme, platform owners select their own inventory of assets and make them available for sharing. Further, they can integrate the supply side with the provision of complementary products or services (Hagiu & Altmann, 2017).

Table 1 below summarizes the abovementioned mechanisms.

The adoption of the above mechanisms is not without cost. Strategic platform integration may be expensive for platforms lacking sufficient users or volume of transactions. In other words, the sustainability of a platform strategy may rely on conditions of high frequency, which in turn depend on the repetition and overall volume of transactions taking place on the platform.

Table 1. Platform integration mechanisms

Measurement Mechanisms
Pre-selection of goods/services to be exchanged on the platform
Collection and exchange of information on products and platform members
Development of trust and reputation-building of platform members
Adaptation Mechanisms (Third-Party Administrative Support)
Rules-setting, definition of the terms of service, safety, and quality
Administration of transactions and contracts
Price definition and management of payments
Safeguarding Mechanisms
Asset protection and provision of warranties and insurance coverage
Supply of complementary products
Direct supply/demand of products

(Source: authors' own)

STRATEGIC GOVERNANCE OF TRANSACTIONS AND PLATFORM INTEGRATION: A GALLERY OF CASES

This section provides an empirical exploration of strategic platform integration processes. We examine three sharing platforms operating in different sectors: Airbnb (accommodation services), Lyft (car mobility) and TaskRabbit (professional services). Airbnb is characterized by impressive growth and the progressive adoption of integration mechanisms and by the recent launch of new sharing categories, such as Airbnb Plus. In 2017, the platform generated a positive net profit for the first time. Lyft is following a similar growth path; however, its strategic evolution reflects the persistent need to catch-up with the market leader, Uber. Further, the platform is not yet viable and is still suffering significant losses. Lastly, TaskRabbit is a sharing platform that has not, thus far, been able to grow to a significant size and this may be considered the main reason that it has been sold to Ikea and is being integrated in the retailer's business model.

Airbnb

Of all sharing platforms, Airbnb stands alongside Uber in public consciousness as being an iconic representation of the emergence of the sharing platform economy. In 2017, Airbnb generated 2.6 billion USD in revenue (rising by one billion USD from the previous year), with a profit of 93 million USD (Bort, 2018). Table 2 below provides a brief timeline of Airbnb's corporate and business development.

The impressive growth of the platform has followed two parallel drivers: organic growth and acquisitions. Airbnb's acquisitions were primarily aimed at consolidating its size and increasing its transaction volumes as well as at broadening its portfolio of assets/services (Crunchbase, 2018). To mention a few of its most significant acquisitions, in May 2011 Airbnb acquired a German competitor, Accoleo, and the following year Airbnb acquired London-based rival CrashPadder. To enhance its integration of destination services, the platform has acquired assets in numerous areas. For example, it acquired NabeWise in November 2012, a city guide that aggregates curated information for specific locations

Table 2. Corporate and business development of Airbnb (Source: Airbnb)

2008	Airbnb is founded
Feb. 2011	1 million nights booked
Jan. 2012	Five million nights booked
June 2012	Ten million nights booked
H2 2016	Airbnb first becomes profitable
End of 2017	150 million guests and over 300 million nights booked since platform establishment Over 5 million lodging listings in 81,000 cities and 191 countries. 4 million listings worldwide 1.9 million instant book listings (allows hosts to offer their homes to be booked immediately, without prior approval of a specific guest)

(source: Airbnb corporate website)

where Airbnb has listings. In December 2012, Airbnb acquired Localmind, a location-based question and answer platform that allows users to post questions about specific locations online. More recently, in 2017, Airbnb invested 13 million USD in restaurant reservation-booking app, Resy. Further, Airbnb acquired Luxury Retreats International, a Canadian-based villa rental company, for approximately 300 million USD in a combination of cash and stock. In addition, Airbnb also acquired Tilt, a social payment startup that enables users to split payments with up to 16 other travelers. On November 16, 2017, Airbnb acquired Accomable, a startup focused on travel accessibility.

The platform's organic growth and its many acquisitions have generated a significant increase in the transaction volume. Simultaneously, the provision of complementary services and the integration of additional inventories of assets directly owned by Airbnb has generated an increase in the average level of asset specificity, which has, in turn, positively impacted the platform size. Alongside the changes in platform size, Airbnb has also adopted a progressively higher level of strategic platform integration by providing safeguarding, adaptation, and measurement mechanisms.

Measurement Mechanisms

Airbnb requires each member to complete a profile and upload photos so that members can learn about their hosts and guests ahead of time. In particular, before booking, users must provide a valid name, email address, telephone number, photo, and payment information. Any Airbnb host can require their prospective guests to scan a government-issued ID to verify their identity. Platform users can search for lodging using a variety of filters including lodging type, dates, location, and price. Guests and hosts use Airbnb to confirm travel dates, expectations, and cost. Further, an Airbnb account can be linked to accounts on social networking services such as Facebook, thereby providing the host with data on common friends and interests. Airbnb builds trust mechanisms on the platform to enable hosts and guests to learn about each other based on past reviews, connections on Facebook, and personal communication through Airbnb. In the same vein, upon completion of the stay, the host and guest are able to post testimonials for each other as well as provide publicly available reviews of their stay. Without identity assurances, no reviews can be attached to the member nor the member to any review.

Adaptation Mechanisms (Third-Party Administrative Support)

The platform provides a logged private messaging system as a channel for users to message one another privately, before booking and accepting reservations. Pricing is determined by the host, with recommendations from Airbnb. All financial transactions are facilitated though a secure payments system managed by the platform. Airbnb holds the payment in escrow for 24 hours after the reservation begins. Hosts retain 87% of booking fees, and guests pay a 6–12% fee to Airbnb. For destination services, such as walking tours, the company takes a 20% commission from the host. Regulatory requirements have increased over time—particularly on the fiscal aspects of income generation for hosts. For this reason, in the United States, Airbnb issues tax forms to hosts that have earned over 20,000 USD in rental income and/or received over 200 reservations via Airbnb in a calendar year.

Safeguarding Mechanisms

Beyond the direct provision of complementary services and the direct acquisition of accommodation capacity, Airbnb encourages hosts to purchase insurance that covers property damage due to vandalism and theft caused by guests during their stay. Airbnb called this its "host guarantee". First launched in August 2011, the program originally covered up to 50,000 USD but subsequently the maximum coverage has been increased to 1 million USD (Source: Airbnb).

Lyft

Initially founded as Zimride in 2012, the company quickly changed its name to become Lyft in 2013. The company operates in approximately 300 US cities and towns and provides over a million rides per day. In December 2017, Lyft expanded into Canada. As a privately held enterprise, Lyft does not publish detailed financial statements. According to Bloomberg, while increasing its revenue by 250% for 2016, Lyft lost 600 million USD in the same year (Newcomer, 2017). With 1 billion USD in cash reserves, Lyft is expected to have achieved profitability by the end of 2018. In early 2016, Lyft formed a strategic alliance with US automaker General Motors, which provided half a billion USD. The partnership is intended to aid both companies to develop market positions in the ride-sharing market, as well as anticipating the arrival of the autonomous car sector. A year later, Lyft announced that Alphabet Inc. (the Google holding company) acquired a 1 billion USD stake in the company via its investment arm CapitalG. The company received an 11.5 billion USD valuation as of December 2017, raising over 4 billion USD from the capital markets.

Table 3 below outlines the explosive organic growth of Lyft since its establishment.

As in the case of Airbnb, Lyft's growth has been aimed at generating economies of scale for the platform and has been characterized by a progressive increase in transaction frequency. Simultaneously, there has been a progressive increase in the degree of asset specificity, by providing additional and complementary services to the platform's actual and prospective users with the intent of better segmenting and serving the market. In particular, Lyft currently offers several types of rides. The first is the basic and most popular Lyft offering that matches passengers with nearby drivers. The second is Lyft Line, currently available in a limited number of cities, that is a low-priced option that matches passengers with other riders travelling in the same direction. The third is Lyft Plus; it matches passengers with larger six-seater vehicles. The fourth is Lyft Premier and Lyft Lux, which match passengers with

Table 3. Business growth at Lyft

2013	2.7 Million Rides
2014	18.1 Million Rides
2015	53 Million Rides
2016	160 Million Rides
2017	375.5 Million Rides

(Source: Carson, 2017)

premium rides with enhanced, more comfortable vehicles and drivers with high ratings. Fifth, in March 2018, Lyft formed an alliance with electronic health records company Allscripts to develop a service that permits healthcare providers to provide rides for patients who do not have a means of transportation to go to their appointments. This service encompasses 2,500 hospitals, 180,000 physicians, and approximately 7 million patients.

Measurement Mechanisms

Lyft has consciously sought to integrate numerous integration mechanisms to enhance the user experience of the platform. To use Lyft, riders download a mobile app and register themselves by providing a valid phone number and a valid form of payment (either a credit card or link to an Apple Pay, Google Wallet, or PayPal account). Optionally, drivers and passengers can add personal information to their profiles, including their hometown, music preferences, and other details to encourage drivers and passengers to converse during the ride. The platform also operates on trust-building mechanisms through extensive screening of drivers. Drivers must be aged 21 or over and have had a driver's license for over one year. Further, they are required to undertake in-person interviews with the company before being allowed to join the platform. They also undergo rigorous background checks focusing on criminal and sex offender records available from law enforcement authorities. When passengers request a ride from a nearby driver and the ride is confirmed, the app reveals the driver's name, his/her ratings from past passengers, and photos of the driver and car. After a ride is completed, drivers and passengers are encouraged to rate each other on a scale of one to five stars. Lyft drivers must maintain a minimum rating or face being dropped from the service. Ratings below 4 or 5 mean that the passenger was not up to par, and Lyft undertakes a process to understand why. Rating 3 or lower means the driver will not be matched with the same passenger again. Unlike Uber, Lyft does not allow passengers to know their rating.

Adaptation Mechanisms (Third-Party Administrative Support)

Upon ride completion, Lyft debits the funding source in the rider's profile. Riders are encouraged to offer a gratuity to the driver, which is billed to the rider's payment method. Lyft retains 20% commission from drivers who joined before January 2016 and 25% percent commission from those who joined after January 2016.

Table 4. TaskRabbit: Corporate history

2008	Founded as RunMyErrand
2009	The firm accumulates 1.8 million USD in seed funding from venture capital firms
2010	Changes its name to TaskRabbit
May 2011	Closes a 5 million USD Series A financing round from Shasta Ventures, First Round Capital, Baseline Ventures, Floodgate Fund, Collaborative Fund, 500 Startups, and The Mesh author Lisa Gansky
December 2011	Raises an additional 17.8 million USD in a Series B round of funding
March 2013	"TaskRabbit Business" is introduced, which allows businesses to hire temporary workers
November 2013	Launches in London
2014	TaskRabbit receives 4,000 applications to be a Tasker.
2015	The number of Taskers grows to 15,000
September 2017	IKEA Group announces its acquisition of TaskRabbit
March 2018	IKEA launches a furniture assembly service from TaskRabbit

(source: Taskrabbit corporate website)

Safeguarding Mechanisms

While Lyft drivers are legally acting as independent contractors, Lyft insures each driver with a one million USD commercial liability policy that is primary to a driver's personal policy. Additional coverage provisions include contingent comprehensive and collision coverage, liability coverage, and uninsured/underinsured motorist coverage.

TaskRabbit

Founded in 2008, TaskRabbit matches freelance labor (which we can consider a peculiar type of asset-sharing, where the skills offered by workers are the 'assets' to be shared) with local demand in the US and in the UK. The platform offers individual and business clients a range of domestic and professional services that range from handyman to cleaning, delivery, moving, furniture assembly, and personal assistance. The company has tens of thousands of vetted, background-checked "taskers" available to help consumers across a wide variety of categories. Below, we provide the most significant information regarding its historical evolution to date.

As an attempt to differentiate its offerings, the platform has established TaskRabbit Elite, a pool of high-rated taskers who consistently provide the highest level of service and professionalism. This is a move towards higher "asset" specificity, which—as in the case of Airbnb and Lyft—helped support market segmentation and a more precise market targeting. Despite the platform's initial success and the significant increase in transaction frequency, also owing to the launch of different specific services, the platform has not yet achieved the requisite size to become firmly established in the market. We do not have evidence of any acquisition made by the platform during its history. In 2017, it was sold to Ikea.

Measurement Mechanisms

TaskRabbit has sought to integrate numerous integration mechanisms to enhance the user experience of the platform. Both Customers and Taskers are registered online on the platform. Before Taskers can join the community, they undergo an extensive vetting process. Each one must pass an identity check and is screened for criminal offenses. In addition, all registrants must attend an info session via TaskRabbit's online session or with a representative from TaskRabbit Headquarters before they can begin tasking. They can then download the Tasker app and begin getting jobs on the platform. Constructive user-generated feedback instills trust and improves the quality of the platform. Both Taskers and Customers are encouraged to leave honest and constructive feedback. If either a Customer or a Tasker provides a negative review (thumbs down or 3 stars or below), they will not be paired for tasks again. The TaskRabbit Policies Team reserves the right to remove reviews if they violate the platform's Terms of Service.

Adaptation Mechanisms (Third-Party Administrative Support)

Customers select from a list of popular chores and submit their requests. This enables the platform to instantly find ready-to-help Taskers in the area, which customers can book for same-day jobs for a set hourly rate or contact through an appointment. If plans change, customers can reschedule or cancel any task with a notice of at least 24 hours. Customers manage their booking directly in the app, chat with the Tasker, obtain accurate arrival times, and pay electronically when the task is complete. The TaskRabbit platform notifies Taskers of potential jobs nearby. Taskers select the ones they wish to complete and confirm details with their clients. Once the work is completed, Taskers submit the invoice on the platform. Customers pay directly in the app with their credit or debit cards when the task is completed. The platform's Customer Support team is available 24/7 for any damages, injuries, or invoice disputes.

Safeguarding Mechanisms

The safeguarding of the user's assets (property damage and theft and/or bodily injuries) is a key priority for TaskRabbit. If users fail to resolve an issue between themselves, TaskRabbit offers an insurance coverage in its discretion on a case-by-case basis:

- Up to 1 million USD per occurrence for property damage arising as a direct result of negligence of a Tasker during performance of a task through the TaskRabbit platform.
- Up to 10,000 USD per occurrence for bodily injury sustained by a user who did not cause the injury, as a direct result of negligence by another user during the performance of a task through the TaskRabbit platform.
- Up to 10,000 USD per occurrence for theft of a user's property by a Tasker during performance of a task through the TaskRabbit platform.

DISCUSSION: LESSONS FROM THE CASES

The three cases studied in this chapter highlight systematic attempts by sharing platform owners to strategically manage transaction features and undertake strategic platform integration to achieve the related goals of fostering growth as well as developing sources of competitive advantage. The identification of a series of common traits in the evolution of these platforms have enabled us to formulate a typical pattern. It is evident that by developing a rigorous due diligence process of platform users, all three platforms (Airbnb, Lyft, and Task Rabbit) have managed to overcome transaction uncertainty while enhancing platform reputation (a source of competitive advantage). Moreover, through targeted acquisition and by offering multiple sharing products or services, all three platforms were able to increase transaction volume (although only up to a certain point in the case of TaskRabbit) by bringing in multiple users across different segments. For example, the introduction of Airbnb Plus, Lyft Lux, or TaskRabbit expanding its range of curated services helped attract more users and achieve platform growth. By introducing insurance coverage of assets, all three platforms reduced transaction uncertainty. Further, the introduction of segmentation in services and products has increased asset specificity and served as a source of differentiated advantage. Lyft offering six-seater vehicles, Airbnb making luxury holiday villas available for rent, and Task Rabbit providing highly specialized freelancers all enable the platform owners to respond to the demand for variety among users and enhance growth opportunities for the platform. All these aspects taken together create a virtuous circle of growth for platform owners. First, more users are attracted to the platform via acquisitions and/or the provision of more services/assets. Increased participation on the platform spreads fixed costs of platform operation across more transactions (transaction volume increase) and generates valuable user data to better understand user demands and practices. Second, the increased uncertainty that may be generated by the addition to the platform of the "marginal" transactions (transactions among new and relatively unknown users) is managed by further investments by the platform owner, aimed at increasing trust and reputation and thus enabling an effective control of uncertainty. Third, the progressive collection of user data enables sharing platforms to better segment clients and effectively target users through differentiated products and services (enhanced asset specificity). Figure 1 below illustrates this.

All three case studies revealed a significant degree of active strategic governance of the transaction features by the platform owner, which was aimed at increasing the transaction volume in parallel with an increase in specificity, with the ultimate goal of expanding platform size and consolidating sources of competitive advantage. Further, we observed significant degrees of strategic platform integration, that is, the progressive adoption of integration mechanisms aimed at minimizing transaction costs by offering increasing levels of asset-safeguarding, transaction adaptability, and performance measurement.

CONCLUDING REFLECTIONS

With a view to furthering research on sharing platforms, we provided a concise review of the theoretical issues that relate TCT with sharing platforms. We focused on three TCT variables—transaction frequency, transaction uncertainty, and asset specificity—and analyzed their consequences in terms of transaction governance. We also explored how the above variables can be strategically manipulated by the platform owner and how these could define the adequate degree of strategic platform integration through the adoption of safeguarding, adaptation, and performance measurement mechanisms.

This has enabled us to focus on how platform owners can develop strategies and tactics for building sources of competitive advantage and achieving growth through platform integration, *inter alia* manipulation of transaction costs. First, by building integration mechanisms that enhance trust and reputation, platform owners are reducing transaction uncertainty. Second, by attracting more users to the platform

Figure 1. Platform integration and the virtuous growth cycle
(Source: authors' own)

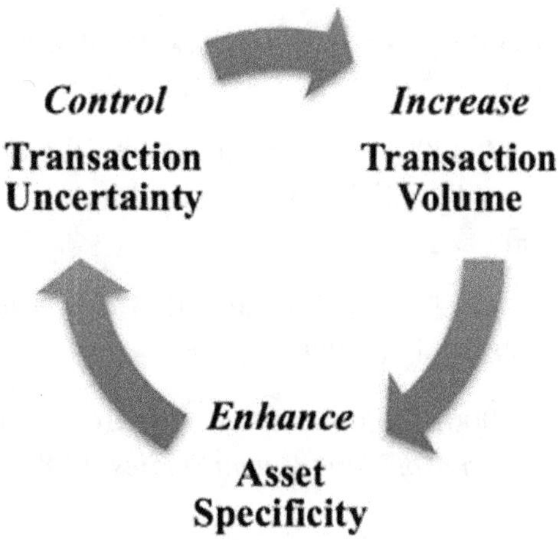

through enhanced trust and product variety, platform owners can spread the costs of operation across a larger number of transactions to lower unit costs and, in the process, collect valuable data regarding users. Third, through astute use of user data and understanding of user practices, platform owners can more effectively segment products and services to provide a source of differentiated advantage for the platform and, in turn, attract more users by enhancing shared asset specificity.

As an increasingly important business phenomenon, sharing platforms appear to have far-reaching consequences for markets, businesses and customers. Sharing platforms appear to combine the benefits of both markets and hierarchies and are simultaneously governed by social and economic motivations (Benkler, 2007; Cook, 2008; Raymond, 1999). If, as in the words of Benkler (2007), these new forms of exchange represent "the dark matter of our economic production universe" (p. 117), TCT's ability to shed light on this darkness represents a critical factor in determining the evolution of sharing platforms (Rindfleish et al., 2010). The role of TCT in explaining this evolution offers great potential for fruitful empirical research.

REFERENCES

Akbar, Y. H., & Tracogna, A. (2018). The sharing economy and the future of the hotel industry: Transaction cost theory and platform economics. *International Journal of Hospitality Management*, *71*, 91–101. doi:10.1016/j.ijhm.2017.12.004

Anderson, E. (1985). The salesperson as outside agent or employee: A transaction cost analysis. *Marketing Science*, *4*(3), 234–254. doi:10.1287/mksc.4.3.234

Anderson, E., & Schmittlein, D. (1984). Integration of the sales force: An empirical examination. *The Rand Journal of Economics*, *15*(3), 385–395. doi:10.2307/2555446

Anderson, J. C., & Narus, J. A. (1990). A model of distributor firm and manufacturing firm working partnerships. *Journal of Marketing*, *54*(1), 42–58. doi:10.1177/002224299005400103

Arthur, W. B. (1989). Competing technologies, increasing returns, and lock-in by historical events. *Economic Journal (London), 89*(394), 116–131. doi:10.2307/2234208

Balakrishnan, S., & Wernerfelt, B. (1986). Technical change, competition and vertical integration. *Strategic Management Journal, 7*(4), 347–359. doi:10.1002mj.4250070405

Baldwin, C. Y., & Woodard, C. J. (2009). The architecture of platforms: A unified view. In A. Gawer (Ed.), *Platforms* (pp. 19–44). Cheltenham, UK: Markets and Innovation, Edgar Elgar. doi:10.4337/9781849803311.00008

Bardhi, F., & Eckhardt, G. (2012). Access-based consumption: The case of car-sharing. *The Journal of Consumer Research, 39*(4), 881–898. doi:10.1086/666376

Barthélemy, J., & Quélin, B. V. (2006). Complexity of outsourcing contracts and ex post transaction costs: An empirical investigation. *Journal of Management Studies, 43*(8), 1775–1797. doi:10.1111/j.1467-6486.2006.00658.x

Belk, R. (2010). Sharing. *The Journal of Consumer Research, 36*(5), 715–734. doi:10.1086/612649

Benkler, Y. (2004). Sharing nicely. On shareable goods and the emergence of sharing as a modality of economic production. *The Yale Law Journal, 114*(2), 273–358. doi:10.2307/4135731

Benkler, Y. (2007). *The Wealth of Networks: How Social Production Transforms Markets and Freedom*. New Haven, CT: Yale University Press.

Bort, J. (2018). Airbnb made $93 million in profit on $2.6 billion in revenue, but an internal clash sent the CFO out the door. *Business Insider*. Accessed on July 30, 2018 at http://www.businessinsider.com/airbnb-profit-revenue-2018-2?IR=T

Botsman, R., & Rogers, R. (2010). *What's Mine Is Yours: The Rise of Collaborative Consumption*. London: Harper Business.

Carson, B. (2017). *Lyft Triped its Rides in 2016*. Accessed on July 30, 2018 at http://www.businessinsider.com/lyft-tripled-its-rides-in-2016-2017-1?IR=T https://www.forbes.com/sites/bizcarson/2018/01/16/lyft-doubled-rides-in-2017/#657fd5a17d6b

Carter, R., & Hodgson, G. M. (2006). The impact of empirical tests of transaction cost economics on the debate on the nature of the firm. *Strategic Management Journal, 27*(5), 461–476. doi:10.1002mj.531

Coase, R. H. (1937). The nature of the firm. *Economica, 4*(16), 386–405. doi:10.1111/j.1468-0335.1937.tb00002.x

Constantia, I., Eaton, B., Tuunainen, V. K., & Sprague, R. H., Jr. (2016). The evolution of a sharing platform into a sustainable business. *Proceedings of the 49th Hawaii International Conference on System Sciences (HICSS 2016)*, 1297-1306.

Cook, S. (2008, October). The contribution revolution. *Harvard Business Review*, 60–69.

Crunchbase. (2018). *Airbnb Acquistions*. Accessed on July 30, 2018 at https://www.crunchbase.com/organization/airbnb/acquisitions/acquisitions_list#section-acquisitions

Davidson, N. M., & Infranca, J. J. (2015). The sharing economy as an urban phenomenon. *Yale Law & Policy Review*, *34*, 215.

Dervojeda, K., Diederik, V., Nagtegaal, F., Lengton, M., Rouwmaat, E., Monfardini, E., & Frideres, L. (2013). *The sharing economy: Accessibility based business models for peer-to-peer markets*. Price Waterhouse Coopers for Business Innovation Observatory. Accessed on July 27, 2018 at http://ec.europa.eu/enterprise/policies/innovation/policy/business-innovation observatory/files/case-studies/12-she-accessibility-based-business-models-for-peer-to-peer-markets_en.pdf

Dyer, J. H. (1996). Specialized supplier networks as a source of competitive advantage: Evidence from the auto industry. *Strategic Management Journal*, *17*(4), 271–291. doi:10.1002/(SICI)1097-0266(199604)17:4<271::AID-SMJ807>3.0.CO;2-Y

Eisenmann, T. R., Parker, G., & Van Alstyne, M. (2006). Strategies for two sided markets. *Harvard Business Review*, *10*, 92–101.

European Commission. (2016). *A European agenda for the collaborative economy*. Communication from the Commission to the European Parliament, the Council, the European Economic and Social Committee, and the Committee of the Regions.

Farrell, J., & Katz, M. L. (2000). Innovation, rent extraction, and integration in systems markets. *The Journal of Industrial Economics*, *48*(4), 413–432. doi:10.1111/1467-6451.00131

Hagiu, A. (2014). Strategic decisions for multisided platforms. *Sloan Management Review*, *55*(2), 71–80.

Hagiu, A., & Altmann, E. (2017). Finding the platform in your product. *Harvard Business Review*, *95*(4), 94–100.

Hagiu, A., & Wright, J. (2011). *Multi-sided platforms*. Harvard Business School Working Chapter, 15-037. Accessed on July 27, 2018 at http://www.hbs.edu/faculty/Publication%20Files/15- 037_cb5afe51-6150-4be9-ace2-39c6a8ace6d4.pdf

Hamari, J., Sjöklint, M., & Ukkonen, A. (2015). The sharing economy: Why people participate in collaborative consumption. *Journal of the Association for Information Science and Technology*, *67*(9), 2047–2059. doi:10.1002/asi.23552

Heide, J. B., & John, G. (1990). Alliances in industrial purchasing: The determinants of joint action in buyer-supplier relationships. *JMR, Journal of Marketing Research*, *27*(1), 24–36. doi:10.1177/002224379002700103

Iansiti, M., & Levien, R. (2004). Strategy as ecology. *Harvard Business Review*, *82*(3), 68–81. PMID:15029791

John, G., & Weitz, B. A. (1988). Forward integration into distribution: An empirical test of transaction cost analysis. *Journal of Law Economics and Organization*, *4*, 337–355.

Joskow, P. (1985). Vertical integration and long-term contracts: The case of coal-burning electric generating plants. *Journal of Law Economics and Organization*, *1*(4), 33–80.

Joskow, P. (1987). Contract duration and relation specific investments: Empirical evidence from coal markets. *The American Economic Review, 17*(3), 168–185.

Joskow, P. (1990). The performance of long-term contracts: Further evidence from coal markets. *The Rand Journal of Economics, 21*(7), 251–274. doi:10.2307/2555423

Katz, M. L., & Shapiro, C. (1986). Technology adoption in the presence of network externalities. *Journal of Political Economy, 94*(4), 822–841. doi:10.1086/261409

Klein, S., & Roth, V. J. (1990). Determinants of export channel structure: The effects of experience and psychic distance reconsidered. *International Marketing Review, 7*(5), 27–38. doi:10.1108/EUM0000000001533

Law, R., Leung, K., & Wong, R. J. (2004). The impact of the Internet on travel agencies. *International Journal of Contemporary Hospitality Management, 1*(2), 100–107. doi:10.1108/09596110410519982

Macher, J. T., & Richman, B. D. (2008). Transaction cost economics: An assessment of empirical research in the social sciences. *Business and Politics, 10*(1), 1–63. doi:10.2202/1469-3569.1210

Maltz, A. (1993). Private fleet use: A transaction cost model. *Transportation Journal, 32*(3), 46–53.

Maltz, A. (1994). Outsourcing the warehousing function. *Logistics and Transportation Review, 30*(3), 245–265.

Mason, P. (2015). *Postcapitalism: A Guide to Our Future*. London: Allen Lane.

Masten, S. E. (1984). The organization of production: Evidence from the aerospace industry. *The Journal of Law & Economics, 27*(2), 403–417. doi:10.1086/467071

Masten, S. E., Meehan, J., & Snyder, E. (1991). The costs of organization. *Journal of Law Economics and Organization, 7*(1), 1–25.

McIntyre, D. P., & Srinivasan, A. (2017). Networks, platforms, and strategy: Emerging views and next steps. *Strategic Management Journal, 38*(1), 141–160. doi:10.1002mj.2596

Minkler, A., & Park, T. (1994). Asset specificity and vertical integration in franchising. *Review of Industrial Organization, 9*(4), 409–423. doi:10.1007/BF01029514

Newcomer, E. (2017). *Lyft Loses $600 Million in 2016 as Revenue Surges*. Retrieved from https://www.bloomberg.com/news/articles/2017-01-12/lyft-loses-600-million-in-2016-as-revenue-surges

Noordewier, T. G., John, G., & Nevin, J. R. (1990). Performance outcomes of purchasing arrangement in industrial buyer-vendor relationships. *Journal of Marketing, 54*(4), 80–93. doi:10.1177/002224299005400407

Olson, M. J., & Connor, A. D. (2013). *The disruption of sharing: an overview of the new peer-to-peer 'sharing economy' and the impact on established internet companies*. Piper Jaffray Investment Research. Accessed on July 27, 2018 at https://piper2.bluematrix.com/ docs/pdf/35ef1fcc-a07b-48cf-ab80-04d80e5665c4.pdf

Owyang, J. (2014). *Sharing is the new buying*. Accessed on July 25, 2018 at http://www.web- strategist.com/blog/2014/03/03/report-sharing-is-the-new-buying-winning-in-the-collaborative-economy

Palay, T. (1984). Comparative institutional economics: The governance of rail freight contracting. *The Journal of Legal Studies*, *13*(6), 265–288. doi:10.1086/467741

Parker, G. G., & Van Alstyne, M. W. (2005). Two-sided network effects: A theory of information product design. *Management Science*, *51*(10), 1494–1504. doi:10.1287/mnsc.1050.0400

Perzanowski, A., & Schultz, J. (2015). Reconciling intellectual property and personal property. *The Notre Dame Law Review*, 90.

Pirrong, S. C. (1993). Contracting practices in bulk shipping markets: A transaction cost explanation. *The Journal of Law & Economics*, *36*(2), 937–976. doi:10.1086/467303

Porter, M. E. (1980). *Competitive Strategy: Techniques for Analyzing Industries and Competitors*. New York: Free Press.

Raymond, E. (1999). *The Cathedral and the Bazaar*. Sebastopol, CA: O'Reilly. doi:10.100712130-999-1026-0

Rifkin, J. (2014). *The Zero Marginal Cost Society: The Internet of Things, the Collaborative Commons, and the Eclipse of Capitalism*. New York: Palgrave Macmillan.

Rindfleisch, A., Antia, K., Bercovitz, J., Brown, J. R., Cannon, J., Carson, S. J., & Wathne, K. H. (2010). Transaction costs, opportunism, and governance: Contextual considerations and future research opportunities. *Marketing Letters*, *21*(3), 211–222. doi:10.100711002-010-9104-3

Rindfleisch, A., & Heide, J. B. (1997). Transaction cost analysis: Past, present and future applications. *Journal of Marketing*, *61*(4), 30–55. doi:10.1177/002224299706100403

Rochet, J., & Tirole, J. (2006). Two-sided markets: A progress report. *The Rand Journal of Economics*, *37*(2), 645–667. doi:10.1111/j.1756-2171.2006.tb00036.x

Schilling, M. A. (2009). Protecting or diffusing a technology platform: tradeoffs in appropriability, network externalities, and architectural control. In A. Gawer (Ed.), *Platforms, Markets and Innovation* (pp. 192–218). Cheltenham, UK: Edward Elgar. doi:10.4337/9781849803311.00015

Schor, J. (2016). Debating the sharing economy. *Journal of Self-Governance and Management Economics*, *4*, 3.

Shapiro, C., & Varian, H. (1999). *Information Rules: A Strategic Guide to the Network Economy*. Cambridge, MA: Harvard Business School Press.

Simon, H. A. (1990). Bounded rationality. In J. Eatwell, M. Milgate, & P. Newman (Eds.), *Utility and Probability. The New Palgrave* (pp. 15–18). London: Palgrave Macmillan. doi:10.1007/978-1-349-20568-4_5

Stump, R. L., & Heide, J. B. (1996). Controlling supplier opportunism in industrial relationships. *JMR, Journal of Marketing Research*, *33*(11), 431–441. doi:10.1177/002224379603300405

Tapscott, D., & Williams, A. D. (2008). *Wikinomics: How mass collaboration changes everything*. London: Penguin.

Tse, A. C. (2003). Disintermediation of travel agents in the hotel industry. *International Journal of Hospitality Management, 22*(4), 453–460. doi:10.1016/S0278-4319(03)00049-5

Varma, A., Jukic, N., Pestek, A., Shultz, C. J., & Nestorov, S. (2016). Airbnb: Exciting innovation or passing fad? *Tourism Management Perspectives, 20*, 228–237. doi:10.1016/j.tmp.2016.09.002

Walker, G., & Weber, D. (1984). A transaction cost approach to make-or-buy decisions. *Administrative Science Quarterly, 29*(3), 373–391. doi:10.2307/2393030

Walker, G., & Weber, D. (1987). Supplier competition, uncertainty and make-or-buy decisions. *Academy of Management Journal, 30*(3), 589–596.

Wallerstein, J., & Shelat, U. (2017). *Learning to Love (or Live with) the Sharing Economy*. BCG Henderson Institute. Accessed on June 14, 2018 at https://www.bcg.com/publications/2017/strategy-technology-digital-learning-love-live-sharing-economy.aspx

Wallsten, S. (2015). The competitive effects of the sharing economy: how is Uber changing taxis. Technology Policy Institute.

Williamson, O. E. (1971). The vertical integration of production: Market failure considerations. *The American Economic Review, 61*(2), 112–123.

Williamson, O. E. (1975). *Markets and Hierarchies*. New York: Free Press.

Williamson, O. E. (1979). Transaction-cost economics: The governance of contractual relations. *The Journal of Law & Economics, 22*(2), 233–261. doi:10.1086/466942

Williamson, O. E. (1985). *The Economic Institutions of Capitalism*. New York: Free Press.

Williamson, O. E. (1991). Comparative economic organization: The analysis of discrete structural alternatives. *Administrative Science Quarterly, 36*(2), 269–296. doi:10.2307/2393356

Williamson, O. E. (2000). The new institutional economics: Taking stock, looking ahead. *Journal of Economic Literature, 38*(3), 595–613. doi:10.1257/jel.38.3.595

Williamson, O. E. (2001). *The theory of the firm as governance structure*. University of California at Berkeley Working Chapter.

Section 3
Collaborative Consumption and Consumer Behavior

Chapter 9
What Pulls Consumers in and What Pushes Consumers Out

Christina Saksanian
https://orcid.org/0000-0003-1327-7554
Esan University, Peru

Myriam Martínez-Fiestas
University of Granada, Spain

Juan S. Timana
Esan University, Peru

ABSTRACT

The recent proliferation of collaborative models of consumption has called attention of organizations, governments, and the academy to understand the impact of these new forms of consumption on the economic scenario. However, specific efforts to understand the changes in consumer behavior are so far scarce. This chapter compiles the available knowledge on how consumers are coping with these new forms of consumption exploring the motivators and obstacles affecting their behavior. Additionally, some relevant information on the current status of the adoption of different forms of collaborative consumption, the collaborative consumer profile, as well as some perspectives for the future are also explored.

INTRODUCTION

Would you share your assets with a stranger? If your answer is yes, then you are a collaborative consumer. This recently spread out behavior reflects a new form of getting access to goods different from the well-established model of ownership. Although a formal definition is still under discussion, one can briefly describe the collaborative consumer as an individual willing to share his/her assets to some unknown person and/or is willing to get access to goods and services that belong to someone strange to his/her inner circle (Bucher, Fieseler, & Lutz, 2016).

DOI: 10.4018/978-1-5225-9928-9.ch009

Copyright © 2020, IGI Global. Copying or distributing in print or electronic forms without written permission of IGI Global is prohibited.

Even though there is no doubt this sharing mode of exchange is gaining more and more attention, the act of sharing is not a novelty as historically individuals have always shared their resources (Belk, 2010). For sure, you have shared, at least once in your lifetime, something with a friend or family member, an entirely standard form of help and support to your inner circle. So, what makes it different now? Currently, strangers are connecting in a chain of users and providers of goods and services activities well outside the frontiers of inner circles, neighborhoods or even countries (Hamari, Sjöklint, & Ukkonen, 2016) mediated by a technology agent, usually a platform (Sutherland & Jarrahi, 2018). This collaborative model of consumption is calling the attention of all, the industry, the academy, and governments as it reflects a change in behavior where individuals are moving from focusing on ownership towards focusing on experience and access to goods and services (Bucher et al., 2016).

Consumers have dramatically changed their behavior in recent years. Economic crisis, concerns with the environment together with the evolution of information and communication technologies with the advent of the internet and social networks created the perfect environment for people to connect to each other and, therefore, built solid grounds for the proliferation of sharing modes of consumption (Edbring, Lehner & Mont, 2016). Although this is a relatively new phenomenon, the impressive fast pace of growth and its global dissemination led collaborative modes of consumption to be considered an alternative economic model which impact on the individuals' life and companies businesses is still unclear (Böcker & Melen, 2017).

Several authors claim collaborative consumption is a radical game changer in the way individuals relate to each other and how the economy moves (Barnes & Mattsson, 2016; Bardhi and Eckhardt, 2012; Belk, 2010; Botsman and Rogers, 2010; Leismann et al., 2013). In the March 2011 issue of Time Magazine, sharing was said to be one of the *ten ideas that will change the world* (Walsh, 2011) as it has the potential to reduce the pressure of consumption in the environment, redefine human interactions, generate new business models and forms of livelihoods and thus, altering the entire marketplace. Therefore, understanding the drivers behind the adoption of collaborative forms of behavior is fundamental and beneficial for all sectors. The industry will be better armed to adjust their plans and course of actions, and the governments will have solid grounds to implement laws and regulations as a way to guarantee adequate protection to all parties involved. Finally, the entire community will benefit from understanding the pros and cons of engaging in a sharing activity as it might change the way individuals live and relate to each other.

Although empirical evidence in the field is still limited, in this chapter, the authors aim to *share* with the reader a comprehensive review of current knowledge regarding the drivers of the adoption of collaborative consumption as well as the key barriers preventing it. The authors reviewed the available literature on Web of Science, and official publications from 2010 through 2019. The chapter seeks to compile current knowledge regarding consumers´ behavior towards CC. Therefore the effects it might have on the economy are not discussed. It starts with a brief background for contextualization, followed by a section with key facts and figures from the consumer standpoint. Next, a review on the key drivers that lead consumers to behave collaboratively, the key barriers preventing them from joining in and the expected growth and penetration of collaborative models of consumption is presented. The chapter concludes with a discussion on implications and future avenues for research in the field.

BACKGROUND

Recent years have witnessed consumers redefine their values and priorities leading to a new way of consumption. Driven by economic, social and environmental pressures, consumers are reassessing their priorities, questioning old conspicuous consumerism behaviors and moving into more conscious, mindful consumption choices. In the search for options to make the most out of personal resources while ensuring access to needed goods, consumers found collaboration to be the answer. Collaborative behavior allows consumers to experience different forms of access to products and services, purchasing what is truly necessary and sharing, renting, reselling or borrowing what is not (Brown & Vergragt, 2016). This behavior represents a significant shift, as consumers are evolving from a previous focus on ownership towards focusing on experience and access (Bucher et al., 2016).

This phenomenon of exchange known as collaborative consumption (CC), is a fast-growing global movement that connects people interested in exchanging unused products and services (Edbring et al., 2016). Collaborative consumption encompasses sharing activities carried out through technology while the commonly interchangeably used "sharing economy" refers to sharing activities dealt directly between individuals (Botsman, 2015). For this reason, CC is characterized as a triadic exchange process involving 1) a platform provider that mediates the exchange; 2) a peer provider who grants temporary access to goods or services and; 3) a peer customer seeking access to goods or services (Benoit, Baker, Bolton, Gruber & Kandampully, 2017). These peer-to-peer (P2P) based activities are the ones that allow individuals to obtain, give or share access to goods and services that may or may not involve monetary transaction (Hamari et al., 2016). They represent a significant change in the market forces as they give to the individuals the power to dictate the way access to goods and services will be defined (Böcker & Melen, 2017).

Although most authors agree that the basic nature of sharing is an act of joined use of a good owned or quasi-owned by at least one of the parties (user/provider), there is so far no consensus on the definition of CC in the literature (Bucher et al., 2016). Belk (2007) defined CC as the "act and process of distributing what is ours to others for their use and/or the act or process of receiving or taking something from others for our use." Meelen & Frenken (2015) defined it as "consumers granting each other temporary access to their under-utilized physical assets ("idle capacity"), possibly for money." Hamari et al. (2016) further specify the definition proposing that CC is "The peer to-peer-based activity of obtaining, giving, or sharing the access to goods and services, coordinated through community-based online services." As this is a relatively new research area, there is a lack of consensus on the many terms used by different authors when refereeing to the same phenomenon. Sutherland and Jarrahi (2018) reviewed 435 Web of Science publications and found the terms "sharing economy", "shareconomy", "collaborative consumption", "collaborative economy", "gig economy", "access-based consumption", "platform economy", "peer-to-peer economy" and "on-demand economy" being used with no clear evidences of the boundaries between them. Therefore, due to the lack of consensus, the authors chose to refer to this phenomenon as collaborative consumption.

In short, CC is a technology-based non-ownership sharing alternative to obtaining product benefits (e.g., Belk, 2010; Botsman & Rogers, 2010; Lamberton & Rose, 2012), as such, CC is often considered more sustainable, ecological and ultimately more profitable than ownership (Bucher et al., 2016). Collaborative consumption may be seen under two perspectives: 1) access over ownership and 2) transfer of ownership. Access over ownership encompasses activities in which individuals may share their goods or services to others for a limited time under the form of renting (for a fee) or lending (for free) (Hamari el al, 2016). Renting is the most common form of access over ownership. Some well-known examples of access over ownership providers are AirBnB (accommodations), Rent the Runway (dresses and accessories) and, Mon Joujou (toys). On the other hand, transfer of ownership encompasses activities such as selling second-hand goods, trading, donating or giving (Hamari et al., 2016). This wide range of activities places a middle ground between sharing economy and marketplace exchange, with elements of both Belk (2014).

The specific CC mode chosen by consumers depends on the nature of what is shared. Tangible or physical goods, such as cars, bicycles, and apartments, and intangible goods, such as knowledge, emotions, and ideas are shared under different modes (Belk, 2007, 2010; Botsman & Rogers, 2010). While tangible goods are mostly shared under the renting mode (for a fee), intangible ones are mostly traded or given for free (Bucher et al., 2016). Additionally, the available literature suggests that behaviors motivations and barriers towards collaborative consumption depend on the specific product being shared (Edbring et al., 2016). In this sense, for the same model of sharing, consumers can show substantially different behaviors depending on the type of product or service. This distinction refers primarily to the type of material the product is made of, the frequency of use, the degree of intimacy as well as the social and emotional values associated with the product or service being shared (Edbring et al., 2016).

For example, goods such as do-it-yourself tools as well as products for an event or party, such as tables and chairs, are some types of products individuals are most likely to share mainly due to their perceived high price and the temporary nature of their use. On the other hand, home textiles, beds and kitchenware are some seen not suitable for sharing with others mostly due to the skepticism regarding hygiene and the potential risk of infection and allergies (Bardhi and Eckhardt, 2012). These differences highlight some motivations that push consumers in, as well as some barriers pulling them out of the different modes of collaborative behavior.

Although the body of literature currently available on collaborative consumption is growing, specific studies exploring consumers' behavior towards sharing activities are scarce either under the scientific or under the professional standpoint. Only recently, studies exploring consumers' behavior towards different activities than ride and home sharing were published (Böcker & Meelen, 2017; Brown & Vergragt, 2016; Edbring et al., 2016; Hamari, 2016) and different motivations and barriers seem to affect consumers' behavior.

Albeit most of the drivers pointed out previously are intrinsic, they might be affected by extrinsic, social factors, hardening or loosening their influence on consumers' behavior. According to the theory of planned behavior (Ajzen, 1991), social pressures influence behavior as people might act accordingly to what they perceive others expect them to. In this sense, if society performs a collaborative behavior assiduously, it is possible that a specific consumer can relativize or ponder a barrier as less critical, and empower, even at a subconscious level, motivation or reason to act collaboratively (Deci, Koestner & Ryan, 1999).

Different theoretical foundations were used to explain the motivations behind the adoption of collaborative forms of consumption (Bellotti, Ambard, Turner, Gossmann, Demkova & Carroll, 2015). Bellotti and colleagues (2015) found that Ajzen's Theory of Planned Behavior (TPB) and Ajzen and Fishbein's Theory of Reasoned Action (TRA) are the most used in studies aimed to understand motivations behind behavioral changes, specifically from popular choices into internet-based, P2P models of consumption. On the other hand, Homans´ Social Exchange Theory (SET) had been used in studies aimed to explain the decision-making process of consumers' engagement into CC modes of consumption, considering the expected rewards as the main motivation. Additionally, Deci & Ryan´s Self-Determination Theory

(SDT) had been mostly used in studies aimed to understand the nature of different motivations that led consumers to adopt a collaborative mode of consumption. In the context of this chapter, the different motivators and barriers will be discussed in light of SDT (Bellotti et al., 2015). However, before that, it is essential to understand the current state of the different CC activities adoption.

CURRENT LEVELS OF AWARENESS AND CONSUMER ENGAGEMENT IN COLLABORATIVE ACTIVITIES: FACTS AND FIGURES

The collaborative consumption is a phenomenon that gathers more and more users across the globe, which, as discussed before, represent a significant change in consumers' behavior, and consequently the way businesses are done. How many people are engaged in CC?, Which are the most used forms of CC?, What is the collaborative consumer's profile? Accurately answering these questions would provide a clear understanding of the current status of collaborative consumption adoption in society and could give a clear perspective of the potential influence of social forces on its adoption. However, the absence of official statistics and consistent measures makes it challenging to address them adequately and, therefore, determine the true scope of collaborative consumption penetration.

Recently some governments and organizations started to monitor consumer's engagement in different CC activities. In this chapter, the authors refer to engagement as an act of usage or participation in a CC activity. While many organizations were interested in having a clear and better understanding of their own clients' behavior, the vast majority of studies focused primarily on the economic impact of the sharing activities in some specific countries (e.g., ING, 2015; Master Card, 2017; PwC, 2015, 2016, 2017). From the available literature, just a few provide broad coverage in terms of both, geographies and CC activities; the Pew Research Center (2015), the European Commission studies (2017) and the Timbro sharing economy index (2018) which results will be further discussed.

Timbro, a Sweedish think-thank organization just published the Timbro Sharing Economy Index (TSEI) as a first attempt to provide a global perspective on the development of sharing activities (Funcke, Bergh & Wernberg, 2018) (Table 1). TSEI was built based on internet traffic volume data, and web scraped data; it comprises 286 sharing platforms offering temporary access to goods and services on 213 countries. Although TSEI does not provide information on how consumers behave towards different activities, it provides some perspective on its development.

According to Funcke and colleagues (2018), countries with a mature internet infrastructure and a tourism-fueled economy have large sharing economies. This fact might help explain why, small countries such as Iceland, the Turks and Caicos Islands, Montenegro, Malta, and New Zealand top Timbro's index. On the other hand, larger economies such as the US, European countries and the BRICKS rank much lower. The US, the largest economy of the world ranks 53 on TSEI while China, the second largest one ranks 150 out of 213 countries (Table 1). At first glance, these results seem odd, and one of the possible explanations is the index nature itself that consider only online activities sharing temporary access to goods and services, leaving behind other important ones. The index provides some light on how these activities are developed world widely; however, it corroborates the need to have a formal definition of what is and what is not considered a sharing activity.

Among the available literature, just a few studies aimed to understand the sharing phenomenon from the consumer behavior standpoint. In this sense, the US and Europe are the two regions leading the ef-

Table 1. G19 Ranking and TSEI index

Rank	Country	TSEI
17	Australia	26.2
19	France	25.1
26	Italy	21.2
27	United Kingdom	20.5
33	Canada	16.6
53	United States	9.5
68	South Africa	4.7
74	Brazil	4.0
77	Germany	3.4
82	Mexico	3.0
84	Argentina	2.9
90	Republic of Korea	1.9
91	Japan	1.9
94	Turkey	1.8
100	Saudi Arabia	1.4
105	Russian Federation	1.2
134	Indonesia	0.6
150	China	0.3
173	India	0.1

Source: Timbro Sharing Economy Index (2018).
G19 consider all G20 members except the European Community.

fort and presenting reliable information on the ground. Therefore, in this section, the authors highlight the critical information available for these two regions.

In the summer of 2016, Pew Research Center (PRC), a nonpartisan US fact tank published a comprehensive study on collaborative consumption - Shared, collaborative and on-demand: The new digital economy. Carried out in December of 2015 amongst a sample of 4,787 internet connected Americans aged over 18, the study aimed to examine Americans' use of – and attitudes toward – the shared, collaborative and on-demand digital economy in eleven different services/activities. Key findings obtained in the study follow.

According to PRC, 72% of Americans have engaged in at least one of the sharing activities studied while 28% have never used any; 22% used four or more different services, and 7% have used six or more services (Pew research center, 2015).

While almost three-fourths of internet users aged over 18 have ever used at least one sharing service, engagement levels vary when it comes to specific activities. Half of adult Americans have purchased second-hand/used goods online, the most used service among the studied ones; 41% made use of expedite same-day delivery programs and; 28% purchased tickets from resellers. Ride-hailing apps and online home-sharing services present lower engagement levels as 15% and 11% respectively of adults Americans have used them (Pew research center, 2015).

There is an apparent concentration of usage of sharing services among people aged 18-44 (Table 2). However, the user profile varies widely among specific demographic characteristics as well as for different sharing activities (Table 3). For example:

- **Education**: Higher educated people are more engaged in sharing activities than lower educated ones. 39% of college graduates have used four or more services, compared with just 8% of those with a high school degree or less.
- **Income**: Higher income households show greater engagement in sharing activities than lower income HH. 41% of Americans earning $100,000 or more per year have used four or more of these services, almost three times the proportion among those earning less than $30,000.
- **Gender**: Even though men and women are equally likely to engage in most sharing activities, women are twice as likely as men to buy handmade or artisanal goods online: (29% vs. 15%).
- **Purchase of Second had Goods**: The most used activity among the studied ones. Nearly two-thirds of Americans under 50 bought used or second-hand goods compared to only 23% of people aged over 65. This activity is also the favorite between higher income and higher educated people.

Table 2. Users of sharing services by age group

Engagement with P2P online platforms	Total internet population	18-24 year olds	25-34 year olds	35-44 year olds	45-54 year olds	55-64 year olds	65 or more year olds
Used in last 12 months	72%	89%	89%	84%	74%	59%	44%
Did not use in last 12 months	28%	11%	11%	16%	26%	41%	56%

Source: Pew research center (2015). Shared, collaborative and on-demand: The new digital economy

- **Home-Sharing Services**: Used predominately by higher income and higher educated people (24% and 25% respectively). Only 12% of users had ever had a bad experience.
- **Ride-Hailing Activities**: Popular among young adults, urbanities and college graduates. Only 16% of users had ever had a bad experience with this activity.

About the same time, on the other side of the Atlantic Ocean, an exploratory study on consumer issues in online peer-to-peer platform markets sponsored by the European Commission (2017) was conducted. This study, held amongst 10,019 individuals aged over 18 in ten EU members (Bulgaria; Denmark; France; Germany; Italy; The Netherlands; Poland; Slovenia; Spain, and the UK) aimed to

Table 3. Profile of sharing services users

	Purchased second-hand/used goods online	Used speedy delivery programs	Purchased tickets from online reseller	Purchased handmade or artisanal products online	Contributed to online fundraising projects	Used ride-hailling apps	Used online home-sharing services	Ordered delivery of groceries online from local store	Worked in a shared office space	Hired someone for errand/task	Rented clothing / other products for a short time online
U.S. internet users 18+	**50%**	**41%**	**28%**	22%	**22%**	**15%**	**11%**	**6%**	**4%**	**4%**	**2%**
Men	52%	43%	31%	15%	19%	16%	10%	5%	4%	5%	2%
Women	48%	39%	26%	29%	24%	14%	13%	6%	4%	4%	3%
Caucasian	53%	41%	31%	25%	24%	14%	13%	5%	3%	4%	1%
Afro-American	36%	33%	19%	10%	19%	15%	5%	5%	7%	4%	3%
Hispanic	48%	39%	24%	20%	16%	18%	9%	5%	5%	5%	2%
18-29	64%	56%	38%	34%	30%	28%	11%	9%	7%	7%	5%
30-49	62%	51%	36%	28%	27%	19%	15%	7%	6%	6%	3%
50-64	42%	30%	23%	15%	18%	8%	10%	3%	2%	2%	1%
65+	23%	20%	11%	7%	8%	4%	6%	2%	1%	2%	<1%
High school or less	37%	26%	15%	11%	11%	6%	4%	3%	3%	4%	3%
Some college	57%	45%	32%	25%	24%	15%	8%	6%	5%	5%	2%
College degree	61%	57%	44%	34%	35%	29%	25%	8%	5%	5%	2%
less than $30,000/year	36%	31%	17%	14%	15%	10%	4%	5%	6%	5%	4%
$30,000 - $74,999	56%	39%	28%	23%	23%	13%	9%	3%	3%	3%	1%
$75,000 or more/year	61%	55%	44%	33%	30%	26%	24%	9%	4%	4%	2%
Urban	51%	43%	29%	24%	25%	21%	14%	7%	5%	5%	3%
Suburban	50%	41%	31%	23%	22%	15%	11%	5%	4%	4%	2%
Rural	46%	34%	20%	17%	14%	3%	6%	2%	3%	3%	2%

Source: Pew research center (2015). Shared, collaborative and on-demand: The new digital economy.

explore consumer issues in five online P2P platform markets: (Re)sale of Goods; Sharing/renting of goods, Sharing/renting accommodation; Sharing/hiring rides; and Odd jobs.

Results of this study show that 77% of EU internet users have used at least one of the five online platforms in the period comprised between May 2015 and May 2016 (Table 4). While 23% have not used any of them, about 17% claimed to be considering the usage of some platform in the future. Based on these findings, an estimate of 191 million Europeans (52.2% of the EU population aged over 18) engaged in at least one of the sharing activities studied.

Awareness and engagement levels vary widely among the different types of sharing platforms. Resale of used goods presents the highest awareness and engagement levels (97% and 73% respectively) while sharing/renting goods and hiring odd jobs present the lowest levels as shown in Table 5.

As expected, the usage frequency of the different platforms also vary. Accommodation sharing was the less frequently used activity (1-2 times per year) while sharing/renting goods and hiring people for odd jobs were the most frequently used ones (Table 6).

Overall, European users are very satisfied/satisfied with the use of P2P activities ranging from the highest 87% with ride sharing to the lowest 73% with sharing/renting goods (Table 7). Additionally, satisfaction levels with the services provided by P2P online platforms are higher when compared to the same services provided by conventional businesses (Table 8). Price, value (price/quality ratio) and quality of service provided present the highest satisfaction levels.

Even though the results of these two studies cannot be directly compared, some patterns emerge from the findings. Engagement levels on sharing activities in both regions are quite high and at similar levels (72% in the US and 77% in Europe), suggesting an intense social pressure exerts on consumers to act collaboratively. This fact might help explain the fast growth of the sharing phenomenon. Noteworthy,

Table 4. Engagement with online P2P platforms

	Total internet population	18-34 year olds	35-54 year olds	55 or more year olds	Men	Women
Used in last 12 months	77%	82%	75%	56%	67%	70%
Did not use in last 12 months	23%	18%	25%	44%	33%	30%

Source: European Commission (2017). An exploratory study of consumer issues in online peer-to-peer platform markets.

Table 5. Awareness and engagement in different sharing platforms

	Resale of goods	Sharing or Renting Goods	Sharing or Renting Accommodation	Sharing or Hiring Rides	Odd jobs
Never heard of	3%	44%	29%	23%	47%
Know but have not used	19%	37%	50%	55%	38%
Used in last 12 months	73%	12%	14%	15%	8%
Have not used but may use in the next 12 months	5%	7%	7%	7%	7%

Source: European Commission (2017). An exploratory study of consumer issues in online peer-to-peer platform markets.

Table 6. Usage frequency of different P2P activities (among users)

	Once a week	Once a month	A couple of times per year	Once a year
Resale of goods	14%	30%	46%	10%
Sharing or Renting Goods	26%	33%	29%	13%
Sharing or Renting Accommodation	11%	15%	34%	39%
Sharing or Hiring Rides	13%	23%	46%	18%
Odd jobs	21%	27%	33%	18%

Source: European Commission (2017). An exploratory study of consumer issues in online peer-to-peer platform markets.

the results suggest that consumers are progressively changing their behavior from traditional ownership into CC. This phenomenon is evidenced by the fact that the purchase/sale of second-hand goods still is the most used activity in both regions (50% in the US and 73% in Europe).

The higher levels of satisfaction with services provided via P2P platforms compared to traditional businesses in Europe suggest there are specific reasons, either intrinsic or extrinsic, driving consumers behavior. According to Deci & Ryan (1985), the motivation to engage in a behavior arises when the individual feels satisfied with (intrinsic motivators) or perceives real benefits (extrinsic motivators) from it. On the other hand, even though a few users of a ride and home sharing service in the US had a bad experience with P2P services, these might indicate some barriers preventing consumers from behaving collaboratively.

Both motivators and barriers affecting consumers' behavior towards collaborative forms of consumption should be carefully understood. The novelty of platform enhanced activities together with the already high levels of awareness and electronic word-of-mouth might influence consumers decision to engage in sharing activities.

Table 7. Overall satisfaction with the use of different P2P activities

	Very satisfied / Satisfied	Neutral	Not / not at all satisfied
All activities	83%	12%	4%
Resale of goods	85%	11%	4%
Sharing or Renting Goods	73%	22%	5%
Sharing or Renting Accommodation	83%	12%	6%
Sharing or Hiring Rides	87%	10%	4%
Odd jobs	74%	21%	5%

Source: European Commission (2017). An exploratory study of consumer issues in online peer-to-peer platform markets.

Table 8. Satisfaction with experience using P2P platforms compared to conventional business

	All Activities		Resale of goods		Sharing or Renting Goods		Sharing or Renting Accommodation		Sharing or Hiring Rides		Odd jobs	
	more / slightly more satisfied	less / slightly less satisfied	more / slightly more satisfied	less / slightly less satisfied	more / slightly more satisfied	less / slightly less satisfied	more / slightly more satisfied	less / slightly less satisfied	more / slightly more satisfied	less / slightly less satisfied	more / slightly more satisfied	less / slightly less satisfied
Price	68%	8%	69%	7%	55%	20%	67%	11%	80%	6%	50%	24%
Availability of offers	58%	12%	57%	11%	52%	20%	64%	11%	62%	13%	50%	20%
Quality of product sold by the peer	40%	11%	39%	11%	50%	16%	n.a.	n.a.	n.a.	n.a.	n.a.	n.a.
Quality of service provided by the peer	60%	10%	n.a.	n.a.	n.a.	n.a.	59%	10%	65%	7%	53%	16%
Price/quality ratio	62%	8%	60%	8%	55%	12%	67%	8%	76%	5%	55%	15%
Trustworthiness	45%	15%	40%	16%	50%	15%	55%	11%	60%	11%	55%	15%

Source: European Commission (2017). An exploratory study of consumer issues in online peer-to-peer platform markets.

MOTIVATORS DRIVING CONSUMERS BEHAVIOR TOWARDS COLLABORATIVE MODELS OF CONSUMPTION

In a broader sense, motivators are the factors that stimulate action, and the Self-Determination Theory (SDT - Deci & Ryan, 1985) is one of the most used to explain how different types of motivations drive behaviors. SDT postulates behaviors are driven by two different types of motivators, intrinsic and extrinsic, that satisfy three essential and universal needs: competence, autonomy, and relatedness. Specifically, intrinsic motivators are those that drive people into a behavior because it is personally rewarding and relates to personal goals like generativity, affiliation, and personal development. On the other hand, extrinsic motivators are those that drive people to engage in an activity to earn a reward or to avoid punishment and relates to personal goals like attractiveness, fame and wealth. The need for competence refers to the pursuit of control over the outcomes and experience mastery when performing a behavior. The need of relatedness refers to the desire to be connected, to interact and to experience caring for and from others and; the need for autonomy refers to the desire to be master of own life and to act upon self-decisions what, according to Deci & Ryan (1985), do not mean to be independent of others.

Although these needs are universal, some may be more important than others at certain times and under certain circumstances. Therefore, the satisfaction of them also depends on the external conditions such as social environment and cultural values that affords and stimulates the performance of a particular behavior (Deci & Ryan, 1985). In the context of collaborative consumption, the different sharing activities promote the achievement of these three essential needs. Through CC consumers can access cheaper goods and services as well as get some extra income from their assets, a clear economic benefit that fulfills the competence need. CC also provides consumers with new, better and faster opportunities to access goods and services, fulfilling the autonomy need. Finally, through CC consumers can build active communities and trust satisfying the need for relatedness (Böcker & Melen, 2017).

However, as collaborative consumption encompasses several different activities, factors affecting consumers' behavior also differ, depending primarily on the nature of the activity and the type of product/service being shared (Edbring et al., 2016). For example, Bucher and colleagues (2016) found that engagement in non-monetized sharing activities presents an active altruistic component derived from the will to help others. On the other hand, monetized sharing activities are strongly influenced by social and economic reasons (Edbring et al., 2016).

Economic Reasons

Although sharing was initially seen as an evolution of the ethical and the mindfulness ways of living suggesting an original intrinsic motivation (Böcker & Melen, 2017), the economic benefits obtained from the monetized activities are found to be stronger motives to engage into sharing activities than environmental reasons (Hamari et al., 2016). According to Tussyadiah (2015), the extrinsic financial rewards obtained from an initially intrinsic motivated behavior undermine the intrinsic motivation as it grows less critical. For example, Bardhi and Eckhardt (2012), found saving money as the primary motivation of Zipcar platform clients to engage in a car sharing activity; Tussyadiah (2015) identified economic motivations as essential drivers for using accommodation sharing in the US while Möhlmann (2015) found that for car and accommodation sharing users "cost savings" increase satisfaction.

The strong economic force affecting consumers' behavior is resultant of the perceived financial benefits obtained out of the sharing activities. From the user perspective, besides being cheaper to rent than to buy some expensive goods, consumers see CC as an excellent option to prevent investing high on goods that might not be of frequent use (Edbring et al., 2016) although Pappas (2019) suggests price acts as a predictor of the quality of the goods and services being shared. For example, Casprini, Di Minin & Paraboschi, (2018) found that BlaBlaCar users see the platform as a reliable reference for ride services fair prices. On the other hand, getting temporary access to certain products offers consumers a unique opportunity to test and experience them before deciding for purchase, thereby reducing the inherent risk of investing in an unfamiliar product (Edbring et al., 2016). Additionally, CC activities seem to be very economically attractive from the provider standpoint as it helps maximize the utility of the investments made. This is evidenced in accommodation sharing activities such as Airbnb where fees are charged to cover not only the costs that arise from the activity itself like the increase in water or electricity use during the sharing period but also to cover for ordinary fees and taxes (Bucher et al., 2016), fulfilling the need of competence.

Economic benefits are particularly essential motivators to younger and low-income consumers (Böcker & Melen, 2017). Specifically, without the opportunity offered by the different sharing activities, these groups would hardly get access to certain goods and services due to their financial limitations. On the other hand, people feel motivated to share seldom used products as they are often considered expensive to buy individually and would make more sense if they were bought with other people. In this sense, people would like to have access to products but do not see the need to own them, mainly if the products in question are considered to lose their value once used (Edbring et al., 2016).

Environmental Reasons

The concern with the environment preservation can potentially be considered the main reason behind the first CC activities (Geissinger, Laurell, Öberg & Sandström, 2019). However, the extrinsic economic rewards obtained from CC activities altered the original intrinsic motivation behind the engagement in CC. Even though, the different collaborative forms of consumption are perceived to have a potentially positive impact on the environment through the increased efficiency in the use of goods, the concern with the environment is not among the most important motivators for consumers to engage into them (Hamari et al., 2016). Bardhi and Eckhardt (2012) found that environmental concern is not among the main motivations of Zipcar users; nor on the intention to use accommodation sharing (Tussyadiah, 2015). Nevertheless, environmental concern appears to be significant and an intrinsic motivation to environmentally and ecologically conscious individuals (Casprini, Di Minin & Paraboschi, 2018; Hamari et al, 2016; Kim, Woo & Nam, 2018) whom prefer to share goods instead of buy new ones as a way to reduce the usage of natural resources, fulfilling their need of autonomy. Geissinger and colleagues (2019) found small CC enterprises such as Swopshop and Freelway offer sustainability as a benefit to environmentally concerned consumers.

Social Reasons

Strengthening social relations with neighbors, meeting people, making friends and getting to know others are also motives for people to engage in CC activities (Bucher et al., 2016) as sharing stimulates user-provider interactions in different ways (Fitzmaurice, Ladegaard, Attwood-Charles, Cansoy, Carfagna, Schor & Wengronowitz, 2016) a robust intrinsic motivation tied to the fulfillment of the relatedness need. Social ties stimulated by CC activities reduces consumers concerns that something might go wrong due to potential risks involved. This way, social integration acts as a source of information that contributes to building trust between peers (Casprini et al., 2018). For example, users of accommodation sharing rely on providers to introduce them to the local community (Pappas, 2019); parents and children enjoy the socialization effect on sharing toys (Böcker & Melen, 2017); TaskRabbit peers claim to have built new social networks and had the opportunity to meet people they would have never met (Fitzmaurice et al., 2016). People report satisfaction with the relations they developed with other people they interact with due to sharing. According to Edbring et al. (2016), "once the economic motive is removed other driving forces emerge and people become more social with their community, indicating that social contact is something that can be seen as a catalyst for sharing resources regardless of the type of product."

Functional Reasons

The possibility to get access to goods either the frequently used ones such as furniture and white goods or the rarely used ones as do-it-yourself tools and garden equipment also drives consumers into sharing activities. The flexibility experienced when renting goods is an essential intrinsic motivator for people to engage in CC activities as individuals may have a sense of freedom by only having access to goods when they need them, (Edbring et al., 2016) fulfilling their need of competence. For example, products that require maintenance or upgrade are more attractive for consumers to rent as they do not need to be concerned with repairs when they break and can always get access to novelties when there are updates

(Edbring et al. 2016). On the other hand, the flexibility to access when needed and the ease of use of most of CC platforms are also essential drivers behind consumers' engagement (Sutherland & Jarrahi, 2018)

Sutherland and Jarrahi (2018) found convenience to be another essential motivator for consumers to engage in CC activities. According to them, platform mediated activities provide both, the convenience to easily connect to others and the freedom from following-up on transaction details for logistics and payment. Users see Kakao Taxi, a popular ride-sharing provider in Korea, as a convenient option for late night rides at isolated locations where public transportation is usually discontinued (Lee, Lee & Kim, 2018). Additionally, CC activities also allow consumers to customize the service according to their specific requirements (Parente, Geleilate & Rong, 2018), an intrinsic motivation that fulfills the need for autonomy.

These pieces of evidence indicate that engaging in CC activities satisfy all three consumers' essential needs, driven primarily by intrinsic motivations, at the exception of the economic, extrinsically motivated reasons. This issue is vital as intrinsic motivations relate to those inner drivers that lead to high psychological health and long-term behavior maintenance (Deci & Ryan, 1985), suggesting CC presents a strong potential to grow further (Möhlmann, 2015). However, on the other hand, some people see sharing as a risky activity enlisting some barriers preventing its adoption.

KEY BARRIERS TO THE ADOPTION OF COLLABORATIVE MODELS OF CONSUMPTION

Even though to engage in CC activities are perceived to bring significant benefits to all people involved, on an individual level it is also perceived to be tied to material and personal risks since they can potentially expose one or one's possessions to the hazards of loss, damage and decreased utility (Bucher et al., 2016).

According to Olsson & Phelps, (2007), learning about potential adverse events is critical in shaping behaviors in a rapidly changing environment. It allows individuals to identify and build associations between external events and motivational states of fear. Fear can be expressed, spread and acquired either through direct experiences or, indirectly, through the social transmission. When fear is experienced either by one or by someone else, it alters individuals' response, mostly in those cases in which individuals see themselves connected. As CC is primarily performed online, any bad experience with a sharing activity is rapidly spread out, with the potential to become a barrier for consumers to engage in the activity.

Lack of Trust

Trust, confidence or faith. Independently of the noun used, belief in someone to be trustworthy when he/she is not, emerges as the most substantial barrier preventing consumers from behaving collaboratively. According to Hawlitschek, Teubner, & Weinhardt (2016), people who are not participating in sharing activities seem to be deterred by the perceived risks involved in these modes of consumption and have difficulties to overcome the trust barrier.

Trust as opposed to perceived risk is one of the fundamental pillars of any relationship and is particularly important in the collaborative forms of consumption. As the basis for the sharing activities rely on the intentions of people to give strangers access to their belongings, the fear of potential damage to goods as well as to endanger personal safety are severe obstacles for people to engage in many sharing activities (ter Huurne, Ronteltap, Corten & Buskens, 2017). Lack of trust makes many individuals not feel comfortable sharing their resources outside the family and closed related ones as they lack some guarantee or insurance as some forms of protection (Edbring, 2016).

On one of her TED talks, Botsman (2016) posits that trust is one of the essential attributes in the sharing environment. She defines trust as "the confident relationship to the unknown" which has the unique capacity to enable people to cope with uncertainty. According to her, trust is built in three different stages. First one needs to believe that engaging in a certain type of CC activity is safe and worth trying; second, one needs to trust in the platform as a form of protection if something goes wrong; and third, people should trust on the ratings provided by previous users. In this sense, trust in sharing platforms emerge as a critical barrier. In the collaborative consumption context, platforms are seen by users as "institutions" that are supposed to "guarantee" the service provided from fraud or any other potential problem, providing consumers with the needed confidence and reliability (Hawlitschek et al., 2016).

Hawlitschek and colleagues (2016) propose three targets of trust in CC, i.e., trust towards the peers, the platform and the product (3P). According to them, trust in the supplier peer refers to the confidence that he/she has the skills and competencies to perform his/her part of the transaction properly, and presents high integrity and benevolence. Trust on the platform also refers to the confidence in its ability, integrity, and benevolence to successfully connect users and providers, secure data integrity and proper information handling (Hawlitschek et al., 2016). Lastly, trust in the product refers to the confidence that the product shared is reliable and performs as expected.

Therefore, trust can affect acceptance, reliance and utilization behaviors (Xu, Zhang, Min, Wang, Zhao & Liu, 2018). For example, Suki and Suki (2017) found that online group buyers are worried of experiencing potential losses due to lack of security with their personal information such as bank accounts, credit card numbers and deposits submitted online. Security and privacy are the most significant factors affecting users trust in accommodation activities as these usually involve additional and more threatening psychological and physical risks (Ert, Fleischer, & Magen, 2016). Unfortunate incidents where hosts attacked guests and vice versa reinforce the critical need of trust (Yang, Lee, Lee, & Koo, 2018). Additionally, older people may seem to be more vulnerable to potential harms when engaging in CC activities (Pappas, 2019).

Lack of Hygiene

Trust, however, is not the only barrier preventing consumers from engaging in sharing activities. It might not be surprising to most people that hygiene appears as another critical barrier that keeps consumers out of collaborative modes of consumption. This issue is particularly crucial amongst those activities that involve sharing goods made out of fabric like apparel, shoes, and furniture as well as those considered of personal use such as kitchen utensils (Edbring et al. 2016). Hygiene can be an even stronger barrier when related to sharing products for children such as toys, seats, and prams. The potential risks of infection, as well as other health-related issues, prevent consumers from sharing this kind of goods (Bardhi and Eckhardt, 2012). Additionally, Edbring and colleagues (2016) found that individuals fear that sharing furniture might bring parasites to their homes that can potentially infect and contaminate their shelter.

Need for Ownership

Another significant barrier for people to engage in sharing activities is the personal desire to own the products needed. The anxiety generated by, either the fear of not being able to get quick access to needed products or that their possessions might be damaged or stolen by others prevent people from engaging in sharing activities (Edbring et al. 2016). In this sense, people would rather have their assets to ensure they are handy and in good shape whenever they need them.

As per the above-discussed factors, it is evident that fear is the fundamental emotion behind all barriers preventing consumers from behaving collaboratively. Thus, establishing durable, trustworthy relations are fundamental to overcome this critical obstacle and promote collaborative consumption growth.

EXPECTED GROWTH AND PENETRATION OF COLLABORATIVE MODELS OF CONSUMPTION

Many claims have been made about sharing becoming a radical game changer in how people make consumption choices and how the economy evolves. However, empirical evidence to support or counteract these claims is still minimal. Are we witnessing signs of behavior changes? Alternatively, is it merely a new business opportunity to profit from seldom-used assets, enabled by the internet and social media technologies? Kathan, Matzler, and Veider (2016) say CC will last and grow as besides presenting significant intrinsic benefits of convenience and flexibility, it also provides extrinsic financial rewards from the optimization of idle capacity.

The expected shifts in lifestyle choices from ownership to experience and access, together with the required adaptations to the current economic realities can stimulate new social practices, more reciprocal interactions and close connections with others building a strong sense of community that might change the understanding of wellbeing (Brown & Vergragt, 2016). Even with clear evidence that consumers motivations to participate in sharing activities vary widely, from altruist to strongly profit-seeking, collaborative forms of consumption will continue to attract more people, providing the perceived benefits outweigh potential additional costs (Hamari 2016). This fact, together with the expected growth in mobile penetration (devices and connections) from 67% in 2018, to 71% of the global population in 2025 (GSM Association, 2019) makes the authors believe collaborative consumption will keep on growing steadily in the future.

Currently, specific estimates on the expected growth in consumers' engagement levels in collaborative activities are not available. Nevertheless, some figures published by Mastercard (2017) project impressive compound annual growth rates (CAGR) up to 2025 for five sharing activities (Figure 1).

Additionally, according to Wosskow (2014), new sharing activities are expected to gain a global presence. For example, DogVacay, a US-based P2P service to take care of dogs while owners are on vacation; bike sharing platforms as Spinlister, currently available in 40 countries and even services for art rental like RiseArt, a UK based platform that allows people to rent works of art they would not afford to buy.

On the other hand, some authors are not as enthusiastic about the future of sharing activities. Frenken & Schor (2017) posit users will become "disenchanted" as they realize their relationships had become more casual and less durable. As time passes, the novelty aura of sharing activities goes away, and the social ties built through them might decline. This scenario, however, does not seem to be the worst. Recent empirical evidence suggests peer to peer activities may increase people discrimination and concentration of wealth.

Empirical evidence found that Afro-American males earn 12% less rent than other Airbnb hosts for the same type of house in the same class of location (Edelman and Luca, 2017). Another field experiment found that hosts more frequently turned down Afro-American guests (Edelman et al., 2015). This news

Figure 1. Projected CAGR (%) for key sharing economy sectors (2013-2025)
Source: MasterCard (2017). The sharing economy: Understanding the opportunities for growth

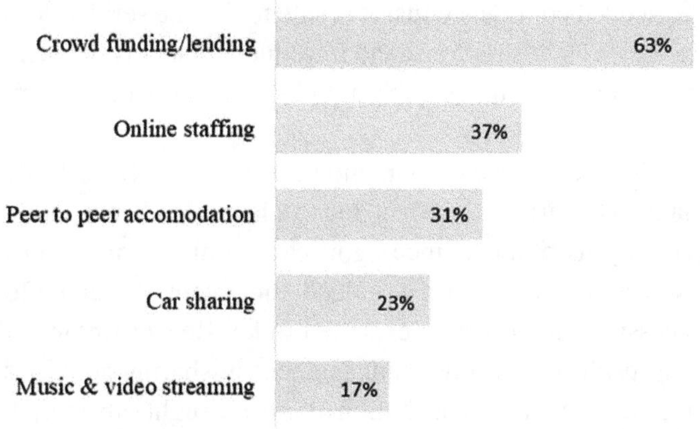

rapidly spread out on social media leading to the establishment of a Black-oriented platform, Noirbnb - A New Lodging Site for Travelers of Color and to Airbnb implement policy changes. A recent analysis carried out by Cansoy and Schor (2017), on more than 200,000 Airbnb listings across the U.S., found evidence of significant racial disadvantage for color peers in ratings, reviews, and prices charged. Ge, Knittel, MacKenzie & Zoepf (2016) found that Uber and Lyft drivers also discriminate Afro-Americans in terms of longer average waiting times and more frequent cancellations. More generally, evidence suggests that people engage in a variety of segregated behaviors when choosing trading partners or collaborators in sharing activities (Schor, Fitzmaurice, Carfagna, Attwood-Charles & Poteat, 2016).

CONCLUSION

Lending, giving, trading and all other forms of sharing are not a novelty. These different forms of collaborative behavior initially confined in inner circles for a long time are now spread-out well beyond any frontier thanks to the advances in technology. The advent of the internet and social media helped individuals connect, even with total strangers, fast and efficiently. They allow people to share properties, resources, time and skills, unlocking previously unused or under-used assets; help people make money from their empty spare rooms and the tools they rarely use.

Although this change on how consumers execute collaborative behaviors is calling the attention of all, academy, industry, governments and society, scientific research that gives light to concepts, models, and theories applicable to this new consumer behavior is scarce. Additionally, the lack of clear definitions of what services should and what should not be classified as sharing activity compromise a deeper understanding of this phenomenon as this lack of definition entails authors to posit his/her definition of sharing.

It is not clear, at this point, how the adoption of these new forms of consumption will evolve, even though some forecasts point out to continuous growth. Although collaborative behavior offers clear benefits for consumers, it is essential that service providers enhance the economic/financial gains in terms of savings as well as stimulate experiences and social ties for users. In addition to that, there are still significant barriers to overcome, mostly related to trust, fear and risk perception. Particular attention should be given to sharing platforms as they have the potential to become ambassadors of trust, providing consumers the needed confidence that it is safe to use the services offered. For that, it is vital for services providers to create clear structures and introduce trustworthy mechanisms for peer reviews and feedback that might help remove this significant obstacle and stimulate more people to engage in sharing activities.

Ultimately, the economic, social and environmental effects of sharing activities are mostly unknown. While the economic/financial benefits are evident due to a large number of monetary transactions taking place, revenues are not equally distributed. Since significant earnings come from home sharing activities, already wealthy homeowners get most of profit. Indeed, the potential social effects of sharing activities are complex and not necessarily inclusive as expected to be. Recent findings though suggest adverse effects could emerge as a result of consumers engagement in sharing activities. Potential increases in people discrimination and an unbalanced distribution of profits might substantially withdraw the benefits obtained and, consequently, drive consumers away from collaborative forms of behavior (Malhotra & Van Alstyne, 2014). These considerations apply to the development of any collaborative business model.

The future of collaborative forms of consumption depends partially on the providers' capacity to consider the motivators valued by consumers, especially the social and economic ones when designing their business models (Chen & Chang, 2018). Finally, yet importantly, providers should build and maintain confidence in their services establishing trustworthy, long-term relations with users while governments must establish clear rules and regulations to ensure adequate protection for all sharing players. Specific actions on fraud detection and punishment, avoidance of discrimination and attribution of responsibility should be implemented. These actions will make consumers feel more secure about their rights and protected by law, creating solid grounds for the evolution of this new way of consumption.

REFERENCES

Ajzen, I. (1991). The theory of planned behavior. *Organizational Behavior and Human Decision Processes*, *50*(2), 179–211. doi:10.1016/0749-5978(91)90020-T

Association, G. S. M. (2019). *The mobile economy*. Retrieved from: https://www.gsmaintelligence.com/research/?file=b9a6e6202ee1d5f787cfebb95d3639c5&download

Bardhi, F., & Eckhardt, G. M. (2012). Access-based consumption: The case of car sharing. *The Journal of Consumer Research*, *39*(4), 881–898. doi:10.1086/666376

Barnes, S. J., & Mattsson, J. (2016). Understanding current and future issues in collaborative consumption: A four-stage Delphi study. *Technological Forecasting and Social Change*, *104*, 200–211. doi:10.1016/j.techfore.2016.01.006

Belk, R. (2007). Why not share rather than own? *The Annals of the American Academy of Political and Social Science*, *611*(1), 126–140. doi:10.1177/0002716206298483

Belk, R. (2010). Sharing. *The Journal of Consumer Research*, *36*(5), 715–734. doi:10.1086/612649

Belk, R. (2014). Sharing versus pseudo-sharing in Web 2.0. *The Anthropologist*, *18*(1), 7–23. doi:10.1080/09720073.2014.11891518

Bellotti, V., Ambard, A., Turner, D., Gossmann, C., Demkova, K., & Carroll, J. M. (2015, April). A muddle of models of motivation for using peer-to-peer economy systems. In *Proceedings of the 33rd Annual ACM Conference on Human Factors in Computing Systems* (pp. 1085-1094). ACM. 10.1145/2702123.2702272

Böcker, L., & Meelen, T. (2017). Sharing for people, planet or profit? Analyzing motivations for intended sharing economy participation. *Environmental Innovation and Societal Transitions*, *23*, 28–39. doi:10.1016/j.eist.2016.09.004

Botsman, R. (2012). We've stopped trusting institutions and started trusting strangers. *TED Talks.* Retrieved from: https://www.ted.com/talks/rachel_botsman_we_ve_stopped_trusting_institutions_and_started_trusting_strangers

Botsman, R. (2015). *Defining the sharing economy: What is collaborative consumption - and what isn't?* Retrieved from: https://www.fastcompany.com/3046119/defining-the-sharing-economy-what-is-collaborative-consumption-and-what-isnt

Botsman, R., & Rogers, R. (2011). *What's mine is yours: how collaborative consumption is changing the way we live* (Vol. 5). London: Collins.

Brown, H. S., & Vergragt, P. J. (2016). From consumerism to wellbeing: Toward a cultural transition? *Journal of Cleaner Production*, *132*, 308–317. doi:10.1016/j.jclepro.2015.04.107

Bucher, E., Fieseler, C., & Lutz, C. (2016). What's mine is yours (for a nominal fee)–Exploring the spectrum of utilitarian to altruistic motives for Internet-mediated sharing. *Computers in Human Behavior*, *62*, 316–326. doi:10.1016/j.chb.2016.04.002

Cansoy, M., & Schor, J. (2017). *Who gets to share in the sharing economy: Racial discrimination on Airbnb.* Working paper, Boston College.

Casprini, E., Di Minin, A., & Paraboschi, A. (2018). How do companies organize nascent markets? The BlaBlaCar case in the inter-city shared mobility market. *Technological Forecasting and Social Change.*

Chen, C. C., & Chang, Y. C. (2018). What drives purchase intention on Airbnb? Perspectives of consumer reviews, information quality, and media richness. *Telematics and Informatics*, *35*(5), 1512–1523. doi:10.1016/j.tele.2018.03.019

Deci, E. L. (1971). Effects of externally mediated rewards on intrinsic motivation. *Journal of Personality and Social Psychology*, *18*(1), 105–115. doi:10.1037/h0030644

Deci, E. L., Koestner, R., & Ryan, R. M. (1999). A meta-analytic review of experiments examining the effects of extrinsic rewards on intrinsic motivation. *Psychological Bulletin*, *125*(6), 627–668. doi:10.1037/0033-2909.125.6.627 PMID:10589297

Deci, E. L., & Ryan, R. M. (1985). Intrinsic motivation and self-determination in human behavior. New York: Springer Science+Business Media. doi:10.1007/978-1-4899-2271-7

Edbring, E. G., Lehner, M., & Mont, O. (2016). Exploring consumer attitudes to alternative models of consumption: Motivations and barriers. *Journal of Cleaner Production*, *123*, 5–15. doi:10.1016/j.jclepro.2015.10.107

Edelman, B., Luca, M., & Svirsky, D. (2017). Racial discrimination in the sharing economy: Evidence from a field experiment. *American Economic Journal. Applied Economics*, *9*(2), 1–22. doi:10.1257/app.20160213

Ert, E., Fleischer, A., & Magen, N. (2016). Trust and reputation in the sharing economy: The role of personal photos in Airbnb. *Tourism Management*, *55*, 62–73. doi:10.1016/j.tourman.2016.01.013

European Commission. (2017). *An exploratory study of consumer issues in online peer-to-peer platform markets*. Retrieved from: https://ec.europa.eu/info/sites/info/files/final_report_may_2017.pdf

Fitzmaurice, C. J., Ladegaard, I., Attwood-Charles, W., Cansoy, M., Carfagna, L. B., Schor, J. B., & Wengronowitz, R. (2016). Domesticating the market: Moral exchange and the sharing economy. *Socio-economic Review*.

Funcke, A., Bergh, A., & Wernberg, J. (2018). Timbro Sharing Economy Index (TSEI). *Timbro*. Retrieved from: https://timbro.se/allmant/timbro-sharing-economy-index/

Ge, Y., Knittel, C. R., MacKenzie, D., & Zoepf, S. (2016). *Racial and gender discrimination in transportation network companies* (No. w22776). Working paper, National Bureau of Economic Research.

Geissinger, A., Laurell, C., Öberg, C., & Sandström, C. (2019). How sustainable is the sharing economy? On the sustainability connotations of sharing economy platforms. *Journal of Cleaner Production*, *206*, 419–429. doi:10.1016/j.jclepro.2018.09.196

Hamari, J., Sjöklint, M., & Ukkonen, A. (2016). The sharing economy: Why people participate in collaborative consumption. *Journal of the Association for Information Science and Technology*, *67*(9), 2047–2059. doi:10.1002/asi.23552

Hawlitschek, F., Teubner, T., & Gimpel, H. (2018). Consumer motives for peer-to-peer sharing. *Journal of Cleaner Production*, *204*, 144–157. doi:10.1016/j.jclepro.2018.08.326

Hawlitschek, F., Teubner, T., & Weinhardt, C. (2016). Trust in the sharing economy. *Die Unternehmung*, *70*(1), 26–44. doi:10.5771/0042-059X-2016-1-26

Kathan, W., Matzler, K., & Veider, V. (2016). The sharing economy: Your business model's friend or foe? *Business Horizons*, *59*(6), 663–672. doi:10.1016/j.bushor.2016.06.006

Kim, Y. G., Woo, E., & Nam, J. (2018). Sharing economy perspective on an integrative framework of the NAM and TPB. *International Journal of Hospitality Management*, *72*, 109–117. doi:10.1016/j.ijhm.2018.01.008

Lee, S. H., Lee, B. Y., & Kim, H. W. (2018). Decisional factors leading to the reuse of an on-demand ride service. *Information & Management*.

Malhotra, A., & Van Alstyne, M. (2014). The dark side of the sharing economy… and how to lighten it. *Communications of the ACM*, *57*(11), 24–27. doi:10.1145/2668893

MasterCard. (2017). *The sharing economy: Understanding the opportunities for growth*. Retrieved from: https://newsroom.mastercard.com/eu/files/2017/06/Mastercard_Sharing-Economy_v7.compressed2.pdf

Meelen, T., & Frenken, K. (2015). *Stop saying UBER is part of the sharing economy*. Retrieved from: http://www.fastcoexist.com/3040863/stop-saying-uber-is-part-of-the-sharing-economy

Möhlmann, M. (2015). Collaborative consumption: Determinants of satisfaction and the likelihood of using a sharing economy option again. *Journal of Consumer Behaviour, 14*(3), 193–207. doi:10.1002/cb.1512

Olsson, A., & Phelps, E. A. (2007). Social learning of fear. *Nature Neuroscience, 10*(9), 1095–1102. doi:10.1038/nn1968 PMID:17726475

Pappas, N. (2019). The complexity of consumer experience formulation in the sharing economy. *International Journal of Hospitality Management, 77*, 415–424. doi:10.1016/j.ijhm.2018.08.005

Parente, R. C., Geleilate, J. M. G., & Rong, K. (2018). The sharing economy globalization phenomenon: A research agenda. *Journal of International Management, 24*(1), 52–64. doi:10.1016/j.intman.2017.10.001

Pew Research Center. (2016). *Shared, Collaborative and On Demand: The New Digital Economy*. Retrieved from: http://www.pewresearch.org/wp-content/uploads/sites/9/2016/05/PI_2016.05.19_Sharing-Economy_FINAL.pdf

Schor, J. B., Fitzmaurice, C., Carfagna, L. B., Attwood-Charles, W., & Poteat, E. D. (2016). Paradoxes of openness and distinction in the sharing economy. *Poetics, 54*, 66–81. doi:10.1016/j.poetic.2015.11.001

Suki, N. M., & Suki, N. M. (2017). Modeling the determinants of consumers' attitudes toward online group buying: Do risks and trusts matters? *Journal of Retailing and Consumer Services, 36*, 180–188. doi:10.1016/j.jretconser.2017.02.002

Sutherland, W., & Jarrahi, M. H. (2018). The sharing economy and digital platforms: A review and research agenda. *International Journal of Information Management, 43*, 328–341. doi:10.1016/j.ijinfomgt.2018.07.004

ter Huurne, M., Ronteltap, A., Corten, R., & Buskens, V. (2017). Antecedents of trust in the sharing economy: A systematic review. *Journal of Consumer Behaviour, 16*(6), 485–498. doi:10.1002/cb.1667

Tussyadiah, I. P. (2015). An exploratory study on drivers and deterrents of collaborative consumption in travel. In *Information and communication technologies in tourism* (pp. 817–830). Cham: Springer.

Walsh, B. (in press). Today's Smart Choices. Don't Own. Share. *Time Magazine*. Available: http://content.time.com/time/specials/packages/article/0,28804,2059521_2059717,00.html

Wosskow, D. (2014). *Unlocking the sharing economy: An independent review*. London: Department for Business, Innovation and Skills.

Xu, Z., Zhang, K., Min, H., Wang, Z., Zhao, X., & Liu, P. (2018). What drives people to accept automated vehicles? Findings from a field experiment. *Transportation Research Part C, Emerging Technologies, 95*, 320–334. doi:10.1016/j.trc.2018.07.024

Yang, S. B., Lee, K., Lee, H., & Koo, C. (2018). *Airbnb we trust: Understanding consumers' trust-attachment building mechanisms in the sharing economy*. International Journal of Hospitality Management. doi:10.1016/j.ijhm.2018.10.016

ADDITIONAL READING

ING. (2015). What's mine is yours – for a price. Rapid growth tipped for the sharing economy. Available: https://www.ing.com/Newsroom/All-news/European-sharing-economy-to-grow-by-a-third-in-the-next-12-months.htm

PwC. (2016) Assessing the size and presence of the collaborative economy in Europe. Available: https://www.google.com/url?sa=t&rct=j&q=&esrc=s&source=web&cd=1&ved=2ahUKEwiolIqaovDhAhWCv1kKHSKyANIQFjAAegQIAhAC&url=https%3A%2F%2Fec.europa.eu%2Fdocsroom%2Fdocuments%2F16952%2Fattachments%2F1%2Ftranslations%2Fen%2Frenditions%2Fnative&usg=AOvVaw3dhIt2XkIasY17azofHrxq

PwC US. (2015). Consumer Intelligence Series – the Sharing Economy. [online] pwc.com. Available at: https://www.pwc.com/us/en/technology/publications/assets/pwc-consumer-intelligence-series-the-sharing-economy.pdf

PwC US. (2017). Share Economy 2017. The New Business Model. Available: https://www.pwc.de/de/digitale-transformation/share-economy-report-2017.pdf

KEY TERMS AND DEFINITIONS

Access Over Ownership: Activities that provide temporary access to goods with or without monetary transactions.

Collaborative Behavior: The practice of getting or providing access to goods and services through sharing, reselling/purchasing used goods, renting, giving or trading activities.

Engagement: The act of usage or participation in sharing activities.

Peer-to-Peer (P2P): A computer-based platform that connects users and providers of goods and services.

Self-Determination Theory: Macro theory of human motivation and sources of satisfaction.

Transfer of Ownership: Sale of second hand/used goods.

Trust: Firm belief on the character, ability, and honesty of someone or something.

Chapter 10
Why Rideshare?
An Analysis of Factors Influencing Intention to Use

Rafael Anaya-Sánchez
https://orcid.org/0000-0003-3327-2793
University of Malaga, Spain

Rocío Aguilar-Illescas
University of Malaga, Spain

Milagros Nasiff-Seiffert
University of Malaga, Spain

Sebastian Molinillo
University of Malaga, Spain

ABSTRACT

The growth in the use of online platforms in the sharing economy is generating great interest in the scientific community. This study seeks to discover what causes travelers to use ridesharing platforms. A theoretical model of causal relationships, evaluated with data collected in an online survey, using partial least squares structural equation modelling (PLS-SEM) is proposed. The results show that attitude towards ridesharing is a critical antecedent of intention to use. Travelers develop positive attitudes mainly due to the economic reward of making savings in travel costs. In addition, attitude is also positively influenced, although to a lesser extent, by perceptions of security and by the moral motivation to help other people. In contrast, the influence of social motivation is not significant. Practical implications guide platform managers in the design of their commercial strategies.

DOI: 10.4018/978-1-5225-9928-9.ch010

Copyright © 2020, IGI Global. Copying or distributing in print or electronic forms without written permission of IGI Global is prohibited.

INTRODUCTION

The new internet-based technologies are an engine for collaborative economies. They give consumers easy access to information and communication platforms that promote shared use, and which have made this type of consumption grow exponentially (Botsman & Rogers, 2011). The sharing economy has changed the way people share and carry out transactions in digital spaces (Sutherland & Jarrahi, 2018). Exchange-based economies are not new, since barter systems and communal lifestyles have a long history. This strong growth is due to the introduction of new technologies, to the late economic crisis, trends towards urbanization, consumers' inclinations towards sustainable consumption and the possibility of enjoying new experiences (Bardhi & Eckhardt, 2012; Kathan, Matzler, & Veider, 2016).

Many digital companies are active in the collaborative economy, in many industrial sectors, and with international presence (Parente, Geleilate, & Kong, 2018). Available services include animal care, tour guiding, parking and storage rental. Although the main companies focus on the hospitality sector (e.g., Airbnb and CouchSurfing), other widely used collaborative economy websites offer ridesharing systems, such as BlaBlaCar and Amicoche.com. BlaBlaCar, on whose business model this work focuses, works by connecting travellers who have common destinations and facilitating their relationship so that they travel together (Casprini, Di Minin, & Paraboschi, 2018).

Collaborative economies are attracting increasing research attention (e.g., Kathan et al., 2016; Parente et al.; 2018; Sutherland, & Jarrahi, 2018). Previous studies have analysed the phenomenon of sharing from a macro-economic perspective, analysing the role played by intermediaries and behaviours and implications at an economic and sociological level (ethics, non-commercial areas, economic implications, etc.). However, few studies have analysed the individual behaviour of users (Bucher, Fieseler, & Lutz, 2016). In addition, most studies focus on the tourism sector, especially on motivations for use (Geissinger, Laurell, Öberg, & Sandström, 2019), and largely do not consider other sectors. In the field of transport, the motivation for car sharing has been investigated (e.g., Bardhi, & Eckhardt, 2012), and studies have analysed its ecological effects and its impact on traditional sectors, such as Uber on taxis (e.g., Casprini et al., 2018; Geissinger et al., 2019). However, the question as to what leads a collaborative economy user to rideshare remains unaddressed. In other words, what are the motivations that lead a person to prefer to share a trip with other users? Thus, the objective of this research is to identify what motivates travellers to rideshare, through an analysis of four classic motivations of consumer behaviour: economic, social, moral and security (see Bucher et al., 2016; Lee, Lee, & Kim, 2018).

LITERATURE REVIEW AND HYPOTHESES DEVELOPMENT

Sharing is a process in which one party shares an object (or experience) that they own with another party for joint use, and/or vice versa, to obtain the benefits of a product without having to own it (Belk, 2007; Belk, 2010). The scientific community agrees that the basic nature of sharing is that it is an act of joint use of an object that is owned by at least one of the sharing parties. Changes in social technologies and societal attitudes have encouraged the growth of online sharing economy models (Bucher et al., 2016). In many cases the consumer values having access to an experience rather than owning the product that facilitates the experience (Bardhi & Eckhart, 2012; Belk, 2013). This practice has increased due to the trend among consumers to use internet-based platforms and to establish new relationships of trust via the medium (Bucher et al., 2016).

Despite its growth, knowledge of the consumer's motivations to participate in the sharing economy is still limited (Belk, 2010). It is considered that people who have sharing motivations sit within two main motivational groups: utilitarian motivation and hedonic motivation (Bucher et al., 2016). These include motivations that are related to prosocial and altruistic behaviours, group membership and support for causes (social, environmental, etc.) (Bucher et al., 2016; Lamberton & Rose, 2012). These motivations are based on acquiring economic and social rewards, as in the potential to feel better about oneself and with one's behaviours. On the other hand, people also find reasons not to share, such as possible negative effects on them personally or on their property (Belk, 2010). The consumer looks for security when accessing a product/experience, so this is a variable of great importance in sharing behaviour (Belk, 2010). These motivations, according to the theory of reasoned action (TRA) and the theory of planned behaviour (TPB), are antecedents of the consumer's attitude, which, in turn, mediates the effect of the motivations for intention to rideshare (Ajzen, 1991; Ajzen & Fishbein, 1980). Thus, a theoretical model is formulated to explore, from a consumer behavioural approach, how motivations shape attitude, and influence intention to rideshare.

Attitudes Towards the Sharing Economy

Attitude results from the organization of beliefs about an object that predisposes an individual to act in a certain way (Rokeach, 1968). An individual's attitude creates a predisposition to evaluate something specific favourably or unfavourably. This attitude must be framed at a general level, that is, it must arise as a result of one's overall view of the object (Van Raaij & Antonides, 1998). Thus, attitude is not innate. Attitudes have three basic components (Rosenberg & Hovland, 1960): the cognitive component, which reflects the individual's information, beliefs or knowledge about an object; the affective component, which reflects the individual's feelings and emotions towards an object; and the conative component, which represents the individual's action tendency, the tendency to respond in a specific way to an object. Thus, if an individual has a strong belief that (s)he will achieve positive results from the performance of a certain behaviour, (s)he will have a positive attitude towards the behaviour (Kim, Woo, et al., 2018).

The TRA and the TPB propose that attitudes towards an object affect the individual's behavioural intentions towards it (Ajzen, 1991; Ajzen & Fishbein, 1980). The study of attitudes in the context of the sharing economy has become more important, as they are fundamental in the explanation of the use of these exchange systems. Hamari, Sjöklint and Ukkonen (2015), Kim, Woo et al. (2018) and Bucher et al. (2016) showed that attitudes towards these platforms clearly affect intentions to use them, and are their principal explanatory factor.

Motivations to Participate in Sharing Economies

Motivation can be described as the internal force that pushes individuals towards action; it exists as a result of an unfulfilled need (Schiffman & Lazar, 1991). The literature on motivation in sharing economies points to the existence of three types, economic, social and moral (Böcker & Meelen, 2017; Bucher et al., 2016). Contradictory results have been obtained as to the importance of each motivation. Greater weight is given to one factor or another, depending on the context, and there are even suggestions that not all the factors are explanatory (Böcker & Meelen, 2017). This present research follows the approach of Bucher et al. (2016), who argue that the three traditional motivations explain the individual's decision-making in online sharing economy contexts as they lead the consumer to adopt positive attitudes. Also included is a variable related to security in decision-making. According to protective motivation theory (PMT) (Rogers, 1975), fear-linked factors shape the attitude of individuals in certain situations in order to minimise the effects of an unpleasant situation. This variable is perceived security, which is considered of great importance in the hiring of online and sharing economy services because it influences trust in the platforms themselves and their users (see Lee et al., 2018; Yang, Lee, Lee, & Koo, 2018). Unlike perceived risk, this variable is measured positively, in line with the other motivations in the model.

Economic Motivation

Economic or monetary motivation is understood as the motivation of users to reduce costs or obtain extra income. Thus, sharing economy users participate, among other reasons, to save money by dividing the costs of contracted services (Bucher et al., 2016). In addition, in open exchange systems, monetary rewards are common (Lamberton & Rose, 2012). However, studies differ in the importance they give to economic motivations. Böcker & Meelen (2017) argue that there is no empirical support for the proposition that the sharing economy has grown mainly due to economic factors, given that it emerged during the economic crisis. Similarly, Möhlmann (2015) notes that, although the economic factor increases customer satisfaction, it does not drive repeat purchase of these services. The importance of economic motivation is highlighted by Tussyadiah (2016) in the accommodation field, by Hamari et al. (2015) in collaborative economies in general and by Bucher et al., (2016). The last study, however, suggests that the effect of economic motivation is positive but the weakest in explaining attitude. Similarly, in the transport context, Bardhi and Eckhardt (2012) demonstrated the importance of economic motivation for car sharing. In accordance with this last approach, the first research hypothesis is proposed:

Hypothesis 1: Economic motivation positively influences attitude towards ridesharing through sharing economy platforms.

Social Motivation

Social and hedonic motivations are considered as consumer behaviours motivated by an interest in interacting with other people. The social aspect of the collaborative economy derives from the unique nature of the sharing economy, which is supported by relationships established between users and between users and platforms; this contrasts with traditional economies, where the focus is more on relations between businesses and consumers (Böcker & Meelen, 2017; Botsman, 2013). According to Botsman and Rogers (2011), the collaborative economy stimulates the individual and helps him/her establish connections and meet people, which seems to be the major trigger for this form of consumption. Tussyadiah and Inversini (2015) note that the social factor is paramount in collaborative tourism; they highlight that meeting hosts, who offer up their homes, and exchanging information with them, enriches the visitor experience. Similarly, Bucher et al. (2016) suggested it is the key factor in creating positive attitudes towards the sharing economy. In ridesharing, this would suggest that users are predisposed to socialise during their journeys. In line with these points, the second hypothesis is proposed:

Hypothesis 2: Social motivation positively influences attitude towards ridesharing through sharing economy platforms.

Moral Motivation

Moral motivation refers to behaviour undertaken based on what the consumer thinks accords with social values. The moral factor can be explained from two standpoints: contributions to the care of the planet and towards helping others (Bucher et al., 2016). Most of the moral factor literature focusses on the environment. Tussyadiah (2016), in the accommodation field, Möhlmann (2015) in accommodation and transport, and Bardhi and Eckhardt (2012) in transport, show that environmental factors are of little importance in decision-making. In contrast, authors such as Schor (2014) and Lawson (2010) have identified a more positive trend in the impact of this factor as a determinant of decisions on collaborative consumption. In fact, the different ways of sharing car journeys (car sharing and ridesharing) seem to be the form of collaborative economy that contributes most to the protection of the environment, since the reduction of pollution through using fewer cars is indisputable (Böcker & Meelen, 2017).

As to the second contribution, helping other people, Belk (2010) noted that the collaborative economy is characterized by its great altruism. Bucher et al. (2016) stated that the moral motives that lead to collaborative consumption can be ethical, ecological, altruistic or based on community support, which all have positive effects on attitude towards participation in sharing economies. The present research focusses on the motivation to help other people. Thus, the third hypothesis is proposed:

Hypothesis 3: Moral motivation positively influences attitude towards ridesharing through sharing economy platforms.

Perceived Security

Consumers feel at risk when buying products, which generates insecurity (Forsythe, Liu, Shannon, & Gardner, 2006). Perceptions of security have been considered in many studies into online consumer behaviour. Suki and Suki (2017), in their study of joint purchasing websites, concluded that the consumer is influenced by perceived risk in terms of product characteristics and the trust (s)he has in the website. Similarly, Chen and Chang (2018) suggested these platforms must offer consumer review systems to help users feel more secure about the services offered; Yang et al. (2018) focussed on the importance of guaranteeing security and privacy. In the sharing economy it is important to take into account the risks to the parties (Pappas, 2018). Authors, such as Belk (2010), have pointed out that the consumer perceives material and personal risks when sharing goods and services but, in turn, shared systems promote a sense of security thanks to the mechanisms of mutual obligation.

Risk and security have been studied in the literature regarding choice of transport. Mehdizadeh, Nordfjaern, Mamdoohi, and Mohaymany (2017) analysed the decision-making processes of parents in whether or not to use transport, based on the perceived risk of schoolchildren making a journey from home to school; and Xu, Zhang, Min, Wang, Zhao, and Liu (2018) consider it a key variable in the acceptance of autonomous cars. This present research proposes that Bucher et al. (2016)'s model must be complemented with a variable that considers the security that the user must feel in order to generate a positive attitude towards this type of shared transport. Based on these points, the fourth study hypothesis is proposed:

Hypothesis 4: The perceived security of the user positively influences attitude towards ridesharing through sharing economy platforms.

Intention to Share

Consumer attitudes change continuously. This, and the fact that sharing economies are very new, means that there is still little understanding of consumer attitudes towards these systems and their effects on behavioural intentions (Bucher et al., 2016). Attitude towards the sharing economy can be defined as the tendency to act favourably or unfavourably towards these type of companies / systems. Previous research mainly focusses on knowledge sharing through the Internet (e.g., Tamjidyamcholo, Bin Baba, Tamjid, & Gholipour, 2013; Zhang, Liu, Deng, & Chen, 2017); few works have examined how intentions to participate in sharing economy systems are generated (see Akbar, Mai, & Hoffmann, 2016; Bucher et al., 2016).

The TPB establishes that positive attitudes positively affect behavioural intentions (Ajzen, 1991). The attitude of an individual towards a specific behaviour, such as sharing, helps to predict their intention to carry out that behaviour (Tamjidyamcholo et al., 2013). Therefore, when there is a very positive attitude towards exchange, this translates into an almost equally high intention to share (Bucher et al., 2016): based on this, the last study hypothesis is proposed:

Hypothesis 5: Positive attitude towards ridesharing through sharing economy platforms generates positive behavioural intentions.

Figure 1 shows the proposed research model, which establishes how different types of consumer motivations and perceptions lead them to develop positive attitudes towards ridesharing; and this, in turn, affects behavioural intentions.

METHODOLOGY

Sample

The data were collected through an online questionnaire aimed at regular users of ridesharing applications (e.g., Blablacar, Amicoche.com). The link to the questionnaire was placed in forums where rideshares exchange information about their experiences and search for fellow travellers. In the event, 162 questionnaires were received; of these, 150 were considered valid after elimination of incomplete returns and those which failed a series of filter questions.

The respondents were all Spanish citizens, 60% female. Regarding formal education levels, 58% had completed secondary/high school and 30.7% had university degrees (30.7%). The largest group were students (39.3%), 13.3% studied and worked, and 38.7% worked, some self-employed and others as employees. The average age was 30.57 years.

Measurements

The measurements used to assess the constructs were adopted from previous research into the sharing economy. From Bucher et al. (2016), the following variables were adapted: economic motivation (5 items), social motivation (4 items), moral motivation (6 items), attitude towards ridesharing (5 items) and ridesharing intention (5 items). Perceived security was measured by adapting 3 items from Xu et

Figure 1. Research model.

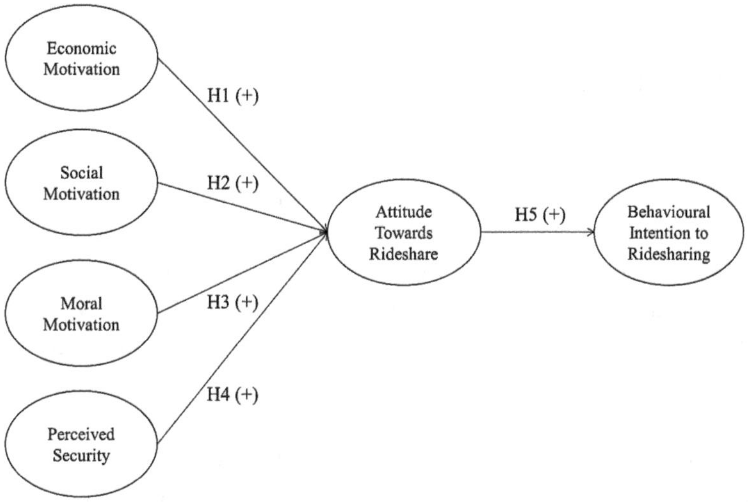

al. (2018). In all cases, 5-point Likert type scales were used, ranging from "totally disagree" to "totally agree", except for the attitude towards ridesharing variable, where bipolar adjectives were used (e.g., good / not good; useful / not useful) (see Appendix). In addition, filter questions were posed to ensure that the respondents were regular ridesharers, and sociodemographic questions (e.g., age and gender) to establish the profile of the sample.

To ensure that the questionnaire was fully comprehensible, a pre-test was carried out with 21 frequent ride sharers. After evaluating and refining the survey and verifying the levels of acceptance, dimensionality, reliability and validity of the proposed scales, data was collected to validate the model.

RESULTS

The data were analysed using partial least squares (PLS) in a structural equation model (SEM). SmartPls 3.2.7 software was used (Ringle, Wende, & Becker, 2015). Unlike SEM models, PLS models are based on covariances, and are appropriate for analyses with small samples (Hair, Hult, Ringle & Sarstedt, 2013). In addition, PLS is valid in cases in which the work continues to be emergent, without being able to ensure the normal distribution of the data. This technique permits efficient analysis of samples smaller than those required in structural equations models based on covariance (CB-SEM or SEM). The sample size (150) can be considered sufficient for PLS-SEM as it greatly exceeds the minimum size of 50 suggested by Iacobucci (2010), and the more restrictive limit of 100 recommended by Bagozzi and Yi (2012), for the analysis of structural equations. The sample size also exceeds the minimum recommended by Hair et al (2011, p. 144): "PLS-SEM minimum sample size should be equal to the larger of the following: (1) ten times the largest number of formative indicators used to measure one construct or (2) ten times the largest number of structural paths directed at a particular latent construct in the structural model."

The study constructs were measured reflexively, so it is more appropriate to use the Consistent PLS algorithm. In addition, bootstrapping was used to verify the significance of the coefficients and blindfolding was used to analyse the predictive capacity of the model. Thereafter, the measurement model's goodness-of-fit was examined to verify that the scales were valid. Thereafter, the structural model and the global goodness-of-fit were tested.

Assessment of the Measurement Model

First, as this is a confirmatory model, its fit was analysed by studying the saturated model (Henseler, Hubona, & Ray, 2016). The measurement model may be valid where the SRMR (saturated) inferential statistic has a fit lower than 0.08, and the values obtained by bootstrapping the three exact goodness-of-fit tests SRMR, D_ULS and D_G2 show significance levels lower than 0.05, or a value lower than the 95th percentile (Dijkstra & Henseler 2015a, b). In our case, the SRMR of the saturated model had a value of 0.053 <0.08, and the p-values of SRMR, D_ULS and D_G2 obtained through boostrapping were less than 0.05.

The reliability of the items was reviewed by studying the loads of each of the indicators / items against their corresponding variables. Where the value is greater than 0.7, the variables are considered well measured, since this shows that the variance between each construct and its indicators is greater than the variance error (Barclay et al.,1995). In our model, all the indicators exceeded the values recommended in the literature, except for one item of the moral motivation variable (MOR2), which was eliminated.

Similarly, Cronbach's *alpha* and Composite Reliability (CR) values were used to measure the reliability of the scales (Cronbach, 1951; Nunnally & Bernstein, 1994). The values of both must exceed 0.7, as they do in the present study. Average variance extracted (AVE) was used to measure convergent validity; this allows us to measure how much variance a construct captures from its indicators compared to that obtained by the measurement error (Fornell & Larcker, 1981). Values above 0.5 confirm that there is convergent validity. Table 1 shows the results of the reliability of the scales and the convergent validity.

Finally, discriminant validity was verified through three procedures. First, through an analysis of the cross-loadings to discover if the variance between each construct and its items is greater than that of the construct with the other model items (Barclay et al. al., 1995). Second, by using the Fornell-Larcker criterion to establish whether the correlations between the variables are less than the square root of their AVEs (Fornell & Larcker, 1981). Third, by using the heterotrait-monotrait ratio (HTMT) to establish whether the inter-construct correlations have values lower than 0.9 (Henseler, Ringle & Sarstedt, 2015). It was also found that in the confidence intervals of the HTMT values obtained by bootstrapping, the value 1 is outside the intervals; thus, discriminant validity is ensured. In all cases the values are within the limits recommended by the literature (see Tables 2 and 3).

Table 1. Assessment of the measurement model: Cronbach's alpha, Composite Reliability (CR) and Average Variance Extracted (AVE)

Construct	Cronbach's Alpha	CR	AVE
Economic Motivation (ECO)	0.952	0.953	0.803
Social Motivation (SOC)	0.912	0.914	0.728
Moral Motivation (MOR)	0.943	0.941	0.763
Perceived Security (SEC)	0.833	0.834	0.626
Attitude Towards Ridesharing (ATT)	0.930	0.930	0.725
Behavioural Intention to Rideshare (INT)	0.976	0.976	0.890

Table 2. Discriminant validity: Cross-loadings

Item	ECO	SOC	MOR	SEC	ATT	INT
ECO1	**0.981**	0.623	0.184	0.435	0.577	0.577
ECO2	**0.942**	0.644	0.147	0.346	0.554	0.564
ECO3	**0.874**	0.696	0.130	0.420	0.514	0.511
ECO4	**0.790**	0.537	0.266	0.424	0.464	0.497
ECO5	**0.880**	0.641	0.102	0.330	0.517	0.520
SOC1	0.619	**0.922**	0.307	0.394	0.500	0.516
SOC2	0.616	**0.881**	0.265	0.421	0.478	0.480
SOC3	0.621	**0.889**	0.268	0.419	0.482	0.461
SOC4	0.637	**0.704**	0.129	0.397	0.382	0.400
MOR1	0.235	0.364	**0.998**	0.343	0.328	0.406
MOR3	0.077	0.190	**0.741**	0.207	0.243	0.295
MOR4	0.142	0.216	**0.771**	0.213	0.253	0.237
MOR5	0.127	0.226	**0.940**	0.256	0.309	0.350
MOR6	0.199	0.251	**0.889**	0.239	0.292	0.310
SEC1	0.304	0.392	0.220	**0.750**	0.366	0.350
SEC2	0.332	0.407	0.173	**0.775**	0.379	0.437
SEC3	0.392	0.337	0.295	**0.846**	0.413	0.442
ATT1	0.474	0.456	0.273	0.331	**0.822**	0.696
ATT2	0.466	0.397	0.305	0.467	**0.833**	0.716
ATT3	0.543	0.482	0.250	0.390	**0.848**	0.717
ATT4	0.547	0.487	0.306	0.431	**0.901**	0.767
ATT5	0.471	0.486	0.264	0.458	**0.870**	0.760
INT1	0.571	0.549	0.366	0.512	0.801	**0.932**
INT2	0.550	0.488	0.346	0.491	0.796	**0.973**
INT3	0.580	0.543	0.337	0.456	0.810	**0.955**
INT4	0.572	0.477	0.334	0.503	0.809	**0.942**
INT5	0.540	0.520	0.364	0.486	0.785	**0.914**

The results confirm that the constructs and scales are reliable and convergent, so the measurement model is validated.

Assessment of the Structural Model

Following the analysis of the measurement model, the structural model was examined. First, multicollinearity was reviewed by examining the VIF values between the related model variables. The values are all within the recommended limits (VIF <0.5). Second, the values of the square roots of the multiple-correlation coefficients (R^2) were examined. This allows us to discover the amount of variance of a construct that can explain the model through its antecedent variables. In this case, the R^2 value of attitude

Table 3. Discriminant validity: Fornell-Larckert criterion (above the main diagonal) and HTMT ratio (below the main diagonal)

Construct	ECO	SOC	MOR	SEC	ATT	INT
Economic Motivation (ECO)	**0.896**	0.726	0.183	0.435	0.588	0.596
Social Motivation (SOC)	0.733	**0.853**	0.290	0.473	0.542	0.546
Moral Motivation (MOR)	0.181	0.279	**0.873**	0.292	0.328	0.370
Perceived Security (SEC)	0.436	0.483	0.285	**0.791**	0.489	0.519
Attitude Towards Rideshare (ATT)	0.587	0.541	0.325	0.487	**0.852**	0.819
Behavioural Intention to Ridesharing (INT)	0.597	0.546	0.365	0.518	0.818	**0.943**

Note: Square root of the AVE in bold (main diagonal).

towards ridesharing is 0.446 and the R^2 of intention to rideshare is 0.738 (see Table 4). Therefore, the explanatory power of the model is considered to be moderate and high, respectively. Both values are clearly higher than the minimum recommended value of 0.1 (Falk & Miller, 1992).

By examining the standardized regression (β) coefficients it is possible to assess the importance that each exogenous variable has for the endogenous variable that explains it. In this case, the coefficient that relates attitude towards ridesharing and intention to rideshare is, as expected, the highest. Similarly, the regression coefficient between economic motivation and attitude towards ridesharing is high and significant. On the other hand, the coefficients between moral motivation and security with respect to attitude towards ridesharing present small but significant values, while the social motivation and attitude coefficient is small and not significant (see Table 4).

On the other hand, the predictive capacity of the dependent constructs was measured by means of the Stone-Geisser, or Q^2 test, obtained through blindfolding (omission distance equal to 7) (Geisser, 1975; Stone, 1974). In cases where values above 0 are obtained, the predictive capacity of the model is confirmed. As can be seen in Table 4, the Q^2 of attitude towards ridesharing is 0.288, while for intention to rideshare it is 0.570. Consequently, the model has high predictive capacity for the dependent variables.

The observed f^2 value (which measures the size of the effect of each exogenous variable on the endogenous variables that it explains) suggests that attitude has the bigger effect size on intention to rideshare (see Table 4). Regarding the explanatory variables of attitude, it was observed that economic motivation ($f^2 = 0.118$), security ($f^2 = 0.065$) and moral motivation ($f^2 = 0.041$) have small but significant effects (Chin, 1998), while the effect of social motivation on attitude is not significant. This result, together with the non-significance of the value of the standardized regression coefficient, means that it is not possible to verify that there is a relationship between these two variables, rejecting hypothesis 2. On the other hand, hypotheses 1, 3, 4 and 5 are accepted. Thus, attitude towards ridesharing is positively influenced mainly by economic motivation, and much less by social motivation and perceived security. In turn, attitude towards ridesharing positively influences intention to rideshare.

Finally, the global goodness-of-fit of the model was tested. The Standardized Root Mean Square Residual, or SRMR, was first used; this allows us to compare the differences between the observed and predicted correlations (Henseler et al., 2014). The value in this case is 0.06, less than the maximum recommended limit of 0.08. In addition, bootstrap-based exact goodness-of-fit tests of the estimated model were applied, that is, SRMR, D_ULS and D_G2 (Dijkstra & Henseler 2015a, b). The values are

Table 4. Assessment of the structural model (bootstrapping=5000; blindfolding=omission distance 7)

Relationship	Path	f^2	Q^2	R^2
Economic Motivation→Attitude Towards Ridesharing	0.378***	0.118		
Social Motivation → Attitude Towards Ridesharing	0.116 n.s.	0.010		
Moral Motivation → Attitude Towards Ridesharing	0.161**	0.041		
Perceived Security → Attitude Towards Ridesharing	0.222**	0.065		
Attitude Towards Rideshare → Behavioural Intention to Rideshare	0.859***	0.814		
Attitude Towards Rideshare			0.288	0.446
Behavioural Intention to Ridesharing			0.570	0.738

Note: *** $p<0.001$, ** $p<0.05$, n.s. (not significant)

significant (p-value <0.05), so the goodness-of-fit of the global model is adequate. Consequently, it can be said that the model has adequate goodness-of-fit for the data.

DISCUSSION

In recent years many internet-based economies have boomed. Among them, the so-called sharing economies stand out (Botsman & Rogers, 2011; Sutherland, & Jarrahi, 2018). In the transport context there are platforms where users offer to convey other travellers in their private cars (e.g., Uber), share a car with other drivers (e.g., Zipcar) and where users contact each other to share a journey (e.g., BlaBlaCar). Although sharing economies have attracted the attention of the scientific community (Kathan et al., 2016; Parente et al., 2018; Sutherland, & Jarrahi, 2018), few studies particularly focus on the transport sector, and they do not closely examine the motivations that lead to ridesharing.

Consequently, this study aims to explore how the positive attitudes that lead consumers to rideshare are generated. To achieve this goal, Bucher et al. (2016)'s model was used; this explains how economic, social and moral motivations cause sharing economy users to develop positive attitudes, which, in turn, lead them to participate in them. In addition to these three motivations, this research includes perceived security as a factor necessary for the consumer to want to participate. The present study evaluated the model in a service and country culturally distinct from that examined by Bucher et al. (2016). While the United States is characterised by higher levels of individualism, masculinity, and indulgence, Spain is characterised by power distance, uncertainty avoidance, and long-term orientation (Hofstede Insights, 2019). In addition, the present study focuses on ridesharing while Bucher et al. focussed on internet-mediated sharing. This study contributes to the literature on consumer behaviour in the sharing economy in two ways. First, because it questions the universal validity of the effect of social motivation on consumer attitude; and, second, because it demonstrates the effect of a variable specifically adapted to ridesharing, that is, "perceived security".

To test the five hypotheses, data from a sample of frequent sharing economy participants were used, treated with PLS. The results confirm that, for the users, the economic motivation is the most important. This implies that the main reason for the generation of positive attitudes towards ridesharing is the saving in transportation costs, which would be higher if the trip was made through another means of transport or in a car on an individual basis. The great importance of the economic factor is discussed in prior studies into the sharing economy; some (e.g., Böcker & Meelen, 2017; Möhlmann, 2015) suggested that monetary reward has little effect on attitude, while others, as the present study, argued that it is, at least, one of the main motivating factors (e.g., Bucher et al., 2016; Hamari et al., 2015; Tussyadiah, 2016).

Moral motivations have a minor, but significant effect. That is, users develop more positive attitudes towards these platforms to the extent that they consider that they can help other users. Previous studies into the sharing economy indicate that these motivations are barely relevant (e.g., Bardhi and Eckhardt, 2012; Möhlmann, 2015; Tussyadiah, 2016), but this could be because they focus on the environmental component of moral motivation. Thus, it seems that ridesharing platform users are more conscious of the help given to others than the associated reduction in pollution. Similarly, it is demonstrated that perceived security affects, although to a limited extent, specific attitudes towards ridesharing. This effect could have, a priori, two explanations: users consider ridesharing platforms and the means of transport for hire to be as least as safe as more traditional systems, allowing economic motivations to prevail; or that the user profile has lower risk aversion, which would limit its effect on attitudes. Our results do not provide support for the contention that social motivations have an effect on attitude, contrary to the findings of previous sharing economy studies (e.g., Bucher et al., 2016; Tussyadiah, & Inversini, 2015). These studies argued that social motivations were not only explanatory factors of attitudes, but that the socialization processes generated through participation in these platforms could be key triggers for the use of collaborative economies. It seems, therefore, that in the ridesharing context, users give scant importance to the establishment of relationships or, at least, not beyond what might be established by using alternative means of transport. This fact may be associated with the distinction that Bucher et al. (2016) make between commercial users (majority group) and non-commercial users. The first group is guided by economic reasons while the second is guided by moral and social reasons. The results of the present study suggest that users of ridesharing platforms are more aligned with users with commercial purposes, as their social motivations are not significant. This observation is particularly valid in the context of Spain; the late economic crisis encouraged the development of the sharing economy as a way of maintaining a certain level of consumption, despite falls in income. From this perspective the consumer is more motivated by the convenience of the mode of transport than social interaction, such that (s)he shares the transport almost in the same way as if (s)he were using public transport. In other words, the value of the shared journey is in its convenience and the saving of money, and to a lesser extent moral aspects, such as environmental protection; the purpose of ridesharing is not to initiate social relationships with other passengers, but simply to share the same transport.

The discrepancies in the previous literature regarding significant motivations and their importance in attitude generation may stem from the nature of the sectors analysed. Specifically, many studies focus on the tourism sector, where it is observed that some accommodation offered on sharing economy platforms (e.g., Airbnb) involve costs similar to other, traditional lodging, and the establishment of relations between hosts and guests might fulfil one's needs to help others and provide a more social component. On the other hand, in shared transport costs are significantly reduced in all cases, and socialization with others may not be an objective, but a mandatory associated feature, whether desired or not. In addition, the user can value and feel that ridesharing helps others to reach their destinations and that the service is secure, even if these are not the main triggers that lead him/her to rideshare. Thus, the managers of platforms such as BlaBlacar or Amicoche.com should focus their commercial strategies on stressing the economic benefits of sharing private transport (lower fuel and maintenance costs, tariffs of other transport, etc.), without forgetting to emphasise the security element, that users can trust those with whom they rideshare, and that they will reach their destination under the stipulated conditions. On the contrary, they should reduce their current strong strategic focus on social functions. These platforms, thus, should realise that other transport providers, such as Uber, Cabify or Zipcar, compete with their services more closely than they might think, as the prospective traveller in many cases will make his/her decision based on cost and not socialisation opportunities. This, possibly, points towards using platforms such Uber and Cabify for urban travel and platforms such as BlaBlacar and Amicoche.com for longer journeys, for cost reasons.

LIMITATIONS AND FUTURE RESEARCH LINES

This work has limitations that should be discussed. First, the sample's responses were based mainly on their experiences with one ridesharing platform, BlaBlaCar. This can influence their perceptions and attitudes. Future studies might include services with different contracting and operational modes. Second, the sample, while representative of users of these platforms, is small and mainly made up of young people living in Spain; it thus largely disregards other regular users of these platforms and other regions / countries with different sociocultural contexts. Third, the study uses cross-sectional data, which limits the ability to analyse causal relationships. Therefore, future research might perform longitudinal studies to strengthen the validity of the results. Finally, the study follows a micro- approach to consumer behaviour. Future research might take a macro-approach to better understand the social effects of ridesharing.

ACKNOWLEDGEMENT

This study was partly funded by the Plan Andaluz de Investigación, Desarrollo e Innovación (Convocatoria 2017), Grupo SEJ-567.

REFERENCES

Ajzen, I. (1991). The theory of planned Behavior. *Organizational Behavior and Human Decision Processes*, *50*(2), 179–211. doi:10.1016/0749-5978(91)90020-T

Akbar, P., Mai, R., & Hoffmann, S. (2016). When do materialistic consumers join commercial sharing systems. *Journal of Business Research*, *69*(10), 4215–4224. doi:10.1016/j.jbusres.2016.03.003

Barclay, D., Higgins, C., & Thompson, R. (1995). The Partial Least Squares (PLS) Approach to Causal Modeling: Personal Computer Adoption and Use as an Illustration. *Technology Studies*, *2*(2), 285–309.

Bardhi, F., & Eckhardt, G. M. (2012). Access-based consumption: The case of car sharing. *The Journal of Consumer Research*, *39*(4), 881–898. doi:10.1086/666376

Belk, R. (2007). Why not share rather than own? *The Annals of the American Academy of Political and Social Science*, *611*(1), 126–140. doi:10.1177/0002716206298483

Belk, R. (2010). Sharing. *The Journal of Consumer Research*, *36*(5), 715–734. doi:10.1086/612649

Belk, R. (2014). You are what you can access: Sharing and collaborative consumption online. *Journal of Business Research*, *67*(8), 1595–1600. doi:10.1016/j.jbusres.2013.10.001

Belk, R. W. (2013). Extended self in a digital world. *The Journal of Consumer Research*, *40*(3), 477–500. doi:10.1086/671052

Böcker, L., & Meelen, T. (2017). Sharing for people, planet or profit? Analysing motivations for intended sharing economy participation. *Environmental Innovation and Societal Transitions*, *23*, 28–39. doi:10.1016/j.eist.2016.09.004

Botsman, R. (2013). *The sharing economy lacks a shared definition*. Retrieved from: https://www.fastcoexist.com/3022028/the-sharing-economy-lacks-a-shared-definition

Botsman, R., & Rogers, R. (2011). *What's mine is yours: how collaborative consumption is changing the way we live*. Collins.

Bucher, E., Fieseler, C., & Lutz, C. (2016). What's mine is yours (fora nominal fee) – Exploring the spectrum of utilitarian to altruistic motives for Internet- mediated sharing. *Computers in Human Behavior*, *62*, 316–326. doi:10.1016/j.chb.2016.04.002

Casprini, E., Di Minin, A., & Paraboschi, A. (2018). (in press). How do companies organize nascent markets? The BlaBlaCar case in the inter-city shared mobility market. *Technological Forecasting and Social Change*.

Chen, C.-C., & Chang, Y.-C. (2018). What drives purchase intention on Airbnb? Perspectives of consumer reviews, information quality, and media richness. *Telematics and Informatics*, *35*(5), 1512–1523. doi:10.1016/j.tele.2018.03.019

Chin, W. W. (1998). The Partial Least Squares Approach to Structural Equation Modeling. In G. A. Marcoulides (Ed.), *Modern Methods for Business Research* (pp. 295–336). Mahwah, NJ: Lawrence Erlbaum Associates Publishers.

Cronbach, L. J. (1951). Coefficient Alpha and the Internal Structure of Tests. *Psychometrika*, *16*(3), 297–334. doi:10.1007/BF02310555

Dijkstra, T. K., & Henseler, J. (2015a). Consistent and asymptotically normal PLS estimators for linear structural equations. *Computational Statistics & Data Analysis*, *81*, 10–23. doi:10.1016/j.csda.2014.07.008

Dijkstra, T. K., & Henseler, J. (2015b). Consistent partial least squares path modeling. *Management Information Systems Quarterly*, *39*(2), 297–316. doi:10.25300/MISQ/2015/39.2.02

Falk, R. F., & Miller, N. B. (1992). *A Primer for Soft Modeling*. University of Akron Press.

Fornell, C., & Larcker, D. F. (1981). Evaluating Structural Equation Models with Unobservable Variables and Measurement Error. *JMR, Journal of Marketing Research*, *18*(1), 39–50. doi:10.1177/002224378101800104

Forsythe, S., Liu, C., Shannon, D., & Gardner, L. C. (2006). Development of a scale to measure the perceived benefits and risks of online shopping. *Journal of Interactive Marketing*, *20*(2), 55–75. doi:10.1002/dir.20061

Geisser, S. (1975). The Predictive Sample Reuse Method with Applications. *Journal of the American Statistical Association, 70*(350), 320–328. doi:10.1080/01621459.1975.10479865

Geissinger, A., Laurell, C., Öberg, C., & Sandström, C. (2019). How sustainable is the sharing economy? On the sustainability connotations of sharing economy platforms. *Journal of Cleaner Production, 206*(1), 419–429. doi:10.1016/j.jclepro.2018.09.196

Hair, F., Hult, G. T. M., Ringle, C., & Sarstedt, M. (2013). *A Primer on Partial Least Squares Structural Equation Modeling (PLS-SEM)*. Thousand Oaks, CA: Sage Publications.

Hamari, J., Sjöklint, M., & Ukkonen, A. (2015). The sharing economy: Why people participate in collaborative consumption. *Journal of the Association for Information Science and Technology, 67*(9), 2047–2059. doi:10.1002/asi.23552

Henseler, J., Dijkstra, T. K., Sarstedt, M., Ringle, C. M., Diamantopoulos, A., Straub, D. W., & Calantone, R. J. (2014). Common Beliefs and Reality about PLS Comments on Rönkkö and Evermann (2013). *Organizational Research Methods, 17*(2), 182–209. doi:10.1177/1094428114526928

Henseler, J., Hubona, G., & Ray, P. A. (2016). Using PLS path modeling in new technology research: Updated guidelines. *Industrial Management & Data Systems, 116*(1), 2–20. doi:10.1108/IMDS-09-2015-0382

Henseler, J., Ringle, C. M., & Sarstedt, M. (2015). A New Criterion for Assessing Discriminant Validity in Variance-Based Structural Equation Modeling. *Journal of the Academy of Marketing Science, 43*(1), 115–135. doi:10.100711747-014-0403-8

Hofstede Insights. (2019). *Compare countries*. Retrieve from https://www.hofstede-insights.com/product/compare-countries/

Kathan, W., Matzler, K., & Veider, V. (2016). The sharing economy: Your business model's friend or foe? *Business Horizons, 59*(6), 663–762. doi:10.1016/j.bushor.2016.06.006

Kim, Y. G., Woo, E., & Nam, J. (2018). Sharing economy perspective on an integrative framework of the NAM and TPB. *International Journal of Hospitality Management, 72*, 109–117. doi:10.1016/j.ijhm.2018.01.008

Lamberton, C. P., & Rose, R. L. (2012). When Is Ours Better Than Mine? A Framework for Understanding and Altering Participation in Commercial Sharing Systems. *Journal of Marketing, 76*(4), 109–125. doi:10.1509/jm.10.0368

Lawson, S. (2010). Transumers: motivations of non-ownership consumption. In M. C. Campbell, J. Inman, & R. Pieters (Eds.), NA - Advances in Consumer Research (pp. 842-853). Duluth, MN: Association for Consumer Research.

Lee, S.-H., Lee, B.-Y., & Kim, H.-W. (2018). (in press). Decisional factors leading to the reuse of an on-demand ride service. *Information & Management*.

Mehdizadeh, M., Nordfjaern, T., Mamdoohi, A. R., & Mohaymany, A. S. (2017). The role of parental risk judgements, transport safety attitudes, transport priorities and accident experiences on pupils' walking to school. *Accident; Analysis and Prevention, 102*, 60–71. doi:10.1016/j.aap.2017.02.020 PMID:28259829

Möhlmann, M. (2015). Collaborative consumption: Determinants of satisfaction and the likelihood of using a sharing economy option again. *Journal of Consumer Behaviour, 14*(3), 193–207. doi:10.1002/cb.1512

Nunnally, J. C., & Bernstein, I. H. (1994). *Psychometric Theory*. New York: McGraw-Hill.

Pappas, N. (2018). (in press). The complexity of consumer experience formulation in the sharing economy. *International Journal of Hospitality Management.*

Parente, R. C., Geleilate, J.-M. G., & Kong, K. (2018). The Sharing Economy Globalization Phenomenon: A Research Agenda. *Journal of International Management, 24*(1), 52–64. doi:10.1016/j.intman.2017.10.001

Ringle, C. M., Wende, S., & Becker, J. M. (2015). *SmartPLS 3*. Bönningstedt: SmartPLS.

Rogers, R. W. (1975). A protection motivation theory of fear appeals and attitude change1. *The Journal of Psychology, 91*(1), 93–114. doi:10.1080/00223980.1975.9915803 PMID:28136248

Rokeach, M. (1968). The role of values in public opinion research. *Public Opinion Quarterly, 32*(4), 547–559. doi:10.1086/267645

Rosenberg, M. J., & Hovland, C. I. (1960). *Cognitive, affective, and behavioral components of attitude. Attitude Organization and Change*. Yale University.

Schor, J. B. (2014). *Debating the sharing economy*. Retrieved from: http://www.greattransition.org/publication/debating-the-sharing-economy

Stone, M. (1974). Cross-Validatory Choice and Assessment of Statistical Predictions. *Journal of the Royal Statistical Society. Series B. Methodological, 36*(2), 111–147. doi:10.1111/j.2517-6161.1974.tb00994.x

Suki, N. M., & Suki, N. M. (2017). Modeling the determinants of consumers' attitudes toward online group buying: Do risks and trusts matters? *Journal of Retailing and Consumer Services, 12*, 1–9.

Sutherland, W., & Jarrahi, M. H. (2018). The sharing economy and digital platforms: A review and research agenda. *International Journal of Information Management, 43*, 328–341. doi:10.1016/j.ijinfomgt.2018.07.004

Tamjidyamcholo, A., Bin Baba, M. S., Tamjid, H., & Gholipour, R. (2013). Information security – Professional perceptions of knowledge-sharing intention under self-efficacy, trust, reciprocity, and shared-language. *Computers & Education, 68*, 223–232. doi:10.1016/j.compedu.2013.05.010

Tussyadiah, L. P. (2016). Determinants of Satisfaction and Future Intention to Use Peer-to-Peer Accommodation International. *Journal of Hospitality Management, 36*, 24–40.

Tussyadiah, L. P., & Inversini, A. (2015). Information and Communication Technologies in Tourism 2015. In *Proceedings of the International Conference in Lugano*, Switzerland. Springer. 10.1007/978-3-319-14343-9

Van Raaij, W. F., & Antonides, G. (1998). *Consumer behaviour: a european perspective*. Wiley.

Xu, Z., Zhang, K., Min, H., Wang, Z., Zhao, X., & Liu, P. (2018). What drives people to accept automated vehicles? Findings from a field experiment. *Transportation Research Part C, Emerging Technologies*, *95*, 320–334. doi:10.1016/j.trc.2018.07.024

Yang, S.-B., Lee, K., Lee, H., & Koo, C. (2018). (in press). In Airbnb we trust: Understanding consumers' trust-attachment building mechanisms in the sharing economy. *International Journal of Hospitality Management*. doi:10.1016/j.ijhm.2018.10.016

Zhang, X., Liu, S., Deng, Z., & Chen, X. (2017). Knowledge sharing motivations in online health communities: A comparative study of health professionals and normal users. *Computers in Human Behavior*, *75*, 797–810. doi:10.1016/j.chb.2017.06.028

ADDITIONAL READING

Banerjee, S., & Johari, R. (2019). Ride Sharing. In M. Hu (Ed.), Sharing Economy. Making Supply Meet Demand (pp. 73-97). Springer Series in Supply Chain Management (SSSCM, vol. 6). Springer. doi:10.1007/978-3-030-01863-4_5

Botsman, R. (2010). *What's Mine Is Yours: The Rise of Collaborative Consumption*. New York, NY: Harper Collins.

Cruz, I., Ganga, R., & Wahlen, S. (Eds.). (2018). *Contemporary Collaborative Consumption. Trust and Reciprocity Revisited*. Springer. doi:10.1007/978-3-658-21346-6

European Commission. (2016). *A European agenda for the collaborative economy*. Brussels, Belgium: Office for Official Publications of the European Communities.

Handke, V., & Jonuschat, E. (2013). *Flexible Ridesharing New Opportunities and Service Concepts for Sustainable Mobility*. Berlin, Heidelberg: Springer.

Mckee, D., Makela, F., & Scassa, T. (2018). *Law and the "Sharing Economy"*. University of Ottowa Press. doi:10.2307/j.ctv5vdczv

Meyer, G., & Shaheen, S. (Eds.). (2017). *Disrupting Mobility Impacts of Sharing Economy and Innovative Transportation on Cities*. Cham: Springer International Publishing. doi:10.1007/978-3-319-51602-8

Sundararajan, A. (2017). *The Sharing Economy. The End of Employment and the Rise of Crowd-Based Capitalism*. Cambridge, MA: The MIT Press.

KEY TERMS AND DEFINITIONS

Attitude: The organization of beliefs about an object that inclines an individual to act in a certain manner.

Collaborative Economy: An economic model of decentralized systems and marketplaces among peers that allow the use of underused assets.

Intention: Explicit decisions to act in a convinced manner based on a personal motivation.

Motivation: The internal state that makes persons act in a determined way, mainly based on an unfulfilled need.

Perceived Security: Feeling of protection against risks resulting from the use of certain objects and services. Usually measured as a degree.

Ridesharing: A mode of transport in which individuals share a private means of transportation for a trip, sharing costs.

Sharing Economy: Economy based on sharing underutilized possessions. Nowadays, sharing economy are aided by ITC-based technologies.

APPENDIX

Table 5. Measures

Items	Construct	Source
ECO1: I rideshare because it pays well ECO2: Ridesharing helps me pay my bills ECO3: Earning extra money is an important factor when I rideshare ECO4: Ridesharing is a good way to supplement my income ECO5: Ridesharing allows me to make money from something I own	Economic	Bucher *et al.* (2016)
MOR1: I rideshare because I want to help others MOR2: I find ridesharing a generous thing to do MOR3: Ridesharing is a decent thing to do MOR4: Ridesharing allows me to do something meaningful.	Moral	Bucher *et al.* (2016)
SOC1: Ridesharing is a good way to meet new people SOC2: Through ridesharing there is a good chance that I will meet like-minded people SOC3: Ridesharing makes me feel part of a community SOC4: Ridesharing is a good way to find company SOC5: Ridesharing is fun SOC6: I rideshare because it is an adventure	Social	Bucher *et al.* (2016)
SEC1: I felt relaxed riding in a shared vehicle SEC2: I felt safe riding in a shared vehicle SEC3: I did not feel at risk riding in a shared vehicle	Perceived Security	Xu *et al.* (2018)
ATT1: Ridesharing is not good/good ATT2: Ridesharing is not useful/useful ATT3: Ridesharing is not valuable/valuable ATT4: Ridesharing is not worthwhile/worthwhile ATT5: Ridesharing is not helpful/helpful	Attitude	Bucher *et al.* (2016)
INT1: If the circumstances allow it, I will rideshare in the future INT2: I may rideshare with others in the future INCT3: It is likely that I will continue to rideshare in the future INT4: I intend to rideshare with others in the future INT5: I will try to rideshare in the future	Intention to Share	Bucher *et al.* (2016)

Chapter 11
Determining Factors of User Satisfaction for Bicycle-Sharing Systems:
MalagaBici Case Study

Sebastian Molinillo
University of Malaga, Spain

Francisco Liébana-Cabanillas
University of Granada, Spain

Miguel Ruiz-Montañez
https://orcid.org/0000-0003-2211-8694
Malagueña Transportation Company (EMT), Spain

Guadalupe González-Sánchez
University of Malaga, Spain

ABSTRACT

With the development of new shared transportation services, changes are occurring in the habitual consumption of these kinds of services, and it is expected that this trend will continue in the coming years. Given the rise of public bicycle-sharing systems (PBSS) and the increase in their use as a new mode of transportation in many cities, it is considered necessary to analyze and understand the main aspects that determine satisfaction with PBSS. This chapter proposes 10 aspects related to PBSS, grouped according to service infrastructure and other factors that are typical of this service. The results show that all the variables maintain a significant relationship with the established levels of satisfaction. In addition, it has been demonstrated that concessionaires and town halls must take special interest in the quality of the city's bicycles, bike lanes, and network of stations.

DOI: 10.4018/978-1-5225-9928-9.ch011

Copyright © 2020, IGI Global. Copying or distributing in print or electronic forms without written permission of IGI Global is prohibited.

INTRODUCTION

Technological development has facilitated the appearance of new business models based on the sharing economy in diverse sectors, such as tourism, retail and education. One of the sectors that has been impacted the most by this process is passenger transportation. With the development of new shared transportation services (e.g., bicycles, scooters, cars, taxis), users' habits are rapidly changing and the growth in demand is expected to increase in the coming years.

In the field of urban transportation, bicycle-sharing systems (BSS) have become a key element of the multimodal network of urban public transportation in cities all over the world, valued as an effective component of sustainable urban mobility strategies. Studies have shown that these systems have had a rapid rate of diffusion as compared to other transportation innovations, as they are associated with both social and environmental benefits (Parkes, Marsden, Shaheen, & Cohen, 2013). For example, there is evidence that using BSS largely substitutes for traditional modes of transportation, such as private vehicles (Fishman, Washington, & Haworth, 2015; Shaheen, Guzman, & Zhang, 2010). The decreased dependence on private vehicles thanks to the use of BSS implies a reduction in gas emissions and traffic congestion. Furthermore, BSS improve public transportation connectivity and intermodality, improving the capacity of bus and train networks in major cities (Shaheen, Martin, & Cohen, 2013). Therefore, BSS help cities encourage more sustainable mobility (Jäppinen, Toivonen, & Salonen, 2013).

BSS also has the potential to further promote the image of bicycles by increasing the practice of cycling and contributing to normalizing its use (Ricci, 2015). This also favors changes in behavior towards a greater use of bicycles for daily mobility and an improved perception of bicycles as a convenient, competitive mode of transportation (Shaheen et al., 2010). It also contributes to improving local economies by connecting people with employment opportunities, retail trade and other places where they can carry out economic activity (Ricci, 2015).

BSS offers numerous benefits for users, including improving their health and physical activity, offering a wider variety of transportation options, decreased time and costs for getting around, and a better travel experience. Users do not need to worry about typical issues associated with privately owned bicycles, such as maintenance, theft protection and finding a place to park it (Mátrai & Tóth, 2016).

Some authors have identified that the users' level of satisfaction with BSS is one of the main variables that influences their use of the system (Chen et al., 2017). Given its importance, various studies have attempted to identify the factors that determine user satisfaction, highlighting those related to infrastructure and service features. However, studies on satisfaction cannot be generalized because the impact of these factors largely depends on the BSS environment. Accordingly, bicycle use varies greatly between different countries and even municipalities (Rietveld & Daniel, 2004). Use is influenced by various aspects such as culture, socioeconomic inequality, climate, topography, cycling infrastructure and protection from road traffic, public policy, bicycle promotion activities, and even drivers' behavior towards cyclists on the road (Pucher, Garrard, & Greaves, 2011). A greater understanding of the use of BSS is therefore necessary (Shaheen et al., 2010).

Until now, most studies have focused on countries in Northern and Central Europe and, recently, in Asia. However, few studies have analyzed user satisfaction with BSS installed in Southern European cities, which have substantially different cultural, socioeconomic, weather, and orographic conditions. Specifically, Spain is one of the countries with the most BSS programs launched in the world (Fishman, 2016), although many have had to close in recent years (Meddin & De Maio, 2017). The objective of this study is to analyze the factors that affect the satisfaction of PBSS users in the sixth largest city in Spain (by number of inhabitants) and one of the largest in Southern Europe: Malaga. This study contributes to improving knowledge of the factors that influence user satisfaction for a PBSS in a geographic area where the climate and orography are favorable for bicycle use, and where bicycle culture as a mode of transportation is still emerging. The study has also developed a methodology that can be applied to other geographic areas, thereby contributing to the design of strategies aimed at promoting sustainable public transportation.

BACKGROUND

Bicycle-Sharing Systems Users' Satisfaction

From the customer's perspective, a service relationship is a value-based relationship, i.e. the relationship is a function of the costs and benefits that accrue from that relationship. A customer's assessment of a service depends on the balance between sacrifices and benefits, both monetary and non-monetary (Mouwen, 2015). This study defines satisfaction as the user's general attitude towards the accumulated behavioral experience.

Transportation service quality is an aspect that significantly influences users' choices. Customers who have a good experience with transportation will probably use those services again, while customers who experience problems may not use those services the next time. Improving service quality is therefore important for retaining current users and for attracting new users. Moreover, the need for supplying high-quality services ensures competition among transportation agencies, and, consequently, users benefit from better services (Eboli & Mazzulla, 2009). To achieve these goals, transportation agencies must evaluate their performance. Customer satisfaction represents a measure of company performance according to customer needs (Hill, Brierley, & MacDougall, 2003); therefore, the measure of customer satisfaction provides a measure of service quality.

Prior studies on BSS have identified a number of factors that affect user satisfaction. According to Li, Zhang, Li, and Shi (2018), the bicycle itself and its characteristics have the greatest impact on user satisfaction. Other authors have highlighted specific aspects of the bicycle, such as its modernity (Bachand-Marleau, Lee, & El-Geneidy, 2012) and mechanics (Manzi & Saibene, 2018). The network of stations also has a significant influence on satisfaction, particularly depending on how close they are to the user's home, work or other frequented destinations (Bachand-Marleau et al., 2012; Fishman, Washington, Haworth, & Mazzei, 2014; Fishman, 2016), where they perceive the service negatively if it requires more than a ten-minute walk to access a station (Bordagaray, dell'Olio, Ibeas, Barreda, & Alonso, 2015).

Other authors highlight the importance of the connectivity of BSS with public transportation (Oh, Kim, & Lee, 2014) and its integration in a multimodal network (Fishman et al., 2014). Other factors have been associated with the infrastructure required for service development, such as bike lanes (Ricci, 2015; Soltani, Allan, Anh Nguyen, & Berry, 2019) and travel times (Fishman et al., 2014). Other factors have also been identified that are related to cost savings (Oh et al., 2014; Soltani et al., 2019), safety (Bordagaray et al., 2015; Soltani et al., 2019) and theft prevention for privately-owned bicycles (Bachand-Marleau et al., 2012). Other studies have identified important factors for satisfaction with PBSS, such as: available service information (Bordagaray et al., 2015), relative difficulty of the registration process (Fishman et al., 2014) and the system for picking up and dropping off the bicycles (Manzi & Saibene,

2018). Lastly, other influential factors include comfort, convenience and reliability (Fishman et al., 2014; Fishman, 2016; Oh et al., 2014; Soltani et al., 2019).

MALAGABICI CASE STUDY

Malaga is a Mediterranean city in Southern Europe. With an area of 398 Km^2 and a population of approximately 600,000 inhabitants, Malaga is the second most populated city in Andalucía and the sixth most populated in Spain.

In 2010, the local government decided to implement the city's first BSS. They conducted a detailed study of relevant factors such as accessibility to local transportation stations, the ease of connectivity between different modes of transportation and how to make BSS stations more accessible in order to integrate them in a future network that would be fully intermodal. The service was launched in 2012 with the brand MalagaBici and managed by the municipal public entity Malagueña Transportation Company (EMT).

In order to participate in the integrated system, MalagaBici customers first have to acquire a personal, nontransferable smartcard. Malaga's travel card incorporates Near Field Communication (NFC) technology, which can be used on a physical or virtual card using a mobile app. In both cases, in order to access the service, in addition to acquiring the travel card, the user must register on the MalagaBici website and pay the yearly fee and a civil liability insurance policy. The card (physical or virtual) is the same that is used to access other modes of public transportation in the city, such as city buses, the metro and commuter trains, thereby encouraging intermodality.

Once registered, to use the BSS, users just have to present their smartcard or smartphone at a transportation post with an available bicycle at a docking station. It is important to keep in mind that the system is designed for use by travelers that intend to use the PBSS as part of the intermodal network and not for leisure; in fact, it is not available for tourists. Other private companies offer bicycle rentals to tourists visiting the city.

In 2018, the number of people registered reached 42,000 users. At that time, the system had 400 bicycles and 23 stations distributed throughout the city. The stations are located on highly populated streets and in neighborhoods with diverse socioeconomic structures. The most widely used stations are those that are located near other modes of transportation, such as train stations, the main bus station, metro lines and the main local bus stops. The high usage rate of the bicycles located at stations in the city center is noteworthy. The bicycles are available 365 days a year from 7:00 a.m. to 11:00 p.m. Trips longer than 30 minutes are unusual, accounting for less than 5% of the total trips, mainly because usage is free for the first 30 minutes. This makes the BSS convenient for the first and last mile of travel until users can access another mode of transportation or their destination (Mátrai & Tóth, 2016).

At the present time, Malaga's PBSS is fully integrated in the public transportation network (city buses, metro, metropolitan area buses and commuter trains). Anticipating the system's expansion, the local government intends to improve PBSS operations, connectivity and performance before launching the system's second phase.

METHODOLOGICAL APPROACH

Measurement Instrument

A survey was conducted to evaluate user satisfaction. The questionnaire includes the main factors identified in the literature, classified in two blocks: (1) factors related to service infrastructure, including aspects of the station and the bike lane; (2) factors derived from the service, such as information, price, and quality. In total, ten factors were included (Figure 1).

Sample and Data Collection

The data for the evaluation of user satisfaction was collected through a face-to-face survey of users with experience using the service, selected through a simple random sample procedure. The survey was conducted at various stations during the months of September and October in 2016, Monday through Sunday, in different time slots during the service hours of operation (7:00 a.m. to 11:00 p.m.). By the end of the data collection period, a total of 1,984 valid surveys were collected. The obtained sample allows for the results to be extrapolated to the general population with a sample margin of error of ±2.14% and a confidence interval of 95%.

Data Analysis

First of all, in order to verify the effects of certain variables on satisfaction with the BSS service, a one-way analysis of variance (ANOVA) was conducted with SPSS 20.0 software. The ANOVA test allowed us to verify the proposed dimensions of satisfaction according to a Likert scale (1-7), reclassified in three dimensions (low, medium and high). The Fisher-Snedecor distribution was used (Snedecor's F distribution) to verify the existing level of influence between the proposed variables and satisfaction. Based on the significance relationship, it was necessary to know how users score each of these variables, and then

Figure 1. Factors for evaluating BSS user satisfaction

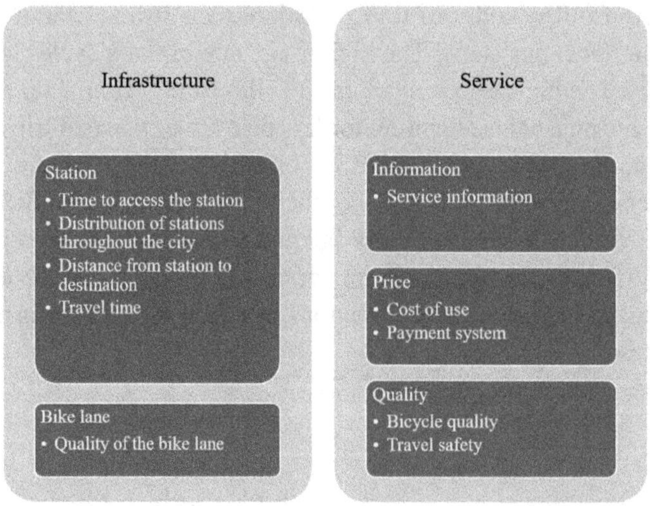

conduct a detailed comparison between the three proposed levels of satisfaction (low, medium and high) as well as the level of each of the proposed variables (very low, low, medium, and high).

Once the importance of each of the proposed variables was verified, an analysis of the possible differences was conducted according to the sample's main sociodemographic variables: age, gender, employment, educational level, immediate family members, average income, place of residence, and experience using BSS. A multivariate analysis of variance (MANOVA) was conducted to determine the effects of the interactions on satisfaction.

RESULTS

In regard to the demographic profile of the survey participants, it is noteworthy that 59.02% were men, 68.75% were between the ages of 14 and 44, and 40.22% had completed university studies (Table 1).

All the factors included in the analysis are significant in the determination of user satisfaction ($p= 0.000$) (Table 2). The results reveal that the quality of the bicycle is the most highly-valued factor according to the survey participants ($F= 311.783$; $p= 0.000$), followed by safety during travel ($F= 180.200$; $p= 0.000$), the distribution of the stations throughout the city ($F= 163.149$; $p= 0.000$), the quality of the bike lane ($F= 151.624$; $p= 0.000$), service information ($F= 151.478$; $p= 0.000$), the distance from station to destination ($F= 130.004$; $p= 0.000$), time to access the station ($F= 128.453$; $p= 0.000$), travel time ($F= 85.912$; $p= 0.000$), cost of use ($F= 59.315$; $p= 0.000$) and, lastly, the payment system ($F= 56.607$; $p= 0.000$).

Table 3 shows the joint analysis of the three levels of satisfaction considered (low, medium and high) and the four levels of each of the proposed variables (very low, low, medium, and high). Figure 2 shows how bicycle quality (the most influential factor on user satisfaction) was given a very low score by MalagaBici users. Secondly, safety during travel is also an especially important determining factor of satisfaction, although in this case its score was medium. Thirdly, the network BSS stations was given a medium-low score. Users gave the quality of the bike lane infrastructure a low score. Service information, distance from station to destination, time to access the station, and travel time all received medium scores. Lastly, the cost of service and selected payment system received medium or good scores, but their importance in determining satisfaction was low.

The multivariate analysis of variance of the proposed factors (Table 4), reveals that they all have significant effects up to 95% ($p<0.05$), both simple and in their interactions, except in the case of average income, place of residence and experience using BSS ($p>0.05$); we can therefore confirm that satisfaction depends on other variables such as age, gender, employment, educational level, and immediate family members.

DISCUSSION AND IMPLICATIONS

The prior scientific literature establishes different factors that determine the level of user satisfaction for public transportation services (Cats et al., 2015; Del Castillo & Benitez, 2013; Diab et al., 2017; Eboli & Mazzulla, 2007, 2009; Joewono & Kubota, 2007; Tyrinopoulos & Antoniou, 2008) and PBSS in particular (Bachand-Marleau et al., 2012; Bordagaray et al., 2015; Fishman et al., 2014; Fishman, 2016; Li et al., 2018; Manzi & Saibene, 2018; Oh et al., 2014; Ricci, 2015; Soltani et al., 2019). This study

Table 1. Demographic profile of respondents

	Frequency	Percentage
Gender		
Man	1171	59.02%
Woman	813	40.98%
Age		
14 – 17	5	0.25%
18 – 24	203	10.23%
25 – 34	583	29.39%
35 – 44	573	28.88%
45 – 54	366	18.45%
55 – 65	198	9.98%
Over 65	56	2.82%
Level of Studies		
No studies	3	0.15%
Primary studies	67	3.38%
Secondary studies (High School and Vocational Training)	563	28.38%
Undergraduate university studies (Bachelor's degree, Engineering…)	798	40.22%
Graduate university studies (Master, PhD)	539	27.17%
Others	14	0.71%
Income Level		
No income	106	5.34%
Less than 650 €	166	8.37%
651 a 900 €	210	10.58%
901 – 1,200 €	327	16.48%
1,201 – 1,500 €	263	13.26%
1,501 – 1,800 €	218	10.99%
1,801 – 2,400 €	283	14.26%
2,401 – 3,000 €	184	9.27%
3,001 – 6,000 €	179	9.02%
Over 6,000 €	48	2.42%
Occupation		
Full-time job	1078	54.33%
Part-time job	208	10.48%
Part-time job and studies	118	5.95%
Studies	170	8.57%
Unemployed	251	12.65%
Retired or early retirement	95	4.79%

continued on following page

Table 3. Detailed scores of the factors influencing user satisfaction

Variable	Level	Satisfaction		
		Low	Medium	Good
Bicycle quality	Very low	306	224	5
	Low	85	620	31
	Medium	22	281	76
	Good	0	11	15
Safety during travel	Very low	116	53	3
	Low	195	386	18
	Medium	97	669	81
	Good	4	31	25
Distribution of stations throughout the city	Very low	120	80	2
	Low	206	448	18
	Medium	85	578	82
	Good	3	34	25
Quality of the bike lane	Very low	179	168	5
	Low	162	443	24
	Medium	67	499	67
	Good	5	27	29
Service information	Very low	83	52	1
	Low	174	286	10
	Medium	145	734	68
	Good	9	67	47
Distance from station to destination	Very low	82	57	1
	Low	157	247	8
	Medium	165	748	77
	Good	10	88	41
Time to access the station	Very low	94	60	5
	Low	146	223	8
	Medium	154	724	66
	Good	18	133	48
Travel time	Very low	31	19	0
	Low	89	98	9
	Medium	271	921	61
	Good	20	99	57
Cost of use	Very low	17	12	0
	Low	62	68	3
	Medium	221	634	27
	Good	112	427	97
Payment system	Very low	29	27	1
	Low	66	93	3
	Medium	229	680	38
	Good	83	337	85

Figure 2. Joint analysis of the main factors and satisfaction

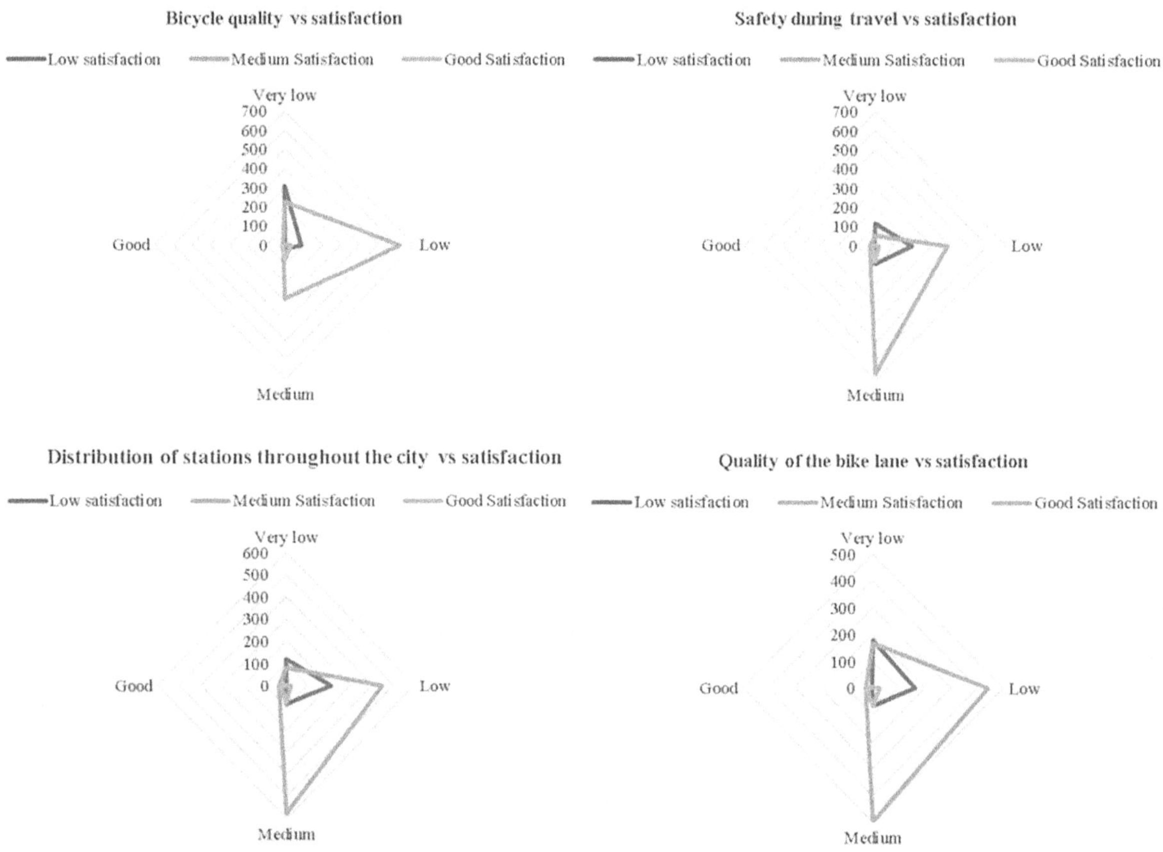

and properly maintained, ensuring appropriate signage, interaction with road traffic, and proper connectivity to access the city's different points of interest.

Service information, the distance from station to destination, the time to access the station, and travel time all received medium scores. Their importance is therefore significant and there is room for improvement. For example, service information could be expanded through different channels (apps, websites, social networks, etc.) and advertising. The distance from station to destination and time to access the station are two factors that are closely related with the network of BSS stations in the city, and to improve them, we reiterate the need to plan strategic station locations in order to minimize travel times and distances from users' start points to their destinations.

Finally, the cost of service and selected payment system received medium and good scores, despite being valued as less important to user satisfaction. Nevertheless, special promotions and discounts could be created to adapt to low income users and other segments of the target market.

In terms of the sociodemographic profile of MalagaBici users, the results reveal that they are mostly men, young adults (25 to 44 years old), employed, with university studies and an average income level, who reside in the city, and usually use private cars as their main form of transportation. These socioeconomic characteristics of BSS users are consistent with prior studies (Fishman, Washington, Haworth, & Watson, 2015; Fishman, 2016; Fuller et al., 2011; Murphy & Usher, 2015).

Table 4. Multivariate analysis of variance

Effect		Valor	F	Gl of the Hypothesis	Gl of the Error	Sig.
Age	Pillai's trace	.054	1.414	60.000	9312.000	.020
	Wilks' lambda	.947	1.416	60.000	8110.270	.019
	Hotelling's trace	.055	1.417	60.000	9272.000	.019
	Roy's largest root	.025	3.825	10.000	1552.000	.000
Gender	Pillai's trace	.027	4.215	10.000	1547.000	.000
	Wilks' lambda	.973	4.215	10.000	1547.000	.000
	Hotelling's trace	.027	4.215	10.000	1547.000	.000
	Roy's largest root	.027	4.215	10.000	1547.000	.000
Employment	Pillai's trace	.075	1.308	90.000	13995.000	.027
	Wilks' lambda	.927	1.310	90.000	10502.523	.027
	Hotelling's trace	.076	1.311	90.000	13907.000	.026
	Roy's largest root	.024	3.792	10.000	1555.000	.000
Educational level	Pillai's trace	.049	1.547	50.000	7755.000	.008
	Wilks' lambda	.951	1.553	50.000	7058.770	.008
	Hotelling's trace	.050	1.560	50.000	7727.000	.007
	Roy's largest root	.030	4.658	10.000	1551.000	.000
Immediate family members	Pillai's trace	.109	1.220	140.000	15560.000	.040
	Wilks' lambda	.896	1.221	140.000	12712.013	.039
	Hotelling's trace	.111	1.222	140.000	15452.000	.039
	Roy's largest root	.033	3.693	14.000	1556.000	.000
Average income	Pillai's trace	.062	1.079	90.000	13995.000	.286
	Wilks' lambda	.939	1.079	90.000	10502.523	.286
	Hotelling's trace	.063	1.079	90.000	13907.000	.286
	Roy's largest root	.019	2.998	10.000	1555.000	.001
Residence	Pillai's trace	.026	1.005	40.000	6200.000	.462
	Wilks' lambda	.974	1.004	40.000	5867.899	.463
	Hotelling's trace	.026	1.004	40.000	6182.000	.463
	Roy's largest root	.012	1.887	10.000	1550.000	.043
Usage experience	Pillai's trace	.038	1.178	50.000	7755.000	.183
	Wilks' lambda	.963	1.181	50.000	7058.770	.180
	Hotelling's trace	.038	1.184	50.000	7727.000	.176
	Roy's largest root	.022	3.424	10.000	1551.000	.000

None of the measures proposed to improve BSS user satisfaction would be effective without the necessary political support to promote bicycle use. The substantial increase in bicycle use requires an integrated package of many different, complementary interventions, including the provision of infrastructure and programs encouraging bicycle use, land-use planning and restrictions on using private vehicles (Pucher, Dill, & Handy, 2010).

LIMITATIONS AND FUTURE RESEARCH

This study has certain limitations that present opportunities for future research. Firstly, although the analyzed data comes from a large user sample, all of the users are evaluating the same BSS. Future studies could replicate this study in other cities. Secondly, the results have been analyzed in regard to a series of sociodemographic characteristics of users. Future research could analyze the impact of users' perceptions, attitudes and preferences, particularly those social groups that are currently underrepresented among users, such as women and older people, as well as social groups with lower levels of income and studies. Lastly, this study only considers the BSS modality organized through loan stations. Future research could expand the study to more recent bicycle loan systems that do not use stations, but rather users are able to leave the bicycles in any location they wish as long as it is not prohibited.

CONCLUSION

Urban planning is intended to meet the mobility needs of the citizens of cities, making it fundamental for the institutions and companies that provide public services to understand the aspects that are more important to transportation users in order to improve their level of satisfaction. Based on this approach, the objective of this study was to understand and analyze the main variables that determine satisfaction with the PBSS service managed by the EMT in Malaga.

The results are important for the system's expansion. The Malaga City Council is currently preparing another public tender for the expansion of this service with new features and more bicycles and stations. Consequently, understanding how current customers perceive the service is essential and will be very helpful to service managers.

This study contributes to the literature on BSS by identifying and evaluating ten factors that influence user satisfaction in a Southern European city. Since few studies previously focused on this geographic area, the results of this research complement prior studies conducted in Central and Northern Europe, China and the United States.

The findings of this research are very useful for institutions and companies that provide public services, allowing them to understand the aspects that users value more in order to improve their level of satisfaction with BSS and, consequently, the aspects that require the most attention. Accordingly, the quality of the bicycles, bike lanes and network of stations are the three most influential factors in satisfaction.

The results of the study provide information to define strategies for attracting new user profiles, as well as to improve the image and perception society has of the bicycle as a competitive mode of transportation in cities. This would promote the use of bicycles, favoring sustainable mobility and thus fulfilling the proposed objectives of the current transportation policy.

ACKNOWLEDGMENT

The authors would like to acknowledge the assistance of the Malaga City Council, Malagueña Transportation Company (EMT) and Cátedra de Gestión del Transporte (Transportation Management Lab) of the University of Malaga, with the data collection. This study was partly funded by the Plan Andaluz de Investigación, Desarrollo e Innovación (Convocatoria 2017), Grupo SEJ-567.

REFERENCES

Ahn, T., Ryu, S., & Han, I. (2007). The impact of Web quality and playfulness on user acceptance of online retailing. *Information & Management*, *44*(3), 263–275. doi:10.1016/j.im.2006.12.008

Bachand-Marleau, J., Lee, B. H. Y., & El-Geneidy, A. M. (2012). Better Understanding of Factors Influencing Likelihood of Using Shared Bicycle Systems and Frequency of Use. *Transportation Research Record: Journal of the Transportation Research Board*, *2314*(1), 66–71. doi:10.3141/2314-09

Bordagaray, M., dell'Olio, L., Ibeas, Á., Barreda, R., & Alonso, B. (2015). Modeling the Service Quality of Public Bicycle Schemes Considering User Heterogeneity. *International Journal of Sustainable Transportation*, *9*(8), 580–591. doi:10.1080/15568318.2013.838722

Cardozo, R. N. (1965). An Experimental Study of Customer Effort, Expectation, and Satisfaction. *JMR, Journal of Marketing Research*, *2*(3), 244–249. doi:10.1177/002224376500200303

Cats, O., Abenoza, R. F., Liu, C., & Susilo, Y. O. (2015). Evolution of Satisfaction with Public Transport and Its Determinants in Sweden. *Transportation Research Record: Journal of the Transportation Research Board*, *2538*(1), 86–95. doi:10.3141/2538-10

Chen, M., Wang, D., Sun, Y., Liu, C., & Bai, Z. (2017). Service Evaluation of Public Bicycle Scheme from a User Perspective: A Case Study in Hangzhou, China. *Transportation Research Record: Journal of the Transportation Research Board*, *2634*(1), 28–34. doi:10.3141/2634-04

Del Castillo, J. M., & Benitez, F. G. (2013). Determining a public transport satisfaction index from user surveys. *Transportmetrica A. Transportation Science*, *9*(8), 713–741. doi:10.1080/18128602.2011.654139

Diab, E., van Lierop, D., & El-Geneidy, A. (2017). Recommending transit: Disentangling users' willingness to recommend transit and their intended continued use. *Travel Behaviour and Society*, *6*, 1–9. doi:10.1016/j.tbs.2016.03.001

Eboli, L., & Mazzulla, G. (2007). Service Quality Attributes Affecting Customer Satisfaction for Bus Transit. *Journal of Public Transportation*, *10*(3), 21–34. doi:10.5038/2375-0901.10.3.2

Eboli, L., & Mazzulla, G. (2009). A New Customer Satisfaction Index for Evaluating Transit Service Quality. *Journal of Public Transportation*, *12*(3), 21–37. doi:10.5038/2375-0901.12.3.2

Fishman, E. (2016). Bikeshare: A Review of Recent Literature. *Transport Reviews*, *36*(1), 92–113. doi:10.1080/01441647.2015.1033036

Fishman, E., Washington, S., & Haworth, N. (2015). Bikeshare's impact on active travel: Evidence from the United States, Great Britain, and Australia. *Journal of Transport & Health*, *2*(2), 135–142. doi:10.1016/j.jth.2015.03.004

Fishman, E., Washington, S., Haworth, N., & Mazzei, A. (2014). Barriers to bikesharing: An analysis from Melbourne and Brisbane. *Journal of Transport Geography*, *41*, 325–337. doi:10.1016/j.jtrangeo.2014.08.005

Fishman, E., Washington, S., Haworth, N., & Watson, A. (2015). Factors influencing bike share membership: An analysis of Melbourne and Brisbane. *Transportation Research Part A, Policy and Practice*, *71*, 17–30. doi:10.1016/j.tra.2014.10.021

Fuller, D., Gauvin, L., Kestens, Y., Daniel, M., Fournier, M., Morency, P., & Drouin, L. (2011). Use of a New Public Bicycle Share Program in Montreal, Canada. *American Journal of Preventive Medicine*, *41*(1), 80–83. doi:10.1016/j.amepre.2011.03.002 PMID:21665067

Giese, J. L., & Cote, J. A. (2000). Defining consumer satisfaction. *Academy of Marketing Science Review*, *2000*(1).

Hill, N., Brierley, J., & MacDougall, R. (2003). *How to Measure Customer Satisfaction*. Gower Publishing, Ltd.

Howard, J. A. (1974). *The Structure of Buyer Behavior in Consumer Behavior: Theory and Application* (J. U. Farley, J. A. Howard, & L. W. Ring, Eds.). Boston.

Jäppinen, S., Toivonen, T., & Salonen, M. (2013). Modelling the potential effect of shared bicycles on public transport travel times in Greater Helsinki: An open data approach. *Applied Geography (Sevenoaks, England)*, *43*, 13–24. doi:10.1016/j.apgeog.2013.05.010

Joewono, T., & Kubota, H. (2007). User Perceptions of Private Paratransit Operation in Indonesia. *Journal of Public Transportation*, *10*(4), 99–118. doi:10.5038/2375-0901.10.4.5

Li, H., Zhang, J., Li, J., & Shi, Z. (2018). An Investigation of User Satisfaction with Shared Bicycles in Nanjing. *Proceedings of the 18th COTA International Conference of Transportation Professionals*, 967–976. Retrieved from https://ascelibrary.org/doi/10.1061/9780784481523.096

Manzi, G., & Saibene, G. (2018). Are they telling the truth? Revealing hidden traits of satisfaction with a public bike-sharing service. *International Journal of Sustainable Transportation*, *12*(4), 253–270. doi:10.1080/15568318.2017.1353186

Martínez, L., & Zapata, T. I. J. A. (2000). Análisis de la varianza. In T. Luque Martínez (coord.) (Ed.), Técnicas de análisis de datos en investigación de mercados (pp. 281–346). Madrid: Pirámide.

Mátrai, T., & Tóth, J. (2016). Comparative Assessment of Public Bike Sharing Systems. *Transportation Research Procedia*, *14*, 2344–2351. doi:10.1016/j.trpro.2016.05.261

Meddin, R., & De Maio, P. (2017). *The bike-sharing world map*. Retrieved from www.bikesharingworld.com

Mouwen, A. (2015). Drivers of customer satisfaction with public transport services. *Transportation Research Part A, Policy and Practice*, *78*, 1–20. doi:10.1016/j.tra.2015.05.005

Murphy, E., & Usher, J. (2015). The Role of Bicycle-sharing in the City: Analysis of the Irish Experience. *International Journal of Sustainable Transportation*, *9*(2), 116–125. doi:10.1080/15568318.2012.748855

Ogilvie, F., & Goodman, A. (2012). Inequalities in usage of a public bicycle sharing scheme: Sociodemographic predictors of uptake and usage of the London (UK) cycle hire scheme. *Preventive Medicine*, *55*(1), 40–45. doi:10.1016/j.ypmed.2012.05.002 PMID:22588228

Oh, J. S., Kim, M. S., & Lee, C. H. (2014). A Study on Factors Affecting the Satisfaction of Public Bicycle System. *Journal of the Korean Society of Road Engineers*, *16*(2), 107–118. doi:10.7855/IJHE.2014.16.2.107

Parkes, S. D., Marsden, G., Shaheen, S. A., & Cohen, A. P. (2013). Understanding the diffusion of public bikesharing systems: Evidence from Europe and North America. *Journal of Transport Geography*, *31*, 94–103. doi:10.1016/j.jtrangeo.2013.06.003

Pucher, J., Buehler, R., & Seinen, M. (2011). Bicycling renaissance in North America? An update and re-appraisal of cycling trends and policies. *Transportation Research Part A, Policy and Practice*, *45*(6), 451–475. doi:10.1016/j.tra.2011.03.001

Pucher, J., Dill, J., & Handy, S. (2010). Infrastructure, programs, and policies to increase bicycling: An international review. *Preventive Medicine*, *50*, S106–S125. doi:10.1016/j.ypmed.2009.07.028 PMID:19765610

Pucher, J., Garrard, J., & Greaves, S. (2011). Cycling down under: A comparative analysis of bicycling trends and policies in Sydney and Melbourne. *Journal of Transport Geography*, *19*(2), 332–345. doi:10.1016/j.jtrangeo.2010.02.007

Ricci, M. (2015). Bike sharing: A review of evidence on impacts and processes of implementation and operation. *Research in Transportation Business & Management*, *15*, 28–38. doi:10.1016/j.rtbm.2015.03.003

Rietveld, P., & Daniel, V. (2004). Determinants of bicycle use: Do municipal policies matter? *Transportation Research Part A, Policy and Practice*, *38*(7), 531–550. doi:10.1016/j.tra.2004.05.003

Shaheen, S. A., Guzman, S., & Zhang, H. (2010). Bikesharing in Europe, the Americas, and Asia. *Transportation Research Record: Journal of the Transportation Research Board*, *2143*(1), 159–167. doi:10.3141/2143-20

Shaheen, S. A., Martin, E. W., & Cohen, A. P. (2013). Public Bikesharing and Modal Shift Behavior: A Comparative Study of Early Bikesharing Systems in North America. *International Journal of Transportation*, *1*(1), 35–54. doi:10.14257/ijt.2013.1.1.03

Soltani, A., Allan, A., Anh Nguyen, H., & Berry, S. (2019). *Bikesharing experience in the city of Adelaide: Insight from a preliminary study*. Case Studies on Transport Policy; doi:10.1016/j.cstp.2019.01.001

Tyrinopoulos, Y., & Antoniou, C. (2008). Public transit user satisfaction: Variability and policy implications. *Transport Policy*, *15*(4), 260–272. doi:10.1016/j.tranpol.2008.06.002

Uriel Jiménez, E., & Aldás Manzano, J. (2005). *Análisis multivariante aplicado* (T. Editores, Ed.). Madrid.

ADDITIONAL READING

Bachand-Marleau, J., Lee, B. H. Y., & El-Geneidy, A. M. (2012). Better Understanding of Factors Influencing Likelihood of Using Shared Bicycle Systems and Frequency of Use. *Transportation Research Record: Journal of the Transportation Research Board*, *2314*(1), 66–71. doi:10.3141/2314-09

Bordagaray, M., dell'Olio, L., Ibeas, Á., Barreda, R., & Alonso, B. (2015). Modeling the Service Quality of Public Bicycle Schemes Considering User Heterogeneity. *International Journal of Sustainable Transportation*, *9*(8), 580–591. doi:10.1080/15568318.2013.838722

Fishman, E. (2016). Bikeshare: A Review of Recent Literature. *Transport Reviews*, *36*(1), 92–113. doi:10.1080/01441647.2015.1033036

Fishman, E., Washington, S., Haworth, N., & Mazzei, A. (2014). Barriers to bikesharing: An analysis from Melbourne and Brisbane. *Journal of Transport Geography*, *41*, 325–337. doi:10.1016/j.jtrangeo.2014.08.005

Li, H., Zhang, J., Li, J., & Shi, Z. 2018. An Investigation of User Satisfaction with Shared Bicycles in Nanjing. Proc. 18th COTA Int. Conf. Transp. Prof. 967–976.

Manzi, G., & Saibene, G. (2018). Are they telling the truth? Revealing hidden traits of satisfaction with a public bike-sharing service. *International Journal of Sustainable Transportation*, *12*(4), 253–270. doi:10.1080/15568318.2017.1353186

Oh, J. S., Kim, M. S., & Lee, C. H. (2014). A Study on Factors Affecting the Satisfaction of Public Bicycle System. *J. Korean Soc. Road Eng.*, *16*, 107–118. doi:10.7855/IJHE.2014.16.2.107

Ricci, M. (2015). Bike sharing: A review of evidence on impacts and processes of implementation and operation. *Research in Transportation Business & Management*, *15*, 28–38. doi:10.1016/j.rtbm.2015.03.003

Soltani, A., Allan, A., Anh Nguyen, H., & Berry, S. (2019). *Bikesharing experience in the city of Adelaide: Insight from a preliminary study*. Case Stud. Transp. Policy; doi:10.1016/j.cstp.2019.01.001

KEY TERMS AND DEFINITIONS

ANOVA: An analysis of variance (ANOVA) evaluates the importance of one or more factors by comparing the averages of the response variable at different levels of the factors.

Quality: The result of the evaluation of service compliance made by users or consumers.

Satisfaction: Response of users or consumers when comparing their expectations prior to acquiring a service with their subsequent evaluation after using it.

Chapter 12
How Do Food Delivery Platforms Affect Urban Logistics?
The Case of Glovo in Barcelona as a Preliminary Study

Eduard Josep Alvarez-Palau
Universitat Oberta de Catalunya, Spain

Marta Viu-Roig
Universitat Oberta de Catalunya, Spain

Josep Reixach Molet
Universitat Oberta de Catalunya, Spain

ABSTRACT

The rise of the platform economy is rapidly changing the traditional economic and business environment. The phenomenon is being widely studied in academia, although so far this has taken a general approach. Lack of precise data and differences in markets hinder more specific analyses that could illustrate the real impact of these trends. This chapter offers an exploratory study of the impact of food-delivery platforms on urban logistics. The study is based on data scraped from the app of the Barcelona-based Glovo, consisting of affiliated restaurants, delivery times, and cost of the delivery. The physical premises identified for the restaurants were georeferenced to study how they are spread and clustered in the city. Restaurants were also matched to their parent companies to obtain economic data from the specialist SABI database. The research questions aim to provide understanding of what types of restaurants have joined the platform, how this has affected their annual turnover, where their physical premises are located, and how the consumer's location affects the service.

DOI: 10.4018/978-1-5225-9928-9.ch012

Copyright © 2020, IGI Global. Copying or distributing in print or electronic forms without written permission of IGI Global is prohibited.

INTRODUCTION

Since it first emerged, the sharing economy has been associated with a new consumption model capable of changing the way we relate to one another. Botsman and Rogers (2010) argue that economic peer-to-peer (P2P) interaction can reduce environmental impact, strengthen local communities and extend the idea of sharing. It is in this context that the concept of *prosumption* has arisen, associated with the idea that citizens can be both producers and consumers at the same time (Ritzer, 2014). Of course, such relations are not new. They have existed in the past, although almost always in the local context and in networks of contacts sharing common characteristics, where sharing was an important factor and monetary transaction was often not an incentive for consumption. It was the arrival of the gig economy that perverted the essence of sharing. Well known start-ups have generated huge amounts of money by offering technological mediation platforms while defining themselves as part of the sharing ecosystem. Their supporters claim they promote P2P exchange and use of idle assets, thereby aligning them with the original idea of the sharing economy. At the other extreme, authors such as Oskam (2016) define these mediation companies as platform capitalism. This is where one of the great ambiguities of the sharing concept lies (Frenken & Schor, 2017).

This study aims to investigate how the gig platforms operate in a specific sector: takeaway food delivery. Specifically, the authors analyze a recent start-up, Glovo, to understand its impact on the city of Barcelona and the last-mile urban distribution logistics model[1]. Although the study focuses on a single city, the choice is considered significant, as Barcelona is an open, global city. It is the 6th largest urban area in Europe and the 23rd largest in the world (Eurostat, 2016; Hales, 2019) and its dedication to technological innovation is evident[2].

The purpose of urban freight distribution is to supply goods at a specific time and in a specific form, guaranteeing low costs and offering good customer services. With the rise of e-commerce, the number of package deliveries to homes in Spain has increased significantly, multiplying the number of orders requiring delivery[3]. Distribution and transport logistics companies have increased their business considerably but have also hit a major obstacle: the last mile. In terms of logistics, the last mile refers to the final stretch of goods delivery. And this stretch involves the highest operating costs and greatest organizational difficulties. On top of this, food distribution involves significant operational factors, largely due to the need to maintain the cold chain (Morganti & Gonzalez-Feliu, 2015). The explosion of gig platforms for urban food distribution has highlighted these challenges and thus requires greater academic analysis and understanding.

Placing the activity of the Barcelona start-up Glovo within the general concept of the sharing economy is not straightforward. However, there are two important reasons for doing so. Firstly, by definition, including gig platforms in the sharing economy creates ambiguity. Secondly, a specific aspect of the business model favors its inclusion: Glovo acts as an intermediary between three parties—restaurants, customers and couriers. The work of its employees is only to develop the technological platform and attract new users. Restaurants announce their services through an app in the form of a culinary offer and consumers buy what appeals. The novelty of this case is the appearance of a new actor, the couriers, who operate as freelancers and provide the service of taking the food from the restaurant (B2C) to the consumer (P2P), using their own transport. In other words, couriers load up orders in thermal backpacks stamped with the Glovo logo, using their own vehicles to make last-mile deliveries.

The differential value of Glovo is the offer of a cheap, easy, personalized and, most of all, fast service (the average delivery time is 25 minutes). As providing fast service is a priority, Glovo's app integrates

GPS geolocation into its operation. This allows the app to detect the closest courier and assign him the delivery service, which translates into optimized resources by minimizing traveled distances and reducing the environmental impact. However, it also guarantees the user's safety and trust, as the merchandise is secured and users are able to use the mobile app to track the order along the route.

In exchange for all this, Glovo charges a service fee. It also takes a commission from its partners based on the cost of the meal[4]. This business model opens itself up to significant criticism due to its lack of economic viability in the short term, still relying on investors to square the annual accounts. This is not rare for a start-up that is still expanding, but it poses a serious problem to the couriers, the weaker party. A review of contemporary printed media reflects the contradictions in this business model, which relies on ambiguity in classifying couriers as freelancers or the falsely self-employed (and thus company employees). The case is being analyzed by the Spanish Government's Social Security Department and in a number of courts of justice. What is clear, though, is the increasing instability for laborers and the precariousness of the model as a whole (Muntaner, 2018).

This situation poses a major challenge to logistics, not just because of route and fleet management, a problem efficiently resolved by platform engineers using state-of-the-art algorithms, but also because of the potential impact of such operations on the urban space, traffic and compatibility with other forms of transport. Operating by bicycle clearly helps control noise and emissions, yet by switching to motorcycles, some couriers are undermining the model.

Given this context, the research questions discussed in this study are:

- How has use of the distribution platform affected the financial results of restaurant companies?
- What types of restaurants have adopted this new distribution system?
- Is there a geographical pattern in the location of the physical premises?
- How does the consumer's location affect delivery costs and times?

This study is structured into an initial introductory section, followed by a review of current literature on the sharing economy, digital platforms and the impact of takeaway food e-commerce on urban logistics. The data and methods used for the research are then described, followed by a section containing the discussion of results and ending with the conclusions.

BACKGROUND

Social penetration of the sharing economy has increased exponentially since the concept first emerged. Attitudes towards consumption have changed in recent years and concern for its ecological, social and developmental impact has increased (Botsman & Rogers, 2010). The sharing economy is an emerging economic-technological phenomenon boosted by the development of ICT, growing consumer awareness and the proliferation of web-based collaborative and social exchange communities (Bostman & Rogers, 2010; Kaplan & Haenlein, 2010; Wang & Zhang, 2012). Hamari (2016) considers the sharing economy an umbrella concept covering a variety of technological developments, including the idea of collaborative consumption, defined as sharing consumption of goods and services over online platforms.

However, such digital platforms have enormous technological potential and, jumping on the sharing economy bandwagon, have been used to develop typical private business initiatives (Stephany, 2015). In practice, day-to-day reality has transformed the original groundbreaking ideas. Large Silicon Valley companies have developed powerful technological platforms to mediate in this new economic context. Claiming that technology is neutral and part of the collaborative ecosystem, their activity has produced a striking contradiction by operating outside existing regulations in the physical market and ignoring the numerous externalities this generates. Significantly, Oskam (2016) defines these online intermediaries as platform capitalism, whereby they establish networks with clearly commercial goals, based on bilateral markets.

The emergence of the platform economy is a very new phenomenon. Airbnb and Uber were created in 2008 and 2009, respectively, and Glovo in 2015. However, the presence of operators on both sides of these bilateral markets continues to grow (Rysman, 2009). Numbers of users of digital platforms that facilitate collaborative consumption through mediation between suppliers and customers are constantly rising (Hamari et al., 2016). The phenomenon has facilitated innovation in new business models (e.g. Airbnb in accommodation, Uber in transport and Amazon in logistics), while also having an impact on operations in cities. Focusing on urban logistics, the expansion of e-commerce has revolutionized distribution of physical goods (Savelsbergh & Van Woensel, 2016). Yet research on the intersection between the last mile and models of the sharing economy is notably lacking (Lim et al., 2018). Aspects such as asset and capacity exchange to increase use and reduce transport, horizontal and vertical cooperation between different stakeholders and the impact of crowdsourcing models in last-mile operations have barely been studied (Wang et al., 2016).

In addition, online shopping and home delivery are current trends with a major impact on freight movement (Visser et al., 2014). Providing a good urban distribution service is becoming extremely difficult due to increased complexity, dynamics and uncertainty (Savelsbergh et al., 2016). The logistics of e-commerce, data infrastructures and information management are crucial to optimizing routes, deliveries, efficiency and operational capacities in the distribution system, recovering costs of breaking down volume and reducing environmental impact (Fikar, 2018). In this context, the problem for e-commerce lies in responding to a growing number of orders that are constantly arriving from different locations, ranging from a few meters to a few miles, requiring very short delivery times (Gharehgozli et al., 2017). According to Morganti and Gonzalez-Feliu (2015), the main obstacles to the successful application of these systems in the sector are: size of delivery (small) and frequency (high); network organization (large number of recipients spread throughout the city); and the complexity of logistic activities (involving wholesalers, suppliers and retailers). This requires a process of continual innovation. According to Giannikas et al. (2017), last-mile innovation can be divided into three categories: organizational, technology-enabled and data-driven innovations. The first, organizational, includes implementation of innovative organizational models or methods for last-mile deliveries. A good example of this is crowd logistics, which is likely to experience significant growth in the future (Carbone et al., 2017). To date, turnover and market share from such initiatives, including food distribution service platforms, have generally been considered insignificant or have not been calculated. Consequently, crowd logistics are likely to have a disruptive influence on traditional business models such as logistics service providers, which focus on last-mile delivery and retailers.

Online food shopping, a type of B2C e-commerce, has increased dramatically in the last decade thanks to the sharp rise in online orders, and forecasts suggest it will continue to grow in the next few years, becoming a very attractive market for urban logistics suppliers (Mortimer et al., 2016). It involves delivery within the urban area over relatively short distances, using smaller freight vehicles, usually delivering single packages to private addresses. Consumers' expectations of local delivery in terms of speed have become increasingly demanding, thus requiring new alternative and innovative forms of product distribution in urban areas (Kin et al., 2018). Research in the field of food delivery focuses on minimizing distances, a cost-based approach, and maximizing product shelf-life on delivery to the customer, a consumer satisfaction-based approach (Fikar, 2018). As Hubber et al. (2016) conclude, although research has so far focused on customer and service-related aspects, success does not depend solely on customer acceptance but also goes hand in hand with an appropriate, scalable and profitable model of fulfillment and delivery.

The whole grocery supply chain is moving towards connection and large amounts of data are being collected, which, if properly used, will help optimize decision-making. Stakeholders can use all such data and connections to increase their adaptability and efficiency, reduce environmental impact and avoid interruptions in food transport (Gharehgozli et al., 2017). In this context, digital food-delivery platforms host the websites and databases of retailers behind online stores and send orders to retailers via a link to the store database. The store collects, packages and delivers the products. The advantage for the store lies in savings on the costs of developing their own online store and certain aspects of marketing. A well-designed and easy-to-use ordering app is essential to the overall customer experience: from the accuracy of photos to order management and online payment. However, retailers can outsource other aspects of their operations to the digital platform, such as logistic support and the carrier (Murphy, 2007). Another advantage of digital platforms is that they let customers choose the time slot that best suits them, ensuring they are at home when the delivery is made and avoid missing it through their own fault or because of delays. This resolves one of the main problems in home delivery in recent years faced by hotels, restaurants and cafés (Ho.Re.Ca), which is particularly important since it involves perishable food requiring specific transport and storage conditions (Hsu et al., 2017).

Minimizing the negative impact of freight transport in urban areas and optimizing efficiency in freight flow are the main objectives of city logistics. However, identifying the main problems in urban transport distribution is not the only relevant issue; the first step in successfully planning city logistics is to analyze possible solutions for different stakeholders (Fancello et al., 2017). Urban logistics and mobility policies will not be successfully implemented without understanding the interests of the stakeholders involved. Failing to do so could discourage their implementation. In this context, it has been noted in the literature that measurement and assessment methodologies are lacking to help policymakers understand the operation and performance of urban food distribution and thus help define integrated policies that improve its efficiency and reduce related negative externalities (Fancello et al., 2017). Indeed these authors also highlight how lack of knowledge combined with significant limitations in the cold chain discourage public policymakers from implementing measures in urban logistics for this type of chain. However, it is worth stressing that public authorities need to adopt the role of mediators between the interested parties rather than imposing authority (Morganti & Gonzalez-Feliu, 2015).

Practically no work has been done on digital platforms in takeaway food delivery as a phenomenon worthy of analysis. For this reason, this literature review offers a more general discussion of aspects of the sharing economy, digital platforms and the impact of home food e-commerce on urban logistics, thereby providing a broader perspective to the analysis of its concepts.

DATA AND METHOD

The main subject of study is the Glovo technological mediation platform for the purchase, collection and home delivery of products. Via this platform, users can buy different types of products, with a guaranteed maximum waiting time of one hour. Specifically, our study focuses on services associated with home delivery of prepared meals. Geographically the analysis focuses on the city of Barcelona. Although this is a limited area, its choice is not trivial. The Glovo start-up was created in the city and established its headquarters and center of operations there, from where it now operates globally. The city's characteristics (such as size, internationalization and levels of innovation) make it suitable for this type of exploratory analysis, which could later be broadened to other cities.

Data from the Glovo platform were obtained on Thursday, February 7, 2019, between 1:45 and 2:15 pm. Manual scraping of advertised restaurants was used to obtain the data. The reason for limiting this process to a specific day and time was to maintain comparability. Some of the variables that appear in the application can change during the course of the day, hence, limiting the time interval for obtaining data guarantees greater homogeneity in the sample.

The variables obtained were the names of restaurants affiliated with the platform, waiting times and delivery costs. The process was repeated at different locations in the city for subsequent comparison. The geographical distribution of the physical premises and limiting waiting times to a maximum of one hour mean results differ depending on where the order is placed. In our case, the following locations were chosen: Plaça Catalunya, 1 (Eixample - Ciutat Vella districts), Plaça Major de Nou Barris, 1 (Nou Barris district) and Carrer d'Anglí, 31 (Sarrià-Sant Gervasi district). The choice of locations is justified by the aim of obtaining different socioeconomic and geographical characteristics. Plaça Catalunya represents the most central point in the city, situated between the Eixample and Ciutat Vella districts, with a large concentration of tertiary activity and average income levels. By contrast, Plaça Major in Nou Barris and Carrer d'Anglí in Sarrià-Sant Gervasi are the outer districts with the lowest and highest income levels, respectively (Barcelona City Council, 2019).

The restaurants found on the app were georeferenced on a map to study the location of their physical premises[5]. Google Earth was used for georeferencing, as this enabled most existing physical premises of restaurants to be identified. The coordinates were exported for subsequent analysis using Geographical Information Systems (GIS). Once in shapefile format, the data were compared geographically with the inventory of restaurants available from the Barcelona City Council Open Data portal (Open Data BCN, 2019), containing over 2,300 premises. Geographical comparison between both databases also helped identify which areas of the city had pioneered digitalization and early access to the technology. The Hot Spot Analysis tool was used to calculate the Getid-Ord Gi* statistic for each element in the database. From this, the geographical clustering of physical premises in the city was compared with premises on the Glovo platform.

Out of a total of 419 restaurants available on the platform, 8 could not be georeferenced. This means that some of the restaurant names available on the platform do not have physical premises of the same name. Other restaurants that could not be located were those operating as food trucks (e.g. Killer Burrito and Ïnta). These vehicles have no permanent physical address, as they move to different locations to provide their services at events. For all restaurants located, a total of 706 physical premises were found (almost 30% of total premises used as restaurants in the city). With regard to numbers of physical premises, it should be stressed that several restaurants have physical premises at several sites (e.g. Enrique Tomás [26], La Tagliatella [20] and McDonald's [18]), representing restaurant chains with multiple premises or franchises. The opposite situation also occurs in cases such as that of Keatz. The premises are associated with six different restaurants on the Glovo platform: Gringo Burrito, Moody Monkey, OnoOno Poké, Green Gurus, Spoony Soups and Convoy BBQ. The interesting point about this case is the company does not even have its own restaurant open to the public. There are also examples of business groups with different restaurants, such as the Soloh and Tragaluz groups. In this case, each restaurant has one or more physical premises, while their financial results are calculated jointly.

With regard to businesses, the authors chose to link restaurants to their parent companies. In doing so, accounting and financial data could be extracted from the specialist SABI database[6]. Not all restaurants had a website, nor did they all offer full information in this regard. Furthermore, not all companies are included in the SABI database. In total, a sample of 104 companies was obtained, with their business name, headquarters, tax identification number, date of founding, number of employees, operating income and before-tax profits. As Glovo only started operating in 2015, data were limited to the period 2015-2017[7].

In the analysis, the quantitative data from SABI were compared to aggregate values for the sector, known as "Food and drink services". For this comparison, growth in operating income for each company was calculated, and then the average value established. In this context, it is worth noting that not all restaurants' parent companies have headquarters in Barcelona. It is also striking that many companies have physical premises outside the city. To avoid forcing the comparison, aggregate values by city and for the whole of Spain were used.

To process all the information, a table was drawn up containing the different restaurants and data extracted for each. These data include: commercial name, type of food, number of physical premises, business name, headquarters, tax identification number, date of founding, cost and delivery time from each location, operating income and profits from 2015 to 2017, and a binary variable indicating whether the restaurant is georeferenced. The table was used to create reports, dynamic tables and graphs, while applying different exploratory statistical methods.

RESULTS AND DISCUSSION

This section presents and discusses the results to provide a better understanding of the context of the study, answering the questions first given above:

RQ1: How Has Use of the Distribution Platform Affected the Financial Results of Restaurants?

To answer this question, the authors analyzed the accounts of the companies associated with the restaurants on the Glovo platform and compared them to all restaurant companies. The data were taken from the SABI business database, together with city and country-wide aggregate information.

Table 1 shows changes to operating income for companies participating on the platform compared to all companies operating in the city and country. The results are as expected, showing steady year-on-year growth between 2015 and 2017. Possibly more surprising, although also expected, is the rise of over 25% operating income for companies on Glovo between 2015 and 2016. This effect could not only be due to an increase in turnover among affiliated companies, but also to an increase in the number of restaurants affiliated with the app shortly after its creation.

An additional exercise would be to look at average growth for the companies studied. Table 2 shows percentage growth, comparing the last two periods for which information is available, 2015-16 and 2016-17. The values obtained show that the average growth of restaurant parent companies on the platform is higher than for all companies in Barcelona and Spain. In the period 2015-16, average growth was three times higher than for Barcelona and twice as high as Spain. Clearly, joining the platform may have

Table 1. Change in aggregate operating income of restaurant companies

Companies	Operating Income in Thousands of EUR		
	2015	2016	2017
Restaurant companies (Barcelona)	1,618,842.00	1,757,788.00	1,832,830.00
Restaurant companies (Spain)	11,103,348.53	12,227,077.99	13,269,040.97
Restaurant companies with premises in Barcelona affiliated with the Glovo platform	848,487.37	1,079,553.85	1,098,885.41

Source: The authors, based on data from SABI.

contributed to higher sales, as it means the area of service can be extended, thereby exceeding the diner capacity of the physical premises.

Possibly the most surprising thing in the table is not the sharp growth among companies advertising on Glovo, but the comparatively low growth in the sector in Barcelona. A detailed analysis of the results for 1,162 companies operating in the city in 2017 shows that 490 experienced negative growth, i.e. lower income than in 2016. This negative growth among 42% of companies contrasts with only 16% for those operating on Glovo with lower operating income at the end of the same period. This raises the question of whether the sector entered a process of internal restructuring, in which case companies affiliated with the platform would be in a preferential position. However, this hypothesis requires further research to document it adequately. Furthermore, using aggregate data by company can create some biases in the results, which will also require further analysis in the future.

Given that physical premises have a limited diner capacity, the possibility of home delivery permits greater use of fixed production factors and labor. Higher turnover goes hand in hand with higher sales, requiring a greater logistic effort in procurement, production and delivery. Greater procurement need not mean a greater impact on urban traffic, as it can easily be absorbed by current suppliers. Increasing production while maintaining standards is only possible if excess space is available in the kitchen. Otherwise, potential expansion or other imaginative solutions have to be explored[8]. Finally, the emergence of an external operator responsible for transporting and distributing orders is a factor that does not affect the restaurant, but which does have an impact on the city. When the service is provided by bicycle, impact is minimal. However, the situation changes when couriers use motorcycles. Although the latter have little impact on congestion, they do however contribute to other externalities such as noise and atmospheric pollution.

Table 2. Change in average operating income of restaurant companies

Operating Income	Growth	
	2015-16	2016-17
Restaurant sector (Barcelona)	5.7%	1.9%
Restaurant sector (Spain)	8.6%	7.0%
Glovo companies	16.2%	8.5%

Source: The authors, based on data from SABI.

RQ2: What Types of Restaurants Have Adopted This New Distribution System?

Restaurants advertising on the platform are difficult to classify. Firstly, this is because of the difficulty in associating restaurant details with their parent companies, but also due to lack of information on their business model. Nevertheless, this question aims to establish whether restaurants advertising on the Glovo platform are more closely associated with the concept of traditional restaurant or with large business groups.

What is clear is that 317 (77%) of restaurants on Glovo have physical premises at just one site, while 23% have more than one (Table 3). In global terms, however, these 317 restaurants represent only 44% of all premises, less than half the total. These data show that business groups have a lower representation on the platform than is the case with their geographical presence. However, these groups seem to have adapted more quickly to using the platform and could be considered early adopters.

Further indicators suggest a preponderance of large business groups to the detriment of traditional restaurants. Most of the restaurants advertising on Glovo have names in a foreign language for Barcelona, such as The Pan's Club, Sushi Way and Burger Shack. Although this is not enough to provide a value judgment on the matter, it is also true that such names do not match the normal standards for traditional Barcelona restaurants. Such restaurants may just have arrived in the city, ready for future expansion. Another case is restaurants with physical premises at only one site in Barcelona but others elsewhere in Catalonia (e.g. Teikit), Spain (e.g. New York Burger) or abroad (e.g. Salad Stop). Logically, such restaurants also fall into the category of business groups. Also of interest is the date on which companies were founded. Many companies with premises at just one site were founded after 2015, suggesting they represent new business models adapted to this type of operation, with good medium-term prospects for expansion. Another indicator is registered company offices outside the city of Barcelona, as occurs in several cases such as La Chelinda, La Taberna del Volapié and Juicy Avenue. Finally, a qualitative aspect to bear in mind is the type of cuisine offered by restaurants. Although healthy options are available, fast food predominates, in the form of burgers, pizza and Asian food. This type of cuisine is also found more frequently among business groups than traditional restaurant companies.

The impact of this trend on urban logistics is obvious. Franchises and business groups tend to operate to specific standards under an integrated supply chain. This simplifies management, as processes such as menu design, marketing campaigns, product procurement and equipment maintenance are all centralized. Thus, there seems to be progress towards a more specialized model, even though this entails greater industrialization of production and a more limited culinary offer. This could also affect the distribution model. Volume of sales increases and product variety drops considerably, which could limit access for small producers and local distributors.

Table 3. Number of restaurants and physical premises by number of associated premises

Condition	Restaurants	Physical Premises
Physical premises at ≤ 1 site	317	307
Physical premises at >1 site	94	399
Total ≤	411	706

Source: The authors, based on data from Glovo.

RQ3: Is There a Geographical Pattern in the Location of Physical Premises?

Business location in cities is a much-studied issue. Shopping streets in historic centers, malls in outer urban districts and even the compact urban fabric with a mix of uses (e.g. commercial use on the ground floor) are a few of the more common models in European cities. This section discusses whether there is a pattern in the geographical location of restaurants affiliated with the Glovo platform.

Two conclusions may be drawn from Table 4. First of all, if one focuses on the number of restaurants located in malls advertised on Glovo in relation to the buyer's location, the results are relatively low. In percentage terms, these are 9% from Plaça Catalunya, 16% from Nou Barris and 9% from Sarrià-Sant Gervasi. It is however interesting to see how the lower income outer district, Nou Barris, has almost twice as many as the central and high-income districts.

Secondly, when considered in terms of number of premises associated with these restaurants, a very different picture emerges. The above figures rise to 32% for Plaça Catalunya, 48% for Nou Barris and 32% for Sarrià-Sant Gervasi. These results show a clear link between presence on the platform and geographical concentration. This is to be expected, given that malls are home to large business groups. Yet it is still surprising that malls such as Heron City and La Maquinista concentrate almost half of all restaurant premises advertising on Glovo for Nou Barris.

A further analysis of interest is the geographical spread of premises by district in the city, in relation to the incorporation on the platform. Here the authors used the georeferenced database of physical premises and matched them geographically with the districts in the city of Barcelona. The percentage of premises in each district was then calculated. The results are shown in Table 5.

The results show a high concentration of premises in the more central districts (Eixample and Ciutat Vella), making up over half the total. In terms of premise density per square kilometer and per inhabitant, the difference is even clearer. If one compares this to premises advertised on Glovo, Eixample remains in first place, while Ciutat Vella drops considerably. This could be explained by the fact that the historic city center is less accessible, but also more informal with a larger degree of casual economic activity. The Sarrià-Sant Gervasi district is also an interesting case, as it is better represented on the platform than its position in the total would indicate. This could be explained by a greater presence of business groups, many of whom have set up in this part of the city and for whom the digitalization process would be simpler. Finally, the case of Nou Barris is paradigmatic. The district contains a residual 1% of all restaurant premises, with regard to the total and those represented on Glovo.

Table 4. Restaurants advertising on Glovo with physical premises present in malls, by buyer's location

	Plaça Catalunya	Nou Barris	Sarrià-Sant Gervasi
Restaurants advertising on Glovo, with premises in malls	37	33	31
Physical premises of those restaurants advertising on Glovo present in malls	222	208	196
All physical premises advertising on Glovo	693	435	619
Percentage of physical premises advertising on Glovo located in malls	32%	48%	32%

Source: The authors, based on data from Glovo.

Table 5. Geographical spread of physical restaurant premises by urban district, in relation to their incorporation on the platform

Districts	Premises	Premises / km²	Premises*10³ / inhab.	% Total	% Glovo	Dif.
Ciutat Vella	519	0.12	5.07	22%	14%	-8%
Eixample	755	0.10	2.83	32%	35%	3%
Gràcia	189	0.09	1.56	8%	7%	-1%
Horta-Guinardó	47	0.09	0.28	2%	0%	-2%
Les Corts	140	0.01	1.70	6%	7%	1%
Nou Barris	24	0.01	0.14	1%	1%	0%
Sant Andreu	61	0.01	0.41	3%	4%	1%
Sant Martí	178	0.02	0.76	8%	10%	2%
Sants-Montjuïc	178	0.03	0.97	8%	7%	-1%
Sarrià-Sant Gervasi	263	0.03	1.78	11%	14%	3%
Total	**2354**			**100%**	**100%**	

Source: The authors, based on data from Glovo and Barcelona City Council.

However, a closer analysis of the clustering of restaurant premises in the city reveals an interesting trend. Figure 1 shows the results of the Hot Spot Analysis applied to all physical premises in the city (left) compared to those whose restaurants advertise on Glovo (right). The map for all premises shows strong clustering in the central area of the city (99% confidence), which includes the urban center, Eixample and neighboring districts. The clustering of premises on Glovo shows a very different pattern. Firstly, the central cluster is smaller and, secondly, additional clusters appear in malls such as Glòries, Diagonal Mar and La Maquinista (95% confidence).

Clearly, there is a pattern in the geographical location of restaurants affiliated with the Glovo platform. There are numerous physical premises in malls, especially in outer urban districts.

The impact of this phenomenon on urban logistics is not clear. Procurement logistics in malls is better organized than in urban centers. Malls have specific infrastructure and spaces reserved for the loading and unloading of heavy vehicles, which thus have less impact on urban traffic. In city streets, operations are less straightforward, due to high traffic levels, limited loading and unloading areas and changing regulations on urban freight distribution. By contrast, urban centers are better positioned than malls for the process of collecting and delivering orders. Bicycle access to malls is rarely allowed, and motorcycle access is impossible. Specific spaces need to be prepared if this model is to spread.

RQ4: How Does the Consumer's Location Affect Delivery Costs and Times?

This question aims to explore differences in the offer of services in relation to consumer location. The previous question focused on the geographical concentration of physical restaurant premises in different districts of the city. Here, the authors analyze the number of restaurants serving a consumer located in the three previously mentioned locations, the cost of delivery and average waiting times. The results are shown in Table 6.

Figure 1. Geographical clustering map of restaurant premises in Barcelona. Source: The authors, based on data from Glovo and Barcelona City Council.

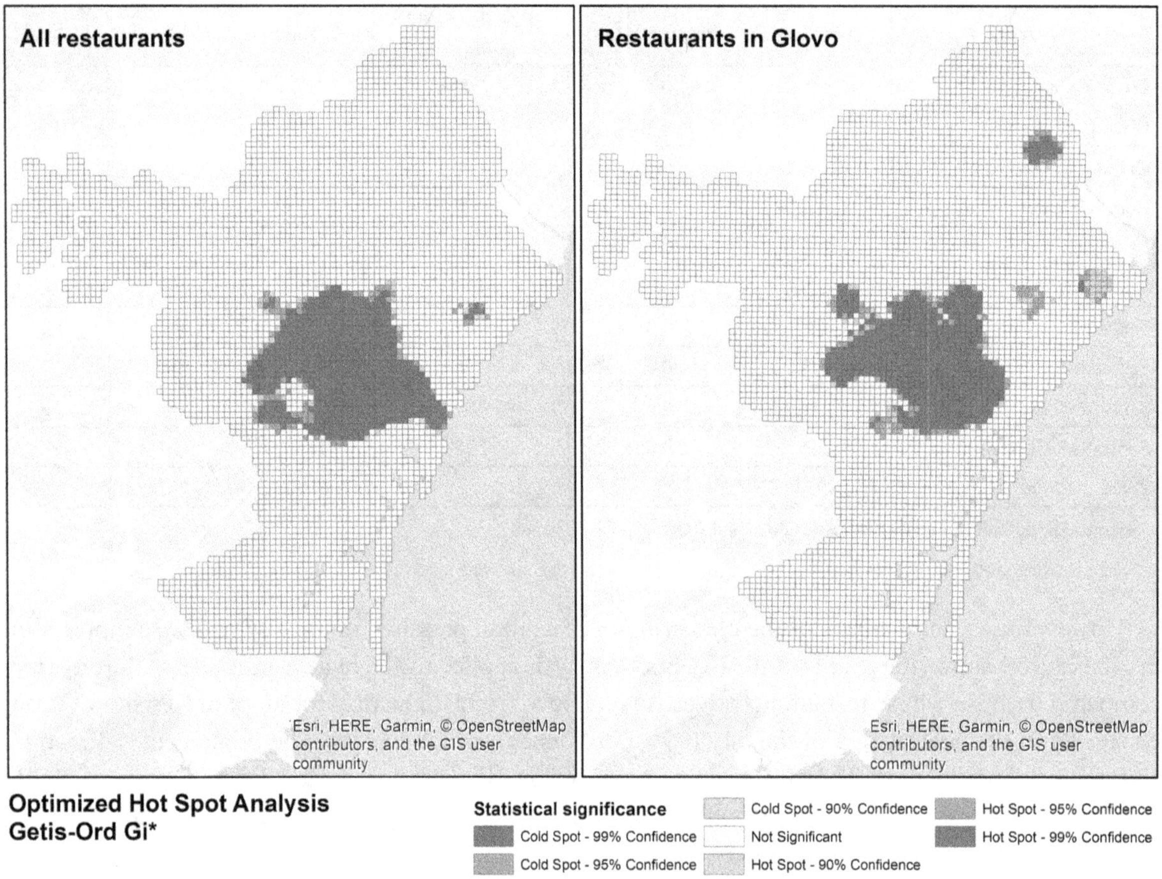

The number of restaurants available when placing an order from a central point such as Plaça Catalunya is clearly higher than at the other locations. There are a total of 408 restaurants, compared to 352 in Sarrià-Sant Gervasi and 208 in Nou Barris. The latter case is particularly concerning, as although the district is largely residential, the service offer is almost half that of the center.

Table 6. Number of restaurants, cost of delivery and average waiting times by district

	Plaça Catalunya	**Nou Barris**	**Sarrià-Sant Gervasi**
Restaurants advertising on Glovo, with premises in malls	37	33	31
Physical premises of those restaurants advertising on Glovo present in malls	222	208	196
All physical premises advertising on Glovo	693	435	619
Percentage of physical premises advertising on Glovo located in malls	32%	48%	32%

Source: The authors, based on data from Glovo.

There are also significant differences between the three locations with regard to average waiting times. From an average 31 minutes after placing an order in Plaça Catalunya, the waiting time increases to 37 minutes in Sarrià-Sant Gervasi and 46 minutes in Nou Barris. This variable could well be associated with the previous one: fewer physical premises from which to provide a service could lead to longer average waiting times. However, other factors should also be explored, such as a hillier topography and the geographical spread of physical premises, which could both contribute to this effect. The previous research question showed there is a proliferation of physical premises based in malls in outer districts. Such concentration of the offer could mean that longer average journey times are required.

Finally, the average cost of delivery shows the same pattern as the previous two variables. It is much lower in Plaça Catalunya, €2.2, rising to €2.6 in Sarrià-Sant Gervasi and €3.2 in Nou Barris. In other words, residents in the poorer outer district pay 50% more than in the city center for a similar order. How the platform contributes to increasing socioeconomic inequalities is not clear, but this is certainly a factor of special interest for future study.

Overall, one can see how the core-periphery model is reinforced, with a clear increase in urban inequalities. The best-located premises extend their area of service and gain market share over competitors located in the outer districts. In addition, consumers in outlying, less well-off districts have to pay more to access this type of order.

Turning to transport, it is also worth bearing in mind that bicycles work well over short, flat distances. However, motorcycles are more suitable for operating in large cities with a hilly topography. Thus, providing a good service in outer urban districts within the established time (under an hour) requires the latter. Work on electrifying the transport fleet and road safety campaigns are needed to solve problems of noise, emissions and accidents associated with motorcycles.

CONCLUSION

This paper provides an exploratory analysis of the potential impact of a food-delivery platform on urban logistics. Data for analysis, restaurants advertising on Glovo in Barcelona in three different locations in the city, were obtained by data scraping from the platform's app. The data were then georeferenced and supplemented with business and financial information.

In economic terms, the results show higher growth in turnover among companies with restaurants affiliated with the platform, compared to restaurant companies overall.

This increase in turnover is associated with the rise in e-commerce experienced in all sectors in Spain, which is likely to continue in the medium term until reaching average market shares for the EU. The doubt in this respect is how much each of these companies can grow. The restaurant sector requires high levels of procurement and food processing. Given that storage and kitchen space in physical premises is limited, there is a threshold past which they cannot grow except by expanding to new premises. With regard to order delivery, as this process is outsourced, it has a limited impact on activity at physical premises. The impact on the city depends on the type of vehicle used and distances involved. Bicycles certainly seem to be the most appropriate vehicle, yet, depending on the distance and urban topography, motorcycles can become essential if delivery in less than an hour is to be guaranteed.

The analysis of business models shows a predominance of specialist restaurant business groups. Although this trend is not visible in terms of restaurants affiliated with the platform, nor in the financial data obtained from SABI's database, it becomes evident when one analyzes the number of physical premises from which they operate. By further analyzing other qualitative variables (restaurant names, type of food, headquarters and date of founding), the trend becomes even clearer.

This greater prevalence of large business groups is an indication of the increasing impact of globalization. The trend in the sector is towards standardization, leading to unification of logistic processes and industrialization in food preparation. Operations become simpler for managers of such premises, but the city loses diversity in its restaurants. Furthermore, higher sales among business groups permit economies of scale. This can affect the business of small producers and local distributors who struggle to compete with larger operators.

On the managerial side, the fact that companies joining the platform are experiencing higher turnovers should encourage traditional restaurants too. The lack of digital skills should be overcome and laborers should be trained on how to use the new systems. This is key in becoming more competitive and not being left behind. The alternative is to let specialist business groups to enjoy ever increasing market shares.

Two trends can be seen with regard to the geographical location of restaurants on the Glovo platform. In the city's central districts, one sees a larger number of physical premises located in the main streets, especially Eixample and Ciutat Vella. In outer districts, however, there is a greater clustering of physical premises in malls. However, analyzing presence on the platform by district shows that Ciutat Vella is highly underrepresented (-7%), while other districts, such as Eixample, Sarrià-Sant Gervasi and Sant Martí, are overrepresented.

Increasing the volume of operations would lead to greater logistic requirements. For districts with a prevalence of premises in urban centers and shopping streets, the task of procurement tends of have a greater impact on urban traffic. This can lead to more journeys or higher demand for parking space for loading and unloading operations. All of this generates externalities such as noise, emissions and congestion. In malls, these operations are better organized, as specific spaces and infrastructure are provided. The main doubt lies in the process of collecting and delivering orders. In this case, ease of access and parking for bicycles and motorcycles in streets means couriers can operate much faster and more efficiently than in malls.

Analyzing the offer of services by consumer location shows that central locations have a greater offer of restaurants. At the same time, average costs and waiting times are up to 50% lower compared to outer districts.

Providing outer districts with an adequate service to limit socioeconomic inequalities requires a comprehensive strategy from government authorities. Longer distances combined with a hillier topography in Barcelona hinder the bicycle delivery model. The need to use motorcycles to reach certain zones has a number of associated externalities (noise, emissions, and accidents, among others) which need to be tackled.

The social impacts of this new consumption model are still to be determined. Although some debates are raising concerning the precarious working conditions platforms impose over couriers, the truth is that more research is required along these lines. In our case, the lack of specific data on employment relationships prevents us from making conclusive statements in this regard. This does not mean, however, that this is not a crucial issue that needs to be tackled in the coming years.

REFERENCES

Barcelona City Council. (n.d.). *Distribució territorial de la renda familiar, 2000-2017*. Retrieved February 2019 from http://www.bcn.cat/estadistica/catala/dades/economia/renda/rdfamiliar/evo/rfdte.htm

Botsman, R., & Rogers, R. (2011). *What's mine is yours: how collaborative consumption is changing the way we live*. London: Collins.

Carbone, V., Rouquet, A., & Roussat, C. (2017). The Rise of Crowd Logistics: A New Way to Co-create Logistics Value. *Journal of Business Logistics*, *38*(4), 238–252. doi:10.1111/jbl.12164

Centre for Retail Research. (2018). *Online Retailing: Britain, Europe, US and Canada 2017*. Retrieved April 2019 from http://www.retailresearch.org/onlineretailing.php

Eurostat. (2016). *Urban Europe statistics on cities, towns and suburbs*. Luxembourg: Publications Office of the European Union.

Fancello, G., Paddeu, D., & Fadda, P. (2017). Investigating last food mile deliveries: A case study approach to identify needs for food delivery demand. *Research in Transportation Economics*, *65*, 56–66. doi:10.1016/j.retrec.2017.09.004

Fikar, C. (2018). A decision support system to investigate food losses in e-grocery deliveries. *Computers & Industrial Engineering*, *117*, 282–290. doi:10.1016/j.cie.2018.02.014

Frenken, K., & Schor, J. (2017). Putting the sharing economy into perspective. *Environmental Innovation and Societal Transitions*, *2*, 3–10. doi:10.1016/j.eist.2017.01.003

Gharehgozli, A., Iakovou, E., Chang, Y., & Swaney, R. (2017). Trends in global E-food supply chain and implications for transport: Literature review and research directions. *Research in Transportation Business & Management*, *25*, 2–14. doi:10.1016/j.rtbm.2017.10.002

Hales, M., Peterson, E., Mendoza, A., & Dessibourg-Free, N. (2019). *2018 Global Cities Report*. A.T. Kearney.

Hamari, J., Sjöklint, M., & Ukkonen, A. (2016). The Sharing Economy: Why People Participate in Collaborative Consumption. *Journal of the Association for Information Science and Technology*, *67*(9), 2047–2059. doi:10.1002/asi.23552

Hsu, C.-I., Hung, S.-F., & Li, H.-C. (2007). Vehicle routing problem with time-windows for perishable food delivery. *Journal of Food Engineering*, *80*(2), 465–475. doi:10.1016/j.jfoodeng.2006.05.029

Hübner, A., Kühn, H., & Wollenburg, J. (2016). Last mile fulfilment and distribution in omni-channel grocery retailing: A strategic planning framework. *International Journal of Retail & Distribution Management*, *44*(3), 228–247. doi:10.1108/IJRDM-11-2014-0154

Kaplan, A. M., & Haenlein, M. (2010). Users of the world, unite! The challenges and opportunities of Social Media. *Business Horizons*, *53*(1), 59–68. doi:10.1016/j.bushor.2009.09.003

Kin, B., Spoor, J., Verlinde, S., Macharis, C., & Van Woensel, T. (2018). Modelling alternative distribution set-ups for fragmented last mile transport: Towards more efficient and sustainable urban freight transport. *Case Studies on Transport Policy*, *6*(1), 125–132. doi:10.1016/j.cstp.2017.11.009

Lim, F., Jin, X., & Srai, J. S. (2018). Consumer-driven e-commerce: A literature review, design framework, and research agenda on last-mile logistics models. *International Journal of Physical Distribution & Logistics Management*, *48*(3), 308–332. doi:10.1108/IJPDLM-02-2017-0081

Morganti, E., & Gonzalez-Feliu, J. (2015). The last food concept as a city logistics solution for perishable products. In Enterprise interoperability: Interoperability for agility, resilience and plasticity of collaborations. ISTE and Wiley. doi:10.1002/9781119081418.ch28

Mortimer, G., Fazal, E., Hasan, S., Andrews, L., & Martin, J. (2016). Online grocery shopping: The impact of shopping frequency on perceived risk. *International Review of Retail, Distribution and Consumer Research*, *26*(2), 202–223. doi:10.1080/09593969.2015.1130737

Muntaner, C. (2018). Digital Platforms. Gig Economy, Precarious Employment, and the Invisible Hand of Social Class. *International Journal of Health Services*, *48*(4), 597–600. doi:10.1177/0020731418801413 PMID:30213247

Murphy, A. J. (2007). Grounding the virtual: The material effects of electronic grocery shopping. *Geoforum*, *38*(5), 941–953. doi:10.1016/j.geoforum.2006.12.012

Open Data BCN. (n.d.). *Llista d'equipaments de resta urants de la ciutat de Barcelona*. Retrieved February 2019 from https://opendata-ajuntament.barcelona.cat/data/ca/dataset/equipament-restaurants

Oskam, J., & Boswijk, A. (2016). Airbnb: The future of networked hospitality businesses. *Journal of tourism. Futures*, *2*(1), 22–42.

Ritzer, G. (2014). Prosumption: Evolution, revolution, or eternal return of the same? *Journal of Consumer Culture*, *14*(1), 3–24. doi:10.1177/1469540513509641

Rysman, M. (2009). The Economics of Two-Sided Markets. *The Journal of Economic Perspectives*, *23*(3), 125–143. doi:10.1257/jep.23.3.125

Savelsbergh, M., & Van Woensel, T. (2016). City Logistics: Challenges and Opportunities. *Transportation Science*, *50*(2), 579–590. doi:10.1287/trsc.2016.0675

Stephany, A. (2015). *The business of sharing: Making it in the new sharing economy*. New York: Palgrave Macmillan. doi:10.1057/9781137376183

Visser, J., Nemoto, T., & Browne, M. (2014). Home delivery and the impacts on urban freight transport: A Review. *Procedia: Social and Behavioral Sciences*, *125*, 15–27. doi:10.1016/j.sbspro.2014.01.1452

Wang, C., & Zhang, P. (2012). The evolution of social commerce: The people, management, technology, and information dimensions. *Communications of the Association for Information Systems*, *31*(1), 105–127.

Wang, Y., Zhang, D., Liu, Q., Shen, F., & Lee, L. H. (2016). Towards enhancing the last-mile delivery: An effective crowd-tasking model with scalable solutions. *Transportation Research Part E, Logistics and Transportation Review*, *93*, 279–293. doi:10.1016/j.tre.2016.06.002

KEY TERMS AND DEFINITIONS

Courier: A person who offers food delivery services as a freelancer, normally using its own bike or motorcycle.

Geographical Information Systems (GIS): Software designed to work with geographic data. It allows to introduce, store, modify, analyze and visualize spatial information.

Last Mile Logistics: Final step of the logistic process of delivering a product. It normally goes from an urban distribution center to the customer or final user.

Parent Company: Company that owns, or manages, a number of subsidiary companies. In our case, companies mainly control restaurants.

Physical Premises: Part of a house, or building, occupied by a business. In our case, the businesses are mainly restaurants.

Restaurant: Food-related business advertised in Glovo's platform. It can operate from single premises or with multiple franchises.

Sharing Economy: Economic system that relies on the relationship between individuals to share assets or services. It can entail or not monetary transactions, and it is normally internet-based.

Technological Platform: System that relies on technology to become a base for developing other applications, processes or technologies. In our case, we consider Glovo as a technological platform.

ENDNOTES

1 For more information see: https://glovoapp.com.

2 Every year, dozens of fairs and congresses on technological innovation are organized there. The biggest event is the Mobile World Congress, but others include 4FYN, Automobile Barcelona, the Retail and Brand Experience World Congress, SIL Barcelona, the IoT Solutions World Congress, In(3D)ustry and the Smart City Expo World Congress.

3 As stated by the Centre for Retail Research (2018), Spanish online shares of retail trade were 4.8% in 2017, considerably below the EU average of 8.8% and trailing behind the leading country, the UK, with a market share of 17.8%. In terms of 2016-17 growth, Spain shows a much higher percentage, 19.2%, clearly above the EU average of 14.2%. Nonetheless, it seems clear that this upward trend will continue in Spain, eventually reaching values that are closer to the European average.

4 The authors have not been able to find the exact amount Glovo charges the restaurants on its website; however, some external sources state it can be somewhere between 15 and 40% of the sale.

5 It should be noted here that our analysis defines restaurants as businesses with their own profile in the Glovo platform, while physical premises are the physical locations used by the restaurants in the city. The concept of restaurant parent company is also discussed below.

6 SABI stands for the Iberian Balance Sheet Analysis System (Sistema de Análisis de Balances Ibéricos, in Spanish), available at https://sabi.bvdinfo.com. SABI's database contains general and financial information for over 2.5 million companies in Spain. The data is gathered from annual accounts deposited by each company in Spain's Companies Registry. It includes company's identification details, operational data, annual turnover and tax and financial data, among others.

7 Last available year in the database at the tie of data extraction.

8 In the United Kingdom there has been considerable debate with regard to so-called "black kitchens". The Deliveroo platform offers spaces in maritime containers fitted out as kitchens, located at different points in the city's outer districts, where orders are met when the restaurant is unable to cover the request.

Chapter 13
Collaborative Finance and Its Hurdles to Overcome

Elisabet Ruiz-Dotras
https://orcid.org/0000-0001-5595-6446
Universitat Oberta de Catalunya (UOC), Spain

Krystyna Mitręga-Niestrój
University of Economics in Katowice, Poland

ABSTRACT

Using survey data from an online Spanish university, real and perceived financial literacy levels, social interactions and personal trust with the social network are measured as key elements for collaborative finance development. This is the first study regarding the factors that may affect the use of collaborative finance. Results show levels of financial literacy are quiet low as in prior studies and individuals consider that the bank manager, friends, and parents can manage financial issues better than them, with the last two peers being those who most trust to discuss financial issues. The findings also provide information about how little individuals trust online networks when it comes to financial matters. Besides, respondents interact moderately with their social network missing the benefits of peer-to-peer learning. Overall, lack of financial literacy, low social interaction, and personal trust may be affecting the short use of collaborative financial services.

INTRODUCTION

With the development of today's new economy -global, networked and digital- a new way of social action is emerging, based on cooperation and sharing. This phenomenon is manifested, among other things, by the development of the collaborative economy, which also could be seen in finance through the increase of alleged collaborative finance. This phenomenon is also driven by the socio-economic consequences of the last global economic and financial crisis. The crisis raised uncertainties about the current economic system and its function and triggered off a lack of trust in financial institutions and governments as well. Additionally, this crisis generated awareness about the deficiency of financial literacy around the world.

DOI: 10.4018/978-1-5225-9928-9.ch013

Copyright © 2020, IGI Global. Copying or distributing in print or electronic forms without written permission of IGI Global is prohibited.

Since social networks and collaboration fuel collaborative consumption, direct peer-to-peer interactions and the sharing of personal experiences allow individuals to create and maintain social connections with others. Hence, while studying collaborative finance, we cannot neglect the role of social interactions when analysing financial literacy. According to Hirshleifer and Teoh (2009), most individuals watch each other's behaviour and learn about each other's choices and beliefs through dialogue. Many studies have shown that social interactions can have a meaningful influence on the process of making financial decision, demonstrating that individual financial decisions can be affected by the behaviour and outcomes of individuals' social network.

In the context of financial system and other financial decisions, the role of trust, social interactions and the level of financial literacy have become a focus, particularly among low-income households. Trust and financial literacy are both important factors in the development of the collaborative finance. Collaborative finance is a significant piece of the collaborative economy and it is understood as a financial transaction which occurs peer-to-peer without the intermediation of a traditional financial institution. However, this new system has not expanded as fast as other types of collaborative economies. There are different factors that may influence the development of collaborative finance. While there is some research regarding crowdfunding (for review of the academic research on crowdfunding see e.g. (Moritz & Block, 2015), alternative currencies (e.g. Diniz et al., 2016; Place, 2013) or P2P lending (Bachmann & Funk, 2011), a lack of research on the determinants of collaborative finance development in general could be observed. Collaborative finance is still a novel phenomenon and it should be understood in a broader sense, including all different kinds of financial transactions. To the best of authors' knowledge, this is the first study that relates the level of financial literacy with social networks interaction and trust and how all these elements could affect the development of collaborative finance.

The study uses a data set collected by a Spanish university during the academic year of 2015/2016. Financial literacy is measured using questions from Lusardi & Mitchell (2011). As in prior research, data shows that the majority of respondents display low financial knowledge, failing to distinguish basic concepts such as the difference between a credit and a debit card or understanding the time value of money or the annual interest rate. Additionally, subjective measures of perceived financial knowledge of seven groups in individual's social network have been included in the survey, as well as the intensity of their relation when it comes to financial issues.

The findings of this research suggest individuals don't use their online social network regarding financial matters and they prefer to trust these topics with those who are closer to them, such as friends, parents and co-workers. Likewise, although respondents perceive their bank manager with the highest financial knowledge, they don't relate to them very often. These conditions could be a real hindrance to expanding collaborative finance services. So that, higher levels of financial literacy may reduce the cost barriers, increasing trust and encouraging participation in the financial sector, either through a more regulated or more collaborative system. The contribution of this research is an attempt to paint a picture of financial literacy, financial social interaction and personal trust in order to reach conclusions concerning the conditions for collaborative finance development.

The remainder of this paper is organized as follows. A review of the related literature is provided in Section 2, followed in Section 3 by an analysis of trust and financial literacy and how they affect collaborative finance. A description of the methodology is presented in Section 4. Measures of financial knowledge, sociability and trust are defined in Section 5. Data analysis and results are provided in Section 6. Finally, future research directions and conclusions drawn from this study are presented in Section 7 and 8.

LITERATURE REVIEW

The term collaborative finance lacks an unambiguous definition in literature. Certainly, the phenomenon of collaborative finance is of an emergent nature and its research is still very novel. It evolves in practice and is the result of various interactions of many entities and factors, and is leading to appear of new, diverse and often unpredictable effects.

According to Baldassarri (2011), the author of the site CollaborativeFinance.org, the term collaborative finance refers to "a specific category of financial transaction which occurs directly between individuals without the intermediation of a traditional financial institution". A similar understanding of this term could be found in the publication prepared by Nesta for the European Commission (2016), where collaborative finance encompasses financial services (i.e. funding, lending and investment) offered outside the traditional financial institutions, especially banks. Vaughan & Daverio (2016) describe this term as financial transactions -such as investing, lending and borrowing- executed directly between individuals or businesses. Likewise, Vanoverschelde, Delancray, & Bartolo (2015) notice that in case of collaborative finance, individuals are bypassing traditional banks and financial institutions and use online platforms to lend each other money, finance innovations, etc. Finally, Botsmann (2016) understands collaborative finance as person-to-person and crowd-driven funding, lending, currency and investment models and stresses its role in decentralising and democratising finance, money and insurance.

Collaborative finance alongside with collaborative consumption, collaborative production and collaborative education is a component, or as Stokes, Clarence, Anderson, and Rinne (2014) refers after Botsman and Rogers (2011), a "pillar" of the collaborative economy. The collaborative economy is a system built on distributed networks of individuals and communities, connected through internet technologies and which unlocks value from underused assets by matching "needs" and "haves" (Botsmann, 2015; Stokes et al., 2014).

Collaborative economy and collaborative consumption should be distinguished from sharing economy, which according to Botsmann (2015) is an economic model based on sharing underutilized assets or services (e.g. spaces, skills, stuff) for monetary or non-monetary benefits. Görög (2018) states that sharing economy is narrower than collaborative consumption as the latter includes not only "re-use of underutilised assets" but also renting, lending, swapping, bartering and gifting. Likewise, Gössling & Michael Hall (2019) point out that "sharing refers to predominantly private, and often non-commercial transactions". Besides, due to the emergent nature of collaborative finance, there is no such typology that is universally accepted and used (see Figure 1 for a proposed one).

The development of collaborative finance is driven by many factors. The critical determinant seems to be the technological development and evolving digital technologies in the era of fourth industrial revolution (Industry 4.0), with Internet as the "natural environment" for the collaborative finance. The "crisis of trust" in traditional financial institutions -especially banks- resulting from the after-effects of the last global financial and economic crisis and financial needs of less favoured individuals and households are also among factors influencing the growth of collaborative finance. Additionally, demographic trends must also be considered -generations Y (millennials) and Z (linkers, screenagers)- redefining the process of creating and using financial services. Moreover, a new "philosophy of life" of the modern society based on i.a. "more cooperation than competition" and "more sharing than possessing" is emerging. There is also an important factor that may not have been widely recognised yet, namely: financial literacy. Collaborative finance is a fairly recent phenomenon, which should be properly understood and used, allowing the peers to fully grasp the benefits and minimise the risks associated. It is even more important

Figure 1. Typology of collaborative finance
Source: Botsman (2016). Collaborative Finance 2016 Update. Retrieved from https://www.slideshare.net/RBotsman/collaborative-finance-2016-update.

considering that the collaborative finance services providers could use non-transparent practices or even "predatory" strategies aimed at achieving profits in the short term, in not always a regulated environment. Lack of financial literacy of collaborative finance could lead to the wrong financial decisions or misallocation of resources, resulting in negative consequences for an individual's financial situation.

Over the last two decades, researchers have started to explore whether individuals are well-equipped to make financial decisions. Abundant evidence indicates that many households make suboptimal financial decisions. A major cause of poor financial decision making is a limited knowledge of financial literacy. Despite a huge growth and development of financial markets and products in the last years, growing literature has documented the average person's understanding of basic economic and financial concepts remain relatively low around the world (Klapper, Lusardi, & Van Oudheusden, 2015; A. Lusardi & Mitchell, 2011; Annamaria Lusardi & Mitchell, 2007c, 2014). These findings are robust to different levels of financial market development as well as the type of pension system prevalent in the country.

Less financial literate individuals have been found to save less, accumulate more debt, pay higher interest rates, have higher mortgage delinquency rates, plan less for retirement, and accumulate less wealth (Disney & Gathergood, 2013; Annamaria Lusardi & Mitchell, 2007c, 2007a, 2008, 2014; Annamaria Lusardi et al., 2011; van Rooij, Lusardi, & Alessie, 2012). Further studies have shown that lack of financial literacy leads to a range of other suboptimal financial outcomes including under-saving and deficient portfolio allocations (Annamaria Lusardi & Mitchell, 2007c; Annamaria Lusardi & Tufano, 2015; van Rooij, Lusardi, & Alessie, 2011b; van Rooij et al., 2012).

Fonseca, Mullen, Zamarro, & Zissimopoulos (2012) study the determinants of financial literacy in the U.S. They show that variables like gender, race, age, education, family income, and marital status can explain about 40% of the variation in financial literacy levels. Researchers have also shown that social interactions can have a significant impact on financial decision making in a wide variety of contexts. For example, peers can affect stock market participation (Brown, Ivković, Smith, & Weisbenner, 2008; Hong, Kubik, & Stein, 2004; Hvide & Östberg, 2015; van Rooij, Lusardi, & Alessie, 2011a), retirement saving decisions (Beshears, Choi, Laibson, Madrian, & Milkman, 2015; Duflo & Saez, 2003), investment in mutual funds (Hong et al., 2005; Pool et al., 2014) and trading decisions (Bursztyn, Ederer, Ferman, & Yuchtman, 2014; Ivković & Weisbenner, 2007). A negative relationship follows from the assumption that low levels of literacy are linked to a greater difficulty to gather and process information. Likewise, trust in the financial system plays a significant role in financial market participation (Balloch, Nicolae, & Philip, 2015; Guiso et al., 2008; Von Gaudecker, 2015), and may increase the likelihood of seeking advice on financial decisions (Calcagno & Monticone, 2015; Gennaioli et al., 2015; van Ooijen & van Rooij, 2016; Von Gaudecker, 2015).

TRUST AND FINANCIAL LITERACY

Trust is an essential condition for the functioning of modern societies and economies or as Arrow (1974) stated "is an important lubricant of a social system". There are numerous definitions, interpretations and classifications of trust from various perspectives. Trust depends on many factors, changes during time and as Luhmann states "is a solution for specific problems of risk" (Luhmann, 2000).

The problem of trust is growing in importance with the development of modern society, equipped with innovative communication and self-organization tools and with the emergence of a new economic system based on a global network of interactions and the growing importance of social networks. Based on the definition proposed by Singh & Bawa (2007), it can be concluded that trust means there is an expectation that a trustor will behave in an anticipated way, despite the trustee is not able to monitor or control either the trustor or the environment in which he or she operates. According to Newton (2001), trust is probably the main element of social capital and it increases the possibility of cooperation between members of society in practice.

Trust is crucial for the financial services sector (Leyshon, Thrift, & Pratt, 1998) and as Assadourian et al. (2004) note, it "facilitates financial transactions by creating a climate of confidence in contractual relationships". According to Balloch, Nicolae, & Philip (2015a) trusting households are more likely to invest in the stock market, and for a given level of trust, lack of financial literacy additionally acts as a barrier to stock market participation. Likewise, Fairholm (1994) states that trust could increase through acquisition of more real, truthful knowledge of the person or situation. Hence financial literacy and trust concurrently explain better financial decisions. This relation should be taken into account while considering the development of collaborative finance. Therefore, better levels of financial literacy could improve trust in both, traditional financial sector and collaborative finance one; and trust is a cornerstone of the collaborative finance.

The collaborative economy as a whole is based on cooperation, and without trust the cooperation is extremely difficult. The more peers trust, the more they cooperate. The more they cooperate, the more they trust. The more knowledge peers have, the more they trust. In the case of collaborative finance, understanding of the peer-to-peer online platforms functioning and the risks associated with them is essential for market participants. The development of collaborative finance is closely related to expansion of development of "digital economy" which is based on digital technologies. It is therefore important to promote the digital financial literacy, i.e. the skills needed to access and use digital devices for financial transactions (G20/OECD, 2017). However, this should be emphasized given that the technology itself also contributes to increasing trust among peers (Botsman, 2012b).

METHODOLOGY

Data from a Spanish university during the academic year of 2015/2016 have been collected for this study. An online survey for the Universitat Oberta de Catalunya (Open University of Catalonia, UOC) was designed. The UOC is widely recognized for providing high quality online university education in Spain, and it aims for lifelong learning with an educational model based on the intensive use of ITC. On its virtual campus, students, tutors, academics advisors and professors interact to teach, learn, and research. All of its higher education programmes are offered virtually and the University is made up of a large online community in over 50 countries. The profile of a typical UOC student is an adult, who works during the day and has family responsibilities.

The questionnaire was sent to students, tutors and academic advisors in different degrees, masters and other undergraduate programs. After removing participants with missing values, the final sample consists of 866 contestants. The age of the respondents in the sample varies from 18 to 74, being more than 86% between 25 and 54 years old; 43.4% of respondents are male. Regarding household composition, 73.4% are married or living with a partner, and around half of them have children living at home. Overall, 76.3% of respondents are employed, 12.3% are self-employed and 9% are unemployed. 46% of the respondents have a bachelor's degree or a master's degree completed and 29% have no university education finished. In general, the household annual net income is between E10,000 and E59,999 for around 56% of the sample and 27% of them have higher annual net income. The characteristics of the sample are presented in Table 1.

Table 1. Demographic profile of the respondents

Distribution	Frequency Total: 866	100.0%
	Gender	
Male	376	43.4%
Female	490	56.6%
	Age	
18-24 years old	60	6.9%
25-34 years old	246	28.4%
35-44 years old	282	32.6%
45-54 years old	219	25.3%
55-64 years old	50	5.8%
Above 65 years old	9	1.0%
	Education	
High school graduate	135	15.6%
Some college credit, no degree	115	13.3%
Trade/technical/vocational training	90	10.4%
Bachelor's degree	219	25.3%

continued on following page

Table 1. Continued

Distribution	Frequency Total: 866	100.0%
Master's degree	181	20.9%
Doctorate degree	126	14.5%
Marital Status		
Single	175	20.2%
Married	379	43.8%
Living with partner	257	29.7%
Separated/Divorced	50	5.8%
Widow	5	0.6%
Number of children		
None	433	50.0%
1	158	18.2%
2	214	24.7%
More than 2	61	7.0%
Household size		
1	89	10.3%
2	299	34.5%
3	208	24.0%
4	209	24.1%
More than 4	61	7.0%
Labour status		
Employed for wages	661	76.3%
Self-employed	107	12.4%
Out of work and looking for work	69	8.0%
Out of work but not currently looking for work	12	1.4%
A homemaker	7	0.8%
Retired	4	0.5%
Unable to work	6	0.7%
Anual Income		
Below E10,000	48	5.5%
E10,000 to E29,999	242	27.9%
E30,000 to E49,999	242	27.9%
E50,000 to E69,999	149	17.2%
E70,000 to E89,999	45	5.2%
E90,000 to E109,999	26	3.0%
Above E110,000	17	2.0%
Refuse to answer	97	11.2%

The survey includes social-demographic questions, basic and advanced financial literacy questions based on Lusardi & Mitchell (2011c) scale. It also includes some social relationship questions as a measure for sociability and the financial perceived knowledge of these people they relate most.

MEASURES OF FINANCIAL KNOWLEDGE, SOCIABILITY, AND TRUST

Financial Knowledge

In order to capture different levels of financial literacy, three measures have been designed: basic, advanced and overall index. These measures are mainly based on van Rooij et al. (2011) index and the questions included are an objective measure of financial literacy to assess how people deal with fundamental concepts at the root of saving and investment decisions.

The survey comprises two sets of questions aimed at assessing financial literacy (see Appendix 1 for the exact wording of these questions). The first set of questions measures basic financial literacy, essentially the ability to perform simple financial calculations. It includes seven items measuring numeracy, inflation, money illusion, time value of money, credit card and understanding of compound interest[1].

The second set of questions computes advanced financial literacy, in particular familiarity with financial products and concepts. It aims to measure a higher level of financial knowledge related to investment and portfolio choice. It includes topics to assess knowledge of financial assets such as stocks, bonds, mutual funds; the returns and riskiness of different assets; the function of the stock market and the concept of risk diversification.

Most of these questions have previously been used in other studies such as English Longitudinal Study of Ageing (Banks & Oldfield, 2007; Steptoe, Breeze, Banks, & Nazroo, 2013), the US Health and Retirement Survey (HRS) and the Rand American Life Panel (Annamaria Lusardi & Mitchell, 2007b).

Personal Financial Confidence

The previous financial knowledge measure is an objective measure and reveals individuals' actual knowledge, since is based on correct answers. However, it doesn't necessary show people's self-assessed financial knowledge. Subjective measures rely on questions asking people to indicate their self-assessed level and there could be a discrepancy between an individual's actual knowledge and their self-perception.

Studies show that particular subjective data help to explain better psychological drivers affecting the individual's financial decisions, since individuals' perceptions of their financial knowledge may differ from their actual level of knowledge. Both an individual's actual financial knowledge and perceived financial knowledge influence investments (Kyrychenko & Shum, 2009), retirement planning (Parker, de Bruin, Yoong, & Willis, 2012), and credit card behaviours (Allgood & Walstad, 2013). Therefore, a subjective measure of financial literacy has been included in the questionnaire in order to measure the self-financial confidence. Participants rated their own financial knowledge on a 5-point scale, whereby a "1" reflects low levels of financial knowledge and a "5" reflects high levels of financial knowledge.

The question about self-financial confidence, as presented in the survey, state:

- On a scale from 1 to 5, where 1 means very low and 5 means very high, how would you assess your overall financial knowledge?

In order to value better the difference between the subjective and objective measure for each individual, an overconfidence measure is created. A common method of measuring overconfidence involves comparing measures of subjective confidence with objective performance. Following Biais, Hilton, Mazurier, & Pouget (2005) and Asaad (2015), a composite overconfidence measure is generated.

Peers' Financial Confidence

Since sharing personal practices and knowledge lead individuals to generate and maintain social connections with others, the research also comprises the financial confidence that individuals associate to the people within their social network. As pointed out earlier, different studies demonstrate that individual financial decisions are affected by the behaviour and outcomes of other formal or informal sources such as neighbours, co-workers, family members or professional advice, amongst other peers. Bucher-Koenen & Lusardi, (2011) suggest in their paper that "those exposed to financially knowledgeable people become more financially knowledgeable themselves". Hence, the financial knowledge of those people surrounding an individual should be considered when analysing the plausible elements which could affect the advance of collaborative finance. In an attempt to go further, this study includes the financial knowledge perception of seven different groups of people with whom individuals usually relate the most: parents, siblings, relatives, friends, co-workers, online networks and personal bank manager. Henceforth, the term "social networks" refers to these seven groups of people.

Participants rated financial knowledge of their social network on a 5-point scale. The exact wording of the question about their social network's financial confidence included in the survey is the following:

- On a scale from 1 to 5, where 1 means very low and 5 means very high, how would you assess the understanding of financial matters of [*parents / siblings / relatives / friends / co-workers / online networks / bank manager*] with whom you discuss financial issues?

Financial Sociability and Personal Trust

After the 2008 financial crisis, people's trust in public institutions dropped sharply in most countries and it has not completely recovered to its pre-crisis levels yet. Trust in other people and trust in institutions are crucial elements for social and economic progress (*OECD Guidel. Meas. Trust*, 2017). Prior works assess the joint importance of trust and sociability on the financial market participation and the findings show that both elements, trust and sociability, affect financial market participation (Balloch et al., 2015; Georgarakos & Pasini, 2011).

According to Unger (1998), sociability refers to the ease and urgency with which individuals pursue common goals, which will otherwise be impossible or expensive to achieve if individuals operate in isolation. Sociability is the set of social interactions that an individual develops on a daily basis (Nguyen & Lethiais, 2016) and these interactions are an important requirement for the collaborative economy development, and thus collaborative finance. As Fehrer et al. (2018) state, the collaborative economy transforms modern economy i.a. by increasing social interaction among peers. And new forms of value and creation are produced by interactions – not only individuals but also communities and businesses (Pattinson, 2016). Emerging of "collaborative lifestyles" promotes the raise of social interactions, in which trust plays an important role (Botsman, 2012a; van den Bos, van Dijk, & Crone, 2012). Links which are created during social interactions form the interconnected basis for social network creation (Sfetcu, 2017). Furthermore, social interactions, allowing peer-to-peer learning, have a positive impact on financial literacy (Hong et al., 2004).

Since individuals' social network can trigger better financial literacy levels and financial literacy may be a key element in the development of collaborative finance, it is necessary to consider both components. In an attempt to analyse how collaborative finance could be influenced by these variables, the questionnaire includes a measure that combines social network interaction and perceived financial knowledge. This research assumes that the more financial knowledge a person is supposed to have, the more reliable they can be in financial matters; yet certain level of interaction is also required. Hence, the present study considers the level of interaction of an individual with their social network as well as the assigned perception of financial knowledge as a measure of personal trust.

In former studies, measures of personal trust are based on broad statements such as whether the respondents are trusting of other people. But such instruments have been criticized as being too vague and perhaps unrelated to specific behaviours (Glaeser, Laibson, Scheinkman, & Soutter, 2000). Since trust can be different depending on the domain, the included trust variable focuses only on the financial context. While previous works analyse trust and sociability as independent and uncorrelated variables, the current research includes as a proxy for trust, the interaction term of sociability and perceived financial knowledge of individuals' social network.

The surveyors are asked to measure on a 5-point scale how often they talk about financial matters with their trusted social environment such as parents, siblings, relatives, friends, colleagues, online networks and their bank manager.

The question about the frequency with which the respondent talks to different groups of people is as follows:

- How frequently in a month do you talk about financial matters with your [*parents / siblings / relatives / friends / co-workers / online networks / bank manager*]? (Select your answer on a 5-pointscale, where 1 means "very low" and 5 means "very high")

Finally, the personal trust measure presented in this research is based on the combination of the frequency of talking with their social network and the level of financial knowledge perceived with respect to their self-assessment level. Therefore, not only it is considered whether or not financial issues are discussed, but also the level of knowledge that the respondent assigns to their peer subject to their own level.

DATA ANALYSIS AND RESULTS

Responses considering the basic and advanced financial knowledge are reported in Table 2 (Panel A and B). A dummy variable is created for each question whereby 1 represents a correct response and 0 represents an incorrect response, a "don't know", or a refusal to answer.

Regarding questions included in the basic section, most respondents answer the first, third and fifth questions correctly; the percentage of incorrect or don't know responses is lower than 25%. However, the proportion of correct answers decreases considerably, to around 50%, when questions on interest compounding, time value of money, and credit and debit card are considered. With reference to the last question about annual interest rate, the percentage of correct answers is the lowest, 36% only, and the proportion of "don't know" answers is the highest in this set, being around 26%. Note also that, while many respondents answer each individual question correctly, the fraction of respondents who answered all seven questions correctly is only 6.4%. The average number of basic questions answered correctly is around 4. Thus, while many respondents display knowledge of a few financial concepts, basic financial literacy is not common.

Table 2. Basic, advanced and overall financial literacy. Panel A and B reports the proportion of surveyors providing correct, incorrect, and 'do not know' answers to each of the basic and advanced literacy questions. Panel C reports the distribution of the number of correct answers on the overall financial literacy questions.

	Correct	Incorrect	Don't Know
Panel A: Basic Financial Literacy Weighted percentages of correct, incorrect and do not know answers (N=866)			
Numeracy	85.7%	09.3%	05.0%
Interest Compounding	53.6%	40.7%	05.7%
Inflation	75.3%	07.7%	17.0%
Time Value of Money	48.0%	39.2%	12.8%
Money Illusion	75.4%	18.0%	06.5%
Credit and Debit Card	44.4%	51.9%	03.7%
Annual Interest Rate	36.6%	36.7%	26.6%
Summary of responses; Weighted number of correct, incorrect and do not know answers (Out of Seven Questions) (N=866)			
None	02.5	11.7	59.1
1	03.8	23.9	21.1
2	09.4	28.2	07.5
3	15.5	20.1	03.6
4	18.8	09.0	01.8
5	24.1	03.1	01.2
6	16.1	00.2	01.3
All	06.4	00.3	00.9
Mean	04.2	02.0	00.8
Note: Correct, Incorrect, and Don't Know responses do not sum up to 100% because of refusals.			
Panel B: Advanced Financial Literacy Weighted percentages of correct, incorrect and do not know answers (N=866)			
Stocks	10.4%	73.3%	14.9%
Mutual Funds	35.3%	49.8%	39.1%
Return	33.0%	28.0%	02.9%
Risk	16.2%	80.9%	11.8%
Diversification	12.5%	75.8%	52.6%
Bonds	33.6%	13.8%	45.8%
Relation Bond Prices and Interest Rates	38.2%	16.0%	00.0%
Summary of responses; Weighted number of correct, incorrect and do not know answers (Out of Seven Questions) (N=866)			
None	06.8	20.1	37.5
1	08.0	20.8	16.6
2	12.5	24.0	15.0
3	23.2	21.6	07.7
4	21.6	07.5	07.7
5	14.3	02.1	04.7
6	05.2	00.5	03.7

continued on following page

Table 2. Continued

	Correct	Incorrect	Don't Know
All	05.1	00.1	03.6
Mean	03.4	01.8	01.8
Note: Correct, Incorrect, and Don't Know responses do not sum up to 100% because of refusals.			
Panel C: Overall Financial Literacy Index Summary of responses; Weighted number of correct, incorrect and do not know answers (N=866)			
None	01.5%	05.5%	32.2%
1	01.7%	07.0%	14.3%
2	01.5%	12.9%	11.3%
3	04.6%	17.1%	10.2%
4	05.4%	18.0%	06.9%
5	08.3%	13.9%	05.0%
6	09.4%	09.8%	04.8%
7	11.1%	05.3%	03.3%
8	11.5%	02.5%	01.5%
9	13.6%	01.4%	01.3%
10	11.1%	00.7%	01.0%
11	06.6%	00.2%	00.7%
12	03.8%	00.1%	00.0%
13	02.5%	00.0%	01.2%
All	01.8%	00.0%	00.8%
Mean	07.5971	03.8620	02.5409
Note: Correct, Incorrect, and Don't Know responses do not sum up to 100% because of refusals.			

The survey also contains another module of advanced questions in order to measure the degree of familiarity with financial products, investment and financial concepts (see Panel B of Table 2). The pattern of answers is different than that from the previous questions, being the proportion of "don't know" and refusals answers on each question much higher. The maximum percentage of correct answers is only 51% for the risk diversification question. Respondents display high levels of difficulty in grasping the concept of long-term returns, how bonds work and the relation between interest rates and bond prices. For instance, almost 40% of respondents are incorrect about which asset (among savings accounts, bonds, and stocks) gives the highest return over a long time period and an additional 33% do not know the answer to this question. Likewise, more than 45% are incorrect about the relationship between bond prices and interest rates, and 38% state they do not know the answer to that question. Similarly, less than 14% know how long-term bonds work and more than 52% of respondents are incorrect. Regarding questions about stocks, risk and diversification, more than 70% respond correctly but the proportion of do not know is higher than 10%. Concerning the mutual funds question, around 50% of respondents know how they work but 35% state they do not know the answer.

Results show that only a small portion of respondents, 5%, is able to answer all the advanced literacy questions correctly, most of them answer between three and four questions right out of seven. The percentage of incorrect responses or ''do not know'' answers is noticeable. These findings are very similar to other prior studies about financial literacy.

Panel C of Table 2 provides the findings for the overall financial literacy index. About half of the respondents answered correctly seven or less individual questions (46%). Around 12% of the respondents answered correctly 10 out of 14 questions and less than 2% answered all the questions correctly. Note that, while many respondents answered each individual question correctly, the portion of respondents who answered questions correctly increases until 9 individual questions and decreases from 10 questions and beyond. The average number of individual questions answered correctly is between 7 and 8, confirming low levels of financial literacy as in previous works.

Table 3 provides the results concerning the personal financial confidence. Panel A indicates that almost 65% of the respondents consider their financial knowledge medium or high. As pointed out before, around 63% of them can answer correctly between 6 to 11 questions. Thus, these results show coherence between the real level of financial knowledge and the subjective one.

Results obtained in the overall financial literacy index and the self-assessment of the participants are compared in order to measure the overconfidence index. A dummy variable is created when the respondent indicates a higher perceived financial literacy level than the real one. Panel B of Table 3 shows that only less than one third of the respondents (30.6%) are overconfidence, considering themselves more knowledgeable than what they really are.

Findings concerning the perceived financial knowledge that respondents assign to different groups of people are provided in Table 4. Note that participants are more able to determine the level of financial literacy for parents, siblings and friends, who are individuals that they usually socialize more often. However, respondents have a little more difficulty in assessing perceived knowledge of relatives and co-workers. Almost 23% of the respondents don't know the financial knowledge of their bank manager. Yet, around 50% of the participants are not able to gauge the level of financial knowledge for the online networks they use.

Analysing the perceived financial literacy for the different groups, Table 4 shows that participants think that parents, siblings, relatives, friends, co-workers and personal bank manager have, in general, medium or a lit bit lower level of financial knowledge. Out of all this seven groups, the bank manager is considered the one with the highest knowledge. On the other hand, online networks are considered the worst source of knowledge, either because they don't know, or they think the level of knowledge on these networks is very low.

Table 3. Perceived financial knowledge or confidence for one-self and for other groups of people (N=866)

Panel A: Self-assessed financial literacy		
	Very Low (1)	00.2
	Low (2)	16.9
	Medium (3)	31.4
	High (4)	32.9
	Very High (5)	14.8
	Don't Know	03.8
	Mean	02.5658
Panel B: Financial overconfidence measure		
	Frequency	Percent
Overconfidence	265	030.6
Non-overconfidence	601	069.4
Total	866	100.0

Table 4. Perceived financial literacy for different groups (N=866)

	Parents	Siblings	Relatives	Friends	Co-workers	Online Networks	Bank Manager
Very Low (1)	18.1%	10.9%	8.8%	3.5%	6.3%	18.3%	4.4%
Low (2)	20.2%	22.0%	26.3%	18.2%	18.6%	11.5%	4.7%
Medium (3)	26.5%	31.7%	33.9%	37.9%	32.3%	13.7%	14.2%
High (4)	22.2%	22.2%	11.8%	26.3%	19.6%	5.9%	27.8%
Very High (5)	10.8%	8.3%	4.2%	7.0%	8.0%	1.5%	26.1%
Don't Know	2.3%	5.0%	15.0%	7.1%	15.2%	49.1%	22.8%
Mean	2.8	2.8	2.3	2.9	2.6	1.1	3.0

Note: Percentages may not sum up to 100% due to refusals.

Similar to the previous overconfidence measure, perceived financial knowledge of individuals' peers is compared to their self-assessment financial knowledge. Following a similar methodology, a composite knowledge measure is created. First, "high" and "low" groups are established for perceived financial knowledge between the respondent and the different groups of people. Those peers with greater score respect to the individual self-assessment financial literacy are categorized as "high" and those peers with worse score respect to the individual self-assessment financial literacy are categorized as "low". Those groups with equal score respect to the individual self-assessment financial literacy are considered as "similar". Finally, three additional variables for each group of their social network are created.

Regarding the perceived financial knowledge of the social network compared to the individual's self-assessment, findings are provided in Table 5. Results suggest that the personal bank manager is the group whom participants perceive a higher financial knowledge compared to them, followed by friends and parents. Respondents consider that 47.6% of their friends demonstrate to manage financial issues better than them, and almost 28% can do it in the same way that they do. This percentage is not very different from the personal bank manager, whom only 51% of individuals think their bank manager show a greater financial knowledge. These results are interesting since they can be affected by the lack of trust in the financial system. Bank managers deal with financial matters every day and they are supposed to be experts in the field of finance. Around 40% of the participants consider their relatives and their co-workers with higher levels of financial literacy than them. Only between 25% and 30% of the respondents think that their parents, their relatives or their online social networks present lower levels of financial knowledge compared to them. Clearly the bank manager is the peer considered with better financial knowledge and online social networks are the ones with the worse understanding of financial issues. However, friends are better positioned in terms of financial literacy respect to family members (parents, siblings and relatives), who around 50% of the participants think they have similar or lower ability than them for financial matters. Hence, these results could give a key concerning the low level of development in collaborative finance. Little or unawareness perceived knowledge in online networks along with low levels of financial literacy may be two reasons that explain why individuals have some reservations to access to the collaborative financial sector.

Results concerning the frequency of talking about financial issues are presented in Table 6. The findings show that respondents discuss financial issues mostly with their parents and friends, followed by colleagues, siblings and their bank manager. However, the frequency of these discussions is moderate.

Table 5. Difference between perceived financial literacy and self-assessment for different groups (N=866)

	Parents	Siblings	Relatives	Friends	Co-workers	Online Networks	Bank Manager
Lower	29.9%	23.9%	27.9%	16.2%	17.8%	24.7%	10.0%
Similar	20.6%	24.0%	22.5%	27.8%	25.9%	11.3%	12.6%
Higher	44.3%	40.5%	33.0%	47.6%	38.9%	11.5%	51.8%
Total	94.8%	88.5%	83.5%	91.6%	82.6%	47.6%	74.5%

Note: Percentages do not sum up to 100% due to do not know answers and refusals are excluded.

Besides, practically never they have financial conversation with the online networks (78.2%) and very few times with their relatives (48.1%). In general, the levels of financial dialogs with their peers are relatively low, which is worrisome considering the fact that individuals display short levels of financial literacy and they could learn from their social interactions.

Finally, Table 7 provides the computed financial trust measure for each social network. Analyzing individuals who discuss financial issues with a moderate or higher frequency, results points out the low level of personal trust on online networks when it comes to financial matters, preferring friends and parents almost indistinctly (55.7% and 54.3%), since both are considered to have similar o better ability to manage financial issues. Co-workers and siblings are also selected ahead of their bank manager (41.3% and 37.5% respectively against 33.9%) to trust personal finance, although respondents perceive bank managers with higher knowledge compared to them. Relatives is one of the less used social networks, but their perceived knowledge is quite good. Hence, the findings show that individuals favor family members, friends and co-workers before their bank manager or online networks to discuss financial questions, reflecting that they trust more with those whom they are closer or spend more time. Therefore, the preceding conditions may have a limiting effect on the development of collaborative finance. As mentioned previously, financial literacy, peer-to-peer learning by means of social interactions and personal trust are three drivers in the collaborative finance development.

Table 6. Frequency of talking about financial issues with different peers (N=866)

	Parents	Siblings	Relatives	Friends	Co-workers	Online Networks	Bank Manager
Very Low (1)	23.6%	31.9%	48.1%	13.4%	26.9%	78.2%	37.8%
Low (2)	21.1%	27.7%	26.0%	29.3%	28.8%	12.3%	24.9%
Medium (3)	23.3%	21.6%	15.6%	29.1%	22.0%	5.2%	17.4%
High (4)	17.4%	13.8%	6.2%	18.4%	11.4%	1.5%	10.9%
Very High (5)	14.7%	3.6%	3.3%	9.3%	9.7%	1.7%	7.1%
Don't Know	0.0%	1.4%	0.9%	0.5%	1.2%	1.0%	1.8%
Mean	2.8	2.3	1.9	2.8	2.4	1.3	2.2

Table 7. Talking about financial issues with different peers considering the perceived knowledge (N=866)

	Parents	Siblings	Relatives	Friends	Co-workers	Online Networks	Bank Manager
Frequency talking medium, high or very high	54.3%	37.5%	23.7%	55.7%	41.3%	7.7%	33.9%
Perceived Knowledge							
Lower	11.9%	7.7%	6.8%	7.2%	5.9%	2.3%	2.4%
Similar	10.9%	10.2%	6.2%	16.3%	14.0%	2.5%	5.2%
Higher	31.5%	19.6%	10.6%	32.2%	21.5%	2.9%	26.3%
Frequency talking low or very low	45.7%	62.5%	76.3%	44.3%	58.7%	92.3%	66.1%

DIRECTIONS FOR FUTURE RESEARCH

The phenomenon of collaborative finance is of an emergent nature. Further research could be directed towards analyzing the impact of technology on trust in social networks in terms of collaborative finance expansion. Because, as mentioned in the article, technology itself also contributes to increasing trust among peers, what is crucial for collaborative finance. It is also worthwhile, in the light of the above, to examine the level of digital financial literacy and to investigate people's awareness of collaborative finance phenomenon and the benefits and risks associated with it. This seems to be important given the state of development of collaborative finance in Spain. As Olivier states on the example of crowdfunding, it is still "often misunderstood and underused" and the skepticism of society must be overcome (Wardrop, Zhang, Rau, & Gray, 2015). Further research in the area of collaborative finance in the context of hurdles to their development is necessary, whether in the field of technology, financial literacy, trust between others.

CONCLUSION

The contribution of this paper is to review three singular elements but related that could be affecting the use of collaborative financial services: financial literacy, social interactions and personal trust. To the best authors' knowledge, there are no previous studies analysing the hurdles that could limit collaborative finance expansion.

Data from an online Spanish university have been collected to measure financial knowledge, perceived knowledge, sociability and personal trust when it comes to financial matters. Lack of financial literacy has been proved it can lead to wrong financing decisions. The findings from this study are similar to previous works, pointing out that individuals are not well-equipped to make sound financial decisions. They are not able to answer properly basic questions related to the interest rate, time value of money or credit/debit cards. And the results are even worse for advanced questions related to investment, diversification or risk. Hence, they fail to grasp essential concepts for their daily life. This lack of financial knowledge could be limiting them from using collaborative financial service.

Cooperation and sharing are the baseline of this new collaborative economy. Besides, interactions and sharing personal experiences allow individuals to create and maintain social connections with others. Since different works demonstrate that individual financial decisions can be affected by their social network, the role of social interactions and their peers' perceived knowledge cannot be neglected while analysing different factors influencing the expansion of collaborative finance. After considering the perceived knowledge of seven diverse groups of people (different family members, friends, colleagues, online networks and their bank manager), results show that the majority of respondents are unware of their online network's knowledge and identify their bank manager, friends, parents and siblings more capable of understanding financial matters compare to them. Regarding the perceived financial knowledge, individuals are more aware of it the closer their social network is. It is to say, they are able to score better those who are closer or spend more time such as family, friends and colleagues. When considering talking about financial issues, they also prefer to discuss these topics with parents, friends and co-workers mainly, instead of the bank manager or their online networks.

Finally, a measure of personal financial trust has been included in this study. For that, it has been taken into account the perceived financial knowledge of their social networks and the frequency with which they discuss financial issues. Results display individuals prefer to debate financial questions with those who are closer such as friends, parents and colleagues, acknowledging them mostly with similar or higher financial knowledge. Therefore, considering the low levels of financial literacy and the evidence individuals don't know how to assess their online networks, the use of collaborative finance could be affected by the fact individuals choose to treat financial issues with who trust the most. As a conclusion, better levels of financial literacy could improve trust in both, traditional financial sector and collaborative finance one. Collaborative economy, as a whole, is based on cooperation and trust is a key driver. The more knowledge peers have, the more they trust; and the more peers trust, the more they cooperate. Social interactions and sharing personal experiences allow individuals to generate social connections with others, and at the same time, social interactions can have a positive impact on individual financial literacy, being surrounded by people with greater financial knowledge.

REFERENCES

G20/OECD. (2017). *G20/OECD INFE core competencies framework on financial literacy for adults*. Author.

Allgood, S., & Walstad, W. (2013). Financial literacy and credit card behaviors: A cross-sectional analysis by age. *Numeracy, 6*(2).

Arrow, K. J. (1974). *The limits of organization (Fels lectu)*. New York: Norton : The Murray Printing Company.

Asaad, C. T. (2015). Financial literacy and financial behavior: Assessing knowledge and confidence. *Financial Services Review*, *24*, 101–117.

Assadourian, E., Flavin, C., French, H., Gardner, G., Halweil, B., & Mastny, L. … Vickers, A. (2004). State of the world state of the world: A worldwatch institute report on progress toward a sustainable society. New York: W.W. Norton & Company.

Bachmann, A., & Funk, B. (2011). Online peer-to-peer lending: A literature review. *Journal of Internet Banking and Commerce*, *16*(2).

Baldassarri, S. (2011). *Collaborative Finance*. Retrieved from http://www.collaborativefinance.org/

Balloch, A., Nicolae, A., & Philip, D. (2015). Stock Market Literacy, Trust and Participation. *Review of Finance, 19*(5), 1925–1963. doi:10.1093/rof/rfu040

Banks, J., & Oldfield, Z. (2007). Understanding pensions: Cognitive function, numerical ability and retirement saving. *Fiscal Studies, 28*(2), 143–170. doi:10.1111/j.1475-5890.2007.00052.x

Beshears, J., Choi, J. J., Laibson, D., Madrian, B. C., & Milkman, K. L. (2015). The effect of providing peer information on retirement savings decisions. *The Journal of Finance, 70*(3), 1161–1201. doi:10.1111/jofi.12258 PMID:26045629

Biais, B., Hilton, D., Mazurier, K., & Pouget, S. (2005). Judgemental overconfidence, self-monitoring, and trading performance in an experimental financial market. *The Review of Economic Studies, 72*(2), 287–312. doi:10.1111/j.1467-937X.2005.00333.x

Botsman, R. (2012a). *Rachel Botsman: The case for collaborative consumption.* TED.com.

Botsman, R. (2012b). *Rachel Botsman: the currency of the new economy is trust.* TED.com.

Botsman, R. (2016). *Collaborative Finance 2016 Update.* Retrieved from https://www.slideshare.net/RBotsman/collaborative-finance-2016-update

Botsman, R., & Rogers, R. (2011). *What's mine is yours : how collaborative consumption is changing the way we live*. Collins.

Botsmann, R. (2015). *The Sharing Economy: Dictionary of Commonly Used Terms - Rachel Botsman.* Retrieved from https://rachelbotsman.com/blog/the-sharing-economy-dictionary-of-commonly-used-terms/

Brown, J. R., Ivković, Z., Smith, P. A., & Weisbenner, S. (2008). Neighbours matter: Causal community effects and stock market participation. *The Journal of Finance, 63*(3), 1509–1531. doi:10.1111/j.1540-6261.2008.01364.x

Bucher-Koenen, T., & Lusardi, A. (2011). Financial literacy and retirement planning in Germany. *Journal of Pension Economics and Finance, 10*(4), 565–584. doi:10.1017/S1474747211000485

Bursztyn, L., Ederer, F., Ferman, B., & Yuchtman, N. (2014). Understanding peer effects in financial decisions: Evidence from a field experiment. *Econometrica, 82*(4), 1273–1301. doi:10.3982/ECTA11991

Calcagno, R., & Monticone, C. (2015). Financial literacy and the demand for financial advice. *Journal of Banking & Finance, 50*, 363–380. doi:10.1016/j.jbankfin.2014.03.013

Diniz, E. H., Siqueira, E. S., & Van Heck, E. (2016). *Taxonomy for understanding digital community currencies: digital payment platforms and virtual community feelings* (Vol. 10). Academic Press.

Disney, R., & Gathergood, J. (2013). Financial literacy and consumer credit portfolios. *Journal of Banking & Finance, 37*(7), 2246–2254. doi:10.1016/j.jbankfin.2013.01.013

Duflo, E., & Saez, E. (2003). The role of information and social interactions in retirement plan decisions: Evidence from a randomized experiment. *The Quarterly Journal of Economics, 118*(August), 815–842. doi:10.1162/00335530360698432

European Commission. (2016). *More than profit: a collaborative economy with a social purpose* (No. Ref. Ares(2016)4889203-31/08/2016). Author.

Fairholm, G. W. (1994). *Leadership and the culture of trust. Choice Reviews Online* (Vol. 32). Greenwood Publishing Group.

Fehrer, J. A., Benoit, S., Aksoy, L., Baker, T. L., Bell, S. J., Brodie, R. J., & Marimuthu, M. (2018). Future scenarios of the collaborative economy: Centrally orchestrated, social bubbles or decentralized autonomous? *Journal of Service Management, 29*(5), 859–882. doi:10.1108/JOSM-04-2018-0118

Fonseca, R., Mullen, K. J., Zamarro, G., & Zissimopoulos, J. (2012). What explains the gender gap in financial literacy? The role of household decision making. *The Journal of Consumer Affairs, 46*(1), 90–106. doi:10.1111/j.1745-6606.2011.01221.x PMID:23049140

Gennaioli, N., Shleifer, A., Vishny, R., Gennaioli, N., Shleifer, A., & Vishny, R. (2015). Money doctors. *The Journal of Finance, 70*(1), 91–114. doi:10.1111/jofi.12188

Georgarakos, D., & Pasini, G. (2011). Trust, sociability, and stock market participation. *Review of Finance, 15*(4), 693–725. doi:10.1093/rof/rfr028

Glaeser, E. L., Laibson, D. I., Scheinkman, J. A., & Soutter, C. L. (2000). Measuring trust. *The Quarterly Journal of Economics, 115*(3), 811–846. doi:10.1162/003355300554926

Görög, G. (2018). The Definitions of Sharing Economy: A Systematic Literature Review. *Management, University of Primorska. Faculty of Management Koper, 13*(2), 175–189.

Gössling, S., & Michael Hall, C. (2019). Sharing versus collaborative economy: How to align ICT developments and the SDGs in tourism? *Journal of Sustainable Tourism, 27*(1), 74–96. doi:10.1080/09669582.2018.1560455

Guiso, L., Sapienza, P., Zingales, L., Guiso, L., Sapienza, P., & Zingales, L. (2008). Trusting the stock market. *The Journal of Finance, 63*(6), 2557–2600. doi:10.1111/j.1540-6261.2008.01408.x

Hirshleifer, D., & Teoh, S. H. (2009). *Thought and behavior contagion in capital markets. Handbook of Financial Markets: Dynamics and Evolution.* The Paul Merage School of Business, University of California-Irvine: Elsevier Inc.

Hong, H., Kubik, J. D., & Stein, J. C. (2004). Social interaction and stock-market participation. *The Journal of Finance, 59*(1), 137–163. doi:10.1111/j.1540-6261.2004.00629.x

Hvide, H. K., & Östberg, P. (2015). Social interaction at work. *Journal of Financial Economics, 117*(3), 628–652. doi:10.1016/j.jfineco.2015.06.004

Ivković, Z., & Weisbenner, S. (2007). Information diffusion effects in individual investors' common stock purchases: Covet thy neighbors' investment choices. *Review of Financial Studies, 20*(4), 1327–1357. doi:10.1093/revfin/hhm009

Klapper, L., Lusardi, A., & Van Oudheusden, P. (2015). *Financial literacy around the world: Insights from the Standard & Poor's ratings services global financial literacy survey.* Standard & Poor's Ratings Services Global FinLit Survey.

Kyrychenko, V., & Shum, P. (2009). Who holds foreign stocks and bonds? Characteristics of active investors in foreign securities. *Financial Services Review, 18*, 1–21.

Leyshon, A., Thrift, N., & Pratt, J. (1998). Reading financial services: Texts, consumers, and financial literacy. *Environment and Planning. D, Society & Space*, *16*(1), 29–55. doi:10.1068/d160029

Luhmann, N. (2000). Familiarity, confidence, trust: Problems and alternatives. In Trust: Making and Breaking Cooperative Relations (pp. 94–107). Academic Press.

Lusardi, A., & Mitchell, O. S. (2007a). Baby Boomer retirement security: The roles of planning, financial literacy, and housing wealth. *Journal of Monetary Economics*, *54*(1), 205–224. doi:10.1016/j.jmoneco.2006.12.001

Lusardi, A., & Mitchell, O. S. (2007b). *Financial literacy and retirement planning: New evidence from the Rand American life panel*. SSRN Electronic Journal.

Lusardi, A., & Mitchell, O. S. (2007c). Financial literacy and retirement preparedness: Evidence and implications for financial education. *Business Economics (Cleveland, Ohio)*, *42*(1), 35–44. doi:10.2145/20070104

Lusardi, A., & Mitchell, O. S. (2008). Planning and financial literacy: How do women fare? *The American Economic Review*, *98*(2), 413–417. doi:10.1257/aer.98.2.413

Lusardi, A., & Mitchell, O. S. (2011). *Financial literacy around the word: An overview* (Vol. 10). Academic Press.

Lusardi, A., & Mitchell, O. S. (2014). The economic importance of financial literacy: Theory and evidence. *Journal of Economic Literature*, *52*(1), 5–44. doi:10.1257/jel.52.1.5 PMID:28579637

Lusardi, A., Mitchell, O. S., Alesina, A., Alessie, R., Botticini, M., Campbell, J., … Washington, G. (2011). *Financial literacy and planning: Implications for retirement wellbeing* (Working Paper 17078 No. 17078). Cambridge, MA: National Bureau of Economic Research.

Lusardi, A., & Tufano, P. (2015). Debt literacy, financial experiences, and overindebtedness. *Journal of Pension Economics and Finance*, *14*(04), 332–368. doi:10.1017/S1474747215000232

Moritz, A., & Block, J. H. (2015). Crowdfunding: A Literature Review and Research Directions. In D. Brüntje & O. Gajda (Eds.), *Crowdfunding in Europe. FGF Studies in Small Business and Entrepreneurship* (pp. 25–53). Springer.

Newton, K. (2001). Trust, social capital, civil society, and democracy. *International Political Science Review*, *22*(2), 201–214. doi:10.1177/0192512101222004

Nguyen, G. D., & Lethiais, V. (2016). Impact des réseaux sociaux sur la sociabilité. *Reseaux*, *34*(195), 165–195.

OECD Guidelines on Measuring Trust. (2017). *OECD Guidelines on Measuring Trust*. OECD.

Parker, A. M., de Bruin, W. B., Yoong, J., & Willis, R. (2012). Inappropriate confidence and retirement planning: Four studies with a national sample. *Journal of Behavioral Decision Making*, *25*(4), 382–389. doi:10.1002/bdm.745 PMID:23049164

Pattinson, H. M. (2016). *The collaborative economy: Implications for B2B marketing from an IMP perspective*. In *32nd Industrial Marketing And Purchasing Conference*, Poznan, Poland.

Place, C. B. L. (2013). Validating and improving the impact of complementary currency systems through impact assessment frameworks. *International Journal of Oncology*, *2*(November), 243–250.

Sfetcu, N. (2017). *Web 2.0 / Social Media / Social Networks: Black & White Edition* (1st ed.). CreateSpace Independent Publishing Platform.

Singh, S., & Bawa, S. (2007). A privacy, trust and policy based authorization framework for services in distributed environments. *Journal of Computational Science*, *2*(2), 85–92.

Steptoe, A., Breeze, E., Banks, J., & Nazroo, J. (2013). Cohort profile: The English Longitudinal Study of Ageing. *International Journal of Epidemiology*, *42*(6), 1640–1648. doi:10.1093/ije/dys168 PMID:23143611

Stokes, K., Clarence, E., Anderson, L., & Rinne, A. (2014). *Making sense of the UK collaborative economy*. Academic Press.

Unger, D. (1998). *Building social capital in Thailand: fibers, finance, and infrastructure. Cambridge University Press.*

van den Bos, W., van Dijk, E., & Crone, E. A. (2012). Learning whom to trust in repeated social interactions: A developmental perspective. *Group Processes & Intergroup Relations*, *15*(2), 243–256. doi:10.1177/1368430211418698

van Ooijen, R., & van Rooij, M. C. J. (2016). Mortgage risks, debt literacy and financial advice. *Journal of Banking & Finance*, *72*, 201–217. doi:10.1016/j.jbankfin.2016.05.001

van Rooij, M., Lusardi, A., & Alessie, R. (2011a). Financial literacy and stock market participation. *Journal of Financial Economics*, *101*(2), 449–472. doi:10.1016/j.jfineco.2011.03.006

van Rooij, M., Lusardi, A., & Alessie, R. J. (2011b). Financial literacy and retirement planning in the Netherlands. *Journal of Economic Psychology*, *32*(4), 593–608. doi:10.1016/j.joep.2011.02.004

van Rooij, M., Lusardi, A., & Alessie, R. J. (2012). Financial literacy, retirement planning, and household wealth. *Economic Journal (London)*, *122*(560), 449–478. doi:10.1111/j.1468-0297.2012.02501.x

Vanoverschelde, J., Delancray, C., & Bartolo, L. (2015). Collaboration, innovation … regulation ? The disruptive shifts taking our economy by storm. *Deloitte's Inside Magazine*, (10).

Vaughan, R., & Daverio, R. (2016). *Assessing the size and presence of the collaborative economy in Europe*. Brussels: Publications Office of the European Union.

Von Gaudecker, H. M. (2015). How does household portfolio diversification vary with financial literacy and financial advice? *The Journal of Finance*, *70*(2), 489–507. doi:10.1111/jofi.12231

Wardrop, R., Zhang, B., Rau, R., & Gray, M. (2015). *The European alternative finance benchmarking report*. Wardour Drury House.

ENDNOTE

1 Two new basic questions have been included. They are related to the difference between credit and debit cards and the compounding interest rate.

APPENDIX

Basic Financial Literacy Questions

1. Numeracy: Suppose you had €100 in a savings account and the interest rate was 2% per year. After 5 years, how much do you think you would have in the account if you left the money to grow?
    a. More than €102
    b. Exactly €102
    c. Less than €102
    d. Do not know
    e. Choose not to answer
2. Interest compounding: Suppose you had €100 in a savings account and the interest rate is 5% per year and you never withdraw money or interest payments. After 5 years, how much would you have on this account in total?
    a. More than €125
    b. Exactly €125
    c. Less than €125
    d. Do not know
    e. Choose not to answer
3. Inflation: Imagine that the interest rate on your savings account was 1% per year and inflation was 2% per year. After 1 year, how much would you be able to buy with the money in this account?
    a. More than today
    b. Exactly the same
    c. Less than today
    d. Do not know
    e. Choose not to answer
4. Time value of money: Assume a friend inherits €10,000 today and his sibling inherits €10,000 3 years from now. Who is richer because of the inheritance?
    a. My friend
    b. His sibling
    c. They are equally rich
    d. Do not know
    e. Choose not to answer
5. Money illusion: Suppose that in the year 2015, your income has doubled and prices of all goods have doubled too. In 2015, how much will you be able to buy with your income?
    a. More than today
    b. The same
    c. Less than today
    d. Do not know
    e. Choose not to answer

6. Credit and debit card: Which of the following statements is false?
    a. If you pay with a credit card, you are taking a loan from your bank and may have to pay interest.
    b. If you pay with a debit card, the money is deducted from your bank account immediately and you do not pay interest rate.
    c. There is no difference between a credit card and debit card.
    d. Do not know
    e. Choose not to answer
7. Annual interest rate: Suppose that Bank A offers you a loan at an annual interest rate of 5% compounded quarterly, and Bank B offers you the same loan at an annual interest rate of 5% compounded annually. Which bank gives you the better option?
    a. Bank A
    b. Bank B
    c. Both are offering the same
    d. Don't know
    e. Choose not to answer

Advanced Financial Literacy Questions

1. Stocks: Which of the following statements is correct? If somebody buys the stock of firm B in the stock market:
    a. He owns a part of firm B
    b. He has lent money to firm B
    c. He is liable for firm B's debts
    d. None of the above
    e. Do not know
    f. Choose not to answer
2. Mutual funds: Which of the following statements is correct?
    a. Once one invests in a mutual fund, one cannot withdraw the money in the first year
    b. Mutual funds can invest in several assets, for example invest in both stocks and bonds
    c. Mutual funds pay a guaranteed rate of return which depends on their past performance
    d. None of the above
    e. Do not know
    f. Choose not to answer
3. Returns: Considering a long time period (for example 10 or 20 years), which asset normally gives the highest return?
    a. Savings accounts
    b. Bonds
    c. Stock
    d. Do not know
    e. Choose not to answer

4. Risk: Normally, which asset displays the highest fluctuations over time?
    a. Savings accounts
    b. Bonds
    c. Stocks
    d. Do not know
    e. Choose not to answer
5. Diversification: When an investor spreads his money among different assets, does the risk of losing money:
    a. Increase
    b. Decrease
    c. Stay the same
    d. Do not know
    e. Choose not to answer
6. Bonds: If you buy a 10-year bond, it means you cannot sell it after 5 years without incurring a major penalty. True or false?
    a. True
    b. False
    c. Do not know
    d. Choose not to answer
7. Relation bond prices and interest rate: If the interest rate falls, what should happen to bond prices?
    a. Rise
    b. Fall
    c. Stay the same
    d. None of the above
    e. Do not know
    f. Choose not to answer

Chapter 14
We Are All Digital Tourists, but Are All Digital Tourists the Same?
Characterization of Digital Tourists Based on Technology Use

Francesc González-Reverté
Universitat Oberta de Catalunya, Spain

Daniel Liviano-Solís
Universitat Oberta de Catalunya, Spain

ABSTRACT

As the sharing economy is transforming the profile, preferences, and expectations of travel and tourism demand, technology becomes an essential element in understanding how tourists change their behavior and consumption patterns. The digital nature of tourism is determined by 1) analogical by digital tourism useful equipment (TUE), 2) a high acceptance of technology, and 3) a high assessment of the tourist experience obtained through mobile devices (MD). Using a sample of 450 tourists in Barcelona, this chapter tries to identify profiles of digital tourists with different degrees of TUE usage. Findings show that digital tourists are characterized by the combination of the use of MD with other TUE. This method could be of great value for managers that want to gain understanding of the characteristics of digital tourists. The study makes a contribution by proposing a classification of digital tourists based on the use of technology supporting the tourist experience. Besides, different patterns of tourist behavior are distinguished depending on the use they make of their mobile devices.

DOI: 10.4018/978-1-5225-9928-9.ch014

Copyright © 2020, IGI Global. Copying or distributing in print or electronic forms without written permission of IGI Global is prohibited.

INTRODUCTION

The sharing economy is transforming the profile, preferences and expectations of travel and tourism demand. On the one hand, technology is an essential element in understanding how tourists change their behaviour and consumption patterns (Buhalis & O'Connor, 2005). On the other hand, the presence of cultures of connection, where common goals and interests are shared, is considered another key feature of the sharing economy. The creation of network cultures with a degree of connectivity, which is also dependent on technology, is a key element in the emergence of consumers' collaborative strategies (Gymóthy, 2017). In tourism, this is exemplified by the communities of travelers, which express opinions and travel preferences through the creation and consumption of digital content in social networks (Amaro, Duarte & Henriques, 2016). Co-creating experiences is another manifestation, often mediated by technology, of adapting to the current needs of tourists. Through co-creation, the traditional relationship between consumers and producers changes. Co-created experiences are shared between tourists or other actors, thus avoiding unidirectionality in the provision of experiences: from business to consumer (Neuhofer, Buhalis & Ladkin, 2012). Understanding how tourists differ in the use of technology, and how they use it to share experiences and content, is a key issue to better capture their behavior in the tourist destination, as well as to understand their ability to influence the rest of members of travelers' communities. In this study, tourists are characterized in terms of the use of technology (mobile devices) for tourist purposes. This allows us to identify specific profiles which show both the preferences and the risks or rejection of the use of technology (González et al 2018). In the end, these profiles show behaviors that are potentially related to the contemporary way of making tourism raised by the sharing economy.

The extension of the use of technology for tourism purposes is related to the emergence of a new class of digital tourist. This kind of consumer can easily access information and share views, comments and suggestions in an informal and collaborative way, thereby increasing their value and gaining greater power of influence over the choices made by other consumers (Miguéns, Baggio & Costa, 2008).

However, the concept of digital tourists has barely been debated or indeed identified as a distinct social category. Some authors consider that digital tourists are characterized by relying on information technology in general and, in particular, on MD technologies and networks for building their travel experiences (Lamsfus et al., 2015). Similarly, Gretzel et al. (2017) state that the new tourist is not solely characterized by relying on a single type of instrument or technology, but rather he/she is a hybrid tourist who uses different channels and technologies to obtain the information he/she needs. Despite efforts by certain academics to undertake some conceptual approaches to the issue of digital tourists, few empirical attempts have been made to characterize and define this type of tourist on the basis of their daily tourism practices. The purpose of our research is to provide empirical evidence on how tourists use technology when visiting a tourist destination, to enable us to develop an accurate profiling of digital tourists. Our proposal is to examine any differences that may exist between tourists who use technology during their visits to the city of Barcelona so that we can then distinguish digital tourist profiles and check whether they form a homogeneous or heterogeneous social group. The results obtained will allow us to initiate a debate around the concept of digital tourists and the way in which tourist destinations are marketed, one example of which is

the Smart Tourism Destination, which is based on an intensive use of technologies and links attractions and experiences to technology-dependent products.

The aim of this research is to provide a classification method for identifying different profiles of digital tourists, based on a case study of tourists in Barcelona. This method could be of great value for managers as well as for those destinations that want to gain a greater understanding of the characteristics of the different digital tourist profiles, which will enable them to optimize their tourism marketing and management strategies and develop action plans in accordance with the behavior and preferences of digital tourists.

From the point of view of the sharing economy, characterizing digital tourists based on their preferences in the use of mobile devices is a useful tool for understanding their willingness to co-create experiences and to create and share digital content which is commonly generated in the digital travel communities.

LITERATURE REVIEW

Digital Tourism

In today's society, where technology plays an increasingly important role in all spheres of everyday life, tourism is no exception. The use of technology in tourism has increased to the extent that it is considered to contribute to changing tourist behavior (Gretzel, Fesenmaier & O'Leary, 2006; Werthner & Klein, 1999; Porter & Heppelman, 2014). Indeed, this phenomenon is heightened by the use of mobile devices (MD) (Fesenmaier & Xiang, 2014; Gretzel, 2010; Wang, Park & Fesenmaier, 2012). Adopting the use of technology in tourism has radically transformed the tourist industry (Buhalis & Law, 2008) as well as the experience and behavior of tourists, especially in relation to searching for and exchanging information and enjoying the tourist experience (NITB, 2015). Tourists, driven by the new possibilities of communication that technology offers, have abandoned a passive role and have begun to act as opinion leaders, whose opinions, especially those expressed through social networks, influence the behavior of other tourists and the managers of tourist destinations. The overall change has been so radical that digital tourists have been identified and distinguished from traditional tourists.

Using technology and MD during tourist trips is beneficial because they provide additional support to the travel experience. Specifically, smartphones have been referred to as catalysts of the tourist experience (Gretzel, 2010) and travel buddies (Tussyadiah, 2014), and have also been linked to the concept of passionate users (Lalicic & Weismayer, 2016). There are practical, functional and social factors driving the use of MD during tourism trips. From a tourist point of view, the use of information technologies offers different advantages for the tourist experience: it facilitates the search for information, allows innovative ways of traveling through the use of applications for MD (Dickinson et al., 2014), enhances the hedonic aspects of the journey and interaction with local culture (Wang et al, 2014), and improves interaction with the social context (Lamsfus et al., 2015; Tussyadiah, 2014). From the perspective of social capital and the construction of communities, there are other elements that also reinforce the value of technology and the use of MD for tourism purposes. Information technologies and MD allow tourists to be connected with their families and friends and to share their experiences in real time (Gretzel, Feisenmaier & O'Leary, 2006). The traveler network, connected through social media, acts as an element of social cohesion for the traveler community, while allowing travelers to share their status and construct travel narratives framed in a personal and social tourist context. Finally, co-production of experiences is also facilitated by the technology and use of MD, providing tourists with a shared experience dimension and giving them a role beyond that of simple consumers (Hunter et al., 2015).

Recent academic literature on MD and tourism has focused on the marketing possibilities that these instruments have to the extent that they allow consumers to reach anywhere and at any time (Hee &

Law, 2015), but few efforts have been made to assess the preferences of tourists as consumers or identify consumer profiles. Although the new tourist has been identified as a more experienced and demanding individual, there are still few empirical studies addressing socioeconomic differences among these kinds of tourists and whether their digital character gives them a unique and differentiating feature compared to other tourists. In this sense, Minghetti and Buhalis (2010) point out the existence of different tourist profiles based on their ability to access technology, which opens up the debate about the existence of a digital divide between different users. In the same vein, some authors show that technology is used differently by individuals depending on their sociodemographic differences and tourist experiences (Kontogreorgopoulos, 2003; Prideau & Coghlan, 2010).

The Use of Mobile Devices in Tourism

The massive introduction of MD has transformed tourism behavior and understanding of the tourist experience in various ways. MD technologies have altered mobility and connectivity to such an extent that the nature of tourist interaction with the destination has changed completely. In fact, these technologies have become important actors in transforming the behavior of tourists at destinations. The use of technology generates a different perception of time and space; it raises new relationships of power between producers and consumers that turn tourists into prosumers and co-producers of their tourist experiences and makes tourists more creative (Wang, 2002; Gretzel & Jamal, 2009). Tourists do not only have access to traveler networks but are also committed to the shared creation of new content through the use of digital cameras, webcams, smartphones, virtual communities, blogs, etc. during all the phases of travel (Gretzel, Fesenmaier & O'Leary, 2006). In this sense, the generation of content by users plays an increasingly important role in many aspects of tourism, especially in information searches, decision-making behavior and tourism promotion (Zeng & Gerritsen, 2014). In fact, some authors propose the figure of a "new consumer" that can easily access information and share his/her own views, comments and suggestions in an informal and collaborative way, increasing their own value and gaining more power of influence over the choices made by other consumers (Miguéns, Baggio & Costa, 2008). Access to information has a major influence on behavior and travel patterns. Besides, the possibilities of social connection offered by technology facilitate the creation of social and community capital and the sharing of experiences among travelers. Tourism consumption is no longer just a means of expressing wealth or status but also of creating cultural capital by adding meaning to consumption through the construction of narratives and by favoring emotional connection with people and places (Gretzel, Fesenmaier & O'Leary, 2007).

MD have been fully incorporated as travel-useful equipment (TUE) as they offer many benefits to tourists; for example, they provide functional advantages (when searching for information about the destination), foster innovative ways of traveling, increase the hedonic dimension of vacations, facilitate contact with local cultures and other tourists when reading tips and advice about the destination, and enhance prior expectations of the trip (Wang, Park & Fesenmaier, 2012; Wang, Xiang & Fesenmaier, 2014). Research carried out on the use of smartphones has identified the different types of impact that these tools have on the tourist experience. Wang and Fesenmaier (2013) distinguish four types of impact: on communication, on leisure, on the search for information and on the ease of undertaking the tourist visit. As a result of travelers' use of smartphones, these impacts transform the sensations and interpretations of tourists when traveling, allowing them to have more connectivity, information, value and entertainment, and greater security and confidence and less stress in their travel experience.

According to Dinholp and Gretzel (2016), the focus of tourist photography has shifted from capturing what is extraordinary to the production of social relationships. They identify the existence of a new type of tourist behavior that differs from the previous way in which tourist trips were experienced and that is based on the presence of the communities of travelers found on the internet. In the era of social media networks, tourists are not the only ones who are seeing what they photograph; they are also looking with the eyes of an imagined audience, thus becoming both actors and narrators (Dinholp & Gretzel, 2016). Other authors show that the use of geolocation technologies on tourist trips also has an effect on the travel experience, as geographic behavior is related to the emotional connection that people have with places through the deployment of place attachment feelings (Tussyadiah & Zach, 2011).

The advantages of MD compared with conventional tourism tools derive from their ability to gather a lot of information combined with instantaneous communication. The integration of cameras into smartphones and digital photography has transformed the way people share their tourist experience (Prideu & Coghlan, 2010). Similarly, MD have also incorporated benefits derived from technical improvements (adaptation to individual needs, personalized recommendations and context awareness), that increase user interaction and enable the collaborative and social integration of users, as in the case of digital guidebooks (Grün et al., 2008). Despite the growing appeal of digital tool markets, it is not clear whether replacing analog TUE with digital TUE has had a definitive effect on tourism. For example, when using digital guidebooks and digital maps, issues such as usability problems, the digital divide among users and the demand for simplicity may reduce the extent to which these tools are accepted (Evjemo, Akselsen & Schürmann, 2007; Norrie & Signer, 2005).

Digital Tourists and the Use of Travel-Useful Equipment

In this research, we introduce the concept of travel-useful equipment (TUE) in order to explain the use of tools and instruments for tourism purposes while at the destination. A TUE is conceptually defined here as a functional instrument, either digital or analog, mainly used by digital tourists to obtain information about the destination and help them make decisions and enjoy the tourist experience. A digital tourist is defined here as a tourist who uses TUE to help with his/her visit and in interpreting the destination, who prefers digital TUE (especially MD) to analog, given that he/she has a high acceptance of the use of technology and a higher level of satisfaction with the tourism experience when experienced through technology. Among all the tools and instruments that TUE comprises, we pay special attention to the role of MD (tablets and smartphones), as these are the technological devices preferred by tourists.Digital tourists are characterized, for the purpose of this research, by a triple approach construct. The tourist's digital equipment is taken into account, that is, the objects and tools that are carried during the tourist trip. We use the concept of TUE to refer to these travel instruments and appliances. The first premise is that digital tourists carry digital TUE with them when traveling or visiting a destination. The second premise is that digital tourists prefer the use of MD to other traditional TUE (maps, cameras, video cameras, etc.). A third premise for characterizing digital tourists is that they have greater acceptance of the use of MD. Digital tourists are considered to have expertise in the use of technology and a positive perception of technology in general and of MD in particular that gives them a high acceptance of their use in terms of perceived utility, ease of use and future use. Finally, digital tourists are also considered to experience a high level of satisfaction with the tourist experience when this is channeled through the use of MD.

In short, the study focuses on the a priori hypothesis that a digital tourist is characterized by: 1) using MD as a TUE and preferring to use the former rather than other traditional instruments; 2) having a high acceptance of the use of MD; 3) experiencing greater satisfaction of the tourist experience when it is conveyed through MD.

However, digital tourists do not constitute a homogeneous social group just because they use technology as a TUE. In fact, they display different individual responses to the use of technology that can be explained by sociodemographic variables, technical skills and cultural factors that influence their perception of technology.

Data and Variables

The data used in this research comes from a survey conducted among 450 tourists visiting Barcelona in June 2015. All the statements in the survey were addressed to domestic and international tourists visiting the destination during their summer vacation. Hence, the survey focused on tourists' use of MD while visiting a tourist destination. The aim of the questionnaire, which included 41 questions, was to gather information about the respondents' MD usage and preferences regarding the use of different TUE. A structured questionnaire was devised, which included questions about skill in the use of the MD and TUE carried during the tourist visit, preferences regarding the use of MD compared to traditional TUE when visiting the destination, preferences regarding the use of smartphones compared to tablets for tourism purposes and the tourists' acceptance of the use of MD (see Table 1).

All these issues were measured on a 5-point Likert scale, where 1 corresponds to *completely disagree* and 5 to *completely agree*. The survey also posed 10 questions regarding different sociodemographic aspects as well as the tourist's trip and technological skills. The survey was conducted by a team that is specialized in tourism and market research surveys and was randomly conducted among tourists visiting the main attractions or walking in the areas of the city with the highest tourist density. The tourist attractions were chosen on the basis of the number of tourists visiting particular places, and only vacationers aged 18 and over were included in the study. Table 2 shows the main socioeconomic features of the sample, which include gender, origin, education and income level. The sample is made up of 450 tourists, most of who were young people of Western European origin, with a medium-to-high education level and a moderate-to-low income level.

Exploratory Analysis

The first phase of research is an exploratory analysis of TUE, both digital (smartphones, tablets, electronic diaries, laptops, video cameras, cameras and phones without internet connection) and analog (tourist maps, destination maps and guidebooks). Tourists were required to answer which of these types of TUE they carried during their stay at the destination. The 450 tourists employed 1,241 TUE in total, which results in an average of 2.76 TUE per person. Results show that tourists mostly use MD as a TUE, especially smartphones (84.4% of the total sample). However, just 10% of the sample only have a smartphone among their TUE, while 15% combine a smartphone with a tablet. Therefore, the use of smartphones clearly reduces the number of devices taken with them on vacation. However, tourists still carry other types of digital and analog TUE. If we analyze the total TUE that tourists brought with them during their stay in Barcelona, we can see that most tourists carried 3 objects (33.78%) or 2 objects (28%), while only a small number of tourists (13.78%) carried a single object, 4 objects or more than 4 objects (17.56% and 6.89%, respectively). If we take into account the number of users that carried TUE and the total volume of instruments they represent, smartphones are the TUE most used by tourists (84.44%),

Table 1. Questions included in the survey

Question	Description
Q1	When I need guidance or I get lost I prefer to use a map rather than a GPS or Google Maps
Q2	I prefer to use credit card rather than my Smartphone when I have to pay for a good service
Q3	When I have to take a picture or tape something I prefer to use my digital camera rather than my MD
Q4	When I need useful information about the city and sightsees I prefer to use a tourist guide rather than my MD
Q5	When I need tourist information I prefer to use a Tourism Board rather than my MD
Q6	When I want word of mouth information about the city I prefer to ask real people rather than Social Networks
Q7	MD are useful on my trip
Q8	Using MD lets me save time and/or money
Q9	MDs let me do things I couldn't otherwise do
Q10	Smartphones are more useful than tablets when visiting the city
Q11	In general, using MD is simple and easy
Q12	It is easier to get information with MD than to use other systems
Q13	The usability of MD is simple and easy
Q14	The tablet is easier to use and interact with than the smartphone
Q15	The use of MD makes my trip more interesting and pleasant
Q16	I like using MD when I travel for pleasure
Q17	Using MD enhances the experience of my trip
Q18	It's more enjoyable using a tablet than a smartphone when I travel for pleasure
Q19	On subsequent trips, I will use MD
Q20	On my future trips I will again use a tablet
Q21	On my future trips I will again use a smartphone
Q22	On my future trips I will use a tablet more than a smartphone

followed by maps (65.15%), cameras (47.1%) and tourist guidebooks (32.6%). These four TUE represent 24.5% of total instruments and were used by a large number of tourists. On the other hand, we observed that some TUE were underused: electronic diaries, video cameras, phones without internet connection and laptops (see Table 3).

In general terms, a duality can be identified whereby a minority of individuals required only MD (especially smartphones) among the TUE used to organize their tourist visit, and a majority of tourists chose to use different instruments as TUE.

Table 2. Socioeconomic structure of the sample

	Count	Percentage
Sample	450	100.00%
Age		
Young (15 - 36)	238	52.88%
Middle-aged (37 - 50)	94	20.88%
Senior (51+)	118	26.22%
Gender		
Men	210	46.67%
Women	240	53.33%
Origin		
Mediterranean	106	23.56%
Western Europe	108	24.00%
North America	39	8.67%
Other	197	43.78%
Education		
Up to secondary	94	20.89%
Graduate	215	47.78%
Postgraduate	141	31.33%
Income Level		
Low	232	51.56%
Medium	146	32.44%
High	50	11.11%

Cluster Analysis

In this section we perform a segmentation of the sample into sub-groups, based on the sociodemographic profile of the tourists. The aim is to determine whether segments of digital tourists with different degrees of TUE usage could be identified. Specifically, we chose the cluster analysis, since this method is more effective than other methods when dealing with a small sample.

The segmentation bases for obtaining cluster profiles comprised five items measuring sociodemographic differences among tourists (age, gender, origin, education, and income level) and an item measuring the use of a specific TUE. The specific method used was k-means clustering, and the resulting plot of the within groups sum of squares suggested that the optimal number of clusters is 2. The resulting cluster profiles are shown in Table 4.

These groups correspond to a highly differentiated tourist profile. The first cluster was named "Complementary technology users". The second cluster was named "Full engaged technology users". Women who prefer to use the smartphone when organizing and going on their tourist trips but complement the smartphone with the use of other digital and analog devices form the first cluster. This is a group where young females of Mediterranean origin, with a medium-to-low education level and with the lowest income in the sample predominate. Senior North American men, with a high education level

Table 3. Frequency of mobile devices usage

	Count	Percentage
By Class of Device		
Smartphone	380	84.44%
Map	306	68.00%
Photo camera	215	47.78%
Guide	148	32.89%
Tablet	113	25.11%
Cell phone	43	9.56%
Laptop	33	7.33%
Video camera	15	3.3%
None	1	0.22%
By Number of Devices Used Simultaneously		
1 device	62	13.78%
2 devices	126	28.00%
3 devices	152	33.78%
4 devices	79	17.56%
5+ devices	31	6.89%

and high income, mainly form the second cluster. They use tablets as their main TUE, which tend to replace all other TUE, whether digital or analog.

Members of the second cluster make greater use of tablets than smartphones, which is a very distinctive and differentiating feature of this group. Our interpretation of this correlation is that they are mainly high-income people who can therefore afford to purchase both types of MD. There is a sharp contrast between these two profiles. Consequently, it is interesting to analyze the relationship that each of the two digital tourist profiles have with technology and TUE when visiting the destination (see Table 5).

Both clusters show a similar tendency towards replacing analog TUE with digital TUE. The individuals belonging to the first cluster agree that they use credit cards more than the smartphone for making payments (93.52% of individuals in cluster 1 agreed compared to 85.98% in cluster 2). They are also more likely to use mainly guidebooks compared with individuals from the second cluster (45.09% and 43.37%, respectively). Besides, individuals from the first cluster prefer to ask people on the street rather than checking their MD if they need information or get lost, and are much more likely to do so than individuals from the second cluster (63.06% and 49.69%, respectively). To obtain information about the destination, the individuals from the second cluster are more likely to check a tourist information board (on the street) rather than use their MD than the individuals from cluster 1 (32.52% and 28.9%, respectively). Compared with individuals from cluster 1, they also prefer taking pictures or videos using digital cameras rather than using the devices integrated into their MD (43.03% and 39.29%, respectively). Finally, both clusters have very similar preferences in checking maps rather than using MD to obtain information about the places they visit (around 56% in both cases).Statistically significant differences between both clusters were found regarding the use of MD at the destination. In general, the perceived utility and ease of use of MD are very similar in both clusters. However, individuals in cluster 2 have

Table 4. Socioeconomic structure of clusters

	Cluster C_1		Cluster C_2	
Mean age	34.12		46.31	
	% subgroup	% cluster	% subgroup	% cluster
Sample	56.22%	100.00%	43.78%	100.00%
Age				
Young	72.69%	68.38%	27.31%	32.99%
Middle-aged	45.74%	17.00%	54.26%	25.89%
Senior	31.36%	14.62%	68.64%	41.12%
Gender				
Men	40.00%	33.20%	60.00%	63.96%
Women	70.42%	66.80%	29.58%	36.04%
Origin				
Mediterranean	82.08%	34.39%	17.92%	9.64%
Western Europe	55.56%	23.72%	44.44%	24.37%
North America	38.46%	5.93%	61.54%	12.18%
Other	46.19%	35.97%	53.81%	53.81%
Education				
Up to secondary	88.30%	32.81%	11.70%	5.58%
Graduate	63.26%	53.75%	36.74%	40.10%
Postgraduate	24.11%	13.44%	75.89%	54.31%
Income level				
Low	83.62%	76.68%	16.38%	19.29%
Medium	25.34%	14.62%	74.66%	55.33%
High	0.00%	0.00%	100.00%	25.38%
Device				
Smartphone	58.16%	87.35%	41.84%	80.71%
Tablet	42.48%	18.97%	57.52%	32.99%
Cell phone	58.14%	9.88%	41.86%	9.14%
Guide	53.38%	31.23%	46.62%	35.03%
Laptop	57.58%	7.51%	42.42%	7.11%
Map	56.21%	67.98%	43.79%	68.02%
Photo camera	54.42%	46.25%	45.58%	49.75%

a greater consensus in considering that MD are more useful for practical or functional purposes. They state that MD save time (87.34% and 82.19%, respectively) and enable them to do things that would be impossible otherwise (72.22% and 67.74%, respectively). Major differences also exist between the clusters in their assessment of the hedonic value of MD and the ability of these devices to improve their satisfaction with the tourist experience. The individuals in cluster 2 have a more positive perception of the features of MD than the individuals in cluster 1. For example, individuals from cluster 2 are more

Table 5. Patterns of Technology use by clusters

Question	Cluster C_1					Cluster C_2				
	Low	Neutral	High	Mean	% Answers	Low	Neutral	High	Mean	% Answers
Q1	34.08	9.42	56.50	3.27	88.14%	29.52	14.46	56.02	3.35	84.26%
Q2	4.17	2.31	93.52	4.42	85.38%	9.76	4.27	85.98	4.19	83.25%
Q3	48.21	12.50	39.29	2.83	88.54%	47.27	9.70	43.03	2.94	83.76%
Q4	41.96	12.95	45.09	3.01	88.54%	37.95	18.67	43.37	3.10	84.26%
Q5	57.92	13.12	28.96	2.59	87.35%	52.15	15.34	32.52	2.74	82.74%
Q6	17.12	19.82	63.06	3.60	87.75%	27.61	22.70	49.69	3.36	82.74%
Q7	1.79	2.24	95.96	4.54	88.14%	1.86	3.11	95.03	4.57	81.73%
Q8	7.31	10.50	82.19	4.07	86.56%	6.96	5.70	87.34	4.22	80.20%
Q9	17.97	14.29	67.74	3.71	85.77%	14.20	13.58	72.22	3.89	82.23%
Q10	8.42	15.26	76.32	3.87	75.10%	13.16	19.08	67.76	3.81	77.16%
Q11	4.07	4.52	91.40	4.32	87.35%	3.11	5.59	91.30	4.32	81.73%
Q12	20.09	21.00	58.90	3.52	86.56%	18.13	20.63	61.25	3.62	81.22%
Q13	5.94	3.65	90.41	4.22	86.56%	4.35	5.59	90.06	4.22	81.73%
Q14	44.71	30.59	24.71	2.81	67.19%	34.06	28.26	37.68	3.14	70.05%
Q15	25.57	16.44	57.99	3.44	86.56%	8.23	14.56	77.22	3.93	80.20%
Q16	7.34	9.63	83.03	3.94	86.17%	5.00	6.88	88.13	4.16	81.22%
Q17	24.77	12.62	62.62	3.48	84.58%	7.59	15.19	77.22	3.97	80.20%
Q18	56.36	21.82	21.82	2.63	65.22%	45.32	20.14	34.53	2.94	70.56%
Q19	3.27	6.07	90.65	4.46	84.58%	4.40	5.03	90.57	4.45	80.71%
Q20	60.48	12.57	26.95	2.66	66.01%	40.15	12.12	47.73	3.23	67.01%
Q21	3.85	12.50	83.65	4.30	82.21%	5.03	6.92	88.05	4.34	80.71%
Q22	78.41	11.93	9.66	2.19	69.57%	65.67	14.18	20.15	2.50	68.02%

likely to perceive that MD make travel more interesting and fun than individuals from cluster 2 (77.22% and 57.99%, respectively). Their responses are also more positive than those of cluster 1 when asked if they like using MD when traveling for pleasure (88.13% and 83.03%, respectively).

Individuals from cluster 2 prefer tablets to smartphones more than individuals from cluster 1. Thus, they state that tablets are easier to interact with (37.68% and 24.71%, respectively), are more fun (34.53% and 21.82%, respectively) and enrich the travel experience more (77.22% and 62.62%, respectively) than smartphones do.

Finally, both clusters have the same intention of using MD on future tourist trips. However, individuals in cluster 2 stated that they would use tablets in the future more than the individuals in cluster 1 (47.73% and 26.95%, respectively). They also agreed more that they would use the smartphone in the future (88.05% and 83.65%, respectively) and that they would prefer to use digital tablets to smartphones in the future if they had to choose between the two devices (20.15% and 9.66%, respectively).

CONCLUSION

This study offers an initial exploration of how tourists use TUE and also attempts to provide a useful comprehension of digital tourists. Digital tourists are not only characterized by an intensive use of MD, but also by their positive attitude towards technology and the tendency towards substituting analog TUE with digital TUE, especially MD.

The study set out to find empirical evidence for the use that digital tourists make of technology when visiting a destination. The results confirm that there is no single digital tourist profile and that sociodemographic characteristics explain some of the differences found. These results question some points of the debate about tourist behavior. As a result of the increased use of technology among all market segments, traditional variables (age, gender, income level, etc.) have been considered irrelevant for describing and differentiating these segments (Gretzel, Fesenmaier & O'Leary, 2017). However, our research indicates that sociodemographic variables are still relevant for defining and differentiating digital tourists. Cluster analysis confirms the existence of two groups of digital tourists, which are well differentiated and even separated by antagonistic behavior patterns. Young and middle-to-low status women display a complementary use of TUE, in sharp contrast to Senior and high-status men who make an intensive and preferential use of digital TUE during their tourist visits.

The results of this study provide strong evidence that gender, age and income level are factors that influence the different use of TUE by digital tourists.

The results also indicate that, although the use of MD is almost universal among tourists, these devices do not replace analog travel instruments but rather play a complementary role to them. These findings further suggest that the use of tourism equipment tends to be reduced and simplified, based on the total number of tools carried by tourists when they visit the destination. However, there is no evidence that MD completely replace the use of other tools. The use made of MD by tourists is more of a complementary use than a substitutive use. The study also aimed to identify any significant differences among digital tourists and showed that the effect of the reduction of the technology gap among generations is lower than expected. Further analysis of cultural and sociodemographic differences between digital tourist groups could help to explain these differences. Instruction level was an exception, as no statistically significant differences were found when considered with other variables. The reason for this could be the convergence of digital skills among tourists. However, the differences in gender, age, income and technology preferences show that individual sociodemographic characteristics can still be important when analyzing technology preferences and tourist behavior at the destination.

To sum up, the study confirms, as other studies have shown, that age, gender and income should be significant drivers when developing segmentation, targeting and positioning strategies, as the technology patterns of digital tourists groups vary (Persaud & Azhar, 2012). The use of MD is almost universal among tourists who visit Barcelona, so it can be stated that digital tourists are predominant. Nevertheless, individual use of MD is strongly conditioned by cultural and sociodemographic profiles that shape tourists' perceptions of the use of technology for tourism purposes and influence their behavior.

Some practical implications for destinations can be identified from the results obtained. The results suggest a need for different marketing destination strategies that focus on digital tourists according to their specific perceptions of technology and MD. Differences in gender, age and income level suggest that a strategy which only addresses a standard digital tourist profile may be inclined to fail. To some extent, this point contradicts the thesis that tourists' preferences regarding the use of technology reduce the relevance of their sociodemographic characteristics in explaining tourist behavior (Gretzel, Fesenmaier

& O'Leary, 2006). Differences in the extent to which digital tourists accept the use of technology and the future use of MD may indicate different levels of concern over privacy issues and limits to how they use technology for tourism purposes. This issue is also mentioned in different research articles about tourists' risk perceptions of smartphones (Kaasinen, 2003; Anuar & Gretzel, 2011; González et al., 2018). Similarly, regarding the results on the acceptance of the use of technology, some digital tourists may have a different response to the mandatory use of MD for understanding attractions or engaging in the tourist experience. Travel and destination managers should help digital tourists by providing them with useful information that stimulates their interest in using technology to enhance their experiences and engages them in tourism technology experiences by addressing the perceived risks and the extent to which they use MD.

Tourists who make an intensive use of technology are an attractive market segment for travel providers, intermediaries and destinations, not only because of their high level of technological skills, but also because they enjoy enhancing their experiences through the use of technology and MD. These digital tourists would appear to be quite a straightforward market segment for those smart tourism destinations providing targeted product development. Moreover, intensive technology use travellers are a target for those destinations developing tourism products and services on a collaborative basis, using shared information and digital contents. Our analysis identifies two types of tourists: a proactive technology user and a reactive technology user. This distinction is relevant from the point of view of the sharing economy, since these tourists can embrace, respectively, a positive or negative attitude towards collaborative forms of travelling regarding the use of technology.

Future research could replicate the study by surveying tourists from other cities and comparing their responses. Our research suggests that some cultural differences may exist among digital tourists, so a future line of research may be to analyze digital tourists by geographical origin in order to gain more insight into cultural and social differences among them when using TUE. The differences identified during the destination phase may also be identified in the previous tourist phase (planning) and in the use of social media networks during (and after) the visit to the destination. This would then be a second subject for future research.

REFERENCES

Amaro, S., Duarte, P., & Henriques, C. (2016). Traveler's use of social media: A clustering approach. *Annals of Tourism Research, 59*, 1–15. doi:10.1016/j.annals.2016.03.007

Anuar, F., & Gretzel, U. (2011). Privacy concerns in the context of location-based services for tourism. *ENTER Conference 2011. Conference Short Paper. ENTER Vol. 1 (Short Papers).*

Buhalis, D., & Law, R. (2008). Progress in information technology and tourism management: 20 years on and 10 years after the Internet. The state of eTourism research. *Annals of Tourism Research, 29*(4), 609–623.

Buhalis, D., & O'Connor, P. (2006). Information communication technology revolutionizing tourism. *Tourism Recreation Research, 30*(3), 7–16. doi:10.1080/02508281.2005.11081482

Davies, F. (1989). Perceived usefulness, perceived ease of use and user acceptance of Information technology. *Management Information Systems Quarterly, 13*(3), 319–340. doi:10.2307/249008

Dickinson, J. E., Ghali, K., Cherrett, T., Speed, C., Davies, N., & Norgate, S. (2014). Tourism and the smartphone app: Capabilities, emerging practice and scope in the travel domain. *Current Issues in Tourism, 17*(1), 84–101. doi:10.1080/13683500.2012.718323

Dinholp, A., & Gretzel, U. (2016). Selfie-taking as touristic looking. *Annals of Tourism Research, 57*, 126–139. doi:10.1016/j.annals.2015.12.015

Evjemo, B., Sykehusvn, S., & Schürmann, A. (2007). User acceptance of Digital Tourist Guides. Lessons learnt from two field studies. In J. Jacko (Ed.), *Human Computer Interaction, Part I* (pp. 746–755). Berlin: Springer-Verlag. doi:10.1007/978-3-540-73105-4_82

González-Reverté. (2018). Tourists' risk perception and the use of mobile devices in beach tourism destinations. *Sustainability, 10*(2), 413. doi:10.3390u10020413

Gretzel, U. (2010). Travel in the Network: Redirected Gazes, Ubiquitous Connections and New Frontiers. In M. Levina & G. Kien (Eds.), *Post-global Network and Everyday Life* (pp. 41–58). New York: Peter Lang.

Gretzel, U., Fesenmaier, D. R., & O'Leary, J. T. (2006). The transformation of consumer behaviour. In D. Buhalis & C. Costa (Eds.), *Tourism Business Frontier* (pp. 9–18). Oxford, UK: Elsevier. doi:10.1016/B978-0-7506-6377-9.50009-2

Gretzel, U., & Jamal, T. (2009). Conceptualizing the tourist creative class: Technology, mobility and tourism experiences. *Tourism Analysis, 14*(4), 471–481. doi:10.3727/108354209X12596287114219

Grün, C. (2008) Assisting tourists on the move. An evaluation of mobile tourism guides. *Proceedings of the 7th International Conference on Mobile Business*, 171-180.

Gymóthy, S. (2017). Networked cultures in the collaborative economy. In D. Dredge & S. Gymóthy (Eds.), *Collaborative economy and tourism. Perspectives, policies and prospects* (pp. 59–74). Springer.

Hee, H., & Law, R. (2015). Smartphones in Tourism and Hospitality marketing. A literature review. *Journal of Travel & Tourism Marketing, 32*(6), 692–711. doi:10.1080/10548408.2014.943458

Hunter, W., Chung, N., Gretzel, U., & Koo, C. (2015). Contructivist research in smart tourism. *Asia Pacific Journal of Information Systems, 25*(1), 105–120. doi:10.14329/apjis.2015.25.1.105

Kaasinen, E. (2002). User needs for location-aware mobile services. *Personal and Ubiquitous Computing, 7*(1), 70–79. doi:10.100700779-002-0214-7

Lalicic, L., & Weismayer, C. (2016). The passionate use of mobiles phones among tourists. *Information Technology & Tourism, 16*(1), 153–173. doi:10.100740558-015-0042-z

Lamsfus, C., Wang, D., Alzua-Sorzabal, A., & Xiang, Z. (2015). Going mobile: Defining context for on-the-go travelers. *Journal of Travel Research, 54*(6), 691–701. doi:10.1177/0047287514538839

Miguéns, J., Baggio, R., & Costa, C. (2008) Social media and tourism destinations: TripAdvisor case study. *Proceedings of the IASK ATR2008 Advances in Tourism Research Conference 2008*, 26-28.

Minghetti, V., & Buhalis, D. (2010). Digital divide in Tourism. *Journal of Travel Research, 49*(3), 267–281. doi:10.1177/0047287509346843

Neuhofer, B., Buhalis, D., & Ladkin, A. (2012). Conceptualising Technology enhanced experiences. *Journal of Destination Marketing & Management, 1*(1-2), 36–46. doi:10.1016/j.jdmm.2012.08.001

Norrie, M., & Signer, B. (2005). Overlaying Paper Maps with Digital Information Services for Tourists. In A. J. Frew (Ed.), *Information and Communication Technologies in Tourism*. Vienna: Springer.

Northern Ireland Tourism Board. (2015). *Tourism in the midst of a mobile revolution. How advances in mobile technology will shape Northern Ireland's tourism industry in the next decade*. Belfast: NITB.

Persaud, A., & Azhar, I. (2012). Innovative Mobile Marketing via Smartphones: Are Consumers Ready? *Marketing Intelligence & Planning, 30*(4), 438–443. doi:10.1108/02634501211231883

Porter, M. E., & Heppelmann, J. E. (2014). How smart, connected products are transforming competition. *Harvard Business Review, 92*(11), 64–88.

Prideaux, B., & Coghlan, A. (2010). Digital cameras and photo taking on the Great Barrier Reef. Marketing opprotunities for Reef tour operators. *Journal of Vacation Marketing, 16*(3), 171–183. doi:10.1177/1356766710372244

Tussyadiah, I. (2014). Social actor attribution to mobile phones: The case of tourists. *Information Technology & Tourism, 14*(1), 21–47. doi:10.100740558-013-0002-4

Tussyadiah, I., & Zach, F. (2011). The role of geo-based technology in place experiences. *Annals of Tourism Research, 39*(2), 780–800. doi:10.1016/j.annals.2011.10.003

Wang, D., & Fesenmaier, D. R. (2013). Transforming the travel experience: the use of smartphones for travel. In L. Cantoni & Z. Xiang (Eds.), *Information and Communication Technologies in Tourism 2013* (pp. 58–69). Berlin: Springer-Verlag. doi:10.1007/978-3-642-36309-2_6

Wang, D., Park, S., & Fesenmaier, D. R. (2012). The Role of Smartphones in Mediating the Touristic Experience. *Journal of Travel Research, 51*(4), 371–387. doi:10.1177/0047287511426341

Wang, D., Xiang, Z., & Fesenmaier, D. (2014). Smartphone use in everyday life and travel. *Journal of Travel Research, 55*(1), 52–63. doi:10.1177/0047287514535847

Wang, N. (2002). The tourist as peak consumer. In G. Dann (Ed.), *The tourist as a metaphor of the social world* (pp. 281–296). Oxford, UK: CABI. doi:10.1079/9780851996066.0281

Werther, H., & Klein, S. (1999). ICT and the Changing Landscape of Global Tourism Distribution. *Electronic Markets, 9*(4), 256–262. doi:10.1080/101967899358941

Zeng, B., & Gerritsen, R. (2014). What do we know about social media in tourism? A review. *Tourism Management Perspectives, 10*, 27–36. doi:10.1016/j.tmp.2014.01.001

Compilation of References

Aarikka-Stenroos, L., & Jaakkola, E. (2012). Value co-creation in knowledge intensive business services: A dyadic perspective on the joint problem solving process. *Industrial Marketing Management*, *41*(1), 15–26. doi:10.1016/j.indmarman.2011.11.008

About, I. G. G. (n.d.). Retrieved March 10, 2019, from https://www.indiegogo.com/about/our-story

Abrate, G., & And Viglia, G. (2016). Strategic and tactical price decisions in hotel revenue management. *Tourism Management*, *55*, 123–132. doi:10.1016/j.tourman.2016.02.006

Acevedo, D. D. (2016). Regulating employment relationships in the sharing economy. *Employee Rights & Employment Policy Journal*, *20*(1), 1–36.

Acquier, A., Daudigeos, T., & Pinkse, J. (2017). Promises and paradoxes of the sharing economy: An organizing framework. *Technological Forecasting and Social Change*, *125*, 1–10. doi:10.1016/j.techfore.2017.07.006

Adamiak, C. (2018). Mapping Airbnb supply in European cities. *Annals of Tourism Research*, *71*(C), 67–71. doi:10.1016/j.annals.2018.02.008

Agencia Tributaria. (n.d.). Statistics of the taxpayers of the income tax of individuals of the largest municipalities by zip code. *Agencia Tributaria*. Retrieved from: https://www.agenciatributaria.es/AEAT.internet/datosabiertos/catalogo/hacienda/Estadistica_del_IRPF_por_codigo_postal.shtml

Agyeman, J., McLaren, D., & Schaefer-Borrego, A. (2013). Sharing cities. *Friends of the Earth Briefing*, 1-32.

Ahn, T., Ryu, S., & Han, I. (2007). The impact of Web quality and playfulness on user acceptance of online retailing. *Information & Management*, *44*(3), 263–275. doi:10.1016/j.im.2006.12.008

Airbnb. (2013). *New study: Airbnb community contributes $175 million to Barcelona's economy*. Available at: www.airbnb.nl/press/news/new-study-airbnb-community-contributes-175million-to-barcelona-s-economy

Airbnb. (2015). *El impacto del alojamiento compartido en Madrid*. Available at: https://blog.atairbnb.com/el-impacto-del-alojamiento-compartido-en-madrid/

Airbnb. (2019a). *Trust & Safety*. Retrieved from https://www.airbnb.com/trust

Airbnb. (2019b). *What are Airbnb's rules about electronic surveillance devices in listings?* Retrieved from https://www.airbnb.com/help/article/887/what-are-airbnb-s-rules-about-electronic-surveillance-devices-in-listings

Ajzen, I. (1991). The theory of planned behavior. *Organizational Behavior and Human Decision Processes*, *50*(2), 179–211. doi:10.1016/0749-5978(91)90020-T

Akbar, P., Mai, R., & Hoffmann, S. (2016). When do materialistic consumers join commercial sharing systems. *Journal of Business Research*, *69*(10), 4215–4224. doi:10.1016/j.jbusres.2016.03.003

Akbar, Y. H., & Tracogna, A. (2018). The sharing economy and the future of the hotel industry: Transaction cost theory and platform economics. *International Journal of Hospitality Management*, *71*, 91–101. doi:10.1016/j.ijhm.2017.12.004

Allgood, S., & Walstad, W. (2013). Financial literacy and credit card behaviors: A cross-sectional analysis by age. *Numeracy, 6*(2).

Amaro, S., Duarte, P., & Henriques, C. (2016). Traveler's use of social media: A clustering approach. *Annals of Tourism Research*, *59*, 1–15. doi:10.1016/j.annals.2016.03.007

Anderson, E. (1985). The salesperson as outside agent or employee: A transaction cost analysis. *Marketing Science*, *4*(3), 234–254. doi:10.1287/mksc.4.3.234

Anderson, E., & Schmittlein, D. (1984). Integration of the sales force: An empirical examination. *The Rand Journal of Economics*, *15*(3), 385–395. doi:10.2307/2555446

Anderson, J. C., & Narus, J. A. (1990). A model of distributor firm and manufacturing firm working partnerships. *Journal of Marketing*, *54*(1), 42–58. doi:10.1177/002224299005400103

Anuar, F., & Gretzel, U. (2011). Privacy concerns in the context of location-based services for tourism. *ENTER Conference 2011. Conference Short Paper. ENTER Vol. 1 (Short Papers).*

Arias Sans, A. (2015). *Desmuntant Airbnb. Apunts crítics sobre el cas de Barcelona*. Available at: http://latramaurbana.net/2015/07/01/desmuntant-airbnb-apunts-critics-sobre-el-cas-de-barcelona/#more-1245

Arrow, K. J. (1974). *The limits of organization (Fels lectu)*. New York: Norton : The Murray Printing Company.

Arthur, W. B. (1989). Competing technologies, increasing returns, and lock-in by historical events. *Economic Journal (London)*, *89*(394), 116–131. doi:10.2307/2234208

Asaad, C. T. (2015). Financial literacy and financial behavior: Assessing knowledge and confidence. *Financial Services Review*, *24*, 101–117.

Assadourian, E., Flavin, C., French, H., Gardner, G., Halweil, B., & Mastny, L. … Vickers, A. (2004). State of the world state of the world: A worldwatch institute report on progress toward a sustainable society. New York: W.W. Norton & Company.

Association, G. S. M. (2019). *The mobile economy*. Retrieved from: https://www.gsmaintelligence.com/research/?file=b9a6e6202ee1d5f787cfebb95d3639c5&download

Attanasio, C., & Pagones, S. (2018). *Uber driver says he was attacked by passenger who accidentally ordered carpool.* Retrieved from https://nypost.com/2018/10/25/uber-driver-says-he-was-attacked-by-passenger-who-accidentally-ordered-carpool/

Ávalos, M. (2015), Baby, you can't drive my car. El caso de Uber en México. Economía informa, (390), 104-112.

Bachand-Marleau, J., Lee, B. H. Y., & El-Geneidy, A. M. (2012). Better Understanding of Factors Influencing Likelihood of Using Shared Bicycle Systems and Frequency of Use. *Transportation Research Record: Journal of the Transportation Research Board*, *2314*(1), 66–71. doi:10.3141/2314-09

Bachmann, A., & Funk, B. (2011). Online peer-to-peer lending: A literature review. *Journal of Internet Banking and Commerce*, *16*(2).

Bakker, M., & Twining-Ward, L. (2018). *Tourism and the Sharing Economy: Policy and Potential of Sustainable Peer-to-Peer Accommodation*. Washington, DC: World Bank. doi:10.1596/30452

Balakrishnan, S., & Wernerfelt, B. (1986). Technical change, competition and vertical integration. *Strategic Management Journal*, *7*(4), 347–359. doi:10.1002mj.4250070405

Baldassarri, S. (2011). *Collaborative Finance*. Retrieved from http://www.collaborativefinance.org/

Baldwin, C. Y., & Woodard, C. J. (2009). The architecture of platforms: A unified view. In A. Gawer (Ed.), *Platforms* (pp. 19–44). Cheltenham, UK: Markets and Innovation, Edgar Elgar. doi:10.4337/9781849803311.00008

Balloch, A., Nicolae, A., & Philip, D. (2015). Stock Market Literacy, Trust and Participation. *Review of Finance*, *19*(5), 1925–1963. doi:10.1093/rof/rfu040

Bamberger, K. A., & Lobel, O. (2017). Platform Market Power. *Berkeley Technology Law Journal*, *32*. Retrieved from https://heinonline.org/HOL/Page?handle=hein.journals/berktech32&id=1095&div=35&collection=journals

Banks, J., & Oldfield, Z. (2007). Understanding pensions: Cognitive function, numerical ability and retirement saving. *Fiscal Studies*, *28*(2), 143–170. doi:10.1111/j.1475-5890.2007.00052.x

Barcelona City Council. (n.d.). *Distribució territorial de la renda familiar, 2000-2017*. Retrieved February 2019 from http://www.bcn.cat/estadistica/catala/dades/economia/renda/rdfamiliar/evo/rfdte.htm

Barclay, D., Higgins, C., & Thompson, R. (1995). The Partial Least Squares (PLS) Approach to Causal Modeling: Personal Computer Adoption and Use as an Illustration. *Technology Studies*, *2*(2), 285–309.

Bardhi, F., & Eckhardt, G. M. (2012). Access-based consumption: The case of car sharing. *The Journal of Consumer Research*, *39*(4), 881–898. doi:10.1086/666376

Bardhi, F., Eckhardt, G. M., & Arnould, E. J. (2012). Liquid relationship to possessions. *The Journal of Consumer Research*, *39*(3), 510–529. doi:10.1086/664037

Barnes, S. J., & Mattsson, J. (2016). Understanding current and future issues in collaborative consumption: A four-stage Delphi study. *Technological Forecasting and Social Change*, *104*, 200–211. doi:10.1016/j.techfore.2016.01.006

Barranco, M. C., & González, M. G. (2016). El transporte intracondominal en la movilidad cotidiana de la periurbanización: el enlace comunitario del Área Metropolitana de Guadalajara. *Revista Transporte y Territorio*, *14*, 167-188. Obtenido de http://revistascientificas.filo.uba .ar/index.php/rtt/article/view/2434/2092

Barron, K., Kung, E., & Proserpio, D. (2018). *The sharing economy and housing affordability: Evidence from Airbnb*. Available at: https://static1.squarespace.com/static/5bb2d447a9ab951efbf6d10a/t/5bea6881562fa7934045a3f0/1542088837594/The+Sharing+Economy+and+Housing+Affordability.pdf

Barthélemy, J., & Quélin, B. V. (2006). Complexity of outsourcing contracts and ex post transaction costs: An empirical investigation. *Journal of Management Studies*, *43*(8), 1775–1797. doi:10.1111/j.1467-6486.2006.00658.x

Barzilay, A. R., & Ben-David, A. (2016). Platform inequality: gender in the gig-economy. *Seton Hall L. Rev.*, *47*, 393.

Belk, R. (2007). Why not share rather than own? *The Annals of the American Academy of Political and Social Science*, *611*(1), 126–140. doi:10.1177/0002716206298483

Belk, R. (2010). Sharing. *The Journal of Consumer Research*, *36*(5), 715–734. doi:10.1086/612649

Belk, R. (2014). Sharing Versus Pseudo-Sharing in Web 2.0. *Anthropologist*, *18*(1), 7–23. doi:10.1080/09720073.2014.11891518

Belk, R. (2014). You are what you can access: Sharing and collaborative consumption online. *Journal of Business Research, 67*(8), 1595–1600. doi:10.1016/j.jbusres.2013.10.001

Belk, R. W. (2013). Extended self in a digital world. *The Journal of Consumer Research, 40*(3), 477–500. doi:10.1086/671052

Bellotti, V., Ambard, A., Turner, D., Gossmann, C., Demkova, K., & Carroll, J. M. (2015, April). A muddle of models of motivation for using peer-to-peer economy systems. In *Proceedings of the 33rd Annual ACM Conference on Human Factors in Computing Systems* (pp. 1085-1094). ACM. 10.1145/2702123.2702272

Benkler, Y. (2004). Sharing nicely. On shareable goods and the emergence of sharing as a modality of economic production. *The Yale Law Journal, 114*(2), 273–358. doi:10.2307/4135731

Benkler, Y. (2007). *The Wealth of Networks: How Social Production Transforms Markets and Freedom*. New Haven, CT: Yale University Press.

Bershidsky, L. (2018). *Gig-Economy Workers Are the Modern Proletariat*. Bloomberg.

Beshears, J., Choi, J. J., Laibson, D., Madrian, B. C., & Milkman, K. L. (2015). The effect of providing peer information on retirement savings decisions. *The Journal of Finance, 70*(3), 1161–1201. doi:10.1111/jofi.12258 PMID:26045629

Biais, B., Hilton, D., Mazurier, K., & Pouget, S. (2005). Judgemental overconfidence, self-monitoring, and trading performance in an experimental financial market. *The Review of Economic Studies, 72*(2), 287–312. doi:10.1111/j.1467-937X.2005.00333.x

Birch, D. G., & Parulava, S. (2017). Ambient Accountability: Shared Ledger Technology and Radical Transparency for Next Generation Digital Financial Services. In Handbook of Blockchain, Digital Finance, and Inclusion (vol. 1, pp. 375–387). Elsevier.

Blal, I., Singal, M., & Templin, J. (2018). Airbnb's effect on hotel sales growth. *International Journal of Hospitality Management, 73*, 85–92. doi:10.1016/j.ijhm.2018.02.006

Blog, K. S. (2017). Celebrating 100,000 Kickstarter Creators. Retrieved from https://www.kickstarter.com/blog/celebrating-100000-kickstarter-creators

Böcker, L., & Meelen, T. (2017). Sharing for people, planet or profit? Analysing motivations for intended sharing economy participation. *Environmental Innovation and Societal Transitions, 23*, 28–39. doi:10.1016/j.eist.2016.09.004

Boltanski, L., & Chiapello, E. (2005). *The new spirit of capitalism*. Verso. doi:10.100710767-006-9006-9

Boltanski, L., & Thévenot, L. (2006). *On justification: economies of worth*. Princeton University Press.

Bordagaray, M., dell'Olio, L., Ibeas, Á., Barreda, R., & Alonso, B. (2015). Modeling the Service Quality of Public Bicycle Schemes Considering User Heterogeneity. *International Journal of Sustainable Transportation, 9*(8), 580–591. doi:10.1080/15568318.2013.838722

Boros, L., Dudás, G., Kovalcsik, T., Papp, S., & Vida, G. (2018). Airbnb in Budapest: Analysing spatial patterns and room rates of hotels and peer-to-peer accommodations. *Geo Journal of Tourism and Geosites, 21*(1), 26–38.

Bort, J. (2018). Airbnb made $93 million in profit on $2.6 billion in revenue, but an internal clash sent the CFO out the door. *Business Insider*. Accessed on July 30, 2018 at http://www.businessinsider.com/airbnb-profit-revenue-2018-2?IR=T

Bostman, R., & Rogers, R. (2010). *What's mine is yours: the rise of collaborative consumption*. New York: Harper Business.

Botsman, R. (2012). We've stopped trusting institutions and started trusting strangers. *TED Talks*. Retrieved from: https://www.ted.com/talks/rachel_botsman_we_ve_stopped_trusting_institutions_and_started_trusting_strangers

Botsman, R. (2012a). *Rachel Botsman: The case for collaborative consumption.* TED.com.

Botsman, R. (2012b). *Rachel Botsman: the currency of the new economy is trust.* TED.com.

Botsman, R. (2013). *The sharing economy lacks a shared definition.* Retrieved from: https://www.fastcoexist.com/3022028/the-sharing-economy-lacks-a-shared-definition

Botsman, R. (2015). *Defining the sharing economy: What is collaborative consumption - and what isn't?* Retrieved from: https://www.fastcompany.com/3046119/defining-the-sharing-economy-what-is-collaborative-consumption-and-what-isnt

Botsman, R. (2016). *Collaborative Finance 2016 Update.* Retrieved from https://www.slideshare.net/RBotsman/collaborative-finance-2016-update

Botsmann, R. (2015). *The Sharing Economy: Dictionary of Commonly Used Terms - Rachel Botsman.* Retrieved from https://rachelbotsman.com/blog/the-sharing-economy-dictionary-of-commonly-used-terms/

Botsman, R., & Rogers, R. (2010). *What's Mine Is Yours: The Rise of Collaborative Consumption.* London: Harper Business.

Botsman, R., & Rogers, R. (2010). *What's mine is yours: The rise of collaborative consumption.* New York: Harper Business.

Botsman, R., & Rogers, R. (2011). *What's mine is yours : how collaborative consumption is changing the way we live.* Collins.

Botsman, R., & Rogers, R. (2011). *What's Mine is Yours. How Collaborative Consumption is Changing the Way We Live.* London: Harper Collins.

Botsman, R., & Rogers, R. (2011). *What's mine is yours: how collaborative consumption is changing the way we live* (Vol. 5). London: Collins.

Botsman, R., & Rogers, R. (2011). *What's mine is yours: How collaborative consumption is changing the way we live.* London: Collins.

Bottomley, K., & Burgess, S. W. (2018). Millennials in Leadership: An Examination of the Practice-Immediacy Model. In *Engaged Leadership* (pp. 223–234). Cham: Springer. doi:10.1007/978-3-319-72221-4_13

Brabham, D. C. (2013). *Crowdsourcing*. Cambridge, MA: The MIT Press. doi:10.7551/mitpress/9693.001.0001

Bradford, C.S. (2012). Crowdfunding and the Federal Securities Laws. *Columbia Business Law Review*, *1*(1), 1-150.

Brauckmann, S. (2017). City tourism and the sharing economy–potential effects of online peer-to-peer marketplaces on urban property markets. *Journal of Tourism Futures*, *3*(2), 114–126. doi:10.1108/JTF-05-2017-0027

Bravo, M. (2015). *Caro y malo, el transporte público en México*. Obtenido de https://meganoticias.mx/tu-ciudad/guadalajara/especiales-meganoticias/item/85874-caro-ymalo- el-transporte-publico-en-mexico.html

Bravo, P. (2019, January 12). De las fake news a las empresas fake: cómo afecta la economía ficción a nuestras ciudades. *Eldiario.Es*. Retrieved from https://www.eldiario.es/desde-mi-bici/fake-empresas-economia-ficcion-ciudades_6_856074416.html

Brown, H. S., & Vergragt, P. J. (2016). From consumerism to wellbeing: Toward a cultural transition? *Journal of Cleaner Production*, *132*, 308–317. doi:10.1016/j.jclepro.2015.04.107

Brown, J. R., Ivković, Z., Smith, P. A., & Weisbenner, S. (2008). Neighbours matter: Causal community effects and stock market participation. *The Journal of Finance*, *63*(3), 1509–1531. doi:10.1111/j.1540-6261.2008.01364.x

Brynjolfsson, E., & McAfee, A. (2016). *The second machine age: work, progress, and prosperity in a time of brilliant technologies*. W. W. Norton Company.

Bucher, E., Fieseler, C., & Lutz, C. (2016). What's mine is yours (for a nominal fee)–Exploring the spectrum of utilitarian to altruistic motives for Internet-mediated sharing. *Computers in Human Behavior*, *62*, 316–326. doi:10.1016/j.chb.2016.04.002

Bucher-Koenen, T., & Lusardi, A. (2011). Financial literacy and retirement planning in Germany. *Journal of Pension Economics and Finance*, *10*(4), 565–584. doi:10.1017/S1474747211000485

Buhalis, D., & Law, R. (2008). Progress in information technology and tourism management: 20 years on and 10 years after the Internet. The state of eTourism research. *Annals of Tourism Research*, *29*(4), 609–623.

Buhalis, D., & O'Connor, P. (2006). Information communication technology revolutionizing tourism. *Tourism Recreation Research*, *30*(3), 7–16. doi:10.1080/02508281.2005.11081482

Burns, M. (2015, November 7). Another $1 million crowdfunded gadget company collapses. *TechCrunch*. Retrieved from https://techcrunch.com/2015/11/07/another-1-million-crowdfunded-gadget-company-collapses/

Bursztyn, L., Ederer, F., Ferman, B., & Yuchtman, N. (2014). Understanding peer effects in financial decisions: Evidence from a field experiment. *Econometrica*, *82*(4), 1273–1301. doi:10.3982/ECTA11991

Bussema, C. (2012, September 5). *Accountability on Kickstarter*. Comment posted to https://www.kickstarter.com/blog/accountability-on-kickstarter

Calcagno, R., & Monticone, C. (2015). Financial literacy and the demand for financial advice. *Journal of Banking & Finance*, *50*, 363–380. doi:10.1016/j.jbankfin.2014.03.013

Calo, R., & Rosenblat, A. (2017). The Taking Economy: Uber, Information, and Power. *Columbia Law Review*, *117*(6), 1623–1690. Retrieved from https://www.jstor.org/stable/44392959?seq=1#page_scan_tab_contents

Canals, J. (1994). *La internacionalización de la empresa*. Madrid: McGraw-Hill.

Cañigueral, A. (2015). Consumo colaborativo. *Leaners Magazine*, 18-22.

Cansoy, M., & Schor, J. (2017). *Who gets to share in the sharing economy: Racial discrimination on Airbnb*. Working paper, Boston College.

Carbaugh, R. J. (2005). La globalización de la actividad económica. In R. J. Carbaugh (Ed.), Economía Internacional (pp. 4-8). Thompson.

Carbone, V., Rouquet, A., & Roussat, C. (2017). The Rise of Crowd Logistics: A New Way to Co-create Logistics Value. *Journal of Business Logistics*, *38*(4), 238–252. doi:10.1111/jbl.12164

Cardozo, R. N. (1965). An Experimental Study of Customer Effort, Expectation, and Satisfaction. *JMR, Journal of Marketing Research*, *2*(3), 244–249. doi:10.1177/002224376500200303

Carson, B. (2017). *Lyft Triped its Rides in 2016*. Accessed on July 30, 2018 at http://www.businessinsider.com/lyft-tripled-its-rides-in-2016-2017-1?IR=T https://www.forbes.com/sites/bizcarson/2018/01/16/lyft-doubled-rides-in-2017/#657fd5a17d6b

Cart. (n.d.). *granadaimedia. Cart*. Retrieved from: https://granadaimedia.carto.com/me

Carter, R., & Hodgson, G. M. (2006). The impact of empirical tests of transaction cost economics on the debate on the nature of the firm. *Strategic Management Journal*, *27*(5), 461–476. doi:10.1002mj.531

Casprini, E., Di Minin, A., & Paraboschi, A. (2018). How do companies organize nascent markets? The BlaBlaCar case in the inter-city shared mobility market. *Technological Forecasting and Social Change*.

Cats, O., Abenoza, R. F., Liu, C., & Susilo, Y. O. (2015). Evolution of Satisfaction with Public Transport and Its Determinants in Sweden. *Transportation Research Record: Journal of the Transportation Research Board*, *2538*(1), 86–95. doi:10.3141/2538-10

Cellon-Jones, R. (2016, January 20). Zano: The rise and fall of Kickstarter's mini-drone. *BBC.com.* Retrieved from https://www.bbc.com/news/technology-35356147

Centre for Retail Research. (2018). *Online Retailing: Britain, Europe, US and Canada 2017*. Retrieved April 2019 from http://www.retailresearch.org/onlineretailing.php

Chafkin, M. (2016). *Fast Company*. Obtenido de Fastcompany.com: http://www.fastcompany.com/3054873/can-airbnb-unite-the-world

Chen, C. C., & Chang, Y. C. (2018). What drives purchase intention on Airbnb? Perspectives of consumer reviews, information quality, and media richness. *Telematics and Informatics*, *35*(5), 1512–1523. doi:10.1016/j.tele.2018.03.019

Cheng, M. (2016). Sharing economy: A review and agenda for future research. *International Journal of Hospitality Management*, *57*, 60–70. doi:10.1016/j.ijhm.2016.06.003

Chen, M., Wang, D., Sun, Y., Liu, C., & Bai, Z. (2017). Service Evaluation of Public Bicycle Scheme from a User Perspective: A Case Study in Hangzhou, China. *Transportation Research Record: Journal of the Transportation Research Board*, *2634*(1), 28–34. doi:10.3141/2634-04

Chin, W. W. (1998). The Partial Least Squares Approach to Structural Equation Modeling. In G. A. Marcoulides (Ed.), *Modern Methods for Business Research* (pp. 295–336). Mahwah, NJ: Lawrence Erlbaum Associates Publishers.

Christensen, C., & Raynor, M. (2003). *The innovator's solution: creating and sustaining successful growth*. Boston: Harvard Business Press.

Chung, J. Y. (2017). Online friendships in a hospitality exchange network: A sharing economy perspective. *International Journal of Contemporary Hospitality Management*, *29*(12), 3177–3190. doi:10.1108/IJCHM-08-2016-0475

Ciulli, F., & Kolk, A. (2019). Incumbents and business model innovation for the sharing economy: Implications for sustainability. *Journal of Cleaner Production*, *214*, 995–1010. doi:10.1016/j.jclepro.2018.12.295

Clifford, C. (2016, January 18). Less than a third of crowdfunding campaigns reach their goals. *The Entrepreneur*. Retrieved from https://www.entrepreneur.com/article/269663

Coase, R. H. (1937). The nature of the firm. *Economica*, *4*(16), 386–405. doi:10.1111/j.1468-0335.1937.tb00002.x

Cócola Gant, A. (2016). Holiday rentals: The new gentrification battlefront. *Sociological Research Online*, *21*(3), 1–9. doi:10.5153ro.4071

Cohen, B., & Kietzmann, J. (2014). Ride on! Mobility business models for the sharing economy. *Organization & Environment*, *27*(3), 279–296. doi:10.1177/1086026614546199

Cohen, B., & Munoz, P. (2016). Sharing cities and sustainable consumption and production: Towards an integrated framework. *Journal of Cleaner Production*, *134*, 87–97. doi:10.1016/j.jclepro.2015.07.133

Constantia, I., Eaton, B., Tuunainen, V. K., & Sprague, R. H., Jr. (2016). The evolution of a sharing platform into a sustainable business. *Proceedings of the 49th Hawaii International Conference on System Sciences (HICSS 2016)*, 1297-1306.

Cook, S. (2008, October). The contribution revolution. *Harvard Business Review*, 60–69.

Cova, B., Dalli, D., & Zwick, D. (2011). Critical perspectives on consumers' role as 'producers': Broadening the debate on value co-creation in marketing processes. *Marketing Theory*, *11*(3), 231–241. doi:10.1177/1470593111408171

Cox, J. (2017). *Hackers are using Uber's 57 million account data breach to steal passwords*. Retrieved from https://www.thedailybeast.com/hackers-are-using-ubers-57-million-account-data-breach-to-steal-passwords?ref=scroll

Coyle, D., & Yeung, T. (2016). *Understanding Airbnb in fourteen European cities*. The Jean-Jacques Laffont Digital Chair Working Papers. Available at: http://www.lcii.eu/wp-content/uploads/2017/03/Yeung-Understanding-Airbnb-in-Fourteen-European-Cities-v4.1-1.pdf

Croft, A. (2015). Airbnb remains symbol of Barcelona's growing unease with tourism. *Skift*. Available at: http://skift.com/2015/08/26/airbnb-remains-symbol-of-barcelonas-growing-unease-withtourism/

Cronbach, L. J. (1951). Coefficient Alpha and the Internal Structure of Tests. *Psychometrika*, *16*(3), 297–334. doi:10.1007/BF02310555

Crunchbase. (2018). *Airbnb Acquistions*. Accessed on July 30, 2018 at https://www.crunchbase.com/organization/airbnb/acquisitions/acquisitions_list#section-acquisitions

Davidson, N. M., & Infranca, J. J. (2015). The sharing economy as an urban phenomenon. *Yale Law & Policy Review*, *34*, 215.

Davis, F. D. (1989). Perceived usefulness, perceived ease of use, and user acceptance of information technology. *Management Information Systems Quarterly*, *13*(3), 319–340. doi:10.2307/249008

De Soto, H. (2000). *The mystery of capital: Why capitalism triumphs in the West and fails everywhere else*. New York: Basic Books.

Deci, E. L., & Ryan, R. M. (1985). Intrinsic motivation and self-determination in human behavior. New York: Springer Science+Business Media. doi:10.1007/978-1-4899-2271-7

Deci, E. L. (1971). Effects of externally mediated rewards on intrinsic motivation. *Journal of Personality and Social Psychology*, *18*(1), 105–115. doi:10.1037/h0030644

Deci, E. L., Koestner, R., & Ryan, R. M. (1999). A meta-analytic review of experiments examining the effects of extrinsic rewards on intrinsic motivation. *Psychological Bulletin*, *125*(6), 627–668. doi:10.1037/0033-2909.125.6.627 PMID:10589297

Del Castillo, J. M., & Benitez, F. G. (2013). Determining a public transport satisfaction index from user surveys. *Transportmetrica A. Transportation Science*, *9*(8), 713–741. doi:10.1080/18128602.2011.654139

Derrida, J. (1992). *Given time: I. Counterfeit Money* (P. Kamuf, Trans.). Chicago: The University of Chicago Press.

Dervojeda, K., Diederik, V., Nagtegaal, F., Lengton, M., Rouwmaat, E., Monfardini, E., & Frideres, L. (2013). *The sharing economy: Accessibility based business models for peer-to-peer markets*. Price Waterhouse Coopers for Business Innovation Observatory. Accessed on July 27, 2018 at http://ec.europa.eu/enterprise/policies/innovation/policy/business-innovation observatory/files/case-studies/12-she-accessibility-based-business-models-for-peer-to-peer-markets_en.pdf

Diab, E., van Lierop, D., & El-Geneidy, A. (2017). Recommending transit: Disentangling users' willingness to recommend transit and their intended continued use. *Travel Behaviour and Society*, *6*, 1–9. doi:10.1016/j.tbs.2016.03.001

Dickinson, J. E., Ghali, K., Cherrett, T., Speed, C., Davies, N., & Norgate, S. (2014). Tourism and the smartphone app: Capabilities, emerging practice and scope in the travel domain. *Current Issues in Tourism, 17*(1), 84–101. doi:10.1080/13683500.2012.718323

Dijkstra, T. K., & Henseler, J. (2015a). Consistent and asymptotically normal PLS estimators for linear structural equations. *Computational Statistics & Data Analysis, 81*, 10–23. doi:10.1016/j.csda.2014.07.008

Dijkstra, T. K., & Henseler, J. (2015b). Consistent partial least squares path modeling. *Management Information Systems Quarterly, 39*(2), 297–316. doi:10.25300/MISQ/2015/39.2.02

Dillahunt, T. R., & Malone, A. R. (2015, April). The promise of the sharing economy among disadvantaged communities. In *Proceedings of the 33rd Annual ACM Conference on Human Factors in Computing Systems* (pp. 2285-2294). ACM. 10.1145/2702123.2702189

Dinholp, A., & Gretzel, U. (2016). Selfie-taking as touristic looking. *Annals of Tourism Research, 57*, 126–139. doi:10.1016/j.annals.2015.12.015

Diniz, E. H., Siqueira, E. S., & Van Heck, E. (2016). *Taxonomy for understanding digital community currencies: digital payment platforms and virtual community feelings* (Vol. 10). Academic Press.

Disney, R., & Gathergood, J. (2013). Financial literacy and consumer credit portfolios. *Journal of Banking & Finance, 37*(7), 2246–2254. doi:10.1016/j.jbankfin.2013.01.013

Dredge, D., Gyimothy, S., Birkbak, A., Jensen, T. E., & Maqdsen, A. K. (2016). The impact of regulatory approaches targeting collaborative economy in the tourism accommodation sector: Barcelona, Berlin, Amsterdam and Paris. Impulse Paper, 9. Aalborg University.

Dredge, D. i S., & Gyimóthy, S. (2015). The collaborative economy and tourism: Critical perspectives, questionable claims and silenced voices. *Tourism Recreation Research, 40*(3), 286–302. doi:10.1080/02508281.2015.1086076

Dudás, G., Boros, L., Kovalcsik, T., & Kovalcsik, B. (2017). The visualisation of the spatiality of Airbnb in Budapest using 3-band raster representation. *Geographia Technica, 12*(1), 23–30. doi:10.21163/GT_2017.121.03

Duflo, E., & Saez, E. (2003). The role of information and social interactions in retirement plan decisions: Evidence from a randomized experiment. *The Quarterly Journal of Economics, 118*(August), 815–842. doi:10.1162/00335530360698432

Dufva, M., Koivisto, R., Ilmola-Sheppard, L., & Junno, S. (2017). Anticipating Alternative Futures for the Platform Economy. *Technology Innovation Management Review, 7*(9), 6–16. doi:10.22215/timreview/1102

Dyer, J. H. (1996). Specialized supplier networks as a source of competitive advantage: Evidence from the auto industry. *Strategic Management Journal, 17*(4), 271–291. doi:10.1002/(SICI)1097-0266(199604)17:4<271::AID-SMJ807>3.0.CO;2-Y

Eboli, L., & Mazzulla, G. (2007). Service Quality Attributes Affecting Customer Satisfaction for Bus Transit. *Journal of Public Transportation, 10*(3), 21–34. doi:10.5038/2375-0901.10.3.2

Eboli, L., & Mazzulla, G. (2009). A New Customer Satisfaction Index for Evaluating Transit Service Quality. *Journal of Public Transportation, 12*(3), 21–37. doi:10.5038/2375-0901.12.3.2

Edbring, E. G., Lehner, M., & Mont, O. (2016). Exploring consumer attitudes to alternative models of consumption: Motivations and barriers. *Journal of Cleaner Production, 123*, 5–15. doi:10.1016/j.jclepro.2015.10.107

Edelman, B. (2017). Uber Can't Be Fixed — It's Time for Regulators to Shut It Down. *Harvard Business Review, 21*. Retrieved from https://hbr.org/2017/06/uber-cant-be-fixed-its-time-for-regulators-to-shut-it-down

Edelman, B. G., & Geradin, D. (2015). Efficiencies and regulatory shortcuts: How should we regulate companies like Airbnb and Uber. *Stanford Technology Law Review: STLR: An Online High-Technology Law Journal from Stanford Law School*, *19*, 293–328.

Edelman, B., Luca, M., & Svirsky, D. (2017). Racial discrimination in the sharing economy: Evidence from a field experiment. *American Economic Journal. Applied Economics*, *9*(2), 1–22. doi:10.1257/app.20160213

Edelstein, S. (2018). *Lyft investigates claim that employees improperly accessed customer data*. Retrieved from https://www.thedrive.com/tech/17993/lyft-investigates-claim-that-employees-improperly-accessed-consumer-data

Edgell, D. L. Sr. (2016). *Managing sustainable tourism: A legacy for the future*. Routledge. doi:10.4324/9781315688343

Edwards, D., Cheng, M., Wong, I. A., Zhang, J., & Wu, Q. (2017). Ambassadors of knowledge sharing: Co-produced travel information through tourist-local social media exchange. *International Journal of Contemporary Hospitality Management*, *29*(2), 690–708. doi:10.1108/IJCHM-10-2015-0607

Eisenmann, T. R., Parker, G., & Van Alstyne, M. (2006). Strategies for two sided markets. *Harvard Business Review*, *10*, 92–101.

Eisenmann, T., Parker, G., & Alstyne, V. W. (2006). Strategies for two-sided markets. *Harvard Business Review*, *84*(10).

Elkington, J. (1998). Partnerships from cannibals with forks: The triple bottom line of 21st-century business. *Environmental Quality Management*, *8*(1), 37–51. doi:10.1002/tqem.3310080106

Ert, E., Fleischer, A., & Magen, N. (2016). Trust and Reputation in the Sharing Economy: The Role of Personal Photos on Airbnb. *Tourism Management*, *55*, 62–71. doi:10.1016/j.tourman.2016.01.013

España, E. Y. (2015). *Impactos derivados del exponencial crecimiento de los alojamientos turísticos en viviendas de alquiler en España, impulsado por los modelos y plataformas ce comercialización*. Madrid: Exceltur.

EU Innovation Observatory. (2014). *Collaborative Economy Collaborative production and the maker economy*. Business Innovation Observatory Contract No 190/PP/ENT/CIP/12/C/N03C01. Available at: https://ec.europa.eu/docsroom/documents/13423/attachments/1/translations/en/renditions/native

Eurofound. (2015). *New forms of employment*. Author.

European Commission. (2016). *A European agenda for the collaborative economy*. Communication from the Commission to the European Parliament, the Council, the European Economic and Social Committee, and the Committee of the Regions.

European Commission. (2016). *More than profit: a collaborative economy with a social purpose* (No. Ref. Ares(2016)4889203-31/08/2016). Author.

European Commission. (2017). *An exploratory study of consumer issues in online peer-to-peer platform markets*. Retrieved from: https://ec.europa.eu/info/sites/info/files/final_report_may_2017.pdf

European Commission. (2017). *The cultural and creative cities monitor*. Available at: https://composite-indicators.jrc.ec.europa.eu/cultural-creative-cities-monitor/

European Commission. (2017). *The cultural and creative cities monitor*. European Commission. Retrieved from: https://composite-indicators.jrc.ec.europa.eu/cultural-creative-cities-monitor/

Eurostat. (2016). *Urban Europe statistics on cities, towns and suburbs*. Luxembourg: Publications Office of the European Union.

Evjemo, B., Sykehusvn, S., & Schürmann, A. (2007). User acceptance of Digital Tourist Guides. Lessons learnt from two field studies. In J. Jacko (Ed.), *Human Computer Interaction, Part I* (pp. 746–755). Berlin: Springer-Verlag. doi:10.1007/978-3-540-73105-4_82

Exceltur. (2016). Urbantur 2016. *Monitor de competitividad turística de los destinos urbanos españoles.* Available at: https://www.exceltur.org/urbantur/

Fairholm, G. W. (1994). *Leadership and the culture of trust. Choice Reviews Online* (Vol. 32). Greenwood Publishing Group.

Falk, R. F., & Miller, N. B. (1992). *A Primer for Soft Modeling*. University of Akron Press.

Fancello, G., Paddeu, D., & Fadda, P. (2017). Investigating last food mile deliveries: A case study approach to identify needs for food delivery demand. *Research in Transportation Economics*, *65*, 56–66. doi:10.1016/j.retrec.2017.09.004

Fang, B., Ye, Q., & Law, R. (2016). Effect of sharing economy on tourism industry employment. *Annals of Tourism Research*, *5*, 264–267. doi:10.1016/j.annals.2015.11.018

FAO, IFAD, UNICEF, WFP, & WHO. (2017). *The State of Food Security and Nutrition in the World 2017. Building resilience for peace and food security.* Rome: FAO.

Farrell, J., & Katz, M. L. (2000). Innovation, rent extraction, and integration in systems markets. *The Journal of Industrial Economics*, *48*(4), 413–432. doi:10.1111/1467-6451.00131

Fehrer, J. A., Benoit, S., Aksoy, L., Baker, T. L., Bell, S. J., Brodie, R. J., & Marimuthu, M. (2018). Future scenarios of the collaborative economy: Centrally orchestrated, social bubbles or decentralized autonomous? *Journal of Service Management*, *29*(5), 859–882. doi:10.1108/JOSM-04-2018-0118

Fellows, N. T., & Pitfield, D. E. (2000). An economic and operational evaluation of urban car-sharing. *Transportation Research Part D, Transport and Environment*, *5*(1), 1–10. doi:10.1016/S1361-9209(99)00016-4

Fergusson, A., Ahlqvist, S. R., & Smith, E. (2017). *Is Airbnb safe for guests? What causes an Airbnb stay to turn into a horror story?* Retrieved from https://www.asherfergusson.com/wp-content/uploads/2017/11/Is-Airbnb-Safe-for-Guests_-Research-Study-Method-Results-Recommendations.pdf

Ferrell, O. C., Ferrell, L., & Huggins, K. (2017). Seismic shifts in the sharing economy: Shaking up marketing channels and supply chains. *Journal of Marketing Channels*, *24*(1–2), 3–12. doi:10.1080/1046669X.2017.1346973

Ferrer, A. (2016). *Taxistas contra Uber: la pelea por los pasajeros en el DF*. Obtenido de http://www.milenio. com/df/conflicto_uber_taxis_df-pelea_uber_taxis_ciudad_mexico-apps_debate_taxis_ df_0_647335583.html

Fikar, C. (2018). A decision support system to investigate food losses in e-grocery deliveries. *Computers & Industrial Engineering*, *117*, 282–290. doi:10.1016/j.cie.2018.02.014

Finley, K. (2013). *Trust in the Sharing Economy: An Exploratory Study*. Warwick, RI: Centre for Cultural Policy Studies, University of Warwick.

Fishman, E. (2016). Bikeshare: A Review of Recent Literature. *Transport Reviews*, *36*(1), 92–113. doi:10.1080/01441647.2015.1033036

Fishman, E., Washington, S., & Haworth, N. (2015). Bikeshare's impact on active travel: Evidence from the United States, Great Britain, and Australia. *Journal of Transport & Health*, *2*(2), 135–142. doi:10.1016/j.jth.2015.03.004

Fishman, E., Washington, S., Haworth, N., & Mazzei, A. (2014). Barriers to bikesharing: An analysis from Melbourne and Brisbane. *Journal of Transport Geography*, *41*, 325–337. doi:10.1016/j.jtrangeo.2014.08.005

Fishman, E., Washington, S., Haworth, N., & Watson, A. (2015). Factors influencing bike share membership: An analysis of Melbourne and Brisbane. *Transportation Research Part A, Policy and Practice*, *71*, 17–30. doi:10.1016/j.tra.2014.10.021

Fitzmaurice, C., Ladegaard, I., Attwood-Charles, W., Cansoy, M., Carfagna, L., Schor, J. B., & Wengronowitz, R. (2018). Domesticating the market: moral exchange and the sharing economy. *Socio-Economic Review, mwy003*. Retrieved from https://academic.oup.com/ser/advance-article-abstract/doi/10.1093/ser/mwy003/4866062?redirectedFrom=fulltext

Fitzmaurice, C. J., Ladegaard, I., Attwood-Charles, W., Cansoy, M., Carfagna, L. B., Schor, J. B., & Wengronowitz, R. (2016). Domesticating the market: Moral exchange and the sharing economy. *Socio-economic Review*.

Fonseca, R., Mullen, K. J., Zamarro, G., & Zissimopoulos, J. (2012). What explains the gender gap in financial literacy? The role of household decision making. *The Journal of Consumer Affairs*, *46*(1), 90–106. doi:10.1111/j.1745-6606.2011.01221.x PMID:23049140

Fornell, C., & Larcker, D. F. (1981). Evaluating Structural Equation Models with Unobservable Variables and Measurement Error. *JMR, Journal of Marketing Research*, *18*(1), 39–50. doi:10.1177/002224378101800104

Forsythe, S., Liu, C., Shannon, D., & Gardner, L. C. (2006). Development of a scale to measure the perceived benefits and risks of online shopping. *Journal of Interactive Marketing*, *20*(2), 55–75. doi:10.1002/dir.20061

Frenken, K. (2017). Political economies and environmental futures for the sharing economy. *Philosophical Transactions of the Royal Society A: Mathematical, Physical and Engineering Sciences, 375*. doi:10.1098/rsta.2016.0367

Frenken, K., & Schor, J. (2017). Putting the sharing economy into perspective. *Environmental Innovation and Societal Transitions*, *23*, 3–10. doi:10.1016/j.eist.2017.01.003

Friedman, M. (1970, September 13). The Social Responsability of Business Is to Increase Profits. *The New York Times Magazine.*

Fukuyama, F. (1995). Social capital and the global economy. *Foreign Affairs*, *74*(5), 89–103. doi:10.2307/20047302

Fukuyama, F. (2014). America in Decay: The Sources of Political Dysfunction. *Foreign Affairs*, 93.

Fuller, D., Gauvin, L., Kestens, Y., Daniel, M., Fournier, M., Morency, P., & Drouin, L. (2011). Use of a New Public Bicycle Share Program in Montreal, Canada. *American Journal of Preventive Medicine*, *41*(1), 80–83. doi:10.1016/j.amepre.2011.03.002 PMID:21665067

Funcke, A., Bergh, A., & Wernberg, J. (2018). Timbro Sharing Economy Index (TSEI). *Timbro*. Retrieved from: https://timbro.se/allmant/timbro-sharing-economy-index/

G20/OECD. (2017). *G20/OECD INFE core competencies framework on financial literacy for adults*. Author.

Gage, D. (2018, April 30). The 10 biggest crowdfunding campaigns: where are they now? *The Wall Street Journal*. Retrieved from https://www.wsj.com/articles/the-10-biggest-crowdfunding-campaigns-where-are-they-now-1525140660

Ganapati, S., & Reddick, C. G. (2018). Prospects and challenges of sharing economy for the public sector. *Government Information Quarterly*, *35*(1), 77–87. doi:10.1016/j.giq.2018.01.001

Garcia-Ayllon, S. (2018). Urban Transformations as an Indicator of Unsustainability in the P2P Mass Tourism Phenomenon: The Airbnb Case in Spain through Three Case Studies. *Sustainability*, *10*(8), 2933. doi:10.3390u10082933

Garth. (2012, September 9). *Accountability on Kickstarter*. Comment posted to https://www.kickstarter.com/blog/accountability-on-kickstarter

Ge, Y., Knittel, C. R., MacKenzie, D., & Zoepf, S. (2016). *Racial and gender discrimination in transportation network companies* (No. w22776). Working paper, National Bureau of Economic Research.

Geisser, S. (1975). The Predictive Sample Reuse Method with Applications. *Journal of the American Statistical Association, 70*(350), 320–328. doi:10.1080/01621459.1975.10479865

Geissinger, A., Laurell, C., Öberg, C., & Sandström, C. (2019). How sustainable is the sharing economy? On the sustainability connotations of sharing economy platforms. *Journal of Cleaner Production, 206*, 419–429. doi:10.1016/j.jclepro.2018.09.196

Gennaioli, N., Shleifer, A., Vishny, R., Gennaioli, N., Shleifer, A., & Vishny, R. (2015). Money doctors. *The Journal of Finance, 70*(1), 91–114. doi:10.1111/jofi.12188

Georgarakos, D., & Pasini, G. (2011). Trust, sociability, and stock market participation. *Review of Finance, 15*(4), 693–725. doi:10.1093/rof/rfr028

Gera, E. (2012, June 27). Why Kickstarter 'can't' and won't protect backers once a project is funded. *Polygon*. Retrieved from https://www.polygon.com/gaming/2012/6/27/3099051/backers-rights-what-kickstarter-funders-can-expect-when-they-pledge

Gharehgozli, A., Iakovou, E., Chang, Y., & Swaney, R. (2017). Trends in global E-food supply chain and implications for transport: Literature review and research directions. *Research in Transportation Business & Management, 25*, 2–14. doi:10.1016/j.rtbm.2017.10.002

Giddens, A. (1999). Risk and responsibility. *The Modern Law Review, 62*(1), 1–10. doi:10.1111/1468-2230.00188

Giese, J. L., & Cote, J. A. (2000). Defining consumer satisfaction. *Academy of Marketing Science Review, 2000*(1).

Gillespie, T. (2010). The politics of 'platforms'. *New Media & Society, 12*(3), 347–364. doi:10.1177/1461444809342738

Glaeser, E. L., Laibson, D. I., Scheinkman, J. A., & Soutter, C. L. (2000). Measuring trust. *The Quarterly Journal of Economics, 115*(3), 811–846. doi:10.1162/003355300554926

Gödecke, T., Stein, A. J., & Qaim, M. (2018). The global burden of chronic and hidden hunger: Trends and determinants. *Global Food Security, 17*, 21–29. doi:10.1016/j.gfs.2018.03.004

Goggin, B. (2018). Apple CEO Tim Cook on privacy: 'we have to admit when the free market is not working'. *Business Insider*. Retrieved from https://www.businessinsider.es/apple-ceo-tim-cook-on-privacy-the-free-market-is-not-working-regulations-2018-11?r=US&IR=T

Gompers, P., & Lerner, J. (2001). The Venture Capital Revolution. *The Journal of Economic Perspectives, 15*(2), 145–168. doi:10.1257/jep.15.2.145

Gonzalez-Padron, T. L. (2017). Ethics in the sharing economy: Creating a legitimate marketing channel. *Journal of Marketing Channels, 24*(1–2), 84–96. doi:10.1080/1046669X.2017.1347005

González-Reverté. (2018). Tourists' risk perception and the use of mobile devices in beach tourism destinations. *Sustainability, 10*(2), 413. doi:10.3390u10020413

Görög, G. (2018). The Definitions of Sharing Economy: A Systematic Literature Review. *Management, University of Primorska. Faculty of Management Koper, 13*(2), 175–189.

Gössling, S., & Michael Hall, C. (2019). Sharing versus collaborative economy: How to align ICT developments and the SDGs in tourism? *Journal of Sustainable Tourism, 27*(1), 74–96. doi:10.1080/09669582.2018.1560455

Gravari-Barbas, M., & Guinand, S. (Eds.). (2017). *Tourism and gentrification in contemporary metropolises: International perspectives*. Taylor & Francis. doi:10.4324/9781315629759

Gretzel, U. (2010). Travel in the Network: Redirected Gazes, Ubiquitous Connections and New Frontiers. In M. Levina & G. Kien (Eds.), *Post-global Network and Everyday Life* (pp. 41–58). New York: Peter Lang.

Gretzel, U., Fesenmaier, D. R., & O'Leary, J. T. (2006). The transformation of consumer behaviour. In D. Buhalis & C. Costa (Eds.), *Tourism Business Frontier* (pp. 9–18). Oxford, UK: Elsevier. doi:10.1016/B978-0-7506-6377-9.50009-2

Gretzel, U., & Jamal, T. (2009). Conceptualizing the tourist creative class: Technology, mobility and tourism experiences. *Tourism Analysis*, *14*(4), 471–481. doi:10.3727/108354209X12596287114219

Grier, S. A., & Perry, V. G. (2018). Dog Parks and Coffee Shops: Faux Diversity and Consumption in Gentrifying Neighborhoods. *Journal of Public Policy & Marketing*, *37*(1), 23–38. doi:10.1509/jppm.16.230

Griffit, E. (2019, January 11). More Start-Ups Have an Unfamiliar Message for Venture Capitalists: Get Lost. *The New York Times*. Retrieved from https://www.nytimes.com/2019/01/11/technology/start-ups-rejecting-venture-capital.html

Grönroos, C. (2008). Service logic revisited: Who creates value? And who co-creates? *European Business Review*, *20*(4), 298–314. doi:10.1108/09555340810886585

Grönroos, C. (2011). Value co-creation in service logic: A critical analysis. *Marketing Theory*, *11*(3), 279–301. doi:10.1177/1470593111408177

Grönroos, C. (2012). Conceptualising value co-creation: A journey to the 1970s and back to the future. *Journal of Marketing Management*, *28*(13–14), 1520–1534. doi:10.1080/0267257X.2012.737357

Grönroos, C., & Voima, P. (2013). Critical service logic: Making sense of value creation and co-creation. *Journal of the Academy of Marketing Science*, *41*(2), 133–150. doi:10.100711747-012-0308-3

Grün, C. (2008) Assisting tourists on the move. An evaluation of mobile tourism guides. *Proceedings of the 7th International Conference on Mobile Business*, 171-180.

Guiso, L., Sapienza, P., Zingales, L., Guiso, L., Sapienza, P., & Zingales, L. (2008). Trusting the stock market. *The Journal of Finance*, *63*(6), 2557–2600. doi:10.1111/j.1540-6261.2008.01408.x

Gutiérrez, J., García-Palomares, J. C., Romanillos, G., & Salas-Olmedo, M. H. (2017). The eruption of Airbnb in tourist cities: Comparing spatial patterns of hotels and peer-to-peer accommodation in Barcelona. *Tourism Management*, *62*, 278–291. doi:10.1016/j.tourman.2017.05.003

Gutt, D., & Herrmann, P. (2015). *Sharing Means Caring? Hosts' Price Reaction to Rating Visibility*. ECIS 2015 Research-in-Progress Papers. Paper 54.

Guttentag, D. (2013). Airbnb: Disruptive innovation and the rise of an informal tourism accommodation sector. *Current Issues in Tourism*, 1–26.

Guttentag, D. (2015). Airbnb: Disruptive innovation and the rise of an informal tourism accommodation sector. *Current Issues in Tourism*, *18*(12), 1192–1217. doi:10.1080/13683500.2013.827159

Guttentag, D. A., & Smith, S. L. (2017). Assessing Airbnb as a disruptive innovation relative to hotels: Substitution and comparative performance expectations. *International Journal of Hospitality Management*, *64*, 1–10. doi:10.1016/j.ijhm.2017.02.003

Gymóthy, S. (2017). Networked cultures in the collaborative economy. In D. Dredge & S. Gymóthy (Eds.), *Collaborative economy and tourism. Perspectives, policies and prospects* (pp. 59–74). Springer.

Hagiu, A., & Wright, J. (2011). *Multi-sided platforms.* Harvard Business School Working Chapter, 15-037. Accessed on July 27, 2018 at http://www.hbs.edu/faculty/Publication%20Files/15- 037_cb5afe51-6150-4be9-ace2-39c6a8ace6d4.pdf

Hagiu, A. (2014). Strategic decisions for multisided platforms. *Sloan Management Review, 55*(2), 71–80.

Hagiu, A., & Altmann, E. (2017). Finding the platform in your product. *Harvard Business Review, 95*(4), 94–100.

Hair, F., Hult, G. T. M., Ringle, C., & Sarstedt, M. (2013). *A Primer on Partial Least Squares Structural Equation Modeling (PLS-SEM).* Thousand Oaks, CA: Sage Publications.

Hales, M., Peterson, E., Mendoza, A., & Dessibourg-Free, N. (2019). *2018 Global Cities Report.* A.T. Kearney.

Hamari, J., Sjöklint, M., & Ukkonen, A. (2016). The sharing economy: Why people participate in collaborative consumption. *Journal of the Association for Information Science and Technology, 67*(9), 2047–2059. doi:10.1002/asi.23552

Hammedi, W., Kandampully, J., Zhang, T. T., & Bouquiaux, L. (2015). Online consumer engagement: Creating social environments through brand community constellations. *Journal of Service Management, 26*(5), 777–806. doi:10.1108/JOSM-11-2014-0295

Harris, B. (2018). *These are the happiest countries in the world.* Retrieved from https://www.weforum.org/agenda/2018/03/these-are-t he-happiest-countries-in-the-world/

Harris, M. (2016). How Zano raised millions on Kickstarter and left most backers with nothing. *Medium.* Retrieved from https://medium.com/kickstarter/how-zano-raised-millions-on-kickstarter-and-left-backers-with-nearly-nothing-85c0abe4a6cb

Hartmans, A. (2017). *Airbnb Now Has More Listings Worldwide than the Top Five Hotel Brands Combined.* Retrieved from https://www.businessinsider.com/airbnb-total-worldwide-listings-2017-8

Hasan, R., & Birgach, M. (2016, June). Critical success factors behind the sustainability of the Sharing Economy. In *2016 IEEE 14th International Conference on Software Engineering Research, Management and Applications (SERA)* (pp. 287-293). IEEE. 10.1109/SERA.2016.7516158

Hawlitschek, F., Teubner, T., Adam, M. T. P., Borchers, N. S., Moehlmann, M., & Weinhardt, C. (2016). Trust in the sharing economy: An experimental framework. *Proceedings of the Thirty-Seventh International Conference on Information Systems (ICIS).*

Hawlitschek, F., Teubner, T., & Gimpel, H. (2018). Consumer motives for peer-to-peer sharing. *Journal of Cleaner Production, 204*, 144–157. doi:10.1016/j.jclepro.2018.08.326

Hawlitschek, F., Teubner, T., & Weinhardt, C. (2016). Trust in the sharing economy. *Die Unternehmung, 70*(1), 26–44. doi:10.5771/0042-059X-2016-1-26

Hee, H., & Law, R. (2015). Smartphones in Tourism and Hospitality marketing. A literature review. *Journal of Travel & Tourism Marketing, 32*(6), 692–711. doi:10.1080/10548408.2014.943458

Heide, J. B., & John, G. (1990). Alliances in industrial purchasing: The determinants of joint action in buyer-supplier relationships. *JMR, Journal of Marketing Research, 27*(1), 24–36. doi:10.1177/002224379002700103

Heinrichs, H. (2013). Sharing economy: A potential new pathway to sustainability. *GAIA-Ecological Perspectives for Science and Society, 22*(4), 228–232. doi:10.14512/gaia.22.4.5

Help, K. S. (n.d.). Retrieved January 24, 2019 from, https://help.kickstarter.com/hc/en-us/articles/115005135574-Are-projects-that-were-not-successfully-funded-browsable-on-Kickstarter-

Henseler, J., Dijkstra, T. K., Sarstedt, M., Ringle, C. M., Diamantopoulos, A., Straub, D. W., & Calantone, R. J. (2014). Common Beliefs and Reality about PLS Comments on Rönkkö and Evermann (2013). *Organizational Research Methods*, *17*(2), 182–209. doi:10.1177/1094428114526928

Henseler, J., Hubona, G., & Ray, P. A. (2016). Using PLS path modeling in new technology research: Updated guidelines. *Industrial Management & Data Systems*, *116*(1), 2–20. doi:10.1108/IMDS-09-2015-0382

Henseler, J., Ringle, C. M., & Sarstedt, M. (2015). A New Criterion for Assessing Discriminant Validity in Variance-Based Structural Equation Modeling. *Journal of the Academy of Marketing Science*, *43*(1), 115–135. doi:10.100711747-014-0403-8

Henten, A. H., & Windekilde, I. M. (2016). Transaction costs and the sharing economy. *Info*, *18*(1), 1–15. doi:10.1108/info-09-2015-0044

Heo, C. Y. (2016). Sharing economy and prospects in tourism research. *Annals of Tourism Research*, *58*, 156–170. doi:10.1016/j.annals.2016.02.002

Heo, C. Y., Blal, I., & Choi, M. (2019). What is happening in Paris? Airbnb, hotels, and the Parisian market: A case study. *Tourism Management*, *70*, 78–88. doi:10.1016/j.tourman.2018.04.003

Hernández, Y., Galindo, S., & Vicente, R. (2015). Conflictividad por la operación del transporte público de pasajeros (modalidad taxi) en conjuntos urbanos de Tecámac, Estado de México, *Revista Espacios Públicos. UAEM*, *18*(42), 135–156.

Hill, D. (2019, January 10). How the world's largest crowdfunder for creativity is kickstarting sustainability. *Forbes*. Retrieved from https://www.forbes.com/sites/edfenergyexchange/2019/01/10/how-the-worlds-largest-crowdfunder-for-creativity-is-kickstarting-sustainability/#40ee17345b2b

Hill, N., Brierley, J., & MacDougall, R. (2003). *How to Measure Customer Satisfaction*. Gower Publishing, Ltd.

Hirschman, E. C. (1984). Experience seeking: A subjectivist perspective of consumption. *Journal of Business Research*, *12*(1), 115–136. doi:10.1016/0148-2963(84)90042-0

Hirshleifer, D., & Teoh, S. H. (2009). *Thought and behavior contagion in capital markets. Handbook of Financial Markets: Dynamics and Evolution*. The Paul Merage School of Business, University of California-Irvine: Elsevier Inc.

Hodge, J. (2016). *Hidden hunger: Approaches to tackling micronutrient deficiencies. In Nourishing millions: Stories of change in nutrition*. Washington, DC: International Food Policy Research Institute (IFPRI). Retrieved from https://www.weforum.org/agenda/2019/01/sharing-economy/

Hofstede Insights. (2019). *Compare countries*. Retrieve from https://www.hofstede-insights.com/product/compare-countries/

Holbrook, M. B., & Hirschman, E. C. (1982). The experiential aspects of consumption: Consumer fantasies, feelings, and fun. *The Journal of Consumer Research*, *9*(2), 132–140. doi:10.1086/208906

Homans, G. C. (1958). Social behavior as exchange. *American Journal of Sociology*, *63*(6), 597–606. doi:10.1086/222355

Hong, H., Kubik, J. D., & Stein, J. C. (2004). Social interaction and stock-market participation. *The Journal of Finance*, *59*(1), 137–163. doi:10.1111/j.1540-6261.2004.00629.x

Horkheimer, M. (1974). *Critique of Instrumental Reason*. New York: Seabury.

Horn, K., & And Merante, M. (2017). Is home sharing driving up rents? Evidence from Airbnb in Boston. *Journal of Housing Economics*, *38*, 14–24. doi:10.1016/j.jhe.2017.08.002

Howard, J. A. (1974). *The Structure of Buyer Behavior in Consumer Behavior: Theory and Application* (J. U. Farley, J. A. Howard, & L. W. Ring, Eds.). Boston.

Hsu, C.-I., Hung, S.-F., & Li, H.-C. (2007). Vehicle routing problem with time-windows for perishable food delivery. *Journal of Food Engineering*, *80*(2), 465–475. doi:10.1016/j.jfoodeng.2006.05.029

Hübner, A., Kühn, H., & Wollenburg, J. (2016). Last mile fulfilment and distribution in omni-channel grocery retailing: A strategic planning framework. *International Journal of Retail & Distribution Management*, *44*(3), 228–247. doi:10.1108/IJRDM-11-2014-0154

Hunter, W., Chung, N., Gretzel, U., & Koo, C. (2015). Contructivist research in smart tourism. *Asia Pacific Journal of Information Systems*, *25*(1), 105–120. doi:10.14329/apjis.2015.25.1.105

Hvide, H. K., & Östberg, P. (2015). Social interaction at work. *Journal of Financial Economics*, *117*(3), 628–652. doi:10.1016/j.jfineco.2015.06.004

Iansiti, M., & Levien, R. (2004). Strategy as ecology. *Harvard Business Review*, *82*(3), 68–81. PMID:15029791

IGG for Entrepreneurs. (n.d.). Retrieved March 10, 2019, from https://entrepreneur.indiegogo.com/how-it-works/

Ikkala, T., & Lampinen, A. (2015). Monetizing network hospitality: hospitality and sociability in the context of Airbnb. *Proceedings of the 18th ACM Conference on Computer Supported Cooperative Work & Social Computing*, 1033-44. 10.1145/2675133.2675274

ILO. (2019). World Employment and Social Outlook: Trends 2019. Geneva: ILO.

Indiegogo vs. Kickstarter. (n.d.). Retrieved March 10, 2019, from https://entrepreneur.indiegogo.com/how-it-works/indiegogo-vs-kickstarter/

INEGI. (2010). *Mexico en cifras*. Recuperado de http://www.inegi.org.mx/

Instituto Nacional de Estadistica. (n.d.). *Hotel occupation survey*. Instituto Nacional de Estadistica. Retrieved from: http://www.ine.es/dynt3/inebase/es/index.htm?padre=238&dh=1

Instituto Nacional de Estadistica. (n.d.). *Methodology*. Instituto Nacional de Estadistica. Retrieved from: https://www.ine.es/daco/daco42/ocuphotel/notaeoh.htm

Instituto Nacional de Estadistica. (n.d.). *Occupancy survey in tourist apartments*. Instituto Nacional de Estadistica. Retrieved from: https://www.ine.es/dynt3/inebase/index.htm?padre=231&capsel=231

Instituto Nacional de Estadistica. (n.d.). *Official population figures resulting from the revision of the Municipal Register on January 1*. Instituto Nacional de Estadistica. Retrieved from: http://www.ine.es/jaxiT3/Datos.htm?t=2871

Interian, J. (2016). Up in the air: Harmonizing economy through airbnb regulations. *Boston College International and Comparative Law Review*, 129–161.

Ivanova, I. (2018). *Uber Reportedly Worth More than Ford, GM, Tesla – Combined*. Retrieved from https://www.msn.com/en-us/money/companies/uber-reportedly-worth-more-than-ford-gm-tesla--combined/ar-BBOtpab

Ivković, Z., & Weisbenner, S. (2007). Information diffusion effects in individual investors' common stock purchases: Covet thy neighbors' investment choices. *Review of Financial Studies*, *20*(4), 1327–1357. doi:10.1093/revfin/hhm009

Jäppinen, S., Toivonen, T., & Salonen, M. (2013). Modelling the potential effect of shared bicycles on public transport travel times in Greater Helsinki: An open data approach. *Applied Geography (Sevenoaks, England)*, *43*, 13–24. doi:10.1016/j.apgeog.2013.05.010

Jeffrey, K., Wheatley, H., & Abdallah, S. (2016). *The Happy Planet Index: 2016. A global index of sustainable well-being*. London: New Economics Foundation.

Jeffries, A. (2013a, August 7). Indie no-go: only one in ten projects gets fully funded on Kickstarter's biggest rival. A comparison of two crowdfunding platforms. *The Verge*. Retrieved from https://www.theverge.com/2013/8/7/4594824/less-than-10-percent-of-projects-on-indiegogo-get-fully-funded

Jeffries, A. (2013b, April 17). Kickstarter is not a store, except when it is: Ouya, Pebble, and the curse of the pre-order. *The Verge*. Retrieved from https://www.theverge.com/2013/4/17/4230440/kickstarter-is-not-a-store-except-when-it-is

Jenkins, H. (2006). *Convergence Culture: Where Old and New Media Collide*. New York: New York University Press.

Joewono, T., & Kubota, H. (2007). User Perceptions of Private Paratransit Operation in Indonesia. *Journal of Public Transportation*, *10*(4), 99–118. doi:10.5038/2375-0901.10.4.5

John, G., & Weitz, B. A. (1988). Forward integration into distribution: An empirical test of transaction cost analysis. *Journal of Law Economics and Organization*, *4*, 337–355.

Joskow, P. (1985). Vertical integration and long-term contracts: The case of coal-burning electric generating plants. *Journal of Law Economics and Organization*, *1*(4), 33–80.

Joskow, P. (1987). Contract duration and relation specific investments: Empirical evidence from coal markets. *The American Economic Review*, *17*(3), 168–185.

Joskow, P. (1990). The performance of long-term contracts: Further evidence from coal markets. *The Rand Journal of Economics*, *21*(7), 251–274. doi:10.2307/2555423

Juul, M. (2015). *The Sharing Economy and Tourism*. Retrieved from http://www.europarl.europa.eu/RegData/etudes/BRIE/2015/568345/EPRS BRI(2015)568345 EN.pdf

Kaasinen, E. (2002). User needs for location-aware mobile services. *Personal and Ubiquitous Computing*, *7*(1), 70–79. doi:10.100700779-002-0214-7

Kamal, P., & Chen, J. Q. (2016). Trust in Sharing Economy. In *Pacific Asia Conference on Information Systems (PACIS)* (pp. 109-119). Association for Information Systems.

Kaplan, A. M., & Haenlein, M. (2010). Users of the world, unite! The challenges and opportunities of Social Media. *Business Horizons*, *53*(1), 59–68. doi:10.1016/j.bushor.2009.09.003

Kathan, W., Matzler, K., & Veider, V. (2016). The sharing economy: Your business model's friend or foe? *Business Horizons*, *59*(6), 663–672. doi:10.1016/j.bushor.2016.06.006

Katz, M. L., & Shapiro, C. (1986). Technology adoption in the presence of network externalities. *Journal of Political Economy*, *94*(4), 822–841. doi:10.1086/261409

Kazmin, A., & Ram, A. (2017). India's Uber drivers feel taken for a ride on earnings promises | Financial Times. *Financial Times*. Retrieved from https://www.ft.com/content/12bf0cce-0d99-11e7-a88c-50ba212dce4d

Kennedy, H. R., Jones, V. C., & Gielen, A. (2018). Reported fire safety and first-aid amenities in Airbnb venues in 16 American cities. *Injury Prevention*, 1–3. Retrieved from https://injuryprevention.bmj.com/content/injuryprev/early/2018/05/28/injuryprev-2018-042740.full.pdf PMID:29735746

Ke, Q. (2017). Sharing Means Renting?: An Entire-marketplace Analysis of Airbnb. Cornell University. *Proceedings of the ACM on Web Science Conference*, 131-139.

Kesar, O., Dezeljin, R., & Bienenfeld, M. (2015). Tourism gentrification in the city of Zagreb: Time for a debate. *Interdisciplinary Management Research, 11*, 657–668.

Kickstarter is not a Store. (2012, September 20). *The Kickstarter Blog*. Retrieved from https://www.kickstarter.com/blog/kickstarter-is-not-a-store

Kim, J., Yoon, Y., & Zo, H. (2015). Why People Participate in the Sharing Economy: A Social Exchange Perspective. In Pacific Asia Conference in Information Systems (PACIS) (pp. 76-84). Association for Information Systems.

Kim, Y. G., Woo, E., & Nam, J. (2018). Sharing economy perspective on an integrative framework of the NAM and TPB. *International Journal of Hospitality Management, 72*, 109–117. doi:10.1016/j.ijhm.2018.01.008

Kin, B., Spoor, J., Verlinde, S., Macharis, C., & Van Woensel, T. (2018). Modelling alternative distribution set-ups for fragmented last mile transport: Towards more efficient and sustainable urban freight transport. *Case Studies on Transport Policy, 6*(1), 125–132. doi:10.1016/j.cstp.2017.11.009

Klapper, L., Lusardi, A., & Van Oudheusden, P. (2015). *Financial literacy around the world: Insights from the Standard & Poor's ratings services global financial literacy survey.* Standard & Poor's Ratings Services Global FinLit Survey.

Klein, S., & Roth, V. J. (1990). Determinants of export channel structure: The effects of experience and psychic distance reconsidered. *International Marketing Review, 7*(5), 27–38. doi:10.1108/EUM0000000001533

Kramer, A. (2015). *Meal-sharing apps fly under the regulatory radar*. Retrieved from https://www.bna.com/mealsharing-apps-fly-b17179934259/

KS PBC 2017. (n.d.). Retrieved from https://www.kickstarter.com/year/2017/benefit-statement

Kyrychenko, V., & Shum, P. (2009). Who holds foreign stocks and bonds? Characteristics of active investors in foreign securities. *Financial Services Review, 18*, 1–21.

La Prensa. (2016). Uber recibirá pago en efectivo. *La Prensa.* Obtenido de http://www.prensa.com/economia/Uber-recibira-pago-efectivo_0_4543795641.html

Lab in Granada. (n.d.). Retrieved from: https://labingranada.org/foroalbaicinsacromonte/

Lafaye, C., & Thevenot, L. (1993). Une justification écologique?: Conflits dans l'aménagement de la nature. *Revue Francaise de Sociologie, 34*(4), 495. doi:10.2307/3321928

Lalicic, L., & Weismayer, C. (2016). The passionate use of mobiles phones among tourists. *Information Technology & Tourism, 16*(1), 153–173. doi:10.100740558-015-0042-z

Lamberton, C. P., & Rose, R. L. (2012). When Is Ours Better Than Mine? A Framework for Understanding and Altering Participation in Commercial Sharing Systems. *Journal of Marketing, 76*(4), 109–125. doi:10.1509/jm.10.0368

Lamsfus, C., Wang, D., Alzua-Sorzabal, A., & Xiang, Z. (2015). Going mobile: Defining context for on-the-go travelers. *Journal of Travel Research, 54*(6), 691–701. doi:10.1177/0047287514538839

Lane, R. E. (2000). *The loss of happiness in market democracies.* Yale University Press.

Law, R., Leung, K., & Wong, R. J. (2004). The impact of the Internet on travel agencies. *International Journal of Contemporary Hospitality Management, 1*(2), 100–107. doi:10.1108/09596110410519982

Lawrence, T. B., & Suddaby, R. (2006). Institutions and Institutional Work. In S. R. Clegg, C. Hardy, T. B. Lawrence, & W. R. Nord (Eds.), *The SAGE Handbook of Organization Studies* (2nd ed.; pp. 215–264). doi:10.4135/9781848608030.n7

Lawson, S. (2010). Transumers: motivations of non-ownership consumption. In M. C. Campbell, J. Inman, & R. Pieters (Eds.), NA - Advances in Consumer Research (pp. 842-853). Duluth, MN: Association for Consumer Research.

Lee, S. H., Lee, B. Y., & Kim, H. W. (2018). Decisional factors leading to the reuse of an on-demand ride service. *Information & Management.*

Lees, L., Shin, H. B., & López-MORALES, E. (2016). *Planetary gentrification.* Cambridge, UK: Polity Press.

Lee, Z. W., Chan, T. K., Balaji, M. S., & Chong, A. Y.-L. (2016). Technology-mediated sharing economy: Understanding user participation in collaborative consumption through the benefit-cost perspective. *Proceedings of the 20th Pacific Asia Conference on Information Systems (PACIS).*

Lehr, D. D. (2015). *An analysis of the changing competitive landscape in the hotel industry regarding Airbnb* (Master thesis). Dominican University of California, San Rafael, CA.

Leiber, R. (2015). *Airbnb Horror Story Points to Need for Precautions.* Retrieved from https://www.nytimes.com/2015/08/15/your-money/airbnb-horror-story-points-to-need-for-precautions.html

Leonhardt, D. (2018). The Monopolization of America. *The New York Times.* Retrieved from https://www.nytimes.com/2018/11/25/opinion/monopolies-in-the-us.html

Leung, X. Y., Xue, L., & Wen, H. (2019). Framing the sharing economy: Toward a sustainable ecosystem. *Tourism Management, 71*, 44–53. doi:10.1016/j.tourman.2018.09.021

Levin, S. (2017). *Airbnb sued by woman who says she was sexually assaulted by 'superhost'.* Retrieved from https://www.theguardian.com/technology/2017/jul/27/airbnb-guest-sexual-assault-allegation

Leyshon, A., Thrift, N., & Pratt, J. (1998). Reading financial services: Texts, consumers, and financial literacy. *Environment and Planning. D, Society & Space, 16*(1), 29–55. doi:10.1068/d160029

Li, H., Zhang, J., Li, J., & Shi, Z. (2018). An Investigation of User Satisfaction with Shared Bicycles in Nanjing. *Proceedings of the 18th COTA International Conference of Transportation Professionals*, 967–976. Retrieved from https://ascelibrary.org/doi/10.1061/9780784481523.096

Li, J., Moreno, A., & Zhang, D. J. (2015). *Agent behavior in the sharing economy: evidence from Airbnb.* Working Paper 1298, Ross School of Business, University of Michigan.

Liang, Choi, & Joppe. (2017). Understanding repurchase intention of Airbnb consumers: perceived authenticity, electronic word-of-mouth, and price sensitivity. *Journal of Travel & Tourism Marketing.* doi:10.1080/10548408.2016.1224750

Lim, F., Jin, X., & Srai, J. S. (2018). Consumer-driven e-commerce: A literature review, design framework, and research agenda on last-mile logistics models. *International Journal of Physical Distribution & Logistics Management, 48*(3), 308–332. doi:10.1108/IJPDLM-02-2017-0081

Luhmann, N. (2000). Familiarity, confidence, trust: Problems and alternatives. In Trust: Making and Breaking Cooperative Relations (pp. 94–107). Academic Press.

Lusardi, A., & Mitchell, O. S. (2011). *Financial literacy around the word: An overview* (Vol. 10). Academic Press.

Lusardi, A., Mitchell, O. S., Alesina, A., Alessie, R., Botticini, M., Campbell, J., … Washington, G. (2011). *Financial literacy and planning: Implications for retirement wellbeing* (Working Paper 17078 No. 17078). Cambridge, MA: National Bureau of Economic Research.

Lusardi, A., & Mitchell, O. S. (2007a). Baby Boomer retirement security: The roles of planning, financial literacy, and housing wealth. *Journal of Monetary Economics, 54*(1), 205–224. doi:10.1016/j.jmoneco.2006.12.001

Lusardi, A., & Mitchell, O. S. (2007b). *Financial literacy and retirement planning: New evidence from the Rand American life panel*. SSRN Electronic Journal.

Lusardi, A., & Mitchell, O. S. (2007c). Financial literacy and retirement preparedness: Evidence and implications for financial education. *Business Economics (Cleveland, Ohio)*, *42*(1), 35–44. doi:10.2145/20070104

Lusardi, A., & Mitchell, O. S. (2008). Planning and financial literacy: How do women fare? *The American Economic Review*, *98*(2), 413–417. doi:10.1257/aer.98.2.413

Lusardi, A., & Mitchell, O. S. (2014). The economic importance of financial literacy: Theory and evidence. *Journal of Economic Literature*, *52*(1), 5–44. doi:10.1257/jel.52.1.5 PMID:28579637

Lusardi, A., & Tufano, P. (2015). Debt literacy, financial experiences, and overindebtedness. *Journal of Pension Economics and Finance*, *14*(04), 332–368. doi:10.1017/S1474747215000232

Lusch, R. F., & Vargo, S. L. (2006). Service-dominant logic: Reactions, reflections and refinements. *Marketing Theory*, *6*(3), 281–288. doi:10.1177/1470593106066781

Lutz, C., Hoffmann, C. P., Bucher, E., & Fieseler, C. (2018). The role of privacy concerns in the sharing economy. *Information Communication and Society*, *21*(10), 1472–1492. doi:10.1080/1369118X.2017.1339726

Lutz, C., & Newlands, G. (2018). Consumer segmentation within the sharing economy: The case of Airbnb. *Journal of Business Research*, *88*, 187–196. doi:10.1016/j.jbusres.2018.03.019

Macher, J. T., & Richman, B. D. (2008). Transaction cost economics: An assessment of empirical research in the social sciences. *Business and Politics*, *10*(1), 1–63. doi:10.2202/1469-3569.1210

Malhotra, A., & Van Alstyne, M. (2014). The dark side of the sharing economy… and how to lighten it. *Communications of the ACM*, *57*(11), 24–27. doi:10.1145/2668893

Maltz, A. (1993). Private fleet use: A transaction cost model. *Transportation Journal*, *32*(3), 46–53.

Maltz, A. (1994). Outsourcing the warehousing function. *Logistics and Transportation Review*, *30*(3), 245–265.

Manzi, G., & Saibene, G. (2018). Are they telling the truth? Revealing hidden traits of satisfaction with a public bike-sharing service. *International Journal of Sustainable Transportation*, *12*(4), 253–270. doi:10.1080/15568318.2017.1353186

Marin, Y. (2019, March 17). *Piqo Pocket Projector*. Comment posted to https://www.indiegogo.com/projects/piqo-worlds-most-powerful-1080p-pocket-projector/x/151186

Marketplace. (n.d.). Retrieved February 11, 2019, from https://www.indiegogo.com/explore/all?project_type=product&project_timing=all&sort=trending

Martin, C. J. (2016). The sharing economy: A pathway to sustainability or a nightmarish form of neoliberal capitalism? *Ecological Economics*, *121*, 149–159. doi:10.1016/j.ecolecon.2015.11.027

Martínez, L., & Zapata, T. I. J. A. (2000). Análisis de la varianza. In T. Luque Martínez (coord.) (Ed.), Técnicas de análisis de datos en investigación de mercados (pp. 281–346). Madrid: Pirámide.

Mason, P. (2015). *Postcapitalism: A Guide to Our Future*. London: Allen Lane.

Masten, S. E. (1984). The organization of production: Evidence from the aerospace industry. *The Journal of Law & Economics*, *27*(2), 403–417. doi:10.1086/467071

Masten, S. E., Meehan, J., & Snyder, E. (1991). The costs of organization. *Journal of Law Economics and Organization*, *7*(1), 1–25.

MasterCard. (2017). *The sharing economy: Understanding the opportunities for growth.* Retrieved from: https://newsroom.mastercard.com/eu/files/2017/06/Mastercard_Sharing-Economy_v7.compressed2.pdf

Mátrai, T., & Tóth, J. (2016). Comparative Assessment of Public Bike Sharing Systems. *Transportation Research Procedia, 14*, 2344–2351. doi:10.1016/j.trpro.2016.05.261

Mauss, M. (1990). *The Gift, The Form and reason for exchange in Archaic societies.* London: Routledge.

McCann, D. (2018). *Digital Power Players: Power and Accountability in the Digital Economy. Part 4: The Problem and the Power of Tech Monopolies.* Retrieved from https://neweconomics.org/uploads/files/Digital-Power-Players_181113_155656.pdf

McIntyre, D. P., & Srinivasan, A. (2017). Networks, platforms, and strategy: Emerging views and next steps. *Strategic Management Journal, 38*(1), 141–160. doi:10.1002mj.2596

McLaren, D., & Agyeman, J. (2015). *Sharing cities: a case for truly smart and sustainable cities.* MIT Press.

Meddin, R., & De Maio, P. (2017). *The bike-sharing world map.* Retrieved from www.bikesharingworld.com

Meelen, T., & Frenken, K. (2015). *Stop saying UBER is part of the sharing economy.* Retrieved from: http://www.fastcoexist.com/3040863/stop-saying-uber-is-part-of-the-sharing-economy

Megalab, U. G. R. (n.d.). *Laboratory for research on culture and society digital.* Universidad de Granada. Retrieved from: https://medialab.ugr.es/

Mehdizadeh, M., Nordfjaern, T., Mamdoohi, A. R., & Mohaymany, A. S. (2017). The role of parental risk judgements, transport safety attitudes, transport priorities and accident experiences on pupils' walking to school. *Accident; Analysis and Prevention, 102*, 60–71. doi:10.1016/j.aap.2017.02.020 PMID:28259829

Midgett, C., Bendickson, J. S., Muldoon, J., & Solomon, S. J. (2017). The Sharing Economy and Sustainability: A Case for Airbnb. *Small Business Institute Journal, 13*(2), 51–71.

Miguéns, J., Baggio, R., & Costa, C. (2008) Social media and tourism destinations: TripAdvisor case study. *Proceedings of the IASK ATR2008 Advances in Tourism Research Conference 2008*, 26-28.

Minghetti, V., & Buhalis, D. (2010). Digital divide in Tourism. *Journal of Travel Research, 49*(3), 267–281. doi:10.1177/0047287509346843

Mingming, C., & Xin, J. (n.d.). What do Airbnb users care about? An analysis of online review comments. *International Journal of Hospitality Management, 76*, 58–70.

Minkler, A., & Park, T. (1994). Asset specificity and vertical integration in franchising. *Review of Industrial Organization, 9*(4), 409–423. doi:10.1007/BF01029514

Mission, K. S. (n.d.). Retrieved January 23, 2019, from https://www.kickstarter.com/about?ref=global-footer

Mitchell, W. J. (1998). *City of bits: Space, place, and the infobahn.* Cambridge, MA: MIT Press.

Mithun, C. (2012). *National Study Quantifies Reality of the "Sharing Economy" Movement.* Retrieved from https://www.prnewswire.com/news-releases/national-study-quantifies-the-sharing-economy-movement-138949069.html

Mody, M., Suess, C., & Dogru, T. (2019). Not in my backyard? Is the anti-Airbnb discourse truly warranted? *Annals of Tourism Research, 74*(C), 198–203. doi:10.1016/j.annals.2018.05.004

Möhlmann, M. (2016). *Digital Trust and Peer-to-Peer Collaborative Consumption Platforms: A Mediation Analysis.* Retrieved from SSRN: https://ssrn.com/abstract=2813367 or doi:10.2139srn.2813367

Möhlmann, M. (2015). Collaborative consumption: Determinants of satisfaction and the likelihood of using a sharing economy option again. *Journal of Consumer Behaviour, 14*(3), 193–207. doi:10.1002/cb.1512

Mollick, E. R. (2015). *Delivery Rates on Kickstarter.* Retrieved from https://repository.upenn.edu/mgmt_papers/210

Moreno-Izquierdo, L., Ramón-Rodríguez, A. B., Such-Devesa, M. J., & Perles-Ribes, J. F. (2019). Tourist environment and online reputation as a generator of added value in the sharing economy: The case of Airbnb in urban and sun-and-beach holiday destinations. *Journal of Destination Marketing & Management, 11*, 53–66. doi:10.1016/j.jdmm.2018.11.004

Morganti, E., & Gonzalez-Feliu, J. (2015). The last food concept as a city logistics solution for perishable products. In Enterprise interoperability: Interoperability for agility, resilience and plasticity of collaborations. ISTE and Wiley. doi:10.1002/9781119081418.ch28

Moritz, A., & Block, J. H. (2015). Crowdfunding: A Literature Review and Research Directions. In D. Brüntje & O. Gajda (Eds.), *Crowdfunding in Europe. FGF Studies in Small Business and Entrepreneurship* (pp. 25–53). Springer.

Morozov, E. (2013, October 14). *The 'sharing economy' undermines workers rights.* Retrieved from https://evgenymorozov.tumblr.com/post/64038831400/the-sharing-economy-undermines-workers-rights

Morozov, E. (2018). From Airbnb to city bikes, the 'sharing economy' has been seized by big money. *The Guardian.* Retrieved from https://www.theguardian.com/commentisfree/2018/nov/27/airbnb-city-bikes-sharing-economy-big-money

Morozov, E. (2015). Socialize the data centres! *New Left Review*, (91): 45–66.

Morozov, E. (2019). Capitalism's New Clothes. *The Baffler.*

Mortimer, G., Fazal, E., Hasan, S., Andrews, L., & Martin, J. (2016). Online grocery shopping: The impact of shopping frequency on perceived risk. *International Review of Retail, Distribution and Consumer Research, 26*(2), 202–223. doi:10.1080/09593969.2015.1130737

Mouwen, A. (2015). Drivers of customer satisfaction with public transport services. *Transportation Research Part A, Policy and Practice, 78*, 1–20. doi:10.1016/j.tra.2015.05.005

MTJ. (2015). Estudio de oferta y demanda de los servicios de transporte de taxis y las nuevas empresas de redes de transporte UBER y CityDrive en el Área Metropolitana de Guadalajara. *El Informador*. Obtenido de https://issuu.com/el_informador/docs/estudio_taxis_uber

Muntaner, C. (2018). Digital Platforms. Gig Economy, Precarious Employment, and the Invisible Hand of Social Class. *International Journal of Health Services, 48*(4), 597–600. doi:10.1177/0020731418801413 PMID:30213247

Murillo, D., Buckland, H., & Val, E. (2017). When the sharing economy becomes neoliberalism on steroids: Unravelling the controversies. *Technological Forecasting and Social Change, 125*, 66–76. doi:10.1016/j.techfore.2017.05.024

Murphy, A. J. (2007). Grounding the virtual: The material effects of electronic grocery shopping. *Geoforum, 38*(5), 941–953. doi:10.1016/j.geoforum.2006.12.012

Murphy, E., & Usher, J. (2015). The Role of Bicycle-sharing in the City: Analysis of the Irish Experience. *International Journal of Sustainable Transportation, 9*(2), 116–125. doi:10.1080/15568318.2012.748855

Narasimhan, C., Papatla, P., Jiang, B., Kopalle, P. K., Messinger, P. R., Moorthy, S., ... Zhu, T. (2018). Sharing economy: Review of current research and future directions. *Customer Needs and Solutions, 5*(1-2), 93–106. doi:10.100740547-017-0079-6

Neeser, D., Peitz, M., & Stuhler, J. (2015). *Does Airbnb hurt hotel business: Evidence from the Nordic countries.* Universidad Carlos III de Madrid.

Neuhofer, B., Buhalis, D., & Ladkin, A. (2012). Conceptualising Technology enhanced experiences. *Journal of Destination Marketing & Management*, *1*(1-2), 36–46. doi:10.1016/j.jdmm.2012.08.001

Newcomer, E. (2017). *Lyft Loses $600 Million in 2016 as Revenue Surges*. Retrieved from https://www.bloomberg.com/news/articles/2017-01-12/lyft-loses-600-million-in-2016-as-revenue-surges

Newton, K. (2001). Trust, social capital, civil society, and democracy. *International Political Science Review*, *22*(2), 201–214. doi:10.1177/0192512101222004

Nguyen, G. D., & Lethiais, V. (2016). Impact des réseaux sociaux sur la sociabilité. *Reseaux*, *34*(195), 165–195.

Noordewier, T. G., John, G., & Nevin, J. R. (1990). Performance outcomes of purchasing arrangement in industrial buyer-vendor relationships. *Journal of Marketing*, *54*(4), 80–93. doi:10.1177/002224299005400407

Norrie, M., & Signer, B. (2005). Overlaying Paper Maps with Digital Information Services for Tourists. In A. J. Frew (Ed.), *Information and Communication Technologies in Tourism*. Vienna: Springer.

North, D. C. (1990). *Institutions, institutional Change, and economic performance*. New York: Norton. doi:10.1017/CBO9780511808678

North, D. C. (2005). *Understanding the Process of Economic Change*. Princeton, University Press. doi:10.1515/9781400829484

Northern Ireland Tourism Board. (2015). *Tourism in the midst of a mobile revolution. How advances in mobile technology will shape Northern Ireland's tourism industry in the next decade*. Belfast: NITB.

Nunnally, J. C., & Bernstein, I. H. (1994). *Psychometric Theory*. New York: McGraw-Hill.

O'Brien, S. A., Black, N., Devine, C., & Griffin, D. (2018). *CNN investigation: 103 Uber drivers accused of sexual assault or abuse*. Retrieved from https://money.cnn.com/2018/04/30/technology/uber-driver-sexual-assault/index.html

OECD Guidelines on Measuring Trust. (2017). *OECD Guidelines on Measuring Trust*. OECD.

OECD. (2019). *Poverty rate (indicator)*. OECD. doi:10.1787/0fe1315d-en

Ogilvie, F., & Goodman, A. (2012). Inequalities in usage of a public bicycle sharing scheme: Socio-demographic predictors of uptake and usage of the London (UK) cycle hire scheme. *Preventive Medicine*, *55*(1), 40–45. doi:10.1016/j.ypmed.2012.05.002 PMID:22588228

Oh, J. S., Kim, M. S., & Lee, C. H. (2014). A Study on Factors Affecting the Satisfaction of Public Bicycle System. *Journal of the Korean Society of Road Engineers*, *16*(2), 107–118. doi:10.7855/IJHE.2014.16.2.107

Olivares, E. M. (2014). *Sistemas económicos y modelos de economía moderna*. Bogotá: Universidad Autónoma de Colombia.

Olma, S. (2014). *Never Mind the Sharing Economy: Here's Platform Capitalism*. Retrieved from http://networkcultures.org/mycreativity/2014/10/16/never-mind-the-sharing-economy-heres-platform-capitalism/

Olson, M. J., & Connor, A. D. (2013). *The disruption of sharing: an overview of the new peer-to- peer 'sharing economy' and the impact on established internet companies*. Piper Jaffray Investment Research. Accessed on July 27, 2018 at https://piper2.bluematrix.com/ docs/pdf/35ef1fcc-a07b-48cf-ab80-04d80e5665c4.pdf

Olsson, A., & Phelps, E. A. (2007). Social learning of fear. *Nature Neuroscience*, *10*(9), 1095–1102. doi:10.1038/nn1968 PMID:17726475

Oner Kula, S. (2019). Responsibilities of sharing economy platforms for cultivating trust. In B. Tejerina, C. Miranda de Almeida, I. Perugorria (Eds.), *Proceedings of the International Conference Sharing Society. The Impact of Collaborative Collective Actions in the Transformation of Contemporary Societies* (pp. 207-222). Leioa: Universidad del País Vasco/ Euskal Herriko Unibertsitatea.

Open Data BCN. (n.d.). *Llista d'equipaments de resta urants de la ciutat de Barcelona*. Retrieved February 2019 from https://opendata-ajuntament.barcelona.cat/data/ca/dataset/equipament-restaurants

Orsi, J., Eskandari-Qajar, Y., Weissman, E., Hall, M., Mann, A., & Luna, M. (2013). *Policies for Shareable Cities: A sharing economy policy primer for urban leaders*. Shareable and the Sustainable Economies Law Center.

Oskam, J., & Boswijk, A. (2016). Airbnb: The future of networked hospitality businesses. *Journal of Tourism Futures*, *2*(1), 22–42. doi:10.1108/JTF-11-2015-0048

Oskam, J., & Boswijk, A. (2016). Airbnb: The future of networked hospitality businesses. *Journal of tourism. Futures*, *2*(1), 22–42.

Owyang, J. (2014). *Sharing is the new buying*. Accessed on July 25, 2018 at http://www.web- strategist.com/blog/2014/03/03/report-sharing-is-the-new-buying-winning-in-the-collaborative-economy

Owyang, J., Tran, C., & Silva, C. (2013). *The collaborative economy*. Altimeter. Retrieved from: http://www.collaboriamo.org/media/2014/04/collabecon-draft16-130531132802-phpapp02-2.pdf

Palay, T. (1984). Comparative institutional economics: The governance of rail freight contracting. *The Journal of Legal Studies*, *13*(6), 265–288. doi:10.1086/467741

Pallares, M. A. (2016). Uber suma 1.2 millones de usuarios en México. *Periódico El Universal*. Obtenido de http://www.eluniversal.com.mx/articulo/cartera/negocios/2016/03/8/uber-suma-12-millones-de-usuarios-en-mexico

Pappas, N. (2019). The complexity of consumer experience formulation in the sharing economy. *International Journal of Hospitality Management*, *77*, 415–424. doi:10.1016/j.ijhm.2018.08.005

Parasuraman, A., Zeithaml, V. A., & Berry, L. L. (1988). Servqual: A multiple-item scale for measuring consumer perc. *Journal of Retailing*, *64*(1), 12–40.

Parente, R. C., Geleilate, J.-M. G. M. G., & Rong, K. (2018). The Sharing Economy Globalization Phenomenon: A Research Agenda. *Journal of International Management*, *24*(1), 52–64. doi:10.1016/j.intman.2017.10.001

Parigi, P., & State, B. (2014). Disenchanting the world: the impact of technology on relationships. In *International Conference on Social Informatics* (pp. 166-182). Springer. 10.1007/978-3-319-13734-6_12

Parker, A. M., de Bruin, W. B., Yoong, J., & Willis, R. (2012). Inappropriate confidence and retirement planning: Four studies with a national sample. *Journal of Behavioral Decision Making*, *25*(4), 382–389. doi:10.1002/bdm.745 PMID:23049164

Parker, G. G., & Van Alstyne, M. W. (2005). Two-sided network effects: A theory of information product design. *Management Science*, *51*(10), 1494–1504. doi:10.1287/mnsc.1050.0400

Parkes, S. D., Marsden, G., Shaheen, S. A., & Cohen, A. P. (2013). Understanding the diffusion of public bikesharing systems: Evidence from Europe and North America. *Journal of Transport Geography*, *31*, 94–103. doi:10.1016/j.jtrangeo.2013.06.003

Paternot, S. (2012). *Robot Dragonfly*. Comment posted to https://www.indiegogo.com/projects/robot-dragonfly-micro-aerial-vehicle#/

Pattinson, H. M. (2016). *The collaborative economy: Implications for B2B marketing from an IMP perspective*. In *32nd Industrial Marketing And Purchasing Conference*, Poznan, Poland.

Peng, M. W. (2000). *Business strategies in transition economies*. Sage.

Peng, M. W. (2012). *Estrategia global*. Cengage Learning.

Peng, M. W. (2012). *Global Strategy*. Cincinnati, OH: Thomson South-Western.

Persaud, A., & Azhar, I. (2012). Innovative Mobile Marketing via Smartphones: Are Consumers Ready? *Marketing Intelligence & Planning*, *30*(4), 438–443. doi:10.1108/02634501211231883

Perzanowski, A., & Schultz, J. (2015). Reconciling intellectual property and personal property. *The Notre Dame Law Review*, 90.

Pew Research Center. (2016). *Shared, Collaborative and On Demand: The New Digital Economy*. Retrieved from: http://www.pewresearch.org/wp-content/uploads/sites/9/2016/05/PI_2016.05.19_Sharing-Economy_FINAL.pdf

Pirrong, S. C. (1993). Contracting practices in bulk shipping markets: A transaction cost explanation. *The Journal of Law & Economics*, *36*(2), 937–976. doi:10.1086/467303

Place, C. B. L. (2013). Validating and improving the impact of complementary currency systems through impact assessment frameworks. *International Journal of Oncology*, *2*(November), 243–250.

Polanyi, K. (1944). *The great transformation: Economic and political origins of our time*. New York: Rinehart.

Porter, M. E. (1980). *Competitive Strategy: Techniques for Analyzing Industries and Competitors*. New York: Free Press.

Porter, M. E., & Heppelmann, J. E. (2014). How smart, connected products are transforming competition. *Harvard Business Review*, *92*(11), 64–88.

Poy, J. (2019, March 17). *Piqo Pocket Projector*. Comment posted to https://www.indiegogo.com/projects/piqo-worlds-most-powerful-1080p-pocket-projector/x/151186

Prahalad, C. K., & Ramaswamy, V. (2004). Co-creating unique value with consumers. *Strategy and Leadership*, *32*(3), 4–9. doi:10.1108/10878570410699249

Prideaux, B., & Coghlan, A. (2010). Digital cameras and photo taking on the Great Barrier Reef. Marketing opprotunities for Reef tour operators. *Journal of Vacation Marketing*, *16*(3), 171–183. doi:10.1177/1356766710372244

Projects We Love. (n.d.). Retrieved March 12, 2019, from https://www.kickstarter.com/discover/recommended?ref=discovery_overlay

Pucher, J., Buehler, R., & Seinen, M. (2011). Bicycling renaissance in North America? An update and re-appraisal of cycling trends and policies. *Transportation Research Part A, Policy and Practice*, *45*(6), 451–475. doi:10.1016/j.tra.2011.03.001

Pucher, J., Dill, J., & Handy, S. (2010). Infrastructure, programs, and policies to increase bicycling: An international review. *Preventive Medicine*, *50*, S106–S125. doi:10.1016/j.ypmed.2009.07.028 PMID:19765610

Pucher, J., Garrard, J., & Greaves, S. (2011). Cycling down under: A comparative analysis of bicycling trends and policies in Sydney and Melbourne. *Journal of Transport Geography*, *19*(2), 332–345. doi:10.1016/j.jtrangeo.2010.02.007

Quijones, D. (2015). Barcelona just declared war on Airbnb. *Business Insider*. Available at: www.businessinsider.com/barcelona-just-declared-war-on-airbnb-2015-8

Radcliff, D. (2017, October). *Robot Dragonfly*. Comment posted to https://www.indiegogo.com/projects/robot-dragonfly-micro-aerial-vehicle#/

Rauch, D. E., & Schleicher, D. (2015). *Like Uber, but for local governmental policy: The future of local regulation of the "Sharing Economy."* George Mason Law & Economics Research Paper (15-01).

Raymond, E. (1999). *The Cathedral and the Bazaar*. Sebastopol, CA: O'Reilly. doi:10.100712130-999-1026-0

Reuters. (2018). SoftBank's Vision Fund says portfolio reached 65 companies so far. *Reuters*. Retrieved from https://www.reuters.com/article/us-saudi-investment-softbank-group-portf/softbanks-vision-fund-says-portfolio-reached-65-companies-so-far-idUSKCN1MX1DB

Reward. (n.d.). In *Oxford. Living Dictionaries, English*. Retrieved December 12, 2018, from https://en.oxforddictionaries.com/definition/reward

Ricci, M. (2015). Bike sharing: A review of evidence on impacts and processes of implementation and operation. *Research in Transportation Business & Management*, *15*, 28–38. doi:10.1016/j.rtbm.2015.03.003

Richardson, L. (2015). Performing the sharing economy. *Geoforum*, *67*, 121–129. doi:10.1016/j.geoforum.2015.11.004

Riegelsberger, J., Sassei, M. A., & McCarthy, J. D. (2005). The mechanics of trust: A framework for research design. *International Journal of Human-Computer Studies*, *62*(3), 381–422. doi:10.1016/j.ijhcs.2005.01.001

Rietveld, P., & Daniel, V. (2004). Determinants of bicycle use: Do municipal policies matter? *Transportation Research Part A, Policy and Practice*, *38*(7), 531–550. doi:10.1016/j.tra.2004.05.003

Rifkin, J. (2014). *La sociedad de coste marginal cero: el internet de las cosas, el procomún colaborativo y el eclipse del capitalismo*. Barcelona: Paidós.

Rifkin, J. (2014). *The Zero Marginal Cost Society: The Internet of Things, the Collaborative Commons, and the Eclipse of Capitalism*. New York: Palgrave Macmillan.

Rindfleisch, A., Antia, K., Bercovitz, J., Brown, J. R., Cannon, J., Carson, S. J., & Wathne, K. H. (2010). Transaction costs, opportunism, and governance: Contextual considerations and future research opportunities. *Marketing Letters*, *21*(3), 211–222. doi:10.100711002-010-9104-3

Rindfleisch, A., & Heide, J. B. (1997). Transaction cost analysis: Past, present and future applications. *Journal of Marketing*, *61*(4), 30–55. doi:10.1177/002224299706100403

Ringle, C. M., Wende, S., & Becker, J. M. (2015). *SmartPLS 3*. Bönningstedt: SmartPLS.

Rinne, A. (2018). The Dark Side of the Sharing Economy. *World Economic Forum*, 21. Retrieved from https://www.weforum.org/agenda/2018/01/the-dark-side-of-the-sharing-economy/

Ritzer, G. (2014). Prosumption: Evolution, revolution, or eternal return of the same? *Journal of Consumer Culture*, *14*(1), 3–24. doi:10.1177/1469540513509641

Robot Dragonfly. (2012). Retrieved December 21, 2018 from https://www.indiegogo.com/projects/robot-dragonfly-micro-aerial-vehicle#/

Rochet, J., & Tirole, J. (2006). Two-sided markets: A progress report. *The Rand Journal of Economics*, *37*(2), 645–667. doi:10.1111/j.1756-2171.2006.tb00036.x

Rogers, R. W. (1975). A protection motivation theory of fear appeals and attitude change1. *The Journal of Psychology*, *91*(1), 93–114. doi:10.1080/00223980.1975.9915803 PMID:28136248

Rokeach, M. (1968). The role of values in public opinion research. *Public Opinion Quarterly*, *32*(4), 547–559. doi:10.1086/267645

Romero Frías, E. (2018b). Granada Proyecta: ciudadanía y funcionariado por un turismo sostenible. Medialab UGR. In *Gobernanza participativa local. Construyendo un nuevo marco de relación con la ciudadanía* (pp. 179-181). Federación Española de Municipios y Provincias. Retrieved from: http://femp.femp.es/files/3580-1936-fichero/GOBERNANZA%20 PARTICIPATIVA%20LOCAL.pdf

Romero Frías, E. (2018a). «Granada Proyecta»: ciudadanía y funcionariado por un turismo sostenible. In C. Güemes, J. Resina, & C. Cruz-Rubio (Eds.), *Participación ciudadana: experiencias inspiradoras en España* (pp. 95–108). GIGAPP y Centro de Estudios Políticos y Constitucionales. Retrieved from http://www.cepc.gob.es/publicaciones/libros/colecciones?IDP=2738

Rosenberg, M. J., & Hovland, C. I. (1960). *Cognitive, affective, and behavioral components of attitude. Attitude Organization and Change*. Yale University.

Russo, A., & Quaglieri, A. (2014). La lógica espacial del intercambio de casas: una aproximación a las nuevas geografías de lo cotidiano en el turismo contemporáneo. *Revista electrónica de georgrafía y ciencias sociales*, 324-331.

Rysman, M. (2009). The Economics of Two-Sided Markets. *The Journal of Economic Perspectives*, *23*(3), 125–143. doi:10.1257/jep.23.3.125

Saarijärvi, H., Kannan, P. K., & Kuusela, H. (2013). Value co-creation: Theoretical approaches and practical implications. *European Business Review*, *25*(1), 6–19. doi:10.1108/09555341311287718

Savelsbergh, M., & Van Woensel, T. (2016). City Logistics: Challenges and Opportunities. *Transportation Science*, *50*(2), 579–590. doi:10.1287/trsc.2016.0675

Schaefers, T., Lawson, S. J., & Kukar-Kinney, M. (2016). How the burdens of ownership promote consumer usage of access-based services. *Marketing Letters*, *27*(3), 569–577. doi:10.100711002-015-9366-x

Schilling, M. A. (2009). Protecting or diffusing a technology platform: tradeoffs in appropriability, network externalities, and architectural control. In A. Gawer (Ed.), *Platforms, Markets and Innovation* (pp. 192–218). Cheltenham, UK: Edward Elgar. doi:10.4337/9781849803311.00015

Schleifer, T. (2017). Crowdfunding site Indiegogo will now let you sell products as it shifts into commerce. *Recode*. Retrieved from https://www.recode.net/2017/10/16/16474794/indiegogo-crowdfunding-commerce-amazon

Schor, J. (2015). *The sharing economy: Reports from stage one* (Unpublished paper). Boston College. Retrieved from https://www.bc.edu/content/dam/files/schools/cas_sites/sociology/pdf/TheSharingEconomy.pdf

Schor, J. B. (2014). *Debating the sharing economy*. Retrieved from: http://www.greattransition.org/publication/debating-the-sharing-economy

Schor, J. (2016). Debating the sharing economy. *Journal of Self-Governance & Management Economics*, *4*(3), 7–22. doi:10.22381/JSME4320161

Schor, J. (2016). Debating the sharing economy. *Journal of Self-Governance and Management Economics*, *4*, 3.

Schor, J. B., & Attwood-Charles, W. (2017). The "sharing" economy: Labor, inequality, and social connection on for-profit platforms. *Sociology Compass*, *11*(8), e12493. doi:10.1111oc4.12493

Schor, J. B., Fitzmaurice, C., Carfagna, L. B., Attwood-Charles, W., & Poteat, E. D. (2016). Paradoxes of openness and distinction in the sharing economy. *Poetics*, *54*, 66–81. doi:10.1016/j.poetic.2015.11.001

Science Direct. (n.d.). Retrieved March 11, 2019, from https://www.sciencedirect.com/search/advanced?qs=reward%20crowdfunding%20success&show=50&sortBy=relevance

Seign, R., & Bogenberger, K. (2012, March). *Prescriptions for the Successful Diffusion of Carsharing with Electric Vehicles*. Paper presented at the Conference on Future Automotive Technology Focus Electromobility, München, Germany.

Seraphin, H., Sheeran, P., & Pilato, M. (2018). Over-tourism and the fall of Venice as a destination. *Journal of Destination Marketing & Management*, *9*, 374–376. doi:10.1016/j.jdmm.2018.01.011

Sfetcu, N. (2017). *Web 2.0 / Social Media / Social Networks: Black & White Edition* (1st ed.). CreateSpace Independent Publishing Platform.

Shahani, A. (2012, September 3). When a Kickstarter campaign fails, does anyone get the money back? *NPR*. Retrieved from https://www.npr.org/sections/alltechconsidered/2012/09/03/160505449/when-a-kickstarter-campaign-fails-does-anyone-get-their-money-back

Shaheen, S. A., Guzman, S., & Zhang, H. (2010). Bikesharing in Europe, the Americas, and Asia. *Transportation Research Record: Journal of the Transportation Research Board*, *2143*(1), 159–167. doi:10.3141/2143-20

Shaheen, S. A., Martin, E. W., & Cohen, A. P. (2013). Public Bikesharing and Modal Shift Behavior: A Comparative Study of Early Bikesharing Systems in North America. *International Journal of Transportation*, *1*(1), 35–54. doi:10.14257/ijt.2013.1.1.03

Shapiro, C., & Varian, H. (1999). *Information Rules: A Strategic Guide to the Network Economy*. Cambridge, MA: Harvard Business School Press.

Shareable. (2018). *Sharing cities: Activating the urban commons*. Mountain View, CA: Shareable.

Shuptrine, C. (2016). Kickstarter: Crowdfunding portal, or pre-order store? *The Huffington Post*. Retrieved from https://www.huffingtonpost.com/chris-shuptrine/kickstarter-crowdfunding-_b_9609322.html

Siefkes, C. (2008). *From exchange to contributions generalizing peer production into the physical world*. Berlin: Siefkes-Verlag.

Simon. (2015, January 12). *Accountability on Kickstarter*. Comment posted to https://www.kickstarter.com/blog/accountability-on-kickstarter

Simon, H. A. (1990). Bounded rationality. In J. Eatwell, M. Milgate, & P. Newman (Eds.), *Utility and Probability. The New Palgrave* (pp. 15–18). London: Palgrave Macmillan. doi:10.1007/978-1-349-20568-4_5

Singh, S., & Bawa, S. (2007). A privacy, trust and policy based authorization framework for services in distributed environments. *Journal of Computational Science*, *2*(2), 85–92.

Smets, K. (2019, March 17). *Piqo Pocket Projector*. Comment posted to https://www.indiegogo.com/projects/piqo-world-s-most-powerful-1080p-pocket-projector/x/151186

Smith, B. G., & Gallicano, T. D. (2015). Terms of engagement: Analyzing public engagement with organizations through social media. *Computers in Human Behavior*, *53*, 82–90. doi:10.1016/j.chb.2015.05.060

Smith, J. B., & Colgate, M. (2007). Customer value creation: A practical framework. *Journal of Marketing Theory and Practice*, *15*(1), 7–23. doi:10.2753/MTP1069-6679150101

Soltani, A., Allan, A., Anh Nguyen, H., & Berry, S. (2019). *Bikesharing experience in the city of Adelaide: Insight from a preliminary study*. Case Studies on Transport Policy; doi:10.1016/j.cstp.2019.01.001

Span, M. (2015, June 23). Indiegogo users raise $500 million. *Inc.com*. Retrieved from https://www.inc.com/maria-aspan/indiegogo-users-raise-$500-million.html

Spangenberg, E. R., Voss, K. E., & Crowley, A. E. (1997). Measuring the hedonic and utilitarian dimensions of attitude: A generally applicable scale. *Advances in Consumer Research. Association for Consumer Research (U. S.)*, *24*, 235–241.

Srnicek, N. (2016). *Platform Capitalism*. Cambridge, UK: Polity Press.

Srnicek, N. (2017). The challenges of platform capitalism. *Juncture*, *23*(4), 254–257. doi:10.1111/newe.12023

Stallman, R. (2002). *Free software, free society: Selected essays of Richard M. Stallman*. Boston, MA: Free Software Foundation.

Stats, K. S. (2019, March 15). Retrieved March, 15 2019, from https://www.kickstarter.com/help/stats?ref=global-footer

Stephany, A. (2015). *The business of sharing: Making it in the new sharing economy*. Hampshire, UK: Palgrave Macmillan. doi:10.1057/9781137376183

Steptoe, A., Breeze, E., Banks, J., & Nazroo, J. (2013). Cohort profile: The English Longitudinal Study of Ageing. *International Journal of Epidemiology*, *42*(6), 1640–1648. doi:10.1093/ije/dys168 PMID:23143611

Stokes, K., Clarence, E., Anderson, L., & Rinne, A. (2014). *Making sense of the UK collaborative economy*. Academic Press.

Stone, M. (1974). Cross-Validatory Choice and Assessment of Statistical Predictions. *Journal of the Royal Statistical Society. Series B. Methodological*, *36*(2), 111–147. doi:10.1111/j.2517-6161.1974.tb00994.x

Streitfeld, D. (2014, October 15). Airbnb listing mostly illegal. *New York Times*.

Strickler, Y., Chen, P., & Adler, C. (2012a, September 4). Accountability on Kickstarter. *The Kickstarter Blog*. Retrieved from https://www.kickstarter.com/blog/accountability-on-kickstarter

Strickler, Y., Chen, P., & Adler, C. (2012b, September 20). Kickstarter is not a store. *The Kickstarter Blog*. Retrieved from https://www.kickstarter.com/blog/kickstarter-is-not-a-store

Strickler, Y., Chen, P., & Adler, C. (2015a, September 21). Kickstarter is now a benefit corporation. *The Kickstarter Blog*. Retrieved from https://www.kickstarter.com/blog/kickstarter-is-now-a-benefit-corporation

Stump, R. L., & Heide, J. B. (1996). Controlling supplier opportunism in industrial relationships. *JMR, Journal of Marketing Research*, *33*(11), 431–441. doi:10.1177/002224379603300405

Suárez Corujo, B. (2017). The sharing economy: The emerging debate in Spain. *Spanish Labour Law and Employment Relations Journal*, *6*(1-2), 30–41. doi:10.20318llerj.2017.3923

Suki, N. M., & Suki, N. M. (2017). Modeling the determinants of consumers' attitudes toward online group buying: Do risks and trusts matters? *Journal of Retailing and Consumer Services*, *36*, 180–188. doi:10.1016/j.jretconser.2017.02.002

Sundararajan, A. (2016). *The sharing economy: the end of employment and the rise of crowd-based capitalism*. MIT Press.

Supiot, A. (2018). A Labour code for the 21st century. *Le Monde Diplomatique*. Retrieved from https://mondediplo.com/2018/05/17-labourcode

Support, I. G. G. (n.d.). Retrieved March 19, 2019, from https://support.indiegogo.com/hc/en-us/articles/204092046-InDemand-FAQ

Sutherland, W., & Jarrahi, M. H. (2018). The sharing economy and digital platforms: A review and research agenda. *International Journal of Information Management*, *43*, 328–341. doi:10.1016/j.ijinfomgt.2018.07.004

Tamjidyamcholo, A., Bin Baba, M. S., Tamjid, H., & Gholipour, R. (2013). Information security – Professional perceptions of knowledge-sharing intention under self-efficacy, trust, reciprocity, and shared-language. *Computers & Education*, *68*, 223–232. doi:10.1016/j.compedu.2013.05.010

Taneja, H. (2019). The Era of "Move Fast and Break Things" Is Over. *Harvard Business Review*. Retrieved from https://hbr.org/2019/01/the-era-of-move-fast-and-break-things-is-over

Tapscott, D., & Williams, A. D. (2008). *Wikinomics: How mass collaboration changes everything*. London: Penguin.

Team Favorites. (n.d.). Retrieved March 18, 2019, from https://www.indiegogo.com/campaign_collections/staff-picks

TechJect Updates. Robot Dragonfly Project. (n.d.). Retrieved November 27, 2017, from https://www.indiegogo.com/projects/robot-dragonfly-micro-aerial-vehicle/x/151186#/updates/all

TechJect vs. PayPal. (n.d.). Retrieved March 16, 2019, from https://www.pacermonitor.com/public/case/22748927/Techject,Incorporated_v_Paypal_Holdings,Incorporated

ter Huurne, M., Ronteltap, A., Corten, R., & Buskens, V. (2017). Antecedents of trust in the sharing economy: A systematic review. *Journal of Consumer Behaviour*, *16*(6), 485–498. doi:10.1002/cb.1667

Terms, I. G. G. (2018, May 25). Terms of Use. Retrieved January 12, 2019, from https://www.indiegogo.com/about/terms

Teubner, T., Hawlitschek, F., & Dann, D. (2017). Price Determinants on Airbnb: How Reputation Pays Off in the Sharing Economy. *Journal of Self-Governance and Management Economics*, *5*(4), 53–80. doi:10.22381/JSME5420173

Tiongson, J. (2015). Mobile App Marketing Insights: How Consumers Really Find and Use Your Apps. *Think with Google*. Obtenido de https://www.thinkwithgoogle.com/articles/mobile-app-marketing-insights.html

Tirole, J. (2019). Regulating the disrupters. *LiveMint*. Retrieved from https://www.livemint.com/Technology/XsgWUgy9tR4uaoME7xtITI/Regulating-the-disrupters-Jean-Tirole.html

Top Ten, I. G. G. (n.d.). Retrieved March 11, 2019, from https://www.indiegogo.com/campaign_collections/top-10

Traum, A. B. (2015). Sharing Risk in the Sharing Economy: Insurance Regulation in the Age of Uber. *Cardozo Pub. L. Pol'y & Ethics J.*, *14*, 511–544.

Troisi, O., Carrubbo, L., Maione, G., & Torre, C. (2016). The more, the merrier: Co-Working as practical expression of Value Co-Creation in Sharing Economy. In *XXVI RESER conference* (pp. 1130–1144). Naples: European Association for Research on Services.

Trust, I. G. I. (n.d.). Retrieved March 21, 2019, from https://learn.indiegogo.com/trust/

Tse, A. C. (2003). Disintermediation of travel agents in the hotel industry. *International Journal of Hospitality Management*, *22*(4), 453–460. doi:10.1016/S0278-4319(03)00049-5

Tussyadiah, I. P., & Zach, F. (2015, May). *Hotels vs. peer-to-peer accommodationrentals: Text analytics of consumer reviews in Portland, Oregon*. Paper presented at the Travel and Tourism Research Association (TTRA) 46th Annual, Portland, OR.

Tussyadiah, I. (2014). Social actor attribution to mobile phones: The case of tourists. *Information Technology & Tourism*, *14*(1), 21–47. doi:10.100740558-013-0002-4

Tussyadiah, I. P. (2015). An exploratory study on drivers and deterrents of collaborative consumption in travel. In *Information and communication technologies in tourism* (pp. 817–830). Cham: Springer.

Tussyadiah, I. P. (2015). An exploratory study on drivers and deterrents of collaborative consumption in travel. In *Information and Communication Technologies in Tourism* (pp. 817–830). Cham: Springer.

Tussyadiah, I. P., & Pesonen, J. (2016). Impacts of peer-to-peer accommodation use on travel patterns. *Journal of Travel Research, 55*(8), 1022–1040. doi:10.1177/0047287515608505

Tussyadiah, I., & Zach, F. (2011). The role of geo-based technology in place experiences. *Annals of Tourism Research, 39*(2), 780–800. doi:10.1016/j.annals.2011.10.003

Tussyadiah, L. P. (2016). Determinants of Satisfaction and Future Intention to Use Peer-to-Peer Accommodation International. *Journal of Hospitality Management, 36*, 24–40.

Tussyadiah, L. P., & Inversini, A. (2015). Information and Communication Technologies in Tourism 2015. In *Proceedings of the International Conference in Lugano*, Switzerland. Springer. 10.1007/978-3-319-14343-9

Tyrinopoulos, Y., & Antoniou, C. (2008). Public transit user satisfaction: Variability and policy implications. *Transport Policy, 15*(4), 260–272. doi:10.1016/j.tranpol.2008.06.002

Uber. (2016a). *Uber mueve a Guadalajara*. Obtenido de https://www.uber.com/es-US/cities/guadalajara/

Uber. (2016b). Recuperado de https://www.uber.com

Uber. (2017). *Sala de redacción*. Obtenido de https://newsroom. uber.com/locations/#na-region

Uber. (2019). *Our Commitment to Safety*. Retrieved from https://www.uber.com/safety/

UNDP. (2008). *Making the Law work for everyone* (Vol. 2). Working Group Reports.

UNEP. (2015). *Sustainable Consumption and Production: A Handbook for Policymakers*. Retrieved from http://wedocs.unep.org/bitstream/handle/20.500.118 22/9660/-Sustainable_Consumption_and_Production_a_Handbook_for_PolicymakersSustainable_Consumptio.pdf?sequence=2&isAllowed=y

Unger, D. (1998). *Building social capital in Thailand: fibers, finance, and infrastructure. Cambridge University Press.*

United Nations General Assembly. (2015). *Transforming Our World: The 2030 Agenda for Sustainable Development*. Draft resolution referred to the United Nations summit for the adoption of the post 2015 development agenda by the General Assembly at its sixty-ninth session. UN Doc. A/70/L.1 of 18 September 2015.

United Nations. (2018). *The Sustainable Development Goals Report 2018*. New York: United Nations Publication.

Urbado, D., Díaz, J., & Hernández, R. (2007). Evolución y principios de la teoría económica institucional. Una propuesta de aplicación para el análisis de los factores condicionantes de la creación de empresas. *Investigaciones Europeas de Dirección y Economía de la Empresa, 13*(3), 183–198.

Uriel Jiménez, E., & Aldás Manzano, J. (2005). *Análisis multivariante aplicado* (T. Editores, Ed.). Madrid.

Valdivia, A. (2017). *La turistificación en Granada*. Retrieved from: https://valdilab.wordpress.com/2017/07/18/turistificacion-en-granada/

van den Bos, W., van Dijk, E., & Crone, E. A. (2012). Learning whom to trust in repeated social interactions: A developmental perspective. *Group Processes & Intergroup Relations, 15*(2), 243–256. doi:10.1177/1368430211418698 van Dijck, J., Poell, T., & de Waal, M. (2018). *The platform society: public values in a connective world.* Oxford University Press. doi:10.1093/oso/9780190889760.001.0001

van Ooijen, R., & van Rooij, M. C. J. (2016). Mortgage risks, debt literacy and financial advice. *Journal of Banking & Finance, 72*, 201–217. doi:10.1016/j.jbankfin.2016.05.001

Van Raaij, W. F., & Antonides, G. (1998). *Consumer behaviour: a european perspective.* Wiley.

van Rooij, M., Lusardi, A., & Alessie, R. (2011a). Financial literacy and stock market participation. *Journal of Financial Economics, 101*(2), 449–472. doi:10.1016/j.jfineco.2011.03.006

van Rooij, M., Lusardi, A., & Alessie, R. J. (2011b). Financial literacy and retirement planning in the Netherlands. *Journal of Economic Psychology, 32*(4), 593–608. doi:10.1016/j.joep.2011.02.004

van Rooij, M., Lusardi, A., & Alessie, R. J. (2012). Financial literacy, retirement planning, and household wealth. *Economic Journal (London), 122*(560), 449–478. doi:10.1111/j.1468-0297.2012.02501.x

Vanoverschelde, J., Delancray, C., & Bartolo, L. (2015). Collaboration, innovation … regulation ? The disruptive shifts taking our economy by storm. *Deloitte's Inside Magazine*, (10).

Vargo, S. L., & Lusch, R. F. (2008). Service-dominant logic: Continuing the evolution. *Journal of the Academy of Marketing Science, 36*(1), 1–10. doi:10.100711747-007-0069-6

Vargo, S. L., & Lusch, R. F. (2010). From repeat patronage to value co-creation in service ecosystems: A transcending conceptualization of relationship. *Journal of Business Market Management, 4*(4), 169–179. doi:10.100712087-010-0046-0

Vargo, S. L., Maglio, P. P., & Akaka, M. A. (2008). On value and value co-creation: A service systems and service logic perspective. *European Management Journal, 26*(3), 145–152. doi:10.1016/j.emj.2008.04.003

Varma, A., Jukic, N., Pestek, A., Shultz, C. J., & Nestorov, S. (2016). Airbnb: Exciting innovation or passing fad? *Tourism Management Perspectives, 20*, 228–237. doi:10.1016/j.tmp.2016.09.002

Vaughan, R., & Daverio, R. (2016). *Assessing the size and presence of the collaborative economy in Europe.* Brussels: Publications Office of the European Union.

Veblen, T. (1965). *La teoría der la empresa de negocios (1904).* Buenos Aires: Eudeba.

Villarreal, O. (2005). La internacionalización de la empresa y la empresa multinacional: Una revisión conceptual contemporánea. *Cuadernos de Gestión, 5*(2), 55–73.

Visser, J., Nemoto, T., & Browne, M. (2014). Home delivery and the impacts on urban freight transport: A Review. *Procedia: Social and Behavioral Sciences, 125*, 15–27. doi:10.1016/j.sbspro.2014.01.1452

Von Gaudecker, H. M. (2015). How does household portfolio diversification vary with financial literacy and financial advice? *The Journal of Finance, 70*(2), 489–507. doi:10.1111/jofi.12231

Wachsmuth, D., & Weisler, A. (2018). Airbnb and the Rent Gap: Gentrification Through the Sharing Economy. *Environment and Planning A: Economy and Space, 50*(6).

Walker, G., & Weber, D. (1984). A transaction cost approach to make-or-buy decisions. *Administrative Science Quarterly, 29*(3), 373–391. doi:10.2307/2393030

Walker, G., & Weber, D. (1987). Supplier competition, uncertainty and make-or-buy decisions. *Academy of Management Journal, 30*(3), 589–596.

Wallerstein, J., & Shelat, U. (2017). *Learning to Love (or Live with) the Sharing Economy*. BCG Henderson Institute. Accessed on June 14, 2018 at https://www.bcg.com/publications/2017/strategy-technology-digital-learning-love-live-sharing-economy.aspx

Wallis, O. F. (Interviewer) & Strickler, Y. (Interviewee). (2017). Kickstarter's Yancey Strickler: tech companies need to be better citizens. *Wired*. Retrieved from http://www.wired.co.uk/article/yancey-strickler-kickstarter-video-interview

Wallsten, S. (2015). The competitive effects of the sharing economy: how is Uber changing taxis. Technology Policy Institute.

Walsh, B. (in press). Today's Smart Choices. Don't Own. Share. *Time Magazine*. Available: http://content.time.com/time/specials/packages/article/0,28804,2059521_2059717,00.html

Wang, C., & Zhang, P. (2012). The evolution of social commerce: The people, management, technology, and information dimensions. *Communications of the Association for Information Systems*, *31*(1), 105–127.

Wang, D., & Fesenmaier, D. R. (2013). Transforming the travel experience: the use of smartphones for travel. In L. Cantoni & Z. Xiang (Eds.), *Information and Communication Technologies in Tourism 2013* (pp. 58–69). Berlin: Springer-Verlag. doi:10.1007/978-3-642-36309-2_6

Wang, D., & Nicolau, J. L. (2017). Price determinants of sharing economy based accommodation rental: A study of listings from 33 cities on Airbnb.com. *International Journal of Hospitality Management*, *62*, 120–131. doi:10.1016/j.ijhm.2016.12.007

Wang, D., Park, S., & Fesenmaier, D. R. (2012). The Role of Smartphones in Mediating the Touristic Experience. *Journal of Travel Research*, *51*(4), 371–387. doi:10.1177/0047287511426341

Wang, D., Xiang, Z., & Fesenmaier, D. (2014). Smartphone use in everyday life and travel. *Journal of Travel Research*, *55*(1), 52–63. doi:10.1177/0047287514535847

Wang, N. (2002). The tourist as peak consumer. In G. Dann (Ed.), *The tourist as a metaphor of the social world* (pp. 281–296). Oxford, UK: CABI. doi:10.1079/9780851996066.0281

Wang, Y., Zhang, D., Liu, Q., Shen, F., & Lee, L. H. (2016). Towards enhancing the last-mile delivery: An effective crowd-tasking model with scalable solutions. *Transportation Research Part E, Logistics and Transportation Review*, *93*, 279–293. doi:10.1016/j.tre.2016.06.002

Wardrop, R., Zhang, B., Rau, R., & Gray, M. (2015). *The European alternative finance benchmarking report*. Wardour Drury House.

WCED. (1987). *Our Common Future* (1st ed.). Oxford, UK: Oxford University Press.

Weber, T. A. (2014). Intermediation in a sharing economy: Insurance, moral hazard, and rent extraction. *Journal of Management Information Systems*, *31*(3), 35–71. doi:10.1080/07421222.2014.995520

Wen, I. (2009). Factors affecting the online travel buying decision: A review. *International Journal of Contemporary Hospitality Management*, *21*(6), 752–765. doi:10.1108/09596110910975990

Werther, H., & Klein, S. (1999). ICT and the Changing Landscape of Global Tourism Distribution. *Electronic Markets*, *9*(4), 256–262. doi:10.1080/101967899358941

Williamson, O. E. (1971). The vertical integration of production: Market failure considerations. *The American Economic Review*, *61*(2), 112–123.

Williamson, O. E. (1975). *Markets and Hierarchies*. New York: Free Press.

Williamson, O. E. (1979). Transaction-cost economics: The governance of contractual relations. *The Journal of Law & Economics, 22*(2), 233–261. doi:10.1086/466942

Williamson, O. E. (1985). *The Economic Institutions of Capitalism.* New York: Free Press.

Williamson, O. E. (1991). Comparative economic organization: The analysis of discrete structural alternatives. *Administrative Science Quarterly, 36*(2), 269–296. doi:10.2307/2393356

Williamson, O. E. (2000). The new institutional economics: Taking stock, looking ahead. *Journal of Economic Literature, 38*(3), 595–613. doi:10.1257/jel.38.3.595

Williamson, O. E. (2001). *The theory of the firm as governance structure.* University of California at Berkeley Working Chapter.

World Bank Group. (n.d.). *CPIA database.* Retrieved from http://www.worldbank.org/ida

Wosskow, D. (2014). *Unlocking the sharing economy: An independent review.* London: Department for Business, Innovation and Skills.

Xu, Z., Zhang, K., Min, H., Wang, Z., Zhao, X., & Liu, P. (2018). What drives people to accept automated vehicles? Findings from a field experiment. *Transportation Research Part C, Emerging Technologies, 95*, 320–334. doi:10.1016/j.trc.2018.07.024

Yang, S. B., Lee, K., Lee, H., & Koo, C. (2018). *Airbnb we trust: Understanding consumers' trust-attachment building mechanisms in the sharing economy.* International Journal of Hospitality Management. doi:10.1016/j.ijhm.2018.10.016

Yeung, E. (2012). How to Launch Your App in an International Market. *Mashable.* Obtenido de http://mashable.com/2012/02/13/mobile-apps-international/#aeYWOgIPIOq8

Zano Drone. (2014). *Kickstarter.* Retrieved May 12, 2018, from https://www.kickstarter.com/projects/torquing/zano-autonomous-intelligent-swarming-nano-drone/community

Zeithaml, V. A. (1988). Consumer perceptions of price, quality, and value: A means-end model and synthesis of evidence. *Journal of Marketing, 52*(3), 2–22. doi:10.1177/002224298805200302

Zeng, B., & Gerritsen, R. (2014). What do we know about social media in tourism? A review. *Tourism Management Perspectives, 10*, 27–36. doi:10.1016/j.tmp.2014.01.001

Zervas, G., Proserpio, D., & Byers, J. (2017). The Rise of the Sharing Economy: Estimating the Impact of Airbnb on the Hotel Industry. *JMR, Journal of Marketing Research, 54*(5), 687–705. doi:10.1509/jmr.15.0204

Zhang, T. C., Gu, H., & Jahromi, M. F. (2018a). What Makes the Sharing Economy Successful? An Empirical Examination of Competitive Consumer Value Propositions. *Computers in Human Behavior, 95*, 275–283. doi:10.1016/j.chb.2018.03.019

Zhang, T. C., Jahromi, M. F., & Kizildag, M. (2018b). Value co-creation in a sharing economy: The end of price wars? *International Journal of Hospitality Management, 71*, 51–58. doi:10.1016/j.ijhm.2017.11.010

Zhang, X., Liu, S., Deng, Z., & Chen, X. (2017). Knowledge sharing motivations in online health communities: A comparative study of health professionals and normal users. *Computers in Human Behavior, 75*, 797–810. doi:10.1016/j.chb.2017.06.028

Zhang, Z., Chen, R. J. C., Han, L. D., & Yang, L. (2017). Key Factors Affecting the Price of Airbnb Listings: A Geographically Weighted Approach. *Sustainability, 9*(1635).

Zhu, G., So, K. K. F., & Hudson, S. (2017). Inside the sharing economy: Understanding consumer motivations behind the adoption of mobile applications. *International Journal of Contemporary Hospitality Management*, *29*(9), 2218–2239. doi:10.1108/IJCHM-09-2016-0496

Zuboff, S. (2018). *The age of surveillance capitalism: The fight for a human future at the new frontier of power*. New York: Public Affairs. Retrieved from https://www.publicaffairsbooks.com/titles/shoshana-zuboff/the-age-of-surveillance-capitalism/9781610395694/

Zucman, G. (2015). *The hidden wealth of nations : the scourge of tax havens*. University of Chicago Press. doi:10.7208/chicago/9780226245560.001.0001

Zvolska, L., Palgan, Y. V., & Mont, O. (2019). How do sharing organisations create and disrupt institutions? Towards a framework for institutional work in the sharing economy. *Journal of Cleaner Production*, *219*, 667–676. doi:10.1016/j.jclepro.2019.02.057 PMID:31080321

About the Contributors

Iviane Ramos de Luna is an Assistant professor in the Economic and Business Studies Department at the Open University of Catalonia (Spain). She holds a Ph.D. in Business Sciences and a Master's degree in Marketing and consumer behavior from the University of Granada (Spain), and has a degree in Business Administration from CESED - Higher Education and Development Center (Brazil). She is a member of the Digital Business Research Group (DigiBiz), officially recognized as a Consolidated Research Group, and collaborates as a researcher in the "Gestão Empresarial" research group from the State University of Paraíba-UEPB (Brazil). Currently, her research focuses on consumer behavior in relation to technological innovations, especially in matters related to e-commerce, m-commerce, mobile payments, financial applications/platforms and sharing services. The results of her research have been published in relevant journals in the scientific environment (Technological Forecasting and Social Change, Journal Economic Research-Ekonomska Istraživanja, Technology Analysis & Strategic Management, etc.) and in various national and international conferences (International Marketing Conference AEMARK, 8th International Scientific Conference: Challenges of the 21st Century Economy - Krakow, EMAC Conference, etc.).

Àngels Fitó-Bertran is the Vice president for Competitiveness and Employability at UOC since February 2019. Previously she was the Director of the Economics and Business Department in the Universitat Obertade Catalunya (UOC) since 2010. Previously she tought in many other spanish universities as an Associated professor while she worked as consultant in the financial and accounting area. She has published several papers indexed in data bases like JCR, Scopus or ABS. Her research interests are e-learning, management accounting and accounting education. She attends regularly to accounting and education national and international conferences.

Josep Llados-Masllorens has a PhD Degree on Economics and Business Science and Master Degree on Regional Economics and Tax Management by the University of Barcelona (Spain). Associate Professor of the Economics and Business Department and director of the Phd Program on Business Management at the Open University of Catalonia (UOC). Previously, he was director of the Internet Interdisciplinary Institue (IN3, vice-rector for Faculty and Academic Organization and vice-director for Research of the Economics and Business Department (UOC).

Francisco Liébana-Cabanillas holds a PhD in Business Sciences from the University of Granada (Spain). His main area of research and interest in the field is the effectiveness of mobile and online banking, Internet consumer Behavior, e-banking acceptance, social media and tourism. He has published articles on these topics in various academic journals, such as Tourism Management, International Journal of Information Management, Computers in Human Behavior, Expert Systems with Applications, Industrial Management & Data Systems, Technological Forecasting and Social Change among others, as well as in national and international conferences (EMAC, AEMARK, Hispanic-Lusitanian Congress in Scientific Management, AEDEM, GIKA, Global Management, etc.).

* * *

Rocío Aguilar-Illescas is B.Sc. in Business and Management and Ph.D. in Marketing. She has been an Assistant Professor of Marketing and Market Research at the University of Malaga (Spain) since 2009. Her research interests are in social networks, online brand communities, branding, retailing, among others topics. Her research has resulted in a number of papers published in peer-review journals such as Electronic Commerce Research and Applications or Tourism Review, and books and book chapters of publishers as Springer or ESIC.

Yusaf H. Akbar is Associate Professor in Management at the Department of Economics and Business of Central European University. With extensive teaching, research and consulting experience in emerging markets - specifically of the Central and East European (CEE) region (currently engaged in consulting and executive education in Bulgaria, China, Hungary, Latvia, Lithuania, Morocco, Poland, Russia and Ukraine) - Yusaf's current research interests are focused on three topics (a) the internationalization capabilities of SMEs into emerging markets; (b) non-market strategies of multinational firms and (c) strategic impacts of the Sharing Economy. His current roles in the Academy and beyond include Founding Editor of the International Journal of Emerging Markets and an advisor to governmental authorities. His consulting and professional references include Citibank, Deutsche Telekom, Siemens and Toyota. He completed Visiting Researcher positions at University of Trieste and the Wirtschaftsuniversiteit in Vienna in 2013. He has published in peer-reviewed journals including Journal of International Management, International Journal of Hospitality Management, Journal of World Business, Business and Politics, Cross-Cultural Management, Global Governance, Global Business and Organizational Excellence, Harvard Business Review, International Business Review, Thunderbird International Business Review, Journal of Air Transport Management and World Competition.

Eduard J. Alvarez Palau is Senior Lecturer in Economics and Business Studies at Universitat Oberta de Catalunya (UOC). He holds a PhD in Engineering and Transport Infrastructure and an MSc in Civil Engineering from Universitat Politècnica de Catalunya (UPC). He also holds a Masters Degree in Organisation Management from UOC. Previously, he was research associate at Cambridge University, Blue-Book trainee at European Commission (DG MOVE), part-time teacher at UPC and course instructor at UOC. He also has experience in project management in civil engineering, regional planning and transport consultancy in the private sector.

Rafael Anaya-Sánchez is B.Sc. in Business and Management, Ph.D. in marketing and Assistant Professors of marketing at the University of Málaga, Spain. His research interests are in online brand communities, social networks, retailing, branding, among others topics. His research has resulted in a number of paper published in peer-review journals as Computers in Human Behavior, Electronic Commerce Research and Applications or Tourism Management, and books and book chapters of publishers as Springer or ESIC.

Melissa Farboudi Jahromi is a PhD candidate of Hospitality Management at the Rosen College of Hospitality Management, University of Central Florida, USA. Her research interests include consumer behavior, sharing economy, and human resources. Melissa got her Master's degree in Tourism Management and her Bachelor's in English Language and Literature in Iran. In 2016, she moved to USA to pursue her doctorate and conduct impactful research.

Guadalupe González Sánchez is a Technical Engineer in Industrial Design, University Master's Degree in Occupational Risk Prevention by the University of Malaga, Master in Logistics, Transportation and Road Safety by the National University of Distance Education. She is a researcher at the Transportation Management Lab of the University of Malaga since 2005, where she works in different closely related lines of research, which mainly refer to passenger and freight transport, sustainable mobility and road safety. On these topics, she develops her research activity, being reflected in projects, conferences and seminars in which she has participated as well as in various publications. It also belongs to the Research Group "Work and Transport Management" (Andalusian Research Plan SEJ-424).

Francesc González-Reverté PhD in Geography from the UAB and professor of the Economics and Business Studies at UOC. He is Director of the Degree in Tourism and Lecturer in the Master of Tourism, Sustainability and New Technologies. He is a researcher at the NOUTUR research group (UOC). His main lines of research are focused on beach cities, cultural events, the relationship between technology and tourism and sustainability in tourism.

Erhan İşcan is an Assistant Professor in the Department of Economics at Cukurova University. He has been there since 2002 and he received his Bachelor's degree in Economics. Then he served as research assistant at Cukurova University. He received his M.Sc. and Ph.D. from Cukurova University. After receiving Ph.D. He started lectures at Cukurova University, Nigde University, and Osmaniye Korkut Ata University. He served as vice-dean of the Faculty, vice-chair of the Department of Economics and Chair of the Department of Economics. He is still serving as Editor of Journal of FEAS that is the official journal of Faculty. His research interests are on bioeconomy, sharing economy, digital economy, and commodity markets.

Charalampos Leontidis is a graduate of the faculty of Electrical and Computer Engineering of the National Technological University of Athens.

Daniel Liviano-Solís has a degree in Business Management from the Universitat Rovira i Virgili (URV), and a PhD in Economics from the same university. He has taught at the URV and the University of Barcelona (UB), and is currently a lecturer of mathematics and statistics at the Universitat Oberta de Catalunya (UOC). His research focuses on the fields of econometrics, quantitative economics, regional economics and demography.

Myriam Martínez-Fiestas is a PhD. in Business Sciences (Marketing) at the University of Granada. She is a Professor by The University of Granada (Spain). Her main research interests are in the fields of Perceived Risk, Mobile payments, Psychophysiology, Emotions, Neuromarketing, Social Marketing and Consumer Behavior. She has published his research work in several journals such as, "Journal of Advertising Research","Food Quality and Preference ", "Journal of Environmental Management ", "Service Industries Journal", "Fire Technology", "ASCE's Journal of Construction Engineering and Management", among others. Additionally, she has developed research projects with diverse companies and public administrations.

Antoni Meseguer-Artola has a PhD Degree on Economics and Business Sciences and a Master Degree on Economic Analysis by the Universitat Autònoma de Barcelona. He is Associate Professor of Quantitative Methods for Economics and Business at the Faculty of Economics and Business of the Universitat Oberta de Catalunya (UOC). Previously, he has been Director of Studies (Dean) of that Faculty (2006-2010), and Director of the Bachelor's Degree Programme in Work Sciences (2001-2006). He is author of several articles and conferences on Digital Marketing, Consumer Behavior, Game Theory and E-learning. He has also authored several teaching books in Mathematics and Statistics. He has a merit in research and four merits in teaching.

Krystyna Mitręga-Niestrój holds a Ph.D. in Economics and currently is an Assistant Professor at the Department of Banking and Financial Markets, University of Economics in Katowice (Poland). She is a Vice-Dean for Master's Degree Programmes at the Faculty of Finance and Insurance, University of Economics in Katowice (from 2012). She conducts lectures and seminars on bachelor and master level of study (in Polish and English languages) and on postgraduate studies as well. She is a lecturer in International Finance. She was the Programme Leader of the Joint Msc Degree in European Business and Finance in Katowice, studies conducted together with The Nottingham Trent University in Nottingham and University of Technology in Brno (2010-2018). Her scientific interest is focused on the contemporary problems of the international financial system and development of alternative financial services.

Sebastian Molinillo is an Associate Professor of Marketing at the University of Malaga (Spain) and the Lead for the Digital Marketing Research Group SEJ-567. His key research interests lie in consumer behaviour, internet, technology adoption, sustainable transportation, and branding. His work has been published in journals such as Journal of Business Research, Journal of Retailing and Consumer Services, Tourism Management, Computers in Human Behavior, Technological Forecasting & Social Change, Electronic Commerce Research and Applications, Industrial Management & Data Systems, Computers & Education, International Journal of Contemporary Hospitality Management, and International Journal of Sustainable Transportation, among others. He was appointed a visiting research fellow at Oxford Brookes University, University of Reading, University of Greenwich, and University of Portsmouth (UK).

David Murillo holds a Ph.D. in sociology and a B.Sc. in humanities and in business administration. He is Lecturer at the Department of Social Sciences at ESADE Business School, Ramon Llull University, Barcelona; and he conducts research at the Institute for Social Innovation of the same school in areas like social innovation, business ethics, and critical management studies. His latest works are From Walmart to Al Qaeda. An interdisciplinary Approach to Globalization, published by Greenleaf (Routledge) in 2015 which received the Axiom Business Book Award 2016 (Bronze Medal Winner in the International Business/Globalization category). With S. Vallentin, he has published 'The Business School's Right to Operate: Responsibilization and Resistance' in Journal of Business Ethics (2016); and with H. Buckland

and E. Val., 'When the sharing economy becomes neoliberalism on steroids: Unravelling the controversies' in Technological Forecasting and Social Change (2017).

Milagros Nasiff-Seiffert holds a Bachelor of Science (BS) in Business Administration and Management (University of Málaga) and a Bachelor of Arts (BA) in International Business Management (Hochschule Furtwangen University).

Selin Öner Kula has recently completed her Ph.D. in Communication at Bilgi University, where she specialized in platform economics, exploring online sharing economy and crowdfunding platforms with a focus on trust-formation. She carries an interdisciplinary background with 13 years of professional experience in economics and finance with key responsibilities in corporate finance, equity research, and project finance, coordinating investment analysis and fundraising. Her extensive exposure to traditional financial markets and methods also stimulated her research, helping her see the gaps that the sharing eco-system can fill if internet's potential is utilized in right ways for facilitating more equal access and sustainable collaborative systems. Kula is also an Independent Expert for European Commission - Innovation Council's SME program. She holds a BA in Economics (with a minor in Mathematics) from Sabanci University in Istanbul and MSc in Finance from University Pompeu Fabra in Barcelona where she also taught practice classes in Economic Theory, Statistics, and Financial Management.

Josep Reixach Molet is Research Assistant in Economics and Business Studies at Universitat Oberta de Catalunya (UOC). He holds a Bachelor's Degree in Politican and Administration Science from Universitat Pompeu Fabra (UPF). Previously he worked as an accountant and financial consultant in the private sector.

Esteban Romero-Frías is a Bachelor of Business Administration and Management, Doctor in Accounting and Senior Lecturer at the Department of Accountancy and Finance at the University of Granada. He teaches business creation, business information technologies, accountancy and finance at grade and master level. His research is based on the use of digital methods in Social Science and Humanities, particularly on science and technology studies, learning and business. He has published research works in top journals in Communication (i.e. Comunicar) and Information Science (i.e. Scientometrics, JASIST, JIS). In 2015 he founded Medialab UGR - Research Laboratory for Digital Culture and Society, within the Vice-Rectorate for Research and Transfer of the University of Granada.

Elisabet Ruiz-Dotras is an Associate Professor of Finance at the Universitat Oberta de Catalunya (UOC) in Barcelona. She was a Visiting Professor at City University of Hong Kong for the academic year 2014/2015. Until 2014, she was also a partner in MuntAudit, SL., a company specialized in auditing, consulting and forensic economic. At the UOC, she was the Head of the Bachelor's Degree in Business and Administration (2001-2005) and the Head of the Bachelor's Degree in Marketing and Market Research (2006-2014) and the Director of the Master Science in Financial Markets (1999-2015). She is an expert in economic valuations, mainly in financial products. Her research interests lie in the areas of international finance, financial literacy and e-learning education. She has published several papers and participated in different international conferences and seminars on Finance and e-learning. She has also developed several teaching materials, designed and created many courses and collaborated in different books and projects related to the financial sector. During the academic year 2010/11, she was at the University of California Los Angeles, as a Visiting Professor.

Miguel Ruiz-Montañez is the president of the Spanish association for public transport (Madrid), and general manager of the public transport operator in the city of Malaga, Spain. He is honorary professor and holds a Ph.D. in Business Sciences from the University of Malaga. He has a degree in Business and Administration Science, and also on Industrial Engineering. At the same time, he holds a diploma from INSEAD Business School, Fontainebleau, France, and Master in Marketing and Sales from ESEM Madrid. He has published articles mainly in the transport area of knowledge, not only regarding operations, but also in strategic and finance in journals such as Technological Forecasting & Social Change, and International Journal of Sustainable Transportation, among others. He is a visiting professor at several Latin America Universities.

Christina Saksanian is PhD candidate on Management Sciences and holds a Master degree in Research in Management Sciences by ESAN. Member of the Marketing Faculty of ESAN Graduate School of Business and Universidad del Pacifico in Lima Perú. Market Intelligence executive with more than 20 years of top managerial responsibilities with Consumer Goods / Retail / Pharmaceutical multinational companies in Brazil, Chile, Argentina, Venezuela, Mexico and Peru. Over 15 years on top management positions applying Advanced Analytics for the thorough understanding of markets and consumers generating powerful insights that led to outstanding business results. Expertise on: leading business units, regional and global projects, multifunctional teams, market and consumer understanding and, capabilities building.

Juan S. Timaná holds the degree of Doctor of Philosophy (Ph.D.) in Business Administration granted in 1992 by The Pennsylvania State University and an MBA degree issued in 1984 by The Graduate School of Business at ESAN University. In 1979, The National University of Engineering awarded him a Bachelor of Science degree. At present, he is a full-time ESAN professor. He has more than 30 years of experience as a professor of graduate and executive programs. He has specialized in the area of applied statistics, quantitative research methodology, quantitative methods for management, statistical models, models for decision making, and market research.

Andrea Tracogna is Full Professor of Strategic Management at the University of Trieste, Italy, where he was the Head of the Department of Business Administration and a member of the Academic Senate. In the same University he launched the first Business Plan competition and coordinated a EU-funded project aimed at promoting innovation and technology transfer in the Adriatic macro-Region. In the last years he has contributed to the establishment of a business accelerator and has been a member of the Advisory Board for a major Venture Capital Fund. He is also Deputy Dean at MIB Trieste School of Management, Italy, where he heads the Full-time Master Programs Division, and directs the MBA in International Business program. His current research interests range from Internationalisation Strategies of SMEs, to Business Model Innovation, New Entrepreneurship and Digital Sharing Platforms.

José G. Vargas-Hernández, M.B.A., Ph.D., Member of the National System of Researchers of Mexico and a research professor at University Center for Economic and Managerial Sciences, University of Guadalajara. Professor Vargas-Hernández has a Ph. D. in Public Administration and a Ph.D. in

Organizational Economics. He has undertaken studies in Organisational Behaviour and has a Master of Business Administration, published four books and more than 200 papers in international journals and reviews (some translated to English, French, German, Portuguese, Farsi, Chinese, etc.) and more than 300 essays in national journals and reviews. He has obtained several international Awards and recognition.

Marta Viu-Roig holds a PhD in Business and a BA in Economics and Business Studies from the University of Barcelona (UB). Academic Director of the Masters Degree in Logistics Management. Co-director of the Executive Masters in Operations, Logistics & SCM (EADA-UOC). She is member of the MeL research group, and her research focuses mainly on logistics and e-learning.

Tingting (Christina) Zhang is an Assistant Professor at Rosen College of Hospitality Management at University of Central Florida, Florida, USA. Her research interests include sharing economy, value co-creation, and customer engagement. Dr. Zhang received her Ph.D. degree and Master's degree in Hospitality Management from the Ohio State University. She received her Master's degree in Translation and Interpretation from Beijing Foreign Studies University, China. She also received her Bachelor of Science degree in Marketing with emphasis on Hospitality and Tourism Management from Beijing International Studies University, China.

Index

T

U

V

Recommended Reference Books

IGI Global's reference books are available in three unique pricing formats: Print Only, E-Book Only, or Print + E-Book.

Shipping fees may apply.

www.igi-global.com

ISBN: 978-1-7998-1048-3
EISBN: 978-1-7998-1049-0
© 2020; 605 pp.
List Price: US$ **285**

ISBN: 978-1-5225-8933-4
EISBN: 978-1-5225-8934-1
© 2020; 667 pp.
List Price: US$ **295**

ISBN: 978-1-7998-0357-7
EISBN: 978-1-7998-0359-1
© 2020; 451 pp.
List Price: US$ **235**

ISBN: 978-1-7998-0070-5
EISBN: 978-1-7998-0071-2
© 2020; 144 pp.
List Price: US$ **175**

ISBN: 978-1-5225-6980-0
EISBN: 978-1-5225-6981-7
© 2019; 339 pp.
List Price: US$ **235**

ISBN: 978-1-5225-5390-8
EISBN: 978-1-5225-5391-5
© 2018; 125 pp.
List Price: US$ **165**

Do you want to stay current on the latest research trends, product announcements, news, and special offers?

Join IGI Global's mailing list to receive customized recommendations, exclusive discounts, and more.
Sign up at: **www.igi-global.com/newsletters.**

Publisher of Peer-Reviewed, Timely, and Innovative Academic Research

IGI Global PUBLISHER of TIMELY KNOWLEDGE

www.igi-global.com Sign up at www.igi-global.com/newsletters facebook.com/igiglobal twitter.com/igiglobal linkedin.com/igiglobal

Ensure Quality Research is Introduced to the Academic Community

Become an Evaluator for IGI Global Authored Book Projects

The overall success of an authored book project is dependent on quality and timely manuscript evaluations.

Applications and Inquiries may be sent to:
development@igi-global.com

Applicants must have a doctorate (or equivalent degree) as well as publishing, research, and reviewing experience. Authored Book Evaluators are appointed for one-year terms and are expected to complete at least three evaluations per term. Upon successful completion of this term, evaluators can be considered for an additional term.

If you have a colleague that may be interested in this opportunity, we encourage you to share this information with them.

IGI Global Author Services

Providing a high-quality, affordable, and expeditious service, IGI Global's Author Services enable authors to streamline their publishing process, increase chance of acceptance, and adhere to IGI Global's publication standards.

Benefits of Author Services:

- **Professional Service:** All our editors, designers, and translators are experts in their field with years of experience and professional certifications.
- **Quality Guarantee & Certificate:** Each order is returned with a quality guarantee and certificate of professional completion.
- **Timeliness:** All editorial orders have a guaranteed return timeframe of 3-5 business days and translation orders are guaranteed in 7-10 business days.
- **Affordable Pricing:** IGI Global Author Services are competitively priced compared to other industry service providers.
- **APC Reimbursement:** IGI Global authors publishing Open Access (OA) will be able to deduct the cost of editing and other IGI Global author services from their OA APC publishing fee.

Author Services Offered:

English Language Copy Editing
Professional, native English language copy editors improve your manuscript's grammar, spelling, punctuation, terminology, semantics, consistency, flow, formatting, and more.

Scientific & Scholarly Editing
A Ph.D. level review for qualities such as originality and significance, interest to researchers, level of methodology and analysis, coverage of literature, organization, quality of writing, and strengths and weaknesses.

Figure, Table, Chart & Equation Conversions
Work with IGI Global's graphic designers before submission to enhance and design all figures and charts to IGI Global's specific standards for clarity.

Translation
Providing 70 language options, including Simplified and Traditional Chinese, Spanish, Arabic, German, French, and more.

Hear What the Experts Are Saying About IGI Global's Author Services

"Publishing with IGI Global has been ***an amazing experience*** *for me for sharing my research. The* ***strong academic production*** *support ensures quality and timely completion."* **– Prof. Margaret Niess, Oregon State University, USA**

"The service was ***very fast, very thorough, and very helpful*** *in ensuring our chapter meets the criteria and requirements of the book's editors. I was* ***quite impressed and happy*** *with your service."* **– Prof. Tom Brinthaupt, Middle Tennessee State University, USA**

Learn More or Get Started Here:

For Questions, Contact IGI Global's Customer Service Team at cust@igi-global.com or 717-533-8845

IGI Global
PUBLISHER of TIMELY KNOWLEDGE
www.igi-global.com

IGI Global
PUBLISHER of TIMELY KNOWLEDGE
www.igi-global.com

Celebrating Over 30 Years of Scholarly Knowledge Creation & Dissemination

InfoSci®-Books

A Database of Nearly 6,000 Reference Books Containing Over 105,000+ Chapters Focusing on Emerging Research

InfoSci®-Books Database

The **InfoSci®-Books** is a database of nearly 6,000 IGI Global single and multi-volume reference books, handbooks of research, and encyclopedias, encompassing groundbreaking research from prominent experts worldwide that spans over 350+ topics in 11 core subject areas including business, computer science, education, science and engineering, social sciences, and more.

Open Access Fee Waiver (Read & Publish) Initiative

For any library that invests in IGI Global's InfoSci-Books and/or InfoSci-Journals (175+ scholarly journals) databases, IGI Global will match the library's investment with a fund of equal value to go toward **subsidizing the OA article processing charges (APCs) for their students, faculty, and staff** at that institution when their work is submitted and accepted under OA into an IGI Global journal.*

INFOSCI® PLATFORM FEATURES

- Unlimited Simultaneous Access
- No DRM
- No Set-Up or Maintenance Fees
- A Guarantee of No More Than a 5% Annual Increase for Subscriptions
- Full-Text HTML and PDF Viewing Options
- Downloadable MARC Records
- COUNTER 5 Compliant Reports
- Formatted Citations With Ability to Export to RefWorks and EasyBib
- No Embargo of Content (Research is Available Months in Advance of the Print Release)

**The fund will be offered on an annual basis and expire at the end of the subscription period. The fund would renew as the subscription is renewed for each year thereafter. The open access fees will be waived after the student, faculty, or staff's paper has been vetted and accepted into an IGI Global journal and the fund can only be used toward publishing OA in an IGI Global journal. Libraries in developing countries will have the match on their investment doubled.*

To Recommend or Request a Free Trial:
www.igi-global.com/infosci-books
eresources@igi-global.com • Toll Free: 1-866-342-6657 ext. 100 • Phone: 717-533-8845 x100

IGI Global
PUBLISHER of TIMELY KNOWLEDGE
www.igi-global.com

www.ingramcontent.com/pod-product-compliance
Lightning Source LLC
LaVergne TN
LVHW060421300926
849162LV00006B/1489